Baedeker's

SPAIN

S0-ADD-387

Cover picture: Segovia Cathedral

156 colour photographs
47 maps and plans
1 large road map

Text:
Rosemarie Arnold (History)
Gerald Sawade (Climate)
Dr Hans K. Weiler (Spain from A to Z)
Christine Wessely (Art)

Editorial work:
Baedeker Stuttgart
English language: Alec Court

Cartography:
Ingenieurbüro für Kartographie
Huber & Oberländer, Munich

Design and layout:
HF Ottmann,
Atelier für Buchgestaltung
und Grafik-Design, Leonberg

Conception and general direction:
Dr Peter Baumgarten,
Baedeker Stuttgart

English translation:
James Hogarth

2nd English edition

© Baedeker Stuttgart
Original German edition

© The Automobile Association 57396
United Kingdom and Ireland

© Jarrold and Sons Ltd
English language edition worldwide

Licensed user:
Mairs Geographischer Verlg GmbH & Co.,
Ostfildern-Kemnat bei Stuttgart

Reproductions:
Gölz Repro-Service GmbH,
Ludwigsburg

The name *Baedeker* is a registered trademark

In a time of rapid change it is difficult to ensure that all the information given is entirely accurate and up to date and the possibility of error can never be entirely eliminated. Although the publishers can accept no responsibility for inaccuracies and omissions they are always grateful for corrections and suggestions for improvement.

Printed in Italy by G. Canale & C. S.p.A. - Turin.

0-13-055913-X US and Canada
0 86145 060 4 UK

Source of illustrations:

Most of the colour photographs were provided by the Spanish National Tourist Office, Madrid and Frankfurt am Main.

Others:
Allianz-Archiv (p. 252)
Hans Baedeker (p. 129, right)
Bavaria-Verlag, Gauting (pp. 49, 55, 58, top; 79, 114, bottom; 115, 126, 135, 168, 174, 178, 236, 247, 285, bottom)
González Byass, Jerez de la Frontera (pp. 143, 264)
Continentale Verlags- und Werbegesellschaft GmbH, Frankfurt am Main (p. 80)
Willi Fischer, Esslingen am Neckar (p. 69)
FOAT, Spain (pp. 51, 61, 89, 103, 127 (two), 134, bottom; 137, 140, 142, 149, 170, 171, 188, 239, 244)
F. Gabin (p. 82)
Dieter Grathwohl, Stuttgart (pp. 7, 45, 54 (two), 55, 62, 65, 66, top; 92, 93 (three), 125, 132, left; 148 (two), 176, 189, 209, 211, 213, bottom; 251, 280, 286, 287, 288)
F. Hecker (pp. 75, 86, 87, 119, 120, 158, 164, 234)
Frank J. Klug, Neuhausen (pp. 56, 71, 139, 175, 184, 197)
Bildagentur Mauritius, Mittenwald (p. 207)
Bildarchiv Kh. Schuster, Frankfurt am Main (pp. 81, 99, 114, 122, 134, top; 213, top)
A. Subirats Casanovas, Valencia (p. 107, two)
Zentrale Farbbild Agentur GmbH (ZEFA), Düsseldorf (pp. 113, 123, 154, 158, 161, 253, 254)

The panorama of Benidorm (pp. 80–81) was drawn by Monika Dostler, Schwäbisch Hall

How to Use this Guide

Europe uses the metric system of measurement. Since this is the only system you will encounter in your travels, many of the measurements in this guide are expressed in metric terms. Conversion is easy. Multiply metres by 3·3 to get the approximate dimensions in feet. A kilometre (1000 m) is approximately 0·62 mile.

The principal towns and areas of tourist interest are described in alphabetical order. The names of other places referred to under these general headings can be found in the very full Index.

Following the tradition established by Karl Baedeker in 1844, sights of particular interest and hotels and restaurants of particular quality are distinguished by either one or two asterisks.

In the lists of hotels b. = beds, r. = rooms and SP = swimming pool. Hotels are classified in the categories shown on p. 262.

A glossary of common geographical, architectural, etc., terms is given on p. 260.

The symbol ⓘ at the beginning of an entry or on a town plan indicates the local tourist office or other organisation from which further information can be obtained. The post-horn symbol on a town plan indicates a post office.

Only a selection of hotels and restaurants can be given: no reflection is implied, therefore, on establishments not included.

This guidebook forms part of a completely new series of the world-famous Baedeker Guides to Europe.

Each volume is the result of long and careful preparation and, true to the traditions of Baedeker, is designed in every respect to meet the needs and expectations of the modern traveller.

The name of Baedeker has long been identified in the field of guidebooks with reliable, comprehensive and up-to-date information, prepared by expert writers who work from detailed, first-hand knowledge of the country concerned. Following a tradition that goes back over 150 years to the date when Karl Baedeker published the first of his handbooks for travellers, these guides have been planned to give the tourist all the essential information about the country and its inhabitants: where to go, how to get there and what to see. Baedeker's account of a country was always based on his personal observation and experience during his travels in that country. This tradition of writing a guidebook in the field rather than at an office desk has been maintained by Baedeker ever since.

Lavishly illustrated with superb colour photographs and numerous specially drawn maps and street plans of the major towns, the new Baedeker Guides concentrate on making available to the modern traveller all the information he needs in a format that is both attractive and easy to follow. For every place that appears in the gazetteer, the principal features of architectural, artistic and historic interest are described, as are its main areas of scenic beauty. Selected hotels and restaurants are also included. Features of exceptional merit are indicated by either one or two asterisks.

A special section at the end of each book contains practical information, details of leisure activities and useful addresses. The separate road map will prove an invaluable aid to planning your route and your travel within the country.

Introduction to Spain

NOTE

Following the recent political reorganisation, especially the division of Spain into autonomous regions (see p. 8), the names of many places and streets, and even of buildings and institutions have been changed.

This is particularly true of those parts of the country in which the Catalan, Basque and Gallic languages take precedence.

As this development is still going on, and as a consequence official approval has not everywhere been uniform, the Spanish names which until now have been generally used have been retained in this book.

Windmills in Castile

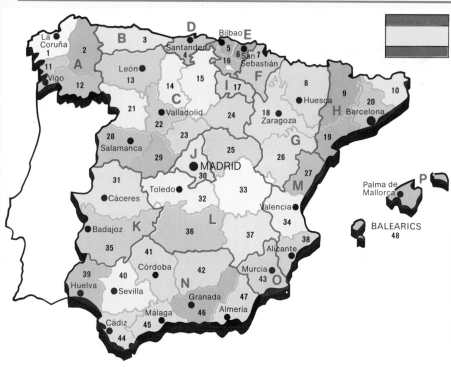

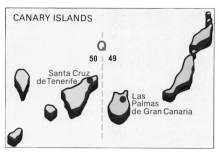

Spain

Borders of Autonomous Regions ————

Borders of Provinces ~~~~~~

Autonomous Regions

	Autonomous Region	Area (sq. km)	Population	Pop. per sq. km
A	Galicia	29,434	2,812,000	96
B	Asturias	10,565	1,159,000	110
C	Castile-León (Castilla y León)	94,147	2,610,000	28
D	Cantabria	5,289	517,000	98
E	Basque Region (País Vasco)	7,261	2,135,000	294
F	Navarre (Navarra)	10,421	509,000	49
G	Aragon	47,669	1,227,000	26
H	Catalonia (Cataluña)	31,930	5,656,000	177
I	La Rioja	5,034	251,000	50
J	Madrid	7,995	4,632,000	579
K	Estremadura (Extremadura)	41,602	1,083,000	26
L	Castile-La Mancha (Castilla-La-Mancha)	79,226	1,683,000	21
M	Valencia	23,305	3,655,000	157
N	Andalusia (Andalucia)	87,260	6,441,000	74
O	Murcia	11,317	935,000	83
P	Balearics (Islas Baleares)	5,014	685,000	137
Q	Canary Islands (Canarias)	7,273	1,523,000	209

Provinces and Other Territories

Provinces	Area (sq. km)	Population	Pop. per sq. km
1 La Coruña	7,876	1,083,000	138
2 Lugo	9,803	399,000	41
3 Asturias	10,565	1,127,000	107
4 Cantabria	5,298	511,000	97
5 Vizcaya	2,217	1,181,000	532
6 Guipúzcoa	1,997	693,000	347
7 Navarra	10,421	507,000	49
8 Huesca	15,613	220,000	14
9 Lérida	12,028	355,000	30
10 Gerona	5,886	468,000	80
11 Pontevedra	4,477	860,000	192
12 Orense	7,278	411,000	57
13 León	15,468	518,000	33
14 Palencia	8,035	187,000	23
15 Burgos	14,309	363,000	25
16 Álava	3,047	261,000	86
17 La Rioja	5,034	253,000	50
18 Zaragoza	17,252	842,000	49
19 Tarragona	6,283	516,000	82
20 Barcelona	7,733	4,619,000	597
21 Zamora	10,559	224,000	21
22 Valladolid	8,202	489,000	60
23 Segovia	6,949	149,000	21
24 Soria	10,287	99,000	10
25 Guadalajara	12,190	143,000	12
26 Teruel	14,785	151,000	10
27 Castellón	6,679	432,000	65
28 Salamanca	12,336	368,000	30
29 Àvila	8,048	179,000	22
30 Madrid	7,995	4,727,000	591
31 Cáceres	19,945	415,000	21
32 Toledo	15,368	472,000	31
33 Cuenca	17,061	210,000	12
34 Valencia	10,763	2,066,000	192
35 Badajoz	21,657	635,000	29
36 Ciudad Real	19,749	468,000	24
37 Albacete	14,862	334,000	23
38 Alicante	5,863	1,149,000	196
39 Huelva	10,085	414,000	41
40 Sevilla	14,001	1,477,000	106
41 Córdoba	13,718	717,000	52
42 Jaén	13,498	628,000	46
43 Murcia	11,317	958,000	85
44 Cádiz	7,385	1,002,000	136
45 Málaga	7,276	1,036,000	142
46 Granada	12,531	762,000	61
47 Almería	8,774	405,000	46
48 Baleares	5,014	685,000	137
49 Las Palmas de Gran Canaria	4,072	756,000	186
50 Santa Cruz de Tenerife	3,170	688,000	217
African Territories			
Ceuta	19	71,000	3,736
Melilla	12	58,000	4,833
SPAIN (Mainland)	504,751	38,330,000	76
Andorra	462	45,000	88
Gibraltar	6·5	31,000	5,172

Spain is one of the great holiday countries; but is has much more to offer than its endless beaches and its southern sun. Its attractions lie not only along its coasts but inland: not only world-famous sights like the Alhambra in Granada and the monastery of Montserrat but a variety of beautiful scenery, many picturesque villages and towns and a profusion of splendid churches and castles, many of them awaiting discovery well away from the beaten tourist track.

Spain (*España*), with about 492,463 sq. km, makes up four-fifths of the Iberian peninsula, which has a total area of 595,000 sq. kilometres. It is separated from the rest of Europe by the 430 km long chain of the Pyrenees, which forms a natural frontier with France, and its long coastline is washed by the Atlantic and the Mediterranean. Off the E coast, the Levante, lie the Balearic Islands, while a good 1000 km SW of Cádiz are the Canaries, off the W coast of Africa. While the almost continuous bastion of the Pyrenees in the N has been both geographically and historically a barrier between Spain and the rest of Europe, the Straits of Gibraltar in the S, only 14 km wide, have served rather to link Spain with Africa than to separate the one from the other.

The Iberian peninsula forms a compact mass, roughly pentagonal in shape – a conformation which led to its being compared in antiquity with an ox-hide. The diagonals measure between 700 and 800 km, so that the distances from the centre to the coasts are very considerable. The most prominent feature of the peninsula's morphology is the central Meseta, framed by much folded mountains. The Meseta is a vast plateau ranging in height between 600 and 1000 m, with the surrounding mountains rising considerably higher: in the N the Cantabrian Mountains (Peña de Cerredo, 2678 m), in the E the rugged Iberian Mountains (Moncayo, 2315 m), in the S the Sierra Moreno and the Sierra de Alcaraz (1798 m). In Extremadura, to the SW, the Meseta slopes down towards Portugal and the Atlantic coast. Across the centre run a series of mountain ranges (Sierra de Gata, Sierra de Gredos, Sierra de Guadarrama) which divide it into two parts, Old Castile to the N and New Castile to the S.

Round the plateau are a variety of fringe regions. To the E the Aragon basin, a region of sedimentary rock watered by the River Ebro, extends to the Mediterranean. In the N the plateau is bounded by the high peaks of the Pyrenees (Pico de Aneto, 3404 m) and outliers of the Cantabrian Mountains. In the S it is separated by the deeply slashed basin of the Guadalquivir from the considerable peaks of the Cordillera Bética, which ends abruptly in sheer rock faces along the Mediterranean coast and rises in the Sierra Nevada to the highest point in the Iberian peninsula (3478 m). In the NE the mountains of Galicia, extending southwards into Portugal, form irregular ranges never exceeding 2000 m in height, much indented by the rías – the fjord-like estuaries of the rivers flowing into the Atlantic – so that the coast is fringed by sandy beaches and rugged cliffs. The peninsula as a whole is thus fairly mountainous in character, with an average altitude of around 600 m.

CATALONIA (Cataluña) is the most northerly of the Mediterranean regions of Spain, different in character and historical development from Castile and the interior. The *Catalonian Mountains* run parallel with the coast, linking the eastern Pyrenees with the hills bordering the Meseta on the NE. Originally a continous range, they were later divided by tectonic disturbances into isolated massifs, such as *Montseny* (1745 m) in the N and the famous *Montserrat* (1241 m), with its monastic buildings, and *Montsant* (1071 m) in the S.

Between the main range of mountains and a lower coastal chain extends the *Catalonian Longitudinal Valley*, a syncline filled with later Tertiary deposits. This is the heart of the region, densely populated and covered with olive-groves, vineyards, market gardens and (particularly round Gerona) plantations of cork-oaks. The rivers flowing down from the Pyrenees, particularly the *Llobregat*, cut through the hills in narrow gorges; their abundant flow of water, long used for irrigation, is now also harnessed to provide electric energy for industry. In the W Catalonia extends also into the Ebro basin.

Catalonia also includes a region of sparse population and rugged mountain scenery in the *Pyrenees*. In the mountains, near the source of the Río Segre, is the remote

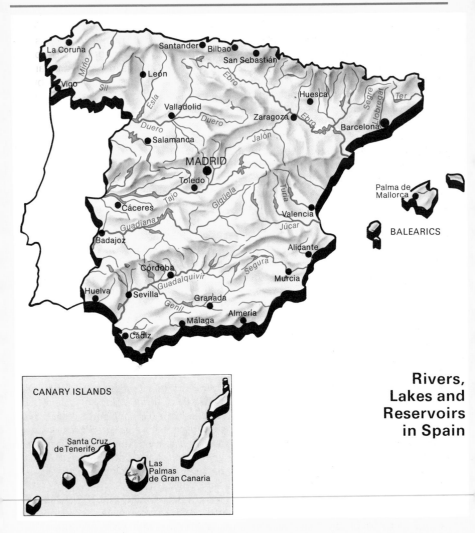

Rivers, Lakes and Reservoirs in Spain

little republic of ANDORRA, which has maintained its separate existence since the 9th c. In the E the Pyrenees run down in a number of separate ridges to the *Ampurdán* uplands, where olive-groves, vineyards and woods of cork-oak fringe the base of the hills.

The Catalonian capital, **Barcelona**, situated in the fertile area round the mouth of the Llobregat, has developed into a major centre of commerce and industry, while the beautiful *Costa Brava* to the N has become one of the great Meccas of mass tourism. Off a rugged stretch of coast lie the Islas Medas, a popular place for diving.

As *Hispania Tarraconensis*, Catalonia was the first nucleus of Roman Spain. After periods of Visigothic and Moorish rule it became the Spanish March of the Frankish kingdom, until Wilfred the Hairy

broke free of Frankish control and established the Condado de Barcelona in 874. In the middle of the 12th c. it was united with Aragon by marriage, and in 1469, together with Aragon, it was joined to Castile, losing political and economic importance but preserving its constitutional freedom and many special rights and privileges (*fueros*). In 1640, when Philip IV levied troops for war with France and demanded oppressive taxes, the Catalans resisted, and with French help held out for some time against Spanish troops. The surrender of Barcelona in 1652, however, was followed by the re-establishment of Spanish authority, though the Catalan *fueros* were renewed. Not until the wars of liberation against Napoleon was Catalonia finally united with Spain. The flowering of the Catalan dialect and writing, however, demonstrated that Catalonia's separate political and cultural consciousness was still very much alive.

The Catalans – unlike the more conservative Castilians – are vigorous, progressive and businesslike by nature. Their energy and resourcefulness have made this mountainous region the main economic centre and a densely populated and most progressive part of the Iberian peninsula. The Catalan language (*Català*) is an independent Romance language related to Provençal which achived a considerable renaissance (*renaxensa*) in the 19th c. and in recent years, after many decades of suppression, has enjoyed a fresh burst of vigour which has also been reflected in literature.

The old kingdoms of **ARAGON** and **NAVARRE** fall mainly within the *Ebro basin*, a depression formed by late Tertiary limestones, clays and marls lying between the Pyrenees in the N and the scarplands bordering the Meseta in the SW, forming a sharp angle in the NW and cut off from the Mediterranean by the Catalonian Mountains. The *Ebro*, flowing down from the Cantabrian Mountains, enters the basin through the *Conchas de Haro*, continues with a fairly gentle gradient and carves a narrow passage through the Catalonian Mountains to the sea. In contrast to the busy activity of Catalonia and the almost central European character of the Basque provinces, the featureless uplands of Aragon have an austerity, isolation and spareness reminiscent of Castile. Enclosed by hills, they have a continental climate like that of the Meseta, with arid summers during which an oppressive heat haze (*calina*) hangs over the whitish-grey plain. With a high salt and gypsum content, the soil is infertile, nourishing only a steppeland of esparto grass and meagre grazing for sheep. The growing of corn, vegetables and other crops is confined to the land bordering the rivers, particularly the ˌEbro and the Segre. Almost the only source of irrigation is the *Canal Imperial*, which runs along the right bank of the Ebro for a distance of some 90 km. The few settlements of any size in this sparsely populated land are to be found in these long oases bordering the rivers, the *huertas*. The capital of Aragon, **Zaragoza**, lies in one of these huertas, in which almonds, olives, figs and vines all flourish.

To the N Aragon and Navarre extend to the main ridge of the **Pyrenees**. At the W end, where they adjoin the Cantabrian Mountains, these ˌare still of medium height, rising to not much over 1500 m and passable at many points without difficulty. In this region, where the Basques are settled on both sides of the mountains, the little kingdom of Navarre developed, strategically situated in command of the passes. Its capital, **Pamplona**, lies in a treeless basin between the main Pyrenean ridge and the sierra zone. To the E of the *Somport pass* (1631 m) the Pyrenees form a mighty mountain barrier with few passes which reaches its highest point in the *Pico de Aneto* (3404 m), in the Maladeta group, a granite massif on the Spanish side of the range. The central ridge, made up of metamorphic and magnetic rock, shows signs of considerable glaciation in the form of small mountain lakes and valleys. The gentler scarps on the S side, contrasting with the steep rock faces on the French side, consist mainly of much-folded Cretaceous and Tertiary rocks, as does *Monte Perdido* (Mont Perdu, 3352 m) in the main ridge. To the S are the sierras, built of the same rocks and carved by a series of rivers into separate ranges (the Sierra de la Peña, etc.). The Spanish side of the Pyrenees has little rain and therefore lacks the green mantle of forest found on the northern slopes, the slopes of the valleys being clad only with meagre mountain pastures and macchia.

The **BASQUE PROVINCES** of **Guipúzcoa, Vizcaya** and **Álava** occupy the eastern part of the *Cantabrian Mountains*, between the valley of the Nervión, which reaches the sea at Bilbao, and the Pyrenees. It is an upland region of medium height, with only a few peaks rising higher, such as the *Peña de Gorbea* (1475 m). The coastal hills are separated from the main ridge of the Cantabrian Mountains by longitudinal valleys along which the E–W traffic passes. Under the influence of the moist N and NW winds this coastal tract produces a rich growth of vegetation. At the higher altitudes there are forests of oak, beech and chestnut or, where these have been destroyed, a dense growth of bracken or plantations of pines and eucalyptus. The hills and valleys are covered with meadows, fields of maize and plantations of walnuts and fruit-trees. In certain favoured areas a light country wine (Chacolí) is produced, but the usual drink is cider (Basque *sagardúa*, Spanish *sidra*). The northern slopes of the Cantabrian Mountains are a pleasant region, with a climate which is agreeable even in summer and a landscape of lush green fields and picturesque Basque farms (*caseríos*). The coast is particularly attractive, with cliffs frequently rising to over 300 m and little fishing towns, many of which have developed into popular seaside resorts. The beaches with the best sand in this area are enclosed by rocks.

The southern slopes of the Cantabrian Mountains differ in landscape and economy from the coastal regions. Wide open valleys alternate with larger basins; the rainfall is considerably lower, and wheat rather than maize is grown. In the open landscapes of the province of Álava the pattern of settlement takes the form of compact villages rather than the separate farmsteads of the coast.

The economic life of the Basque provinces is closely bound up with the products of their soil. In addition to agriculture – still to some extent carried on by archaic methods – there is a well-developed metal-working industry based on the iron ores of Bilbao, and the abundance of timber provides the raw material for a furniture-making industry which has a national reputation. A plentiful supply of water favours paper-making, particularly in Guipúzcoa, and the mountain streams have been harnessed to supply electric power.

The Basques (Basque *Euskaldunak*, Spanish *Vascos*) are a pre-Indo-European people which managed to preserve a considerable degree of independence until the 19th c. They repelled the onslaughts of the Franks and the Moors, and submitted to the authority of León and Navarre, and later of Castile, only on condition that their special rights and privileges – recorded, in the case of Vizcaya, in a document dating as far back as 1342 – were recognised. These privileges remained in force until 1876, when, with the exception of one or two particular provisions, they were abolished. The Basque language (*Euskara*) is spoken, in a number of dialects, mainly in the provinces of Vizcaya and Guipúzcoa and in the Basque region of France. Practically the only relic of the traditional Basque costume is the typical beret (*boina*) of red, blue or white woollen cloth. The Basques are prosperous, attached to their native soil and their traditions, and ready to fight for their ancient rights, as is evidenced by the ETA separatist movement. The Basque national sport is pelota, the vigorous ball game which is also played in other parts of Spain.

The former principality of **ASTURIAS**, now an autonomous region with its capital, **Oviedo**, is a mountainous area extending along the Bay of Biscay W of Santander province, almost completely occupied by the *Cantabrian Mountains*, here rising to Alpine altitudes and reaching a height of 2646 m in the *Picos de Europa*. In the W they are wild and rugged, offering romantic mountain scenery. High passes run S through the range, but only the *Puerto de Pajares* (1364 m), which is followed by the road from Oviedo to León, links Asturias with central Spain.

In the centre of Asturias – covered, thanks to its oceanic climate, with a green mantle of vegetation – is the *Oviedo basin*, a fertile upland region extending to the coast. Asturias has few towns, the only one of any size apart from Oviedo being the port of **Gijón**. Along the picturesque coast with its sheer cliffs are many small fishing settlements which have in most cases developed in recent years into lively little seaside resorts.

The economy of Asturias is based on the growing of maize and fruit and on stock-farming (particularly pigs: the ham of Asturias is renowned). The agricultural population live in small villages, individual farms and, most commonly, in straggling hamlets. Beside the dwelling-house stands a small granary (*hórreo*) borne on four posts which protects the maize crop from vermin. The coal-mines of Asturias are also of major economic importance, supplying half Spain's total output of coal. Other minerals are fluorspar, zinc and iron, which have promoted the industrial development of the region. The lowlands yield peat and amber.

GALICIA occupies the NW corner of the Iberian peninsula, extending S to the frontier with Portugal. The mountain chains which dominate so much of Spain are lacking here. The extensive areas of granite and other crystalline rocks have militated against the development of any particular line of folding, so that the river systems have played a more important part in determining the topography of the region than in the Cantabrian Mountains.

Here wooded valleys (pine, oak, euca-lyptus), in the form of elongated basins like that of the *Miño*, are enclosed by ridges of hills, between which are pla-teaux traversed by numerous rivers flow-ing through steep narrow valleys.

A particular feature of Galicia is the series of long fjord-like inlets at the mouths of the rivers known as **rías** (the Rías Altas on the N coast, the Rías Bajas on the W coast). These arms of the sea, often with beautiful sandy beaches, provide safe havens on the storm-swept coast, and some of them contain important Atlantic ports such as **Vigo** and **La Coruña**.

Fishing, particularly for sardines, plays an important part in the economy of this rather backward region. The hills along the rías are covered with forests and a variety of crops. In the interior the tenant farmers gain a modest subsistence on their small and heavily burdened hold-ings, growing maize, corn and, in the SW, wine. The mild damp climate also favours stock-farming. Recently the extraction of tin and wolfram has also made a consider-able contribution to the economy.

The Galicians (Galacian *Galegos*, Spa-nish *Gallegos*), who were exposed for many centuries to the influence of suc-cessive conquerors – Romans, Vandals, Suevi, Visigoths, Moors, Castilians – are similar in character and language to the Portuguese. They are attached to their homeland (VPG separatist movement) and hard-working, but have the re-putation among other Spaniards of being rather slow and stolid. The heavy taxes payable by the smallholders have led many Galicians to move to other parts of Spain or to emigrate to South America or Portugal.

CASTILE, the heartland of Spain, is an inland region, the **Meseta** (the "large table"), bordered by ranges of hills, with most of its area lying far from the sea. The plateau, formerly defended by a string of castles, is divided by the *Central Castilian Range*, consisting of the Sierra de Gua-darrama, the Sierra de Gredos and the Sierra de Gata, into **Old Castile** (*Castilla la Vieja*) in the N and **New Castile** (*Castilla la Nueva*) to the SE. The two parts of the plateau, in which the base-ment rock is covered by more recent deposits, slope down towards the W and

are traversed by large but non-navigable rivers, which cut through the western rim in rocky gorges. The northern scarp, in the province of Santander, a region of oceanic climate, is formed by the *Cantabrian Mountains*, which here, as in the Basque provinces, are of no more than medium height.

The considerable altitude of the Meseta (900 m and over in Old Castile, 600–700 m in New Castile) gives the climate a continental character, with hot summers and severe winters. Most of the land was formerly left unused as a result of the low rainfall (400 mm – $15\frac{3}{4}$ in.), lack of trees and scanty population, but more recently has been brought under cultivation (wheat, etc.) following the construction of reservoirs to provide irrigation and the planting of quickly growing eucalyptus trees. The spring and autumn rains produce grazing for the merino sheep from Extremadura which are brought here in the summer. On the large expanses of fertile steppeland in León, around **Palen-cia, Valladolid** and **Zamora**, and on the *Mesa de Ocaña* in New Castile (with artificial irrigation in some areas), corn is grown, as well as the popular *garbanzos* (chick peas), an essential ingredient of the national dish, *cocido*. Along the eastern and northern edges of the Meseta are the bleak and empty *Páramos* or *parameras*, high and arid limestone pla-teaux, lashed by wind in winter, formed of rocks which are older than those in the lower-lying areas and older than the dusty limestone expanses of Don Quixote's La Mancha.

Monotonous and colourless as the central Spanish plateau may be, however, it has its moments of scenic grandeur when the sun sinks down in the W and the red colouring of the soil merges into the varying hues of the sunset sky.

On these endless expanses of the Cas-tilian plains the character of the Spaniard was formed. The villages built of sun-dried bricks (adobes) have the same tawny colour as the earth. Here and in the modest little country towns live the peasants (*labradores*) displaced by the large landowners – generous and hospit-able people of the kind portrayed by Cervantes and Calderón.

VALENCIA occupies a narrow coastal area extending from the Ebro delta to the mouth of the Río Segura – although the province of Alicante, S of Cabo de la Nao, belongs geographically to Murcia. Here the treeless reddish-grey limestone and sandstone plateaux of the Meseta approach the sea and terminate in sheep and rugged coastal cliffs slashed by narrow river gorges. The rivers flowing down from the interior, such as the *Guadalaviar* and the *Júcar*, which surge down in spate after thunder showers or when the snow melts depositing fertile alluvial soil along the coast, provide water for the irrigation of the thirsty lands lying in the rain shadow of the hills. The irrigation system, first constructed by the Romans and later developed by the Moors, makes Valencia the most fertile part of Spain. An ancient code of regulations provides for the equitable distribution of the precious water, which is carried far and wide throughout the region in a network of countless canals and smaller channels and stored up during the winter in reservoirs (*pantanos*) against the summer drought. The irrigated areas (the *campo de regadío*) form the *huertas*, in which crops grow and ripen so rapidly that several harvests can be taken in a year. The main crops are wheat, maize, lucerne, vegetables and, particularly round the marshy *Albufera* lagoon, rice, which requires to grow in water for many weeks. In the shade of the orange-, apricot-, almond- and fig-trees, melons, tomatoes and other vegetables are grown. More attractive than the huertas, on which the fruit-trees are frequently set out in regular geometric formation, are the areas where the fruit orchards are planted on terraces, with clumps of slender palms and cypresses adding variety to the scene. On the non-irrigated land, the *campo secano*, olives, vines and carobs flourish. – The little white houses of the peasants (*hortelanos*) are scattered about at regular intervals in the green of the huertas. The creaking water-wheels (*norias*) of the Moors, powered by donkeys, are increasingly giving place to electric pumps. – The capital, **Valencia**, is one of the most attractive towns in Spain. Its port, *El Grao*, exports the produce of the huertas.

Adjoining Valencia on the S is **MURCIA**, where the Andalusian Mountains reach the sea. The northern ranges run parallel to the coast, ending in the limestone promontory of *Cabo de la Nao*; much of the southern range has sunk and only isolated fragments like the Sierra de Cartagena still rise out of the coastal plain, formed of soil deposited by the rivers, which with the exception of the *Río Seguara* are short and have a poor flow.

The climate is very hot and dry. From the end of July until the end of September the dreaded *calina* (heat haze) blankets the countryside: the sky appears bluish grey, and the rising sun and moon gleam redly through the brownish haze on the horizon. Thinly populated except in the oases along the river valleys, the region is a desert-like salt steppe on which only esparto grass and a meagre covering of scrub can grow. Some cultivation is made possible by irrigation, but this is limited by the shortage of water. In the huertas of **Murcia**, *Totana* and *Lorca* oranges, lemons, mulberries and dates are grown, and **Elche** is famous for its forest of date-palms, originally planted by the Arabs.

In the area around Valencia industry as well as agriculture is well developed – silk and wool, papermaking, the extraction of salt from the coastal lagoons, fishing and the processing and canning of agricultural produce. There are also lead, zinc and iron mines, particularly in the *Sierra de Cartagena*. – As a result of the levelling influence of tourism along the coasts the inhabitants have lost much of their distinctive individuality, now preserved only in traditional folk events.

EXTREMADURA is the western continuation of the Meseta, but in this region the tableland is more deeply slashed by the trough valleys of the *Tajo* (Tagus) and *Guadiana* and their tributaries. On the N it is separated from León and Old Castile by the *Sierra de Gata* (1735 m), the *Sierra de Béjar* and the *Sierra de Gredos* (2592 m), falls away towards Andalusia in the gently sloping *Sierra Morena*, and is divided by the *Sierra de Guadalupe* (1736 m) into **Extremadura Alta** (Upper Extremadura: Taja valley, Cáceres province) and **Extremadura Baja** (Lower Extremadura: Guadiana valley, Badajoz province).

The region is dry, and much of it is covered with stony moorland (*jarales* or *tomillares*), particularly at the foot of the Sierra de Gata (the area known as *Las Hurdes*, where wheat-growing has recently been developed on a considerable scale). The most interesting town in Extremadura is

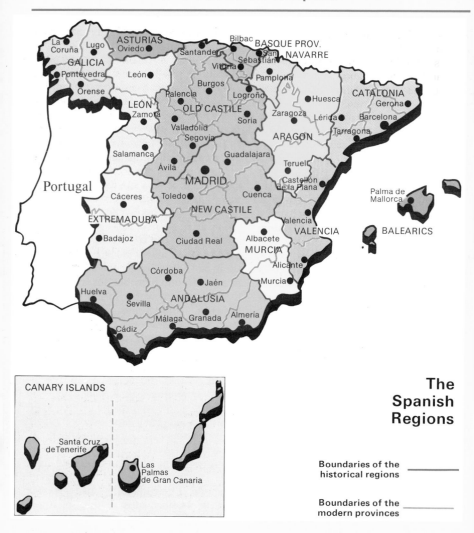

The Spanish Regions

Boundaries of the historical regions _____

Boundaries of the modern provinces _____

Mérida, with numerous remains of the Roman period. Other places well worth visiting are **Plasencia, Badajoz, Cáceres** and **Trujuillo**, with their fine buildings of the period of the Conquistadors, and the monasteries of _Guadalupe_ and _Yuste_.

The growing of corn and pulses is confined to the Cáceres area and Extremadura Baja, always subject to the hazards of inundation by the rivers and devastation by swarms of migratory locusts (_langostas_) from the moorland regions. Vines, olives, figs and almonds grow in the valleys, mulberries only in the Plasencia area, where the hillsides are terraced to form orchards. Pig-farming flourishes in the oak-forests of Extremadura, and the hams produced here are reckoned to be the best in Spain. – From time immemorial Extremadura has been traversed in the winter months by flocks of transhumant merino sheep, which come down from the Meseta in the autumn to seek fresh grazing, under the system known as the _Mesta_. In order to avoid conflicts between the settled peasant farmers and the owners of the sheep a special court, the Consejo de la Mesta, was set up in 1526, and in 1834 it was provided by statute that a strip of grazing land 90 yards wide (the _cañada_) must be left on either side of main roads for the use of the sheep-drovers.

In recent years many rivers have been dammed to form reservoirs (_embalses_) which supply water for irrigation and the production of hydroelectric power. Thus under the "Badajoz Plan" some 1150 sq. km of land in the Guadiana valley were brought into cultivation in a project which involved the building of several dams, the construction of 350 km of irrigation channels and the provision of roads, railways, industrial plants and some 1500 villages and townships.

ANDALUSIA (Andalucía) is still, in spite of the extensive developments along its coasts, the Spain of our imagination. It is a land of fascinating contrasts – of snow-capped mountains and massive coastal dunes, of sun-scorched plateaux and lush green huertas along the rivers, of palm-groves and heaths covered with rock roses. To all this it adds the monuments of a glorious past, culminating in the forest of columns in the Mosque in **Córdoba** and the gleaming red towers and beautiful patios of the Alhambra in **Granada**.

The southern part of Andalusia is dominated by the Andalusian Mountains or *Cordillera Bética*. This range of folded mountains running from the S towards the main Iberian land-mass consists of an inner zone of crystalline schists and an outer zone of Mesozoic and Tertiary sedimentary rocks, which begins at the limestone rock of Gibraltar and extends N to the Jaèn uplands. Later tectonic disturbances have produced collapse basins like the fertile vega of Granada and formed a sheer scarp to the Mediterranean. Although the range includes Spain's highest peak, Mulhacén (3481 m) in the **Sierra Nevada**, it consists mainly of rounded mountains of medium height. The higher altitudes, with large areas of scree, are covered with steppe vegetation, grazing suitable only for goats, and with macchia-like scrub. At lower levels are forests of cork-oaks and chestnuts. The region is thinly populated, and the high valley of the *Alpujarras* has afforded refuge to a population which still shows strong Moorish traits. Very different is the more densely populated coastal strip to the S, which is subject to the influence of the moist sea winds and has become a Mecca of international tourism. This is a region of fruit orchards, plantations of sugar-cane and bananas, vineyards and cotton fields laid out on terraces. **Málaga** has considerable industry and its port handles a large export trade, particularly in its famous wine. **Algeciras** and **Cádiz** are also busy industrial towns.

Between the Andalusian Mountains and the Sierra Morena are the *Andalusian Lowlands*, a former inlet of the sea filled with Tertiary and alluvial deposits and watered by the River *Guadalquivir*. The eastern part of the Guadalquivir basin is a much dissected upland region: only below Seville is it a genuine lowland area.

In this area are the **Marismas**, great expanses of fenland occupied by waterfowl and herds of bulls. The hot dry uplands are still largely covered with steppe country and areas of grazing for fighting bulls and Andalusian horses. Wheat and vegetables, vines and citrus fruits are grown only in those areas where irrigation is available. Andalusia's capital, **Seville**, lies in a fertile garden landscape of this kind. The province of Cádiz, turned towards the sea, is a region of large landowners and sharp contrasts in the social structure.

Side by side with agriculture mining plays a major part in the economy of Andalusia. The Sierra Moreno produces copper (Río Tinto) and zinc (Linares), the Andalusian Mountains lead, silver and iron (Almería). Stock-farming (horses, mules, cattle, fighting bulls) also makes an important contribution.

The Andalusians have preserved many characteristics from their Moorish past. In contrast to the sedate and dignified Castilians, they are noted for their carefree gaiety and a vein of almost Oriental fantasy. The women of Andalusia are renowned for their grace and their ready wit (*sal* or "salt"); the men are born to play the character of Gracioso in the Spanish theatre, the Figaro of the operas, the toreador (in Spanish actually *torero*) in the bullring.

The **BALEARIC ISLANDS**, lying off the SE coast of Spain in the western Mediterranean, between 1° and 4° longitude E and between 38° and 40° latitude N, consist of the Balearics proper, the *Islas Baleares* – the two main islands of **Majorca** (*Mallorca*, 3640 sq. km) and **Minorca** (*Menorca*, 700 sq. km) – and the smaller group of the *Islas Pitiusas*, made up of **Ibiza** (in the local dialect *Eivissa*, 572 sq. km) and **Formentera** (100 sq. km), together with some 150 smaller islands, including *Cabrera* (17 sq. km), off the S coast of Majorca, and numbers of rocky islets, some used for military or nautical purposes, others totally unoccupied. The whole group of islands makes up the provinces of the Balearics (*Baleares:* total area 5014 sq. km), the capital of which is **Palma de Mallorca**, on a bay in the island of Majorca. – The name of the Balearics is derived from the Latin *balearii* ("slingsmen"), which may come either from the Greek *ballein* ("throw") or the Semitic *ba'al yarah* ("skilled in using the sling"). Pitiusas comes from the Greek name, meaning "islands of pines".

The Balearics are the continuation, broken off from the main mass, of the Andalusian Mountains, which extend on the mainland of Spain from Gibraltar by way of the Sierra Nevada to Cabo de la Nao. In the late Tertiary era the islands were cut off from the Iberian peninsula by tectonic movements which resulted in massive collapses of the land and marine transgressions. The archipelago is now separated from the mainland by a trough up to 1500 m deep. The Balearics and the Pitiusas each have their own continental shelf.

The main island, **Majorca**, is made up of three distinct parts. In the NW is the Sierra del Norte, a range of wooded heights some 90 km long and rising to 1443 m in *Puig Mayor* which falls to the sea in steep and rugged cliffs, forming picturesque rocky inlets known as *calas*. To the SE are the hills of the Serranía de Levante, with stalactitic caves, which rise to a height of 509 m in San Salvador and form numerous *calas* along the coast. Between these two ranges, in which Mesozoic limestones predominate, is the Llanura del Centro, a central plain of pluvial red earth deeply indented on the N by the large bays of Alcudia and Pollensa and to the SW by Palma Bay, with a number of individual hills of some height like Randa (542 m) and Santa Magdalena (304 m).

North-western **Minorca** is occupied by gently rolling uplands, rising to 357 m in *Monte Toro* and cut by fjord-like inlets along the NW coast. The SW of the island is made up of an extensive plain fringed by cliffs and small rocky coves.

Ibiza is a hilly island, with a number of hills rising above 400 m (Atalayasa, 476 m) and numerous bays round the coast. **Formentera**, separated from Ibiza by a strait only 4 km across, is mainly flat, rising gently in the E to 192 m (La Mola) and in the W to 107 m (Guillen).

In view of the sparse flow of the rivers (with the exception of the Río de Santa Eulalia on Ibiza) the islands long depended for their water supply on rainwater or ground-water collected in cisterns and raised to the surface by windmills (smaller than those used for grinding corn or pressing olives) or norias (a type of water-wheel worked by animal power which was introduced by the Moors). Nowadays these primitive but efficient and economical methods are being replaced by modern irrigation systems fed by water under pressure. Majorca and Ibiza have abundant reserves of fresh water, Minorca only small reserves, Formentera hardly any.

The maritime situation of the Balearics gives them a temperate Meditrerranean climate, with mild, wet and almost always frost-free winters and dry and not unduly hot summers. There are, however, considerable differences between the various islands. Cold dry winds blowing from the N (the *tramontana*) create relatively severe conditions on Minorca and Formentera, reflected in the typical wind-blown vegetation. On Majorca they come up against the barrier of the Sierra del Norte, and during the summer they take the form of fresh winds blowing down from the hills (the *mestral*) which bring some coolness to the central plain.

Of all the Balearic Islands Ibiza has the steadiest climate, with the temperature seldom rising above 30 °C (86 °F) in summer and rarely falling below freezing point in winter. The average annual rainfall decreases steadily from Minorca to the more southerly islands (Mahón 580 mm (23 in.), Palma de Mallorca 480 mm (19 in.), Ibiza 350 mm (13¾ in.), Formentera under 200 mm (8 in.)). On Majorca the Sierra del Norte acts as a weather barrier: while in the hills, at the monastery of Lluch, the precipitation (in winter frequently in the form of snow) exceeds 1460 mm (57½ in.), in the plain it is only between 400 and 500 mm (15¾ and 19¾ in.).

The province of the Balearics has a population of 685,000, almost all Roman Catholics – 530,000 on Majorca, 56,000 on Minorca, 54,000 on Ibiza and Formentera. The highest density is in Palma de Mallorca; the most sparsely populated of the major islands is Formentera, the inhabitants of which – no doubt in consequence of the climate – have the highest life expectancy in Spain.

The inhabitants of the islands differ both in type and in character from the people of mainland Spain. They are stolid and straightforward people, whose qualities and peculiarities can be seen most easily during the winter, when the swarms of additional workers who come in during the main tourist season have departed. The vicissitudes of history, on these islands lying on the main Mediterranean traffic routes, have produced, from the mingling of Moorish, Jewish and Catalan ethnic groups of roughly comparable size and smaller numbers of Italians, Basques, French, Greeks (particularly on Ibiza) and British (particularly on Minorca) a distinctive dark-haired thickset human type; and the most recent influx of immigrants has brought in fresh influences from Central Europe, Scandinavia and North America.

The original inhabitants of the Balearics, renowned in antiquity for their skill with the sling, were Iberians, who were subjugated by the Carthaginians in the 3rd c. B.C. and in 123 B.C. came under Roman rule. The Roman consul Quintus Caecilius Metellus, who after conquering the islands was granted the style of Balearicus, founded Pollentia (near Alcudia) and Palmaria (Palma) on Majorca. Later the islands fell successively into the hands of the Vandals, the Visigoths, the Byzantines, the Franks and the Moors (798). In 1229 King Jaime I of Aragon, el Conquistador, conquered Majorca and gave it to his younger son as an independent kingdom. In the 14th c., however, it was reunited with Aragon. From 1708 to 1782 and from 1798 to 1802 Minorca was occupied by Britain, with a brief period of French rule after a naval victory in 1756.

There are important archaeological remains dating from prehistoric and early historical times on Majorca and Minorca. They belong mainly to the Talayot Culture (from the Arabic *atalaya*, "watchtower"), a megalithic culture which flourished between 1500 B.C. and the Roman occupation, building the *talayots* (round towers constructed of massive blocks of stone) from which it gets its name. – Other monuments of the Talayot Culture are the *taulas* (from Latin *tabula*, "table") which are found only on Minorca. These are T-shaped stone structures consisting of an upright monolith supporting a horizontal slab. – Also notable are the *navetas* ("little boats") found particularly on Minorca but also on Majorca – the tombs of tribal leaders, built of stone in the form of an uptured boat, which may have been used for habitation in a later period.

The **CANARY ISLANDS** (*Islas Canarias*, "Dog Islands"), also known as the *Islas Afortunadas* ("Fortunate Islands"), which have belonged to Spain since the 15th c., lie between 100 and 500 km from the NW coast of Africa (Cape Juby), between longitude 13° and 18° W and between latitude 27° and 29° N (like Cairo and Florida). There are 13 islands, with a total area of 7273 sq. km and a population of 1,520,000, which form the provinces of Tenerife and Las Palmas. The province of Tenerife includes the *western group* of islands, with **Tenerife, Gomera, La Palma** and **Hierro** (*Ferro*), the province of Las Palmas the *eastern group*, comprising **Gran Canaria, Lanzarote, Fuerteventura** and five minor islands (*Alegranza, Graciosa*, etc.).

The Canaries are of volcanic formation. Above the diabase formations which are frequently found, particularly on Fuerteventura, as outcrops, are layers of scories and lava deposited by a long series of eruptions which have taken place since the Miocene period, leaving huge calderas on La Palma and Tenerife and also on Hierro and Gran Canaria. Later eruptions of stones, ash and lava filled up almost completely the huge cavity of Tenerife known as the Cañadas and built up the *Pico de Teide*, a volcanic cone rising to 3718 m above sea level. Subsequent major eruptions devastated La Palma in 1677, Lanzarote in 1730–36 and 1824 and the NW coast of Tenerife in 1705, 1706, 1796 and 1798. The most recent eruption on the Canaries was on La Palma in 1971. The effects of erosion are everywhere to be seen in the wide valleys, rich in humus, and the deeply indented gorges (*barrancos*), particularly on the islands to the W, which are almost without natural harbours, being edged by steep cliffs with only occasional stretches of sandy beach.

The climate of the coastal regions of the Canaries, under the influence of the sea, is mild and equable. The average winter temperature in Las Palmas, Puerto de la Cruz and Santa Cruz de la Palma is 16–18 °C (61–64 °F), the same as the French Riviera in May, while the average for August is 23–24 °C (73–75 °F) barely higher than on the Riviera. The humidity of the air in the coastal regions is low, as is the rainfall (an annual 450 mm ($17\frac{3}{4}$ in.) in Puerto de la Cruz, some 600 mm ($22\frac{3}{4}$ in.) at Laguna), with practically no rain in summer. The prevailing winds are the NE trades, which blow mainly in summer, forming a bank of cloud on the N side of the islands between about 700 and 1600 m and driving back the cloud-bringing winds off the sea as they pursue their course down the S side.

In the dry summit regions the blazing heat of the day is followed almost without transition by a sharp drop in temperature at night. In winter the northern limit of the trade winds sometimes moves S, and the SW counter-trade wind blowing above them comes down to the N coasts as a parching S wind: this is the *tiempo de sur*. In periods of low atmospheric pressure there are also dry SE winds which carry with them clouds of yellow desert dust and occasionally swarms of locusts, reaching as far as Gran Canaria. These afflict particularly the arid islands to the E, Lanzarote and Fuerteventura, whose winters, thanks to the colder sea water, are less mild than on the more westerly islands.

The existence of the archipelago of the Canary Islands was known in ancient times. In the course of their voyages of exploration along the West African coast the Phoenicians, and later the Carthaginians visited the islands. The Romans, to whom the Canaries were known as the "Happy Islands" or "The Islands of the Blessed", must have sent ships there, as is verified by finds of amphora. However, little is known about the history of the islands before the arrival of the Spaniards. The ancient inhabitants (called *Guanches* in Tenerife) continued until well into the 15th c. to live in the style of the New

Stone Age. In 1402–06 a Norman nobleman named Jean de Béthencourt, a feudal vassal of the crown of Castile, conquered Lanzarote, Fuerteventura, Gomera and Hierro and converted the inhabitants to Christianity. The conquest of Gran Canaria and Tenerife by the Spaniards began only in the second half of the 15th c. The last island to be subjugated was Tenerife. Those of the native population who were not sold into slavery soon became assimilated into the stratum of their Spanish conquerors. Little survived of the culture of the ancient people of the Canaries; however a curious method of communication still exists today on Gomera – a whistling language which is audible over a distance of 4–6 km and the *gofio*, a kind of gruel made of roasted wheat or maize, still forms an important element of the diet, as it did in the time of the earliest inhabitants.

In 1797 a British fleet commanded by Nelson attacked the town of Santa Cruz de Tenerife but were compelled to withdraw after suffering severe losses. It was here that Nelson lost his arm.

The present population of the islands consists mainly of the descendants of Norman, Flemish, southern Spanish and Irish settlers, whose blood became mingled in due course with that of the native Guanches. In recent years there has been a movement in favour of separation from Spain. – Since 1982 the Canary Islands have formed an autonomous region, the capital of which alternates between Las Palmas and Santa Cruz de Tenerife.

Climate

The climate of the Iberian peninsula, reflecting its varied topography, shows striking contrasts. The *central uplands*, enclosed by mountains, and including the Ebro basin, have all the characteristics of a continental climate, with hot summers and cold winters, wide variations in *temperature* and, in the rain shadow of the Atlantic W winds, low rainfall and moderate humidity. Madrid (alt. 667 m (2188 ft), average annual temperature 13·2 °C (56 °F), January 4·5° (40°), August 23·5° (74°), lowest recorded −11·9° (11°), highest recorded 43·3° (110°)) is said to have "nine months of winter and three months of hell". Zaragoza (alt. 205 m (673 ft)), in the Ebro basin: annual 14·1 °C (57 °F), January 6° (43°), August 23° (73°). An oppressive feature of the exceptionally dry summers is the notorious heat haze (*calina:* see below). – The *rainfall* is mainly in spring and autumn, with a marked low point in July and

August Madrid annual 412 m (16¼ in.), January 27 mm (1$\frac{1}{16}$ in.), February 45 mm (1¾ in.), July 7 mm (¼ in.), August 5 mm ($\frac{3}{16}$ in.), November 57 mm (2¼ in.); Zaragoza annual 312 mm (12¼ in.), January 16 mm ($\frac{5}{8}$ in.), May 43 mm (1¾ in.), August 15 mm ($\frac{5}{8}$ in.), October 36 mm (1¾ in.): – The mountains surrounding the central plateau and rising out of it have a high annual rainfall (between 800 (31½ in.) and 2000 mm (78¾ in.)) from the clouds driven against the hills, and in winter have a deep covering of snow (winter sports).

(Bilbao annual 14·7 °C (58 °F), January 8° (46°), July and August 21·5° (71°), annual rainfall 1212 mm (47¾ in.), minimum August 55 mm (2¼ in.), maximum November 140 mm (5½ in.), 163 days with rain. The Spanish town with the highest rainfall is Santiago de Compostela (annual 1637 mm (64½ in.), maximum January 180 mm (7$\frac{1}{16}$ in.), September to May between 100 mm (4 in.) and 180 mm (7$\frac{1}{16}$ in.) in the month, minimum August 48 mm (1$\frac{7}{8}$ in.)).

The most equable climate on the mainland of Spain is that of the *Mediterranean coast of Catalonia and Valencia*, which is similar to that of the French Riviera but with a milder winter (Barcelona annual 16 °C (61 °F), January 8° (46°); Valencia annual 16·6° (62°), January 10° (50°), August 24·5° (76°); Nice, on the Riviera, annual 13·6° (56°), January 6·5° (44°), July 21·3° (70°)). – *Surface temperature of the sea* on the Costa Brava and Costa Blanca: April 14–15 °C (57–59 °F), May 17° (63°), June 20° (68°), July 23–24° (73–75°), August 25° (77°), September 23–24° (73–75°), October 21° (70°). – As on the Riviera, the *rainfall* occurs in spring and autumn, when it is at its highest (Barcelona annual 600 mm ($23\frac{5}{8}$ in.), minimum January 26 mm (1 in.), July 30 mm ($1\frac{3}{16}$ in.), maximum May 55 mm ($2\frac{1}{4}$ in.), October 95 mm ($3\frac{3}{4}$ in.); Valencia annual 406 mm (16 in.), minimum January 18 mm ($\frac{3}{4}$ in.), August 8 mm ($\frac{3}{8}$ in.), maximum February 35 mm ($1\frac{3}{8}$ in.), November 83 mm ($3\frac{1}{4}$ in.); Nice annual 805 mm ($31\frac{3}{4}$ in.), minimum January 53 mm ($2\frac{1}{8}$ in.), July 23 mm (1 in.), maximum March 68 mm ($2\frac{5}{8}$ in.), October 135 mm ($5\frac{1}{4}$ in.)). At the monastery of Montserrat (alt. 760 m (2493 ft)), however, there is a marked spring maximum (annual 697 mm ($27\frac{1}{2}$ in.), May 100 mm (4 in.), October 74 mm ($2\frac{7}{8}$ in.)).

The *Balearics*, with their maritime situation, have a very equable *Mediterranean climate*, with mild, rainy and almost always frost-free winters, and summers which are dry and not unduly hot (Palma de Mallorca: annual average 16·8 °C (62 °F), January 10·1° (50°), August 24·7° (76°); annual rainfall 480 mm ($18\frac{7}{8}$ in.), minimum July 8 mm ($\frac{3}{8}$ in.), maximum October 63 mm ($2\frac{1}{2}$ in.); Punta Grossa de Sóller, on the N coast of Majorca, which has a high rainfall in winter: annual 757 mm ($29\frac{3}{4}$ in.), minumum July 9 mm ($\frac{3}{8}$ in.), maximum October 135 mm ($5\frac{1}{4}$ in.)). The wettest area is in the mountains near the monastery of Lluc, with annual precipitation (in winter frequently in the form of snow) of 1460 mm ($57\frac{1}{2}$ in.). Mahón on Minorca has temperatures similar to Palma de Mallorca; annual rainfall 580 mm ($22\frac{3}{4}$ in.), April 60 mm ($2\frac{3}{8}$ in.), July 7 mm ($\frac{1}{4}$ in.), October 90 mm ($3\frac{1}{2}$ in.). Towards the S the rainfall decreases: Ibiza annual 350 mm ($13\frac{3}{4}$ in.), Formentera under 200 mm ($7\frac{7}{8}$ in.). – The temperature of the sea in the Balearics is similar to that of the Costa Blanca (see above).

The province of *Murcia*, where palms grow in profusion, has a climate of African type (Murcia annual 17·9 °C (64 °F), January 10·5° (51°), August 26·5° (80°), absolute maximum 44·8° (113°); Almería annual 18·5° (65°), January 12·5° (55°), August 26° (79°)). From the end of July to the end of September the dreaded *calina* (heat haze) settles down oppressively on the landscape; the sky appears bluish grey, and the rising and setting sun and moon gleam redly through the brownish haze on the horizon. *Rainfall* is low even in winter: Murcia annual 354 mm (14 in.), minimum July 4 mm ($\frac{3}{16}$ in.), maximum October 44 mm ($1\frac{3}{4}$ in.); Almería annual 205 mm (8 in.), July and August each 2 mm ($\frac{1}{16}$ in.), November 35 mm ($1\frac{3}{8}$ in.); Cabo de Gata, SE of Almería, annual 122 mm ($4\frac{3}{4}$ in.), July and August each 2 mm ($\frac{1}{16}$ in.), November 25 mm (1 in.).

The *southern Mediterranean coast* of Spain, thanks to its hothouse situation on a narrow strip of land under high mountains which are snow-clad in winter, has the *warmest winter on the mainland of Europe*: Málaga annual 18·6 °C (65 °F), January 13° (55°), August 26° (79°), absolute minimum 0° (32°), maximum 43·2° (110°). The *rainfall* occurs almost entirely from autumn to spring (Málaga annual 600 mm ($23\frac{5}{8}$ in.), minumum July 3 mm ($\frac{3}{32}$ in.), maximum November 88 mm ($3\frac{1}{2}$ in.)). At Málaga the sky is overcast on only 40 days in the year, and 195 days are absolutely cloudless. – The climate of *Gibraltar* is somewhat cooler, with higher rainfall in winter (annual 17·3 °C (63 °F), January 13° (55°), August 23·5° (74°); annual rainfall 845 mm ($33\frac{1}{4}$ in.), minumum July 1 mm ($\frac{1}{32}$ in.), maximum November 180 mm ($7\frac{1}{8}$ in.)). – The Spanish enclave of *Melilla* in North Africa, lying opposite Almería, has similar temperatures to Almería but a higher rainfall: annual 18·3 °C (65 °F), January 13° (55°), August 25° (77°); annual rainfall 389 mm ($15\frac{1}{4}$ in.), minimum August 3 mm ($\frac{3}{32}$ in.), maximum November 70 mm ($2\frac{3}{4}$ in.).

On the *Atlantic coast of Andalusia* the summers are less hot and the average annual temperature accordingly lower: Tarifa annual average 16·9 °C (62 °F), January 12·5° (55°), August 23° (73°). Rainfall is heavy in winter: Tarifa annual 683 mm ($26\frac{7}{8}$ in.), minimum July and August each 1 mm ($\frac{1}{32}$ in.), maximum November 120 mm ($4\frac{3}{4}$ in.).

In *inland Andalusia* the heat increases again and the rainfall decreases: Seville annual average 19·6 °C (67 °F), January 11·5° (53°), August 28·5° (83°), absolute maximum 47·8° (118°); annual rainfall 493 mm ($19\frac{1}{2}$ in.), minimum July 2 mm ($\frac{1}{16}$ in.), August 3 mm ($\frac{3}{32}$ in.), maximum November 74 mm ($2\frac{7}{8}$ in.); the nights are, however, distinctly cool in winter in Seville. The town of Écija, E of Seville, is known as the "frying-pan (*sartén*) of Andalusia" on account of its scorching summer heat.

The climate of the *Canary Islands*, lying between latitude 27° and 29° N, is mild and equable in the coastal regions, thanks to the influence of the sea. *Air temperatures* at sea level show little variation on all the islands (minimum January and February 17–18 °C (63–64 °F)), but *sea temperatures* vary over the year between about 18° and 24° (64° and 75°). In the arid summit regions on Tenerife the blazing heat of the day is followed almost immediately by a sharp drop in temperature. The Pico de Teide (3707 m – 12,190 ft) is capped with snow in winter. – The *rainfall* occurs almost entirely in winter, from about October to March, particularly on the N and E sides of the islands (Santa Cruz de la Palma annual 439 mm ($17\frac{1}{4}$ in.), minimum July and August each 3 mm ($\frac{3}{32}$ in.), maximum November 125 mm ($4\frac{7}{8}$ in.); Puerto de Orotava, on Tenerife, annual 453 mm ($17\frac{7}{8}$ in.), minimum June and July each 2 mm ($\frac{1}{16}$ in.), maximum January 90 mm ($3\frac{1}{2}$ in.); Santa Cruz de Tenerife annual 290 mm ($11\frac{1}{2}$ in.), minimum July and August each 1 mm ($\frac{1}{32}$ in.), maximum November 68 mm ($2\frac{3}{4}$ in.); Las Palmas, on Gran Canaria, annual 243 mm ($9\frac{1}{2}$ in.), minimum June 2 mm ($\frac{1}{16}$ in.), maximum November 56 mm ($2\frac{1}{4}$ in.); La Laguna, on Tenerife, alt. 547 m (1795 ft), annual 594 mm ($23\frac{3}{8}$ in.), minimum August 3 mm ($\frac{3}{32}$ in.), maximum November 98 mm ($3\frac{3}{4}$ in.)). – The prevailing NE trade winds, which blow throughout the year but more particularly in summer, form a *bank of cloud* which clings throughout the day to the wooded hillsides between about 700 and 1600 m (2297 and 5250 ft). The S and W sides of the islands, lying in the wind shadow, have little rain and in places are of desert character. This applies to the whole of Lanzarote and Fuerteventura, with no hills of any great heights and colder sea-water: Tefia (on the W coast of Fuertaventura) annual rainfall 112 mm ($4\frac{1}{2}$ in.), minimum July 1 mm ($\frac{1}{32}$ in.), maximum January 36 mm ($1\frac{3}{8}$ in.); Punta Orchilla (on the S coast of Hierro) annual 157 mm ($6\frac{1}{4}$ in.), minimum July 1 mm ($\frac{1}{32}$ in.), maximum November 43 mm ($1\frac{3}{4}$ in.).

State and Government

After Franco's death in November 1975 Juan Carlos became king of Spain. Franco, who had reigned as a dictator since the Spanish Civil War (1936–39), had designated him as his successor. The monarchy is descended from the Bourbon-Anjou house. From 1978 Spain (Estado Español) has been a constitutional monarchy with a parliamentary system of government (Reino de España).

Parliament, the *Cortes*, consists of two houses, the lower houses, *Congreso*, and the Senate, *Senado*. There are 350 members of the Congreso elected for four years. The members of the Senate, who represent the 50 Spanish provinces, number 248 of whom 207 are elected by the provinces and 41 chosen by the king. The Head of State, the President, is also named by the king on the proposal of the Cortes. The provinces are governed by a provincial council ("Diputación Provincial") and a civil governor ("Gobernador"), who represents the central government in Madrid.

After a transitional period, during which concessions had to be made to the Right, Juan Carlos named the politician Adolfo Suárez González as Head of State in 1976. With the latter's help he began to introduce the long overdue reforms. Democratic parties and the Communist party ("Partido Comunista Español", PCE) as well as independent trade unions were again permitted.

In the parliamentary elections of 1977 the victors were the Union of the Democratic Centre ("Unión del Centro Democrático", UCD) under Suárez. In 1982 the majority of votes in the parliamentary elections were cast for the Socialist Workers' Party ("Partido Socialista Obrero Español, PSOE) under Felipe González Márquez, a development for which the regional elections had paved the way. In the parliamentary elections of 1986 the PSOE were the victors. González was confirmed in the office of Prime Minister.

The new constitution of 1978 guarantees the citizens of the country basic democratic rights including universal suffrage from the age of 18, freedom of opinion and religion (the population is mainly Roman Catholic) as well as the right of divorce. The death penalty – with the exception of military law – was abolished.

From now on each individual region sought greater independence from the central government in Madrid. At first the independence movements arose principally in those regions where the inhabitants by reason of language and culture differed greatly from the Castilian-speaking Spaniards. These ethnic groups are the Basques ("Euskaldun"), the Galicians ("Gallegos") and the largest group, the Catalans ("Catalanes"). In order to put an end to the increasing discontent of the minorities, Catalonian ("Catalan", "Catala"), Galician ("Gallego", "Galego") and Basque ("Vascuence", "Euskera") were recognised as

national languages beside the official language of Castilian. Catalonian dialects are not only spoken in Catalonia but also in the neighbouring southern provinces of Valencia and in the Balearics.

In addition regionalisation of the country was put into operation. The process which began in 1979 was completed in 1983. Spain today is divided into 17 autonomous regions (see p. 8). Each autonomous region has its own parliament consisting of a single chamber and its own regional government. The North African towns of Ceuta and Melilla, which are claimed by Morocco, have belonged to Spain since the 15th/16th c. They now form part of the Spanish provinces of Cádiz and Málaga respectively.

In size, density of population and economic development the autonomous regions reveal considerable differences. Highly developed areas – as for example Catalonia – contrast sharply with poorly developed territories such as Estremadura.

Side by side with the historical regions of Spain there were in places shifts in territorial relationship. In the north of Old Castile the former province of Santander has declared itself the autonomous region of Cantabria; in the north-east the former province of Longroño has become an autonomous region under the name of La Rioja. The union of the other provinces of Old Castile with the provinces of the old kingdom of León has given rise to the autonomous region of Castile-León. New Castile in the south was joined to the province of Albacete, belonging to the historic region of Murcia and which included a large part of the territory of "La Mancha". The original provinces of New Castile and Albacete were united to form the autonomous region of Castile-La Mancha. Madrid, the capital, situated in New Castile forms an independent autonomous region. – The inhabitants of the autonomous regions are seeking a federal state. Only in the Basque country, where there are strong "nationalist" undercurrents, has there been a long-lasting aim of complete independence from the motherland. Acts of violence by the separatist movement ETA (a military organisation) often cause unrest and lead to anti-terrorist measures by their opponents.

Spain is a member of a number of international organisations, including the United Nations (UN), the North Atlantic Treaty Organisation (NATO) and the European Economic Community (EEC). The entry of Spain into the EEC had been delayed again and again, as other EEC countries, which also marketed agricultural produce, regarded Spain as an unwelcome competitor. France and Italy in particular, as wine producing countries, opposed the application of Spain for membership of the community. Since Spain's membership of NATO and the presence of American military bases on Spanish soil is opposed by the population, a referendum was held in 1986 to determine whether Spain should remain in NATO. A majority of the electorate voted in favour. González, the head of the government, declared the result of the referendum to be "a success for the entire Spanish nation". Rural regions, such as Andalusia and Estremadura were the strongest supporters of the government's request to approve membership.

History

From the prehistoric period to the Moorish conquest (c. 10000 B.C.–A.D. 711). – The territory of Spain was already populated in the Palaeolithic period. The earliest attested inhabitants are the **Ligurians** on the NE coast and the **Iberians**, probably immigrants from North Africa, in the E and S. The **Basques**, in the western Pyrenean region, are thought to be the remnant of a pre-Indo-European population.

About 1000 B.C. Late Palaeolithic: notable cave paintings (Altamira, El Castillo, etc.).

5000–2000 Neolithic: cave paintings (scenes of war and hunting) in E Spain.

2000–1600 **Megalithic culture** (Copper Age): monumental tombs and cult structures.

About 1100 The **Phoenicians** establish trading posts on the S coast – Gadri (Cádiz), Malaka (Málaga), Tartessos, etc.

After 1000 The **Celts**, who in subsequent centuries mingle with the Iberians to become **Celtiberians**, thrust into the interior of the country.

700 onwards A number of ports – Emporion (Ampurias), Mainake (at Torre del Mar, 30 km E of Málaga), etc. – are established by **Greeks**, mainly Ionians from the Phocaean colony of Massalia (Marseilles).

600 onwards The **Carthaginians** drive out the Greeks.

236–206 After the First Punic War the Carthaginians under Hamilcar Barca, Hasdrubal and Hannibal extend their colonial power from the Tajo (Tagus) to the Ebro.

About 225 Foundation of Carthago Nova (Cartagena).

219 At the beginning of the Second Punic War Hannibal destroys Saguntum, an ally of **Rome**.

201 Under a peace treaty with Rome Carthage gives up its Spanish possessions.

197 Establishment of the Roman provinces of Hispania Citerior in the NE and Hispania Ulterior in the SW.
A series of risings – by the Lusitanians under the leadership of Viriathus (154–139); the Celtiberians (143–133), the Asturians, Cantabrians and other tribes (25–19), etc. – hamper the complete subjection of the peninsula but not the rapid linguistic and cultural Romanisation of the country (with the exception of the Basque territories).

81–72 The Roman praetor Sertorius, a supporter of Marius, tries to establish an independent Celtiberian state.

45 Julius Caesar defeats Pompey's sons and supporters at Munda (SW of Córdoba) and becomes dictator. His veterans are settled on the properties of his defeated rivals.

27 Spain is divided into the provinces of Hispania Tarraconensis (in the N and E), Lusitania (in the W between the Duero/Douro and the Guadiana) and Baetica (the original Hispania Ulterior).

19 The Iberian peninsula is fully incorporated into the Roman Empire by Augustus.

The Romanised population of Spain produces writers like Seneca, Lucan and Martial and the Emperors Trajan, Hadrian and Theodosius (the Great).

A.D. 74 Vespasian grants the principal towns the ius Latii (municipal charters).

100 onwards Beginning of the Christianisation of the Iberian peninsula.

After 400 During the Great Migrations the **Alans** (a tribe from the Iranian steppe) settle in what is now Portugal, the **Vandals** (an East Germanic people) in southern Spain, the **Suevi** (from southern Germany) in the NW.

414 The Visigoths (West Goths), led by King Athaulf, advance into Catalonia (Gotalonia).

429 The Vandals move on into Africa.

466–484 King Eurich, ruler of the Visigothic kingdom of Tolosa, defeats the Suevi and establishes Visigothic rule throughout Spain (except the NW). The oldest Germanic code of law, the "Codex Euricianus", written in Latin, is compiled during his reign.

507–711 After the fall of the kingdom of Tolosa the Visigoths continue to rule Spain, with their capital at Toledo.

551 Under Justinian the **Byzantines** conquer the S coast of Spain, but lose it again by 624.

587 The conversion of the Arian Visigoths to orthodox Catholicism is followed by their rapid amalgamation with the Romanised population.

711 The Arab general Tarik defeats a Visigothic army led by Roderick at Jerez de la Frontera.

Spain under the Moors (711–1492). – During the period of Arab rule the peninsula enjoys an economic and cultural flowering. Eastern and Hellenistic learning is transmitted through Spain to the Christian West.

From 714 Spain (with the exception of the upland regions of Asturias, Galicia and the Basque country) is a province of the Umayyad Caliphate of Damascus.

732 Through his victory at Tours and Poitiers Charles Martel drives the Arabs out of Gaul.

756 The Umayyad Abderrahman I flees to Spain and founds the Emirate of Córdoba, which extends over the whole of the peninsula. The introduction of new crops (rice, sugar, etc.), irrigation and the growing output of silk and weapons make possible a period of great economic prosperity and high cultural achievement. The Arabs show religious tolerance to Christians and Jews. Many Christians become converts to Islam and adopt the Arabic language and Arab customs (the Mozarabs).

778 Charlemagne loses his Spanish conquests after the defeat of his rearguard in the pass of Roncesvalles, in which Roland (hero of the "Chanson de Roland") is killed.

929–1031 **Caliphate of Córdoba.** Abderrahman III assumes the title of Caliph in 929. This was the heyday of Moorish culture in Spain (mosques, terraced gardens adjoining the Alhambra, large library, new palace at Medina Azahara, etc.).

930 The Caliph conquers Toledo, and in the following year NW Africa to beyond Tahert (lost in 979).

985–997 *Almansor* ("the Victorious"), grand vizier of Caliph Hisham II, conquers Barcelona (985), León (987) and Santiago de Compostela (997) – the farthest expansion of Moorish military power in Spain.

1031 Fall of the last Umayyad Caliph, *Hisham III*. The Caliphate of Córdoba is split up into more than 20 independent petty states (*taifas*), later to be reunited by the Almoravides.

1085 *Alfonso VI of Castile* takes Toledo after a five years' siege.

From 1086 The **Almoravides**, a Berber sect from North Africa, responding to a call for help from the Moorish Emirs, defend the Moorish states against Christian attacks under the leadership of Yusuf ibn Tashfin and unite the Muslim S of Spain with their kingdom in North Africa.

1146 The Almoravid kingdom in North Africa is conquered by the Almohades, a fanatical Berber sect, who maintain their position in Spain from 1195 to 1225, continually at war with the Christian kingdoms.

1212 Caliph *Mohammad en-Nasir* suffers a heavy defeat at Las Navas de Tolosa at the hands of the combined armies of Castile, Aragon and Navarre. A number of petty Muslim states are established but cannot prevent the decline of the Almohad empire. The Moors lose Córdoba (1236), Seville (1248), Cádiz (1263) and other towns.

1238–1492 The **Emirate of Granada**, under the Nasrid dynasty.

1238 *Mohammed ibn al-Ahmar*, of the Beni Nasr tribe, establishes the Emirate of Granada (incorporating Málaga and Almería). Granada becomes the wealthiest town in the peninsula and its cultural centre.

1246 Granada is required to pay tribute to the king of Castile.

1275 *Mohammed II*, with the help of the Merinden Sultan Abu Yusuf of Morocco, defeats the Castilians at Éjica and Martos.

1292 The Emirate loses Tarifa to Castile, followed by Gibraltar in 1309 and Algeciras in 1344.

1300–1400 Granada's brilliant cultural heyday (construction of the Alhambra).

1333 Recovery of Gibraltar (until 1462).

1340 *Yusuf I*, allied with the Sultan of Morocco, suffers a heavy defeat on the Salado.

1481 Beginning of the war between Granada and Castile, which gradually conquers the whole of Granadian territory.

1492 After the fall of Málaga (1487) and Granada (1492) Emir *Abdallah Mohammad XI*, known to the Spaniards as Boabdil, retires to North Africa. This is followed by the expulsion of the Moors and the Jews, seriously hampering the further economic development of Spain.

The rise of the Christian states until the union of the two leading kingdoms, Castile and Aragon (c. 718–1516). – The *Reconquista* (recovery by the Christian kingdoms) of the Iberian peninsula, starting in the N, ends in the final *expulsion of the Moors* and the formation of a Spanish national state. The medieval culture of Spain bears the mark of its contact with Islam as well as with the Christian West.

722 *Pelayo*, a Goth, defeats the Moors at Covadonga and founds the **kingdom of Asturias** in the Asturian hills.

About 750 *Alfonso I* unites Asturias with Cantabria and acquires León, Old Castile and Galicia. Under *Alfonso III* León becomes capital.

After 778 The Counties of *Catalonia* (capital Barcelona) and *Navarre* are formed out of Charlemagne's Spanish March.

About 900 The County of *Castile* (named after the castles built for defence against the Moors) comes into being.

After 910 Alfonso III's sons divide the kingdom into Galicia, Asturias and León.

1029 King *Sancho III of Navarre* inherits the County of Castile. The division of his kingdom between his three sons leads to the formation of the **kingdoms of Castile, Navarre** and **Aragon**.

1037 *Ferdinand I* (Fernando I), the Great, of Castile wins León.

1072 *Alfonso VI of Castile* reunites the kingdom (which had again been split up), enlarges it by the addition of part of Navarre and in 1085 conquers New Castile and Toledo. *Rodrigo Diaz*, the Cid (from Arabic *sayyid*, "lord"), later to become the Spanish national hero, briefly enters the service of the Moors; in 1094 he conquers Valencia.

1109 Portugal becomes an independent County (from 1139 a kingdom).

1118 *Alfonso I of Aragon* extends his kingdom during his wars with the Moors and conquers Zaragoza (later his capital). Failure of attempts to unite Castile and Aragon.

1130 *Alfonso VII of Castille* becomes emperor, with authority over all the Christian states in Spain, but his empire is divided up again by the laws of succession into Castile and León.

1137 Union of Aragon and Catalonia.

1212 In the battle of *Las Navas de Tolosa* the combined knightly armies of Castile, Aragon and Navarre win a decisive victory over the Almohad Caliph.

1229–38 *Jaime I of Aragon* victorious over the Moors. Conquest of the Balearics (1229–35), Valencia (1238), etc.

1230 *Ferdinand III of Castile* finally unites Castile and León, and conquers Córdoba (1236), Murcia (1243) and Seville (1248).

1234–1441 Navarre under French rule.

1263 *Alfonso X of Castile* (from 1257 also king of Germany) conquers Cádiz and Cartagena.

1282 *Pedro III of Aragon* gains possession of Sicily.

1295 Under the peace of Anagni *Jaime II of Aragon* gives up Sicily, and in return receives Sardinia and Corsica from the Pope.

From 1307 The Cortes (the estates representing the Church, the nobility and the towns) of Aragon, Catalonia and Valencia meet together.

1443 Aragon acquires the kingdom of Naples.

1458 *Juan II*, king of Navarre since 1425, becomes king of Aragon on the death of his brother Alfonso V.

1469 The marriage of **Ferdinand II of Aragon** (1479–1516) and **Isabel of Castile** (1474–

1504) unites the two kingdoms. Under the *"Catholic Monarchs"* the transition to an absolute monarchy takes place.

1486–88 Reorganisation of the Inquisition in Aragon and Castile by *Jiménez de Cisneros* (from 1495 Archbishop of Toledo).

1492 The *conquest of Granada* ends the Reconquista. Thereafter the fanatical expulsion of the Moors and Jews begins.
Isabella gives her support to *Christopher Columbus* (Cristóbal Colón), whose voyages of exploration prepare the way for the establishment of the Spanish colonial empire in America.

1494 Under the *Treaty of Tordesillas* a demarcation line between Spanish and Portuguese colonial interests in America is laid down.

1504 Ferdinand II recovers Naples and Sicily after the fall of the royal house (a collateral line of the Aragonese kings).

1515 Navarre up to the Pyrenees falls to Spain.

Spain as a world power – until the Peninsular war (1516–1813). – Spain rises to international importance in the 16th c. through the enormous expansion of its territories in Europe and the colonies and as a centre of the *Counter-Reformation*. After the death of Philip II it loses its dominating position, since the numerous wars it fights to maintain the Catholic faith ruin the country economically and financially.

1516 *Charles I*, a Habsburg, becomes king of Castile and Aragon. After the death of his grandfather Maximilian I he inherits the Habsburg territories and becomes in 1519 Holy Roman Emperor as **Charles V** (coronation in Rome 1530). He is now ruler of Spain, the Netherlands, Sardinia, Naples, Sicily, Milan, Franche-Comté and numerous American colonies. He hands over the Habsburg possessions in Germany to his brother *Ferdinand* in 1521.

1519–35 **Establishment of colonial rule in America**. The Spanish conquistadors *Cortés* and *Pizarro* conquer Mexico (1519–21), Peru (1531–34) and Chile (from 1535). Vast quantities of gold and silver are brought back to Spain.

1520–21 The rising of the *Comuneros* (the towns of Castile) is repressed, and **absolutism** prevails: the Cortes lose their importance.

1521–56 Charles V fights *five wars against France* in order to maintain Spanish hegemony in Italy and Burgundy.

1534 *Ignacio de Loyola* founds the Jesuit order (the Society of Jesus).

1535–41 Charles V occupies Tunis and Algiers.

1556 Charles V abdicates and withdraws to the monastery of Yuste.

1556–98 *Philip II*, Charles's son, assumes the leadership of the *Counter-Reformation* in Europe. With the help of the **Inquisition** he fights heresy in Spain and has the Christianised Moors (Moriscos) in Andalusia almost completely exterminated.

1559 The Treaty of Câteau-Cambrésis ends the war with France for supremacy in Italy and Burgundy.

1563–84 Building of the Escorial.

1565–72 Conquest of the Philippines.

1571 in the naval battle of *Lepanto* the Turkish fleet is annihilated by Spanish warships.

1580 Spain is united with Portugal in a personal union (which lasts until 1640). The acquisition of the Portuguese colonial possessions enlarges the Spanish empire to its greatest extent.

1581 The fanatical severity with which Philip II and his general the *Duke of Alba* seek to repress the Protestant and patriotic *rising in the Netherlands* leads to the secession of the northern Netherlands under *William of Orange*.

1588 With the destruction of the Armada in the Channel Spain loses the fight with Britain for command of the sea.

1609–10 Expulsion of the last Moriscos and Jews (c. 600,000) from southern Spain in the reign of *Philip III*.

1618–48 Spain takes part in the *Thirty Years War* on the side of the Austrian Habsburgs.

1621 Resumption of the fight against the free Netherlands (whose independence Spain has later to recognise under the Treaty of Westphalia).

1640 Portugal dissolves its union with Spain.

1652 The *rising of the Catalans* (which had begun in 1640) is repressed.

1659 Under the Peace of the Pyrenees Spain cedes Roussillon, Cerdagne and part of Flanders to France.

1678 Spain gives up the Franche-Comté, now conquered by France.

1701–13 In the **War of the Spanish Succession** the Bourbon claimant, *Philip of Anjou*, a grandson of Louis XIV, fights for recognition against the Austrian Habsburgs, Britain and the Netherlands.

1713 Under the Treaty of Utrecht *Philip V* cedes Spanish territory in the Netherlands, Milan and Naples to Austria, Sicily to Savoy, Minorca (until 1783) and Gibraltar to Britain, but retains the Spanish colonies.

1717–30 Unsuccessful *conflicts with Austria* for Sardinia and Sicily.

1735 The kingdom of Naples and Sicily passes to a collateral line of the Spanish Bourbons, as does the Duchy of Parma and Piacenza in 1748.

1759–88 The Bourbon *Charles III* (Duke of Parma 1731–35, King of Naples and Sicily 1723–59) rules in the spirit of enlightened absolutism.

1763 At the end of the *Seven Years War* Spain loses Florida to Britain but acquires W Louisiana from France.

1767 Expulsion of the Jesuits.

1783 Under the Treaty of Versailles at the end of the War of American Independence Spain recovers Florida and Minorca from Britain.

1788–1808 Advised by his favourite *Manuel de Godoy, Charles IV* leads Spain into total dependence on *Napoleon*.

1801 Return of Louisiana to France.

1805 Destruction of the French and Spanish fleet by Nelson at Trafalgar.

1808 A rising in Aranjuez overthrows the Francophile Godoy and compels Charles IV to abdicate in favour of his son *Ferdinand* (Fernando) in March. Seeing his interests in the Iberian peninsula in jeopardy, Napoleon occupies Spain and compels both Charles and *Ferdinand VII* to abdicate. Napoleon's brother Joseph becomes King of Spain, his brother-in-law Murat king of Naples.

A revolt by the people of Madrid against Marshal Murat's troops on 2 May marks the beginning of a *Spanish national rising*. Juntas (committees) are formed to organise a guerilla war against French rule. A French army surrenders at Bailén in July, and Joseph flees from Madrid. A British army commanded by General Wellesley (later Duke of Wellington) supports the Spanish war of liberation, and Napoleon then intervenes personally in the war.

1808–09 Napoleon occupies Madrid, takes Zaragoza and enables Joseph to return. Spain is almost completely occupied.

1810–25 The Spanish colonies in South America declare their independence.

1812 The Cortes, meeting in Cádiz, adopt the *first Spanish constitution*.

1813 Wellington's victory in the decisive battle of Vitoria frees Spain from foreign rule.

From the Restoration to the establishment of the Second Republic (1813–1931). – The history of Spain in the 19th c. is marked by a series of civil wars, caused by the reactionary policies of the restored monarchy, the country's economic backwardness and a number of misadventures in foreign policy. Although Spain remains neutral in the First World War and prospers economically, the country's internal conflicts become more acute for lack of the necessary economic and social reforms.

1814 *Ferdinand VII* returns to the throne, rejects the liberal constitution of 1812 and rules as an absolute monarch.

1820 *Liberal revolution* in Cádiz, led by Colonel *Rafael del Riego Núñez*. The king thereupon recognises the 1812 constitution. The Liberals soon fall into two schools of thought, the Moderados and the Exaltados (radicals), who are constantly at odds.

1823 On behalf of the Holy Alliance France represses the revolution by military intervention. Absolutism is restored.

1830 In the "Pragmatic Sanction" Ferdinand VII provides for his daughter Isabella to succeed him on the throne.

1834 Introduction of a moderately liberal constitution.

1834–39 **First Carlist War**. *Don Carlos*, Ferdinand VII's brother, declares himself king (Charles V) in opposition to the regency of the Queen Mother, María Cristina of Naples, during the minority of *Isabella II*. He is supported by the Basque provinces, Aragon and Catalonia, but the enterprise fails and he flees to France (1839).

1843 Isabella comes of age.

1845 Reactionary constitutional reform.

1847–49 The **Second Carlist War** and republican risings aggravate internal conflicts.

1851 Concordat with the Pope confirming the exclusive status of the Roman Catholic region in Spain.

1859–60 War with Morocco: Spain's only gain is Tetuán.

1861–62 Spain participates in the unsuccessful French expedition to Mexico.

1868 Revolt led by General *Prim* and Marshal Serrano: Isabella II is deposed and flees to France.

1869 The Cortes appoint Serrano Regent pending the choice of a new king. The candidature of Prince Leopold of Hohenzollern fails because of French resistance.

1871–73 *Amadeo II*, son of Victor Emmanuel II of Italy, abdicates because of opposition by the Left. *First Republic* established by the Cortes.

1872–76 The **Third Carlist War**, initiated by Don Carlos's grandson is directed against Amadeo I and the First Republic. Mass socialist risings.

1874 Serrano becomes Dictator; end of the First Republic. Restoration of the Bourbons following a military putsch led by General *Martinez de Campos*.

1874–85 *Alfonso XI*, son of Isabella II, makes possible a quieter course of internal political development.

1876 A *new constitution* provides for freedom of association and freedom of the press, but does away with jury trial and civil marriage. End of the Carlist War.

1879–88 Foundation of the Spanish Socialist Workers Party and the General Workers' Union.

1885 Regency (until 1902) of the Queen Mother, María Cristina of Austria, during the minority of *Alfonso XIII*.

1890 Introduction of universal suffrage.

From 1890 Autonomist movements in Catalonia, the Basque country and Galicia.

1898 *Spanish-American War*. Spain loses its last large colonies (Cuba, the Philippines, Puerto Rico).

1899 Spain sells the Mariana, Caroline and Pelew Islands to Germany.

1904 Agreement on Morocco between Spain and France.

1909 Beginning of campaign in Morocco against the *Rif rising*, which is not quelled until 1926. – Anarcho-syndicalist (from Anarcho *sindicato*, trade union) rising in Barcelona.

1910–12 Prime Minister *Canalejas* develops a liberal cultural policy, but fails to undertake economic or social reform. Increasing emigration to America.

1914–18 Spain remains neutral in the First World War.

1923 General *Primo de Rivera* establishes a military dictatorship, with Alfonso XIII's approval. *Dissolution of the Cortes*.

1925 Primo de Rivera transforms his military dictatorship into a civil **dictatorship**. Reform of financial and tax system; attempted land reform. Increasing opposition in the country.

1926 Spain leaves the League of Nations (readmitted 1928).

1930 Revolutionary and republican disturbances lead to Primo de Rivera's resignation; he dies in Paris on 16 March.

1931 After a Republican victory in the local government elections Alfonso XIII leaves the country. Beginning of the **Second Republic**.

From the Second Republic to the present day

(1931–87). – Since the European democracies do nothing to help the new Spanish republic, and even the Soviet Union believes that the time is not ripe for a social revolution in Spain, the Republican forces are defeated by the *Fascist dictatorship* of General Franco, with support from Hitler and Mussolini. After the Second World War the Franco regime is unable to lead the country out of its political and economic isolation: only after Franco's death is the way clear for the *liberalisation* and *democratisation* of the country.

1931 Spain receives a *new constitution*, liberal and progressive in its provisions: separation of Church and state, a unified state, regional self-government for Catalonia (1932) and the Basque country (1936), a limited degree of land reform.

1932–33 Foundation of the Confederation of the Autonomous Right (CEDA) and the Falange.

1933 Election victory for CEDA which forms a coalition government with the Republicans. During the next three years there are a succession of government crises and serious disturbances, which lead to the dissolution of Parliament.

1936 After the victory of the *Popular Front* (Republicans, Socialists, Syndicalists and Communists) there is much social unrest (splitting up of large estates, occupation of factories).

1936–39 The **Spanish Civil War** breaks out following the murder of the Monarchist member of Parliament *Calvo Sotelo* (13 July) and the military rising (17 July) led by General *Francisco* (**Franco** *y Bahamonde*) (1892–1975) in Spanish Morocco. Franco and other generals set up a government in Burgos, and the Junta de Defensa Nacional (Committee of National Defence) appoint him as their leader (Caudillo) and supreme commander of the rebel forces (30 September). As leader of the Fascist Falange he is supported by the Monarchists and the conservative clergy. While Franco's forces receive military support from Germany, Italy and Portugal, the Republican government receives help only from Mexico and the Soviet Union and from the volunteers of the International Brigade. Germany and Italy recognise the Franco government (18 November 1936).

1937 Amalgamation of the Falange Española and the Traditionalists to form the Falange Española Tradicionalista, led by Franco.

1939 Recognition of Franco's regime by France, Britain (27 February) and the United States (1 April). With the entry of Fascist troops into Madrid (28 March) the Civil War comes to an end. Spain joins the Anti-Comintern Pact (7 April) and leaves the League of Nations (8 May).

1939–45 During the *Second World War* Spain remains neutral in spite of its links with the Berlin – Rome Axis.

1940 The Spanish government occupies the International Zone of Tangier (3 November). The Syndicate Law (6 December) prohibits strikes and free trade unions, which are replaced by paternalistic corporative organisations. Wage freeze, leading to an upturn in the economy.

1945 Spain is obliged to restore the International Zone of Tangier (11 October).

From 1945 Spain is politically and economically isolated as a result of Franco's authoritarian regime. It is not a founding member of the United Nations and receives no aid under the Marshall Plan.

1947 A national referendum approves Franco's plan to restore the monarchy at a later date.

1950 The economic and diplomatic sanctions imposed on Spain by the United Nations in 1946 are lifted on the initiative of the United States.; Spain grants the United States military bases.

From 1951 Opposition to Franco's dictatorship grows. Major strikes, largely promoted by separatist movements (Aragon, Basque provinces, Asturias), and student revolts, and from 1962 battles over pay, directed against lack of political freedom and social abuses.

1953 *Agreement on US bases:* Spain receives economic and military aid worth 1,000 million dollars which promotes economic development.

1955 Spain becomes a member of the United Nations.

1956 Loss of Spain's North African possessions (except the ports of Ceuta and Melilla) to Morocco.

1958 Ifni, Spanish Guinea and the Spanish Sahara are declared to be Spanish overseas provinces.

1959–60 Spain becomes a member of the OEEC and OECD.

From 1960 Spain enjoys a considerable economic upturn thanks to mass tourism, much foreign investment and the remittances of Spanish workers in Western Europe.

1962 Spain applies for association with the EEC.

1962–63 Miners' strikes in Asturias.

1966 A new *Organic Law of the State* is promulgated as a substitute for a new constitution.

1966–68 Students and priests demonstrate in support of liberalisation.

1968 Madrid closes the frontier with Gibraltar at La Línea after the introduction of a new constitution in Gibraltar.

1969–73 The Roman Catholic Opus Dei holds important posts in the government.

1969 *Juan Carlos* (b. 1938 in Rome), grandson of the last king, Alfonso XIII, is nominated as successor (and from 1971 deputy) to Franco and as the country's future king. – Spain cedes Ifni to Morocco.

1970 Military agreement with France and renewal of the agreement on US bases. Basque rising (led by the militant ETA) against political repression. The Falange, whose influence had been steadily reduced by Franco since the 1950s, is renamed the Movimiento Nacional.

1972–73 Strikes in Asturias and Catalonia.

1973 *Carrero Blanco*, appointed Prime Minister in June, is murdered by supporters of the illegal Basque separatist movement ETA (Dec.).

1974 The new Prime Minister, *Arias Navarro*, introduces minor political reforms. Spain, which is not a member of NATO, signs a "NATO parallel declaration".

From 1974 The effects of the world-wide *energy crisis* and the economic *recession* aggravate Spain's internal difficulties: increased unemployment, high inflation, budgetary and balance of payments deficits. Increased **terrorist activity** by extremist organisations of the left and the right, harsh anti-terrorist laws and wildcat strikes reflect the country's *political and social insecurity*.

1975 State visit by US President Ford (June); renewal of agreement on US bases (October).
On Franco's death (20 November) Prince Juan Carlos becomes king of Spain as *Juan Carlos I*. Basque, Catalan and Galician are recognised as teaching and official languages.

1976 The withdrawal of the last troops from the former province of Spanish Sahara marks the end of Spanish colonial rule (12 January). Treaty of friendship with the United States: Spain is now in practice integrated into the NATO defence system (June). Arias Navarro is succeeded as Prime Minister by *Suárez Gonzalez*, who promotes the process of *democratisation* (July). Two-thirds of the country's political prisoners are freed under an amnesty (2 August).

1977 Resumption of diplomatic relations with the Soviet Union (9 February). Dissolution of the Movimiento Nacional and legalisation of the Communist Party (PCE: April). The first democratic election since 1936 is held on 15 June. The new Cabinet, headed by Suárez, consists almost exclusively of members of the UCD (Unión del Centro Democrático: 4 July). Spain applies formally for membership of the European Community (July). In order to stimulate the economy and reduce unemployment the peseta is devalued by 20% against the US dollar: measures to promote employment are introduced at the same time (24 July).

1978 Spain becomes a member of the Council of Europe (24 February). Amalgamation of the socialist parties (30 April). – There is a further wave of violence by Basque separatists.
After a plebiscite on 6–7 December a new *democratic constitution* comes into force: **constitutional monarchy**, abolition of the death penalty, reintroduction of civil marriage (with the possibility of divorce).

1979 In the second Parliamentary election since the liberalisation of the country (2 March) the UCD, led by Prime Minister Suárez, maintain their lead over the Socialists. The Basque provinces elect members associated with the extreme separatists, leading high military officers to express alarm and utter threats. – Free local government elections are held for the first time since the Civil War. In a referendum Basques and Catalans decide on far-reaching self-government for their regions (October); in November the Spanish Lower House grants by a majority decision a Statute of Autonomy to Guernica (Basque region) and Sau (Catalonia).

1980 In the Basque region and in Catalonia regional parliaments are elected. Other regions seek a statute of autonomy. A law of religious freedom comes into force; Catholicism is no longer the state religion.

1981 Resignation of President Adolfo Suarez Gonzalez (29 January). – During the voting for the election of the UCD candidate Leopold Calvo-Sotelo y Bustelo as President, more than 200 soldiers of the Civil Guard invade parliament and hold the members prisoner for ten hours (23 February). On 25 February Calvo-Sotelo is elected

Head of State. – Renewed acts of violence by the ETA, striving for complete independence of their region from Spain.
The two largest Spanish parties, UCD and PSOE (Partido Socialista Obrero Español), combine to promote a "pact of autonomy" (plan for the conversion of Spain into an extensive decentralised state; 2 August).

1982 Spain becomes the sixteenth member country of NATO (30 May). Passing of a "Law for the Harmonisation of the Process of Autonomy", 30 June, which has been the subject of renewed dispute between the UCD and the PSOE. Dissolution of parliament (August); In the election for the Cortes on 28 October the PSOE is victorious. In November Pope John Paul II visits Spain. – On 1 December the socialist Filipe Gonzalez Marquez is elected President.

1983 Dissolution of the UCD. – President Gonzalez pays a state visit to the USA to seek aid for the Spanish economy (June). In the regional elections on 8 May which confirmed the shift in power in favour of the Socialists, the process of autonomy for the regions reaches a formal conclusion. In all, 17 "Autonomous Communities" now possess a regional constitution (State of Autonomy) as well as elected representative bodies. Summit meeting of the Portuguese (Soares) and the Spanish Presidents in Lisbon (December).

1984 Demonstration against the Spanish membership of NATO and the presence of US military bases on Spanish soil (19 February). – In Brussels there are differences of opinion between the EEC states and Spain concerning the entry of Spain into the EEC (February).

1985 On 5 February the frontier between Spain and Gibraltar was reopened after 16 years.
In July a law came into effect, by which the Muslim inhabitants of Mellila and Ceuta, the Spanish enclaves in North Africa, are treated as foreigners; this can lead to their being deported to Morocco. As a consequence there are demonstrations.

1986 On 1 January Spain joins the Common Market (EEC).
Following an agreement between the Spanish government and the towns of Mellila and Ceuta the Muslim inhabitants of these places can obtain Spanish citizenship more quickly (February).
In a referendum a majority votes for remaining in NATO (12 March).
In the parliamentary elections on 22 June the Spanish Socialist Labour Party (PSOE) again gains a majority of votes; Felipe González is elected Prime Minister and President of the Council for a further four years.

1987 The Spanish Socialist Labour Party (PSOE), which has been in power in most regions with an absolute majority since 1982, suffers significant losses in the local and regional elections (June).
Several people die as a result of a bomb attack on a store in Barcelona by the ETA.

Art

Although it lies on the edge of Europe, separated from the rest of the continent by the Pyrenees, Spain has been inhabited by man since a very early period. The art of the late *Palaeolithic period* is represented, mainly in northern Spain, by numerous cave paintings, many of them of astonishing beauty and great expressive force, with a stylisation which is often reminiscent of modern art. They depict hunting scenes which probably served some cult purpose. The most impressive are in the Altamira caves near Santander (bisons, mammoths, wild horses). These animal figures, belonging to the Magdalenian culture, are the finest examples known of Franco-Cantabrian cave painting; estimates of their date range between 20,000 and 10,000 years B.C. In the later rock paintings found in the coastal hills of eastern Spain (*c.* 5000 B.C.) human figures are now shown in social groups (hunters and warriors), even more strongly stylised, with an almost impressionistic effect; possible influences from North Africa can be detected.

From the *Bronze Age* (2000 B.C. onwards) date the *talayots* (round towers), *taulas* (T-shaped megalithic structures) and *navetas* (chamber tombs in the shape of an upturned boat) found in the Balearics.

The original inhabitants of Spain, Ligurians and Iberians, mingled with the Celts who thrust into Spain about 550 B.C. to produce the race known as *Celtiberians*. Their culture is represented by two striking pieces of sculpture, the "Lady of Elche" with her characteristic disc headdress (4th or 3rd c. B.C.) and the "Lady of Baza", discovered as recently as 1971 (both in the Archaeological Museum, Madrid).

The various colonial peoples of the ancient Mediterranean world have left traces of their passage at many places in Spain – the *Phoenicians* at Cádiz, the *Carthaginians* on Ibiza, the *Greeks* at Ampurias and above all the **Romans.** There are considerable remains of Roman buidings of the colonial period at Mérida, Segovia, Tarragona and elsewhere, and numerous smaller objects dating from this period have been found. So firmly was Roman culture established in Spain that in A.D. 74 the population, then completely

The Lady of Elche

Romanised, was granted Roman civil rights.

During the period of the great migrations the *Visigoths*, among other peoples, established theselves in Spain (A.D. 415 onwards) and mingled with the indigenous population. One of the very few surviving examples of Germanic stone architecture is to be seen at Naranco: a great hall, which was later converted into a Christian church, built by the Visigothic king Ramiro I, showing the influence of Roman architecture.

After their victory at Jerez de la Frontera in 711 the **Moors** set up various caliphates in Spain which, particularly in the S of the country, enjoyed a great flowering of intellectual life, accompanied by a splendid development of architecture. Many features of later Spanish art are derived from this earlier Islamic art (glazed earthenware; *azulejos*, brightly coloured majolica tiles; *artesonados*, carved coffered ceilings). The old Caliphal capital of Córdoba still betrays the original Moorish layout, and its houses often show Eastern architectural features. The finest monument of Moorish art and architecture in Córdoba, however, is the gigantic Mezquita (785–999), the principal mosque of the western Moslem world, with its seemingly endless rows of red and white double horseshoe arches stretching away in the dim light of the interior, borne on 856 columns and forming 19 aisles. After the Reconquista it was converted into a cathdral and thereby preserved. Moorish religious architecture is also represented by the Giralda (*c.* 1190), the 93 m high tower of Seville Cathedral, orginally a minaret of the Great Mosque, and the Patio de los Naranjos (Court of Orange-Trees) outside the Cathedral, formerly the courtyard of the mosque. The old Moorish Alcázar of Seville, rebuilt in Mudéjar style after the Reconquista, shows the skill of Moorish masters in its beautiful inner courtyards and gardens; in its present form it dates from the second half of the 14th c.

The finest achievement of Moorish secular architecture in Spain is the Alhambra, begun under Yusuf I in the mid 14th c., which towers above Granada on a rocky crag. Externally unimpressive, like all Moorish secular buildings, it contains inner courtyards (Court of Myrtles, Court of Lions) of magical beauty, with charming fountains and ornamental ponds. The interior decoration is mainly of wood and stucco, with colourful azulejos and rich arabesque ornament. Since Islam banned the representation of nature the decoration shows a strong tendency to abstraction. All the wall surfaces are framed in Arabic inscriptions, mostly in praise of Allah. The palace, long neglected, was much dilapidated by the 18th c., but was restored in the 19th.

A mingling of Christian and Moorish elements produced two hybrid styles, *Mozarabic* and *Mudéjar.* The Mozarabic style arose in the Moorish regions of Spain from the mingling of early Romanesque and Moorish features in buildings erected mainly by Christians under Moorish rule. The more important Mudéjar style was the architectural and decorative style developed by the Mudéjars (the Moors who were "authorised to remain") and Christian architects influenced by the Moors in the Spanish territories recovered from the Moors, which reached its peak in the 14th c. Although the Mudéjar style contains considerble Gothic elements the Moorish influence prevails (horse-shoe arches, majolica tiles, etc.). The ceramic products of this period are also of great beauty.

The steady advance of the Reconquista, beginning round A.D. 1000 in northern Spain and continuing for almost 500 years, was accompanied by the conversion of Moorish buildings to Christian uses and the gradual displacement of the Moorish style. The beginnings of a distinctive Spanish art can be dated roughly to the 11th c. Under French and Lombard influence the **Romanesque** style established itself in Spain. Spain's finest Romanesque building is the Cathedral of Santiago de Compostela, the great medieval pilgrimage centre, built between 1060 and 1096, which shows southern French influence. Particularly beautiful is the S doorway, the Puerta de las Platerías (12th–13th c.). The W front, the Obradoiro, was remodelled in lavish Baroque style in the 18th c. Under the high altar is a crypt containing the tomb of the Apostle James (Santiago).

In Catalonia Lombard influence was introduced into Spanish architecture by the Benedictines in their famous monastery of Santa María de Ripoll (founded 874). Most churches built in northern Spain during this period are modest in size and decoration, but Romanesque sculpture achieved a great flowering, particularly in the decoration of doorways (Santa María de Ripoll; figures on the doorway of San Vicente, Ávila; Pórtico de la Gloria, Santiago de Compostela, begun in 1168 by Maestro Mateo; reliefs in cloister, Santo Domingo de Silos). Splendid fescoes, mainly of the 12th c., have been preserved in towns and villages lying off the main through roads. Catalan painting, showing a stylisation reminiscent of Byzantine art, set a pattern which was much imitated (Museo de Arte de Cataluña, Barcelona). Less rigid and other-worldly are the frescoes in the Panteón Real in San Isidoro, León. The book illumination of the period is also of splendid quality (Apocalypse manuscripts of the 10th and 11th c.).

In Spain as in other countries the displacement of Romanesque by **Gothic** was a gradual process. The Burgundian form of Gothic, with its pointed arches, was brought to Spain by the Cistercians (Las Huelgas, Burgos). For long the Transitional style prevailed, a blending of Romanesque and Gothic in which for the first time a typically Spanish spirit comes to the fore (Old Cathedral, Salamanca). The buildings of this period still have a plain earth-bound heaviness, combined with an impressive spatial effect; but the

Gothic striving towards greater height and opening up of the wall surfaces to produce quite new effects of light becomes steadily more evident. The three cathedrals of Burgos, Toledo and León show the complete assimilation of the French style of cathedral architecture which had been brought in by foreign masters. Burgos Cathedral (1221), with Norman towers, was followed in 1227 by Toledo, seen as a "protest against Moorish architecture". The masterpiece of this French style was León Cathedral (c. 1250), with an over-abundance of tracery and, on the model of Burgos, double lateral aisles.

After the Reconquista cathedrals of hall-church type were built on the site of Moorish mosques at Zaragoza (begun 1188) and Seville (begun 1402). Seville Cathedral, with its five huge aisles, is one of the largest Gothic churches every built.

Other outstanding examples of 14th and 15th c. Gothic church architecture are Ávila Cathedral with its rich girdle of chapels, the churches of Santa María in Antigua and San Benito in Valladolid and the cathedrals of Astorga, Segovia, Pamplona and Barcelona. In Catalonia a special type was developed under the influence of southern France, the aisleless hall-church (Gerona Cathedral).

The moving of the choir (coro) into the nave (trascoro) is a feature found in many Spanish churches which detracts seriously from the spatial effect of the interior – a fault which is not redeemed by the rich sculptured adornment of the choir walls. Sometimes, too, the wide windows and openwork walls are concealed behind masonry, severely reducing the amount of light admitted (Ávila Cathedral).

The Mudéjar style, enriched by the incorporation of late Gothic and ancient forms, developed into the **Plateresque** style, a highly charged decorative style in which the façades of buildings are covered with a riot of variegated and intricate details. The earliest example is the Colegio de Santa Cruz in Valladolid (1480–92) by the silversmith (platero) Pedro Díez. The cathedrals of Salamanca (1513) and Segovia (1525), built by the brothers Juan and Rodrigo Gil de Hontañón in sumptuous style, with a super-abundance of decoration, are the last

great creations of Gothic architecture in Spain, already giving expression to a sense of national pride enhanced by the successful completion of the Reconquista and reflecting also the rising national prosperity due to the shipments of gold and silver from the newly discovered territories in America.

Spain's Gothic sculpture, like the architecture, was strongly influenced by France. Monumental sculpture is seen at its finest in the cathedrals of Vitoria, León and Burgos, in the Apostles' Doorway of Valencia Cathedral and in Tarragona. Leading figures of the period are Maestro Bartolomé (active 1278) and Castayls (1375). The beautiful Gothic statues of the Virgin usually show particularly strong French influence, if indeed they are not actually of French origin (Seville, Toledo).

Catalonia, where the rich flowering of art continued – here too showing strong French influence – is notable for its large retablos, made up of numerous separate carved scenes (fine examples in Barcelona, Vich and Lérida museums; high altar of Tarragona Cathedral, by Johan de Valfogona, c. 1430), and fine tombs (tomb of Archbishop Lope Fernández de Luna, Zaragoza Cathedral, after 1382).

In sculpture as in architecture the 15th c. brought a trend towards a luxuriant proliferation of forms, promoted by the example of Dutch and German masters – Gil de Siloé (an architect and sculptor from Nuremberg), Anequin de Egas, Juan Alemán, Enrique and Juan Guas, Rodrigo Alemán. The huge retablo in Toledo Cathedral (1504) was the work of 17 foreign masters.

Gothic painting too was subject to French influence; later it was also influenced by Italy and in the 15th c. by Dutch artists. Many Italian painters worked in Spain (Gherardo Starnina, Nicolás Florentino), and the Sienese school was particularly influential (Vich, Barcelona, Valencia and Palma de Mallorca museums). The Barcelona school of painters, which developed in the 15th c. under Dutch influence, nevertheless achieved vigorous characteristics of its own, a marked realism and considerable magnificence (Luis Dalmau, Jaime Huguet, Bartolomeo Vermejo). In the later 15th c. schools of painting also developed in Valencia and in

Castile, the latter school showing strong North German influence (Fernando Gallegos). A number of artists from the Netherlands also worked in Spain, among them Francisco de Amberes (=Antwerp), Juan de Flandes, Juan de Holanda and Juan de Borgoña. In Seville there were Juan Sánchez de Castro and a German artist. Alejo Fernández; while Pedro Berruguete was the first artist in whom distinctively Spanish characteristics can be detected. The emerging national spirit in painting, however, was to suffer a setback as a result of the powerful impulses sent out by the Italian Renaissance.

In architecture the forms of the **Renaissance** were at first applied to purely decorative purposes, the buildings themselves being still influenced by the Gothic spirit. Extraordinary minglings of styles – Plateresque (late Gothic), Moorish, Renaissance – are found, for example, in the cloister at Santiago de Compostela (1521–86), the largest in Spain; the Casa de Pilatos, Seville; and the courtyard of the University and the Casa de Las Conchas (1514) in Salamanca. The summer palace built for Charles V on the Alhambra hill in Granada (by Pedro Machuca, 1526) is the finest example of Spanish High Renaissance architecture already radiating imperial greatness. Burgos became a centre of the new architectural style under the leadership of Diego de Siloé, son of Gil. More attuned to the Spanish national character than the uncluttered forms of the Roman Renaissance, however, were the Mannerist and early Baroque grotesqueries of the "Estilo monstruoso". Only under the influence of the Counter-Reformation, which was opposed to an excessive proliferation of ornament, was it possible for a new style of imposing austerity and rigour to come to the fore. The masterpiece of this new severe style is the huge Escorial (completed by Juan de Herrera in 1584), a convent, a fortress and a palace all in one, which already shows the influence of the early Baroque. Valladolid Cathedral (begun 1580), also by Herrara, was planned on such a gigantic scale that it was never completed.

In sculpture too the Renaissance style displaced Gothic only very gradually. A particularly impressive example of a free-standing tomb with a recumbent figure is the monument of Ferdinand and Isabella,

the Catholic monarchs, in the Capilla Real in Granada. The leading names in 16th c. sculpture are Alonso Berruguete, Felipe Vigarní (also known as Felipe de Borgoña) and Damián Forment. Like Berruguete, Forment developed a Renaissance style of wholly Italian stamp (altar of N.S. del Pilar, Zaragoza). With Berrugeuete was associated Juan de Juni, who was probably of French origin. The "Romanist" reaction which reflected the severity and austerity of the Counter-Reformation toned down the fervid emotionalism of the previous style in favour of lofty grandeur and rigidity (cf. the retablos of northern Spain, which sometimes cover the whole of the choir wall up to the vaulting; retablo in Astorga Cathedral by Gaspar Becerra, c. 1560). The Arfe family of sculptors created mainly works of small sculpture and liturgical utensils.

Many painters, like Juan de Juanes, Juan Fernández Navarrette (surnamed El Mudo, the Dumb), Bartolomé Gonzalez and Luis de Morales, modelled themselves on the great Italian Renaissance masters (Leonardo da Vinci, Michelangelo).

The Spanish **Baroque** introduced into the vocabulary of architectural form created by Borromini the elaborately decorative style known as *Churrigueresque* after its originator José de Churriguera – a riot of fanciful ornament, often totally uncontrolled, which catered for the characteristic Spanish penchant for unrestrained richness of decoration and was frequently carried to the pitch of extravagance and to the very verge of tastelessness (sacristy of the Cartuja, Granada, 1727–64; Plaza Mayor, Salamanca).

In the second half of the 18th c., under the Bourbons, a reaction set in, and the sober lines of **neo-classicism** came into fashion. An early masterpiece in this style is the Royal Palace in Madrid, designed by an Italian, Filippo Juvara, and built by another Italian, Giovanni Battista Sacchetti. The most celebrated pioneer of neo-classicism in Spain, however, was Francisco Sabatini, also an Italian. Ventura Rodríguez continued to work on Nuestra Señora del Pilar in Zaragoza, while Juan de Villanueva built the finest example of the neo-classical style in Spain, the Prado in Madrid (1785–1819).

Spanish Baroque sculpture is almost exclusively confined to religious themes, which are treated with great realism, and sometimes in an exaggeratedly naturalistic manner, in order to achieve a dramatic – and on occasion, indeed, distressing – effect (the statues are clad in fabric garments and wigs; they have eyes inserted into the sockets, artificial tears and realistically depicted wound-marks). Gregario Hernández worked in Castile, Martinez Montañés in Seville. Celebrated examples of the sculpture of this period are the *pasos* (figures associated with the Passion) which are carried in the great religious processions, like the "Cristo del Gran Poder" in San Lorenzo, Alonso Cano and Pedro de Mena were talented successors to Martínez Montañés.

Spainish **PAINTING of the Baroque period** counts among the supreme achievements of European art. In his visionary pictures the great Mannerist painter **El Greco** ("the Greek": born in Crete as Domenikos Theotokopoulos) gives expression to the religious experience with the greatest intensity and a very personal style "Burial of Count Orgaz", Santo Tomé, Toledo). Although closely attuned to the Spanish character, he did not form a school. More typical of Spanish Baroque painting were Francisco Ribalta and Jusepe de Ribera (teacher of Velázquez), Zurbarán and Murillo. Francisco Zurbarán is mainly known for his portraits of monks and his sharp chiaroscuro effects in the manner of Caravaggio.

Diego **Velázquez** (1599–1660) was the outstanding painter of the Spanish Baroque, a great realist who, as court painter to Philip IV, painted unflattering portraits of the courtiers, which are notable for their expressiveness and acute delineation of character, as well as charming portraits of children (the Infante Baltasar Carlos on horseback, the little Infanta Margarita Teresa), but painted practically no religious pictures.

Perhaps Spain's most popular painter is Bartolomé Esteban Murillo, whose works can be seen in Seville and in the Prado in Madrid. He painted religious visions and ecstacies, but also charming genre pictures, appealing little street-boys and sorrowful figures of Christ ("Purísima", Prado; "St Antony", baptistery of Seville Cathedral).

After the flowering of Baroque painting in the 17th c., the 18th c. produced no artists of any consequence. The German painter Anton Raphael Mengs attempted, as court painter, to develop the neo-classical style in painting, but without great success. Nor did Giovanni Battista Tiepolo, who lived in Madrid from 1761 to 1770, have any great effect on Spanish painting.

It was not until the turn of the 18th and 19th c. that the painter and graphic artist Francisco de **Goya** (1746–1828), standing alone at the beginning of a new development, broke out of the stagnation of the 18th c. and gave a powerful new impetus to European art. A man of profound humanity, with a sharp eye for the seamy sides and cruelties of life, he produced a series of works of great emotional effect, among them his series of etchings, "Desastres de la Guerra", "Proverbios" and "Caprichos". His great skill as a portrait painter found ample scope in the corrupt world of Charles IV's court ("Charles IV and his Family"). His masterpieces (over 120 pictures) are in the Prado in Madrid ("Maja Nude" and "Maja Clothed", "The Shootings of 3rd May 1808"). As a portraitist Goya had a number of successors (Vicente López, Federico Madrazo, Leonardo Alenza, José de Madrazo). During this period there was also a notable school of historical painters.

In the first half of the 20th c. Ignacio Zuloaga painted in a very personal style, showing affinities with realism, while José María Sert achieved international reputation as a fresco-painter.

The architecture of the 19th c., as in other European countries, showed a mingling of the most diverse historical styles, in the manner practised by the exponents of *historicism*. An excellent example of this trend is the Almudena Cathedral in Madrid, designed by the Marqués de Cubas (begun 1895). The Catalan architects Luis Doménech i Montaner and Antonio Gaudí, representatives of the *Neo-Catalan* style, went their own ways. Gaudí's Templo de la Sagrada Familia in Barcelona, begun in 1882 and still under construction, is a monumental cathedral in a fantastic style which owes something to Art Nouveau, with forms reminiscent of Gothic and others of almost organic

In the El Greco Museum, Toledo

effect based on vegetable forms. Purely functional buildings have made their appearance in Spain only during the economic upswing of the last few decades, particularly in the large cities of Madrid and Barcelona. The extremely rapid development of the resorts on the Mediterranean coasts of Spain has led to a building boom of extraordinary dimensions and to the urbanisation of whole stretches of the coast which become dead towns during the off-season. Often of poor architectural quality, these new developments represent an assault on the landscape, the full effects of which cannot yet be measured.

The sculpture of the 19th c. was influenced by the principles of historicism ("Dos de Mayo" monument, Madrid, 1840), but the old traditions of Catalonian sculpture were still maintained by the Vallmitjana brothers in Barcelona, Julio Antonio and José Llimona.

The first half of the 20th c. produced the remarkable metal sculpture of Julio González and Eduardo Chillida. Pablo Picasso initiated a radical break with tradition in the field of sculpture: the dependence of Cubist sculpture on painting is very evident. Instead of the traditional material the artists of this period preferred montages of papier-mâché, plywood and miscellaneous objects of all kinds.

In parallel with the political, social and economic changes of the period the 20th c. saw a profound revolution in the arts, in which Spain played an important part together with France and Germany. Art now began to diverge ever farther from the reproduction of reality.

Pablo **Picasso** (1881–1973), living in Paris, became the leading exponent of the new trend. After the earlier phases of his long artistic development (the Blue Period, the Rose Period) he was associated with Georges Braque in creating *Cubism*, in which geometric planes bounded by straight lines combine to form structures of three-dimensional effect, which frequently offer few clues to permit objective interpretation. Picasso developed into the most important painter of our century, a great experimenter with a profound concern for human values (as in "Guernica", commemorating the destruction of that little town by a Fascist air attack during the Civil War; now in a wing of the Prado Museum in Madrid), transforming affliction and calamity into anarchic and revolutionary art.

Juan Gris was another exponent of Cubism, while Joan Miró became a leading representative of *Surrealism*, which came to the fore in Paris in the 1920s. His gay and subtly elegant pictures are among the most attractive creations of modern art. Salvador Dalí, who was influenced by the Italian "Pittura metafisica" and Freudian psychoanalysis, is now the most celebrated of the Surrealists ("The Burning Giraffe"), with a strong leaning towards the morbid and occasionally the obscene.

The artistic impoverishment which resulted from the Spanish Civil War is being gradually overcome since the end of the Franco regime. The young Spanish *avantgarde* led by Antonio Tàpies (1948 cofounder of the "Dau al Set" group), developed a radically modern school of painting of specifically Spanish stamp. While preserving the freedom of the various individual styles, this group has been concerned to explore the dramatic effects which can be derived from the material. Centred in Madrid and Barcelona, it forms one of the most interesting schools of painting of the present day, with such artists as M. Cuixart, J. J. Tharrats, Antonio Saura, Luis Feito, Rafael Canogar and the still younger generation consisting of E. Alcoy, F. de Echevarría, G. Rueda, J. M. de Vidales, Edùardo Arroyo and others.

Literature

Spain can look back with pride on a literature almost 2000 years old. The first literary works produced on Spanish soil were written by *Romans*, in a Latin noted for its purity. Among them were **Seneca the Elder**, known as the Rhetor (54 B.C.–A.D. 39), his son *Seneca the Stoic* (4 B.C.–A.D. 65), the epic poet *Lucan* (A.D. 39–65) and the epigrammatist *Martial* (A.D. 42–104).

Christian literature in Latin, starting in the 4th c., was cut off before reaching its full flowering by the Moorish conquest (711). Its principal representatives were *Juvencus* (*c.* 330), *Prudentius* (348–410), *St Damasus* (Pope 367–384), *Paulus Orosius*, a universal historian and disciple of St Augustine, and *St Isidore of Seville* (*c.* 570–636), who compiled the first encyclopaedia in his "Etimologías". Under the very tolerant Moorish regime there were also Christian theologians such as the Biblical commentator *Juan Hispalense* (*c.* 839) and *Alvare de Córdoba*, known as the "Indiculus Luminosus", the most learned of the Mozarabs. The Christians not under Moorish rule produced only the "Cronicones", which are of very limited literary value.

Of greater importance were the writings of *Arabs* living in Spain, since the Moorish kingdoms of the Iberian peninsula achieved a considerable flowering of learning and literature. Scholars and writers at the Arab universities preserved and extended the heritage of antiquity which the Christian scholars of the early Middle Ages rejected. Early thinkers influenced by Plato, like *Aben Masarra* (833–931) and *Aben Hazam* (994–1064), were followed by an Aristotelian school whose principal representative Ibn Rushd, in Latin **Averroes** (1126–98), wrote commentaries on Aristotle transmitting and enlarging much scientific knowledge. The most important historians of the period were *Abdelmelic ben Habib* (d. about 853) and *Ahmed Arrazi* (887–955). Among leading geographers were *El Becri* ("The Roads and the Province", one of the earliest geographical works) and *Idrisi* (1100–69), known as the Arab Strabo. – Jewish writers, like *Abraham ibn Ezra* (1092–1167) and the great *Moses ben Maimon*, known as Maimonides (1135–1204), wrote both in Hebrew and in Arabic.

Even before Castilian had developed into a written language *Galician* had become the language of poetry (Alfonso the Wise's "Cantigas de Santa María"), used even at the Castilian court. – *Catalan* became a literary language when the Majorcan philosopher, poet and missionary Ramón Llull (Raimundus Llullus, 1233–1314) wrote his copious works not only in Latin and Arabic but also in the vernacular. Earlier, in the 12th and 13th c., the Catalan troubadours had used the related Provençal language.

Castilian achieved its predominant position only with the development of epic poetry. The earliest work of this kind which has come down to us in written form is the **"Cantar de Mio Cid"**, written about 1140, which recounts the life and deeds of Roy Díaz de Vivar, the Cid, and became the prototype of the Spanish heroic epic. Other anonymous heroic poems, surviving only in incomplete form, are "The Seven Infantes of Lara" and "The Deeds of Sancho II of Castile", together with fragments of the epic of Roncesvalles, an early form of the Song of Roland.

The minstrel poetry of the *mester de juglaría*, mostly transmitted only in oral form, was followed in the 13th c. by the learned genre of the *mester de clerecía*, which is recorded in writing. At first it was mainly concerned with Christian themes (poems on the life of the Virgin by Gonzalo de Berceo); then came subjects taken from antiquity ("Libro de Alexandre") and from Spanish history ("Poema de Fernán González"). This learned poetry culminated in the works, notable both for their quantity and their content, of **Alfonso X** of Castile, the Wise (1252–84). They comprised works on Spanish and universal history, collections of laws and voluminous translations of Arabic scientific and didactic works, and provided the basis for the further development of Spanish prose. Alfonso X's nephew the *Infanta Juan Manuel* wrote "El Conde Lucanor", a collection of tales of great stylistic perfection. His contemporary *Juan Ruiz*, Archpriest of Hita, mingled secular themes with mystical ideas in his "Libro del Buen Amor" ("Book of True Love").

The Spanish *drama* developed out of plays on religious themes, the *autos sacramentales*. On the threshold of modern times it reached a first peak in the "Tragicomedy of Calisto and Melibea", usually known as **"La Celestina"** after the bawd Celestina, its principal character, which is attributed to *Fernando de Rojas* (c. 1500).

The Spanish theatre rose to universal significance in the **Siglo de Oro**, the Golden Age, the beginning of which can be set about the middle of the 16th c. After a period of Italian influence, brought back by Spanish noblemen from the campaigns in the kingdom of naples (Juan Boscán, c. 1490–1542, and his friend Garcilaso de la Vega, 1503–36), two main schools came to the fore in a great flowering of drama, the *Salamanca school* (Fray Luis de León, 1527–91) and the *Seville school* (Fernando de Herrera, 1534–97), the former full of mystical and pantheist emotionalism, the latter notable for its fine simplicity. A controversial figure in his day was *Luis de Góngora* (1561–1627), the most typical representative of Baroque poetry, who used complicated metres and affected Latinised diction, founding the school known as *cultismo*. During this period, too, more popular genres came into vogue – the *romance of chivalry* ("Amadís de Gaula", 1508), *pastoral poetry* ("Diana", 1559?) and the more realistic *picaresque novel* ("Lazarillo de Tormes", 1554), which were followed by a whole series of continuations, imitations and translations.

The world-famous novel "Don Quixote" ("Don Quijote de la Mancha") was directed in the first place against the excesses and fashionable follies of the romances of chivalry; but thanks to the genius and literary skill of its author, **Miguel de Cervantes Saavedra** (c. 1547–1616), it developed into a work of high stylistic quality and profound human significance in which Don Quixote incarnates head-in-the-clouds idealism and his squire Sancho Panza matter-of-fact reality Cervantes' other works – short stories ("Novelas Ejemplares", 1613), plays and poems – are also of considerable quality, but tend to be overshadowed by this masterpiece of world literature.

The drama of the Siglo de Oro reached its peak in **Lope de Vega** (1562–1635), the real creator of the Spanish national theatre and one of the world's most prolific playwrights, author of more than 1000 plays. In addition to his *comedias*, in which comedy and tragedy are mingled in a fashion typical of his work, he wrote fine lyric poems. His most celebrated followers were the Mexican *Ruiz de Alarcón y Mendoza* (c. 1580–1639) and *Tirso de Molina* (c. 1571–1648), whose "Burlador de Sevilla" ("The Seducer of Seville") was the prototype of all later treatments of the Don Juan theme. The greatest dramatist after Lope de Vega, however, was **Calderón de la Barca** (1600–81), a typical representative of the Baroque drama. His best known play is the profound "La vida es sueño" ("Life is a Dream").

The religious literature of the Golden Age is notable for its passionate mysticism. In addition to the Dominican *Fray Luis de Granada* (1504–88) and the Augustinian Fray Luis de León, already mentioned as a dramatist, Spain's two greatest mystics belong to this period – *Santa Teresa de Ávila* (1515–82) and her disciple *San Juan de la Cruz* (St John of the Cross, 1542–91), both members of the Carmelite order.

Worlds apart from the fervid piety of the mystics are the worldly wisdom and shrewd satire of *Francisco de Quevedo* (1580–1645): "La Vida del Buscón") and *Baltasar de Gracián* (1601–58: "El Criticón"). whose works, in both content and style, were directed against the symptoms of decadence in the society and literature of their day.

This decadence is reflected in a sharp decline in creative force which began in the second half of the 17th c. and marked the end of the Golden Age. The country's intellectual life was wholly occupied by the conflict between the French influence which became increasingly strong under the Bourbons (Nicolás Fernández de Moratín, 1737–80) and a harking back to the Spanish national tradition. A leader of this latter trend was *Gaspar Melchor de Jovellanos* (1744–1811), poet, philanthropist, economist and statesman, who suffered much persecution for his fierce resistance to French oppression.

At the beginning of the 19th c. the Romantic movement came to Spain. Of enduring value is the lyric poetry – post-Romantic rather than Romantic – of

Gustavo Adolfo Becquér (1836–70), whose life overlapped into the second half of the century, the period of *realism*, marked in Spain by descriptions of the scenery and way of life of the various regions and by the frequent use of dialect and occupational jargons. Outstanding among the realists, who were mostly novelists, were *Pedro de Alarcón* (1833–91: "The Three-Cornered Hat"), *Juan Valera* (1824–1905: "Pepita Jiménez"), *Benito Pérez Galdós* (1843–1920: "Angel Guerra"), *Leopoldo Alas*, better known as *Clarín* (1852–1901: "La Regenta"), and *Vicente Blasco Ibáñez* (1869–1928), an author widely known beyond the bounds of Spain. Compelled to flee from Spain on account of his Republican views, he later became a member of the Cortes of the First Republic. In his novels he describes the life of country people, particularly in his native province of Valencia ("La Barraca", "Sangre y Arena").

At the beginning of the 20th c. the *modernist school* came to the fore, at first very much under French influence. Its real founder was the Nicaraguan *Rubén Darío* (1867–1916: "Cantos de vida y esperanza"), who, like his followers, preferred lyric poetry as a form of expression. By looking back to Spanish folk poetry for their inspiration the members of this school soon broke away from their foreign models and found a distinctive voice. Their leading representatives were *Juan Ramón Jiménez* (1881–1958: Nobel Prize 1956), *Manuel Machado* (1874–1947) and his brother *Antonio Machado* (1875–1939), *Rafael Alberti* (b. 1902) and *Vicente Aleixandre* (1898–1984: Nobel Prize 1977). In prose *Ramón del Valle Inclán* (1866–1936) followed a similar line.

Simultaneously with the emergence of the modernist school a group of writers of about the same age were striving to reintegrate the intellectual life of Spain, rigidly fixed in its isolation, into the mainstream of European thinking and to overcome the inferiority complex which many Spaniards had felt since the end of the 17th c. in relation to the rest of Europe. After the salutary shock of defeat in the Cuban war of 1898 they sought to return to the true spiritual values of Spain and to link them up again with the main trends of European thought.

Although the members of this group, who called themselves the *"Generation of 1898"*, were very different from one another they showed a common preference for the essay and the novel. Their intellectual leader was Miguel de **Unamuno** (1864–1936), a Basque of strong opinions who taught at Salamanca University but was exiled to the Canaries in 1924 for his opposition to the dictatorship and later lived in voluntary exile in France. In his works (essays, interpretations of "Don Quixote", novels, plays) he gave expression to a tragic view of life, making him one of the forerunners of existentialism, and argued not only for the Europeanisation of Spain but also for the Hispanisation of Europe. Other representatives of the Generation of 1898 were *José Martínez Ruiz*, known as *Azorín* (1873–1967), author of essays and novels depicting life in Castile, who also lived in voluntary exile from 1936 to 1939; the deeply pessimistic novelist *Pío Baroja* (1872–1956), who describes interesting aspects of his Basque homeland; and *Ramón Menéndez Pidal* (1869–1968), a scholar who made major contributions in the fields of literary history and Romance linguistics until his premature retirement in 1939.

Outstanding among prose writers of a rather later generation are **José Ortega** y **Gasset** (1883–1955), who developed the essay into a distinctive art form and in works like "The Revolt of the Masses" and "The Modern Theme" had a considerable influence on European thinking; the witty **Salvador de Madariaga** (1886–1978), who received the Prix de Charlemagne in Aachen in 1973, and who went into exile in 1936, becoming the intellectual leader of expatriate Spaniards; and the Catholic essayist, lyric poet and dramatist *José Bergamin* (1897–1983), who also lived in exile for many years.

In the period before the Civil War lyric poetry was given fresh stimulus, particularly in the choice of a new system of metaphors, by the movement called *Ultraísmo* which was initiated by the Chilean *Vicente Huidobro* (1893–1948). To this school belonged *Gerardo Diego* (1896–1987) and **Federico García Lorca** (1898–1936). Soon, however, Lorca broke free from attachment to any particular school and found a distinctive voice of his own. His intricately contrived lyric poetry has its roots in the folk poetry of Andalusia ("Romancero Gitano") and the improvised songs of the flamenco dancers ("Poema del cante jondo" – *cante jondo* being the most melancholy form of flamenco), but in dealing with modern themes he employs bold and surrealist forms of expression ("Poeta en Nueva York"). He was director of the student theatre, La Barraca, and wrote psychologically subtle plays of social criticism in lofty poetical language full of surprising metaphors, employing music, singing, dancing and sometimes puppets to create the total effect. His most important plays are "Bodas de Sangre" ("Blood Marriage"), "Yerma" ("Waste Land") and "La Casa de Bernarda Alba" ("The House of Bernada Alba"). He had perhaps not yet reached the peak of his achievement when he was murdered by fanatical Francoists.

A lyric poet more interested in "poésie pure" was *Jorge Guillén* (1893–1984), who went into exile in the United States at the time of the Civil War, until 1977. *Luis Cernuda* (1902–63), who was influenced by the English Romantic school, died in exile in Mexico. The neo-classicist *Miguel Hernández* (1910–42), another Republican, died in prison.

Spain also lost a number of excellent prose writers as a result of the Civil War, like *Ramón Pérez de Ayala* (1881–1962), until 1936 ambassador of the Spanish Republic in London, who lived in Argentina until 1954, when he returned to Spain. *Ramón Gómez de la Serna* (1888–1963), author of novels and striking epigrams (*greguerías*), lived in Buenos Aires. *Ramón José Sender* (1902–82) spent more time in Guatemala and Mexico before moving to the United States where he died in San Deigo (California).

Alejandro Casona (1903–65), a dramatist influenced by Lorca ("The Trees Die Erect", "The Woman at Break of Day"), also spent many years in exile.

After the Civil War a new generation of writers came forward, mainly novelists. *Juan Antonio de Zunzunegui* (b. 1901) showed a preference for the "roman objectif"; *Camilo José Cela* (b. 1916) founded *Tremendismo*, a school of harsh realism based on the theories of existentialism; while *José María Gironella* (b. 1917) more a trilogy on the Civil War. The novels of *Carmen Laforet* (b. 1921) and *Ana María Matute* (b. 1926) are concerned with contemporary themes. The work of *Rafael Sánchez Ferlosio* (b. 1927) uses a modern montage technique borrowed from the cinema.

The journalist and novelist *Juan Goytisolo* (b. 1931) paints realistic and critical pictures of Spanish society. – Finally there is the dramatist *Fernando Arrabal* (b. 1932), who lives in Paris, author of surrealist and often obscene plays in which he sets out to destroy bourgeois taboos.

Economy

Until the Civil War Spain had the economic structure of an under-developed country – large tracts of land with a backward agriculture and an almost feudal social structure (large landed estates), its mineral resources (particularly in Asturias and Andalusia) mainly in foreign hands. The country was in process of taking the first steps towards the development of its own industries (mining, shipbuilding, textiles), but apart from this most of Spain was still at the stage of traditional craft production and cottage industry: family-owned firms and prosperous farmers tilling their own land were to be found almost exclusively in Catalonia and the Basque provinces.

Launch in a Spanish shipyard

It was just these better-off areas that suffered particularly during the Civil War and in addition – since they had been on the Republican side – were subjected to economic and political sanctions, crippling the efforts of their hard-working populations for years to come. Apart from the destruction of factories and utilities and the large numbers killed on both sides there was the further damage inflicted by the departure of many of the country's best people, who had gone into exile to escape the Franco regime and had made major contributions to intellectual life in their adopted countries (particularly Mexico), while science and learning in Spain had stagnated.

After dealing with the worst of the war damage Franco proceeded to put into effect his conception of a centralised corporative state. His labour legislation (e.g. banning strikes and freezing wages) promoted investment but aggravated social injustices to such an extent that the opposition could be quelled only by the brutal methods of a police state and constant harping on the spectre of Communism and another civil war.

The one-party system also fostered corruption and created an inflated and inflexible bureaucracy. In spite of all these limiting factors, however, the Spanish economy has contrived to show a strong upturn over the last twenty years or so. The negative consequences of Spain's one-sided course of development only began to show up clearly after the democratic process was started.

The gross national product in 1983 amounted to some 183 million dollars of which by far the greatest part fell to the service factor, followed by industrial production; in third place were agriculture, forestry and fishing. The main exports are machinery and vehicles (up to 33% of total exports by value), chemical and petrochemical products (c. 15%) and agricultural produce (oranges, lemons, olives and olive oil, wine). Spain is the world's fourth largest producer of wine (after Italy, France and the Soviet Union), and exports considerable quantities to Great Britain in addition to special products like sherry and malaga. There is also a considerable export trade in canned fish and vegetables. Spain's principal trading partners are the United States, the German Federal Republic and France.

Spain's principal mineral resources are iron (Vizcaya; Asturias, along with coal), pyrites, sulphur (Río Tinto area, Andalusia: processing and shipment, Huelva), copper (Río Tinto, Córdoba), tin and lead (Sierra Morena), mercury (Almadén) and bauxite.

Since the beginning of the 50s tourism has developed into an important factor of the economy and brings the country a considerable income. This is of great importance for the political economy, since the value of imports always exceeds that of exports. In addition the leisure industries have created numerous jobs in a country which suffers from high unemployment.

The coastal zones on the Mediterranean as well as the Balearics and the Canaries are the most visited holiday areas. In 1985 Spain was chosen for holidays by some 47 million foreign visitors of whom 11 million were French, 9·5 million Portuguese, about 6 million British and almost as many West Germans. In addition there were more than a million Belgians and Dutch and about 800,000 from the USA. The island of Majorca alone received more than 3 million holiday-makers. The annual income from tourism is, however, subject to considerable fluctuations, since the number of visitors is dependent on the international situation and the price of fuel.

In order that the Spanish coasts may be even more attractive to holidaymakers, the tourist industry of the country is taking strong measures in the immediate future to combat pollution. A publicity campaign has been mounted to encourage tourists to visit places of interest in the interior of the country.

Spain
A to Z

Giralda, Seville

Aguilar de Campóo

Province: Palencia (P).
Telephone code: 988.
Altitude: 870 m. – Population: 3000.
ⓘ **Oficina de Información de Turismo,**
Plaza Mayor 32;
tel. 12 20 24.

HOTELS. – *Valentín*, Avda. del Generalísimo 21, II, 50 r.; Hostal *Pórtico de Castilla*, Avda. José Antonio, P II, 25 r.; *Comercio*, Plaza de España 14, P III, 10 r.; *Siglo XX*, Plaza de España 11, P III, 10 r.

The ancient little town of Aguilar de Campóo, picturesquely situated on the Río Pisuerga, is believed to have been the Roman settlement of Vellica. It flourished particularly between the 13th and 15th c., when the town and surrounding area were made a marquisate.

SIGHTS. – The most notable features are the ruins of the old castle and the town walls, with the *Puerta de Reinosa* (14th c.). There are also a number of old palaces and the churches of **Santa Cecilia** (Romanesque) and **San Miguel** (early Gothic), both with numerous monuments of the 12th–16th c.

SURROUNDINGS. – 2 km W, on the Pantano de Aguilar, is the former Premonstratensian monastery of **Santa María la Real** (11th c.), a triple-naved church and a Romanesque cloister.

Town gate, Aguilar de Campóo

Albacete

Province: Albacete (AB)
Telephone code: 967.
Altitude: 686 m. – Population: 85,000.
ⓘ **Oficina de Información de Turismo,**
Virrey Morcillo 1;
tel. 21 56 11.

HOTEL. – *Los Llanos* (no rest.), Avenida España 9, I, 102 r.; *Parador Nacional de La Mancha*, Carretera N 301, km 260, II, 70 r., SP, tennis; *Gran Hotel* (no rest.), Marqués de Molíns 1, II, 69 r.; *Albar* (no rest.) Isaac Peral 3, II, 51 r.; etc.

RESTAURANTS. – **Parador Nacional*, in La Mancha style; *Ortega*, Concepción 15; *Surco*, Capitán Cortés 120; *Las Rejas*, Dionisio Guardiola 9; *La Casita*, Carretera N 430, km 248; etc.

EVENTS. – *Ferias y Fiestas de Albacete* (Sept.), in honour of the Virgen de los Llanos, with cavalcade; folk music, sporting events, bullfights, international art competition; *Festivales de España*.

Albacete (Arabic: al-Basita), capital of the province of the same name and the seat of a bishopric, lies in a fertile region in the centre of La Mancha, a large wine-producing area. It is noted for its knives (navajas) and daggers (puñales), often bought by tourists as souvenirs.

SIGHTS. – In the older upper part of the town is the Cathedral of **San Juan Bautista** (16th c.), a Gothic church originally built by Diego de Siloé and continued in Renaissance style: Churrigueresque *high altar* (1726); *sacristy* with fine grisaille painting (1550). – In the newer lower part of the town, in the *Diputación Provincial* (1880), is the **Museo Arqueológico**, with Iberian pottery, which has been declared a national monument by virtue of the importance of its collection.

SURROUNDINGS. – 11 km SE is **Chinchilla de Monte Aragón** (alt. 896 m; pop. 8000), an old Moorish settlement on a steep-sided hill which was the provincial capital until 1833 and has a 15th c. castle and old palaces in Mudéjar style. Plaza Mayor, with the fine Gothic church of Santa María del Salvador (15th–16th c.): Capilla Mayor containing a magnificent retablo. Convento de Santo Domingo (14th c.), with a fine cloister, on a tufa hill 200 m high (old cave dwellings).

Through the Montes de Chinchilla. – The Valencia road (N 430) runs by way of Chinchilla de Monte Aragón through the Montes de Chinchilla and comes in 64 km to a branch road which runs N to *Alpera*. Near this little town is the *Cueva de la Vieja* (key from mayor), a cave with prehistoric rock paintings (10000–2000 B.C.). – The main road continues past the Alpera turning to **Almansa** (alt. 712 m; pop. 16,000), 74 km from Albacete, over which towers a massive Moorish castle on a hill of white limestone. Church of the Asunción (15th c.), which contains pictures by the Colombian painter Carlos Sosa; Palacio de los Condes de Cirat ("Casa Grande"); Convento de las Agustinas, with a Baroque and Renaissance façade (1564).

Castle, Almansa

To Hellín. – The road to Murcia (N 301) runs SE from Albacete through the Huerta de Albacete, passing the little town of *Tobarra* (alt. 631 m), and comes in 61 km to **Hellín** (alt. 566 m; pop. 30,000), a town surrounded by hills which was known to the Romans as *Ilunum*. Near the town are sulphur mines which were worked in Roman times. – 8 km E are the *Cuevas de Minateda*, with interesting prehistoric rock paintings.

Into the Sierra de Alcaraz. – From Albacete follow N 322 SW to *Balazote*, where the Iberian sculpture known as the "Bicha de Balazote" (the "Hind of Balazote"), dating from the 5th c. B.C., was found in 1898. The road then continues through lonely country to **Alcaraz** (alt. 798 m; pop 6000), 79 km from Albacete, a picturesque little town dominated by a Moorish castle on a nearby hill. It has a number of notable churches, including the Trinidad (1486), which has a fine tower, a beautiful doorway and statues by Salzillo and Roque López; Ayuntamiento (Town Hall), with a classical-style façade of 1588. – Nearby, to the N, is the *Santuario de Cortes*.

To La Roda. – N 301 crosses the Canal de Marla Cristina and leads NW by way of *La Gineta* to **La Roda** (alt. 716 m; pop. 13,000), 36 km from Albacete, a little market town in a fertile farming region. The church of El Salvador (16th c.), with a dome covered with dark blue azulejos, contains a Churrigueresque retablo (1721). Museo de Antonio Martinez (history of the town).

Alba de Tormes

Province: Salamanca (SA).
Telephone dialling code: 923.
Altitude: 821 m. – Population: 4000.
ⓘ **Ayuntamiento** (Town Hall),
Plaza del Generalísimo;
tel. Alba de Tormes 1.

HOTELS. – *Benedictino*, Benitas 6, III, 40 r.; Hostal *Alameda*, Avda. Juan Pablo II, P II, 10 r.

EVENT. – *Fiestas de Santa Teresa* (Oct.).

The old-world little town of Alba de Tormes lies 22 km SE of Salamanca

on a hill on the right bank of the Río Tormes. During the Middle Ages it was an important pilgrimage centre, with eighteen churches, of which only four remain.

SIGHTS. – The town has many memories of the great mystic Santa Teresa of Ávila (d. 1582), whose tomb is in the **Convento de Carmelitas**, founded in 1571. – Its finest churches are **San Juan** (12th c.), in Romanesque-Byzantine style, with a Churrigueresque retablo (1771); *Santiago Apóstol*, the oldest church in the town; and **San Miguel** with elaborate tombs and recumbent figures (13th–15th c.).

Alcalá de Henares

Province: Madrid (M).
Telephone dialling code: 91.
Altitude: 587 m. – Population: 140,000.
ⓘ **Oficina de Información de Turismo,**
Callejón de Santa Maria 1;
tel. 8 89 26 94.

HOTELS. – *El Bedel* (no rest.), San Diego 6, II, 51 r.; *Hostal Bari*, Carretera N 11, km 31, P II, 48 r.; *El Torero* (no rest.), Puerta de Madrid 18, P II, 18 r.

RESTAURANTS. – *Hosteria Nacional del Estudiante*, Colegios 3, old *posada* (inn) in Castilian style with an attractive inner courtyard; *Reinosa*, Goya 3; *Nuevo Olivers*, Los Gallegos 15; etc.

The old town of Alcalá de Henares, rebuilt after severe destruction during the Civil War, is beautifully situated on the left bank of the Río Henares. It was the Roman Complutum and the Moorish al-Kal'a ("fortress").

The town was the birthplace of Cervantes and the Emperor Ferdinand I. It had a famous university, founded by Cardinal Jiménez in 1508, which was moved to Madrid in 1836.

SIGHTS. – The town's most notable features is the **Colegio Mayor de San Ildefonso**, built as the University, with a beautiful Plateresque façade (16th c.). The *main doorway* is decorated with statues of warriors. In one of the inner courtyards is a *statue of Cardinal Jiménez* (1670). – A number of the town's medieval posadas still survive.

Alcántara

Province: Cácares (CC).
Telephone code: 927.
Altitude: 240 m. – Population: 4000.
ⓘ **Officina Municipal de Turismo,**
Avenida de Mérida 21;
tel. 39 00 02.

HOTEL. – *Cruz de Alcántara*, General Franco 3, P III,
6 r.

The old-world little frontier town of Alcántara lies above the south bank of the Río Tajo (Tagus), with a recently constructed dam and hydroelectric station (capacity 950,000 kW). The town was founded about A.D. 106. It was the headquarters of the knightly order of Alcántara and the birthplace of the great Spanish saint San Pedro de Alcántara.

SIGHTS. – The town's most important ancient monument is the *****Puente Romano**, the famous Roman bridge (Arabic: al-kantara) built over the Tagus in A.D. 105. The bridge, constructed entirely of granite blocks without the use of mortar, is 188 m long and 8 m wide, with six arches rising to heights of up to 58 m. In the middle is a gate-tower. On the left bank of the river is a small Roman temple. – The Gothic church of **Santa María de la Amocóbar**, built in the 13th c. on the site of an earlier mosque, has fine choirstalls and contains the tombs of the Grand Masters of the Order of Alcántara. – The *Convento de San Benito* (16th c.), once the seat of the Order, has a Gothic tower and cloister.

SURROUNDINGS. – 30 km E is the pretty little town of *Garrovillas*. – 15 km SE on C 523 is the village of **Brozas**, with the church of the Asunción, the finest Gothic church in the diocese.

Alcañiz

Province: Teruel (TE).
Telephone code: 974.
Altitude: 338 m. – Population: 10,000.
ⓘ **Ayuntamienta** (Town Hall),
Plaza de España 1;
tel. 13 11 31.

HOTELS. – *Parador Nacional de la Concordia*, Castillo de los Calatravos, II, 12 r.; *Guadalope*, Plaza de España 8, IV, 15 r.; *Senante*, Carretera N 232, IV, 29 r.; Hostal *Mesequer* (no rest.), Avendi Maestrazgo 9, P II, 30 r.

EVENTS. – *Fiesta de la Virgen de los Pueyos* (Sept.), the town's principal fiesta, with a pilgrimage to a chapel. – *Semana Santa* (Holy Week), with traditional ceremonies.

The ancient little town of Alcañiz, on the Río Guadalope, is the centre of one of the most characteristic regions in lower Aragon, noted for the production of olive oil. It lies on a steeply sloping eminence, surrounded by hills.

A Roman army was annihilated by the Carthaginians here in 212 B.C. In the 12th c. Alfonso I conquered the area and built a castle in Pui Pinos. The town was Jaime I's favourite residence.

SIGHTS. – The handsome 12th c. **Castillo de los Calatravos**, once held by the Templars, is now a parador. The main front is 18th c.; Gothic cloister, 12th c. chapel. – In Plaza de España are the **Ayuntamiento** (Town Hall), a carefully proportioned Renaissance building, and the richly decorated **Lonja** (15th c.), with pointed arches. – The collegiate church of **Santa Maria La Mayor** (1736) is a massive and imposing structure, of cathedral-like dimensions, with an interesting façade.

SURROUNDINGS. – 15 km SE on N 232, at *Venta de Valdealgorfa* (alt. 616 m), is a road junction, to the S of which is the *Cueva del Charco* (cave paintings).

To Zaragoza. – N 232 runs W past a salt lake, the *Estanca de Alcañiz* (on right), and over the bleak plateau *Llano de la Chumilla* (363 m) to *Híjar* (alt. 304 m), a little town lying above the Río Martín. N 232 then turns N to reach **Azaila** (alt. 276 m; pop. 3000), on the *Meseta de Azaila*, with a Celtic cemetery and Ibero-Roman remains.

Alcoy

Province: Alicante (A).
Telephone code: 965.
Altitude: 278 m. – Population: 61,000.
ⓘ **Centro de Iniciativas Turísticas;**
Avenida Puente San Jorge;
tel. 33 28 57.

HOTELS. – *Reconquista*, Puente San Jorge 1, II, 77 r.; *San Jorge*, San Juan de Ribera 11, IV, 86 r.; *Savoy*, Casablanca 5, P III, 44 r.

RESTAURANT. – *Lolo*, Castalla 5; *Venta del Pilar*, 2·5 km NE on the Valencia road.

EVENT. – *Moros y Cristianos* (Apr.), a fiesta commemorating the fighting between Moors and Christians, with mock battles in the streets and a closing firework display and bell-ringing.

The town of Alcoy lies in a picturesque setting at the foot of the Sierra de Montcabrer, surrounded by terraced olive-groves and vineyards. Paper and textiles are important factors in the economy.

SIGHTS. – Two interesting churches, *Santa María* (1767) and *Santo Sepulcro*, with 18th c. tiles. – *Museo Arqueológico*, with a large collection of Iberian pottery, and lead tablets with inscriptions in Ionic Greek which were found in the vicinity.

SURROUNDINGS. – 3 km E, at *La Serreta*, are the remains of an Iberian settlement. Material found here is in the Museo Arqueológico. – 4 km S of Alcoy, on the hill of Carrascal (964 m), is the *Santuario de le Fuente Roja*; beautiful views. – 10 km N on N 340 is **Cocentaina** (alt. 455 m; pop. 8000), an old-world little town with remains of Roman walls and gates, partly rebuilt during the Moorish period, and the *Palacio Condal* (15th c.), under a hill crowned by an old tower. – N 340 runs S from Alcoy over the *Puerto da Carrasqueta* (1020 m), with an impressive *view of the wide coastal plain and the sea, to **Jijona** (alt. 460 m; pop. 6000), noted for its nougat (*turrón*); imposing castle.

Fishing harbour, Algeciras

BOAT SERVICES. – Ferry services to Tangier by Compañia Trasmediterránea, Limadet Ferry; and Comarit Ferry; other ferries to Ceuta by Compañia Trasmediterránea.

The port of Algeciras lies at the southern tip of the Iberian peninsula on the W side of Algeciras Bay, opposite Gibraltar. It is the starting point for a visit to Gibraltar, Ceuta, Tangier and the rest of Morocco, and is also a popular winter holiday resort.

Algeciras

Province: Cádiz (CA).
Telephone code: 956.
Altitude: 2 m. – Population: 100,000.
Ⓘ **Oficina de Información de Turismo,**
Avenida de la Marina (Puente);
tel. 60 09 11.

HOTELS. – *Reina Cristina*, in its own park, on a hill above the sea to the S of the town, I, 135 r., SP, tennis; *Octavia*, San Bernardo 1, I, 80 r.; *Al-Mar*, Avda de la Marina 2, II, 192 r.; *Alarde* (no rest.), Alfonso XI 4, II, 68 r.; *Las Yucas* (no rest), Agustín Balsamo 2, II, 33 r.; *Anglo Hispano*, Avda Villanueva 7, III, 30 r.; *Marina Victoria*, Avda Cañonero Dato 7, III, 49 r.; *Término*, Avda Villanueva 6, III, 45 r. – CAMPING SITE: *Costasol*, 3 km N of the town.

RESTAURANTS. – *La Cazuela*, Castelar 59, rustic atmosphere, Basque specialities; *Marea Baja*, Trafalgar 2 (fish, mussels).

EVENTS. – *Feria and fiestas*, with bullfights (June). – *Fiestas partronales* (Aug.), with under-water fishing competition and bullfights. – *Festivales de España*, with regatta (Aug.).

WATER SPORTS. – Algeciras has a Club Náutico and excellent beaches in the immediate vicinity of the town – El Rinconcillo to the N, Getares (3 km long) to the S, La Atunera in La Línea. SPORT and RECREATION on land: bullfights, golf, tennis, fishing, shooting. (Information on fishing and shooting: Sociedad de Caza y Pesca 'La Oropéndola', Santisimo 1.)

The port handles a considerable export trade in cork from the forests of the *Seirra de los Gazules*, to the W of the town. The town was settled from 1704 onwards by Spanish refugees from Gibraltar and was developed by Charles III.

SIGHTS. – The **Casa Consistorial** (Town Hall), built in 1897, was the scene of the international conference of 1906 which recognised the predominance of France and Spain in Morocco. SW of the town, beyond the Río Miel, are the remains of **Old Algeciras**, founded by the Moors in 713 under the name of Al-Gezira al-Khadra ("green island"), conquered by Alfonso XI of Castile in 1344 and destroyed by Mohammed V of Granada in 1368.

SURROUNDINGS. – **Around Algeciras Bay**: Along the harbour into N 340, than 15 km NE to **San Rogue** (alt. 109 m; pop. 18,000), built by Spanish settlers from Gibraltar from 1704 onwards. It lies on a hill, with wide views. Remains of the Roman colony of *Carteia*. – From here it is another 7 km S to the frontier town of *La Línea de la Concepcíon* (pop. 60,000). On the S side of the town is the Spanish customs post and beyond this the frontier bewteen Spain and **Gibraltar**. (Frontier now open).

Alicante

Province: Alicante (A).
Telephone code: 965.
Altitude: at sea level. – Population: 251,000.

(i) **Oficinia de Información de Turismo,**
Explanada de España 2;
tel. 21 22 85.
Patronato Provincial de Turismo,
Avda, del General Mola 6;
tel. 12 35 31.

HOTELS. – *Sidi San Juan Palace-Sol*, Pda. Cabo la Huerta, L, 176 r., SP., Tennis; *Adoc* (no rest), Finca Adoc Bloque 17–18, I, 93 r., SP., Tennis; *Gran Sol* (no rest.), Avda Méndez Nuñez 3, I, 150 r.; *Colegio Oficial Farmacéuticos* (no rest.), Gravina 9, II, 46 r.; *Covadonga* (no rest.), Plaza de los Luceros 17, II, 83 r.; *Cristal* (no rest.), López Torregrosa 9, II, 54 r.; *Estudio Hotel Alicante*, Poeta Vila y Blanco 4, II, 493 r. (Apartment Hotel); *Leuka* (no rest.), Segura 23, II, 108 r.; *Maya* (no rest.), Canónigo Peñalva s/n, II, 198 r.; *Palas*, Cervantes 5, II, 49 r.; *Bahía* (no rest.), F 14, III, 22 r.; *La Balseta* (no rest.), Manero Molla 9, III, 84 r.; *La Reforma* (no rest.), Reyes Católicos 7, III, 52 r.; *El Álamo* (no rest.), San Fernando 56, IV, 48 r.; *Alfonso el Sabio* (no rest.), Alfonso el Sabio 18, IV, 85 r.; *Marítimo* (no rest.), Calle Valdés N 13, IV, 33 r.; *Navas* (no rest.), Las Navas 26, IV, 40 r.; *San Remo* (no rest.), Las Navas 30, IV, 28 r.; Hostal *Cervantes* (no rest.), Pascual Pérez 19, P I, 30 r.; – CAMPING SITES: *Bahía de Santa Pola*, 4 km E on Playa de la Albufereta; two others in the immediate vicinity, to N and S.

RESTAURANTS in several hotels; also *Delfin*, Explanada de España 12; *Dársena*, Muelle del Puerto; *La Goleta* Explanada de España 8 (well spoken of); *Nou Manolin*, Villegas 3; *La Masía*, Valdés 10, *Quo Vadis*, Plaza de la Santisima Faz 3; *Jumillano*, César Elguezábal 62; *Rincón Castellano*, Mandero Mollá 12; *China*, Avda Dr. Gadea 11; etc.

EVENTS. – *Hogueras de San Juan* (June), a fiesta in honour of St John, with *hogueras* (figures of wood and cardboard which are burned at the end of the fiesta), parades, riding contests, fireworks and colourful booths and stalls. – *Cátedra Mediterránea* (summer), courses for foreigners (information: Cátedra, Ramón y Cajal 4).

CASINO. – *Casino Costa Blanca*, Villajoyosa.

WATER SPORTS. – Several bathing beaches: to the N, near the Valencia road, *Playa de la Albufereta* (4 km) and *Playa de San Juan* (9 km); to the S, *Arenal del Sol* (10 km), on the coast road to Cartagena. All kinds of water sports, including sub-aqua diving. Royal Regatta Club.

SPORT and RECREATION on land. – Shooting and fishing, target shooting, riding, tennis, gliding; *flamenco* at Tablao Flamenco and El Zorongo.

Alicante, known to the Romans as Lucentum and to the Moors as Lecant or Al-Lucant and now a provincial capital, lies on a beautiful bay on the SE coast of Spain, under a hill crowned by the Castillo de Santa Bárbara. With its many hotels and tower blocks, it is a town of modern aspect.

Alicante, at the centre of the Costa Blanca, is a seaside resort which is popular both in summer and in winter. In recent years numerous parks and open spaces have been laid out and some of the streets and boulevards widened. The town has economic importance as a port: varied industries (chemicals, aluminium) and export of wine, raisins, citrus fruits, early vegetables, oil, liquorice and esparto grass.

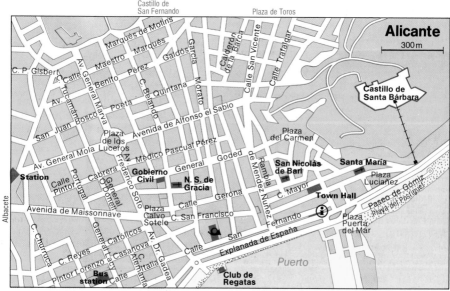

Alicante Harbour

SIGHTS. – The central feature of the town is the *Plaza de Calvo Sotelo*, from which the palm-lined Avenida del Doctor Gadea leads down to the spacious **harbour**, protected by large breakwaters (wide views). Along the front extends the *Explanada de España*, almost 600 m long, also lined with palms, paved in colourful mosaic patterns and flanked by numerous hotels and cafés. From the W and outer breakwaters, and particularly from the lighthouse at the end of the E breakwater, there are beautiful views. – The line of the Explanada de España is continued beyond *Plaza Puerta del Mar* by the *Paseo de Gómiz*, which runs along the *Playa del Postiguet* to the suburban district of Roig and the *Playa de San Juan*.

From the Plaza Puerta de Mar we go left across the park-like *Plaza del Teniente Luciáñez* to reach the older part of the town and the church of **Santa María**, built by the Catholic monarchs and remodelled in the 18th c., with a Rococo doorway and a richly decorated Baroque interior. A little way SW is the fine **Ayuntamiento** (Town Hall), built between 1696 and 1760, with two square towers 35 m high and a Churrigueresque façade. On the steps of the Ayuntamiento is the "zero point" above sea level by reference to which all heights in Spain are measured. – NW of the Ayuntamiento is the 17th c. church of **San Nicolás de Bari**, dedicated to the town's patron saints, also known as the Cathedral. It has an impressive interior, a number of notable retablos and a fine cloister. In the adjoining district of Santa Cruz, on the western slope of the castle hill, is a *Ceramic Museum*.

From *Calle de la Concepción* it is half an hour's walk up the castle hill to the **Castillo de Santa Bárbara** (209 m), from which there are magnificent *views of the town, the coast, the huerta and the hills to the N. There is also a lift to the top of the hill from the E end of the Paseo de Gómiz.

NW of the Plaza de Calvo Sotelo, reached by way of the *Plaza de los Luceros*, is the massive building occupied by the *Diputación Provincial*, in which is the **Museo Arqueológico**. In addition to an interesting archaeological collection, including a figure of the goddess Tanit, this contains a picture gallery and a collection of coins. Close by is the church of *Nuestra Señora de Gracia* (1949).

SURROUNDINGS. – 5 km NE of the Explanada de España on N 332, which leads to the suburban district of San Juan, is the **Convento de Santa Clara** (or *Santa Faz*), with an 18th c. church which houses the *sudario* (handkerchief with the imprint of Christ's face) of St Veronica.

To Villena. – N 330 runs W and then N, over the *Puerto de Pedreras* and through *Monforte del Cid* (230 m), to **Elda** (alt. 416 m: pop. 37,000), lying to the left of the road in a well-cultivated huerta, with a ruined castle high above it on a tabular hill. Important shoe-manufacturing industry. 9 km SW is *Monóvar*, which has a parish church of 1750 with a leaning tower (Torre del Reloj). – Returning to N 330, we continue over the *Peña de la Correta* and past *Sax* (alt. 526 m), on the left of the road, with a ruined castle on a tall crag, to **Villena** (alt. 504 m; pop. 27,000), a picturesquely situated little hill town dominated by a handsome 15th c. castle with a massive keep. The late Gothic church of Santiago (1492), with a square tower, contains a richly carved retablo. Church of Santa María (Gothic). Small archaeological museum with an interesting collection.

To Torrevieja. – The coast road along the Costa Blanca (N 332) runs S to **Santa Pola**, with the *Albufera de Elche*, and continues via the bathing resort of *Guardamar de Segura* to **Torrevieja** (pop. 10,000), an old port which has developed into a modern bathing resort. Considerable quantities of salt are extracted from the nearby *Salinas de la Mata* and *Salinas de Torrevieja*.

Almería

Province: Almería (AL).
Telephone code: 951.
Altitude: 2 m. – Population: 140,000.
(i) **Oficina de Información de Turismo,**
Calle Hermanos Machado
tel. 23 47 05
Delagación Provincial de Turismo,
Calle Hermanos Machado 4;
tel. 23 92 23

HOTELS. – *Gran Hotel Almería* (no rest.), Avda Reina Regente 8, I, 124 r., SP.; *La Parra*, Bahía el Palmer, I, 156 r., SP.; *Torreluz IV*, Plaza Flores 5, I, 56 r., SP.; *Club Alborán*, Alquian Retamar, II, 103 r.; *Costasol* (no rest.), Avda de Almería 58, II, 55 r.; *Hairán* (no rest.), Avda Cabo de Gata 72, II, 40 r.; *Indálico* (no rest.), Dolores R. Sopeña 4, II, 52 r.; *Torreluz II* (no rest.), Plaza Flores 1, II, 67 r.; *Embajador*, Calzado de Castro 4, III, 67 r.; *La Perla* (no rest.), Plaza del Carmen 7, III, 44 r.; *Torreluz* (no rest.), Plaza de Flores 6, III, 24 r.; etc.

CAMPING SITES. – *La Garrofa* (5 km W); *Mar Azul* (9 km W); others in the area.

RESTAURANTS. – *Solymar*, Carretera de Málaga (view of fishing harbour and town); *Rincón de Juan Pedro*, Plaza del Carmen 16, *Club de Mar*, Muelle 1 (view of harbour). – IN AGUADULCE: *El Crucero*, Playa 6 (view of sea).

EVENTS. – **Fiestas de la Ciudad de Almería**, one of the most brilliant fiestas in Andalusia, usually lasting 10 days (Aug.). – *Fiestas de Invierno* (Dec.–Jan.), with cultural events, Nativity crib competition, bull-fights and ceremonial entry of the Three Kings. – *Semana Santa* (Holy Week), with an impressive procession. – *Costa del Sol Rally* (Dec.), a car race through the provinces of Almería, Granada and Málaga.

WATER SPORTS. – Under-water fishing (two diving schools); fishing (boats can be hired for sea angling); sailing, water skiing.

SPORT and RECREATION on land. – Bullfights, golf (two courses), tennis, riding, hang gliding (training school).

Almería, capital of the province of the same name, was already an important Mediterranean port in Roman times, when it was called Portus Magnus. The town, bordered by an area of subtropical vegetation, was known to the Arabs as Al-Mariyya ("mirror of the sea"), a name which it has preserved in slightly altered form.

The town, with two picturesque old castles dominating it, lies in the wide Gulf of Almería, which is enclosed on the W by the *Sierra de Gádor* (1443 m), on the NE by the *Sierra Alhamilla* (1359 m) and on the SE by the *Sierra de Gata* (513 m), named after the Cabo de Gata which juts far out into the Mediterranean. The port handles a considerable export trade in fresh grapes, southern fruits and esparto grass, as well as iron ore and other minerals from mines in the hinterland. A clean town of whitewashed houses, Almería is one of the leading centres on the stretch of coast, so favoured by tourists, where the bountiful climate (with 322 days of sun) gives it the name of Costa del Sol, the Sunshine Coast.

SIGHTS. – The central feature of the old town, reminiscent of an eastern city with its Moorish-style houses, is the *Puerta de Purchena*, in which is the information office. From here Calle de las Tiendas runs SW to the 16th c. church of **Santiago el Viejo**, now designated as a national monument, with a slender Romanesque tower 55 m high. Then along Calle Lope de Vega to the *Plaze Vieja*, with the *Ayuntamiento* (Town Hall). To the S, in Plaza de la Catedral, are the *Palacio Episcopal* (Bishop's Palace) and the *Seminario*.

On the S side of the square is the **Cathedral**, a fortress-like structure with four massive corner towers, a tower-like apse and battlements. It was rebuilt by Diego de Siloé between 1524 and 1543 after destruction in an earthquake. It contains fine carved walnut choir-stalls by Juan de Orea (1558) and a statue of San Indalecio, the town's patron saint, by Salzillo.

On a hill W of the town is a Moorish fortress, the **Alcazaba**, which was begun by Abderrahman III, Caliph of Córdoba, enlarged by Almansor and completed by Hairan, and later extended by the Emperor Charles V. It has a massive 15th c. tower, the *Torreón del Homanaje* (Tower of Homage), with a Gothic gateway and the arms of the Catholic monarchs. Concerts and dramatic performances are given in the castle during the great fiesta in August. – On the adjoining hill, to the N, are the ruins of the **Castillo de San Cristóbal**.

Alcazaba, Almería

Between the Cathedral and the *Avenida* (or Paseo) *de Almería* are the church of *San Pedro*, founded in 1494 on the site of an earlier mosque (present building erected 1795, with frescoes in the dome by Fray Juan García), and the **Santuario de Santo Domingo**, a 17th c. church which has been restored, with a fine Baroque altar and an image of the Virgen del Mar, the town's second patron saint, which was found on the beach at Torre García in 1502.

SURROUNDINGS. – Enclosed by hills and lying within a widely extended bay, Almería offers a wide variety of excursions, both on winding mountain roads and along the coast.

Circuit through the Alpujarras (*c.* 160 km). – The route through this hilly region, also known as the "Road of Grapes and Oranges", runs via *Benahadux* on N 340 and through the rich vega of Almería to the little town of **Gádor** (alt. 158 m; pop. 3600), 17 km from Almería in the foothills of the Sierra de Gádor. Above the town, with its houses sporting coats of arms, is a ruined Moorish castle. – Beyond Gádor N 324 diverges to the left and follows the valley of the *Río Nacimiento*, with numerous gorges, and along the southern slopes of the *Sierra de los Filabres* to Guadix.

A minor road which branches off N 324 runs along the charming valley of the *Río Andarax* and through *Canjáyar* to the picturesque village of *Laujar de Andarax*, with the ruins of a Moorish Alcazaba and the 16th c. church of the Encarnación. It then continues S via *Berja*, with remains of town walls, to **Adra** (pop. 16,000), a long straggling port town, formerly fortified, with bathing beaches.

From here the route continues E on the coast road (N 340) along the foot of the Sierra de Gádor. A secondary road on the right (11 km) runs down to the little fishing port and bathing resort of *Roquetas del Mar*. The main road continues to **Aguadulce**, a major tourist centre a few kilometres W of Almería, with swimming pools, parks, sports facilities and a large bathing beach.

Circuit of the Acantilados (*c.* 270 km). – This route takes in the steep coastal scenery and beaches E of Almería. The road runs past the airport to the *Cabo de Gata*, with its small rocky beaches on either side of the lighthouse, and continues to **San José**, a little fishing port with beautiful beaches separated from one another by steep cliffs. There is ample scope for sub-aqua diving in the adjoining bays of Los Genoveses and Los Escullos.

The road then turns inland to the little town of *Níjar* (pop. 12,000), noted for its potters' workshops and old weaving establishments, skirts the N side of the *Sierra de la Higuera*, returns to the coast and continues via *Carboneras*, with beautiful views, to the pictures-que village of **Mojácar* (alt. 175 m; pop. 2000; Parador Nacional de los Reyes Católicos, I, 98 r., SP). This town of gleaming white houses, known in Arabic as *Murgis-akra*, still preserves Moorish traditions in its architecture and way of life. Nearby is a beach of fine sand, with the Parador Nacional and a camping site. 5 km N are the Castillo de Garrucha and a lighthouse, and there are a number of old watch-towers in the surrounding area.

From Garrucha a side road runs NW to the little town of **Vera** (alt. 94 m; pop. 5000), which has a church with a beautiful retablo. 6 km N are the *Cuevas de Almanzora* (cave dwellings). From Vera we continue on N 340 in the direction of Almería. Off the main road, soon after it crosses the *Río de Águas*, is the charming little town of **Sorbas** (alt. 441 m), on the steep slopes flanking the valley; here too there are cave dwellings. – The road then runs over the vega and follows a fairly level course, in long straight stretches, between the Sierra Alhamilla on the left and the Sierra de los Filabres on the right, to **Tabernas** (alt. 350 m; pop. 4000), a little town of Moorish aspect, with a history going back to Roman times, which straggles round the foot of a hill bearing the ruins of a Moorish castle.

The road then continues over the fertile vega. A minor road on the right runs up to the remote little hill town of *Gérgal* (castle), 18 km away. N 340 runs through the hills of *Rioja* into the green huerta, with large orange-groves, and then joins N 324 coming from Guadix (Granada).

Andalusia (Andalucia)

Autonomous Region.
Organ of Government: Junta de Andalucia.
Provinces: Almería, Cádiz, Córdoba, Granada,
Huelva, Jaén, Málaga and Seville.

**Andalusia, the most southerly part
of the Iberian peninsula, is what
most people think of as the very
incarnation of Spain. It offers an
enchanting counterpoint of snow-
covered mountains and coastal barriers of dunes, sun-scorched expanses of high steppeland and green
huertas, groves of palms and heath-
land gay with rock-roses. To all
this it adds the monuments of a
glorious past, supreme among them
the columns of the Great Mosque in
Córdoba and the vivid red towers
and beautiful patios of the Alhambra
in Granada.**

The southern part of Andalusia is dominated by the **Andalusian Mountains** or
Betic Cordillera (*Cordillera Bética*).
Although this range contains Spain's
highest peak, the Cerro de Mulhacén
(3481 m), in the *Sierra Nevada* with its
covering of eternal snow, it is mainly a
region of rounded mountains of medium
height. Between the Betic Cordillera and
the *Sierra Morena* lies the **Andalusian
plain**, watered by the River Guadalquivir.

Andalusian still-life

The people of Andalusia have preserved
something of their Moorish past in race,
language and culture. In contrast to the
deliberate and dignified Castilian, the
Andalusian is notable for this carefree
cheerfulness and an almost Oriental play
of fancy. The women of Andalusia are
noted for their grace and ready wit (*sal*
"salt"); and to the Spaniard *salero* expresses the very essence of feminine
charm.

Andorra

Principality. – Car nationality letters: AND.
Altitude: 939–2407 m. – Population: 45,000.

ⓘ **Sindicat d'Iniciativa de les Valls
d'Andorra,**
Dr. Vilanova sln, Andorra la Vella;
tel. (9738) 2 02 14.

HOTELS. – IN ANDORRA LA VELLA: *Andorra Palace*, 140
r., SP.; *Andorra Centre*, 150 r., SP.; *Eden Roc*, 55 r.,
President, 88 r., SP.; *Flora*, 45 r., SP.; *Cerqueda*, 75 r.,
SP.; *Pyrénées*, 84 r.; *Internacional*, 50 r.; *Mirador*, 26
r.; *Celler d'En Toni*, 19 r.; *Cornellá*, 90 r.; *Serola*, 60 r.
SP.; *Garden*, 34 r., SP.; *Jaume I*, 70 r., SP.; *Isard*, 55 r.,
etc. – CAMPING SITES. – IN ENCAMP: *De França*, 48 r.
Rosaleda, 74 r., AP.; *Univers*, 40 r.; *Comtes de Foix*, 70
r.; *La Mola*, 45 r.; etc. – IN LES ESCALDAS: *Roc Blanc*
240 r., SP.; *Delfos*, 200 r., SP.; *Comtes d'Urgell*, 200 r.,
SP.; *Carlemany*, 54 r., SP.; *Paris-Londres*, 115 r., SP.
Europa, 70 r.; *Espel*, 102 r.; *Muntanya*, 85 r., SP.
Madriu, 50 r.; etc. – IN SANT JULIÀ DE LÒRIA (many hotels
close winter): *Pol*, 75 r.; *Co-Princeps*, 76 r.; *Sol-Park*,
40 r.; *Sant Eloi*, 88 r.; *Sant Julià*, 100 r.; *Coma Bella*, 28
r.; *Font de Ferro*, 34 r.; *Glòria*, 40 r.; etc.

**The free state of Andorra (Valls
d'Andorra; in French Vallées
d'Andorra; in Spanish Principado de
Andorra), occupying two high valleys of the Valira, is one of the
smallest states in Europe, with an
area of 462 sq. km.**

Vejer de la Frontera, Andalusia

t has preserved its independence for a thousand years and since 1278 has been under the joint protection of its two larger neighbours, France and Spain. Its remoteness has enabled it to maintain its own characteristic patriarchal customs and way of life, though these are how disappearing in face of the rapid development of tourism.

SIGHTS. – *Andorra la Vella** (alt. 1029 m; pop. 16,000; in the town 5500), the chief town, lies in a beautiful setting on the E side of the *Pic d'Enclar* (2317 m), at the junction of two mountain streams, the *Valira del Orient* and the *Valira del Nord*, to form the *Gran Valira*. It has a fine *church* (12th c., enlarged 1969), with beautiful woodcarving. In the centre of the town is the unpretentious *Casa de la Vall* (16th c.), the traditional seat of government, with the council chamber on the first floor. The archives of Andorra (including documents said to date from the time of Charlemagne and his son Louis the Pious) are kept in a wall cupboard (the "Cupboard of the Six Keys") to which each of the six parishes holds a key.

SURROUNDINGS. – Coming from Spain (Seo de Urgel), the first village is **Saint Julià de Lòria** (alt. 939 m): church with Romanesque tower and a beautiful 17th c. crucifix of carved wood.

On the road which runs NE from Andorra la Vella through the valley of the *Valira del Orient* into France is the popular spa (sulphurous springs) of **Les Escaldes** (alt. 1105 m), with the church of *San Miguel d'Engolasters*. – Higher up the valley, where it opens out, is the village of **Encamp** (alt. 1315 m), from which there is a cableway fo *Engolasters*. On a hill to the N is the pilgrimage church of *Notre-Dame de Méritxell*, a national shrine. – Above Encamp (7 km) is **Canillo** (alt. 1560 m), an old-world village of slate-roofed houses dominated by the parish church.

Street scene, Andorra la Vella

Still higher, above the road on the right, is the chapel of *Sant Joan de Caselles* (12th c.), with a beautiful 15th c. retablo. – Further on is **Soldeu** (alt. 1850 m), the highest village in Andorra (chair-lift, winter sports).

From Andorra la Vella a road (partly cut through the rock, with three tunnels) runs 8 km N along the valley of the *Valira del Nord* to **Ordino** (alt. 1305 m), which has a fine church and picturesque houses. – 10 km farther on is the hamlet of **El Serrat** (alt. 1540 m), in a magnificent mountain setting.

Aragon

Autonomous Region.
Organ of Government: Disputación General de Aragón.
Provinces: Huesca, Teruel and Zaragoza.

The old kingdom of Aragon, a relatively featureless upland region, has much the same character of remoteness and bareness as Castile, in contrast to the lively activity of Catalonia and the almost Central European aspect of the Basque country. Enclosed by mountains, it has the same continental climate as the Meseta, with very dry summers during which the whitish-grey plains swelter in the heat. The cultivation of corn and vegetables is confined to the tracts of land along the banks of the rivers.

Aragon, together with Navarre (see p. 175), occupies the Ebro basin, an area of lower ground enclosed by the Pyrenees in the N and the succession of scarps bordering the Meseta in the SW, forming a sharp point in the NW and shut off

A typical high valley in Andorra

Aragonese landscape, near Tremp

from the Mediterranean by the hills of Catalonia. The *Ebro*, coming from the Cantabrian Mountains, flows through the Conchas de Haro into the basin and traverses it in a gentle gradient before breaking through the Catalonian hills in a narrow valley to reach the sea.

The people of Aragon are similar in character to their neighbours of Castile – proud, freedom-loving but demanding little for themselves. Their attachment to freedom was given expression in their *fueros* (charter of rights), which were preserved until their abolition by Philip V in 1707. – The Aragonese have a picturesque traditional costume consisting of a black velvet jacket with slashed sleeves ornamented with buttons, a red or purple sash (*faja*) round the waist, black velvet knee-breeches, long stockings and hemp sandals (*alpargatus*), and a brightly coloured handkerchief on the head.

Aranda de Duero

Province: Burgos (BU).
Telephone code: 947.
Altitude: 798 m. – Population: 30,000.
ⓘ **Ayuntamiento** (Town Hall),
   Plaza Mayor 1;
   tel. 50 00 75.

HOTELS. – *Los Broncos*, Carretera N 1, km 160, II, 29 r.; *Montehermoso*, Carretera N 1, km 163, II, 54 r.; *Juliá*, San Gregorio 2, IV, 65 r.; *Tres Condes* (no rest.), Parcela 4, P I, 35 r.; *Aranda*, Plaza Doctor Costales, P II. 48 r.; *Ulloa*, Plaza de Santa María 1, P 1, 35 r.; etc. – CAMPING SITE: *Costaján*.

RESTAURANTS: *Mesón de la Villa*, Alejandro Rodríguez de Valcárcel 3; *Casa Florencia*, Arias de Miranda 14; *Méson el Roble*, P 1, Primo de Rivera 7; *Chef Fermín*, Avda. Castilla 69; etc.

EVENTS. – *Fiestas* (Sept.), with traditional ceremonies, folk dancing and various contests.

Aranda de Duero, beautifully situated on both banks of the Río Duero in the centre of a fertile vega, is still enclosed by its old walls.

SIGHTS. – The handsome late Gothic church of **Santa María la Real**, begun about 1500 by Simon of Cologne, has a very beautiful façade, an Isabelline doorway and a Plateresque pulpit of walnut wood. The church of *San Juan* dates from the 13th c. – Pilgrimage chapel of the *Virgin de las Viñas*.

SURROUNDINGS. – 3 km NE, on a secondary road, is the little town of **Sinovas**. The church of *San Nicolás de Bari* (national monument) has an elaborate polychrome coffered ceiling in Mudéjar style (13th–14th c.) with representations of human figures.

Aranjuez

Province: Madrid (M).
Telephone code: 91.
Altitude: 492 m. – Population: 35,000.
ⓘ **Oficina de Información de Turismo,**
   Plaza Santiago Rusiñol;
   tel. 8 91 04 27.

HOTELS. – *Las Mercedes*, Carretera N IV, km 46, II, 37 r.; *Hostal Francisco José* (no rest.), Avda del Príncipe 12, P II, 28 r.; *Infantas*, Calle de las Infantas 4, P II, 40 r.; *Príncipe*, Avda del Príncipe 11, P II, 11 r.; etc.

RESTAURANTS. – **El Castillo*, Jardines del Príncipe, in the hall of an old castle; *Casa Pablo*, Alimbar 20, Castilian-style; *Chirón*, Real 10; *La Mina*. Avda del Príncipe 21.

*Aranjuez, formerly a royal summer residence, lies in the basin of the Río Tajo some 50 km S of the Spanish capital. It is noted for its asparagus and strawberries.

SIGHTS. – This favourite resort of the Spanish kings possesses two palaces and extensive parks and gardens. The central point of the town is the *Plaza de San Antonio*, to the S of the bridge over the Tajo, around which are a number of handsome buildings. – To the W of the town is the **Royal Palace** (*Palacio Real*), rebuilt by Philip V in 1727 on the site of an earlier residence destroyed by fires in 1660 and 1665 and subsequently restored after a late fire. It contains some interesting pictures; Museum of Court Dress on the ground floor. – To the E of the palace is the *Parterre*, a beautiful ornamental garden. From here two bridges ead to the *Jardín de la Isla ("Island Garden"), a notable feature of which is ne avenue of plane-trees along the river nown as the *Salón de los Reyes Católios.* – To the NE of the town is the **Jardín del Príncipe**, laid out in the region of Charles IV, which contains magnificent rees, including exotic species. The *Calle de la Reina* leads of the **Casa del Labrador**, a small country house with a umptuous *interior, built in 1803 during he reign of Charles IV.

Arévalo

Province: Ávila (AV).
elephone code: 918.
Altitude: 826 m. – population: 5000.
ⓘ **Ayuntamiento** (Town Hall),
Plaza General Franco 10;
tel. 30 00 01.

HOTELS. – *Fray Juan Gil* (no rest.), Avda Emilio Romero, III, 30 r.; *Hostel El Comercio*, Calle 18 de ulio 2, P III, 20 r.

The little town of Arévalo lies in the N of the province of Ávila at the outflow of the Río Arevalillo into the Río Adaja. A number of churches and convents bear witness to its former importance as one of the keys of Castile.

SIGHTS. – Convent of **Santa María la Real**, in Romanesque-Mudéjar style, built in the 12th c. on the site of a former royal palace. – Parish church of *Santo Domingo*, with a Byzantine apse. – **Castillo de Arévalo**, with a well-preserved *Torre del Homenaje*, where sabel the Catholic spent her early years.

SURROUNDINGS. – 24 km W of Arévalo on C 605 is **Madrigal de las Altas Torres**, birthplace of Isabel he Catholic, with several brick-built Romanesque churches.

Astorga

Province: León (LE).
Telephone code: 987.
Altitude: 869 m. – Population: 13,000.
ⓘ **Oficina de Información de Turismo**,
Plaza de España (in Town Hall);
tel. 61 68 38.

HOTELS. – *Gaudi*, (no rest.), Eduardo de Castro 6, II, 35 r.; *Hostal Las Cadenas*, Pio Gullón 8, P II, 12 r.; *Gallego* (no rest.), Avda Ponferrada 28, P II, 58 r.; *La Peseta* (no rest.), Plaza San Bartolomé 3, P II, 22 r.; *San Narciso* (no rest.), Carretéra Madrid–La Coruña, km 325, P II, 13 r.; *Santana* (no rest.), Plaza Portirio López 12, P II, 18 r.; *Coruna* (no rest.), Avda Ingeniero Ahijon 22, P III, 18 r.; etc.

RESTAURANTS. – *Virginia*, Plaza de Santocildes 16; *La Concha*, General Mola 2; *El Norte*, opposite the station; *Camino de Santiago*, Río Esla; *La Ruta Gallega*, Riego de la Vega; etc.

EVENTS. – *Ferias* (Aug.), with bullfights, riding competitions and tradtional dances of the Maragatos (see below). – *Semana Santa* (Holy Week), with religious procession and parades by the confraternities.

Astorga, still partly surrounded by walls dating from the late Roman period, is an old-world episcopal city occupying a beautiful situation on an outlier of the Manzanal range. Described by Pliny in Roman times as a "splendid city" (*urbs magnifica*), it rose to prosperity and power in the 9th c. as important staging point on the pilgrim road to Santiago de Compostela.

SIGHTS. – The town's finest building is the **Cathedral** (15th–16th c.), which has three Plateresque *doorways* with sculptured scenes from the life of Christ on the W front and two 17th c. *towers*. The high altar has a *retablo* by G. Becerra (1562); fine carved woodwork; *choir-stalls* (1551); Gothic *cloister*, rebuilt in 1780. In the *sacristy* is the valuable cathedral treasury, including an 11th c. chalice.

In the arcaded *Plaza Mayor* are the 17th c. *Casa Consistorial* (Town Hall), with a Maragatos clock, and the *Palacio Episcopal* (Bishop's Palace), a neo-Gothic building by Antonio Gaudí (1893). The Bishop's Palace houses a museum containing pictures of the 14th–17th c., material on the pilgrimage to Santiago and costumes of the Maragatos.

SURROUNDINGS. – NW of Astorga is the region known as the *Maragatería*, on the SE slopes of the *Montes de León*, with some 30 villages occupied by the Maragatos, a people of unknown origin (perhaps Germanic) who were formerly employed as carters. They marry only among themselves and still wear their picturesque traditional costumes on special occasions.

To La Bañeza. – From Astorga N VI runs SE down the valley of the *Río Tuerto* to **La Bañeza** (alt. 771 m; pop. 10,000). There was a settlement here in Roman times, and some remains are still to be seen. In the Ermita de Jesús is an 18th c. figure of Christ by Salzillo.

Asturias

Autonomous Region.
Organ of Government: Consejo de Gobierno del
Principado de Asturias. Province: Asturias.

**The former principality of Asturias
contains few towns, the only ones of
any size being the capital, Oviedo,
and the port and industrial town of
Gijón. Along the picturesque coasts
with their steep cliffs are numerous
little fishing villages, most of which
have developed into popular seaside
resorts.**

Between Oviedo and Luarca

Asturias is a hilly region extending along
the Bay of Biscay to the W of the province
of Cantabria, almost wholly occupied by
the **Cantabrian Mountains** (*Cordillera
Cantábrica*), which here rise to Alpine
altitudes, reaching their highest point in
the *Picos de Europa* (2642 m). High
passes run through the mountains to
the S, but only the *Puerto de Pajares*
(1379 m), which is traversed by the road
from Oviedo to León (N 630), provides a
link between Asturias and central Spain.

Asturias is the centre of the Spanish
mining industry. Among its various minerals coal is of particular importance, and
the Asturian coalfield produces roughly
half the total Spanish output. Other
sources of income for those not engaged
in mining or in industry are fishing, in the
coastal areas, and farming. Those who
make their living from agriculture live
either in villages, on isolated farms or –
most commonly – in straggling hamlets.
The basis of Asturian agriculture is maize
and fruit growing and stock-farming
(particularly pigs, which yield the famous
Asturian ham).

Ávila

Province: Ávila (AV).
Telephone code: 918.
Altitude: 1130 m. – Population: 40,000.
ⓘ **Oficina de Información de Turismo**,
Plaza de la Catedral 4;
tel. 21 13 87.
Delegación Territorial de Turismo,
Avenida de Madrid s/n;
tel. 22 76 00.

HOTELS. – *Palacio de Valderrábanos*, Plaza de l
Catedral 9, I, 73 r.; *Parador Nacional Raimundo d
Borgoña*, Marqués de Canales y Chozas 16, II, 62 r
Cuatro Postes, Carretera Salamanca 23, III, 36 r.; *Do
Carmelo* (no rest.), Paseo D. Carmelo 30, III, 60 r
Encinar (no rest.), Avda del 18 de Julio, III, 20 r.; *Re
Niño* (no rest), Plaza de José Tome 1, III, 24 r.; *Jardir
San Segundo 38, IV, 26 r.; *Reina Isabel*, Avda de Jos
Antonio 17, IV, 44 r.; *Hostal Continental* (no rest.)
Plaza de la Catedral 4, P II, 54 r.; etc.

RESTAURANTS. – *Caballeros*, Estrada 10; *Copa
cabana*, San Millán 9; *El Torreón*, Tostado 1 (in an ol
palacio); *Piquío*, Estrada 6 (first floor); *Mesón El So
on road to Las Navas.

EVENTS. – *Semana Santa* (Holy Week), with proces
sion. – *Fiesta de San Juan* (June), with traditiona
cattle market, folk events and fair. – *Summer Fiest.
(July), with battle of flowers, bullfights, exhibitions
Festival of Spain, folk dancing. – *Fiesta de Sant.
Teresa* (Oct.), the town's principal fiesta, wit
verbenas (open-air celebrations and dancing) and
parade of giant figures and masks.

***Ávila, capital of the province of the
same name in Old Castile and the
seat of a bishop, is situated on a ridge
of high ground, falling steeply down
on three sides, in the middle of a
treeless plateau watered by the Río
Adaja. It is enclosed by high hills
with more open country only on the
N, and accordingly has a notably
harsh climate.**

Town walls, Ávila

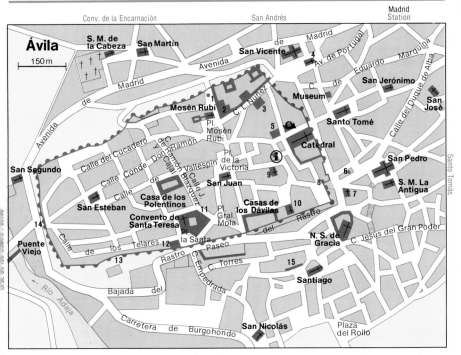

Ávila
150 m

1 Fuente de Sol	5 Casa de Velada	9 Las Nieves	12 Casa de Núñez Vela
2 Casa de Aguila	6 Santa Teresa	10 Santo Tomé	13 Puerta de la Mala Dicha
3 Casa de Verdugc	7 La Magdalena	11 Torreón	14 Puerta del Puente
4 Humilladero	8 Puerta del Alcázar	de los Guzmanes	15 Paneras del Rey

Ávila's wealth of medieval buildings (particularly its well-preserved Romanesque churches and Gothic mansions) and its ancient walls, still enclosing the heart of the old town, make Ávila one of the most interesting cities in Spain.

HISTORY. – Originating as the legendary Roman town of *Avela*, Ávila alternated between Arab and Christian rule for a period of more than three centuries following the coming of the Moors in 714. Its heyday was in the 16th c., when its life was dominated by the presence of Santa Teresa de Jesús (1515–82). With the expulsion of the Moors in 1607–10, during the reign of Philip III, the town fell into decline.

SIGHTS. – Ávila's great treasures are the 2526 m long circuit of its old **town walls**, with their nine gates and 88 semicircular towers and its numerous medieval buildings. – At the E end of the old town is the massive *Cathedral (Catedral de San Salvador)*, begun in 1091 but not completed until the 13th c. The choir is built into the town walls. Of the two towers on the W front only the northern one is complete (14th c.). Particularly notable are the *main doorway* (16th c.) and the *N doorway*, also known as the Apostle's Doorway (*c.* 1200). The interior contains many Gothic tomb recesses. The transept has beautiful 16th c. *stained glass*; good reliefs of *c.* 1530 in

the *trascoro*; richly decorated *choir-stalls* (1547). The *high altar*, with scenes from the life of Christ, was begun by Pedro Berruguete in 1499 and completed in 1508. In the *trassagrario* is the *alabaster tomb* of Bishop Alfonso Tostado de Madrigal (d. 1455), by Vasco de la Zarza (1518). In the S transept is the entrance to the *sacristy* (13th c.) and the *Cathedral Museum*, with many treasures, including a famous monstrance by Juan de Arfe (1571) and works by Berruguete and Juan de Frías. Adjoining, to the S, is the 14th c. *cloister*, entered through a Romanesque doorway. From the tower there are fine views of the town.

Going S from the Cathedral past the cloister and along the town walls, we come to the *Puerta del Alcázar*, partly built with Roman stones. Outside the gate, in *Plaza de Santa Teresa*, is the church of *San Pedro* (12th–13th c.), with a large rose window; *high altar* by Juan de Borgoña, in the N aisle a "Peter in Chains" (1673), by Morán. – Beyond the church the *Paseo de Santo Tomás* runs SE to the Dominican **Convento de Santo Tomás**, founded in 1482, with a late Gothic church containing richly decorated choir-stalls and a notable retablo by Pedro

Berruguete (c. 1500), a masterpiece of the Spanish school. In the transept is the marble tomb of Prince John (d. 1497), only son of the Catholic monarchs (Ferdinand II and Isabella of Castile), by the Italian sculptor Domenico Fancelli (1512). Adjoining the church are three beautiful cloisters, the last of which, the Claustro de los Reyes, contains an interesting *museum of East Asian art*.

It is well worth while walking round the old town to see the remains of the original Roman walls. From the Puerta de Alcázar we go W along the *Paseo del Rastro*, with fine views of the valley of the Río Ambles, to the *Puerta de Santa Teresa*. Inside the gate is the former **Convento de Santa Teresa**, with a *church* built in 1638 on the site of the saint's birthplace. In the N transept are relics of Santa Teresa, who was a nun and later prioress in the Carmelite convent of the Encarnación. – Beyond the convent is the church of **Santo Domingo** (13th c., restored), with a beautiful Gothic crucifix.

Returning outside the walls, we continue W and then N to the *Puerta del Puente*, from which a street runs down to the *Puente Nuevo* (New Bridge) over the Río Adaja. Below, to the left, can be seen the old five-arched bridge (*Puente Viejo*). On the far side of the river the road to Salamanca climbs on the right to a stone cross, the **Crus de los Cuatro Postes**, from which there is a magnificent *view of the town.

From the Puerta del Puente we can either return towards the centre of the town, passing the Romanesque church of *San Esteban* and the Plateresque *Palacio de los Polentinos* on the way to the arcaded *Plaza Mayor*, or continue round the walls. In the latter event we come first to the little Romanesque church of **San Segundo**, with a beautiful doorway (12th c.). Immediately to the right of the main apse is the *tomb of St Secundus*, first bishop of Ávila, by Juan de Juni (1573). – Farther along the N side of the old town is the little church of *San Martín* (Romanesque tower with Mudéjar ornament). To the E, on higher ground, is the church of *San Vicente* (12th–15th c.), which is entered through the richly decorated W doorway. Under the central dome, to the right, is the *sarcophagus*, with carved decoration, of San Vicente and his sisters Sabina and Cristeta (c. 1180–85). In the *crypt* is the

rock on which the saint and his sisters are said to have been martyred in the year 303.

Just to the SW of San Vicente is the *Puerta de San Vicente*, the imposing N gate of the town, from which Calle del Tostado runs S to the Cathedral. – S of San Vicente, outside the town walls, is the **Casa de los Deanes**, in Renaissance style (16th c.), which houses the *Museo Provincial*, with a collection of wooden presses, carpets and tiles. Adjoining is the church of *Santo Tomé*, now a lapidarium.

SURROUNDINGS. – In the S of the province of Ávila, reached from the town on C 502, is the massive rock wall of the *Sierra de Gredos (see p. 212).

To the Puerto de Tornavacas. – N 110 crosses the Río Adaja and leads SW towards the *Sierra de Ávila*, which it traverses by way of the *Puerto de Villatoro* (1356 m), from which there are wide views. The road then continues via the summer resort of *Piedrahita* (alt. 1060 m) to El Barco de Ávila (alt. 1014 m; pop. 2500; Hotel Manila, II, 50 r., fishing) which stands in a beautiful situation on the right bank of the Río Tormes, with the 14th c. Castillo de Valdecorneja and a notable Gothic parish church containing a number of fine pictures.

Beyond El Barco de Ávila N 110 leads up to the *Puerto de Tornavacas* (1275 m), also known as the Puerto de Castilla, since it marks the boundary between Old Castile and Extremadura. From the pass there are fine views.

Over the Puerto de Paramera. – N 403, running S from Ávila, reaches in 22 km the *Puerto de Paramera* (1416 m) and then continues over the *Río Alberche*, with a large artificial lake, the *Embalse de Burgillo*, to El Tiemblo (alt. 980 m; pop. 3800), with a Gothic church. Nearby is the convent of *Guisando* (14th c.), where Isabel the Catholic was proclaimed queen in 1468; and a short distance away are the famous "Toros de Guisando", a group of four bulls carved from granite, of Iberian workmanship (4th–3rd c. B.C.).

Avilés

Province: Asturias.
Telephone code: 985.
Altitude: 4 m. – Population: 85,000.
ⓘ **Oficina de Turismo,**
    Ruiz Gómez 1;
    tel. 54 43 25.

HOTELS. – *Luzana* (no rest.), Fruta 9, II, 73 r.; *San Félix*, Avenida de Lugo 48, III, 18 r.; *Hostal Rivero*, Rivero 39, P II, 7 r. – AT PLAYA DE SALINAS: *Hotel Esperanza*, Príncipe de Asturias 31, III, 35 r.

RESTAURANTS. – *Hostal San Félix*, Avenida de Lugo 48; *Cantina Renfe*, Avenida de los Telares 14. – AT PLAYA DE SALINAS: *Las Conchas*, Edificio Espartal, with sea view.

EVENTS. – *Fiesta del Bullo* (Mar.–Apr.), an Easter festival with folk performances, parades, a regatta and a cattle show. – *Ferias* (Aug.), with a fair.

The port and steel-making town of Avilés lies on the Ría de Avilés, some 6 km from the coast.

SIGHTS. – In addition to its 17th c. *Ayuntamiento* (Town Hall) the town has a number of fine churches and palaces. Among the churches are **San Nicolás de Bari** (14th c.), with the tomb of Pedro Menéndez, the conqueror of Florida, and interesting carved altars; **San Francisco**, with a Romanesque doorway of the 13th–14th c. and a 9th c. frieze in the Capilla de Jesús; and *Santa María* (14th c.). Among secular buildings are the 16th c. *Palacio del Marqués de Santiago* (Baroque) and a number of other aristocratic mansions.

Badajoz

Province:Badajoz (BA).
Telephone code: 924.
Altitude: 155 m. – Population: 110,000.
ⓘ **Oficina de Información de Turismo**,
Pasaje de San Juan 1;
tel. 22 27 63 98.

HOTELS. – *Gran Hotel Zurbarán*, Paseo de Castelar, I, 215 r., SP, tennis; *Lisboa*, Avda de Elvas 13, II, 176 r.; *Río* (no rest.), Avda de Elvas, II, 90 r., SP; *Conde Duque* (no rest.), Muñoz Torrero 27, III, 35 r.; *Hostal Cervantes* (no rest.), Tercio 2, P I, 25 r.; *Victoria*, Luis de Camoens 3, P III, 16 r.; etc.

RESTAURANTS. – *El Caballo Blanco*, Avda General Rodrigo 7; *Dardy's*, Avda de Elvas; *El Águila*, Plaza de España 16 (first floor); *El Sótano*, Virgen de la Soledad 6.

Badajoz, known as the "key to Portugal", lies on a low ridge of hills on the left bank of the Río Guadiana, near the Portuguese frontier. It is the capital of the province of the same name and the seat of a bishop.

HISTORY. – The town was known to the Romans as *Colonia Pacensis*, to the Moors as Badaljóz. After the fall of the Caliphate of Córdoba the Aftassides established a small Moorish kingdom here. In 1229 the town was captured by Alfonso IX of Léon.

SIGHTS. – On a hill to the NE of the town is the **Alcazaba**, once the seat of the town's Moorish rulers, with the octagonal *Torre de Espantaperros* (wide views) and a *Museo Arqueológico*. – The central

Puerta de Palmas, Badajoz

point of the old town is the *Plaza de España*, in which is the *Palacio Municipal* (Town Hall). Opposite it is the **Cathedral** (*San Juan*), a fortress-like structure begun in 1258, with a new Renaissance-style façade and doorway (1619). It has a large *Renaissance choir* with beautiful stalls. In the *Capilla de Santa Ana* (third on right) are a number of over-painted pictures by the Badajoz-born artist Luis de Morales (1509–86). – In the cloister is the *Diocesan Museum*.

NW of the Plaza de España, reached by way of *Calle Hernán Cortés*, is the *Palacio de la Diputación Provincial*, with the **Museo Provincial** (works by Extremadura artists). *Calle de Gabriel* leads to the battlemented **Puerta de Palmas**, built at the end of the 16th c. It stands at the end of the **Puente de Palmas** (1596), a granite bridge of 32 arches, 582 m long, spanning the Río Guadiana, it has frequently been damaged by the river's floods.

Other notable buildings are the churches of the *Concepción* and *San Agustín*, both with tombs of considerable artistic quality, and the *Convento de Santa Ana*.

SURROUNDINGS. – The province of Badajoz contains many places and features of interest which are easily reached from the capital.

C 436 runs S (26 km) to **Olivenza** (alt. 160 m; pop. 10,000), which until 1801 belonged to Portugal. Among a number of notable churches is *Santa María*, with a Gothic retablo depicting the Virgin's ancestry. The Hospital de la Caridad contains Portuguese decorative tiles with Biblical scenes. – C 436 continues beyond Olivenza to *Villanueva del Fresno*, with the ruins of a castle and the Convento de la Luz.

C 530 runs N from Badajoz over the *Puerto de los Conejeros* (340 m) to **Alburquerque** (alt. 750 m; pop. 7800). 44 km away, an old-world little town on a hill with the ruins of a massive castle (13th c.) and the large Gothic church of Santa María del Mercado.

N V runs E over the fertile *Vega del Guadiana*, passing through *Lobón*, an ancient and picturesque little town with a handsome church, to **Mérida** (see p. 169), 62 km from Badajoz.

To Zafra. – N 432 runs SE, skirting the *Sierra de la Calera*, to **Zafra** (alt. 509 m; pop. 12,000; Parador Nacional Hernán Cortés, II, 28 r., SP), an old town with an *Alcázar of the 15th–16th c., a good example of a nobleman's castle of Moorish origin. The Candelaria church (16th c.) has a retablo with a painting by Zurbarán.

Baeza

Province: Jaén (J).
Telephone code: 953.
Altitude: 760 m. – Population: 18,000.
ⓘ **Oficina de Información de Turismo.**
   Casa del Pópulo;
   tel. 74 04 44.

HOTELS. – *Juanito*, III, 21 r.; *Comercio*, P II, 31 r.

The old-world town of Baeza, known to the Romans as Vilvatia, lies in the upper valley of the Guadal-quivir, among the foothills of the Loma de Úbeda. In the Visigothic period it was the seat of a bishop.

SIGHTS. – Gothic **Cathedral**, built on the foundations of an earlier mosque (1567–93), with the Moorish *Puerta de la Luna. Capilla Mayor* with stellate vaulting. Good carved wood. – Handsome Town Hall with Renaissance façade (1559). – Old *University* (1533). – **Casa del Pópulo** (1530), with Plateresque

A Majorcan windmill

façade; nearby is the *Arco del Pópulo*. – With a variety of other old buildings, ranging in date from Romanesque to Renaissance, the town has preserved something of a medieval aspect.

SURROUNDINGS. – 11 km N is **Canena**, with a Moorish castle which was converted into a palace by Vandaelvira in the 16th c.; it is square in plan, with massive round towers. At *Ibros* are Cyclopean walls.

Balearics

Autonomous Region.
Organ of Government: Conseil General Interinsular de les Illes Balears.
Province: Balearics.

The group of islands known as the *Balearics (Islas Baleares), in the western Mediterranean off the SE coast of Spain, comprises the Balearic islands proper of Majorca (Mallorca) and Minorca (Menorca), together with Ibiza and Formentera, which are also known as the Pitiusas ("Pine Islands"). Thanks to their mild climate, their beautiful scenery and the excellent bathing they offer, the Balearics are popular with visitors at almost every time of year.

HISTORY. – The original inhabitants were Iberians, who were famous for their skill with the sling. In the 3rd c. B.C. the islands were conquered by the Carthaginians, and from 123 B.C. were under Roman rule. Later they fell successively into the hands of the Vandals, the Visigoths, the East Roman Empire, the Franks and the Moors (798). In 1229 King Jaime I of Aragon ("el Conquistador") conquered Majorca, which later became the independent kingdom of Majorca but in the 14th c. was reduced to the status of a province of Aragon. Between 1708 and 1782 and again between 1798 and 1802 Minorca was held by Britain.

BOAT SERVICES. – Car ferry services between the islands and from the Spanish mainland (Barcelona, Valencia, Málaga) to the islands; regular services with France (Sète); regular service between Palma de Mallorca and Cabrera.

Majorca (Mallorca)

The largest of the Balearic islands and also the one which attracts the largest numbers of visitors is **Majorca (area 3660 sq. km, pop. 420,000). It is bounded on the NW by the Sierra del Norte, a long range of wooded hills with the island's highest peaks, rising to 1445 m, and on the E by the much lower Sierra de Levante, with hills of up to 562 m in height. **Between the two ranges is an area of plain, deeply indented to the NE by the bays of Alcudia and Pollensa and to the SW by Palma Bay. The fields and fruit orchards on this plain are provided with water with the help of the windmills characteristic of Majorca.**

EVENTS. – *Los Reyes Magos* (Jan.), in honour of the Three Kings, with presents for children. – *Semana Santa* (Holy Week), celebrated in many towns and villages with impressive religious processions. – *Corpus Christi.* – *Fiesta de San Pedro y San Pablo* (SS. Peter and Paul). – *Fiesta de Santiago*, in honour of St James, patron saint of Spain. – *Festival de Música* (Aug.) in Pollensa. – *Moros y Cristianos* (Aug.), the fighting between Moors and Christians, celebrated at many places. – *Dia de la Hispanidad* (Oct.). – *Dijous Bó* (Nov.): "Good Thursday" in Inca, with agricultural show. – *Inmaculada Concepción* (Dec.), with local celebrations.

CASINO.– *Casino Sporting Club de Mallorca*, in the Urbanisation Sol de Mallorca, Calviá.

Palma de Mallorca

Province: Balearics (PM).
Telephone code; 971.
Altitude: at sea level. – Population: 320,000.
(i) **Oficina de Informacion y Turismo,**
Avenida Jaime III 10,
Palma de Mallorca;
tel: 71 22 16.
Fomento de Turismo, Plaza de la Constitución (opposite main post office), Palma de Mallorca; tel: 72 53 96.

HOTELS. – From the enormous range of accommodation available only a small selection can be given here.

IN PALMA: *Vida Sheraton*, L, 170 r., SP.; Golf; *Valparaíso Palace*, L, 138 r., SP.; *Victoria-Sol*, L, 171 r., SP.; *Bellver-Sol*, I, 393 r., SP.; *Palas Atenea-Sol*, I, 370 r., SP.; *Racquet Club*, I, 51 r., SP., Golf; *Uto Palma*, I, 234 r., SP. (Apartment Hotel); *La Almudaina*; (no rest.), II, 80 r.; *La Caleta* (no rest.), II, 19 r., SP.; *Club Nautico* (no rest.), II, 35 r., SP.; *Constelacion*, II, 42 r., SP.; *Costa Azul*, II, 126 r., SP.; *Festival*, II, 216 r., SP.; *Jaime III-Sol*, II, 88 r.; *Majorica*, II, 153 r.; SP.; *Reina Constanza*, II, 97 r., SP.; *Rembrandt*, II, 72 r., SP.; *San Carlos*, II, 46 r., SP.; *Saratoga*, II, 123 r., SP.; *Bonanova*, III, 80 r., SP.; *Borenco*, III, 70 r., SP.; *Villa Río*, III, 83 r., SP.; *Terrono Center*, IV, 69 r., SP.; etc.

AT PLAYA DE PALMA (EL ARENAL): *Delta*, I, 288 r., SP.; *Garonda*, I, 112 r., SP.; *Playa de Palma-Sol*, I, 113 r., SP.; *Río Bravo*, I, 200 r., SP.; *Acapuluco*, II, 109 r., SP.; *Bahía de Palma*, II, 433 r., SP.; *Bali*, II, 264 r., SP.; *Copacabana*, II, 112 r., SP.; *Flamingo*, II, 100, r., SP.; *Gran Fiesta*, II, 241 r., SP.; *Ipanema Park*, II, 210 r., SP.; *Luna Park*, II, 318 r., SP.; *Luxor*, II, 52 r.; *Pamplona*, II, 105 r., SP.; *Playa Golf*, II, 222 r., SP.; *Riviera Sol*, II, 74 r., SP.; *Tropical Sol*, II, 165 r., SP.; *Concordia*, III, 220

r., SP.; *Dunas Blanca*, III, 167 r., SP.; *Lancaster*, III, 318 r., SP.; *Playas Arenal*, III, 90 r.; *Riutort*, III, 180 r., SP.; *Sofia*, III, 328, r., SP.; *Torre Arenal*, III, 143 r., SP.; *Don Miguel*, IV, 84 r., SP.; *Europa*, IV, 134 r., SP.; Hostal *Golondrina*, P I, 59 r., SP.; etc.

AT PLAYA DE PALMA (CA'N PASTILLA): *Alexandra-Sol*, I, 164 r., SP.; *Almendros*, II, 91 r.; *Ambos Mundos*, II, 96 r., SP.; *Calma*, II, 190 r., SP.; *Gran Hotel El Cid*, II, 216 r., SP.; *Las Arenas*, II, 152 r., SP.; *Java*, II, 249 r., SP.; *Leo*, II, 285 r., SP.; *Linda*, II, 189 r., SP.; *Lotus Playa*, II, 127 r., SP.; *Oleander*, II, 264 r., SP.; *Apolo*, III, 151 r., SP.; *Caballero*, III, 308 r., SP.; *Cisne*, III, 116 r., SP.; *Helios*, III, 305 r., SP.; *Orléans*, III, 128 r., SP.; *Playa d'Or*, III, 71 r.; *Covi*, IV, 98 r., etc.

W OF THE TOWN (CALOR MAYOR): *Nixe Palace*, I, 130 r., SP.; *Playa de Cala Mayor*, (no rest.), I, 143 r., SP.; *Atlas*, II, 48 r., SP.; *Belvedere Park*, II, 414 r., SP.; *Cala Mayor*, II, 93 r., SP.; *Gran Mallorca*, 112 r., SP.; *San Augustín* II, 56 r.; *Vista Mar*, II 75 r., SP.; Hostal *Mimosa*, P II, 27 r., SP.; etc.

RESTAURANTS. – IN PALMA *Hermitage*, Moro 6; *Caballito de Mar*, Paseo de Sagrea 5; *Casa Sophie*, Apuntadores 24 (French); *El Gallo*, Teniente Torres 17, *El Puerto*, Paseo de Sagrera 3; *Le Bistrot*, Teodoro Llorente 4 (French); *Los Gauchos*, San magin 78 (S. American); *S'Escudella*, Industria 52; *Ulises*, Paseo Maritimo 3; *Xoriguer*, Fabrica 60. – W OF THE TOWN: *La Caleta*, Marqués de la Cenia 147 (view of the harbour); etc.

*Palma de Mallorca, capital of Majorca and the province of the Balearics, seat of a bishop and since 1967 a university town, lies on a wide bay 20 km deep. With its many palaces it is a tourist attraction in its own right, as well as a popular holiday centre and a good base from which to explore the rest of the island.

SIGHTS. – By the *Harbour* is the palatial ***Lonja**, formerly the Stock Exchange (15th c.), now an exhibition hall. Near the Gothic building is the *Consulado del Mar*. A short distance away in Calle de Apuntadores, to the N, is the *Mansión del Arte* ("House of Art"), with a collection which includes all Goya's etchings in original printing and works by Picasso. – From the Harbour the Avenida Antonio Maura leads to the ***Cathedral** or **Seo**, standing on higher ground. This magnificent building was begun in 1230 in early Gothic style but not completed until the 17th c. W front, with splendid rose window (renewed in 19th c.); richly decorated S doorway (14th c.), from which there are magnificent *views. The interior (120 m long, 56 m wide, 44 m high) has good stained glass and richly appointed chapels; the Old Sacristy contains a valuable collection of relics.

Built on to the massive tower is the Gothic *Casa de la Almoina*. Immediately E of the Cathedral is the *Bishop's Palace* (1616), with the *Diocesan Museum*.

Facing the Cathedral, to the W, is the *Palacio de la Almudaína*, formerly the seat of the Moorish governors and the Christian kings. In the patio is the Gothic *Capilla de Santa Ana*. – From the Plaza de la Reina the *Paseo del Generalísimo Franco*, traditionally known as *El Borne*, the lively street which is Palma's main promenade, runs N, with numerous cafés, clubs and the *Palacio Morell* (Palacio Sollerich, 1763; art museum). – From the N end of the Borne a street runs E to the *Theatre* (1860; restored). From here the tree-lined *Vía Roma* runs NW, with the *Plaza Mayor* (underground shopping centre, garage) at its SE end. From this square Calle San Miguel runs N to the church of *San Miguel*, formerly a mosque. – SW of the Plaza Mayor is the Renaissance *Ayuntamiento* (Town Hall), and near this, to the E, are the Gothic churches of *Santa Eulalia* and *San Francisco* (1281–1317). San Francisco has a Plateresque-Baroque doorway, a charming late Gothic cloister and the tomb of the medieval scholar Ramón Llull (1232–1315), who was born in Palma.

Adjoining Santa Eulalia is the 18th c. *Palacio Vivot*.

EXCURSIONS FROM PALMA. – **To the Castillo de Bellver** (4 km). – From the Paseo Marítimo go W along Calle Andrea Doria to the *Pueblo Español* (Spanish Village: reproductions of characteristic Spanish buildings), in the villa suburb of *El Terreno*; then skirt the Parque de Bellver to reach the well-preserved *Castillo de Bellver (alt. 130 m), a royal castle dating from the 13th c., with a museum, an arcaded patio and a tower (*views).

Circuit via Andraitx and Sóller (125 km). – Go W from Palma on the new motorway or the winding C 719, which join just beyond *Palma Nova* and come (20 km) to the junction leading to **Santa Ponsa (hotels: Pionero, II, 312 r., SP; Rey Don Jaime, II, 417 r., SP; Santa Ponsa Park, II, 269 r., SP, golf course, 18 holes), a rapidly developing holiday centre with good bathing beaches. On a projecting crag is a cross commemorating the landing of Christian troops in 1229. – Continue via *Paguera*, a trim holiday resort with a sheltered beach (many hotels), to **Andraitx** (pop. 6000), a beautifully situated little country town in a fertile agricultural region. 5 km SW is the little port of *Puerto de Andraitx*. – Continue from Andraitx on C 710 to the impressive *W coast of Majorca, with numerous outlook towers, passing through the villages of *Estellencs* and *Bañalbufar*; then a short distance inland to **Valldemosa** (alt. 425 m; pop. 1200), a hillside village dominated by the *Cartuja* (Charterhouse), founded in 1339, in which Chopin spent the winter of 1838–39 (museum, with many mementoes of Chopin). – Then back to the winding coast road. Off the road to the left is the estate of *Miramar*, which belonged to the Austrian Archduke Ludwig Salvator (1847–1915). A short distance farther on is the estate of *Son Morroig*, with a museum. The road continues, with wide views, to

Cathedral, Palma de Mallorca

Palma de Mallorca

300m

Valldemosa   Sóller   Arena

1 Fuente del Sepulcro
2 Fuente de la Princesa
3 Casa Belloto
4 Consulado del Mar
5 Casa Oleo
6 Almudaína Arch
7 Casa Oleza
8 Casa del Marqués de Palmer
9 Baños Árabes (Casa Font y Roig)

Deyá (alt. 185 m; pop. 500), a delightfully situated village on a hill surrounded by orange-groves, which is the home of many artists. – The coast road finally joins the road to **Sóller** (alt. 55 m; pop. 11,000; hotels: Eden, II, 152 r. SP; Eden Park, II, 64 r. Espléndido, II, 104 r.), a popular tourist centre situated amid beautiful orange and lemon groves. 4 km N is the port and seaside resort of *Puerto de Sóller* (tram from Sóller). – The return to Palma is on C711, going over the *Coll de Sóller* (562 m), from which there are fine *views of Palma and its bay. On the far side of the pass are the *Alfabia Gardens.

*Through the hills to Cabo de Formentor (112 km). – Palma to Sóller (30 km): see above. Then turn right off the road to Puerto de Sóller into a magnificent *hill road. This runs past the picturesque hill village of *Fornalutx* (on right, 2 km) and continues, with numerous bends offering extensive views, up to the *Mirador de Ses Barques* (Bellavista restaurant) and then through a 600 m long tunnel (alt. 820 m) and past a small reservoir to the barracks at *Son Torrella*, with the island's highest peak, **Puig Mayor** (1445 m), towering above them to the N. – Continue past the *Gorch Blau* reservoir and then through another tunnel, beyond which the impressive *hill road to La Calobra (14 km) branches off on the left. Near La Calobra is the rocky gorge of the *Torrente de Pareis* (visit recommended). – The main road continues past the

Mirador del Torrente de Pareis (viewpoint, alt. 664 m). Beyond this, off the road to the left, the **Monasterio de Lluc** (museum, restaurant). – Then down towards the plain, through rocky scenery, to **Pollensa** (alt. 70 m; pop. 9000), in a beautiful situation, with a Calvary reached by a flight of 365

Terraced gardens, Bañalbufar

Torrente de Pareis, La Calobra

steps (fine views). 6 km N, attractively situated on the *Bahía de Pollensa*, is the port, now a popular resort, of *Puerto de Pollensa* (hotels: Capri, II, 33 r., SP; Daina, II, 60 r., SP; Illa d'Or, II, 119 r., golf; Miramar, II, 69 r., golf; Pollensa Park, II, 316 r., SP, golf). – From Puerto Pollensa a boldly engineered *road (magnificent viewpoints, some tunnels) runs along the Formentor peninsula, much of which is wooded. In 10 km a road goes off on the right (500 m) to the *Hotel Formentor* (L, 131 r., SP, golf, beach), beautifully situated above the sea. – Then another 11 km to the *Cabo de Formentor* (alt. 189 m), crowned by a 20 m high lighthouse: wide-ranging views.

Palma to Alcudia (54 km). – C 713 runs NE through the huerta by way of *Santa María* and comes in 29 km to **Inca** (alt. 38 m; pop. 18,000), an ancient little town which is believed to have originated as a Roman settlement (bypass). – Continue N beyond the turning for Pollensa to **Alcudia** (alt. 9 m; pop. 3500), an old-world little town situated near the bay of the same name, with well-preserved 14th c. walls. E of the town are the remains of a Roman amphitheatre. 2 km SE of the town centre is *Puerto de Alcudia* (hotels: Princesa (no rest.), I, 102 r., SP, tennis; Condesa de la Bahia, II, 491 r.; Bahia de Alcudia, II, 205 r., SP; Golf, II, 12 r. with a broad sandy beach extending for 10 km round the wide bay. – From Puerto de Alcudia it is possible to continue round the bay to *Ca'n Picafort*.

Cabo de Formentor, Majorca

To the *stalactitic caves of Artá. – C 715 runs over the fertile plain E of Palma (many windmills) and comes in 50 km to **Manacor** (alt. 110 m; pop. 23,000), the second largest town on the island, noted for the manufacture of artificial pearls. 14 km S is the pottery-making town of *Felanitx*, from which it is possible to drive up (5 km) to a pilgrimage chapel (1348) on the hill of *San Salvador* (509 m), with wide *views in all directions. A short distance S is the 13th c. *Castillo de Santueri*, on a rocky crag. – From Manacor it is 11 km E to the attractively situated port and seaside resort of **Porto Cristo** (hotels: Castell Dels Hams, II, 131 r., SP; Drach, III, 70 r., SP). 1 km S are the *Cuevas del Drach** ("Dragon's Caves"), with an underground lake (conducted tours; concerts). 1·5 km W are the *Cuevas dels Hams* ("Fish-hook Caves": conducted tours). 5 km N is the *Reserva Africana**, with African animals living in free conditions (4 km long "photo safari" in visitors' own cars or in safari bus). – NE of Porto Cristo is **Cala Millor**, a hotel colony on the Bahía de Artá (hotels: Borneo, II, 200 r., SP; Flamenco, II, 220 r., SP, beach; Sumba, II, 280 r., SP; Castell de Mar, III, 248 r., SP). From Manacor it is 21 km NE to the picturesque little town of **Artá** (alt. 170 m; pop. 6000), 10 km SE of which are the *Cuevas de Artá**, famous for the length of their stalactites. – From Artá a road runs NE by way of *Capdepera* (medieval fortifications) to **Cala Ratjada** (hotels: Aguait, II, 188 r., SP; Bella Playa, II, 214 r., SP; Cala Gat, III, 44 r., SP; Lux, II, 236 r., SP), a resort surrounded by pine-woods. In the vicinity are a lighthouse (extensive views) and several bathing beaches.

Palma to Santanyí (50 km). – Leave Palma on the motorway to the E, which runs into C 717. This runs through a hilly region and comes in 24 km to **Lluchmayor** (pop. 11,000), an old-world little town. 5 km N is the *Puig de Randa* (548 m: extensive views), with three monasteries. – Continue on C 717 by way of *Campos* (road on right to the southernmost tip of Majorca) to **Santanyí** (alt. 60 m; pop. 5000), near which are the remains of prehistoric cult sites and fortifications. 12 km N are the *Cala d'Or* and the developing resorts of *Calas de Mallorca*.

Minorca (Menorca)

(i) **Oficina de Información y Turismo**, Plaza de la Constitución 13, Mahón; tel. (971) 36 37 90.

HOTELS. – IN MAHÓN: *Port Mahón*, I, 74 r., SP; *Capri* (no rest.), II, 75 r.; *Hostal El Paso*, P II, 40 r.; *Jume*, P III, 35 r. – IN VILLA CARLOS (3 km E): *Agamemnón*, II, 75 r., SP; *Rey Carlos III*, II, 87 r., SP; *Hámilton*, III, 132 r., SP; *Hostal Miramar*, P II, 30 r.; etc.

IN CIUDADELA: *Alfonso III* (no rest.), IV, 54 r.; *Hostal Alhambra*, P III, 14 r. – IN WESTERN DISTRICTS: *Almirante Farragut*, II, 472 r., SP; *Cala Blanca*, II, 147 r., SP; *Calan Blanes*, III, 103 r.; *Los Delfines*, III, 96 r., SP. – IN SOUTHERN DISTRICTS: *Calan Bosch*, II, 174 r., SP; *Ses Voltes*, III, 40 r.; *Cala Bona* (no rest.), IV, 16 r.

RESTAURANTS. – IN MAHÓN AND SURROUNDINGS: *Chez Gaston*, Conde de Cifuentes 13 (French); *El Greco*, Doctor Orfila 49; *Iritón*, Norte 15; *225*, Andén del Muelle; *Mesón del Cid*, Plaza de la Explanada 61; *Rocamar*, Fonduco 16, Villacarlos; etc. – IN CIUDADELA

Ferrerías, Minorca

AND SURROUNDINGS: *Caballito de Mar*, Avda Asunción, Cala Busquet; *Cala Bruch*, Torre del Ram, Cala Bruch; *Cas Quinto*, Alfonso III; *D'es Port*, Marina 105–107; *El Gran Comilón*, Plaza de Colón 48; *Scala*, Mallorca 34; etc.

EVENTS. – *Semana Santa* (Holy Week), with an impressive Good Friday procession in Mahón. – *Fiestas de San Juan* (June) in Ciudadela, an impressive fiesta lasting several days, with a procession to the Ermita de San Juan and riding contests in medieval costume. – *Fiestas de San Martín* (July) in Mercadal, with processions. – *Fiestas de San Jaime* (July) in Villacarlos. – *Fiestas de San Lorenzo* (Aug.) in Alayor, with cavalcades of riders. – *Fiestas de Nuestra Señora de Gracia* (Sept.) in Mahón, with traditional parades, festival of water sports, dance festival, concerts and exhibitions.

BOAT SERVICES. – Car ferries from Mahón to Barcelona and from Ciudadela to Palma de Mallorca and Puerto de Alcudia (Majorca).

Some 40 km NE of Majorca lies the second largest of the Balearic islands, *Minorca (area 686 sq. km; pop. 50,000), also with very attractive scenery, many good bathing beaches and large numbers of prehistoric remains. Its highest point is Monte Toro (360 m).

On the E coast, picturesquely situated in a 6 km long bay under the shelter of the fortified hill of *La Mola*, is the port of **Mahón** (pop. 17,000), which has been capital of the island since 1722. Characteristic houses reminiscent of the period of British occupation; interesting archaeological museum. Airport 5 km SW of the town. 10 km S is *Punta Prima* (hotel), with a good bathing beach. – On the W coast of the island is the former capital, **Ciudadela** (pop. 14,000), the seat of a bishop, with a Gothic Cathedral (begun 1287) and many fine mansions. There are popular bathing beaches in the immediate

vicinity of the town, and also at *Santa Galdana* and *Santo Tomás* on the S coast and *Arenal d'en Castell*, in a wooded bay on the NE coast.

Ibiza

ⓘ **Oficina de Información de Turismo,** Pasco Vara del Rey 13, Ibiza (town); tel. (971) 30 19 00.

HOTELS. – IN IBIZA TOWN AND IMMEDIATE SURROUNDINGS: *Los Molinos*, in Figueretas, I, 147 r., SP; *Royal Plaza* (no rest.), I, 117 r., SP; *Torre del Mar*, I, 217 r., SP; *Algarb*, II, 408 r., SP; *Argos*, II, 106 r., SP; *Corso*, II, 179 r., SP; *Goleta*, II, 225 r., SP; *Ibiza Playa*, II, 155 r., SP; *Simbad*, II, 111 r., SP; Tres Carabelas, II, 245 r., SP; *Copocabana*, III, 110 r.; *Victoria*, III, 140 r., SP; Hostal *Montesol* (no rest.), P II, 60 r.; *Robinson Club*, in Cala Vadella, 320 r., SP; etc. – CAMPING SITES: *Cala Bassa*, at Cala Bassa, San José; *Playa es Canar*, at Santa Eulalia; *San Antonio*, 14·7 km on to San Antonio.

RESTAURANTS. – IN IBIZA TOWN: *Dalt Vila, Luis Tur y Paláu; *El Portalón*, Plaza Desamparados; *Celler Balear*, Ignacio Wallis 18; *Gormand*, Avda Bartolomé Ramón 13; *El Olivo*, Luis Tur y Paláu; *Delfin Verde*, Garijo 3; etc. – IN SAN ANTONIO ABAD: *Celler El Refugio*, Bartolomé Ramón 5; *Celler Es Cubelles*, Ramón y Cajal; *Capri*, Avda Doctor Fleming; etc. – IN SANTA EULALIA: *El Almendro*, Can Fita; *Sa Caleta*, San Jaime 74; *Sa Punta*, Isidoro Macabich 36; *Club de Golf*, Roca Llisa; *Del Mar*, Calla Llonga; *Celler Ca'n Pere*, San Jaime 63; etc.

Ibiza Harbour

EVENTS. – *Fiesta Patronal* (Jan.) in San Antonio Abad. – *Fiesta Patronal* (Feb.) in Santa Eulalia. – *Fiestas de San Juan* (June), with folk events and fireworks. – *Sea Procession* (July) in Ibiza, with regatta and water sports. – *Fiestas Patronales* (Aug.) in Ibiza. – *Fiesta Popular* (Aug.) in San Antonio Abad. – *Semana Santa* (Holy Week) in almost every town and village on the island, with religious processions; in Ibiza procession on night of Good Friday. – *Folk dancing* in front of the parish church in San Miguel (every Thursday at 6 p.m.).

CASINO. – *Casino de Ibiza* at the new pleasure harbour (Ibiza Nueva).

BOAT SERVICES. – Car ferries to Palma de Mallorca and to Spanish mainland (Barcelona, Valencia).

Some 85 km SW of Majorca is *Ibiza (in the local dialect Eivissa), which has an area of 593 sq. km and a population of 45,000. It is an island of fruit orchards and beautiful wooded scenery, reaching its highest point in Atalayasa (476 m).

On the SE coast is the island's capital, **Ibiza** (pop. 16,000), rising above its busy harbour and attractive fishermen's quarter, with an airport 8 km SW. In the old town (*Dalt Vila*) higher up the hill, which was fortified in the 16th c., is the 18th c. *Cathedral* (view). The **Museo Arqueológico* contains material from the Punic *cemetery of more than 5000 tombs on the Puig des Molins ("Windmill Hill"), including terracottas of the 5th–2nd c. B.C., among them a bust of the Carthaginian goddess Tanit, and Hellenistic and Roman objects. There are bathing beaches at *Figueretas* and *Playa d'en Bossa*, W of the town, and at *Talamanca*, across the bay. – The most popular tourist centres apart from the capital are the two coastal towns of **San Antonio Abad** (pop. 1500), the Roman *Portus Magnus* and **Santa Eulalia del Río** (pop. 1500). In the vicinity of both these towns are many bays which offer excellent bathing.

Formentera

(i) **Oficina Municipal de Turismo**,
Town Hall, San Francisco Javier;
tel. (971) – 32 00 32.

HOTELS in San Francisco Javier: *La Mola*, I, 328 r., SP.; *Formentera Playa*, II, 211 r., SP.; Hostal *Sa Volta* (no rest.), P I, 18 r.; *Cala Sahona*, P II, 69 r., SP.; *Casbah* (no rest.), P II, 29 r., etc.

EVENTS. – *Fiesta Patronal* (July).

BOAT SERVICES. – Ferry service between L Sabina and Ibiza (1 hour: several daily in summer).

A channel 4 km wide separates Ibiza from Formentera (area 93 sq. km, pop. 3500), the smallest inhabited island in the Balearics, with cornfields, salt-pans and a number of windmills still in use.

The chief place on the island is *San Francisco Javier* (pop. 800). On the S coast is a 4 km long bathing beach, the *Playa de Mitjorn*; on the N coast is the *Playa d'es Pujols*. At the E end of the island, with large areas of pine forest, is its highest point, *La Mola* (192 m), from which there are magnificent *views of Ibiza. On the eastern slope of the hill is *Nuestra Señora del Pilar*, with a church and a lighthouse on the *Punta de la Ruda*.

Barcelona

Province: Barcelona (B).
Telephone code: 93.
Altitude: at sea level. – Population: 1,755,000.
(i) **Oficina de Información de Turismo**,
Gran Via de les Corts Catalanes 658;
tel: 3 01 74 43.
Patronat Municipal de Turismo, Avenida Parallel 202;
tel: 2 23 24 20.
Oficina Municipal d'Información,
Estación de França;
tel: 3 19 27 91.
Centro Iniciativas y Turismo,
Avda. Cristina (Palacio de Congresos);
tel: 2 23 31 01.

HOTELS. – IN THE AREA OF PLAZA CATALUNA: **Avendi Palace*, Gran Via de les Corts Catalanes 605, L, 211 r.; **Diplomatic*, Paul Claris 122, L, 213 r., SP.; **Ritz*, Gran Vía de les Corts Catalanes 668, L 195 r.; *Barcelona* (no rest.), Caspe 1–13, I, 64 r.; *Colón*, Avda Catedral 7, I, 161 r.; *Cristal* (no rest.), Diputación 257, I, 148 r.; *Gran Hotel Calderón*, Rambla de Cataluña 26, I, 244 r.; *Manila* (no rest.), Ramblas 111, I, 210 r.; *Regente*, Rambla de Cataluña 76, I, 78 r., SP.; *Royal* (no rest.), Ramblas 117, I, 108 r.; *Gran Via*, Gran Vía de les Corts Catalanes 642, II, 48 r.; *Habane* (no rest.), Gran Via de les Corts Catalane 647, II, 65 r.; *Montecarlo* (no rest.), Rambla de los Estudios 124, II, 73 r.; *Regina* (no rest.), Vergara 2, II, 102 r.; *Lloret*, (no rest.), Rambla Canaletas 125, IV, 53 r.; *Principal* (no rest.), Junta de Comercio 8, IV, 46 r.; etc.

BETWEEN THE CATHEDRAL AND THE PUERTA DE LA PAZ: **Princesa Sofía*, Plaza Papa Pio XII 4, L, 505 r.; SP; *Guardí*, Carrer Nou de la Rambia 12, II, 71 r.; *Oriente*, Ramblas 45–47, II, 142 r.; *Suizo*, Plaza del Angel 12, II, 50 r.; *San Agustin*, Plaza de San Augustin 3, III, 71 r.; *Cosmos* (no rest.), Escudellers 19, IV, 67 r.; *España*, San Pablo 9/11, IV, 87 r.; *Inglés* (no rest.), Boquería 17 IV, 29, r.; 17, IV, 29 r.; *Internacional* (no rest.), Ramblas 78, IV, 62 r.; *Hostal Cuatro Naciones*, Ramblas 40, P I, 34 r.; *Aragonés* (no rest.), San Pablo 34, P III, 80 r.; etc.

OTHER PARTS OF THE CITY: **Gran Hotel Sarría Sol*, Avda. Sarríe 50, L, 314 r.; **Presidente*, Avenida de la Diagonal 570, L, 161 r., SP. **Balmoral* (no rest.), Via Augusta 5, I, 94 r.; *Dante* (no rest.), Mallorca 181, I, 81 r.; *Derby* (no rest.), Loreto 21, I, 116 r.; *Europark* (no rest.), Aragón 325, I, 66 r.; *Gran Hotel Cristina* (no rest.), Avda de la Diagonal 458, I, 123 r.; *Majestic*, Paseo de Gracia 70, I, 344 r., SP.; *Astoria* (no rest.), Paris 203, II4 r.; *Condado*, Aribau 201, II, 89 r.; *Expo Hotel*, Mallorca 1, II, 423 r.; *Tres Torres* (no rest.), Calatrava 32–34, II, 56 r.; *Zenit* (no rest.), Sanatalo 8, II, 61 r.; *Antibes* (no rest.), Diputación 394, III, 65 r.; *Mesón Castilla* (no rest.), Valdoncella 5, III, 56 r.; *Park Hotel*, Avda Marqués de Argentera 11, IV, 95 r.; etc.

Templo de la Sagrada Familia, Barcelona ▶

CAMPING SITES. – *Camping Internacional Barcino*, Esplugues de Llobregat; *Cala Gogó*, El Prat del Llobregat; *Toro Bravo*, Viladecans; and a number of other sites along the coast within easy reach of the city.

RESTAURANTS. – In hotels; also the following. ROUND PLAZA CATALUÑA: *Milán*, Paseo de Gracia 44; *Lutecia*, Ausías March 17; *Buenavista*, Ronda da San Antonio 84; *Soley*, Bailén 29; *Petit Soley*, Plaza Villa de Madrid; *Luna*, Plaza de Cataluña 9; *Navara*, Paseo de Gracia 4; *Orotava*, Consejo de Ciento 335; *Oro del Rhin*, Avda de José Antonio 601; *Baviera*, Rambla de Canaletas 127; etc. – BETWEEN THE CATHEDRAL AND THE PUERTA DE LA PAZ: *Glaciar*, Plaza Real 3; *Can Solé*, Paseo de Colón 17; *Amaya*, Rambla de Santa Mónica 24; *China Gran Dragón*, Ciudad 5; *Los Caracoles*, Escudillers 14; *Siete Puertas*, Paseo de Isabell II 14. – OTHER PARTS OF THE CITY: *Atalaya, Avda de la Diagonal 523 (23rd floor); *Reno, Tuset 27; *Via Véneto*, Granduxer 10; *Tres Coronas*, Buenos Aires 54; *La Pérgola*, Avda de la Reina María Cristina; *Carballeira*, Avda de la Reina María Cristina 3 (seafood); *Guría*, Casanova 97 (Basque); *Finisterre*, Avda de la Diagonal 469; etc.

CAFÉS. – *Monza*, Rambla de Cataluña 86; *Piazza*, Plaza de Cataluña 15; *Liceo*, Rambla de los Capuchinos; *Moka*, Rambla de los Estudios 8; etc.

SHOPPING. – Barcelona is an excellent shopping centre, where visitors can buy the products of Catalonian industries and crafts as well as those of other parts of Spain, in great variety and usually of excellent quality.

Department stores: Arias, corner of Calles Tamarit and Villaroel; Capitol, Pelayo 20; Cortefiel, Avda de la Puerta del Ángel 38; El Corte Inglés, Plaza de Cataluña 14; El Corte Inglés, Avda de la Diagonal 619; El Siglo, Pelayo 54; Jorba-Preciados, Avda de la Puerta del Ángel 19; Sears, Avda de la Diagonal 471; Sears (Meridiana), Avda de la Meridiana 352; Sepu, Rambla de los Estudios 120; Simago, Rambla de los Estudios 113. Leather clothing and shoes are particularly good buys.

Fashion shops (many boutiques): Paseo de Gracia, Avenida de la Diagonal, Calle Tuset.

Antiques: Calle de la Paja, Pino, Baños Neuvos, Aviño and above all the Barrio Gótico.

Handicrafts and souvenirs: The best and most genuine articles are to be found in the Pueblo Español, where visitors can watch many of them being made.

Flowers can be bought in the flower market in Rambla de les Flors, *birds* and small animals in Rambla dels Ocells, Spanish and foreign *books* and *newspapers* in kiosks.

EVENTS. – *Fiesta de San Antonio* (Jan.), with blessing of animals, parade of riders and decorated floats. – *Palm Market* in Rambla de Cataluña during the week before Palm Sunday, followed on Palm Sunday by the hanging of the palm leaves, after they have been blessed, from the balconies of houses. – *Semana Santa* (Holy Week), with Good Friday procession on the Ramblas; on Easter Saturday lamb market in Paseo de San Juan. – *Corpus Christi*, with a great procession, starting from the Cathedral. – *Fiesta*

Mayor (Sept.), patronal festival of Virgen de la Merced. – Bonfires in the Paseo de San Juan and other streets on St John's day and the feast of SS. Peter and Paul.

CASINO. – *Gran Casino de Barcelona*, San Pedro de Ribes.

BOAT SERVICES. – Barcelona is the main port for car ferry services to the Balearics (Palma de Mallorca, Mahon, Ibiza), and it also has regular connections with Genoa, Marseilles, Le Havre, Hamburg, and all the major Mediterranean ports, as well as with New York, Central and South America. Reservations for the car ferry services: *Compañía Trasmediterránea*, Vía Layetana 2 (Barcelona).

WATER SPORTS. – Barcelona has good bathing beaches within easy reach of the city as well as a magnificent swimming stadium on Montjuich. Facilities for other water sports (sailing, motorboating, etc.) are available through the Club Náutico and Club Marítimo.

SPORT and RECREATION on land. – Numerous clubs catering for all kinds of sports – golf, riding, tennis, racing, football, polo, hockey, etc. Bullfighting in the Plaza Monumental (22,000 seats) and Arena Plaza España (15,000 seats).

Barcelona is the old and the new capital of Catalonia, the seat of a university and a bishopric, Spain's second city and its leading industrial and commercial centre, one of the largest ports in the Mediterranean and a major centre of international air traffic.

The town is attractively situated in a wide coastal plain which rises gradually from the sea to the ridge of Tibidabo, bounded on the NE by the Montaña Pelada and on the SW by Montjuich. Beyond the Montaña Pelada is the valley which the Río Besós has carved through the hills; to the S of Montjuich the Río Llobregat reaches the sea after flowing through a wide and fertile valley which provides Barcelona with its vegetables and fruit.

HISTORY. – Barcelona first appears in history under the Iberian name of *Barcino*. In the time of Augustus it became a Roman colony under the style of *Iulia Faventia*. The Visigoths captured "Barcinona" in the years 414 and 531 and made it their capital. The Moors conquered the town in 716, and in 801 it was retaken by Charlemagne's son Louis the Pious. From 874 onwards the Counts of Barcelona were independent rulers. During this period, and also after the union of Catalonia with Aragon, Barcelona ranked with Genoa and Venice as one of the leading commercial cities of the Mediterranean. Its power was destroyed, however, by the union with Castile in the 15th c., and particularly by the exclusion of Catalonia from trade with the New World. During the War of the Spanish Succession it supported the cause of Archduke Charles, from whom it hoped for greater liberties, and much of the town was destroyed when it was stormed by the French in the autumn of 1714.

During the reign of Charles III, who opened up trade with America in 1778, Barcelona began to prosper again and was able to re-establish its old pre-eminence in the course of the 19th c. During the Spanish Civil War (1936–39) the city was held by the Republicans.

SIGHTS. – This great international city has so much to offer the visitor that it is not possible to include everything in a single itinerary. In the following description the main features of interest are grouped together in convenient sections.

Harbour area. – The **Harbour** (*Puerto*), which including the outer harbour (*ante-puerto*) covers an area of 741 acres, ranks with those of Gijón and Bilbao as one of the largest and most modern in Spain, handling some 17 million tons of goods annually. The main imports are coal, corn and cotton, the main exports wine, olive oil and corks. There are trips round the harbour from the Plaza Pùerta de la Paz; but it is also well worth while strolling along the quays, or better still along the outer breakwater, reached from Barcelona.

Barcelona Harbour

Just off the harbour, in the *Plaza de la Paz*, is the **Columbus Monument**, erected in 1888, 60 m high, with an iron column (lift to top: restricted view) bearing a bronze statue of Columbus 8 m high. – On the harbour side of the square is a reproduction (1951) of the caravel *Santa María* in which Columbus sailed to America in 1492. On the S side of the square are the handsome *Aduana* (Custom House) and the **Reales Atarazanas**, the old royal shipyards (13th–14th c.), which now house the *Museo Marítimo*, with an interesting collection of model ships and much other material on the sea and ships.

From the Plaza de la Paz the *Paseo de Colón*, 42 m wide and lined with palms, runs SW along the edge of the harbour to the foot of Montjuich and NE to the Head

Post Office. Just off this wider section is the handsome domed **church of the Merced**, built in the mid 18th c., with the much venerated statue of the Virgen de la Merced (13th c.), patroness of Barcelona, on the high altar. At the NE end of the Paseo, which here widens out into the *Plaza de Antonio López*, is the **Head Post Office** (*Correos*), built in 1928. – From here the line of the Paseo de Colón is continued by the short Paseo de Isabel II into the *Plaza Palacio*, centre of Barcelona's maritime trade, with the *Gobierno Civil* and numerous offices and commercial houses. On the W side of the square is the **Lonja** (Exchange), founded in 1382, with a fine Gothic exchange hall (Sala de Contrataciones).

A little way N of the Lonja is the Gothic church of ***Santa María del Mar** (1329–83), after the Cathedral Barcelona's most important medieval church, with a Gothic rose window and richly decorated doorways; spacious interior, with 15th–17th c. stained glass. Beyond the church is the *Plaza del Borne*, a ceremonial square around which a number of narrow old-world streets have been preserved, such as the *Calle Moncada*, once an aristocratic address. At No. 20 is the *Casa Dalmases*, with a beautiful patio and a Renaissance staircase. No 15, the *Palacio Berenguer de Aguilar*, now houses the **Picasso Museum** (opened 1963), with one of the most important collections of pictures by Picasso (who lived mainly in Barcelona between 1895 and 1903), including works of the blue and rose periods and the 1957 paraphrases of Velázquez's "Meninas".

SE of the Plaza Palacio is the fishermen's quarter, **Barceloneta**, laid out on a regular plan on a projecting tongue of land, where visitors can see something of the busy everyday life of the people. In this district is the church of *San Miguel del Puerto*, built in 1755 and enlarged in 1863. From the *Torre de San Sebastián* (96 m high: restaurant) on the "New Breakwater" there is a *cableway over the harbour to the *Torre de Jaime I* (158 m) and on to the *Balcón de Miramar* viewpoint on Montjuich.

The Ramblas. – The *Ramblas are a succession of wide avenues lined with plane-trees; they run from the Columbus Monument to the Plaza de Cataluña, a total distance of 1180 m. At the near end,

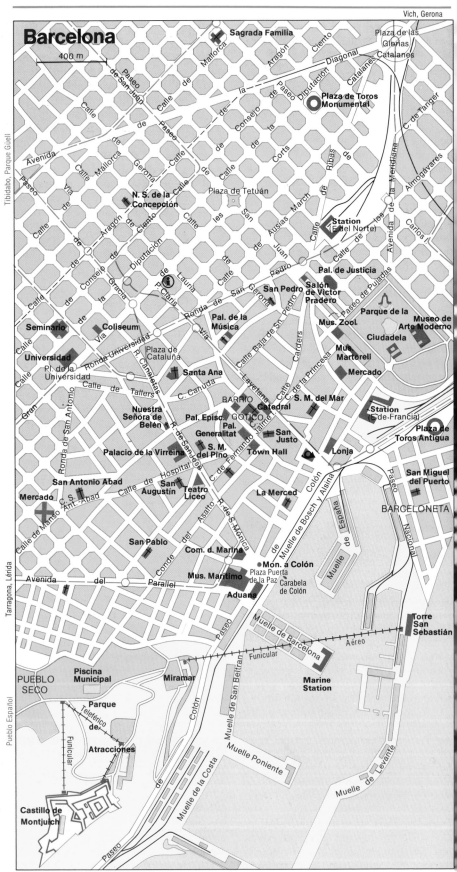

Vich, Gerona

Barcelona

400 m

Sagrada Familia

Plaza de las Glorias Catalanes

Diagonal

Plaza de Toros Monumental

Tibidabo, Parque Güell

Paseo de San Juan

Calle

Calle

de

Calle

de

Mallorca

Aragón

Ciento

de

la

Consejo

de

Paseo

Diputación

de

las

Corts

C. de Tánger

Avenida

Vía

Paseo

de

Calle

Mallorca

Gerona

Calle

Calle

de

de

Ribas

de

Almogávares

de

N. S. de la Concepción

Plaza de Tetuán

Calle

San

Avenida de la Meridiana

Carlos

Calle

de

Aragón

de

Ciento

les

Juan

March

Ausias

Pedro

de

Station (E. del Norte)

Calle

de

los

Diputación

Consejo

de

Diputación

San Gerona

de

San

Pedro

Pal. de Justicia

Paseo de Pujadas

Calle

Laura

San Pedro

Salón de Victor Pradero

Mus. Zool.

Parque de la Ciudadela

Museo de Arte Moderno

de

Ronda

Pal. de la Música

Via

Calle

Baja de Sn. Pedro

Carders

de la Princesa

Mus. Martorell

Seminario

Coliseum

Ronda Universidad

Calle

Plaza de Cataluña

Santa Ana

Lavetana

Calle

Mercado

Universidad

de

Calle

R. Canaletas

Calle

de

Talleres

C. Canuda

BARRIO

Calle

S. M. del Mar

Pl. de la Universidad

Gran

Ronda de San Antonio

Nuestra Señora de Belén

Catedral

GOTICO

Pal. Episc.

Jaime I

Station (E.-de-France)

Plaza de Toros Antigua

Pal. Generalitat

Calle de Fernando

San Justo

Paseo

de Sepúlveda

S. M. del Pino

Town Hall

Lonja

San Miguel del Puerto

Palacio de la Virreina

Calle

de

Hospital

San Agustín

Teatro Liceo

Asalto

R. de S. Mónica

La Merced

Colón

Muelle de Bosch y Alsina

Muelle de España

Muelle de Nacional

BARCELONETA

San Antonio Abad

C. S. Ant. Abad

Mercado

Calle de Manso

San Pablo

Conde del

Com. d. Marina

Mon. a Colón

Plaza Puerta de la Paz

Carabela de Colón

Avenida

del

Parallel

Paseo

Muelle de Barcelona

Aéreo

Funicular

Torre San Sebastián

Mus. Maritimo

Aduana

Colón

Muelle de San Beltrán

PUEBLO SECO

Piscina Municipal

Miramar

Marine Station

Tarragona, Lérida

Parque

Teleférico

de

Funicular

Atracciones

Muelle de la Costa

Muelle Poniente

Muelle de Levante

Pueblo Español

Castillo de Montjuich

Paseo

Metro

on the left-hand side of the *Rambla de Santa Mónica*, is the **Comandancia de Marina** (Naval Command Headquarters). – The Rambla de Santa Mónica joins the very busy *Rambla de los Capuchinos* (formerly Rambla del Centro). In Calle del Conde de Asalto, on the left, is the **Palacio Güell** (by Antonio Guadí, 1885–89), now a *Museum of the Theatre*. To the right, along the short Calle de Colón, is the *Plaza Real*, an arcaded square planted with palms which is a scene of bustling activity all day long. The next street on the right is *Calle de Fernando*, much frequented in the evening, which leads to the Plaza de San Jaime. – Beyond the **Gran Teatro del Liceo** (1848: 500 seats) used for opera and concerts, *Calle de San Pablo* goes off on the left to the Romanesque church of **San Pablo del Campo**, built in 1117, when it lay outside the town (hence "del Campo", "in the Fields"). It has an octagonal dome over the crossing, a beautiful main doorway and a fine interior. Adjoining the church to the SE is a charming little 13th c. cloister.

The Rambla de los Capuchinos ends at a busy traffic intersection, the *Llano de la Bouqería*, from which Calle del Cardenal Casañas runs N to the *Plaza del Pino*, with the 15th c. church of **Santa María del Pino** (large rose window in W end, beautiful modern stained glass). In the surrounding area are many antique shops.

From the Llano de la Boquería the Rambla de San José – also known as the *Rambla de las Flores* on account of the flower market held here in the morning – continues NW. On the left is a large market hall, the **Mercado de la Boquería**, and adjoining it on the N the **Palacio de la Virreina** (1778), the former palace of the Vicereine of Peru, now housing the *Museo de Artes Decorativas* (furniture, carpets, porcelain, and also pictures by Italian and Spanish artists, including Titian, El Greco and Goya). – The line of the ramblas is continued by the *Rambla de los Estudios*, in which a bird market is held in the morning. Immediately left, at the end of Calle del Carmen, is the former Jesuit church of **Nuestra Señora de Belén** (1681–1729).

The ramblas end in the *Plaza de Cataluña*, Barcelona's largest and busiest square with gardens and fountains and the main junction point of the underground railway

system. On the E side is the massive *Telephone Building* (Telefónica). On the SE side, near the end of the rambla, is the entrance to the old church of **Santa Ana**, founded 1146, with a charming two-storey cloister (14th c.).

From the Plaza de Cataluña Calle Pelayo, a busy shopping street, and the Ronda de la Universidad run W to the *Plaza de la Universidad*, in which is the **University**, founded in 1450 (present building 1863–73). Two beautiful courtyards; University Library.

The line of the ramblas is continued NW from the Plaza de Cataluña by the *Rambla de Cataluña*, which extends to the Avenida de la Diagonal – Parallel to it on the NE is the *Paseo de Gracia*, a splendid promenade 61·5 m wide and 1200 m long lined by a fourfold row of plane-trees, with elegant shops. In Calle de Aragón, off the Paseo de Gracia on the right, is the church of **Nuestra Señora de la Concepción**, brought here from the old town in 1869, with a 14th c. cloister (badly damaged in 1936). Farther along the Paseo de Gracia, on the right (No. 92), is the **Casa Milá** (by Guadí, 1910). – At the N end of the Paseo de Gracia is the *Plaza de la Victoria*, with an obelisk commemorating the entry of Franco's troops (1939) Here we cut across the *Avenida de la Diagonal*, the main traffic artery of the new town, more than 10 km long. Near its W end are the *Stadium* of the Barcelona Football Club, with seating for 125,000 spectators, and the *University City* (Ciudad Universitaria).

The Cathedral and the Barrio Gótico. – 500 m SE of the Plaza de Cataluña, on the highest point in the old town, known as Monte Tabor, stands the ****Cathedral** (*Santa Cruz* or *Santa Eulalia*), begun in 1298 and completed in 1448, apart from the main front (1898) and the dome tower (1913). It occupies the site of an earlier Romanesque building, some reliefs from which have been preserved in the NE side doorway.

The magnificent INTERIOR (83·3 m long, 37·2 m wide, 25·5 m high) contains brilliantly coloured *stained glass*, dating in part from the 15th c., fine 15th c. *choir-stalls* and a beautiful *pulpit* of 1403. The **Capilla Mayor** has a late Gothic *retablo* (16th c.). Of the numerous side chapels the finest is the **Capilla del Santísimo Sacramento** or *Capilla del Santo Cristo de Lapanto* (on the right, near the high altar),

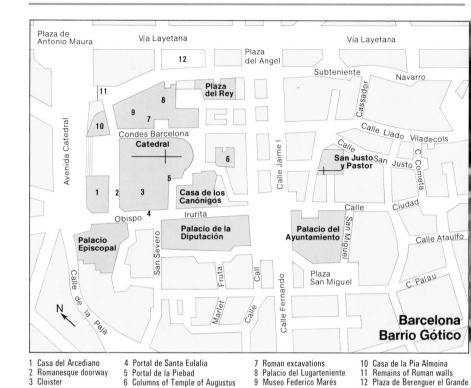

Plaza de Antonio Maura · Via Layetana · Plaza del Angel · Via Layetana · Subteniente · Navarro · Cassador · 12 · 11 · 8 · 9 · 7 · 10 · Condes Barcelona · Calle Llado · Viladecols · Catedral · Calle · Calle Jaime I · San Justo · San Justo · San Justo y Pastor · C. Cometa · 5 · 6 · Calle · Ciudad · 1 · 2 · 3 · Casa de los Canónigos · Obispo · 4 · Irurita · San Miguel · Calle Ataulfo · San Severo · Palacio de la Diputación · Palacio del Ayuntamiento · Palacio Episcopal · Fruta · Call · Plaza San Miguel · C. Palau · N · Calle de la Paja · Marlet · Calle · Calle Fernando

Barcelona
Barrio Gótico

1 Casa del Arcediano	4 Portal de Santa Eulalia	7 Roman excavations	10 Casa de la Pía Almoina
2 Romanesque doorway	5 Portal de la Piebad	8 Palacio del Lugarteniente	11 Remains of Roman walls
3 Cloister	6 Columns of Temple of Augustus	9 Museo Federico Marés	12 Plaza de Berenguer el Grande

formerly the chapterhouse, which contains the *alabaster tomb* (15th–16th c.) of St Olegarius, archbishop of Tarragona (d. 1136), and the "Christ of Lepanto", which Don John of Austria is said to have carried -on the prow of his flagship during his victorious battle with the Turks at Lepanto in 1571. The other 26 chapels, which contain a number of fine monuments, mostly date from the 16th and 17th c. – From the Capila Mayor steps lead down to the **Crypt**, with the *alabaster sarcophagus* (Italian workmanship, c. 1330) of St Eulalia (3rd c.?). In the **Sacristy** is the valuable Cathedral Treasury (Tesoro). – From the *SW tower* (entrance inside the Cathedral: 210 steps) there are very fine *views. – Adjoining the Cathedral on the SW is the magnificent *Cloister* (Claustro) of 1380–1451, the inner courtyard of which is planted

with palms and magnolias. In the SW corner of the cloister is the *Capilla de Santa Lucía*, founded 1270, and adjoining it the *Chapterhouse* (Sala Capitular), now the Cathedral Museum, with pictures by Spanish masters of the 14th and 15th c.

Around the Cathedral is the *Barrio Gótico (Gothic Quarter)*, the most important surviving part of the medieval town, now occupied by many antique shops. From the Plaza de la Catedral Calle de Santa Lucía runs S, passing the 15th c. **Casa del Arcediano**, with a beautiful patio, which houses the *Municipal Archives*, to the **Bishop's Palace**, first mentioned in the records in 926 (several times rebuilt). At the N end of the Plaza de la Catedral is the 15th c. **Casa Canónica** (Canons' House), which contains the interesting *Diocesan Museum* (altarpieces, sculpture, vestments). Adjoining, in Calle Condes de Barcelona, are the **Museo Marés**, with a rich collection of sculpture, and the *Archives of the Crown of Aragon* (Archiva General de la Corona de Aragón). To the NE is the *Plaza del Rey*, once the centre of the palace of the counts of Barcelona and kings of Aragon, to which belonged the five-storey **Mirador** (outlook tower) of the 16th c. and the *Salón del Tinell* (1370), the former reception hall of the counts, with arcades supporting the ceiling, also belonged. The palace chapel also survives

Barcelona Cathedral

– the Gothic *Capilla de Santa Águeda* (13th c.); in front of it is a column from the Roman temple which once stood here. On the E side of the square is the **Casa Padellas**, with the *Municipal Historical Museum* (Museo de Historia de la Ciudad).

Calle del Obispo Irurita, which skirts the SW side of the Cathedral, runs S to the *Plaza de San Jaime*, on the NW side of which is the 15th c. **Casa de la Diputación**, formerly the seat of the parliament of Catalonia, now the headquarters of the provincial administration. Beautiful Gothic *patio*; on the first floor the Gothic *St George's Chapel*; to the rear of the building the charming *Patio de los Naranjos* (Court of Orange-Trees). Adjoining the Casa de la Diputación on the N is the old **Audiencia** (Law Courts), with a beautiful Gothic façade on Calle del Obispo Irurita. – On the SE side of the Plaza de San Jaime is the **Casa Consistorial** or *Ayuntamiento* (Town Hall), built 1369–78 (main front 1847). The main features of the interior are the large 14th c. Council Chamber (*Salón de Ciento*) and the Salón de las Crónicas, with paintings by José María Sert. – A short distance E is the Gothic church of *Santos Justo y Pastor* (begun *c.* 1345).

From the Plaza de San Jaime *Calle de Jaime I* runs NE to the *Plaza del Ángel*, where it intersects *Vía Layetana* which is lined with banks and the offices of insurance companies. This street leads from the harbour in the SE to Calle de Córcega in the NW. In Calle Alta de San Pedro, which runs NE from the northern section of Vía Layetana, is the **Palau** (*Palacio*) **de la Música**, a concert hall in neo-Catalan style (by Domènech i Montaner, 1908). Calle Alta de San Pedro continues to the *Arco del Triunfo*, built in 1888 as the entrance to the International Exhibition, and the **Palacio de Justicia** (Law Courts) of 1903 (murals by J. M. Sert in the interior). From here Calle de los Almogávares runs NE; to the SE is the Municipal Park.

Municipal Park. – From the Plaza Palacio the wide Avenida del Marqués de Argentera runs NE past the *Estación de Francia* to the **Municipal Park** (*Parque y Jardines de la Ciudadela*), an area of 74 acres on the site of the former Citadel, with avenues of trees, terraced flower-beds, ornamental ponds and various

Paseo de Carlos I, Barcelona

monuments. In the W corner of the park, occupying a building designed by Domènech i Montaner, is the **Zoological Museum** (*Museo de Zoología*). To the SE, beyond the palm-house, is the **Geological Museum**, also known as the **Museo Martorell** after its founder. On the NE side of the park is the **Zoological Garden** (*Jardín Zoológico*). At the N corner of the park is a fantastic grotto structure, the *Cascada del Parque*, opposite which is a café-restaurant. – To the SE are a number of buildings which formed part of the old Citadel. In the 18th c. **Palacio Real** and its modern additions is the *Museum of Modern Art* (Museo de Arte Monderno), which offers a good general survey of Spanish painting and sculpture of the 19th and 20th c., including works by Dalí, Miró and Tapies. – In Calle de los Almogávares (No. 99) is a *collection of historic hearses* (*carros fúnebres*) of the 17th–19th c.

Montjuich and the Pueblo Español. – On the S side of the city is *Montjuich, a hill (213 m) which falls steeply down to the sea. It is reached by cableway, funicular and a road from the *Avenida del Parallel* which skirts the N side of the hill and has numerous places of entertainment. On top of the hill stands the **Castillo de Montjuich**, with the *Military Museum* and fine *views from the bastions. On its NW slopes is a **park** containing the pavilions of the 1929 International Exhibition, now museums, and the *Centro de Estudios de Arte Contemporáneo*, founded by Joán Miró.

At the W end of the Avenida del Parallel is the *Plaza de España*, with a large fountain,

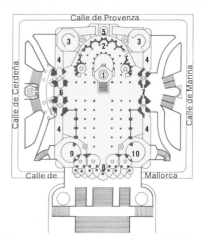

1 Altar
2 Apsidal chapel
3 Sacristies (towers above)
4 Cloister
5 Chapel of Resurrection of
  Virgin
6 Doorway of the Passion
7 Doorway of the Nativity
8 Doorway of Majesty
9 Baptistery (tower above)
10 Chapel of Sacrament
   (tower above)

"Spain offered to God", *illuminated in summer with 4730 lights in ten colours. From here the *Avenida de la Reina María Cristina* runs up between the exhibition pavilions (on the right the reconstructed World Exhibition Pavilion by Mies van der Rohe, 1929), via a series of staircases and terraces, to the **Palacio Nacional**, with a hall seating 10,000 and the ***Museum of Catalan Art** (*Museo de Arte de Cataluña*). The museum contains an outstanding collection of Spanish art from the 11th to the 18th c., including Romanesque and Gothic painting and sculpture, wall and ceiling paintings from Catalan churches and works by El Greco, Velázquez, Zurbarán and Ribera. E of the Palacio Nacional is the *Museum of Ethnology* (Museo Etnológico). To the NE of this is the richly stocked *Archaeological Museum* (Museo Arqueológico). Close by, to the E, is the *Greek Theatre* (Teatro Griego), in an old quarry (2000 seats; performances in summer). – In the western part of the park is the ***Pueblo Español** (Spanish Village), originally built for the 1929 International Exhibition, with reproductions of typical houses from the various parts of Spain, each region being represented by a street (handicrafts on sale). In the Plaza Mayor (No. 6) is the *Spanish section of the Museum of Ethnology*, with examples of decorative art and craft and industrial products.

From the Pueblo Español the *Avenida del Estadio* runs E, affording fine views, past the *Stadium* (seating for 60,000). It is continued by the *Avenida de Miramar* (total length of the two avenues 3 km) to

the funicular station and the *Miramar viewing terrace* (60 m), with a restaurant and the upper station of the cableway from the harbour. From here it is possible to reach the E end of the Paseo de Colón and the harbour in a few minutes, either by walking down a flight of steps or by driving down the Carretera de Montjuich. On the NE slopes of Montjuich lies the *Parque de Atracciones* (amusement park).

The northern districts. – In the N of the city, beyond the Avenida de la Diagonal stands the imposing ***Templo de la Sagrada Familia**, a monumental church in neo-Catalan style designed by Gaudí (begun 1882), the cost of which was met by the alms and public subscription. The church is planned to have a total length of 110 m and a height of 45 m, with twelve towers between 100 and 115 m high and a principal dome 160 m high. So far only the four-towered E doorway (the "Nativity front"), the apse and the crypt (used for services) have been completed.

From the N terminus of Metro line III in Plaza Lesseps it is only a short walk up through the suburban district of Gracia to the **Parque Güell**, designed by Antonio Gaudí between 1900 and 1914, with a series of fantastic buildings in neo-Catalan style (market hall, Greek theatre, tower blocks, galleries, viaducts). Gaudí lived here from 1906 until shortly before his death (Casa-Museo Gaudí).

An attractive drive of 12 km leads N into *Calle de Balmes*, which starts between the Plaza de Cataluña and the Plaza de la Universidad, and continues on a road affording magnificent views to the hill of *Tibidabo* (532 m), which can also be reached by a funicular (1·2 km) from the end of the "Tranvía Azul" tramline near the Tibidabo Metro station. On the hill are hotels and restaurants, an amusement park and the church of the *Sagrado Corazón de Jesús* (completed 1961), with a large statue of the Sacred Heart (1935). On the summit are a water-tower 45 m high (lift) and the Barcelona radio and television transmitter. The view embraces the surroundings of the city with some 80 towns and villages (impressive also after dark), a wide expanse of sea (extending in clear weather as far as the Balearics) and, inland, Montserrat, Montseny and on the northern horizon the Pyrenees. – There is an attractive return route by way of the villa suburb of **Vallvidrera** (alt. 375 m), 2 km W, with a prettily situated parish church, and then either by tram to Barcelona (12 km) or by funicular to the suburb of Sarriá, or from the Sarriá church (tram; Metro line III from Roma station) westward on the Paseo de la Reina Elisenda to **Pedralbes**, where the Gothic conventual church of *Santa María* (1326) contains the fine alabaster monument of Queen Elisenda de Montcada (d. 1364), wife of Jaime II. In the three-storey cloister is the Capilla de San Miguel, with notable Gothic *wall paintings by Ferrer Bassa (1346).

In the Parque Güell, Barcelona

SURROUNDINGS. – There are many places of interest within reach of Barcelona, some of them lying well off the main roads.

Via Sabadell to Tarrasa. – Leave Barcelona on the new motorway to the NW or N 150, which lead in 21 km to **Sabadell** (alt. 190 m; pop. 145,000), an industrial town on the Río Ripoll, with an interesting *museum* (prehistory, early historical period, history of the town). *Ermita La Salud*, on a hill. – Then continue on N 150, almost due W, to **Tarrasa** (see p. 221).

To San Cugat de Vallés. – 12 km NW of Barcelona, reached by a secondary road via *Tibidabo*, is **San Cugat de Vallés** (alt. 210 m; pop. 20,000), a villa suburb in a well-wooded area, with a fine abbey of the 11th–12th c. (Romanesque cloister, 9th c. graves) and a 15th c. abbey church.

Along the coast road to the Costa Brava. – Leave Barcelona by way of the Plaza de las Grlorias on A 19, the motorway, going NE over the *Río Besós* to **Badalona** (alt. 7 m; pop. 160,000), a long, straggling industrial town (oil refinery, steel plant, etc.).

From Badalona on the N 11 via *Mongat* over the higher ground and along a beautiful stretch of road skirting the beaches of the *Costa Dorada* ("Golden Coast"), separated from them only by the railway. Beyond *Masnóu* the road continues dead straight alongside the sea by way of *Premiá de Mar* and *Vilasar de Mar* (hotels and camping sites) to **Mataró** (alt. 23 m; pop. 68,000; hotels: Castell de Mata, II, 52 r., SP;

Colón (no rest.), P I, 55 r.), another straggling industrial town with a harbour and a bathing beach. The first railway in Spain (1848) ran between here and Barcelona.

N II continues along the coast. Off the road on the left is *San Andrés de Llavaneras* (alt. 114 m; hotels); then comes *Caldas de Estrach* (alt. 33 m; hotels), with a thermal spring (41 °C – 106 °F) and a bathing beach. Then on, with beautiful views to **Arenys de Mar** (alt. 13 m; pop. 9000; hotels: *Raymond, II, 33 r.; Titus, III, 44 r., SP), a picturesquely situated little port (bypass) with a yacht harbour and bathing beaches. The road then continues, with many bends, along the steeply scarped coast formed by the hills of *La Serp* and *Las Rosas*, passes through *Canet de Mar* and *San Pol de Mar*, dominated by the battlemented tower of its castle (both with hotels), and runs along the rocky coast to **Calella** (alt. 5 m; pop. 9000; numerous hotels, mostly closed in winter; camping site), a popular seaside resort near the foot of the *Sierra de Montnegre*.

Beyond *Pineda* the road forks. The coast road, to the right, continues by way of *Malgrat* (pop. 9000) to the **Costa Brava** (see p. 111), while N II, to the left, crosses the provincial boundary to **Gerona** (see p. 123), 104 km from Barcelona.

To Puigcerdá. – From the Plaza de las Glorias take the motorway which runs N in the direction of Gerona and then turn off into N 152 to reach (28 km from Barcelona) **Granollers** (alt. 145 m; pop. 30,000), a busy town with a well-known cattle market. Church of *San Esteban* (14th c.), with a Romanesque doorway. – From Granollers it is well worth while making a detour (33 or 41 km) to the mighty *Sierra del Montseny* (1745 m) and the *Ermita Santa Fé*, in a beautiful setting (extensive views) on the southern slope of the hills.

The road continues through *La Garriga* (alt. 260 m), in a rocky valley, and climbs, with many bends, to *Ayguafreda* and *Tona* (alt. 491 m), with a large ruined castle above the village on the left; then over the Vich plain to the old episcopal city of **Vich** (see p. 239).

N 152 leads, via *La Gleva*, with a view of *Montserrat* to the rear, to *Montesquiú*, with the *Castillo de Besora* dominating it on the right. It then continues over the boundary between the provinces of Barcelona and Gerona to the little town of **Ripoll** (see p. 189), after which there is a beautiful stretch of road (waterfall) to the health resort of *Aguas de Ribas* and the larger township of **Ribas de Freser** (alt. 926 m; pop. 9000), a very popular summer resort in a wooded setting on the *Río Freser*. – 8 km N is the winter sports centre of *Nuria* (alt. 2000 m; hotels), which can also be reached by a mountain railway.

N 152 climbs up between *Puigmal* (2912 m) on the right and the *Sierra de Cardí* on the left to the **Puerto de Tosas** (1800 m), and then descends from the pass, with many bends, to the little village of **Urtg** (alt. 1190 m), from which a side road goes off into the magnificent winter sports area of *La Molina* (1600–2500 m; hotels), with several ski-lifts and cableways. – Soon afterwards C 1313 diverges on the left to **Seo de Urgel** (see p. 206).

Just after the junction with C 1313 the main road enters the old fortified frontier town of **Puigcerdá** (alt. 1147 m; pop. 5400), beautifully situated on a hill at the confluence of the *Río Segre* and the *Río Carol*, in the middle of the Pyrenees. Thanks to this situation it is much frequented both as a summer holiday resort and for its winter sports (numerous hotels and *hostales*). – 5 km NE is the little medieval town (protected as a national monument) of *Llivia*, a Spanish enclave in French territory. – 5 km N on N 152 is *Ur* (alt. 1135 m), with the Spanish customs post.

Coast road along the Costa de Garraf. – The motorway which runs SW from Barcelona and joins C 245 is the coast road to Tarragona, which affords magnificent views. After passing through the industrial suburb of *Hospitalet* (pop. 230,000) it leaves the city and eventually comes, near the junction of the motorway and C 245, to **Castelldefels** (pop. 11,000; many hotels, some of them closed in winter; camping site), which attracts many visitors with its beautiful beach and pine-woods: small Romanesque church, old castle (dramatic performances in summer) and watch-towers.

The road runs past the village of *Garraf*: then follows a magnificent stretch, with many bends, along the steep and rocky coast of the *Costas de Garraf*, the most beautiful part of the Costa Dorada, to **Sitges** (see p. 215), an elegant bathing resort of international standing.

Over the Cruz de Ordal pass. – The road traverses the western industrial districts of Barcelona and comes (17 km from the city centre) to the industrial suburb of *Molins de Rey* (alt. 140 m). Soon after this, at *Cuatro Caminos*, N 340 goes off on the left and ascends the valley by way of *Vallirana* (alt. 205 m), through beautiful wooded country, to the *Viaducto del Lladoner*, with two tiers of arches, which spans a gorge 22 m deep and continues up to the **Cruz de Ordal** pass (510 m), marked by a crucifix (panoramic views). – After many undulations the road passes between cultivated fields and comes, beyond the motorway access road, to **Villafranca del Panadés** (alt. 224 m; pop. 16,000), in the wine-growing district of *Panadés*, with old palaces, the 13th c. Gothic church of Santa María (pictures, monuments) and a wine museum (samples) in the old palaces of the kings of Aragon.

N 340 again cuts across the motorway and comes to *Arbós*. At the entrance to the town is the three-towered church of San Julián, with a handsome façade decorated with statues and a good retablo. In the town itself is a palacio with a tower similar to the Giralda in Seville.

To Martorell. – Leave Barcelona, as in the preceding route, through the western industrial districts, but at *Cuatro Caminos* continue NW on N II, which passes through *San Andrés de la Barca* and runs along the right bank of the *Río Llobregat* to **Martorell** (alt. 160 m; pop. 13,000), an ancient little town at the outflow of the *Río Noya* into the *Río Llobregat*, here spanned by the *Puente del Diablo*, which is said to have been built by the Carthaginian general Hannibal in 218 B.C. and has a triumphal arch erected by him in honour of his father Hamilcar Barca.

To Andorra. – Leave Barcelona on N 11, in a westerly direction to *Igualada* (alt. 315 m; pop. 27,000; Hotel América, II, 52 r., SP), an industrial town (spinning mills, tanneries). A few kilometres beyond the town turn right into C 1412, which runs N to *Prats del Rey* (alt. 435 m) and *Calaf* (alt. 470 m), at the foot of the sierra of the same name, with a ruined castle overlooking it. The road descends, with many bends, to *Castellfullit* (alt. 410 m), dominated by the towers of an old castle. It then enters the province of Lérida

and continues NW to **Pons** (alt. 360 m; pop. 2000), on the left bank of the Río Segre, with an early Gothic parish church. Here C 1412 joins C 1313, coming from Lérida. Turning right into this road, we continue N up the beautiful Segre valley towards the Pyrenees, which are seen in the background. At the village of **Basella** a road goes off on the right (25 km) to *Solsona* (alt. 665 m; pop. 5500), an old episcopal city with a Gothic church (14th–15th c.) of Romanesque origin (late Romanesque "Virgen del Claustro").

C 1313 continues to *Oliana* (alt. 460 m) and then runs through a gorge enclosed between high rock walls, the *Grau de la Granta*, to the *Embalse de Oliana*, an artificial lake more than 10 km long. At its N end, in a picturesque setting, is the village of *Coll de Nargó* (alt. 530 m). After passing through *Organá* the road climbs through a gorge, the Garganta de Organá, passes a number of villages and comes to **Seo de Urgel** (see p. 206). Continuing N from Seo de Urgel on C 145, in 10 km, beyond the Spanish village of *Farga de Moles*, we arrive at the frontier of **Andorra** (see p. 54).

The Basque Provinces

Autonomous Region.
Organ of Government: Gobierno Vasco.

Provinces (with capitals): Guipúzcoa (San Sebastián), Vizcaya (Bilbao) and Álava (Victoria).

The three Basque provinces (Provincias Vascongadas) on the Bay of Biscay have a Central European type of landscape untypical of Spain. The hills and valleys are covered with fresh green meadows, fields of maize and plantations of walnut-trees and fruit-trees, and the climate, which is agreeable even in summer, combines with the lush greenery and the picturesque Basque farms (caseríos) to give the northern slopes of the Cantabrian Mountains a friendly and appealing character. Particularly attractive is the Basque coast, with cliffs rising to over 300 m in places and little fishing towns, many of them now popular resorts.

The Basque region is bounded on the E by Navarre and the Pyrenees, on the W by the province of Santander. It takes in the eastern part of the **Cantabrian Mountains** (*Cordillera Cantábrica*), an upland region of medium height, with only a few peaks rearing up to greater altitude, among them the *Peña de Gorbea* (1475 m). The coastal hills are separated from the main ridge of the Cantabrian Mountains by longitudinal valleys used by traffic from E to W.

Basque wood-chopping contest

Part of it now accommodates the *Museo Municipal*. Church of *Santa María* (13th c.), with a "Virgen de las Angustias" by Luis Salvador Carmona. – Above the town is the *Santuario El Castañar* (alt. 1050 m), with the "Virgen del Castañar", the town's patroness: beautiful view.

SURROUNDINGS. – **Baños de Montemayor** (alt. 750 m), a spa with a sulphurous thermal spring (48 °C – 118 °F), situated at the head of the *Río Ambroz* valley.

Through the Sierra de Peña de Francia. – A trip through the hills, with attractive scenery. Take C 515, which runs NW from Béjar, and turn off into the road to **Miranda del Castañar**, an interesting little town with defensive walls, old castles and houses decked with coats of arms. Important *Fiesta de las Águedas* (Feb.), with characteristic local folk dancing during the evening. – Nearby is *San Martín de Castañar*, with a handsome castle.

Continue on minor roads to (10 km) **La Alberca** (protected as a national monument), one of the most charming villages in Spain, with something of an Arab aspect. Its principal fiesta is the *Ofertorio* to Nuestra Señora de la Asunción (Aug.), with a performance of the "Loa", a mystery play, in front of the church. – A mountain road (7 km) leads up to the old pilgrimage chapel of *Nuestra Señora de la Peña de Francia* (alt. 1725 m).

The inhabitants, the **Basques** (Spanish *Vascos*, Basque *Euskaldunak*), are a pre-Indo-European race who preserved a large measure of independence until the 19th c. The Basque language, *Euskara*, is still spoken, in a number of dialectal variants, mainly in the two coastal provinces of Guipúzcoa and Vizcaya, in parts of Navarre and in the Basque regions of France, in which some 110,000 Basques live. The Basques, whose old traditional costume is now represented, for all practical purposes, only by the well-known beret (*boina*), are stubbornly attached to their native soil and way of life and are struggling for complete independence from Spain (separatist movement ETA).

Belmonte

Province: Cuenca (CU).
Telephone: via operator.
Altitude: 79 m. – Population: 4000.
ⓘ **Ayuntamiento** (Town Hall),
Plaza del Caudillo;
tel. Belmonte 8.

The whole of the ancient little fortified town of Belmonte, a few kilometres off N 301 to the N, has been declared a monument of tourist interest. It was the birthplace of Fray Luis de León (1527–91).

SIGHTS. – Belmonte has a large and well-preserved ***castle** (national monument) of the mid 15th c. on a hill commanding the surrounding area, with handsome towers, bastions and battlements. It has a fine **collegiate church**, which is also a national monument, with beautiful choir-stalls, Gothic retablos and the font at which Luis de León was christened.

SURROUNDINGS. – 6 km N of the town is *Villaescusa de Haro*, with the Gothic chapel of Nuestra Señora de la Asunción; the interior has fine Gothic decoration and a beautiful retablo.

Béjar

Province: Salamanca (SA).
Telephone code: 923.
Altitude: 950 m. – Population: 20,000.
ⓘ **Oficina Municipal de Turismo,**
Paseo de Cervantes 6;
tel. 40 30 05.

HOTELS. – *Colón*, Colón 42, II, 54 r.; *Comercio*, Puerta de Ávila 5, IV, 13 r.; *Hostal España*, Mariano Zúñiga 4, P III, 27 r.

EVENTS. – *Fiestas Patronales* (Sept.), in honour of the Nativity of the Virgin. – *Ferias de San Miguel* (Sept.).

Béjar, an important centre of cloth manufacture, lies in an attractive situation on a hill above a valley in the western foothills of the Sierra de Gredos. Its agreeable climate makes it a popular summer resort.

SIGHTS. – The town's most notable building is the 16th c. **Palacio Ducal**, with a beautiful Renaissance courtyard.

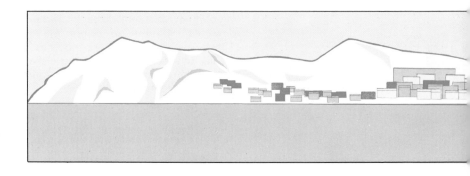

Benavente

Province: Zamora (ZA).
Telephone code: 988.
Altitude: 729 m. – Population: 11,000.
ⓘ **Ayuntamiento** (Town Hall),
Plaza de España;
　　tel. 63 03 71 and 63 12 89.

HOTELS. – *Parador Nacional Fernando II de León*,
Paseo Ramón y Cajal, I, 30 r.; *Arenas*, Carretera de
Madrid, km 261, IV, 50 r.; *Martín*, Carretera de Madrid,
km 26, IV, 46 r.; *Hostal Benavente*, Avda Federico
Silva, P II, 8 r.; etc.

**The little town of Benavente, on the
right bank of the Río Esla, formerly
the seat of the noble Pimentel family, is an important road junction. It
was probably the Roman town of
Brigeto which is mentioned in the
Antonine Itinerary.**

SIGHTS. – The town, of Medieval aspect,
has a number of interesting Romanesque
buildings. – Church of *San Juan del
Mercado* (begun 1182 as a conventual
church; S doorway 12th c.), with Gothic
vaulting and a 13th c. crucifix. – Church of
Santa María del Azogue (12th c.), with
five apses, sculptured doorways and
Baroque retablo. – Ruins of the palatial
Castillo de los Pimentel, destroyed by
Napoleon, with the 16th c. Torre del
Caracol. – Other fine buildings include the
Ayuntamiento or Casa Consistorial
(Town Hall) and the *Hospital de la
Piedad*, with a 15th c. façade and a
beautiful inner courtyard.

SURROUNDINGS. – 27 km SE on N V is **Villalpando**
(alt. 690 m; pop. 3000), a little fortified town with
medieval walls, a handsome town gate, the Puerta de
San Andrés (rebuilt in the 16th c.). the brick-built
Romanesque church of Santa María la Antigua
(12th c.) and two other churches dating from the
Moorish period.

Benidorm

Province: Alicante (A).
Telephone code: 965.
Altitude: 4 m. – Population: 40,000.
ⓘ **Oficina Municipal de Información
Turistica**,
　　Avenida de Martínez Alejos 16;
　　tel. 85 13 11

HOTELS. – *Gran Hotel Delfin*, L, 87 r., SP *Avenida*,
I, 144 r., SP; *Belroy Palace*, I, 102 r., SP; *Cimbel*, I, 144
r., SP; *Costa Blanca-Sol*, I, 190 r., SP; *Los Dálmatas*,
I, 270 r., SP; *Don Pancho*, I, 251 r.; *Selomar*, I, 246 r.,
SP; *Alameda*, II, 68 r.; *Los Alamos* (no rest.), II, 127 r.,
SP; *Bali*, II, 349 r., SP; *Benilux Park*, II, 216 r., SP;
Brisa, II, 70 r., SP; *Bristol Park*, II, 77 r., SP; *Didac*, II,
100 r., SP; *Les Dunes*, II, 110 r., SP; *Madeira*, II, 81 r.,
SP; *Marconi*, II, 130 r., SP; *Los Pelicanos*, II, 476 r., SP;
Royal, II, 88 r., SP; *Tres Coronas* (no rest.), II, 80 r., SP;
Voramar, II, 136 r., SP; *Acapulco*, III, 128 r., SP;
Bonanza, III, 52 r.; *Calypso*, III, 303 r., SP; *Don Rolf*,
III, 154 r., SP; *Esmeralda* (no rest.), III, 66 r.; *Golden*,
III, 50 r., SP; *Montemar*, III, 93 r.; *Mont Park*, III, 112 r.,
SP; *Regente*, III, 189 r.; *Torre Dorada*, IV, 240 r., SP;
etc. – *Numerous pensiones*. – Several CAMPING
SITES close to the town.

RESTAURANTS. – *Caserola*, Bruselas 7, charming
terrace, French cuisine; *Mesón Felipe V*, Horno 1, fine
view of sea; *El Cisne*, 4 km N, rustic style; *El Molino*,
2 km N; *Pampa Grill*, Ricardo 16, rustic style; *La
Trattorie*, Avda Bilbao 3; *La Parrilla*, Rincón de Lois.

The beach, Benidorm

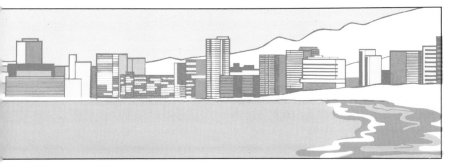

Panorama of Benidorm (Costa Blanca)

CASINO. – *Casino Costa Blanca*, Villajoyosa.

WATER SPORTS. – Facilities for all kinds of water sports (rowing, sailing, water skiing, etc.) at a number of beaches, including the extensive Playa de Poniente in the W and the Playa de Levante in the E; sub-aqua diving.

SPORT and RECREATION on land. – Bullfights, tennis, donkey rides, football, riding, etc.

Once a small fishing village, Benidorm has now become an internationally known resort, one of the most popular holiday centres on the Costa Blanca ("White Coast").

Although now surrounded by more than 150 hotels and numbers of villas and apartment blocks on both sides of the coast road, the old fishing village still stands on a rocky promontory above the sea, with its castle, church (blue cupolas) and a terrace from which there are extensive views; picturesque little lanes can still be found in the older part of the town. N of the town lies the 'Aqualand' recreation park (waterchutes, waterfalls, etc.).

SURROUNDINGS. – There are numerous excursions from Benidorm along the Mediterranean coast and into the hills of the *Sierra de Aitana*: for example by way of *Callosa de Ensarriá* to **Guadalest**, 18 km from Benidorm, a mountain village with a castle of the Moorish period (with bell-tower) perched on a crag. Nearby is an artificial lake on the *Río Guadalest*.

Along the coast to the N. – N 332 runs by way of *Altea*, beautifully situated on the hillside to the left of the road, to the cliff-fringed coast, with magnificent *views of the Peñón de Ifach and the sea; then through two tunnels and into a side road on the right to reach **Calpe** (alt. 20 m; pop. 3000), a charming little fishing town with old defensive walls and a small church in Mudéjar style. Projecting into the sea is the *Punta de Ifach**, one of the finest natural features on the Spanish Mediterranean coast, with the *Peñón de Ifach* (383 m) rising magnificently out of the sea like a lesser Gibraltar; rewarding climb to the top (about 1½ hours) on a good path. At the foot of the Peñón, to the left is the *Playa de la Fosa*. – Farther N is *Cabo de la Nao*, the most easterly point in the coastal range of hills, reached by way of *Jávea*.

Along the coast to the S. – The road at first runs a little way inland, then returns to the coast at (10 km) **Villajoyosa** (pop. 16,000; hotel: El Montoboli, I, 49 r., SP), in a beautiful situation above the sea, a little seaport with impressive remains of walls and towers and a fortress-like Gothic church.

Guadalest, near Benidorm

Betanzos

Province: La Coruña (C).
Telephone code: 981.
Altitude: 25 m. – Population: 12,000
ⓘ **Ayuntamiento** (Town Hall),
Plaza del Generalísimo 1;
tel. 77 00 11.

HOTELS. – *Los Ángeles*, Los Ángeles 11, IV, 36 r.; *Hostal Barreiros*, P III, 9 r.

RESTAURANTS. – *Casanova*, Soportales del Campo 15; *Casilla*, on N IV, with garden.

EVENTS. – The town has a full programme of events, beginning with an important cattle market on New Year's Day. – *Pilgrimage to Santa Magdalena* (Easter), with folk dances. – *Feria de los Mayos* (May), with children's fiesta. – *Fiesta de los Caneiros* (Aug.), in honour of the town's patroness, with a large fair, parades, a boat pilgrimage and fireworks on the water. – *Fiesta de la Virgin de los Remedios* (Sept.), with a procession carrying the image of the Virgin through the streets.

Attractively situated on a hill beside the Ría de Betanzos, this is an appealing little town, surrounded by vineyards, with craftsmen's workshops open to the street.

Feria in Betanzos

SIGHTS. – The town has preserved remains of its medieval walls, with interesting pointed-arched gates, as well as typical old streets and buildings, including several noteworthy churches. – Church of *San Francisco* (14th c.), with fine monuments, including the tomb of Count Fernán Pérez de Andrade (1387), supported on a bear and a boar. – Church of **Santa María del Azogue** (14th–15th c.), with monuments of members of noble families and a medieval *ratablo* of Flemish origin. – Parish church of **Santiago** (15th c.), the town's mother-church, with a number of notable chapels, one of which has a *retablo* in Isabelline style and a fine Gothic grille.

Bilbao

Province: Vizcaya (BI).
Telephone code: 94
Altitude: 19 m. – Population: 433,000.

ⓘ **Delegado de Cultura y Turísmo en Vizcaya,**
Gran Vía 17;
tel. 4 16 44 11.
Centro de Iniciativas Turísticas,
Alameda Mazarredo;
tel. 4 24 48 19.

HOTELS. – *Villa de Bilbao* (no rest.), Gran Vía de López de Haro 87, L, 142 r.; *Aránzazu* (no rest), Rodríguez Arias 66, I, 173 r.; *Avenida* (no rest.), Avda Zumalacárregui 40, II, 116 r.; *Ercilla* (no rest.), Ercilla 37, I, 350 r.; *Husa Carlton* (no rest.), Plaza de Federico Moyúa 2, I, 142 r.; *Conde Duque* (no rest.), Campo de Volantín 22, II, 67 r.; *Nervión* (no rest.), Campo de Voltantín 11, II, 351 r.; *Cantábrico* (no rest.), Miravilla 8, III, 40 r.; *Excelsior* (no rest.), Hurtado de Amézaga 6, IV, 65 r.; Hostal *San Mamés* (no rest.), Luis Briñas 15, P I, 36 r.; *Zabálburu* (no rest.), Plaza Martinez Artola 8, P I, 32 r.; *Arana* (no rest.), Bidebarrieta 2, P II, 65 r.; *Maroño*, Correo 21, P II, 49 r.; etc.

RESTAURANTS. – In some hotels; also *Artagán* Virgen de Begoña 34 (very elegant); *Guría*, Gran Vía de López de Haro 66 (rustic style); *Casa Vasca*, Avda del Ejército 13 (Basque style); *Colavidas*, Hurtado de Amézaga 1; *Edificio Albia*, San Vicente; *Iturriaga*, Alameda Mazarredo 20; *Señor*, General Eguia 50; *Victor*, Plaza Nueva 2; etc.

CAFÉS. – *Nervión*, Paseo Camp Volantin 11; *Ercilla*, Ercilla 37; *El Corte Inglés*, Gran Vía 9; *Toledo*, Gran Vía 56; *California*, Plaza de Zabálburu; etc.

EVENTS. – *Feria de la Máquina-Herramienta* (Mar.). – *Semana Grande* (Aug.), a crowded programme, with bullfights and sporting contests, concerts, opera performances, folk dancing and a pilgrimage to San Roque, ending with the Feria de Muestras (Trade Fair).

Lying only some 14 km from the sea, Bilbao is capital of the Basque province of Vizcaya and the seat of a bishop. It was founded in 1300 by Diego López de Haro, but became a place of major economic importance only in the 19th c.

Bilbao owes its rise as an important industrial and commercial city, with a large inner harbour and an outer harbour at El Abra, to the broad Río Nervión (Basque *Ibaizábal*, "wide river"), which can take seagoing vessels of up to 4000 tons and has large deposits of iron ore on its left bank. On the right bank of the river lies the cramped Old Town, linked by five bridges with the New Town.

SIGHTS. – In the **Old Town**, a huddle of narrow streets on the slopes of the hill, the main traffic artery is the tree-lined *Paseo del Arenal*. On the SW side of the square is the *Teatro de Arriaga* (1890); at the E end is the church of *San Nicolás de Bari* (15th c.; rebuilt 1756), which contains a notable carved altar and pictures by Juan de Mena. – A little way S is the arcaded *Plaza de los Mártires*, and beyond this is the *Museo Arqueológico*, with Basque ethnographical material and finds from the Basondo cave. To the SW is the Gothic **Cathedral** of *Santiago* (14th c., remodelled in 1571), with a bell-tower, a Renaissance S porch and a Gothic cloister. – In the Plaza del Mercado (Market Square), farther S near the river, is the 15th c. church of **San Antón**, with a Baroque tower added in the 18th c.

Following the river downstream from the N end of the Paseo del Arenal, we come to the handsome **Ayuntamiento** (Town Hall), built in 1892 on the site of an Augustinian monastery; it has a tall central tower and a large ceremonial hall in Moorish style. – From here the *Campo de Volantín* and the *Avenida de las Universidades* follow the right bank of the river, forming an attractive promenade which passes the *Jesuit College* (Universidad Literaria) and the *Commercial University* (Universidad Comercial).

The main connection between the Paseo del Arenal and the **New Town** (*Ensanche*) is the *Puente de la Victoria*, from which there is a fine view of the busy movement of boats on the river. From here *Calle de Navarra* runs past the railway stations to the *Plaza de España*, in which is a monument to Diego López de Haro, the town's founder. From here a magnificent modern street, the *Gran Vía de López de Haro*, 30 m wide, leads W. On its S side is the **Palacio de la Diputación** (by Luis Aladrén, 1897), in which are a small picture gallery and the Provincial Historical Museum. It cuts across the large *Plaza de Federico Moyúa* (formerly Plaza Elíptica) and ends, after a total distance of 1½ km, at the tall memorial in honour of the *Sagrado Corazón de Jesús* (Sacred Heart; 1927). One block N of the Gran Vía is the *Parque Doña Casilda de Iturriza*, named after a great benefactress of the city (monument). At its NE corner are the **Museo de Bellas Artes**, with important works by Dutch and Spanish masters of the 15th and 16th c. (El Greco, Ribalta, Ribera) and Goya, and the *Museo*

San Nicolás de Bari, Bilbao

de Arte Moderno (modern Spanish and particularly Basque artists).

The finest *view of Bilbao and the valley of the Río Nervión is from the 16th c. church in the outlying district of **Begoña**, on a hill to the E (lift from behind the church of **San Nicolás de Bari**; on foot, 20 minutes). The old pilgrimage church of San Nicolás is also worth a visit, with its Plateresque doorway and its pictures, including one of "The Pilgrimage of Begoña".

SURROUNDINGS. – Near Galdacano in the nearby Sierra de Ganguren is the **Parque de Atracciones de Vizcaya**, an amusement park which is open daily (except Mondays) from 4 p.m. to midnight, on Saturdays and Sundays from 11 a.m.

Right bank of the Nervión. – C 6311 descends the valley, through industrial districts with large blast furnaces, to **Las Arenas**, 12 km from Bilbao, a much frequented villa suburb from which a transporter bridge, the *Puente Vizcaya*, crosses the river to Portugalete (see below); from the top of the 62 m high tower (lift) there are panoramic views.

The road continues through the residential and holiday resorts of *Algorta* and *Sopelana* (both with hotels) to **Plencia** (pop. 2500), a little fishing town with a bathing beach at the mouth of the Río Plencia. Then from Plencia along the coast to *Bermeo*.

Left bank of the Nervión. – C 639 traverses industrial districts with blast furnaces and iron foundries to (12 km) **Portugalete** (pop. 40,000), a port at the mouth of the Río Nervión which is a popular resort with the people of Bilbao. At the end of the pier (views) there is a breakwater 1 km long, with a lighthouse at the far end from which there are magnificent *views. Transporter bridge to Las Arenas.

Soon after Portugalete the road comes to the beautifully situated resort of **Santurce**, an interesting little fishing port under the Monte de Serantes. From here the coast road continues, affording fine views, to the little port of *Ciérvana* and then along the right bank of the *Río Barbadún* to *San Juan de Somorrostro*.

To Ondárroa by the coast road. – From the old town of Bilbao take C 6313, which runs N through *Begoña* to *Munguía*. From here the road climbs, with many bends, up to the ridge of *Monte Acherre*, with a picturesque view of Bermeo; to the right is the hill of *Sollube* (684 m), with a television transmitter. The road finally comes down to **Bermeo** (alt. 2 m; pop. 13,000), the main fishing port in the province of Vizcaya, a charming town which rises in tiers above its picturesque harbour and beaches. – 6 km NW is *Cabo Machichaco* (lighthouse; extensive views). Farther W are the romantic rocky islet of *San Juan de Gaztelugache* and the bathing beach of *Baquino*.

From here C 6315 runs SE to *Mundaca*, at the wide mouth of the river, usually known as the *Ría de Guernica*, and continues to *Pedemales* from which there is a bridge to the attractive island of *Charcharramendi* (bathing beach; oysters).
At **Guernica y Luno** (see p. 136) we leave C 6315 and follow C 6212, going N. This runs via *Ereño* to **Lequeitio** (alt. 3 m; pop. 5000), beautifully situated in a bay sheltered by the rocky wooded islet of San Nicolás. This little fishing port, an important centre of the tunny fisheries, is also a holiday resort. Gothic church (14th–15th c.) with sculptured doorway and late Gothic retablo (16th c.).

The road now follows the coast, with views of the Bay of Biscay, to **Ondárroa** (alt. 3 m; pop. 8000), a little fishing port attractively situated in a bay (bathing beach).

To San Sebastián by the direct road. – Bilbao and San Sebastián are connected both by the motorway and by N 634, which runs E through the *Barrio de Achuri* and the industrial district of *Galdácano*. Beyond this N 240 diverges on the right to Vitoria. The main road continues through the fertile valley of the *Río Durango* to **Amorebieta** (alt. 92 m; pop. 5000), with a parish church built between 1555 and 1608 (tower of 1773). 2 km N is the spa of *Echano* (sulphur spring). – Then comes **Durango** (alt. 120 m; pop. 15,000), an industrial town in the wide upper valley of the Río Durango, surrounded by hills; fine churches. Outside the town, to the SW, is the church of San Pedro de Tavira (13th c.), one of the oldest churches in the Basque country. – The road then ascends to the *Puerto de Areitio* (625 m), on the boundary between the provinces of Vizcaya and Guipúzcoa, and continues via **Deva** to **San Sebastián** (see p. 194), 119 km from Bilbao.

Over the Puerto de Orduña. – Leave Bilbao on N 625, which runs through the *Barrio de Achuri* and then S over the Río Nervión to the industrial suburb of *Besauri*. It then continues up the valley of the Río Nervión, heavily industrialised, past *Miravalles* and through *Areta* (alt. 95 m) to **Llodio** (alt. 102 m), a handsome town in the province of Álava, in a beautiful situation. Then comes the little spa (chalybeate water) of *Luyando*, where the valley becomes flatter.
Amurrio (alt. 184 m) has a handsome church. There are beautiful views of the Cantabrian Mountains: on the right the rocky *Peña de Aro* (1178 m), on the left the skilfully engineered railway, which here climbs 440 m in 35 km, and the *Peña de Gorbea* (1475 m).
Orduña (alt. 285 m; pop. 3500) has a charming setting in a depression dominated on the W by the limestone cliffs of the *Peña de Orduna*. This old-world

little town near the source of the Rio Nervión has well-preserved walls, and figures frequently in Basque history.

Beyond Orduña begins the magnificent *pass road, with numerous bends and gradients of up to 13%, which climbs up to the **Puerto de Orduña** (900 m) through the *Cantabrian Mountains*. The road begins with a series of nine hairpin bends (parking place with splendid views). From the top of the pass, which lies on the watershed between the Atlantic and the Mediterranean, there are also wide views.

From here the road runs down to *Berberana* and continues through beautiful hill pastures to *Bergüenda* and *Puentelarrá* (alt. 470 m), where it crosses the River Ebro. Beyond the village of *Encío* with a conspicuous church, N 625 joins N I (San Sebastián to Burgos).

Blanes

Province: Gerona (GE).
Telephone code: 972.
Altitude: 5 m. – Population: 20,000.
ⓘ **Oficina Municipal de Información**,
Plaza de Cataluña s/n;
tel. 33 03 48.

HOTELS. – *Horitzo*, Paseo Marítimo Sabanell 11, II, 122 r.; *Park Blanes*, Playa S'Abanell, II, 131 r., SP; *Lyon Magestic*, Villa Mas Marot 13, III, 120 r., SP; *Ruiz*, Raval 45, III, 59 r.; *Boix Mar*, Avda Villa de Madrid, IV, 170 r., SP; *Costa Brava*, Anselmo Clavé 48, IV, 80 r., SP; *Mar Ski* (no rest.), P. Martimo Sabanell 4, IV, 64 r.; *Rosa*, San Pedro Martín 42, IV, 151 r., SP; *San Antonio*, Paseo Marítimo 63, IV, 156 r.; *San Francisco*, Paseo Marítimo 72, IV, 32 r.; *Soteras* (no rest.), Plaza Estrella del Mar 9, IV, 33 r.; *Stella Maris*, Avda de Madrid 18, IV, 87 r., SP; *Hostal Clivia*, Auguer 44, P II, 45 r.; *Esperanza* (no rest.), Paseo del Mar 61, P II, 36 r.; *S'Arjau*, Paseo del Mar 89, P II, 49 r.; *Burvi* (no rest.), La Muralla 34, P III, 54 r.; etc. – many CAMPING SITES.

EVENT. – *Fiesta de Santa Ana* (July), with folk performances.

Blanes (Costa Brava)

Beautifully situated on the Costa Brava, Blanes is a little fishing town which has developed into a popular seaside resort. It is also noted for its lace.

SIGHTS. – On a small promontory are the ruins of the convent of *Santa Ana*. Inland, on a hill, are the *Castillo de San Juan* and the *Marimurtra Botanic Gardens*, with over 3000 Mediterranean species, laid out by a German named Karl Faust (d. 1952).

El Burgo de Osma

Province: Soria (SO).
Telephone code: 975.
Altitude: 850 m. – Population: 6000.
(i) Ayuntamiento (Town Hall),
Plaza General Franco 7;
tel. 34 01 07.

HOTELS. – *Virrey Palafox*, Travesía de Acosta I, IV, 20 r.; *Hostal Casa Agapito* (no rest.), Universidad 1, P II, 7 r.; *La Perdiz* (no rest.), Universidad 33, P II, 18 r.

RESTAURANT. – *La Perdiz*, Universidad 33.

EVENTS. – *Fiesta de la Virgen del Espino* (Aug.), patronal festival in honour of the town's patroness and St Roch. – *Ferias* (Oct.), with characteristic local dances ("Triscado", "La Rueda", "Los Monitos", "Las Chiclaneras", "Las Palomas").

The old episcopal city of El Burgo de Osma was founded by the Visigoths. Its heyday was in the 16th c.

SIGHTS. – The town's finest building is the Gothic **Cathedral**, begun in Romanesque style in the 12th c., with a Baroque tower (15th c.) which is a notable landmark. *Capilla Mayor*, with a richly decorated retablo by Juan de Juni and his pupil Picardo; wrought-iron *grille* (16th c.) and *monument* of San Juan de Osma; Gothic cloister, *museum* and *library*, with valuable collection of miniatures. – *University of Santa Catalina* (opened 1779, closed down 1841), with Plateresque façade. – *Hospital San Agustín* (17th c.), with a fine Baroque façade. – In the *Plaza Mayor* are a number of handsome buildings, including the *Bishop's Palace* (17th c.), with a curious doorway.

SURROUNDINGS. – S of El Burgo is the old **Osma** the Roman *Uxama Argalae*, with mosaics and fine remains of old buildings. – 16 km N is **Ucero**, with the Romanesque church of San Bartolomé (13th c.) and a handsome castle. – 24 km E is the historic little town of **Berlanga de Duero**, with a magnificent 15th c. castle, two rings of walls and a keep; beautiful collegiate church (1530), with a magnificent retablo incorporating both pictures and sculpture; Palacio de los Marqueses de Berlanga (Plateresque). 9 km S is the *Ermita San Baudelio*, on a curious Mozarabic ground plan. – 12 km SW on N 122 is the ancient little fortified town of **San Esteban de Gormaz**, in an area of historic interest, with the Romanesque church of San Miguel and a Moorish castle on the hill above the town.

Burgos

Province: Burgos (BU).
Telephone code: 947.
Altitude: 860 m. – Population: 150,000.
(i) Centro de Iniciativas Turisticas,
Paseo del Espolon 1;
tel. 20 18 46.
Oficina de Información de Turismo,
Plaza de Alonso Martinez 7;
tel. 20 31 25.

HOTELS. – *Almirante Bonifaz* (no rest.), Vitoria 22, I, 79 r.; *Condestable*, Vitoria 8, 82 r.; *Cordón* (no rest.), La Puebla 6, II, 35 r.; *Corona de Castilla*, Madrid 15, II, 52 r.; *Fernán González*, Calera 17, II, 64 r.; *Mesón del Cid*, Plaza Santa Maria 8, II, 30 r.; *Rice* (no rest.), Reyes Catolicos 30, II, 50 r.; *Conde de Miranda* (no rest.), Miranda 4, III, 14 r.; *España*, Paseo del Espolón 32, III, 69 r.; *Norte y Londres* (no rest.), Plaza Alonso Martínez 10, III, 55 r.; *Villa Jimena*, P. Pisones 47, IV, 23 r.; Hostal *Asubio*, Carmen 6, P I, 30 r.; *Avila* (no rest.), Almirante Bonifaz 13, P II, 57 r.; *Lar* (no rest.), Cardenal Benlloch 1, P II, 10 r.; *Moderno*, General Queipo de Llano 2, P II, 28 r.; etc. OUTSIDE THE TOWN ON THE MADRID ROAD *Landa Palace*, Carretera N-I, km 236, L, 39 r. SP. – CAMPING SITES: *Fuentes Blancas*, 4 km from the town; other sites in surrounding area.

RESTAURANTS. – In hotels; also *Puerta Real*, Plaza Rey San Fernando 5 (first floor); *Casa Ojeda*, Vitoria 5 (first floor), Castilian style; *Pinedo*, Paseo del Espolón 1; *Arriaga*, Laín Calvo 4; *Rincón de España*, Nuño Rasura 11, *Mesón de los Infantes*, Corral de los Infantes, rustic style; etc.

CAFÉS. – *Espolón*, Paseo del Espolón 28; *Iturriaga*, Plaza Santo Domingo de Guzmán 3; *Los Gigantillos*, Avda del Cid 16; etc.

EVENTS. – *Corpus Christi*, with a great procession to the monastery of Las Huelgas, dancing and many-coloured costumes. – *Ferias y Fiestas de San Pedro* (June), with bullfights, ceremonial parades, traditional dances and concerts.

Burgos, famous for its magnificent Cathedral, was capital of Old Castile in the 10th and 11th c. and is now capital of the province of Burgos and the seat of an archbishop. The town lies on both banks of the Río Arlanzón in the middle of the fertile N Castilian plain, under the hill, 100 m high, on which stand the remains of an old castle.

The climate of Burgos, with its long winters and torrid summers, gave rise to the description (also applied to the climate of Madrid), "nine months of winter, three months of hell".

HISTORY. – The town was originally founded in 882 by King Alfonso the Great of León. It was the home of the famous mercenary leader Rodrigo Díaz de Vivar (1026–99), whose victories over the Moors made him a Spanish national hero under the style of *El Cid* (from the Arabic *sidi*, "lord") *Campeador* ("valorous").

SIGHTS. – The central feature of the town is the arcaded *Plaza Mayor* or Plaza de José Antonio, on the S side of which is the **Ayuntamiento** (Town Hall), built in 1791, with a fine interior; it contains the municipal archives.

Burgos: view towards the Cathedral

A little way W of the Plaza Mayor, on a terrace at the foot of the castle hill, is the ****Cathedral** (*Santa María*), in its general structure and its profusion of sculpture one of the most impressive of Gothic cathedrals. Built of white limestone with something of the quality of marble, it was begun in 1221 and largely completed by the mid 13th c. The magnificent open-work spires of the two principal **towers* (84 m high) were built in 1458 by John of Cologne (d. 1480). Above the *Puerta Principal*, the central feature of the W front, is a splendid rose window, over which are eight statues of kings. The other doorways are also very fine – at the end of the N transept the richly decorated *Puerta de la Coronería* or *Puerta de los Apóstoles* (*c.* 1250), to the E of this the *Puerta de la Pellejería*, a lively example of Plateresque by Francis of Cologne (1516), and in the S transept the *Puerta del Sarmental* (*c.* 1230), also richly decorated with sculpture.

Burgos Cathedral

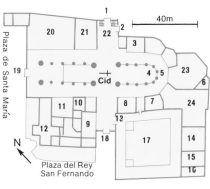

1	Puerta de la Coronería	13	Puerta del Claustro
2	Puerta de la Pellejería	14	Capilla de Santa Catalina
3	Capilla de la Natividad	15	Capilla del Corpus Christi
4	Capilla Mayor	16	Sala Capitular
5	Trassagrario	17	Cloister
6	Sacristy	18	Puerta de Sarmental
7	New Sacristy	19	Main Door
8	Capilla de San Henrique	20	Capilla de Santa Tecla
9	Capilla de la Visitación	21	Capilla de Santa Ana
10	Relicario	22	Gilded Staircase
11	Capilla de la Consolación	23	Capilla del Condestable
12	Capilla del Santisimo Cristo	24	Capilla de Santiago

The INTERIOR is 84 m long (excluding the Capilla del Condestable) and of impressive height. In the centre of the nave is the octagonal **lantern* (*cimborio*), 59 m high and richly decorated with sculpture and coats of arms, a masterpiece of Plateresque art (1568), borne on four massive piers. Under the dome are the remains of the Cid and his wife Jimena, deposited here in 1921. In the *Choir* (1521) are double rows of richly carved stalls (most of the scenes by Felipe Vigarní) and the enamel-decorated *tomb* of Bishop Maurice (d. 1240), founder of the Cathedral. In the *Capilla Mayor* is the richly gilded *high altar* (1580), a Renaissance work by Rodrigo and Martín de la Haya. – The most notable of the numerous *chapels* are the first on the right, the *Capilla del Santísimo Cristo*, with a very old *crucifix* of buffalo hide, the "Cristo de Burgos"; the *Relicario* (third on right), with the much venerated "Virgen de Oca", probably dating from the 16th c.; the *Capilla de Santa Tecla* (first on left), by Churriguera (1736), with a 12th c. *font*, rich and colourful Rococo decoration and a large *high altar*; and the **Capilla del Condestable* (at E end of ambulatory), a sumptuous Plateresque structure built by Simon of Cologne in 1494 for Pedro Hernández de Velasco, Constable of Castile, with the *tomb* of the Constable and his wife, a carved wood *altar* dedicated to St Anne (on right) and old stained glass. In the adjoining *Sacristy* is a good painting of the Magdalene by Gian Petrino, a pupil of Leonardo da Vinci. The other chapels contain numerous tombs, some of them of very high artistic quality. At the end of the N transept is the *Escalera Dorada* (by Diego de Siloé, 1519), a double staircase, decorated with many reliefs, leading up to the Puerta de la Coronería, 8 m above the level of the transept. – The *New Sacristy*, a richly decorated Baroque structure, is the entrance to the two-storey **Cloister* (13th c.), which contains a number of notable *tombs*. In the *Capilla del Corpus Christi* is a wooden chest which El Cid left here as security for a loan. On the upper storey of the cloister is the *Diocesan Museum*, with tapestries of the 16th and 17th c.

Opposite the NW corner of the Cathedral is the little church of **San Nicolás** (1408; completely restored in 1911), with a magnificent *high altar* (fine alabaster reliefs) by Francis of Cologne (1505), beautiful vaulting and a number of notable tombs.

S of the Cathedral is the *Plaza del Rey San Fernando*, on the S side of which is the *Arco de Santa María* (rebuilt 1552), a massive gate flanked by semicircular towers, now containing part of the *Museo Arqueológica*. Beyond it the **Puente de Santa María** crosses the *Río Arlanzón* (on both banks of which are attractive promenades). SE of the bridge, in *Calle de la Calera*, are two imposing palaces – at No. 23 the *Casa de Ángulo* and at No. 25 the ***Casa de Miranda** (1545), an excellent example of a Castilian noble mansion, now occupied by the *Museo Arqueológico* (rich collection of material ranging from Roman times to the 18th c.).

N of the Plaza Mayor, reached by way of side streets, is the 14th c. church of **San Gil**, with stellate vaulting, a sculptured Pietà and a richly decorated retablo. – From here we go along Calle Fernán González, in which are several old noble mansions, and up the second street on the right to reach the Gothic church of **San Esteban** (1280–1350), with a richly sculptured W doorway (beautiful rose window) and an early Gothic cloister. Continuing N through the *Arco de San Esteban*, in Mudéjar style, and turning left along the old *town walls* (begun 1276), we come to the **Castillo** (destroyed by fire in 1736) from the ramparts of which there are fine views. – At the W end of Calle Fernán González, under the ruins of the castle, are three stone pillars marking the position of the *Solar del Cid*, the ancestral home of El Cid. Close by is the 14th c. *Arco de San Martín*, a gate in the old walls running SW from the Castillo. Continuing down towards the S and turning left, we come into the *Paseo de los Cubos*, named after the semicircular towers (*cubos*) set at intervals along the walls – fine examples of Castilian military engineering.

E of the Plaza Mayor, reached by way of Plaza de Prim (on the right, the provincial government offices), is *Plaza Calvo Sotelo*. On the N side of this square is the 15th c. **Casa del Cordón** (named after the Franciscan rope girdle, *cordón*), in

Town gate, Burgos

which Columbus was recieved by the Catholic monarchs in 1497 after his second voyage. Philip I died in this house in 1506. – Farther E, in Plaza de San Juan, is the church of **San Lesmes** (14th-15th c.), with a Gothic doorway; late Gothic altars and tombs. To the SE is the **Museo Marceliano Santa María**, containing works by the painter of that name (d. 1952).

SURROUNDINGS. – There are a number of features of interest in the immediate vicinity of the town. – 1½ km SW is the ***Monasterio de las Huelgas**, originally a country residence of the kings of Castile (*huelga*="repose, relaxation"), which Alfonso VIII converted into a convent of Cistercian nuns in 1187. The Gothic church (1248) contains in the Coro de los Capillanos (on left) the tomb of Alfonso VIII and his wife Eleanor of England, with kneeling figures of the king and queen. Adjoining the church is a Romanesque cloister, full of atmosphere, which now houses a museum of valuable old textiles. – ¾ km W of the monastery is the **Hospital del Rey**, a hostel for pilgrims travelling to Santiago. It was built by Alfonso VIII, and has a Plateresque doorway of 1526.

4 km SE of Burgos, on a wooded hill, is the **Cartuja de Miraflores**, a Carthusian house founded by King John II, which was rebuilt by John of Cologne and his son Simon after a fire in 1452. In the Gothic *church (the only part open to the public), in front of the large gilded high altar (by Gil de Siloé and Diego de la Cruz), is the alabaster tomb of King John and his queen, also by Siloé (1489–93), one of the most elaborate of its kind in Spain. In a recess in the N wall of the church is the alabaster tomb of the Infante Alfonso (d. 1468), again by Siloé. In St Bruno's Chapel is a statue of the saint, a native of Cologne (1032–1101), by Manuel Pereira.

Towards Soria. – Leave Burgos on N 1, going S, and in 8 km turn left into N 234. At *Cuevas de San Clemente* take a secondary road on the right for **Covarrubias** (40 km from Burgos), once capital of a principality in Castile. Collegiate church (12th c.), with triptych of the Three Kings and numerous tombs of infantes and abbots. The sacristy contains an interesting museum, with fine sculpture, pictures and goldsmith's work. Remains of old town walls, including the Torreón de Doña Urraca. – From Coverrubias continue via *San Pedro de Arlanza*, with the ruins of a monastery, to the Benedictine monastery of **Santo Domingo de Silos** (believed to have been founded by the Visigothic king Reccared in 593), an unusual building with fine reliefs and a two-storey *cloister (11th–12th c.); the church is 18th c. The monastery, of which Santo Domingo of Silos was abbot from 1047 to 1073, has a museum containing a valuable treasury. It is notable for its Gregorian chant.

From Cuevas de San Clemente continue on N 234 to *Mazariegos*, beyond which a road goes off on the left to **Quintanilla de las Viñas** (36 km from Burgos), with the Visigothic church of *Santa María de Lara* (7th–8th c.), famous for the unusual threefold band of low relief decoration on the exterior walls.

Towards Madrid. – N I runs S, in long straight stretches, over the undulating Meseta, broken up by small valleys, to **Lerma** (alt. 752 m; pop. 2500), a fortress-like little town on the *Río Arlanza*, with a history going back to the 8th c. Palace of the Duke of Lerma, built in 1614 by Fray Alberto de la Madre de Dios. Collegiate church (1616), with the bronze tomb of Archbishop Cristóbal de Rojas of Seville. Old town walls (12th c.) and medieval town gate with massive round towers.

Then S over the *Río Esgueva* to *Gumiel de Hizán*: church (national monument) with a beautiful retablo.

Towards Valladolid. – From a road junction a few kilometres W of Burgos N 620 runs SW, following the valley of the *Río Arlanzón*. After traversing *Celada del Camino*, with a fine 13th c. fortified church, and passing on the left the *Sierra de Covarrubias*, the road comes to the village of *Villanueva de las Carreteras*. 1 km farther on a road branches off on the left and crosses the river to reach (11 km) the beautifully situated village of **Santa María del Campo** (pop. 1500): parish church (15th c.) with a fine Plateresque tower by Diego de Siloé (1527) and a pulpit and choir-stalls in Mudéjar style. – Off the main road to the right is **Castrogeriz** (pop. 2000), a little town founded by the Goths, with remains of a camp (*Castrum Sigerici*) established by Caesar, a castle and a number of richly furnished churches.

Towards León. – There are a number of places of interest on N 120, which runs W from Burgos. After crossing the *Río Arlanzón* and the *Canal Arlanzón* the road passes through *Villanueva de Argaño* and comes to a crossroads. 2 km N is the ancient little town of **Sasamón**, originally a Roman foundation. Church of Santa María (13th–14th c.), with a doorway modelled on the Puerta del Sarmental in Burgos; fine choir and cloister. – 1 km S of the crossroads is **Olmillos de Sasamón** (alt. 798 m), with the old Castillo de los Cartagena (15th c.) and a Gothic church.

Towards Santander. – N 623, a broad road of motorway standard, runs N from Burgos, passing on the right the little village of *Vivar del Cid*, where Spain's national hero El Cid spent his childhood, and the ruined castle of *Sotopalacios*, to the **Puerto de Páramo de Masa** (1050 m), the highest point of the road.

From the pass the road descends to *Tubilla del Agua* and then climbs again through a wild and romantic valley and up, with many bends (*view of the Ebro valley, enclosed between high rock walls), to the **Puerto de Carrales** (1020 m), above the plateau of Old Castile, with further undulations, and gradients of 7 per cent in places.

Then via *Cilleruello de Bezana* (alt. 935 m) to the large *Ebro reservoir* (*Embalse del Ebro*), with a dam 26 m high. Off the road to the left is the health resort of **Corconte** (alt. 936 m), in a beautiful setting on the shores of the reservoir.

Towards Vitoria. – N I runs NE from Burgos to the *Puerto de la Brújula* (981 m), with a fountain commemorating Queen Isabella (1845), and comes to **Briviesca** (alt. 710 m; pop. 4300), the Roman *Vivovesca*, with old town walls. In the Capilla de Sopraga of the collegiate church and the former conventual church of Santa Clara there are fine carved altars (16th c.); the one in Santa Clara is by Anchieta. – 9 km N of the town is the little village of *Vileña*,. with a Cistercian monastery founded in 1223 (fine monuments).

The road continues through the hilly corn-growing country of Old Castile, runs through *Cubo de Bureba* (alt. 640 m) and comes to **Pancorbo** (alt. 635 m), picturesquely situated in a narrow rocky valley under the ruins of two castles. It then enters the gorge (*desfiladero*) of *Gerganta de Pancorbo*, carved by the *Rio Oroncillo* through the *Montes Obarenes* (Sierra de Pancorbo). Soon afterwards N 625 diverges on the left and runs N to Bilbao.

The main road continues through a barren hilly region flanked by the higher sierras to *Orón*, with a small castle, and **Miranda de Ebro** (alt. 453 m; pop. 33,000), a busy commercial town (road and rail junction) situated on both banks of the River Ebro. The 12th c. church of San Nicolás (formerly a mosque) has a beautiful Arab doorway. On the right bank of the river are the ruins of a castle.

Towards Logroño. – N 120 follows the *Río Arlanzón* in an easterly direction. Beyond *Zalduendo* a secondary road runs N to the little town of **San Juan de Ortega**, a pilgrimage centre. *Parish church* (12th–15th c.), built on Romanesque foundations; *Convento del Jacobeo*, with tomb of San Juan de Ortega.

N 120 climbs to the *Puerto de la Pedraja* (1130 m) and descends to **Villafranca Montes de Oca** (alt. 843 m; pop. 500), on the old pilgrims' route to Santiago. – Then on to **Belorado** (alt. 722 m; pop. 2300), with the remains of an old *castle* (9th c.) and an interesting retablo in the church of the *Virgin de Belén*.

Cáceres

Province: Cáceres (CC).
Telephone code: 927.
Altitude: 471 m. – Population: 70,000.
(i) **Oficina de Información de Turismo**,
Plaza del General Mola 33;
tel. 24 63 47.
Patronato de Promoción de Turismo,
Amargura 1;
tel. 24 37 00

HOTELS. – *Alcántara* (no rest.), Avda Virgen de Guadalupe 14, II, 67 r. *Extremadura*, Avda Virgen de Guadalupe II, 68 r. SP; *Álvarez*, Parras 20, III, 37 r.; *Ara* (no rest.), Juan XXIII 3, IV, 62 r.; *Iberia*, Generalísimo Franco 2, IV, 41 r.; *Metropol* (no rest.), Obispo Segura Sáez 5, IV, 22 r.; *Los Naranjos* (no rest.), Alfonso IX 12, IV, 26 r.; etc.

Casa de las Veletas, Cáceres

RESTAURANTS. – *Hosteria Nacional Comendador*, Ancha 6; *Álvarez*, Carretera de Salamanca, km 208; *El Montero*, Gil Cordero 11; *El Figón de Eustaquio*, Plaza San Juan 12, *Delfos*, Pl. de Albatros; etc.

CAFÉS. – *Acuario*, Avda de España 6; *Fara*, Avda Virgen Montaña; etc.

EVENTS. – *Fiestas de la Candelaria* (Feb.), with a pilgrimage to the Ermita da San Blas. – *Semana Santa* (Holy Week), with an impressive procession through the Ciudad Monumental at dawn on Good Friday. – *Fiesta de San Jorge* (Apr.), in honour of the town's patron saint, with a contest between "Moors and Christians" in the Plaza Mayor. – *Ferias y Fiestas* (May–June), with bullfights and riding contests. – *Festivales de España* (June). – *Feria de San Miguel* (Sept.–Oct.), with bullfights and folk performances.

The busy commercial town of Cáceres, capital of the province of the same name in western Spain and the seat of a bishop, was founded by the Roman consul Caecilius Metellus under the name of Norba Caesarina or Castra Caecilii, probably on the site of an earlier Ibrian settlement.

SIGHTS. – The **Old Town** (*Ciudad* or *Barrio Monumental*) is situated on a hill and separated from the modern part of the town by its circuit of medieval walls, with twelve towers and five gates. In its picturesque narrow streets are many aristocratic mansions of the 16th c., with large patios. – Just outside the walls to the W is the *Plaza Mayor* or Plaza General Mola, with the **Ayuntamiento** (Town Hall). Near the NE corner of the square is

the *Torre del Bujaco* or *Torre del Reloj* (Clock Tower), a relic of the Roman town walls, with a statue of Ceres, and to the right of this is the *Arco de la Estrella* (1723), topped by a figure of the Virgin. Passing through the arch, we enter the Old Town, with the *Plaza de Santa María* straight ahead. On the E side of this square is the late Gothic church of *Santa María la Mayor:* Puerta de la Sacristía, in Renaissance style (by Alonso Torralba, 1527); retablo of 1551 on the high altar.

Round the Plaza Santa María are a number of other aristocratic mansions: the *Bishop's Palace* (1567), opposite the church, with a handsome doorway; adjoining it the *Palacio de Mayoralgo*, with a Gothic Façade (16th c.); and opposite these two, near the church, the *Palacio de los Golfines*, in the Plateresque style of the 15th c.

A little way S of the Plaza Santa María is the 18th c. church of *San Francisco Javier*, and beyond this, on the highest point in the town, is the 15th c. Gothic church of **San Mateo**, built on the site of an earlier mosque, with a fine Baroque retablo and monuments. Nearby, to the NW, is the 15th c. *Casa del Mono*, which now houses the *Museo de Bellas Artes* (pictures, weapons, costume). – From San Mateo we go SE past the *Casa de las Cigüeñas*, occupied by the Gobierno Militar, to the **Casa de las Veletas**, the former Moorish Alcázar, with a deep cistern (10th c.). It now contains the *Museum Arqueológico* (important pre-historic and Roman material; folk arts and crafts).

Two fine churches outside the walls are *San Juan* (13th c.), to the S of Plaza del General Mopla, and *Santiago* (16th c.), to the N of the square, with a retablo by A. Berruguete (1558).

The SW part of Cáceres is occupied by the **New Town**, with large squares and wide avenues. On the SW edge of the town is the *Plaza de América*, where the roads from Plasencia, Valencia de Alcántara and Mérida meet. From here the wide Avenida de España runs NE, continued by other streets in the direction of the Plaza Mayor. – On the S side of the town is the beautiful Gothic church of *San Francisco*, with elaborately decorated chapels and tombs, which belonged to a convent founded at the end of the 15th c.

SURROUNDINGS. – On a hill 1 km SE of Cáceres is the **Ermita de Nuestra Señora de la Montaña** (17th c.): chapel containing a copy of the Black Virgin of Montserrat. From here there are wide views of the Extremadura plateau. – 3 km N of Cáceres is **Cáceres el Viejo**, the site of a Roman fort established by Caecilius Metellus in 79 B.C. during the war with Sertorius, with the remains of ramparts and the *porta praetoria* (excavated).

The road to Portugal. – N 521 runs W from Cáceres, roughly parallel to the *Río Salor*, to *Malpartida de Cáceres*, beyond which N 523 goes off on the right towards Alcántara. 7 km N on this road is the beautiful village of *Arroyo de la Luz*, with a church containing a large carved retablo by Morales. – N 521 continues past the northern foothills of the *Sierra de San Pedro* to the Spanish frontier town of **Valencia de Alcántara** (alt. 462 m; pop. 16,000), with the Spanish customs post for entry into Portugal. It is an attractive little town with a 13th c. Moorish castle and two fine churches, the Encarnación (13th c.) and Roqueamador or Rocamador (16th c.). There is also an Archaeological Museum.

Cádiz

Province: Cádiz (CA).
Telephone code: 956.
Altitude: 5 m. – Population: 150,000.
ⓘ **Oficina de Turismo,**
Calderón de la Barca 1;
tel. 21 13 13.
Patronato para la Promoción Turística,
Plaza de España s/n;
tel. 22 48 00.

Cádiz

HOTELS: – *Atlántico*, Parque Genovés 9, II, 173 r, SP; *Francia y Paris* (no rest.), Plaza Calvo Sotelo 2, III, 69 r.; *Regio* (no rest.), Ana de Viya 11, III, 40 r.; *Regio II* (no rest.), López Pinto 79, III, 40 r.; *San Remo*, Paseo Marítimo, III, 34 r.; *Imares* (no rest.), San Francisco 9, IV, 37 r.; *San Francisco* (no rest.), Valenzuela 1, IV, 35 r.; *Carlos* (no rest.), Plaza de Sevilla s/n, P II, 30 r.; *Apartment Hotel Isecotel*, Paseo Maritimo s/n, II, 33 r.; *La Playa*, Dr Herrera Quevedo 1, IV, 12 r.; etc. – CAMPING SITE: *El Pinar*, Puerto Real.

RESTAURANTS. – In most hotels; also **Mikay*, Plaza San Juan de Dios; **El Tablao*, Santa María de la Cabeza 4 (Andalusian style); *La Palma*, Avda Primo de Rivera; *La Pizzería*, Feduchy 17 (Italian); *El Anteojo*, Alameda Apodaca 22; *Cantábrico*, Avda Ingeniero Lacierva; etc.

EVENTS. – *Semana Santa* (Holy Week), with a spectacular procession. – *Corpus Christi*, with a famous procession, bullfights, sporting events and folk dancing. – *Fiestas Típicas Gaditanas* (May), a characteristic local fiesta. – *Festivales de España* (Aug.), with regatta. – *Trofeo Internacional Ramón de Carranza* (Aug.), an international football competition. – Courses for foreigners run by Seville University (July–Aug.).

CASINO. – *Casino Bahía de Cádiz*, Puerto de Santa María.

WATER SPORTS. – Cádiz has a yacht harbour and a nautical club, excellent beaches at Victoria and Cortadura and the beach of La Caleta in the old part of the town.

SPORT and RECREATION on land. – Bullfights, tennis, football, hockey, shooting, fishing in the Bahía de Cádiz; flamenco in El Tablao.

The Andalusian port of Cádiz, capital of its province and a bishopric, is famed for its beautiful *situation on a limestone rock rearing out of the sea at the end of a promontory which extends for 9 km into the Gulf of Cadiz and the Atlantic Ocean and is linked to the mainland by a bridge.

Strong walls of up to 15 m in height protect the town from the violence of the waves, with tides which have a rise and fall of almost 2 metres (3 metres at the spring tides). The high white flat-roofed houses with their balconies and the characteristic little lookout towers (*miradores*), as well as the parks and gardens with their palms and their extensive sea views, give Cádiz the particular charm which had earned it the name of *una taza de plata*, a "silver bowl".

HISTORY. – Cádiz is probably the oldest town in the Iberian peninsula. Founded by the Phoenicians about 1100 B.C. under the name of *Gadir* ("the "fortress") as an entrepôt for the trade in tin and silver, it was occupied about 500 B.C. by the Carthaginians, who advanced from here into southern Spain. During the Second Punic War (now known as *Gades*) it fell into the hands of the Romans, under whom the town rose to great prosperity. Greek scientists came here to study the movement of the tides, and the cuisine of Cádiz was also widely famed during this period. During the Middle Ages the town, known to the Arabs as *Jeziret Kadis*, declined into insignificance. After its reconquest by Alfonso the Wise in 1262 it began to be repopulated, and after the discovery of America it became an anchorage for the Spanish silver fleet. Subsequent wars, and above all the loss of the American colonies, brought a further period of decline, from which Cádiz has recovered only in comparatively recent times.

SIGHTS. – The town is reached from the mainland either by the toll bridge from *Puerto Real* or by the expressway from *San Fernando*. Entering through the *Puerta de Tierra* (1775), we bear right across Plaza Santa Élena and continue down the Cuesta de las Calesas, past the railway station, to the **Harbour**. On the left is the *Plaza San Juan de Dios*, an attractive square in which stands the imposing *Ayuntamiento* (Town Hall),

built in 1816. Beyond this the beautiful palm-lined *Avenida Ramón de Carranza* extends alongside the harbour to the *Gobierno Civil* (1773), the offices of the provincial administration. The avenue then runs into the spacious *Plaza de España*, in the centre of which is a massive monument commemorating the meeting of the Cortes in Cádiz in 1810–12, Spain's first representative national assembly, which enacted the constitution of 1812.

Beyond the Plaza de España, to the left, are the *Alameda de Apodaca* and its continuation the *Alameda Marqués de Comillas*, with magnificent *views of the N side of the bay. At the end of the Alameda, on the left, is the twin-towered Baroque church of *Nuestra Señora del Carmen* (1737–64), with a beautiful patio and an altarpiece by El Greco.

Map of Cadiz

1 Academia de Bellas Artes
2 San Francisco
3 Santa Cueva
4 San Felipe Neri
5 Hospital de las Mujeres
6 Catedral Nueva
7 Catedral Vieja
8 Santo Domingo

Along the NW side of the rock on which the city stands is the large **Parque de Genovés**, with a *theatre* (used in summer) and a beautiful palm garden. From the platform of a grotto there is an extensive view. – Farther S, beyond the balustrade in front of the *Castillo de Santa Cataline* is the bay of **La Caleta**, with the *Playa de la Palma*. On the left are the Provincial Hospital, the *Hospital de Mora* (1904) and the *Hospicio Provincial*, an orphanage and poorhouse. On the S side of La Caleta, on a promontory reaching far out into the ocean, is the *Castillo de San Sebastián*, with a lighthouse.

Along the town's southern sea-wall extends the long road *Campo del Sur*. A

New Cathedral, Cádiz

little way along this, on the left, is a former Capuchin convent, now a psychiatric hospital. In the conventual church of *Santa Catalina* (entrance through courtyard), on the high altar, is Murillo's last work, the *"Mystic Marriage of St Catherine". While painting this he fell from the scaffolding and died in Seville on 3 April 1682 as a result of his injuries. The church also contains Murillo's "Stigmata of St Francis". – Continuing along the Avenida, with views of the towering S side of the town, we pass the chancel of the New Cathedral and come to the church of the **Sagrario** or Old Cathedral, originally dating from the 13th c. but rebuilt in Renaissance style (1602) after its destruction in 1596. It contains paintings and a richly decorated high altar by Saavedra (*c.* 1650).

From the Sagrario we go NW through narrow streets to the *Plaza Pío XII*, on the S side of which is the **New Cathedral** (*Catedral Nueva*), begun by Vicente de Acero in 1722 but not completed until 1838. The interior, with lateral aisles, is 85 m long and 60 m wide, with massive piers and a magnificent dome (52 m high) over the crossing. Fine 18th c. choir-stalls by Pedro Duque Cornejo; crypt containing tombs of bishops and the composer Manuel de Falla; valuable treasury, with a precious silver monstrance and fine pictures by Murillo and other artists. From the E tower there are far ranging views.

The **Old Town** is an area of narrow streets, with a number of handsome squares, including the *Plaza de Castelar*, shaded by palms, N of the New Cathedral. In this square are the birthplace and a statuette of the statesman Emilio Castelar (1832–99). From here *Calle del Sacremento* runs W through the old town. On the right-hand side of this street is the *Torre del Vigía* (34 m high), occupying the highest point in the town, with fine views. In the chapel of the *Hospital del Carmen de Mujeres*, a short distance S, is a "St Francis" by El Greco. NW of the Torre del Vigía, in Calle Santa Inés, is the chapel of *San Felipe Neri*, an oval building (1671) in which the Cortes met in 1812 (commemorative tablet on W end); on the high altar is an "Immaculate Conception" by Murillo. Adjoining the chapel on the S is the *Municipal Historical Museum*, with interesting models, including one of Cádiz.

Puerto de Santa María

Calle San José runs N, passing close to Plaza de San Antonio (on left), to the *Plaza de Miña*, laid out in gardens. On the E side of the square is the **Museo de Bellas Artes**, with a fine collection of works by Zurbarán and pictures by Murillo, Alonso Cano and contemporary artists. On the ground floor is the *Museo Arqueológico* (relics from the Phoenician cemetery of Cádiz, including a unique sarcophagus). – A little way S of Calle Rosario stands the oval church of *Santa Cueva* (1783), with wall paintings by Goya (1795).

SURROUNDINGS. – The province of Cádiz contains a great range of tourist attractions, including many picturesque old towns, both large and small. The motorway provides easy communication with Seville.

Northern part of the province. – Leave Cádiz by the toll bridge, which leads to the road junction in *Puerto Real* (pop. 21,000), the Roman *Portus Gaditanus*, where the motorway to Seville begins. Then N on N IV to (22 km) **Puerto de Santa María** (alt. 8 m; pop. 51,000; hotels; Meliá Caballo Blanco, I, 84 r., SP; Puertobahía, II, 330 r.; Restaurant Alboronia), a commercial town usually known simply as *El Puerto*. It is one of the oldest settlements in Cádiz Bay (Phoenician tomb 1st c. B.C.). Church of Nuestra Señora de los Milagros and remains of the 13th c. Moorish castle of San Marcos (view). Conducted tours of the famous wine cellars. – W of El Puerto is *Fuentebravía*, with a good beach.

Continue N on N IV to (14 km) **Jerez de la Frontera** (see p. 143). – From here W on C 440, which traverses the Jerez wine-growing area, the Marco de Jerez. A road on the left leads to (21 km) the white township of *Rota* (pop. 25,000), a United States naval and air base.

Continue NW on C 440 to **Sanlúcar de Barrameda** (alt. 30 m; pop. 43,000), a little port, now also a seaside resort, is attractively situated at the mouth of the River *Guadaequivir*. From here Columbus sailed in 1498 on his third voyage to the New World, and from here Magellan set out on his first circumnavigation of the globe in 1519. The town has a number of interesting churches, including the 16th c. *Nuestra*

Señora de la O, with a Mudéjar doorway and magnificent panelling. On the highest point in the town is the Castillo Santiago, with massive square towers (panoramic views). – 10 km SW, on Punta Camerón, is *Chipiona* (pop. 10,000), with a lighthouse and the chapel of the Virgen de la Regla, which contains a figure of the Virgin much venerated by seamen.

The road to Ronda and Málaga (N 342) runs E from Jerez and climbs through a region of vineyards into the Andalusian coastal hills. In 9 km it passes on the right the ruins of the 14th c. Moorish *Castillo de Malgarejo* and continues to (31 km from Jerez) **Arcos de la Frontera** (alt. 160 m; pop. 27,000; Parador Nacional Casa del Corregidor, II, 21 r.), with the castle of the Dukes of Arcos (view) and two interesting churches (unusual retablo in San Pedro). – From here C 344 continues E, passing through the hill village of *El Bosque* (Las Truchas, III, 8 r.) and over the *Puerto del Boyar* (1103 m), to **Ronda** (see p. 189).

Storks' nest, Sanlúcar de Barrameda

A minor road runs SE from Arcos through the *Sierra del Aznar* and over the *Río Majaceite* to the *Puerto de Galis*, and then SW to the picturesque hill village of *Alcalá de los Gazules*, with remains of an Arab castle.

Southern part of the province. – From Cádiz take the expressway, which runs along the narrow spit of sand, past the *Playa Victoria* on the Atlantic coast, to **San Fernando** (alt. 20 m; pop. 60,000), a long straggling naval town and the centre of the Isla de León, founded in the 18th c. on a rocky island in the salt marshes (from which salt was already being extracted in Roman times), with the fine Teatro de las Cortes.

Continue over the *Canal de Sancti Petri* on the Puente Zuazo to a road junction. From here bear right on N 340 to **Chiclana de la Frontera** (alt. 17 m; pop. 27,000), partly built on a hill, a town which has an almost Moorish aspect with its white houses and the mosque-like church of San Juan Bautista. – 8 km W, at the mouth of the Canal de Sancti Petri (with a little island of the same name on which are the remains of a temple of Heracles famed in antiquity), is the popular bathing beach of *La Barrosa*. Continue SE on N 340, passing (3 km off the road) the little port and seaside resort of *Conil de la Frontera* (pop. 2000), with a peaceful sandy beach and the ruined Torre de Guzmán, to the picturesque little hill town (2 km off the road) of *Vejer de la Frontera* (alt. 218 m; pop.

In Chiclana de la Frontera

12,000), high above Cape Trafalgar. See photograph, below. – From here a detour can be made to **Cape Trafalgar**, 14 km S, the Roman *Promontorium Lunosis* and the Moorish *Tarif al-Ghar* ("Cape of the Cave"), off which Nelson gained his famous victory over a French and Spanish fleet on 21 October 1805. 2 km E of the lighthouse is the village of *Los Caños*, with a road along the coast and a long sandy beach.

The road continues over the *Río Barbate* and along the *Sierra del Niño*, with views of the Moroccan hills on the right, and then follows the Gibraltar road to **Tarifa** (alt. 8 m; pop. 20,000), a picturesque little town of Moorish aspect. The Roman *Iulia Traducta*, it was fortified during the Moorish period by Tarif ben Malik. Well-preserved town walls; Castillo de Guzmán (view); church of Santa María y San Mateo. To the S of the town is the ***Punta Marroquí** or *Punta de Tarifa*, the most southerly point on the continent of Europe, at the narrowest part of the Straits of Gibraltar (14 km to Punta Cires), looking across to the coastal hills of Morocco.

N 340 runs up from Tarifa, with gradients of up to 12 per cent, to the **Puerto del Cabrito** (340 m), in the rocky Sierra del Algarrobo, with a magnificent *view over the Straits of Gibraltar to Africa. Then over the *Puerto del Bujeo* (340 m), from which there is a *view of Algeciras Bay and Gibraltar, and down, with many bends, to **Algeciras** (see p. 49).

The Rio Barbate at Vejer de La Frontera

Calatayud

Province: Zaragoza (Z).
Telephone code: 976.
Altitude: 522 m. – Population: 22,000.
ⓘ **Centro de Iniciativas Turisticas,**
   Puerta Alcántara;
   tel. 88 15 20.

HOTELS. – *Calatayud*, Carretera Madrid-Barcelona, km 237, II, 63 r.; *Hostal Fornos*, Paseo Calvo Sotelo 5, P II, 50 r.; *Marivella* (no rest.), Carretera N-11, km 241, P II, 39 r.; *Gimeno* (no rest.), Luis Guedea 9, P III, 15 r.; *La Perla*, San Antón 17, P III, 10 r.

Calatayud, in the valley of the Río Jalón, is an old Aragonese frontier town, in the shadow of Moorish ruins dating from the 8th c.

SIGHTS. – On a hill above the town are the ruins of the Moorish **Kalat-Ayub** ("Castle of Ayub"). Church of **Santa María la Mayor**, a former mosque, with an alabaster doorway (1528; sculptures in Spanish Renaissance style) and an octagonal tower (16th c.). Church of **San Sepulcro** (12th c., later remodelled), once the principal church of the Templars in Spain.

SURROUNDINGS. – 3 km NE of the town, on the left bank of the Río Jalón, are the remains of the Celtiberian town of **Bilbilis** (birthplace of the Roman poet Martial (A.D. 40–100). – 27 km S, also reached by way of C 202, is the **Monasterio de Piedra**, a Cistercian house founded in the 12th c., with a keep, chapterhouse, refectory and the apse of the church: a popular summer resort, surrounded by a magnificent nature park with luxuriant vegetation, waterfalls, lakes and caves.

Canary Islands

Autonomous Region.
Organ of Government: Junta de Canarias.
Provinces: Las Palmas de Gran Canaria, Santa Cruz de Tenerife.

The **Canary Islands (Islas Canarias), lying off the W coast of Africa in the Atlantic Ocean, consist of seven large and a number of smaller islands whose southern latitude gives them a subtropical climate. The archipelago forms two provinces – Las Palmas de Gran Canaria, to which the islands of Gran Canaria, Fuerteventura and Lanzarote belong, and Santa Cruz de Tenerife, which comprises the islands of Tenerife, La Palma, Gomero and Hierro.

HISTORY. – The aboriginal population, the Guanches, were a tall light-skinned race. In 1402 Castile began the process of annexing the islands, and after a series of conflicts the last resistance of the Guanches (on Tenerife) collapsed in 1496. Columbus sailed from Gomera on his first voyage of exploration. Since the 19th c. the economy of the Canaries has been promoted by the establishment of free ports, and the agreeable climate, with its "eternal spring", has created a flourishing tourist trade.

Gran Canaria

Province: Las Palmas (GC).
Telephone code: 928.
ⓘ **Oficina de Información de Turismo,**
   Casa del Turismo, Parque Santa Catalina;
   Las Palmas;
   tel. 26 46 23.
   Patronato Provincial de Turismo,
   León y Castilla 17, Las Palmas;
   tel. 36 24 22.

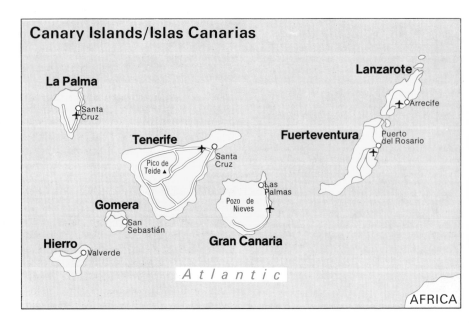

Canary Islands/Islas Canarias

La Palma
  ○Santa
  +Cruz

Tenerife
  Pico de
  Teide ▲   Santa
                   Cruz

Gomera
  ○San
  Sebastián

Hierro
  ○Valverde

Lanzarote
  +○Arrecife

Fuerteventura
                 Puerto
                 del Rosario
                 +

          ○Las
          Palmas
  Pozo de
  Nieves
    +
Gran Canaria

A t l a n t i c

AFRICA

Las Palmas Harbour, Gran Canaria

HOTELS. – Only a small selection from the enormous number of hotels can be given here. IN LAS PALMAS DE GRAN CANARIA: *Cristina, L, 316 r., SP; *Reina Isabel, L, 234 r., SP; *Santa Catalina, L, 208 r., SP; Los Bardinos, I, 215 r., SP; Concorde, I, 127 r., SP; Iberia Sol (no rest.), I, 298 r., SP; Imperial Playa, I, 173 r.; Rocamar, I, 87 r.; Sansofe, I, 101 r.; Tigaday (no rest.), I, 160 r., SP; Astoria Club, II, 160 r., SP; Atlanta (no rest.), II, 58 r.; Bañosol (no rest.), II, 40 r.; Cantur (no rest.), II, 124 r.; Fataga, II, 92 r.; Gran Canaria, II, 90 r.; Lumi (no rest.), II, 61 r.; Miraflor (no rest.), II, 78 r.; Parque (no rest.), II, 119 r.; Rosalia (no rest.), II, 45 r.; Sol (no rest.), II, 35 r.; Trocadero, II, 82 r.; Utica, II, 79 r.; Funchal (no rest.), III, 35 r.; Majorica (no rest.), III, 38 r.; Pez Espada (no rest.), III, 38 r.; Pujol (no rest.), III, 48 r.; Valencia (no rest.), III, 35 r. – IN MASPALOMAS: *Maspalomas Oasis, L, 342 r., SP; Apolo, I, 115 r., SP; Corona Caserio (no rest.), I, 106 r.; Ifa Dunamar, I, 184 r., SP; Ifo Hotel Faro de Maspalomas, I, 188 r., SP; Lucana, I, 167 r., SP; Las Margaritas, I, 323 r., SP; Maspalomas Palm Beach, I, 358 r.; Rio Palmera, I, 231 r., SP; Parque Tropical, II, 235 r., SP; Apartment-Hotel Rey Carlos, II, 160 r.; Inter Club Atlántic (no rest.), III, 105 r., SP; etc.

RESTAURANTS. – Acuario, Plaza de la Victoria 3; Canario, Perojo 2; El Coto, Alfredo Calderón 21; La Guitarra, Dr Miguel Rosas 21; Hamburg, General Orgaz 54 (German); Julio, La Naval 132 (fish dishes); Mesón la Paella, José Maria Durán 47; House Ming, Paseo de las Canteras 30 (Chinese); Montreal, 29 de Abril; Nanking, Francy Roca 11 (Chinese); El Novillo Precoz, Portugal 9; Samoe, Valencia 46; etc.

EVENTS. – Los Reyes Magos (Jan.), Three Kings procession in Las Palmas. – Festivales de Invierno (Feb.–Mar.), with opera and dramatic performances in Las Palmas. – Semana Santa (Holy Week) in Las Plamas. – Festivales de España (Apr.–May), with drama, ballet and concerts in Las Palmas. – Nuestra Señora de la Luz (Oct.), with pilgrimage and procession on the sea.

CASINO. – Casino Tamarindos, San Agustín.

BOAT SERVICES. – Car ferry services between the islands and with the Spanish mainland (Cádiz, Málaga); connections with European and overseas ports.

**Gran Canaria (area 1532 sq. km) is the third largest of the islands, after Tenerife and Fuerteventura. Its main features are the gorges which extend from the central peaks of almost 2000 m to the sea. The highest point on the almost circular island is the Pozo de las Nieves (1949 m). It has many wide beaches of golden yellow sand, including the Playa del Inglés (2·7 km long) and the beach of Maspalomas (6 km long).

*Las Palmas (at sea level; pop 366,000) is a provincial capital and the largest town in the Canaries, with an international port, the Puerto de la Luz. On a peninsula adjoining the town is the Castillo de la Luz (1492). On the opposite side of the town, which at this point is only a few streets wide, is the famous *Playa de las Canteras, (3 km long), with restaurants, cafés, hotels, etc. Farther S, near the pier, is the *Parque de Santa Catalina. From here we continue S past the Playa de las Alcaravaneras to the Ciudad Jardín (Garden City), with handsome houses, the Pueblo Canario and the Museo de Nestor (with works by the painter of that name). Close by is the famous Hotel Santa Catalina, with the Parque Doramas and animal enclosures. Still farther S is the Vegueta (Old

Town), with the Gothic *Cathedral* of Santa Ana (consecrated 1570): Baroque high altar, treasury in sacristy (fine enamel work), picturesque cloisters; fine views from towers. Nearby is the *Museo Canario*, with a large collection of material from the Guanche period. N of the Cathedral is the *Casa de Colón*, in which Columbus lived before setting out on his voyage to America, it has a magnificent doorway, a sumptuous interior and objects dating from the time of the discovery of America. From here it is only a few paces to the *Ermita San Antonio Abad*, a 15th c. chapel rebuilt in the 18th c.

GRAN CANARIA. – 14 km S of Las Palmas is **Telde** (alt. 116 m), in a fertile fruit-growing district, with the basilica of Santo Cristo and the church of San Juan Bautista (carved Flemish Gothic altar, the island's greatest artistic treasure). Nearby are *Tara*, with interesting caves which were occupied by the original inhabitants of the island, and *Cuatro Puertas*, with the sacred hill of the Guanches. – From Telde (45 km) to *Tejeda* (alt. 958 m), the central point of the island. Nearby is the majestic *Roque Nublo*, with the *Cruz de Tejeda* (Parador).

16 km S of Telde is the holiday resort of Agüimes (alt. 259 m), with beaches near the town. From here the road continues, with many bends, to *San Bartolomé de Tirajana* (22 km), in a volcanic crater, surrounded by the island's highest peaks.

48 km from Las Palmas on the coast road C 182 which runs S from the town is the holiday colony of **San Agustín**, with gardens, hotels, bungalows and a recreation centre. Nearby are the *Playa de San Agustín* and the *Playa del Inglés*. – Then we come to **Maspalomas**, a holiday centre with a large beach. 2 km W is *Pasito Blanco*, with a yacht harbour.

Tenerife

Province: Santa Cruz de Tenerife (TF).
Telephone code: 922.
ⓘ **Oficina de Información de Turismo,**
   Calle de la Marina 57, Santa Cruz;
   tel. 28 72 54.
   Oficina de Información de Turismo,
   Plaza de la Iglesia 3, Puerto de la Cruz;
   tel. 38 43 28.

HOTELS. – Only a selection of the large number of hotels can be given here. IN SANTA CRUZ DE TENERIFE: *Mencey*, L, 298 r., SP; Apartment Hotel *Colón Rambla* (no rest.), II, 40 r.; *Diplomático* (no rest.), II, 38 r., SP; Apartment-Hotel *Plaza* (no rest.), II, 64 r.; *Anaga*, III, 126 r.; *Pelinor* (no rest.), III, 67 r.; *Taburiente* (no rest.), III, 90 r.; *Tamaide* (no rest.), III, 65 r.; *Horizonte*, IV, 55 r.; *San José*, IV, 53 r.; Hostal *Peceño* (no rest.), P I, 49 r.; etc. – IN PUERTO DE LA CRUZ: *Botánico*, L, 282 r., SP; *San Felipe*, L, 260 r., SP; *Semiramis*, L, 275 r., SP; *Atalya Gran Hotel*, I, 183 r., SP; *Atlantis Playa*, I, 326 r., SP; *Bonanza Canarife*, I, 411 r., SP; *La Chiripa*, I, 276 r.; *Dania Park*, I, 227 r., SP; *Florida*, I, 315 r., SP; *Gran Hotel los Do gos sol*, I, 237 r., SP; *Interpalace*, I, 291 r., SP; *Meliá Puerto de la*

Cruz, I, 300 r., SP; *Orotava Garden*, I, 241 r., SP; *Parque San Antonio-Sol*, I, 211 r., SP; *Puerto Playa*, I, 168 r., SP; *Tenerife Playa*, I, 339 r., SP; *El Tope*, I, 216 r.; *Las Vegas*, I, 223 r., SP; *Las Aguilas Sol*, II, 500 r., SP; Apartment Hotel *Guajara*, II, 335 r., SP; *Internacional*, II, 111 r.; *Magec-Park*, II, 154 r., SP; *Miramar*, II, 143 r., SP; *Nopal*, II, 68 r., SP; *Los Principes*, II, 55 r.; *San Telmo*, II, 91 r., SP; *Trovador*, II, 80 r., SP; *Maquesa*, III, 92 r.; *Pinocho* (no rest.), III, 29 r., SP; *Alfomar* (no rest.), IV, 25 r.; etc. – IN LAS CAÑADAS DEL TEIDE (La Orotava): *Parador Nacional Cañadas del Teide*, III, 16 r., SP. – IN BAJAMER (La Laguna): *Nautilus*, I, 268 r., SP; *Delfin-Laguna* (no rest.), II, 66 r.; *Neptuno*, II, 97 r., SP; *Tinquaro*, II, 115 r., SP. – IN LOS CRISTIANOS (Arona): *Princesa Dacil*,

Puerto de la Cruz, Tenerife

II, 366 r.; SP; Apartment Hotel *Tenerife-Sur*, II, 137 r., SP; *Andrea* (no rest.), III, 42 r.; etc.

RESTAURANTS. – *La Riviera*, Rambla General Franco 155 (elegant); *La Estancia*, Méndez Núñez 116; *Corynto*, Avda de Anaga 19; and others in Santa Cruz de Tenerife. – *El Pescado*, Avda Venezuela 3; *Marina*, José Antonio 2; *Cockpit*, Cólogan 6; *Cochino de Oro*, Zamora 23 (Belgian); *El Pajar*, Cuesta de la Villa, Santa Úrsula (rustic style, fine view); *Oscar*, Cuesta de la Villa (fine view); and others in Puerto de la Cruz. – *París*, Camino San Bartolomé de Geneto 8, La Laguna.

EVENTS. – *Los Reyes Magos* (Jan.), Three Kings procession in Santa Cruz. – *Carneval* (Feb.), carnaval in Santa Cruz celebrated at great expense. – *Semana Santa* (Holy Week) in Santa Cruz and La Laguna. – *Festivales de España* (Apr.–May), with drama, ballet and concerts in Santa Cruz. – *Fiestas de Primavera* (May), spring festival in Santa Cruz, with opera. – *Fundación de la Ciudad* (May), commemorating the foundation of the town, in Santa Cruz. – *Corpus Christi*, with processions, in La Laguna and La Orotava. – *Virgen del Carmen* (July), popular fiesta in Santa Cruz in honour of the Virgen del Carmen. – *Fiesta del Santísimo Cristo* (Sept.) in La Laguna. – Opera performances in Santa Cruz (Nov.–Dec.).

CASINO. – *Casino de Taoro*, Puerto de la Cruz.

BOAT SERVICES: see under Gran Canaria.

**Tenerife, the largest of the Canaries (area 2053 sq. km), is an island with a great variety of scenery. In the interior is a central mountain range, with a series of wide and fertile valleys along its sides, the most notable being the Orotava and Güimar valleys. In the Cañadas plateau rears up the Pico de Teide

(3718 m), the highest peak in the Canaries, and indeed in the whole of Spain. Round the rocky and in places much indented coast are numerous gently sloping sandy beaches. Tenerife is also notable for the abundance and variety of its flora.

Santa Cruz de Tenerife (at sea level; pop. 191,000) is the capital of the island and the province, with beautiful parks and gardens, including the *García Sanabría Municipal Park*. Adjoining the busy harbour is the *Plaza de España*, with a monument to the dead of the Civil War. To the W is the *Plaza de la Candelaria*, with a monument (1778) to the island's patroness, the Virgen de la Candelaria. N. of this square is the church of *San Francisco* (1680), with a beautiful high altar and ceiling paintings. To the W of the church is the *Museo Municipal*, with important works of art, including pictures by artists of the Canaries. From the Plaza del Príncipe the Calle del Pilar leads to the church of *Nuestra Señora del Pilar* (18th c.), with a statue of the Virgen de las Angustias (1804). – From the Plaza de España the Avenida de Anaga skirts the harbour to the *Castillo de Paso Alto*, where five ancient canon can be seen.

TENERIFE. – 9 km NW of Santa Cruz is the island's second largest town, **La Laguna** (alt. 550 m), formerly the capital, now the seat of a bishop and a university town. The 16th c. Cathedral has interesting carving and pictures. The church of the Concepción, the oldest church in the town (1502), is a protected monument. Many old aristocratic mansions with characteristic balconies. Near the town is the hill of *Las Mercedes*, with magnificent flora. – From La Laguna through the *Bosque de la Esperanza* (58 km) to *Las Cañadas* (Parador); ascent of *Pico de Teide* (cableway and climb).

*__Puerto de la Cruz__ (at sea level; pop. 16,500) is the largest tourist centre on the island, with huge sea-water swimming pools. Church of San Telmo (1626), the town's emblem and landmark, with a statue (copy) of San Telmo, patron saint of fishermen. Church of Nuestra Señora de la Peña (17th c.), with a number of Baroque works of art, including the high altar (by Luis de la Cruz). – On the road to Orotava is the famous *Botanic Garden*, with trees and plants from all over the world. From here it is another 6 km up to

La Orotava (alt. 600 m), centre of the beautiful *Valle de la Orotava*, with scenery of bewitching charm. Features of the town are the numerous old mansions with balconies, the church of the Concepción (Baroque façade) and the 17th c. Casas de los Balcones, housing a collection of decorative and applied art. – From La Orotava a road runs SW between banana groves and cultivated fields to nearby **Los Realejos**, with the church of Nuestra Señora de la Concepción (magnificent Baroque retablo) and the parish church of Santiago (1498), the oldest church on the island. – The road along the N coast continues to **Icod** (alt. 250 m), at the foot of Teide. Famous thousand-year-old dragon-tree; church of San Marcos, with a Renaissance doorway and a Baroque retablo. – Beyond Icod is the little port of **Garachico**, the "Pearl by the Sea", a beautiful little town with the Castillo de San Miguel and natural swimming pools. – In the S of the island are the holiday centres of *Playa de las Américas* and **Los Cristianos**.

Fuerteventura

Province: Las Palmas (GC).
Telephone code: 928.
ⓘ **Oficina de Información de Turismo,** General Franco 33, Puerto del Rosario; tel. 85 10 24.

HOTELS. – *Parador Nacional de Fuerteventura*, II, 50 r., SP; *Las Gabias* (no rest.), II, 64 r.; etc. HOLIDAY VILLAGES: *Club Aldiana, El Castillo*.

Fuerteventura, second largest of the Canaries (area 1722 sq. km), is the one with the longest coastline. It is an island of wide plains and extensive beaches.

The island's capital and principal port is **Puerto del Rosario** (pop. 4300). S of the town is the Playa Blanca, a beautiful bathing beach.

Lanzarote

Province: Las Palmas (GC).
Telephone code: 928.
ⓘ **Oficina de Información de Turismo,** Parque Municipal, Arrecife; tel. 81 18 60.

HOTELS. – *Arrecife Gran Hotel*, I, 150 r., SP; *Lancelot Playa* (no rest.), II, 123 r.; *Miramar* (no-rest.), II, 90 r.; *San Ginés* (no rest.), IV, 28 r.; Hostal *Cardona* (no rest.), P I, 62 r.; *España*, P III, 26 r.; etc.

The most easterly of the Canaries, Lanzarote (area **795** sq. km) is the most unusual and distinctive, with its eerie lunar landscape, created by volcanic eruptions in the 17th and 18th c.

On Lanzarote

Above the island's capital **Arrecife** (pop. 18,000) are the *Castillo San Gabriel* (archaeological museum) and the *Castillo San José* (art museum). The town itself has attractive old streets and an arcaded market square. In the SW of the island are the **Montañas del Fuego** ("Mountains of Fire"), with more than 300 volcanic cones; they can be visited on camel-back (magnificent view from mountain hut).

La Palma

Province: Santa Cruz de Tenerife (TF).
Telephone code: 922
(i) **Oficina de Información de Turismo,**
    Calle O'Daly 22, Santa Cruz de la Palma;
    Tel. 41 21 06.

HOTELS. – *Parador Nacional de Santa Cruz*, II, 32 r.; *San Miguel*, II, 72 r.; etc.

Santa Cruz de la Palma

In the middle of the green island of La Palma (area **728** sq. km) is the Caldera de Taburiente, one of the largest craters in the world, now a national park, with huge forests of pines. The highest peak is the Roque de los Muchachos (**2426** m).

The capital, **Santa Cruz de la Palma** (pop. 15,000), is situated on the edge of a volcanic crater, La Caldera, in the foothills on the E side of the island. The town's main street, the picturesque Calle O'Daly (Calle Real), runs into the Plaza de España, in which are the Renaissance Town Hall and the Salvador church (1503). – On the W coast of the island is the commercial and agricultural centre, **Los Llanos de Aridane**, situated in a beautiful valley. Nearby is *Tazacorte*, with a small harbour and a beach.

Gomera

Province: Santa Cruz de Tenerife (TF).
Telephone code: 922.
(i) **Oficina de Información de Turismo,**
    Calle de la Marina 57, Santa Cruz de Tenerife;
    tel. 28 72 54.

HOTEL. – *Parador Nacional*, I, 40 r., SP.

The almost circular island of Gomera (area 378 sq. km) is covered with luxuriant vegetation. Its highest peak, in the centre of the island, is the Alto de Garajonay (1487 m).

The island's capital and port is **San Sebastián** (pop. 7000), a picturesque little town where Columbus fitted out his ships and took on supplies before his voyage. Church of the Asunción, in which he heard mass before sailing. The most important historical monument is the 16th c. Torre del Conde ("Count's Tower"). – Near the town are several beaches of white sand with crystal-clear water. The valley called *Valle Gran Rey* is extremely popular with visitors.

Hierro

Province: Santa Cruz de Tenerife (TF).
Telephone code: 922.
(i) **Oficina de Información de Turismo,**
    Calle de la Marina 57, Santa Cruz de Tenerife;
    tel. 28 72 54.

HOTEL. – *Parador Nacional*, II, 47 r., SP.

The most westerly of the Canary Islands is Hierro (area 278 sq km), which is roughly triangular in shape. In the middle of the island is a plateau with some 1500 ash cones and its highest point, Mal Paso 1500 m).

The capital is **Valverde** (pop. 5000), a picturesque little town of orchards and ornamental gardens, with an old fortified church.

Near the town, to the E, is the little port of *Puerto de la Estaca*, with a sandy beach.

Cantabria

Autonomous Region.
Organ of Government: Diputación Regional de Cantabria.
Province: Cantabria.

The Spanish region of Cantabria, to the N of the mountains of the same name, borders the Atlantic Ocean on the coast of which lies the capital, Santander (see p. 198).

Cartagena

Province: Murcia (MU).
Telephone code: 968.
Altitude: 2 m. – Population: 173,000.
ⓘ **Oficina de Información del C.I.T.,**
Plaza Castellini 5;
tel. 50 75 49.

HOTELS. – *Cartagonova* (no rest.), Marcos Redondo 3, II, 126 r.; *Alfonso XIII*, Paseo de Alfonso XIII 30, III, 239 r.; *Cartagenera* (no rest.), Jara 32, IV, 46 r.; *Hostal Los Habaneros*, San Diego 60, P II, 70 r.; *Manolo* (no rest.), Muñoz Grandes 7, P II, 95 r.; *Za-Or* (no rest.), Alcalde Zamora 1, P III, 12 r.; etc.

RESTAURANTS. – *Anibal*, Callejón de la Parra; *Mesón Montería*, Pl. Cuartel de Rey 5; *Mare Nostrum*, Paseo de Alfonso XII (at the harbour); etc.

EVENTS. – *Semana Santa* (Holy Week), with a famous procession. – *Virgen del Monte Carmel* (July), patronal festival.

WATER SPORTS. – There are facilities for all kinds of water sports in Cartagena and in the Mar Menor, to the NE. Cartagena has a club Náutico and a Real Club de Regatas.

SPORT and RECREATION on land. – Tennis, riding, football; La Manga golf-course in Los Belones.

CASINO. – *Casino Azarmenor* in San Javier, N of the Mar Menor.

Cartagena, founded by the Carthaginian leader Hasdrubal in 221 B.C., is Spain's leading commercial port and principal naval base, situated in a deeply indented bay which is guarded by two forts on steep rocky promontories. As the Roman Nova Carthago it was for centuries the most important settlement in the Iberian peninsular.

SIGHTS. – The town's main street is the busy *Calle Isaac Peral* (closed to cars), at the S end of which is the *Ayuntamiento* (Town Hall). From here attractive promenades extend along the harbour, separated from it by the railway. The finest views are to be had from the *Avenida* (monument to Columbus), laid out on the line of the old town walls. Passing the ruins of the 13th c. church of **Santa María la Vieja**, we come to the ruined **Castillo de la Concepcíon** (alt. 70 m: approached by a flight of steps), surrounded by beautiful gardens. From here there is a view of the town and harbour, and of the oil refineries on the S coast at *Escombreras*. – To the N of the town is the **Museo Arqueológico**, with a notable collection of Roman matrial.

SURROUNDINGS. – NE of the town is the seaside resort and tourist centre of the Mar Menor (see p. 174). On the way there (N 332) is the old mining town of *La Unión*.

Around the Golfo de Mazarrón. – N 332 runs W from Cartagena to *Cuesta Blanca* and *Puerto de Mazarrón* (15 km), with a bathing beach and tourist centre. From here inland to *Mazarrón* and then along the *Sierra de la Almenara* to **Águilas** (pop. 17,600), a little port with the remains of Roman baths. Bathing beaches on the *Costa Blanca*. Near the town are old fortifications.

An old coastal watch-tower near Cartagena

Castellón de la Plana

Province: Castellón (CS).
Telephone code: 964.
Altitude: 28 m. – Population: 120,000.
ⓘ **Oficina Muncipal de Turismo,**
Plaza Maria Augustina 5;
tel. 22 77 04.

HOTELS.. – *Mindoro* (no rest.), Moyano 4, I, 114 r.;
Del Golf, Playa del Pinar (El Grao), II, 127 r., SP;
Myriam (no rest.), Obispo Salinas 1, II, 25 r.; *Turcosa*
(no rest.), Avda de Buenavista 1, II, 70 r.; *Amat* (no
rest.), Temprado 15, III, 22 r.; *Doña Lola* (no rest.),
Lucena 3, III, 24 r.; *Gabiska* (no rest.), Plaza del Real
2, III, 35 r.; Hostal *Brisamar* (no rest.), Avda
Buenavista 26, P II, 12 r.; *Marti* (no rest.), Herrero 19,
P II, 28 r.; *Bagan*, Pérez Galdos 13, P III, 24 r.; etc. –
CAMPING SITE: *Bonterra*, N in Benicasim; others in the
vicinity.

RESTAURANTS. – *Club Náutico*, Escollera Poniente, El Grao (5 km E); *Electra*, Ronda Mijares 20;
Mesón del Cordero, 10 km NW on the road to Alcora.

EVENTS. – *Fiesta de Santa Magdalena* (Holy Week),
with mass and folk celebrations at the pilgrimage
chapel on the Ermita hill; procession, regatta,
bullfights.

WATER SPORTS. – Two sandy beaches at El Grao;
water sports at the Riff Poniente.

**The attractive provincial capital of
Castellón de la Plana, situated in a
fertile plain, is a centre of the trade
in oranges, large quantities of which
are shipped from the port of El Grao
de Castellón, 5 km E on the beautiful
Costa del Azahar ("Orange-Blossom
Coast").**

SIGHTS. – Church of **Santa María
Mayor**, originally Gothic, with a separate
tower 46 m high (1604, rebuilt after
destruction in 1936). – **Ayuntamiento**
(Town Hall), *c.* 1700. – **Diputación
Provincial**, with the excellent *Museo
Provincial de Bellas Artes*, which has
pictures by the Castellón-born painter
Ribalta. There is a monument to the artist
on the Paseo de Ribalta, with the *Parque
Ribalta.*

SURROUNDINGS. – There are many places of
interest within reach of Castellón. Most of them are
included in the following itineraries.

To the Puerto El Remolcador. – Leave Castellón
on C 232, which runs NW to (34 km) **Lucena del Cid**
(alt. 568 m; pop. 2400), a picturesque little town on a
hill above the valley of the *Río Lucena* which is a
popular summer resort. Castillo del Duque de Hijar;

fine retablo in the parish church. – From here C 232
climbs to the *Puerto El Remolcador* (1018 m), from
which it is possible to continue to Teruel.

The coast road to Tarragona. – There are a number
of roads running N from Castellón – the motorway
A 7, N 340 and a secondary road from El Grac which
joins N 340. The route passes orange-groves and
plantations of olive-trees, with the rugged limestone
crags of the *Peña Golosa* (1831 m) on the left, to
Benicasim (alt. 15 m; pop. 3000), in an attractive
setting amid palm plantations at the foot of the hilly
Desierto de las Palmas, near the sea (beach). The road
then climbs inland and runs along a fairly level stretch
to **Oropesa del Mar** (alt. 33 m), picturesquely
situated on a rocky hill crowned by a ruined castle. Off
the road to the right (1 km), on the coast, are an old
watch-tower, the Toree del Rey, and a signal station,
the Faro de Oropesa; here too is the bathing beach.

The road then runs in long straight stretches between
cultivated fields, with views of the sea to the right, to
Torreblanca (pop. 4000), in the centre of which is
an 18th c. church with an azulejo-covered dome. 3 km
away, on the coast, is the resort of *Torrenostra*.

Beyond Torreblanca N 340 crosses the river bed
(usually dry) of the *Rambla de las Cuevas* and passes
the prominent ruins of the Castillo de Chivert, in the
Sierra de Irta (on right). Then via *Alcalá de Chivert* and
Santa Magdalena de Pulpis (imposing ruined castle)
to an attractive side road (7 km) which runs SW over
the coastal plain to the little rocky peninsula of
*Peñíscola, rearing out of the sea like a fortress and
linked with the mainland by a tongue of land flanked
by popular bathing beaches. The picturesque little
town of *Peñíscola* (pop. 3000; *Hostería del Mar, I,
85 r., SP) is dominated by an old castle which King
Jaime I captured from the Moors in 1233 and which
was occupied by the deposed Antipope Benedict XIII
from 1415 until his death in 1424; from the castle there
are magnificent views.

N 340 continues along the coast from Peñíscola to
Benicarló (alt. 11 m; pop. 14,000; Parador Nacional,
II, 108 r., SP, with sea view; Marynton, III, 26 r.),
which has an old castle and a beautiful church of 1743
(octagonal tower, azulejo dome, magnificent doorway).

The road then traverses the dry valley of the *Río Seco
de Benicarló* and an area of vineyards to **Vinaroz** (alt.
6 m; pop. 14,000), a lively little fishing town.

The coast road to Valencia. – The motorway and N
340 run along the Costa del Azahar. S of Castellón N
340 crosses the *Río Mijares* on the stone Puente de
Ribelles (1794) and comes to **Villarreal de los
Infantes** (alt. 42 m; pop. 30,000), founded in 1272,
where the large principal church (18th c.) has an
azulejo dome.

The road continues through the fertile plain of
Villarreal, irrigated with water from the Río Míjares,
with flowers and orange-groves, to **Nules** (alt. 11 m;
pop. 9700), a little town with remains of its old walls.
– 3½ km W, at the foot of the hills, is the health resort of
Villavieja. 7 km SW is the village of *Vall de Uxó*, with
the magnificent *stalactitic cave of San José (conducted tours, including boat trip; concerts). From Vall
de Uxó it is possible to continue on C 225 over the
Collado de Marienet (400 m) to **Sergorbe**.

Beyond Nules the coast road comes to **Almenara** (alt. 23 m), dominated by a ruined castle on a rocky hill. King Jaime I of Aragon defeated the Moors here in 1238 and was then able to capture Valencia. There are numerous Roman remains in the area, including a camp dating from 217 B.C. on the Monte del Cid, to the left of the road.

Castile

Autonomous Regions: Castile y León; Castile-La Mancha.
Organ of Government: Consejo General de Castilla-León; Junta de Comunidades de Castilla-La Mancha.
Province of Castile-León: Ávila, Burgos, León, Palencia, Salamanca, Segovia, Soria, Valladolid and Zamora.
Province of Castile-La Mancha: Ciudad Real, Albacete, Cuenca, Guadalajara and Toledo.

Castile (Castilla), with its endless plateaux, has long been the heartland of Spain. The austere villages of unbaked brick (adobe) have the same tawny colour as the soil. Here and in most little country towns live the peasants (labradores) who have been displaced by the large landowners: often still the same generous and hospitable people depicted by Cervantes and Calderón. But monotonous as the central Spanish plateau undoubtedly is, it has its moments of astonishing beauty when the sun sinks and the red tones of the earth merge into the varied hues of the sky.

This region, mostly far from the sea, and enclosed by the hills round its borders is known as the *Meseta* ("Table"). This area, once defended by numerous fortresses and castles, is divided by the Castilian watershed, which comprises the Sierra de Guadarrama, Sierra de Grados and Sierra de Gata, into the historic regions of Old Castile (Castilla la Veija) and New Castile (Castilla la Nueva) in the south-east. These two plateaux, tilted towards the W, are traversed by a number of large rivers which cut their way through the western rim in rocky gorges.

The considerable altitude of the Meseta (Old Castile rising to over 900 m, New Castile to 700 m) gives the climate a continental character, with hot summers and severe winters. The spring and autumn rains produce pasture for the merino sheep from Extremadura which graze here in the summer. As in other parts of the country agriculture is in places only possible by artificial irrigation.

Catalonia

Autonomous Region.
Organ of Government: Generalitat de Catalunya.
Provinces: Barcelona, Gerona, Lerida and Tarragona.

Catalonia (Cataluña), the most northerly of Spain's Mediterranean regions, has a distinctive character – the result partly of geography, partly of race and partly of history. Here wild and thinly settled areas are found alongside densely populated fertile valleys, with gardens, olive-groves and vineyards from which the hard-working Catalans draw rich harvests, and busy industrial towns, chief among them as a centre of commerce and industry the great city of Barcelona; and in addition to all this there are the tourist resorts along the Costa Brava.

The *Catalonian Mountains* run parallel to the coast, linking the eastern Pyrenees with the hills bounding the Meseta on the NE. Originally a single chain, they were later broken up into isolated massifs like *Montseny* (1745 m) in the N and the famous *Montserrat* (1241 m) and *Montsant* (1071 m) in the S. – Between the main range and a lower coastal chain extends a longitudinal valley, where olives and vegetables are grown and where wine is produced. The capital of Catalonia, *Barcelona*, situated in the fertile region around the mouth of the *Río Llobregat*, has enjoyed a considerable rise in prosperity. – In the N and W Catalonia takes in part of the Pyrenees and in the S part of the Ebro basin.

This mountainous region has become Spain's economic heart, the most densely populated and most progressive part of the country through the vigour and activity of its people. Its major industry is textiles, centred in Barcelona and also in Sabadell and Tarrasa; other important activities are leather-working, paper-making, the manufacture of soap from olive oil, hardware and the processing of cork. – The Catalans are lively, progressive and efficient. Catalan (Català) is an independent Romance language developed out of Provençal.

Ceuta

Province: Cádiz (CA).
Telephone code: 956.
Altitude: at sea level. – Population: 65,000.
ⓘ **Oficina de Información de Turismo,**
    Avenida Cañonero Data 1;
    tel. 51 13 79.

HOTELŚ. – *La Muralla*, Plaza de África 15, I, 83 r., SP; *Ulises* (no rest.), Camoens 5, I, 124 r., SP; *África* (no rest.), Muelle Cañonero Dato s/n, II, 39 r.; Hostal *Atlante* (no rest.), Paseo de las Palmeras 1, P II, 40 r.; *Miramar* (no rest.), Avda Reyes Católicos 23, P II, 21 r.; *Skol* (no rest.), Avda Reyes Católicos 6, P II, 14 r.

BOAT SERVICES. – Car ferry daily from Algeciras (about 1½ hours).

The town of Ceuta, on the African side of the Straits of Gibraltar, is an area under Spanish sovereignty (plaza de soberanía) with a free port which carries on a lively trade.

Ceuta Harbour, North Africa

SIGHTS. – The central point of the town is the palm-shaded *Plaza de África*, in which are the *Town Hall* and the **Cathedral**, with a black marble Renaissance doorway and a large choir. – Opposite the Town Hall is the church of **Nuestra Señora de África** (18th c.), with a beautiful 15th c. statue of the Virgin, patroness of the town, on the high altar. – At the far end of the tongue of land on which the town stands is the **Foso de Felipe** ("Philip's Ditch"), which separates the old town from the mainland (remains of towers, bastions and battlemented walls). – On the promontory is *Monte Hacho*, with the prominent remains of an old fortress.

SURROUNDINGS. – There are bus services to all the principal towns in the neighbouring kingdom of Morocco.

Ciudad Real

Province: Ciudad Real (CR).
Telephone code: 926.
Altitude: 632 m. – Population: 45,000.
ⓘ **Oficina de Información de Turismo,**
    Avenide Alarcos 31;
    tel. 21 29 25.

HOTELS. – *Castillos* (no rest.), Avda del Rey Santo 18, II, 131 r.; *El Molino*, 242 km on N 420, II, 18 r.; *Almanzor*, Bernardo Balbuena s/n, III, 66 r.; Hostal *Alfonso el Sabio*, Carlos Vázquez 8, P II, 57 r.; *San Millán*, Ronda de Granada 23, P II, 40 r.; etc.

RESTAURANTS. – *Casa Blanca*, Ronda de Granada 23; *Miami Park*, Ronda Ciruela 48; etc.

CAFÉS. – *Los Faroles*, Plaza del Pilar 9; *Manchega*, Tinte 35.

EVENTS. – *Fiestas de la Virgen del Prado* (Aug.), the town's chief patronal festival, with bullfights, flower games, competition for the best decorated floats. – *Festivales de España.*

The provincial capital of Ciudad Real, the seat of a bishop, is the chief town in La Mancha, the home of Don Quixote. The town lies in a fertile region between the Río Guadiana and the Río Jabalón.

HISTORY. – The town was founded in 1252 by Alfonso el Sabio (the Wise) on the site of Alarcos, which had been destroyed by the Moors. Its original name was Villareal. In 1420, during the reign of John II, it received its municipal charter and took the name of Ciudad Real.

SIGHTS. – Ciudad Real has preserved a few monuments of its warlike past, such as the 14th c. **Puerta de Toledo**, one of the old town gates, flanked by two square towers (national monument). It has an imposing Gothic **Cathedral** (1531) dedicated to the Virgen del Prado, with a 12th c. *W doorway* and a *retablo* by Giraldo de Merlo (1616); in the *sacristy* is a picture by Eugenio Cazès, "The Beheading of John the Baptist". From the 17th c. tower of the Cathedral there are extensive views. – Also very fine is the 16th c. church of **San Pedro**, with Gothic and Mudéjar doorways; high altar with statue of St Peter; Subsidiary altar of the Virgen de la Guía, with a silver throne.

SURROUNDINGS. – Two sights of great interest in the immediate vicinity of the town are the old *Ermita de Alarcos* (8 km W), built to commemorate the battle of Alcaros, and the *Castillo de Calatrava* (15 km N), a Moorish fortress which was captured by Alfonso VII of Castile. – There are also many places associated with Don Quixote in the surrounding area.

Lagunas de Ruidera, near Ciudad Real

Sierra de los Molinos. – N 420 runs NE to *Daimiel*, near which Don Quixote encountered the Yanguesian goatherds. – Continue via *Puerto Lápice* (where N IV is crossed) to **Alcázar de San Juan** (alt. 643 m), a little town which has an important collection of Roman mosaics, as well as the church of Santa María (13th c.). – 8 km farther on is **Campo de Criptana**, an attractive village where Don Quixote is supposed to have had his fight with the windmills. Several windmills are still working; some (e.g. El Quimera and El Pilón) contain small museums. – Continue on N 420 to *Pedro Muñoz*, 13 km N of which is the village of *El Toboso*, home of Don Quixote's Dulcinea. – From Pedro Muñoz NE to the typical La Mancha village of *Mota del Cuervo* on N 301, which links Madrid with Albacete and Alicante.

Via Manzanares to the Sierra Morena. – Take N 420, which runs NE to *Daimiel*; from there E on N 430 to (52 km from Ciudad Real) **Manzanares** (alt. 645 m; pop. 16,000), a friendly little town on the *Río Azuer*, built round a castle erected after the battle of Las Navas de Tolosa; *Castillo de Peñas Borras*. Then on a secondary road to (27 km) **Argamasilla de Alba**, where Cervantes began to write "Don Quixote" while in prison. Molino Dulcinea (windmill); Castillo de Peñarroya, a Moorish castle taken by Alonso Pérez de Sanabria in 1198. – Near Argamasilla is **Tomelloso**, the principal La Mancha wine-producing centre. Parish church (16th c.), with a beautiful retablo of the Virgen de la Paz.

N IV runs S from Manzanares (bypass) to **Valdepeñas** (alt. 701 m; pop. 28,000), which is noted for its red wine and its large wine-cellars (*bodegas*). Handsome 18th c. Plaza Mayor; church of Asunción (15th–16th c.), with a fine late Gothic doorway; Museo Gregorio Prieto (in a large windmill), with works by the painter of that name. Excursions can be made to *Almagro* and *Villanueva de los Infantes*.

Continue S on N IV, past the modest little town of *Santa Cruz de Mudela*, founded by Spanish crusaders about 1200, with a 14th c. pilgrimage church. The road then climbs gradually into the *Sierra Morena*, and

at the *Puerto de Despeñapperos* (1009 m), the "Pass of the Overthrow of the Dogs" (i.e. the Moors), crosses the border into Andalusia and continues towards **Jaén** (see p. 141).

To the Campo de Montiel. – C 425 runs E from Ciudad Real to (24 km) **Almagro** (Parador Nacional, I, 55 r., SP) on the site of the ancient *Mariana* in the Campo de Calatrava, once the seat of the knightly Order of Calatrava. Residence of the Grand Master; churches of San Bartolomé el Real and Madre de Dios; Corral de Comedias, a 16th c. theatre (national monument).

Then via *Moral de Calatrava*, with the fine church of La Soledad, to **Valdepeñas**, and from there continue E on C 415 to **Villanueva de los Infantes**, an aristocratic little town. Houses with coats of arms on the doorways, including the Casa del Caballero del Verde Gabán, the House of the Knight of the Green Coat, which features in "Don Quixote". In the Dominican monastery is the tomb of the writer Francisco de Quevedo (1580–1645). – Continue on C 415 to *Villahermosa*, 5 km S of which is the *Castillo de Montiel*, seat of the Order of the Campo de Montiel.

To the Sierra de Almadén. – From Ciudad Real N 420 leads S to *Cañada de Calatrava*, from which a road runs W to Almadén (97 km from Ciudad Real). Continue on N 420 to *Puertollano*, and turn right to reach in 7 km **Almodóvar del Campo**, birthplace of Juan Bautista de la Concepción, reformer of the Carmelite order. Parish church (13th c.), with a fine 14th c. retablo on the high altar; Palacio Juan de Ávila, with chapel of the Trinidad (16th c.); church of Carmen (16th c.).

From Almodóvar C 424 runs NW via *Abenojar* to **Almadén** (alt. 450 m; pop. 15,000), from the Arabic *al-ma'den* (mine). In the surrounding area are rich mercury mines which were worked by the Greeks, Romans and Moors, and between 1525 and 1645 were pledged to the Fugger family of Augsburg as security for a loan; since 1921 they have belonged to the State. The mine is worked by opencast methods at depths of up to 300 m.

Ciudad Rodrigo

Province: Salamanca (SA).
Telephone code: 923.
Altitude: 653 m. – Population: 13,000.
(i) **Oficina de Información de Turismo,**
Arco de las Amayuelas 6,
tel. 46 05 61.
Centro de Iniciativas Turísticas,
Plaza Mayor 1;
tel. 46 01 50.

HOTELS. – *Parador Nacional Enrique II*, Plaza del Castillo 1, II, 27 r.; *Conde Rodrigo*, Plaza de Salvador 9, III, 35 r.; *El Cruce*, Carretera de Lisboa 4, IV, 40 r.; *La Llave del Campo*, Carretera de Lisboa 141, IV, 20 r.; Hostal *Tamarix*, km 319 on Salamanca road, P II, 16 r.; *Fernando Cambronero 'el Pibe'*, Lisboa 10, P III, 13 r.

EVENTS. – *Fiesta de San Blas* (Feb.), with an unusual pilgrimage to the Ermita de la Caridad, 3 km away. – *Fiestas de Carnaval* (Feb.), a cheerful fiesta, with parade of drummers, bullfights and fights with young bulls, which has become a great tourist attraction.

Ciudad Rodrigo, founded in the 12th c. by Count Rodrigo González, was a strong point on the frontier with Portugal, and is still the seat of a bishop. It has a beautiful situation high above the Río Agueda, spanned by a bridge built on Roman foundations.

SIGHTS. – Ciudad Rodrigo, on the site of the Roman *Augustobriga*, is one of the most interesting towns in the province of Salamanca, with many charming old buildings. The whole town is a protected monument. – **Ayuntamiento** (Town Hall), 16th c., with arcades, round turrets and a gallery in Plateresque style. – 12th c. Romanesque **Cathedral**, rebuilt in the 16th c. Two richly decorated doorways; beautiful choir-stalls by Rodrigo Alemán (16th c.); cloister of 13th–14th c.; interesting monuments. – In the **Alcázar**, built in the Middle Ages by Henry II of Trastamara, there is now a Parador Nacional.

Compostela

See Santiago de Compostela.

Córdoba

Province: Córdoba (CO).
Telephone code: 957.
Altitude: 119 m. – Population: 285,000.
(i) **Oficina Municipal de Turismo,**
Plaza de Judá Leví 3,
tel. 29 07 40.
Patronato Provincial de Turismo,
Plaza de Colón 15;
tel. 47 57 85.

HOTELS. – *Adare*, Magistral González Francés 15, I, 103 r.; *Husan Gran Capitán*, Avda América 3–5, I, 99 r.; *Meliá Córdoba*, Jardines de la Victoria, I, 106 r., SP; *El Califa* (no rest.), Lope de Hoces 14, II, 46 r.; *Los Gallos*, Avda de Medina Azahara 7, II, 105 r., SP; *Maimónides* (no rest.), Torrijos 4, II, 61 r.; *Colón* (no rest.), Alhaken II 4, III, 40 r.; *Marisma* (no rest.), Cardenal Herrero 6, III, 28 r.; *Niza Sur* (no rest.), Avda de Cadiz 60, III, 30 r.; *Riviera* (no rest.), Plaza de Aladreros 7, III, 29 r.; *Selu* (no rest.), Eduardo Dato 7, III, 118 r.; *Andalucía* (no rest.), José Zorrilla 3, IV, 40 r.; *Avenida* (no rest.), Avda de Generalísimo 26, IV, 35 r.; *Granada*, Avda de America 17, IV, 27 r.; *El Oasis*, Avda de Cádiz 78, IV, 31 r.; etc. – *Parador Nacional de la Arrruzafa*, I, 83 r., SP (on the Carretera del Brillante, 3 km N), with terrace, gardens and good restaurant.

CAMPING SITES. – *Campamento Municipal del Turismo*, 2 km on Villaviciosa road; *Cerca de Lagartijo*, km 398 on N IV.

RESTAURANTS. – In hotels; also **Caballo Rojo*, Cardenal Herrero 28; *Zoco*, Judíos (Andalusian folk style, with flamenco); *Castillo de la Albaida*, km 4 on Trassierra road (rustic style); *Imperio*, Victoriano Rivera 6; *Primera el Brillante*, Avda del Brillante 26, 2·5 km N (with *hostal*, P II, 27 r.); *El Bosque* (3 km N); etc.

CAFÉS. – *Galerias Presiados*, Avda del Generalísimo; *Gran Capitán*, Avda América 3–5; *Bristol*, Ángel de Saavedra 4; *Tifany's*, General Primo de Rivera 31.

EVENTS. – *Festival de los Patios Cordobeses* (May), celebrating the patios of Córdoba, and also a pilgrimage in honour of the Virgen Conquistadora, with riders and richly decorated horse-drawn carriages, decoration of patios and windows, and flamenco contests, dancing and singing in the streets and squares. – *Feria de Nuestra Señora de la Salud* (May). – *Fiestas de Otoño* (Sep.), autumn fair, with folk dancing.

The provincial capital Córdoba, the seat of a bishop and the most important city in Andalusia after Seville, lies at the foot of the Sierra de Córdoba, an outlier of the Sierra Morena, on a plain which slopes gently down to the river Guadalquivir.

Narrow winding streets, small squares and low whitewashed houses, usually with beautiful patios which can be

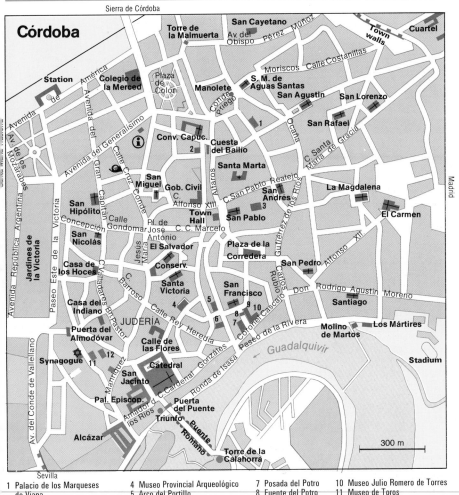

admired from the street, give the town a Moorish character inherited from its past. It is still a kind of Western European Mecca, with the famous Great Mosque, now the Cathedral, which in spite of later alterations ranks with the Alhambra in Granada as one of the two most splendid examples of Islamic art and architecture in Western Europe. In addition to the Cathedral it also has numerous churches and palaces of the 15th and 16th c. Córdoba is also famous for its silver-work.

HISTORY. – *Corduba* was already an important town in Iberian times, and in 152 B.C. it became capital of the Roman province of Hispania Ulterior. Under the Empire it alternated with Hispalis (Seville) and Italica (N of Seville) as capital of the province of Baetica. During the Visigothic period it became a bishopric, but remained a place of little importance. After the defeat of the Visigoths by the Moors in 711, however, the town enjoyed a new period of prosperity under Arab rule, particularly after 756 under the Umayyad ruler Abd ar-Rachman I, who had been driven out of Damascus. As capital of an independent Spanish

Caliphate, Córdoba developed into one of the richest cities in Europe and an important centre of Islamic culture which attracted students from all over the Western world.

With the fall of the Caliphate in 1031 the city's decline began. It fell successively under the control of Seville (1078), the Almoravides (1091) and the Almohades (1148) before returning to Christian hands in 1236. Thereafter the brilliant Arab city fell into oblivion. The magnificent structures created during the Moorish period fell into disrepair: in particular the irrigation system was neglected, and the once so fertile Campiña became an almost barren steppe. Only in recent times has the city recovered some importance as a provincial capital. – Córdoba was the birthplace of the Roman orator *M. Annaeus Seneca* (54 B.C.–A.D. 39), his son the Stoic *Lucius Annaeus Seneca* (4 B.C.–A.D.65) and his grandson the poet *Lucan*; of *Averroes*, the famous translator and interpreter of Aristotle (1126–98), the Jewish scholar *Moses Maimonides* (1135–1204) and the writer *Luis de Góngora* (1561–1627).

SIGHTS. – The city's outstanding monument is the ****Cathedral** (*Mezquita-Catedral*), formerly the principal mosque

Interior of the Mezquita-Catedral, Córdoba

of the western Islamic world and still known as the *Mezquita*. It is one of the largest mosques in the world and the finest achievement of Moorish religious art in Spain. The building of the mosque, on the site of an earlier Visigothic church, was begun in 785 under Abd ar-Rachman I, and it was enlarged to its present size (179 m long, 129 m wide) in the 9th and 10th c. About a third of the total area is taken up by the courtyard. The whole building is surrounded by a battlemented outer wall ranging in height between 9 and 20 m, with countless tower-like buttresses. After the conquest of Córdoba by the Christians the mosque became a church dedicated to the Virgen de la Asunción, but the present high choir which towers over the original building was not inserted until the 16th c. – The principal entrance, on the N side, is the *Puerta del Perdón* (1377), in Mudéjar style. Adjoining it is the *Campanario* (Bell Tower), 60 m high, built in 1593, which is crowned by a statue of the Archangel Raphael, the town's patron saint (1664). The Puerta del Perdón leads into the picturesque ***Patio de los Naranjos** ("Courtyard of Orange-Trees"), planted with orange-trees and palms, originally designed for the ablutions prescribed by Islamic law. From here the Mudéjar *Puerta de las Palmas* (1531) leads into the interior of the Mezquita-Catedral.

The impressive INTERIOR, only 11·5 m high, is seen in the semi-darkness as an apparently endless forest of columns, in vistas changing at every step. There is an astonishing impression of space. Some of the columns – a total of 856, linked longitudinally by red and white horseshoe arches – were taken from ancient buildings and Christian churches. At the Puerta de las Palmas and between the Mihrabs (prayer niches), which mark the direction of Mecca, some of the colourful and richly carved roof structure of the mosque has been exposed. Particularly fine is the third mihrab or **Mihrab Nuevo*, with the vestibule or *maqsura*, in the SE wall of the mosque. – In the heart of the mosque is the Gothic *transverse nave*, used as a choir, with the Capilla Mayor – a church in itself, built between 1523 and 1599, with the removal of 63 columns. The choir has richly carved Baroque stalls (18th c.); on the red marble high altar (1618) is a picture by Palomino. To the S of the choir is the Capilla Real. In the *Sacristy* (Sala Capitular) are nine fine statues of saints by Alonso Cano and a silver tabernacle by Enrique de Arfe (1517). In an adjoining room is the valuable *church treasury*.

Around the Cathedral. – Facing the SW corner of the Cathedral is the *Bishop's Palace* (15th c., restored 1745), built on the ruins of the old Caliph's Palace. Adjoining is the *Seminario de San Pelagio*, and beyond this, to the W, the *Composanto de los Mártires*, said to have been the place of execution of Christian martyrs. On its S side is the **Alcázar** (*Alcázar de los Reyes Cristianos*), with massive walls and towers (well worth walking round them), which was improved and rebuilt as a fortress by Alfonso XI, the Righteous, in the 16th c.; there are some remains of Moorish work. The Alcázar has beautiful gardens, which are illuminated on summer evenings. – S of the Cathedral, on the banks of the Guadalquivir, is the *Triunfo de San Rafael*, a tall column bearing a statue of the Archangel, erected in 1765. Beside it is the *Puerta del Puente*, a Doric triumphal arch (16th c.) at the end of the 16-arched ***Puente Romano** (Roman Bridge). The bridge was originally built after Caesar's triumph over Pompey, and a 200 m long Moorish bridge was later built on its foundations. At the S end of the bridge is the massive Arab *Torre de la Calahorra*, a defensive tower which now houses the Muncipal Museum. Beyond this is the suburban district of *Campo de la Verdad*. From the bridge there is a magnificent *view upstream of the town rising above the right bank of the Guadalquivir and downstream of a number of dilapidated old Moorish watermills (*molinos*).

We now return over the bridge to the town NW of the Cathedral in Plaza Bulas are the 16th c. *Casa Zoco* and the *Synagogue* (14th c.). Farther N is the **Puerta de Almodóvar**, a well-preserved Moorish gate which formerly gave access to the ghetto. NE of the Cathedral is the *Calle de las Flores*, a little lane gay with flowers.

Around the Plaza José Antonio. – In the centre of the town is the Plaza José Antonio, with an equestrian *statue of the "Gran Capitán"* Gonzalo Fernández de Córdoba (1453–1515), who was born at Montilla, near Córdoba. From the NW corner of the square a modern street, the

Roman Bridge, Córdoba

Avenida Cruz Conde, runs into the wide *Ronda de los Tejares*, which (to left) cuts across the *Avenida del Gran Capitán*, a popular promenade, with theatres, clubs, hotels and cafés, which is particularly busy on summer evenings. Towards its S end is the fortress-like collegiate church of **San Hipólito**, built by Alfonso XI in 1340 and rebuilt in 1729, with the modern tombs of Ferdinand IV and Alfonso XI on either side of the high altar. Farther S is the 15th c. church of *San Nicolás*, with an elegant octagonal tower and a fine treasury.

SE of Plaza José Antonio, in Plaza Don Jerónimo Páez, is the interesting *Museo Provincial Arqueológico*, with Iberian, Visigothic and Moorish material. A short distance E, in the picturesque quarter of the *Barrio de la Judería*, is the charming *Plaza del Potro*, in which is a fountain with the figure of a foal (*potro*), the emblem of

A flower-decked lane in Córdoba

Córdoba, which is mentioned in "Don Quixote". On the E side of the square are the **Museo Provincial de Bellas Artes**, in the former Hospital de la Caridad, containing works by Spanish masters, including Ribera, Murillo and Goya, and numerous pictures by the Córdoba-born Antonio del Castillo y Saavedra (1616–68). Adjoining this museum is the *Museo de Julio Romero de Torres* (portraits of women).

E of the Plaza del Potro are the churches of *San Pedro* (13th c.), with Moorish apses and two doorways, and *Santiago*, with a minaret dating from the time of the Reconquista. – To the NE are the church of the *Magdalena* (13th c.), now in ruins; the church of *San Lorenzo*, Romanesque and Gothic, with a splendid rose window and a tower built in 1555; and the *Casa de los Villalones*, a handsome Renaissance mansion. Farther N is the **Palacio de los Marqueses de Viana**, a princely residence with 14 beautiful patios containing a museum of leather-work.

SURROUNDINGS. – There are a number of places of great interest in the immediate neighbourhood of Córdoba.

Ruins of Medina Azahara. – Leave Córdoba by way of the new Puente San Rafael and follow a secondary road which runs SW through the Guadalquivir valley to (10 km) **Medina Azahara** (or *Medina az-Zahra*), the Versailles of Córdoba in the 10th c. – a palace-town built by Abd ar-Rachman III for his favourite (begun in 936), which was said to have accommodation for 30,000 inhabitants. After a very short life it was destroyed in 1010. Finds from the site are in the Archaeological Museum and in the Medina Azahara Museum (buildings at present under restoration).

Las Ermitas. – From the Plaza de Colón, at the NE end of the Ronda de los Tejares, the *Carretera del Brillante* climbs into the *Sierra de Córdoba* (7 km) and comes to **Las Ermitas**, a group of hermitages belonging to the Congregation of Brethren of Our Lady of Bethlehem. 18th c. church (fine view). Pillared courtyard with monument to the writer Antonio Gribo (1928).
Convento de San Gerónimo (9 km), also at the foot of the Sierra de Córdoba: built in 1408, with a beautiful Gothic cloister.
Santa María de Trassierra (16 km), on the NW slopes of the sierra, with a ruined castle enclosing a former mosque; church dating from the Reconquista.

The Ruta del Vino ("Wine Highway"). – This traverses a series of charming villages and towns, with tempting opportunites for visits to wine-cellars, bodegas and wine-tasting rooms. Leave Córdoba by the Puente San Rafael and take N IV, the Seville road, which runs through the rolling corn-growing country of the Campaña to the *Cuesta del Espino*; from here on N 331 to **Montemayor** (pop. 4000), with a castle

which is an interesting example of 14th c. military engineering. Church of Nuestra Señora de la Asunción.

Farther S, off the road to the left, is **Montilla** (alt. 379 m; pop. 22,000), the ancient *Munda Baetica* and birthplace of the famous "Gran Capitán", Gonzalo Fernández de Córdoba. The town has a number of fine churches, including Santa Clara (magnificent bas-reliefs). The principal fiesta is the Vintage Festival (Vendimia) in September, with traditional ceremonies.

N 331 continues to **Aguilar de la Frontera** (alt. 372 m; pop. 13,000), which has a history going back to the Phoenician period. Several churches, including Santa María de Soterraño (beautiful retablo) and Nuestra Señora del Carmen, with a "Jesús Caído" which is probably by Montañés, Plaza San José is a charming octagonal square. – Then via *Monturque*, the ancient *Hispalis*, with the remains of town walls, to **Lucena** (alt. 485 m; pop. 30,000), a town with a long history which is now a centre of the Andalusian wine trade. Torre del Moral, in which Boabdil, last Moorish king of Granada, was held prisoner. Several interesting churches, including the parish church of San Mateo, with the Churrigueresque Capilla del Sagrario.

From Lucena we take C 327, which runs NE to **Cabra** (pop. 20,000), formerly known as Egabro, with the interesting ruins of the Castillo de los Condes and the church of San Juan Bautista (7th c.), one of the oldest churches in Andalusia. On the *Picacho de la Virgen*, in the Fuente del Río nature reserve, is the hermitage of the Virgen de la Sierra.

From Cabra we return to Lucena and take C 338, which runs W to the little industrial town of **Puente Genil** (alt. 171 m; pop. 29,000), noted for its excellent wine and its oil-mills. – The NE on C 329 to Agúilar and so back to Córdoba. Total distance 170 km.

Towards Granada. – Leaving Córdoba by the Puente San Rafael, we follow N 432, which runs SE through the Campiña, passing through *Espejo* and *Castro del Río* with its beautiful gardens, to **Baena** (alt. 407 m; pop. 20,000), picturesquely situated on the slopes of a hill. Torre del Sol, a remnant of the old fortifications. Gothic church of Santa María, with lateral aisles, containing an interesting treasury. Convento de la Madre de Dios, in Mudéjar style, with a carved retablo.

Towards Bailén. – Leave Córdoba on N IV, going NE. Just outside the town, on the left, is the fine campus of the *Universidad Católica Laboral Onésimo Redondo*, the Catholic Workers' University of Córdoba, with some 1500 students.
After crossing the Guadalquivir by an 18th c. bridge of black marble, the *Puente de Alcolea*, and passing the village of *El Carpio* (alt. 183 m), in a valley on the right of the road, N IV comes to the long straggling little town of *Pedro Abad*. It then continues through cotton fields and large plantations of olive-trees to **Montoro** (alt. 195 m; pop. 15,000), on the left bank of the river. This was the Roman *Epora*, and became an important fortress during the Moorish period. Picturesque streets in typical Andalusian style; 16th c. churches. Well-known pilgrimage in honour of Nuestra Señora de la Fuenstanta (April).

The road then continues E to **Villa del Río** (alt. 163 m; pop. 6000), also on the left bank of the Guadalquivir, with a church converted from a Moorish alcázar.

La Coruña (Corunna)

Province: La Coruña (C).
Telephone code: 981.
Altitude: at sea level. – Population 232,000.
ⓘ **Oficina de Información de Turismo,**
Dársena de la Marina; s/n;
tel. 22 18 22.
Delegación Provincial de Turismo,
Meruelos s/n;
tel. 29 81 22.

HOTELS. – *Atlántico*, (no rest.) Jardines de Méndez Nuñez 2, 1, 200 r.; *Finisterre*, Paseo del Parrote, I, 127 r., SP; Apartment hotel *Ciudad de Coruna* (no rest.), II, 131 r., SP; *Riazor* (no rest.), II, 176 r.; *Juana de Vega 7*, III, 84 r.; *Rivas* (no rest.), Avda Fernández Latorre 45, III, 70 r.; *Los Lagos*, Polígono Residencial de Elviña, IV, 35 r., SP; *Hostal Almirante* (no rest.), Paseo de Ronda 54, P I, 20 r.; etc. – AT PLAYA DE SANTA CRISTINA (commune of Perillo, 6 km E.): *Rias Altas*, II, 103 r. – AT PLAYA DE SANTA CRUZ (6 km further E): *Porto Cobo*, II, 58 r., SP. – CAMPING SITE. – *Valdoviño*, Valdoviño near El Ferrol.

RESTAURANTS. – In hotels; also *Coral*, Estrella 5; *Duna* 2, Estrella 2; *El Rápido*, Estrella 7; *Naveiro*, San Andrés 129; etc.

EVENTS. – *Semana Santa* (Holy Week), with procession. – *Fiesta de la Virgen del Carmen* (July), with procession of boats. – *Fiesta de María Pita* (Aug.); also Summer Festival, with sporting contests, battles of flowers, bullfights and concerts. – *Galician Pilgrimage* (Sept.).

WATER SPORTS. – Facilities for a wide range of water sports on the numerous beaches close to the town – *Playa de Riazor* and *Playa de Orzán* in the Ensenada del Orzán, *Ensenada de San Amaro* at the Torre de Hércules, etc. In summer there are boat races. La Coruña has a sailing club and other water sports clubs.

SPORT and RECREATION on land. – Almost every kind of sport, including riding, tennis, golf, fishing, shooting, pelota, etc. Numerous clubs for the various sports.

La Coruña, traditionally known in English as Corunna, is the largest town in Galicia, picturesquely situated on a promontory between two bays on the Atlantic coast, in the NW corner of Spain.

It is capital of the province of the same name, an important commercial town and international port. Characteristic features of the old town are the glazed balconies (*mirandores*) which provide protection from the wind.

HISTORY. – The town, originally an Iberian settlement, was known until the medieval period as *Coronium*. In 1588 the "Invincible Armada" sailed from here, and in the following year an English expedition burned down the whole town, so that La Coruña has few ancient buildings of any importance. It is known in British history as the scene of Sir John Moore's death while withdrawing in face of the French advance during the Peninsular War (1809).

SIGHTS. – On the promontory is the **New Town** or *Pescadería*, originally a fishing village, with the characteristic *miradores*. Along the bay which forms the harbour extends the *Paseo de los Cantones*, continuing the line of the high-level motorway, with the beautiful *Jardines de Méndez Núñez*, containing various monuments, to the S. The Paseo joins two busy streets, Calle Real and Riego de Agua, which lead to the *Plaz de María Pita*. On the N side of the square is the *Palacio Municipal* (Town Hall), with a gallery of paintings by contemporary artists and the archives of the Real Academia Gallega. W of the Town Hall is the church of *San Nicolás* (18th c.), with a figure of the Virgen de los Coruñeses. Farther W again is the *Museo Provincial*, with pictures and china, antiquities and a library on overseas trade. Near the museum is the Baroque church of the *Capuchinas*, with a "St Francis" by Zurbarán.

Torre de Hércules, La Coruña

E of the Plaza de María Pita, on high ground to the N of the harbour, is the cramped **Old Town** (*Ciudad Vieja*), centred on the *Plaza de la Harina*. To the S is the *Capitanía General* (1748), which also houses law courts. To the W is the church of *Santiago*, a Romanesque church of basilican type (12th–13th c.), the oldest church in the town, with an impressive treasury. A little way N stands the church of *Santa María del Campo* (13th–15th c.), with a 14th c. tower, sculptured doorways and an interesting rose window. To the E is the church of *Santo Domingo*, with a Baroque façade and Churrigueresque altar. Here too is the *Jardín de San Carlos*, with a view of the harbour. To the S of the park is the *Castillo San Antón*, containing the *Museo Histórico-Arqueológico*.

From the Plaza de María Pita a road goes up past the cemetery to the lighthouse known as the *Torre de Hércules*, 2 km N on a rocky hill (58 m) on the NW coast of the peninsula. From the tower there are magnificent panoramic *views. The lower part of the tower is Roman (with a large inscription naming the Roman architect); the upper part dates from 1792. – W of the town are the elegant bathing beaches in the *Ensenada del Orzán*, and nearby is the attractive *Ciudad Jardín* ("Garden City").

SURROUNDINGS. – The extensive coastal strip adjoining La Coruña and the beautiful rías offer a variety of interesting excursions in the immediate vicinity of the town and farther afield.

To Lugo. – Lugo lies SE of La Coruña on N VI, the main road to Madrid, from which various secondary roads branch off. – Leave La Coruña by way of the Avenida del General Sanjurjo. Soon the road crosses the *Río Mero*, here enlarged into a ría, passes through *El Burgo* and continues through an attractive garden landscape. A road goes off on the left to El Ferrol, and N VI then crosses the *Río Mendo* and enters **Betanzos** (see p. 81), beautifully situated on a hill.

Beyond Betanzos the road passes on the left the ruined 12th c. church of *La Espenuca*, on a projecting spur of high ground. After the *Monte del Gato* (on right) there is an uphill stretch through wooded country, with many bends, after which the road continues up the valley of the *Río Mandeo* to the *Portobello* pass (510 m), the boundary between the provinces of La Coruña and Lugo. – Then via *Baamonde* to **Lugo** (see p. 150). 98 km from La Coruña.

To El Ferrol. – Leave La Coruña on N VI, and some 13 km from the town centre turn left into a side road which passes through *Bergondo* and then joins a branch of N VI. This follows a winding course to **Puentedeume** (pop. 5000), a fishing town and port on the Ría de Ares. Church of Santiago, with the tomb of Fernando de Andrade; ruins of a palace and a castle belonging to the Condes de Andrade.

The road continues N, crosses the *Río Eume* on the 14th c. *Puente de Andrade*, passes the summer resort of *Cabañas* and comes to **El Ferrol** (alt. 15 m; pop. 87,000; hotels; Parador Nacional, II, 39 r.; Almirante, II, 122 r.), founded in 1726. As the birthplace of General Franco it bears the honorific style of *El Ferrol del Caudillo*. Concealed and sheltered in its bay, it is Spain's principal naval base on the Atlantic, with shipyards, docks, a Naval Academy, etc. It has interesting fortifications and an old town of little narrow streets. – From El Ferrol a detour can be made to *Cabo Prioriño*, with the Castillo de San Felipe. On

the other bank of the Ría del Ferrol is an old fort, the *Castello La Palma*.

From El Ferrol continue N on C 646 to *Valdoviño* (bathing beach and camping site; fine views from Punta Frouzeira), beyond which is a winding stretch to *Cedeira*, with a bathing beach of fine sand in a fjord-like branch of the Ría de Cedeira. The road then continues, still with many bends, to rejoin the direct road from El Ferrol via *San Saturnino* which runs N and then E along the *Ría de Santa Marta* to **Ortigueira** (pop. 22,000), a little fishing town on a peninsula in the ría.

The road continues along the coast to the *Ría del Barquero*. 7 km N is the *Estaca de Bares*, the most northerly point in Spain, with a lighthouse. – The ría, which forms the boundary between the provinces of La Coruña and Lugo, is spanned by a railway bridge. The road continues via **Vivero**.

To Santiago de Compostela. – Leave La Coruña on N 550, which runs almost due S. In a short distance there is a fine view of the bay. The undulating road then winds up through fertile upland country, and climbs via *Rutis* and *Carral* to the *Montes del Xalo* (440 m). It then continues over the wooded *Monte de Chamarde* to **Ordenes** (alt. 285 m), a little country town situated above the Río Lavandeira. Then on to *Siquerio*, where the *Río Tambre* is crossed on a Roman bridge. 10 km beyond this is **Santiago de Compostela** (see p. 200).

To Cape Finisterre. – Leave La Coruña by way of the Avenida de Finisterre and C 552, which in a short distance affords a fine general view of the town. It then continues SW at some distance from the sea, with side roads leading down to the beaches of the Rías Bajas, to *Carballo* (pop. 22,000) and *Bayo*, where it crosses the *Río del Puerto*. Soon afterwards a minor road goes off on the right to (16 km) the *Ría Camariñas*, with the resort of the same name (hotel), noted for its pillow-lace (*encajes*). – C 552 continues to **Corcubión** (pop. 1500; Hotel El Hórreo, II, 40 r., beautifully situated above the bay), a little port with the Parque and Palacio del Príncipe. From here it is 12 km on a road along the coast, with fine views, to *Cape Finisterre ("end of the land"), a rocky promontory (lighthouse) which is Spain's most westerly point.

From a point just N of Corcubión C 550 runs S along the coast, with magnificent views of the sea. It passes through *Ezaro* and *Louro*, both with beaches, to the charming little port of *Muros* (pop. 11,000), with a Gothic church. Then along the *Ría de Muros y Noya* and, near *Cando*, over the *Río Tambre* on the medieval *Puente Alonso* (in Galician *Nafonso*), restored during the 19th c., to **Noya** (pop. 10,000), an ancient little town, beautifully situated on the bay of the same name, with three notable churches and a number of noble mansions (arcades, pointed windows), including the Casa de los Churruchaos, once the residence of the feudal lords of the town.

From Noya it is possible to continue down the coast on C 550, to *Cabo Corrubedo* and then return via Padrón to Santiago de Compostela, or alternatively to take the inland road (C 543) from Noya to Santiago (36 km).

Costa Blanca

ⓘ **Patronato Provincial de Turismo,**
Avda. de General Mola 6, Alicante;
tel. (965) 12 35 31.
Dirección Regional de Turismo,
Isidoro de la Cierva 10, Murcia;
tel. (968) 21 37 10.

The *Costa Blanca ("White Coast")
extends S from Setla on the promontory
of *La Almadraba*, at the end of the Costa
del Azahar, to the *Cabo de Gata*, taking
in the coastal regions of the provinces
of Alicante and Murcia and part of the
coast of Almería. It is mainly flat and
sandy, with numerous bathing beaches.
Thanks to its excellent climate it attracts
visitors in winter as well as in summer. −
For itineraries see under Alicante and
Cartagena.

Costa Brava

ⓘ **Mancomunidad Turistica de la Costa
Brava,**
Plaça Marqués de Camps 17, Gerona;
tel. (972) 20 84 03.
Consejeria de Turismo,
Travessía de la Creu 1, Gerona;
tel. (972) 20 13 43.
There are local tourist information offices
(*Centros de Iniciativas y Turismo*) in many
places on the Costa Brava.

HOTELS. − IN CADAQUÉS: *Llane Petit* (no rest.), II, 35 r.,
SP; *Playa Sol* (no rest.), II, 49 r., SP; *Rocamar* (no
rest.), II, 70 r., SP; *Port Lligat*, IV, 30 r., SP; several
Hostales; *Clúb Mediterranée*, 7 km outside the town.
CAMPING SITES. − IN ROSAS: *Almadabra Park*, I, 66 r.,
SP; *Bahía*, II, 52 r.; *Canyelles Platja* (no rest.), II, 99 r.;
Coral Playa, II, 128 r.; *Goya Park*, II, 224 r., SP; *Marian*,
II, 145 r., SP; *Montecarlo*, II, 126 r., SP; *Monterrey*, II,
138 r., SP; *Univers*, III, 207 r.; *Victoria*, III, 221 r., SP;
etc. CAMPING SITES. − IN LA ESCALA: *Bonaire-
Juvines*, II, 31 r.; *Nieves Mar*, II, 80 r., SP; *Voramar*, II,
40 r., SP; *Dels Pins*, III, 40 r., SP; *El Rem*, III, 16 r.;
Riomar, IV, 26 r.; Several Hostales. − IN TORROELLA DE
MONTGRI: *Picasso*, IV, 8 r.; *Vila Vella* (no rest.), IV, 26
r.; Hostal *Can Miguel*, P II, 30 r.; *Tres Delfines* (no
rest.), P II, 30 r.; *Las Cañas*, P III, 16 r., SP; *Coll* (no
rest.), P III, 24 r.; *Xicarts*, P III, 26 r., SP; etc.;
CAMPING SITE. − IN ESTARTIT: *Bell Aire* (no rest.), II,
78 r.; *Club de Campo Torre Grau*, III, 10 r., SP; *Coral*,
III, 59 r., SP; *Miramar*, III, 64 r., SP; *Amer* (no rest.), IV,
57 r., SP; *Club el Catalán* (no rest.), IV, 112 r., SP;
Flamingo, IV, 100 r.; *Las Islas*, IV, 35 r.; *Panorama*, IV,
154 r., SP; etc. − IN BAGUR: *Aiguablava*, I, 85 r., SP;
Bonaigua (no rest.), II, 47 r., SP; *Bagur*, III, 34 r.; *Plaja*,
IV, 16 r.; *Rosa* (no rest.), IV, 18 r.; etc. − AT PLAYA SA
RIERA: *Sa Riera*, III, 41 r., SP; etc.; CAMPING SITE. −
IN PALAFRUGELL: *Costa Brava*, IV, 30 r.; Hostal *Anfora*,
P III, 14 r.; *Playa*, P III, 18 r.; *San Sebastián*, P III, 15 r.;
Tamariu Playa (no rest.), P III, 22 r.; CAMPING SITE.
− IN LLAFRANCH: *Paraíso*, II, 55 r., SP; *Terramar*, II, 56 r.;
Casamar, III, 20 r.; *Llevant*, III, 20 r.; *Marinada*, IV, 12
r.; *Montecarlo*, IV, 20 r.; several Hostales. − IN TAMARIU:
Hostalillo, II, 70 r.; *Jano*, III, 49 r.; *Tamariu*, IV, 24 r.;
Hostal *Sol d'Or*, P II, 20 r.; *Vora la Mar* (no rest.), P III,
13 r.; etc. − IN PALAMÓS: *San Luis*, II, 29 r.; *Trias*, II, 81
r., SP; *Vostra Llar*, II, 45 r.; *Ancora*, III, 28 r., SP;
Marina, III, 62 r.; *San Juan*, III, 31 r., SP; *El Sosiego*, IV,
40 r.; Hostal *Vostra Llar*, P I, 30 r.; *Xamary*, P II, 36 r.;
u.a.; CAMPING SITES. − IN PLAYA DE ARO: *Columbus*,
I, 110 r., SP; *Aromar*, II, 167 r., SP; *Claramar* (no rest.),
II, 36 r.; *Cosmopolita*, II, 89 r.; *Rosmar*, II, 61 r.; *Royal
Playa* (no rest.), II, 42 r.; *S'Agoita*, II, 70 r., SP;
Acapulco, III, 64 r.; *Bell Repós*, III, 34 r.; *Costa Brava*
(no rest.). on a crag above the sea, III, 59 r.; *Japet*, III,
48 r.; *Planamar* (no rest.), III, 86 r.; *La Terraza*, III, 72
r.; *Clipper*, IV, 35 r.; several Hostales; CAMPING

Costa Brava, Tossa de Mar

SITES. – IN SAN FELIÚ DE GUIXOLS: *Reina Elisenda*, I, 68 r.; *Caleta Park*, II, 105 r., SP; *Kurhotel Hippocrates*, II, 87 r.; *Eden Roc*, II, 104 r., SP; *Montjoi*, II, 64 r., SP; *Murla Park Hotel*, II, 89 r., SP; *Panorama-Park*, II, 69 r.; *Roca*, II, 70 r., SP; *Avenida* (no rest.), III, 28 r.; *Gesoria* (no rest.), III, 34 r.; *Jecsalis*, III, 64 r.; *Montecarlo*, III, 64 r.; *Nautilus* (no rest.), III, 22 r.; *Les Noies*, III, 45 r.; *Regina*, III, 53 r.; *Rex I* (no rest.), III, 25 r.; *Mediterráneo*, IV, 36 r.; *Regente* (no rest.), IV, 36 r.; several Hostales; CAMPING SITES. – IN TOSSA DE MAR: *Gran Hotel Reymar*, quiet situation, I, 131 r., SP; *Alexandra*, II, 76 r., SP; *Costa Brava*, II, 182 r., SP; *Delfin*, II, 63 r.; *Florida*, II, 45 r.; *Mar Menuda*, II, 40 r., SP; *Vora Mar* (no rest.), II, 63 r.; *Alaska* (no rest.), III, 55 r.; *Ancora*, III, 58 r.; *Avenida*, III, 50 r.; *Cataluña* (no rest.), III, 33 r.; *Continental*, III, 63 r., SP; *Diana*, III, 21 r.; *Flor Tossa*, III, 45 r.; *Mar d'Or*, III, 51 r.; etc.; CAMPING SITES. – IN LLORET DE MAR: *Monterrey*, I, 229 r., SP; *Rigat-Park*, I, 99 r., SP; *Roger de Flor*, I, 98 r., SP; *Santa Marta*, I, 78 r., SP; *Tropic*, I, 40 r., SP; *Alexis*, II, 101 r., SP; *Anabel*, II, 230 r., SP; *Astoria Park*, II, 126 r., SP; *Bahamas*, II, 239 r., SP; *Capri*, II, 155 r., SP; *Clúamarsol*, II, 87 r., SP; *Copacabana*, II, 162 r., SP; *Frigola*, II, 217 r., SP; *Gran Hotel Flamingo*, II, 288 r., SP; *Rosamar*, II, 169 r., SP; *Xaine Park*, II, 183 r., SP; *María del Mar II* (no rest.), III, 207 r., SP; *Oasis Park*, III, 428 r., SP; *Rosamar Park*, III, 306 r., SP; *Samba*, III, 477 r., SP; etc.; CAMPING SITES.

The **Costa Brava ("Wild Coast"), the most northerly stretch of the Spanish Mediterranean coast, is an especially popular tourist area and is particularly attractive to foreign visitors by virtue of its ease of access as well as its beautiful scenery.

The coast is much indented, and for most of its length is rocky, with steeply scarped promontories which often cannot be reached by car, and sometimes only by boat. Between these inhospitable headlands, however, lie picturesque little fishing villages and towns with sandy bays.

The coast road along the Costa Brava is long, and with its many bends can be tiring for motorists. Those who prefer to avoid it can see the most attractive parts of the coast by taking side roads (mostly in good condition) from the main road, N II.

Along the Costa Brava. – Visitors coming from France should take N 114 from *Perpignan* via *Argelès-sur-Mer* to the French frontier town of *Cerbère* (49 km from Perpignan). From here the road climbs, with many bends, to the **Col de Balitres** (173 m), on the French-Spanish frontier, with fine views and the frontier and customs posts of both countries. From here the road winds down to **Port-Bou** (alt. 15 m; pop. 2500), the Spanish frontier town, with an important railway station: in view of the wider gauge of the Spanish railways passengers usually have to change trains here. Port-Bou is also a fishing port, with a church situated above the town.

The road continues S high above the sea, fringed with cliffs and dotted with islands (magnificent *views), to

San Miguel de Colera, picturesquely situated on the coast, below the road on the left. Beyond this is **Llansá** (pop. 2500), off the road on the right, which has preserved its old town walls; fortress-like church tower. Near the town is a flat bathing beach 400 m long.

Continuing along the steep and rocky coast, with beautiful views, the road comes to **Puerto de la Selva** (pop. 900), an attractively situated fishing village at the foot of the *Sierra de Roda*, on which is the ruined Benedictine abbey of San Pedro de Roda (alt. 460 m), with a church originally dating from the 8th c. (example of a Romanesque barrel vault). Above the abbey is the Castillo de San Salvador, with a magnificent *view. The village has a bathing beach.

At the next road junction bear left to reach ***Cadaqués** (alt. 20 m; pop. 1500), an attractive little fishing town, picturesquely situated in a curving bay flanked by rugged cliffs (only limited scope for bathing). The town attracts artists and has an art museum (modern art). 1 km NE is the little promontory of *Port-Lligat*, with a house belonging to the painter Salvador Dalí. – A little farther N (accessible only by boat) is *Cabo Creus (alt. 80 m), a headland known to the Greeks as Cape *Aphrodisium*, the most easterly point on the Iberian peninsula (lighthouse).

From Cadaqués return to the road junction and turn left, continuing SW to a side road on the left which leads to **Rosa** (alt. 55 m; pop. 7000), a little fishing port which was known to the Greeks as *Rhode*.

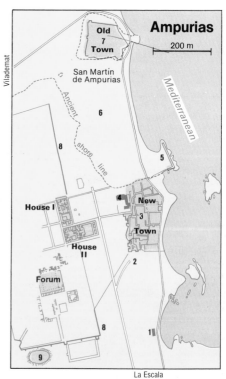

La Escala

1 Hotel Ampurias
2 Car park
3 Neapolis
4 Museum
5 Hellenistic quay
6 Old harbour (silted up)
7 Palaiapolis
8 Town walls
9 Amphitheatre

Fishing boats, Palamós

Attractively situated in a bay on the N side of the *Golfo de Rosas*, it is also a seaside resort, with a broad sandy beach (very suitable for children), a seafront promenade, a pleasure harbour and a camping site.

From Rosas C 260 runs round the Bahía de Rosas to **Castelló de Ampuias** (alt. 18 m; pop. 2000), an old market town with the 14th c. church of Santa María, which has a Gothic altarpiece and other notable works of art. Nearby lies *Ampuriabrava*, a well laid-out holiday complex in the form of a town with lagoons.

From here continue S on a secondary road, which runs through *San Pedro Pescador* (alt. 5 m; hotel), crosses the *Río Fluvía* and continues via *Armentera* to *Vilademat*, where the road runs into C 252, coming from Figueras. Here a road on the left runs down to the coast and (4 km) *Ampurias*, founded in the 6th c. B.C. as the Greek trading station of *Emporion* (="market"). The site, originally on an island but now joined to the mainland, bears the modern name of *San Martín de Ampurias*. Excavations have revealed the S town wall, extensive remains of houses and temples (large mosaic floor) and the harbour quay, constructed of massive blocks of dressed stone. Museum, with much material recovered during excavation. From the car park on the edge of the cliffs there are magnificent *views of the Golfo de Rosas and La Escala (to the right). In the picturesque bay at the foot of the cliffs (numerous caves) is a beautiful sandy beach. – The road continues S from Ampurias to **La Escala** (pop. 3500), attractively situated above the sea on a small promontory in the Golfo de Rosas. Formerly a little fishing port, it is now a popular family holiday centre, with a beach of sand and pebbles.

From La Escala the road continues S and finally joins a secondary road coming from Gerona. A road on the left runs via *Ullá* to **Torroella de Montgrí** (alt. 30 m; pop. 4500), situated on the *Río Ter*, a river with an abundant flow of water, amid rugged coastal scenery. Fine Gothic church (14th–16th c.); Renaissance Palacio Marqués de Robert, with a beautiful inner courtyard; *Castillo de Toroella* (14th c.), on Montgrí, NE of the town; *Ermita de Santa Catalina* on the hill of the same name (310 m). – 5 km NE is the port and bathing resort of *Estartit*, from which there are boat trips to the *Islas Medias* (lighthouse; caves; diving).

From Torroella the road runs through a level region (rice-fields) to *Pals*, an old-world little town picturesquely situated on a hill, *Regencós* and **Bagur** (alt. 220 m; pop. 2000), in an attractive situation above the

Cabo Bagur (lighthouse), on a rugged coast guarded by numerous watch-towers (*atalayas*). – 3 km NE is the beach of *Sa Tuna*. – 3 km S is **Aiguablava.**

SW of Bagur, reached either by a direct road or via *Regencós*, is **Palafrugell** (alt. 65 m; pop. 12,000), which together with the adjoining resorts of Llafranch, Tamariu and Calella de Palafrugell constitutes one of the major tourist centres of the Costa Brava, with beautiful beaches in the neighbouring resorts. Fine Gothic church of San Martín, with 17th c. retablo; remains of old town walls. – Two roads run SE from the town. One goes (3 km) to *Calella*, with a Botanic Garden on Cabo Roig, and *Llafranch* (also reached by a short stretch of motorway); between the two resorts runs the *Avenida del Mar. The other (4 or 5 km) goes to the picturesque *Cabo de San Sebastián* (lighthouse; hermitage) and *Tamariu*, with a number of caves (boat trips). – Beyond Palafrugell the coast road runs into C 255, coming from Gerona, which continues S to **Palamós** (alt. 10 m; pop. 10,000), an old fishing town (fish auctions) prettily situated on an outlying promontory of the *Sierra de las Gabarras*, which is now also a popular resort. Fine 14th c. church of Santa María, with a Flemish altarpiece; small Municipal Museum.

Boating harbour, San Feliú de Guixols

The road continues, at a short distance from the coast, to *San Antonio de Calonge* (with the attractively situated holiday resort of *Calonge* off the road to the right) and **Playa de Aro** (pop. 1300), a smart and popular holiday resort, with tall hotel and apartment blocks and excellent shopping facilities; good beach. – From here it is only a few kilometres S to **San Feliú de Guixols** (alt. 4 m; pop. 12,000), a little port situated in an attractive bay. As the main centre for the export of the cork grown in the surrounding area it is visited by ships of all nations, and it is also one of the most popular seaside resorts on the Costa Brava, with a beautiful seafront promenade and bathing beaches. SW of the town is *Baños de San Telmo*, with a restaurant and public gardens on the *Punta de Garbi*, crowned by the Ermita de San Telmo. 1 km S of the town is the beach of *S'Agaró*, with beautiful gardens. – In the town are remains of a 13th c. church, with the 11th c. *Porta Ferrada*, brought to light in 1931. In the Casa Barraguer is a small museum. Parish church of San Feliú (14th c., Romanesque and Gothic). – From San Feliù de Guixols the coast road runs SW, high up on the slopes of the *Puig de Cadiretas* (519 m), and continues, with an endless succession of bends and magnificent *views, to *Tossa de Mar* (pop. 2500), a popular seaside resort (bypass) delightfully situated in a bay, with a good beach and a seafront promenade with beautiful views. Remains of Roman buildings; imposing medieval walls and towers enclosing the interesting old town (Vila Vella; museum), above the modern part of the town. On a rocky spur above the town is a lighthouse.

The road continues SW, with many bends, and then runs gently downhill, with a beautiful view of **Lloret de Mar** (alt. 5 m; pop. 5000), a busy little fishing town which is also a very popular holiday resort, with a long beach, a palm-shaded promenade, numerous villas, restaurants, places of entertainment and shops.

The coast road finally reaches **Blanes** (see p. 84) and with it the boundary between the provinces of Gerona and Barcelona. Soon afterwards it joins N II, coming from the French frontier.

On the Peñiscola peninsula

Costa de la Luz

(i) **Patronato para la Promoción Turistica,**
Plaza de España s/n, Cadiz;
tel. (956) 22 48 00.

The ***Costa de la Luz** ("Coast of Light") is the stretch of the southern Spanish Atlantic coast which extends from the mouth of the *Río Guadiana* on the Portuguese frontier to the promontory of *Tarifa* on the Straits of Gibraltar. Along the coastal region, almost perpetually bathed in the warm light of the sun, are a whole succession of huge sandy beaches, well away from main roads and traffic routes. The coast of the province of Huelva in particular, with the extensive Playa de Castilla, is a bathers' paradise, bounded on the landward side by eucalyptus trees. Inland from the coast round Cádiz are vineyards and gnarled olive-trees. Almost all the villages along the coast live by fishing. – For itineraries see under Algeciras, Cádiz and Huelva.

Costa del Azahar

(i) **Servicio Territorial de Turismo,**
Plaza María Agustina 5, Castellón de la Plana;
tel. (964) 22 74 04.
Asociación Provincial de Promoción del Turismo,
Gregorio Mayans 3, Valencia;
tel. (96) 3 34 16 02.

The ***Costa del Azahar** ("Orange Blossom Coast") is the beautiful espanse of coast which extends in a wide arc along the shores of the provinces of Castellón de la Plana and Valencia. The longest and flattest stretch of coast in Spain, it gets its name from the countless orange- and lemon-trees which grow all along the coast, pervading the whole region with the delicate fragrance of their blossoms. The mild climate makes this stretch of coast ideal for both summer and winter holidays. – For itineraries see under Castellón de la Plana and Valencia.

The Balcón de Europa, on the Costa del Sol

Costa del Sol

ⓘ **Patronato Provincial de Turismo
de la Costa del Sol,**
Palacio Nacional de Congresos, Torremolinos;
tel. (952) 38 57 31.

The *Costa del Sol ("Coast of the Sun") extends along almost the whole of the Mediterranean coast of Andalusia, from *Cabo de Gata*, where the Costa Blanca ends, to the most southerly point in Spain at *Tarifa*, where the Costa de la Luz begins. The mild climate of this region (average annual temperature over 18°C) has led to the development of a densely populated holiday and tourist region almost 300 km long which attracts hosts of foreign visitors. The vivid colouring of the landscape, the abundance of trees and woodland and the luxuriant flora give the Costa de Sol its particular stamp. With its whitewashed houses, its agaves and cactuses, its farms and its cheerful villages, it is the very image of Andalusia. – For itineraries see under Almería, Algeciras and Málaga.

The beach of Salou, Costa Dorada

Costa Dorada

ⓘ **Comunidad Turistica
de la Costa Dorado,**
Levante 10, Salou (bei Tarragona);
tel. (977) 36 15 33.

The stretch of Mediterranean coast to the S of the Costa Brava is known as the *Costa Dorada ("Golden Coast"); it includes almost all the coastal area of the two provinces of Barcelona and Tarragona. This area, extending some 260 km along the Mediterranean coast, is notable for its smooth beaches with fine golden sand and is particularly popular because of its mild climate. Among the numerous seaside resorts in this region is Sitges (see p. 215). For suggested routes see Barcelona and Tarragona.

Cuenca

Province: Cuenca (CU).
Telephone code: 966.
Altitude: 998 m. – Population: 40,000.

ⓘ **Oficina de Información de Turismo,**
Dalmacio Garcia Izcarra 8;
tel. 22 22 31.

HOTELS. – *Torremanga, San Ignacio de Loyalo 9, I, 115 r.; Alfonso VIII (no rest.), Parque de San Julián 3, II, 48 r.; Figón de Pedro (no rest.), Cervantes 17, III, 28 r.; Francabel (no rest.), División Azul 7, III, 30 r.; Hostal Avenida, Avda José Antonio 39, P II, 33 r.; etc.

RESTAURANTS. – Casas Colgadas, Canónigos (impressive view); Figón de Pedro, Cervantes 15 (old Castilian style); Togar, República Argentina 3; Casa Marlo, Colón 57.

EVENTS. – Semana Santa (Holy Week), with solemn procession and concerts. – Fiesta de Nuestra Señora de la Luz (May–June), with singing competition in which groups from all over the province take part. – Fiesta de San Julián (Sept.), with bullfights, sporting contests and art exhibitions.

The provincial capital of Cuenca, which is also the seat of a bishop, is picturesquely situated on the steep rocky slopes of the Serranía de Cuenca above the deep valleys of the Río Júcar and the Río Huécar. It is one of the most picturesque of Spain's old medieval towns, famous for its Casas Colgadas ("hanging houses").

HISTORY. – This was the Roman Conca, which later fell into the hands of the Visigoths and then of the Moors, from whom it was liberated by Alfonso VIII in 1177. Thereafter it enjoyed special privileges as a frontier town and became the headquarters of the knightly Order of Santiago.

SIGHTS. – The **Old Town** has preserved much of its medieval aspect, with handsome old noble mansions sporting the coats of arms of the families to whom they once belonged. – The Gothic **Cathedral** (12th–13th c.), now declared a national monument, has a richly decorated *interior. High altar by Ventura Rodríguez (18th c.), with magnificent grilles dating from 1557. Two particularly fine works of art are a statue of the Virgen del Sagrario and a Crucifixion, both 12th c. The valuable treasury contains among much else two pictures by El Greco. – On the W side of the square is the Ayuntamiento (Town Hall) of 1762. To the S of the Plaza Mayor are the famous **Casas Colgadas** ("hanging houses") above the

The Casas Colgadas, Cuenca

Río Huécar (here spanned by eight bridges), with their balconies projecting over the abyss. They contain a small museum of Spanish abstract art and a restaurant. – N of the Plaza Mayor is the church of *San Miguel*, high above the gorge of the Río Júcar, with a Mudéjar ceiling. – At the foot of the old town, on the right bank of the Huécar, is the *Museo Arqueológico*, with a collection of coins, Roman mosaics and pottery.

SURROUNDINGS. – There are numerous interesting places to visit in the immediate surroundings of the town. – 36 km N through the Júcar valley is the **Ciudad Encantada** ("Enchanted City"), a natural rock labyrinth which looks like a ruined city, with caves, lakes and waterfalls. From here it is possible to continue to *Uña* (viewpoint) and an artificial lake, the *Embalse La Toba*. – 22 km away (SE on N 420, then a side road) is the group of curious natural features known as **Las Torcas**: funnel-shaped depressions up to 700 m in diameter produced by subterranean erosion of the rock.

To the Rincón de Ademuz. – N 420 leads SE from Cuenca via Las Torcas (above) and continues through the beautiful wooded landscape of the southern part of the *Serranía de Cuenca*. It passes through the ancient little fortified town of *Cañete* (alt. 1074 m), with a 15th c. castle, to the **Rincón de Ademuz**, an enclave of the province of Valencia caught between Cuenca and Teruel. The highest peak in this area is the *Pico Calderón* (1834 m), and the chief place is the picturesquely situated little town of *Ademuz*. Near the Río Turia is the *Ermita de Nuestra Señora de la Huerta* (13th c.), built by Jaime I.

Over the Puerto de Tordiga. – Leave Cuenca on N 320, which runs SE and climb, with many bends, to the *Puerto de Tordiga* (1200 m) , beyond which (36 km from Cuenca) a road goes off on the right to (12 km) *Valera de Arriba*, with the remains of the Roman town of *Valeria* (seat of a bishop until the 7th c.). Another 12 km S is a large artificial lake, the *Embalse de Alarcón*.

Continuing on N 320, we pass through *Almodóvar del Pinar* and come to the little town of **Motilla del Palancar** (alt. 900 m), on the *Río Valdemembro*, at the meeting-place of a number of roads. From here

N III leads E over the *Puerto de Contreras* to **Valencia**. Going W along N III, we come in 18 km to **Alarcón** (alt. 837 m), beautifully situated to the S of the road in a bend on the Río Júcar; it has a fine church and a castle (Parador Nacional Marqués de Villena, II, 11 r.). To the N of the road is the *Embalse de Alarcón*, an artificial lake 25 km long formed by the damming of the Río Júcar; the road cuts across its S end.

Over the Puerto de Cabrejas. – N 400 runs W from Cuenca, crosses the valley of the Júcar and winds up to the *Puerto de Cabrejas* (1150 m). It then runs through a thinly populated area, with many ruined churches and castles, to *Carrascosa del Campo* (alt. 898 m), passes the *Santuario de Riánsares* and comes to **Tarancón** (alt. 700 m; pop. 7000), a little country town with a Gothic church and a mansion built by Queen María Cristina. Several roads meet here. Going SE along N III, we come to **Saelices**, with the remains of a Roman aqueduct which served the town of *Segobriga*, 3 km SW. Segobriga was founded in the 2nd c. B.C. and rose to considerable importance, became a Visigothic archbishopric between the 6th and 8th c. and was then destroyed by the Moors. Excavations have brought to light the remains of an amphitheatre and a Visigothic basilica; small museum. – Half way between Saelices and Tarancón a minor road runs N to **Uclés**, with a monastery known as the "Escorial of La Mancha" which was at one time held by the knightly Order of Santiago. Refectory with magnificent panelling (16th c.); church of 1529.

Denia

Province: Alicante (A)
Telephone code: 965.
Altitude: 12 m. – Population: 17,000.
ⓘ **Oficina de Información de Turismo,**
Petrocinio Ferrandiz;
tel. 78 09 57.

HOTELS. – IN DENIA: *Denia*, Partida Suertes del Mar, II, 280 r., SP; *Los Ángeles*, Playa de las Marinas 649, III, 59 r., SP; *Costa Blanca*, Pintor Llorens 3, IV, 53 r.; *Las Rotas*, Partida les Rotes 47, IV, 27 r.; Hostal *Rosa* (no rest.), Partida Marines 197, P II, 19 r., SP; *Villa Amor*, Partida Marines 752, P II, 20 r.; etc.; CAMPING SITE at *Punta de los Molinos* and others in the area. – IN JÁVEA: *Parador Nacional Costa Blanca*, Playa de Arenal 2, I, 65 r., SP; *Toscamar*, on road to Cabo de la Nao, 5 km S, II, 140 r., SP (apartment hotel); *Miramar* (no rest.), Almirante Bastarreche 12, III, 26 r.; *Plata*, Avda Montañar 83, III, 34 r.; Villa *Naranjos*, Carretera Montañar, III, 145 r., SP; *Jávea* (no rest.), Pío X 5, IV, 19 r.; Hostal *Costa Mar*, Caleta 4, P II, 18 r.; *Portichol*, Partida Portichol 157, P II, 11 r.; etc.

Denia, now a seaside resort on the Mediterranean, has a history going back to Greek and Roman times. It was known to the Greeks (8th c. B.C.) as Hemeroskopeion, to the Romans as Dianium. During the Moorish period, between 715 and 1253, it was a flourishing port, which at one time was in control of Majorca. It is today of importance as a port for the shipment of raisins.

SIGHTS.– The town, dominated on the S by the limestone bulk of *Mongó* (735 m), lies at the foot of a hill crowned by a castle, from which there are extensive views (open-air theatre). It has two large sandy beaches and a water sports club. – Baroque church of Santa María (1734), with tile decoration.

SURROUNDINGS. – Rewarding climb to the top of *Mongó*, with the ruins of the *Casa de Biot* and magnificent *views of the coast and the sea; the climb takes about 4 hours. – Farther S is the seaside resort of *Jávea*, a little port at the mouth of the *Río Jalón*, with walls and towers, the Castillo de San Juan and a fortified Gothic church (14th c.) – 2 km E of Jávea is *Cabo de San Antonio* (alt. 174 m), with a lighthouse from which there are far-ranging views. – 4 km S of Jávea is *Cabo de la Nao*, the most easterly point in the range of coastal hills, to the S of which is the *Punta de Ifach*, with the rocky mass of the *Peñón de Ifach* rearing out of the sea to a height of 383 m: see under Benidorm. – Near Jávea are stalactitic caves, the *Cueva del Órgano* and the *Cueva del Oro*.

Écija

Province: Seville (SE).
Telephone code: 954.
Altitude: 101 m. – Population: 53,000.
ⓘ Oficina de Información de Turismo,
Avenida Andalucia s/n;
tel. 83 02 50.

HOTELS.– *Hostal Astigi*, km 450 on N IV, P II, 18 r.; *Ciudad del Sol* (no rest.), Miguel de Cervantes 42, P II, 34 r.; *Santiago* (no rest.), km 455 on N IV, P II, 24 r.; *Vega de la Hermanos* (no rest.), km 461 on N IV, P III, 12 r.

EVENTS. – *Fiesta de la Primavera* (May), with parades, bullfights, and a full programme of folk celebrations. – *Fiesta de San Mateo* (Sept.), with traditional processions.

Écija, situated on the left bank of the Río Genil (which is navigable at this point), is an old town – the Roman Astigi – with considerable industries. It has picturesque narrow streets and a number of notable churches.

SIGHTS. – Church of **Santa Cruz** (17th c.), with remains of an Arab tower and a figure of Nuestra Señora del Valle (probably 6th c.). – Church of **San Juan** (19th c.), with a tower reminiscent of the Giralda in Seville; figure of Christ by Montañés. – **Palacio del Marqués de Cortés**, with a Plateresque doorway; two other interesting noble mansions. – The church of *La Merced*, originally conventual, has a 16th c. retablo.

Elche

Province: Alicante (A).
Telephone code: 965.
Altitude: 88 m. – Population: 160,000.
ⓘ Oficina de Información de Turismo,
Parque Municipal;
tel. 45 27 47.

HOTELS. – *Huerto del Cura*, García Sanchiz 14, I, 59 r., SP.; *Cartagena* (no rest.), Residencia Cartagena, II, 34, r.; *Don Jaime*, Avda Primo de Rivera, 5, III, 64 r.; *Hostal Candilejas*, (no rest.), Dr Ferrán 19, P II, 24 r.; *Galicia*, Playa de Pinet 1, P II, 24 r.; *Quesada* (no rest.), Pérez Galdós 2, P II, 13 r.; *Maruja*, Playa del Pinet 46, P III, 30 r.; etc. – Good CAMPING SITE in the Palm Forest (with open-air swimming pool); two others SW of the town.

RESTAURANT. – *Parque Municipal*, 7 in idyllic surroundings, Paseo Alfonso XIII; etc.

EVENTS. – *Misterio de Elche* (Aug.), a 13th c. mystery play, performed in the church of Santa María on the basis of a special privilege granted by Pope Urban VIII: a fascinating performance, with music.

Elche, situated on both banks of the Río Vinalopó in one of the hottest parts of Spain, is noted for its *Palm Forest, a feature unique in Europe. With its flat-roofed whitewashed houses and the domes of its churches, it has the air of an Oriental town set down on the edge of an oasis planted with palms.

In the Municipal Park, Elche

SIGHTS. – The 17th c. church of **Santa María**, dedicated to the Virgen de la Asunción, has a richly decorated *main doorway* and a Baroque façade (by Nicolás de Bussi). The mystery play on the subject of the Assumption of the Virgin, the *Misterio de Elche*, is performed here. From the *tower* (37 m high) there are good views of the town and the Palm Forest. – N of the church is the *Palacia de Altamira* (15th c.), now declared a national monument, which provided a lodging for the kings of Spain, including Ferdinand the Catholic. – Farther N again is the *Parque Municipal*, with the adjoining

Museo Arqueológico, which has a collection of prehistoric and Greco-Roman antiquities, including a copy of the "Lady of Elche" (see p. 29), an Iberian figure dating from the 4th or 3rd c. B.C. which was found near Elche in 1897; the original is in the Archaeological Museum in Madrid. – There is a very fine view of the town from the *Puente de Santa Teresa*, a bridge in Gothic style (1705) which crosses the Río Vinalopó a little way SW of the Plaza Baix. Farther S is the *Museo de Arte Contemporáneo*.

Immediately E of the town is the ***Palmeral de Europa**, the largest forest of palms in Europe. A visit takes about 2 hours; the best time is the early morning (guide advisable). The plantations, originally established by the Moors, are surrounded by walls or hedges. Water for irrigation comes from a reservoir in the Vinalopó valley, 5 km away. – The palms, most of them between 20 and 25 m in height and some as high as 33 m, stand with "their feet in water and their heads in the fires of heaven", in the words of an Arab saying. Among them are planted pomegranate trees, in the shade of which fodder crops and vegetables are grown. Particular features of interest are the *Palmera Imperial*, a male palm said to be 200 years old, with seven lateral stems branching off the main trunks (in the *Huerto del Cura* or "Priest's Garden"); the *Palmeras Romeo y Julieta*; and the *Villa Carmen*, with a belvedere (view). – The date palm (*Phoenix dactylifera*; Spanish (*palmera*) requires careful cultivation. The dates (which are inferior in quality to those of the Sahara) are harvested between November and the spring; each tree bears dates (about 77 lb) only every other year. From April onwards some of the male palms are bound up so that they become bleached; the bleached palms (*ramillets*) are then sold all over Spain for Palm Sunday, and after being blessed are hung from the balconies of houses.

SURROUNDINGS. – 2·5 km S of Elche on the secondary road to Dolores is the excavation site of **La Alcudia de Elche**, where the famous "Lady of Elche" was found. The small *site museum* contains Iberian and Roman material found in the area.

14 km SE of Elche, on the coast road (N 332), is the **Albufera de Elche**, a lagoon N of the *Golfo de Santa Pola* from which sea-salt is extracted. Nearby is **Santa Pola** (pop. 8700; hotels: Pola-Mar, II, 76 r., beach; Rocas Blancas (no rest.), II, 100 r.; Espinosa, IV, 39 r.), a fishing port from which a boat trip can be taken to the island of *Tabarca* (lighthouse). For further excursions see under Alicante.

El Escorial

Province: Madrid (M).
Telephone code: 91.
Altitude: 1028 m. – Population: 8000.

(i) **Oficina de Información de Turismo,**
Floridablanca 10, San Lorenzo de el Escorial;
tel. 8 90 15 54
Administración del Patrimonio Nacional,
Real Monasterio;
tel. 8 96 15 12.

HOTELS. – *Victoria Palace*, Juan de Toledo 4, I, 89 r.; SP; *Miranda Suizo*, Floridablanca 20, III, 47 r.; *Hostal Cristina*, Juan de Toledo 6, P II 16 r.; *Jardín*, Leandro Rubio 2, P II, 22 r.; *Malagón*, San Francisco 2, P II, 10 r.; *Vasco*, Plaza de Santiago 11, P II, 20 r.

RESTAURANTS. – *Mesón la Cueva, Sant Anton 4 (typical Castilian style), *Alaska*, Plaza San Lorenzo 4; *Mesón Serrano*, Floridablanca 4; *Castilla*, Plaza de la Constitución 2; *El Parque*, Plaza Virgen de Gracia 1 (garden restaurant, summer only); *Charolés*, Floridablanca 24; etc.

San Lorenzo de el Escorial, or El Escorial for short, consists of the old village of El Escorial de Abajo (alt. 923 m) and the upper part of the town to the W, El Escorial de Arriba (alt. 1028 m), a summer resort popular with the people of Madrid which originally grew up round the famous palace-cum-monastery, the most monumental complex of buildings in Spain.

The **Monasterio de San Lorenzo de el Escorial, built by King Philip II in fulfilment of a vow to St Lawrence, was designed both as the burial-place of his father Charles V and as a summer residence. It was begun in 1563 to the plans of Juan Bautista de Toledo, an architect who had been trained in Italy, and after his death in 1567 was completed by Juan de Herrera (1584). The decoration was the work of numerous Spanish painters and of a number of Italian artists, including Pellegrino Tibaldi and Luca Giordano and the sculptor Pompeo Leone. – The massive pile, built of greyish-white granite in the form of a rectangle 207 m long by 161 m wide, with four corner towers, is more like a fortress than a princely residence. Although conceived in the spirit of 16th c. Italian classicism, it marks the beginnings of Spanish Baroque architecture. – The heart of the whole structure is the *church*, with its two tall towers and dome. At the W end of the church is the entrance courtyard; on the S side is the *cloister*, with the sacristy and

The monastery of San Lorenzo de el Escorial

chapter rooms; to the E and N extends the *royal palace*. Altogether the Escorial has 16 courtyards, 2673 windows, 1250 doors, 86 staircases and 88 fountains, and the corridors have a total length of 16 km.

TOUR. – On the W side of the monastery complex is the *Plaza del Monasterio* or *Lonja*, bounded on the W by the former *Casa de la Compaña* (17th c.), now the Augustinian University. On the S side of the square is the *Galería de Convalecientes*, a two-storey pillared loggia opening into the beautiful monastery garden. – From the E side of the square we pass through the main entrance, the *Puerta Principal*, into the *Patio de los Reyes*, an outer courtyard 64 m by 38 m, flanked on the left by the *Colegio* and on the right by the *Convento* (the actual monastic buildings) and the Library. On the far side is the *Church (Basilika)*, with two towers 72 m high and six massive statues of kings of Israel (1584) on the façade.

The INTERIOR is entered through the *Coro Bajo* (lower choir). On the spherical vaulting are frescoes by Luca Giordano (*c.* 1695. – The high altar in the *Capilla Mayor*, 26 m high, is made of precious marbles, with *gilded bronze figures (1598). In a chapel in the *Coro Alto* (upper choir) is a life-size marble crucifix by Benvenuto Cellini (1562). – Under the Capilla Mayor is the *Panteón de los Reyes, begun by Philip II but not completed until 1654, with the sarcophagi of the kings of Spain (only a few of the 26 sarcophagi being still unoccupied). Under the Sacristy is the **Panteón de los Infantes** (1862–88). – From the S aisle we pass through the *Ante-Sacristy* (ceiling painting by Nicolás Granelo) into the *Sacristy*, which contains Claudio Coello's finest work, including the "Feast of the Sacred Host" (1684).

From the Sacristy or the vestibule of the church we enter the **Lower Cloister** (*Claustro Principal Bajo*), decorated with frescoes. The courtyard is known as the *Patio de los Evangelistas*, from the statues of the four Evangelists on the little temple in the centre. – On the S side of the cloister are the **Chapter Rooms** (*Salas Capitulares*). In the SW corner is the *Old Church* (Inglesia Vieja), used while the monastery was under construction, with

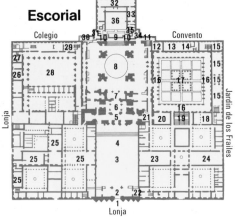

Escorial

Colegio   Convento

Lonja

Jardín de los Frailes

Lonja

1 Main entrance
2 Vestibule (Library above)
3 Patio de los Reyes
4 Steps leading up to church
5 Narthex (western porch)
6 Coro Bajo (Lower Choir)
7 Choir for collegians
8 Basilica
9 Presbytery and high altar
10 Royal oratories
11 Steps up to Coro Alto and down to Panteón
12 Ante-Sacristy
13 Sacristy
14 Altar of Sagrada Forma
15 Chapter Rooms
16 Lower Cloister
17 Patio de los Evangelistas
18 Old Church
19 Grand Staircase
20 Sala de la Trinidad
21 Sala de los Secretos (formerly porter's lodge)

22 Entrance to Library (over Vestibule)
23 Manuscript Library
24 Refectory
25 Colegio
26 Entrance to Bourbon palace
27 Palace staircase
28 Apartments of palace
29 Exit from palace and entrance to 16th c. apartments
30 Sala de Batallas
31 Apartments of the Infanta Isabel Clara Eugenia
32 Gallery of royal apartments
33 Throne Room
34 Philip II's Cell
35 Alcoves and Philip II's oratory
36 Patio de los Mascarones

Titian's "Martyrdom of St Lawrence" (1564). – The *Grand Staircase* (Escalera Principal) has a ceiling painting by Luca Giordano.

On the S side of the Patio de los Reyes is the ***Library** (*Biblioteca de Impresos*), 54 m long, richly decorated with frescoes by Pellegrino Tibaldi and Bartolommeo Carducci. It contains 40,000 volumes, including the "Codex Aureus" written by the German Emperor Conrad II (completed in 1039).

Adjoining the N side of the church is the **Royal Palace** (*Palacio Real*), sumptuously decorated and furnished by Philip II's successors in the styles of the 17th and 18th c. Its principal treasures are its 338 tapestries, including 150 Spanish (some after cartoons by Goya) and 163 Flemish. On the ground floor is the *Picture Gallery, with many important works, including pictures by Velázquez,

El Greco, Ribera, Titian, Tintoretto, Veronese, Giordano, Palma Giovane, Rubens, Bosch and Roger van der Weyden. In the basement is the *Museum of Architecture*, with a collection which includes plans by J. de Herrera.

In *Philip II's Cell* (Habitación de Felipe II) are Bosch's "Seven Deadly Sins" and 11 watercolours ascribed to Albrecht Dürer. In an adjoining alcove Philip II died on 13 September 1598.

To the E of the monastery are the **Jardines del Príncipe**, with beautiful avenues of trees including individual specimens of gigantic size, some 250 years old. In the lower part of the gardens is the **Casita del Príncipe*, a country house built in 1772 for the prince who later became Charles IV, with valuable furniture and numerous pictures.

SURROUNDINGS. – 3 km S of the Escorial is the little hill known as the *Silla de Felipe II*, with steps hewn from the rock, from which Philip used to contemplate the building of the Escorial.

To the Valle de los Caídos. – 13 km N of the Escorial on C 600, also accessible from the motorway or N VI (5 km), is the **Valle de los Caídos** ("Valley of the Fallen"), officially the *Monumento Nacional de Santa Cruz del Valle de los Caídos*, a memorial to those who died in the Spanish Civil War (1936–39). Here too are buried José Antonio Primo de Riviera, founder of the Falange, and Generalísimo Franco. Built 1950–59, the memorial consists of a crypt (the Basilica) hewn from the rock and extensive conventual buildings laid out round a large courtyard. Above this, on a rocky hill, the Risco de la Nava (1393 m), is a cross 150 m high, a landmark visible from afar.

In the Escorial

Estella

Province: Navarre (NA).
Telephone code: 948.
Altitude: 426 m. – Population: 10,000.

ⓘ **Oficiana de Información de Turismo,**
Bajos del Ayuntamiento (Town Hall),
Paseo de la Inmaculada 1;
tel. 55 08 14.

HOTELS. – Hostal *San Andrés*, Plaza Santiago 58, P
III, 28 r.; *San Andrés* (no rest), José Antonio 1, P III,
10 r.

RESTAURANTS. – *El Bordón*, San Andrés 6, 1st floor;
La Cepa, Plaza de los Fueros 18, 1st floor; *Tatana*, Don
García el Restaurador 3.

EVENTS. – *Patronal festival* (Aug.) in honour of the
Virgen del Puy and San Andrés.

**The ancient little town of Estella,
situated on the Río Ega, off the main
road, was the residence of the kings
of Navarre during the Middle Ages
and a staging point for pilgrims
travelling to Santiago de Compostela.**

SIGHTS. – The town has a number of
handsome mansions of the 16th–18th c.
and many old churches and palaces. –
Church of **San Pedro de la Rúa** (12th
c.), with an interesting façade and a
beautiful cloister. – Church of **San
Miguel** (12th c.), with fine sculpture and
a 14th c. *retablo*. – Church of *San
Sepulcro*, with a Gothic doorway (13th
c.). – Notable among the many palaces are
the *Palacio Real*, an important building of
the late 12th c., the *Palacio de los Reyes
de Navarra* and the *Palacio del Duque de
Granada* (12th c.).

SURROUNDINGS. – 3 km SE, off N 111, is the
Monasterio de Santa María de Irache (12th c.),
with a 16th c. Plateresque cloister and a notable
Romanesque apse.

Estepona

Province: Málaga (MA).
Telephone code: 952.
Altitude: 21 m. – Population: 24,000.

ⓘ **Oficina de Información de Turismo,**
Avenida Miguel Cano 1, Marbella;
tel. 77 14 42.
Oficina de Información de Turismo,
Paseo Marítimo Pedro Manrique s/n;
tel. 80 09 13.

HOTELS. – *Atalaya Park*, km 168 on N 340, I, 239 r.,
SP, golf; *Golf el Paraiso*, km 167 on N 340, I, 201 r.,
SP, golf; *Santa Marta*, Apardo 2, II, 37 r., SP; *Caracas*,
Avda San Lorenzo 50, III, 27 r.; *Dobar* (no rest.), Avda

de Espana 117, III, 39 r.; *Hostal Buenavista*, Paseo
Marítimo, P II, 38 r.; *Las Delicias* (no rest.), Delfin 10,
P II, 26 r. – CAMPING SITE. – *La Chimenea*, km 162·8
on N 340.

RESTAURANTS. – *Molino*, Urb. El Saladillo, 10 km E
(French cuisine); *El Carrusel*, Urb. El Saladillo, 10 km
E (French cuisine); *Le Castel*, Bahía Dorada, 7 km W
(French cuisine); *Bahía Dorada*, 7 km W.

EVENTS. – *Fiestas de San Isidro* (May), with an
Andalusian procession of riders. – *Fiestas de San Juan*
(June), with a fair, fireworks and processions. –
Fiestas de la Virgen del Carmen, with sea procession,
fair and fireworks over the water (July).

WATER SPORTS. – Facilities for many kinds of water
sports on several beaches (4 km long); modern marina
with 900 berths; sailing club; fishing, regattas, water
skiing.

SPORT and RECREATION on land. – Two golf-
courses (18 holes), tennis, riding.

**This little fishing port on the coast
road (N 340) along the Costa del Sol,
at the foot of the Sierra Bermeja, has
a history going back to Roman times.
In the neighbourhood are the ruins
of the thousand-year-old aqueduct
of Salduba, and in the town itself are
remains of an Arab fortress and
medieval watch-towers. Estepona
is now a tourist and holiday centre
which attracts many foreign visitors.**

Extremadura

Autonomous Region.
Organ of Government: Junta Regional de
Extremadura.
Provinces: Cáceres and Badajoz.

**Extremadura (in English tradi-
tionally Estremadura) is a barren
region, often called the ''Ceni-
cienta'' (Cinderella) of Spain. It is
arid, with large areas of stony moorland (jarales or tomillares), particularly at the foot of the Sierra de
Gata (the district of Las Hurdes,
formerly one of the poorest parts of
Spain, with some recent development of wheat-growing). Perhaps
because of its very poverty Extremadura produced many conquistadors, who on returning to their
homeland employed the wealth they
had acquired overseas in the building of magnificent palaces.**

Extremadura is the western continuation
of the Meseta, bounded on the W by
Portugal. In this area, however, the

Monument to Pizarro in Trujillo (Extremadura)

plateau is more deeply slashed by the valleys of the *Tajo* (Tagus) and *Guadiana* and their tributaries. It is separated from León and Old Castile to the N by the *Sierra de Gata* (1735 m), the *Béjar* uplands and the *Sierra de Gredos* (2592 m); in the S it slopes down towards Andalusia in the gentle gradients of the *Sierra Morena*; and it is divided into *Extremadura Alta* (the Tajo Basin) and *Extremadura Baja* (the Guadiana basin) by the *Sierra de Guadalupe* (1736 m).

The region's main source of revenue is the growing of corn and legumes (only in the Cáceres area and Extremadura Baja). Vines, olives, figs and almonds flourish in the valleys. Pigs are herded in the oak-forests, and Extremadura hams (*jamones*) are reputed to be best in Spain. – From time immemorial Extremadura has been traversed during the winter months by flocks of merino sheep, which come down from the Meseta in autumn to seek fresh grazing – a transhumant system known as the *Mesta*. In order to avoid disputes between the settled farmers and the sheep-owners a special court, the Consejo de la Mesta, was established in 1526, and a law passed in 1834 provided that a strip of grazing land (*cordel, cañada*) 90 yards wide should be left on either side of main roads for the benefit of the passing flocks.

In recent years many dams have been built in Extremadura Baja, creating large artificial lakes (*embalses*). Under the Badajoz Plan an extensive area in the Guadiana valley is to be brought into cultivation by the construction of five artificial lakes and 350 km of irrigation canals, together with roads, railways and farming settlements.

Fuengirola

Province: Málaga (MA).
Telephone code: 952.
Altitude: at sea level. – Population: 30,000.
(i) **Oficina de Información de Turismo**.
Plaza de España;
tel. 47 61 66.

HOTELS. – *Las Palmeras*, Paseo Marítimo Fuengirola, I, 398 r., SP, golf; *Las Pirámides*, Paseo Marítimo, I, 320 r., SP; *Ángela*, Paseo Príncipe de España, II, 260 r., SP; *Florida*, Paseo Marítimo, II, 116 r., SP; *Mare Nostrum*, km 207 on N 340; II, 257 r., SP; *Torreblanca*, Urb. Torreblanca del Sol, II, 198 r., SP; *El Cid* (no rest.), Avda del Ejército, III, 46 r.; *Mas Playa*, Urb. Torreblanca del Sol, III, 108 r., SP; *Stella Maris*, Paseo Príncipe de España, III, 196 r., SP. – CAMPING SITES: *Calazul*, km 200·3 on N 340; *Playa la Debla*, km 200·5 on N 340.

RESTAURANTS. – *Fuengirola Playa*, Paseo Marítimo; *Don Bigote*, Calvo Sotelo 39 (Andalusian style); *La Langosta*, Francisco Cano 1; *Sin Igual*, Ramón y Cajal.

EVENTS. – *Holiday courses* for foreigners, run by the University of Granada (summer). – *Fiestas* (Oct.), with fair, pilgrimage and bullfights.

WATER SPORTS. – Facilities for a variety of water sports on the beaches (total length 6·5 km); wide seafront promenade; marina; Club Náutico (hire of boats).

SPORT and RECREATION on land. – Golf in Mare Nostrum and Mijas (4 km); bullfights.

The seaside resort on Fuengirola on the Costa del Sol, 29 km from Málaga on N 340, lies in the shelter of the Sierra de Mijas. Known to the Romans as Suel, it has the ruined Moorish Castillo de Sohail, and there are a number of old watch-towers in the surrounding area.

SURROUNDINGS. – From the neighbouring resort of *Santa Fé de los Boliches*, to the E, a road runs inland (9 km) to the picturesque village of *Mijas*, on the southern slopes of the Sierra de Mijas.

Galicia

Autonomous Region.
Organ of Government: Xunta de Galicia.
Provinces: La Coruña, Lugo, Orense and Pontevedra.

Galicia is given its particular character by the numerous bays and estuaries (rías) which cut deep into the land at the mouths of the rivers – the Rías Altas on the N coast and the Rías Bajas on the W coast. These inlets, many of which have beautiful sandy beaches, not only provide

refuges for shipping in the storms which frequently sweep this coast but also accommodate major international ports such as Vigo and La Coruña.

Galicia occupies the whole of the northwestern corner of the Iberian peninsula, extending S to the Portuguese frontier. Here there are none of the high mountain ranges found elsewhere in Spain. It is a region of wooded valleys (pines, oaks, eucalyptus), forming elongated basins such as that of the *Miño*, bounded by chains of hills; between them lie plateaux, slashed by numerous rivers flowing through narrow steep-sided valleys.

Fishing plays an important part in the economy of this rather backward region, and every day the sardine fishermen can be seen sailing out to sea in small fleets. In the interior peasants gain a modest subsistence on small and heavily burdened tenant holdings, growing maize, cereals and (in southern Galicia) vines. The mild, damp climate also favours stock-farming. – The Galicians (Spanish *Gallegos*, Galician *Galegos*) resemble the Portuguese in language and character. They are proud of their own country – there is a separatist movement, the VPG – but have the reputation among other Spaniards of being rather slow and stolid.

View of the Ría de Vigo

Gandía

Province: Valencia (V).
Telephone code: 96.
Altitude: 22 m. – Population: 48,000.
Oficina Municipal de Turismo,
Parque de la Estación;
tel. 2 84 24 07.

HOTELS. – *Bayren I*, Paseo de Neptuno, I, 164 r., SP, *Bayren II*, Mallorca 19, II, 125 r.; *Madrid*, Castilla la Nueva 22, II, 108 r., SP, *Porto* (no rest.), Avda María Angeles Suarez, II, 135 r.; *Riviera* (no rest.), Paseo de Neptuno 29, II, 72 r.; *Los Robles*, Formentera, II, 240 r., SP; *Safari*, Legazpi 3, II, 113 r., SP; *San Luis*, Paseo de Neptuno 6, II, 72 r.; *Tres Anclas*, Playa, II, 332 r., SP; *Gandia Playa*, Devesa 17, III, 90 r., SP; *Ernesto*, Valencia 40, IV, 86 r.; *Europa*, Levante 12, IV, 23 r.; *Los Naranjos* (no rest.), Pio XI 57, IV, 35 r.; *Hostal Duque Carlos* (no rest.), P II, 28 r.; *Mavi*, P II, 40 r.; etc. – Two CAMPING SITES on the beach.

RESTAURANTS. – *Club Náutico*, Paseo de Neptuno (magnificent view); *Marisquería As de Oros*, Alcira 4 (fish specialities); *Mesón de los Reyes*, Calle Mallorca 39.

EVENTS. – *Fallas de San José* (Mar.), fiesta in honour of St Joseph. – *Beach Festival* (mid Aug.).

SPORT. – Facilities for a variety of water sports (water skiing, etc.) on the beaches round the port of *Grao de Gandía*; riding, tennis.

Gandía, once the seat of a dukedom granted to the Borja (Borgia) family, is situated in the richest and most populous huerta in the former kingdom of Valencia, with beautiful beaches which have enabled it to develop into a lively tourist centre.

SIGHTS. – Fine Gothic **collegiate church** (c. 1400), with richly decorated doorways, including the 15th c. *S doorway* and the *Apostles' Doorway*. – **Palacio de los Duques de Gandía** (Ducal Palace), built in the 16th and 18th c.; residence of the Borja family (charming Patio de Armas, decorated with coats of arms; state apartments; small museum).

Gerona

Province: Gerona (GE).
Telephone code: 972.
Altitude: 70 m. – Population: 87,000.
Oficina de Información de Turismo,
Ciudadanos 12;
tel. 20 16 94.
Consejeria de Turismo,
Travessía de la Creu 1,
tel. 20 13 43
Oficina Municipal de Turismo,
Plaza del Ví 1;
tel. 20 16 94

HOTELS. – *Costabella* (no rest.), Avda Franca 61, II, 22 r.; *Immortal Gerona* (no rest.), Carretera Barcelona 31, II, 76 r.; *Ultonia* (no rest.), Avda Jaime I 22, II, 45 r.; *Europa* (no rest.), Carrer Julio Garreta 23, III, 26 r.; *Condal* (no rest.), Juan Maragall 10, IV, 39 r.; *Peninsular* (no rest.), Nou 3, IV, 68 r. – IN FORNELLS DE LA SELVA (5 km): *Fornells Park* II, 36 r. – CAMPING SITES: numerous sites in the immediate vicinity on the Costa Brava. – IN FIGUERAS: *Ampurdan*, km 763 on

Plaza de Cataluña, Gerona

N 11, 42 r.; *Durán*, Lasauna 5, II, 67 r.; *Pirineos*, Ronda Barcelona 1, II, 53 r.; *President*, Ronda Ferial 33, II, 75 r.; *Rallye*, Ronda Barcelona, II, 15 r.; *Ronda*, Ronda Barcelona 104, III, 43 r.; *Trave*, Carretera Olot, III, 73 r., SP; *Hostal Bon Retorn*, km 759 on N II, P II, 53 r.; *España*, La Junquera 26, P II, 36 r.; *Bon Repós*, Vilallonga 43, P III, 15 r.; *San Mar*, Rech Arnau 43, P III, 25 r.; etc. – CAMPING SITE: *La Fresca*. – IN JUNQUERA: *Porta Catalana* (no rest.), II, 81 r.; *Puerta de España*, II, 26 r.; *Frontera*, III, 28 r.; *Goya* (no rest.), III, 36 r.; *Junquera* (no rest.), III, 28 r.; Hostales; CAMPING SITE.

RESTAURANTS. – *La Rosaleda*, Parque de la Dehesa; *Saratoga*, San Juan Bautista Lasalle 15; *Casa Marieta*, Plaza de la Independencia 5; *Selva Mart*, Santa Eugenia 81.

EVENTS. – *Fiestas de San Narciso* (Oct.–Nov.), the town's principal fiesta, with a fair.

CASINOS. – *Casino de Lloret de Mar; Casino Castillo de Perelada.*

Gerona, capital of the province of the same name, a bishopric and from the 16th to the 18th c. a university town, lies in the fertile and densely populated upland region of Catalonia roughly half way between Barcelona and the French frontier, near junction of the Río Oñar and the Río Ter.

HISTORY. – Gerona was founded by the Iberians and has preserved remains of its Iberian town walls. In the Roman period it was known as *Gerunda*. During the Arab occupation it was temporarily recaptured by Charlemagne (785), and it later became part of the kingdom of Catalonia and Aragon. In 1809 it held out

for seven months against a superior French force, and thereafter was given the honorific style of "*Inmortal Gerona*".

SIGHTS. – The town is divided into two by the Río Oñar, with the old town on the right bank and the new town on the left. From the principal bridge over the river there is a fine view of the **Old Town**, the main street of which, the tree-lined *Rambla de la Liberta*, runs left from the end of the bridge. To the E is the **Casa Carles**, which houses the *Museo Diocesano*, with a fine collection of Catalan church painting of the 10th–12th c. Beyond this is the old 17th c. *Ayuntamiento* (Town Hall). Both of these buildings are in the *Plaza del Vi*, which runs N into *Calle Ciudadanos*, with old patrician houses and the *Municipal Historical Museum* (No. 13). From here a flight of steps (1690) leads up to the Gothic *****Cathedral** (begun 1312, completed at the end of the 16th c.; façade 1793), with an aisleless nave. Fine *retablo* (1348) in Capilla Mayor; numerous *monuments*. Adjoining the Cathedral is a beautiful 12th c. *cloister* with richly decorated capitals. The *treasury* contains an embroidered *tapestry (11th–12th c.) depicting the creation of the world.

A short distance NW of the Cathedral stands the prominent collegiate church of **San Feliú** (choir completed 1318, W front 17th c.), with a tall *tower*; beside the high altar are Roman and Early Christian sarcophagi. – Near the church are the so-called *Arab Baths* (12th c.). – To the N, beyond the *Río Galligans*, is the Romanesque church (deconsecrated) of **San Pedro de Galligans**, with interesting reliefs; *Museo Arqueológico* in the cloister.

The **New Town** is on the left bank of the *Río Oñar*. Along its N side, beyond the arcaded *Plaza de la Independencia*, extends the large **Parque de la Dehesa**, reaching as far as the *Río Ter*, with fountains, monuments and avenues of palms.

SURROUNDINGS. – 27 km E on C 255 is *La Bisbal* (alt. 39 m; pop. 5000); hotels, with medieval castle walls and Catalan potteries.

To the French frontier. – Take the motorway or N II, going N, N II runs through *Sarriá de Ter*, where C 255 goes off on the right, and through the pretty village of *Mediñá* (alt. 85 m), dominated by its castle. After passing the *Castillo de Orriols* (on right) it comes to *Báscarra*, then crosses the *Río Fluviá* and runs through hilly country, with fine views of the *Ampurdán* plain and its vineyards, to **Figueras** (alt. 38 m; pop. 22,000; bypass), chief town of the Ampurdán district, with the pentagonal Castillo de San Fernando (18th c.) overlooking it on the NW. *Museo del Ampurdán*, with interesting material on the customs and way of life of the district. **Museo Dalí*, containing numerous works by the surrealist painter Salvador Dalí, born in Figueras in 1904.

Beyond Figueras N II continues through the eastern foothills of the Pyrenees to *Pont de Molins* (alt. 85 m; hotels), where the *Río Mugat* is crossed, followed by the *Río Llobregat*. Then via *Balneario de las Mercedes* to **La Junquera** (alt. 112 m; pop. 2000), close to the French frontier, with the Spanish customs-post. – The road then climbs gradually up to the *Col de Perthus* (290 m), which marks the frontier. On both sides of the frontier is the busy little town, half Spanish and half French, to *Le Perthus*. From here it is 31 km to *Perpignan*.

To Barcelona. – The motorway and N II run S over the Río Oñar. In 15 km N II comes to a branch road on the left to (3 km) **Caldas de Malavella** (alt. 95 m; hotels), on the *Riera de Caldas*, with mineral and thermal springs (35 °C–95 °F) which were already frequented in Roman times. – A few kilometres farther on a road leaves N II on the right to another health resort, *Santa Coloma de Farnés*. The main road crosses the boundary between the provinces of Gerona and Barcelona and drops down to the sea, continuing along the coast via *Arenys de Mar* and **Mataró** to **Barcelona** (see p. 68), 104 km from Genoa.

To Ripoll and Puigcerdá. – N of Gerona C 150 branches off N II and runs NW to (18 km) **Bañolas** (alt. 175 m; pop. 10,000), on the *Lago de Bañolas*. Benedictine monastery of San Esteban, with a 16th c. high altar and an 18th c. cloister; Gothic parish church of Santa María; Archaeological Museum.

Besalú

Continue on C 150 to **Besalú** (alt. 151 m), an ancient little town with several Romanesque churches and a bridge which is part Roman and part medieval. – Then up the valley of the *Río Fluviá*, flanked by mountains, to **Olot** (alt. 433 m; pop. 21,000), an industrial town with a number of churches and two interesting museums (Museo Gelabert, natural history). Several hermitages in the surrounding area. – From Olot C 153 runs over the *Puerto de Capsacosta* to *Camprodón*

(alt. 988 m), a Pyrenean summer resort which is a good climbing centre.

C 150 continues W from Olot and then climbs, with many bends, over two passes, the *Collado de Canas* (1130 m) and the *Collado de Coubet* (1010 m), to **Ripoll** (see p. 189), from which N 152 runs N to **Puigcerdá**.

Gibraltar

British territory.
Telephone: via operator.
Altitude: 0 to 425 m. – Population: 29,000.
ⓘ **Gibraltar Government Tourist Office**,
Cathedral Square;
tel. 76400.
Tourist information offices in The Piazza, Main Street.

HOTELS. – *Rock Hotel*, 160 r., SP; *Holiday Inn*, 120 r., SP; *Montarik*, 64 r., SP; *Queen's Hotel*, 62 r.; *Bristol*, 60 r., SP. – ON THE EAST COAST: *Caleta Palace*, 200 r., SP; *Gibraltar Beach Hotel*, 18 r. and 103 apartments.

Gibraltar, the rocky peninsula with an area of only 6·5 sq. km which has been famous for centuries as the "key to the Mediterranean", lies just E of the most southerly point on the Iberian peninsula. It has been British territory since 1704 and since 1969 an autonomous town.

The Rock of Gibraltar (Arabic *Jebel al-Tarik*) rears out of the sea on the E side of Algeciras Bay, linked by a narrow isthmus with the mainland of Spain. The town of Gibraltar lies on the W side of the rock, which rises from the sea in a series of terraces.

The **Straits of Gibraltar**, known in antiquity as the *Fretum Gaditanum* or *Fretum Herculeum*, are a strategically important link between the Atlantic and the Mediterranean. In ancient times they were guarded by the *Pillars of Hercules* – Calpe (Gibraltar) on the European side and Abyla lying opposite it on the African coast.

HISTORY. – The Spanish fortress on Gibraltar was taken by British forces in 1704, during the War of the Spanish Succession, and has remained in British hands ever since. Spain's efforts to recover what it regards as a piece of Spanish territory have so far been unsuccessful, and Gibraltar remains a contentious issue between Britain and Spain. From 1969 until 1985 the frontier at La Linea was closed.

SIGHTS. – The old town, **North Town**, begins beyond the British airfield on the level isthmus, with *Casemates Square*, above which, to the E, is the 14th c. *Moorish Castle*. To the NW is the *Market*, and beyond this is the **Harbour**, with the *Old Mole* (1309). – From Casemates Square *Main Street*, in which are most of the hotels, shops and public buildings, passes the *Post Office* and *Exchange* (with the *Town Hall* to the rear) to the *Roman Catholic Cathedral* (originally a mosque, rebuilt in Gothic style in 1502). To the SW can be found a synagogue and the *Gibraltar Museum*. Farther on, in Cathedral Square, is the *Protestant Cathedral* (Church of England), a Moorish-style building erected in 1821. At the S end of Main Street, on the right, is the *Governor's Palace*, built in 1531 as a Franciscan convent. Beyond it, through the *Southport Gates*, is the **Alameda**, a public garden with luxuriant subtropical vegetation and an open-air theatre. Close by is the cableway to the *Signal Station* (395 m), where there is a restaurant.

Gibraltar

On the E side of the Alameda is the beginning of *Europa Road*, a fine scenic road which climbs steeply up the W side of the rock between the houses and gardens of the **South Town** and then runs down between the jagged rock face of *Europa Pass*. – At the southern tip of the peninsula is ****Europa Point** (*Punta de Europa*), with a restaurant, a lighthouse and the old chapel of *Nuestra Señora de Europa* (magnificent views). – On the E side of the rock a road runs from N to S via *Eastern Beach* and *Catalan Bay Village* (tourist centre), under the Water Catchments (for the Collection of rainwater), to Sandy Bay.

From Main Street Willis's Road leads past the Moorish Castle into *Queen's Road*, a narrow road which runs along the rock, half way up, affording fine views. At the

near end of this road, on the left, are the *Upper Galleries*, hewn for military purposes in the 18th c. 1·5 km farther S along Queen's Road is the *Alps' Rock*, with the dens of the Barbary apes, some 30 of which still inhabit the rock. Beyond this, on the left, a flight of steps leads up to the *Highest Point. Farther along Queen's Road is a track on the left leading to *St Michael's Cave*, the largest cave on the rock (used as a concert hall in summer), with fine stalactites and stalagmites. Finally Queen's Road turns down in the right to join Europa Road.

Gijón

Province: Asturias (O).
Telephone code: 985.
Altitude: at sea level. – Population: 260,000.
ⓘ **Oficina de Información de Turismo**.
General Vigón 1;
tel. 34 11 67.
Oficina Municipal de Turismo,
Marqués de San Esteban 1;
tel. 34 60 46

HOTELS. – *Parador Nacional Molino Viejo*, Parque de Isabel la Católica, I, 40 r.; *Hernán Cortés* (no rest.), Fernández Vallín 5, I, 109 r.; *Príncipe de Asturias*, Manso 2, I, 80 r.; *Robledo* (no rest.), Alfredo Truán 2, II, 138 r.; *León*, Carretera de la Costa 45, III, 156 r.; *Pathos* (no rest.), Contracay 5, III, 56 r.; *Asturias* (no rest.), Plaza Mayor 11, IV, 101 r.; *Castilla* (no rest.), Corrida 50, IV, 34 r.; *París* (no rest.), Marqués de Casa Valdés 65, IV, 10 r.; Hostal *América*, Santa Lucia 2, P II, 26 r.; etc. – CAMPING SITE: *Gijón*, E of the town.

RESTAURANTS. – In the hotels, e.g. in the *Parador Molino Viejo*, old mill (rebuilt) with park; *El Faro del Piles*, Avda Garcia Bernado (view of bay); *Bella Vista*, Avda Garcia Bernado (view of bay); *Mercedes*, Libertad 6; *Tino*, Alfredo Trúan 9; *El Trole*, Alvarez Garaya 6.

TYPICAL TAVERNS (all in Cimadevilla). – *Mesón del Gallo*, Vicaria 11; *Posada Jamaica*, Olavarría 10; *Carrizo*, Olavarría 10; *Casa Zabala*, Viz. Campogrande 2.

CAFÉS. – *Arrango*, Menén Pérez 1; *Hernán Cortés*, Fernández Vallín 5; *Lord Jim*, Plaza Piñole 2; *Mayerling*, Corrida 14; *Palermo*, Rufo Rendueles 12; etc.

EVENTS.– Gijón and the surrounding area have an abundance of fiestas and folk events. – *Fiesta Patronal* (June), in honour of San Juan Bautista, with blessing of the sea; opening of the festival season. – **Fiestas de la Soledad** (Sept.) in the old district of Cimadevilla, with decorated streets and squares, folk performances and groups in traditional costume.

The busy port and industrial town of Gijón is the largest city in Asturias, with one of the best harbours on the N coast of Spain. It lies between two sheltered bays on the S side of the

The beach, Gijón

the Campo Valdés, through the fishing quarter of *Cimadevilla*, is the **Monte de Santa Catalina**, from which there are extensive views – W to the Cabo de Peñas, E to the Cabo de San Lorenzo and SE to the Picos de Europa. – On an eminence in the south-eastern outskirts of Gijón, 5 km from the town centre, are the extensive buildings of the *Universidad Laboral* (Workers' University), opened in 1955, with residential accommodation for 2000 students.

SURROUNDINGS. – **To the Cabo de Peñas**: Leave Gijón on N 632, going W, and in 6 km turn into a secondary road (dust-free) which runs NW along the coast to the fishing village of *Candás de Correño*, with a church containing a famous Irish figure of Christ. Then on to *Luanco de Gozón*, with a Museo del Mar (Museum of the Sea), and beyond *Bañagues* take a road on the right which leads to the *Cabo de Peñas (extensive views). From here it is possible to continue via *Podes* to *Avilés*.

former island of Santa Catalina and on the deposits of alluvial soil which now link it with the mainland.

HISTORY. – In the 8th c. Gijón was the residence of the Asturian kings. In 1588 the remnants of the "Invincible Armada" sought refuge here. Largely destroyed during the Civil War (1936–39), the town was later rebuilt on a modern plan, so that practically no ancient buildings have survived.

SIGHTS. – In the centre of the town is the *Plaza del 6 de Agosto*, with a *monument to Gaspar Melchor de Jovellanos* (1744–1811), the statesman and writer who did so much for Gijón. To the NE is the *Instituto Jovellanos*, founded in 1794 as a school for training in the natural sciences, now the Provincial College of Industry and Nautical Science.

From the Plaza 6 Agosto the busy *Corrida* runs N to the **Harbour**, which has been considerably developed in recent years and now extends 4 km W as *Puerto del Musel* (road to the suburban district of Musel, 6 km). This is one of the busiest ports in Spain, as the main exporting point for the output of the Asturian mines, a coal transhipment port and a port of call for foreign shipping lines. On the E side of the harbour is the *Plazuela Marqués*, in which is the *Palacio de Revillajigedo* (15th–16th c.), with two towers.

E of the Plazuela Marqués, across the narrow isthmus leading to the Santa Catalina peninsula, is the *Palacio del Conde de Valdés* (1590), in the Campo Valdés, at the beginning of the **Playa de San Lorenzo**, a beach which extends SE for more than a kilometre to the *Río Piles*, lined by tall modern blocks. – N of

Workers' University, Gijón

Granada

Province: Granada (GR).
Telpehone code: 9 58.
Altitude: 662–780 m. – Population 262,000.
ⓘ **Oficina de Información de Turismo**,
Casa de los Tiros, Pavaneras 19;
tel: 22 59 90.
Delegación Provincial de Turismo,
Plaza de Isabel la Católica 1;
tel. 22 62 89.

Panoramic view of Granada

HOTELS. – ON THE ALHAMBRA HILL: *Parador Nacional San Francisco*, in a former convent (quiet situation) I, 39 r.; *Alhambra Palace*, Peña Partida 2, (fine views), II, 121 r.; *Guadalupe*, Avda de los Alijares, II, 43 r. – IN THE TOWN: *Luz Granada*, Avda de la Constitución 18, I, 174 r., (view of Alhambra); *Meliá Granada*, Ángel Ganivet 7, I, 221 r.; *Carmen* (no rest.), Avda de José Antonio 62, I, 205 r.; *Los Alixares* (no rest.), Avda Alixares del Generalife s/n, II, 148 r., SP; *Los Ángeles*, Cuesta de Escoriaza 17, II, 100 r., SP; *Brasilia* (no rest.), Recogidas 7, II, 68 r.; *Condor* (no rest.), Avda de la Constitución 6, II, 101 r.; *Kenia*, Molinos 65, II, 16 r.; *Rally*, Paseo de Ronda 107, II, 44 r.; *Victoria*, Puerta Real 3, II, 69 r.; *Anacapri* (no rest.), Joaquín Costa 7, III, 32 r.; *Inglaterra* (no rest.), Cetti-Marien 10, III, 40 r.; *Montecarlo* (no rest.), Avda de José Antonio 44, III, 63 r.; *Sacromonte*, (no rest.), Plaza del Lino 1, III, 33 r.; *Sudán*, Avda de José Antonio 60, III, 69 r.; *Niza* (no rest.), Navas 16, IV, 24 r.; etc. – CAMPING SITES. – *El Último*, Camino Huétor-Vega 50; *María Eugenia*, on the Malaga road; *Reina Isabel*, Carretera La Zubia 49, all within easy reach of the town.

RESTAURANTS. – *Los Arcos*, Plaza Gran Capitán 4; *Baroca*, Pedro Antonio de Alarcón 34; *Columbia*, Antequeruela Baja 1; *Cunini*, Pescadería 9 (fish dishes); *Embarcadero*, Paseo de Ronda 100; *Los Leones*, Acera del Darro 10; *Horno de Santiago*, Plaza de los Campos 8; *Sevilla*, Oficios 12, in Andalusian style; etc.

EVENTS. – *Día de la Toma*, celebrating the Reconquista, with procession and service in Capilla de los Reyes Católicos (Jan.). – *Semana Santa* (Holy Week), with splendid procession. – *Fiesta de las Cruces de Mayo* (May), combined with "Carnation Day". – *Festival Internacional de Música y Danza* (June–July), with concerts and dancing displays in the Palacio de Carlos V. – *Semana Deportiva Internacional* (International Sport Week), with skiing competitions in the Sierra Nevada (winter). – *Rallye Costa del Sol* (Dec.), car race through the provinces of Granada, Almería and Málaga.

SPORT and RECREATION. – Winter sports in the Sierra Nevada, from November to May around 2500 m, throughout the year at higher levels (ski-lifts and chair-lifts at the Solynieve winter sports centre); shooting and fishing; scuba diving on the Costa del Sol; bullfights, tennis, riding, target shooting, flying.

The famous old Moorish capital of *Granada, now chief town of a province, the see of an archbishop and a university town, occupies a very beautiful situation at the foot of the Sierra Nevada, between two outlying hills which fall steeply down to the fertile vega of the Río Genil (often waterless in summer).

The more northerly of the two hills is the *Albaicín*, on which the older part of Granada is built; the *Alhambra Hill* to the S is separated from the Albaicín by the deep gorge of the *Río Darro*, a normally meagre stream which flows underground below the town centre to join the Río Genil. Crowned by the unique Alhambra palace on its hill, Granada has been declared a national monument by virtue of numerous well-preserved remains of a rich alien culture and art and as the scene of great events in the history of Spain.

HISTORY. – Probably founded by the Iberians, Granada fell into the hands of the Arabs in 711 after the defeat of the Visigoths. The new rulers of the town, which they called *Gharnatha*, built a fortress on the Alhambra Hill. After the fall of the Caliphate of Córdoba the governor of Granada declared his independence (1031). Thereafter it became subject to the Almoravides and then the Almohades. In 1241 Ibn al-Ahmed, of the Beni Nasr tribe, founded the Nasrite dynasty as Mohamed I and made Granada the wealthiest city in the Iberian peninsula. After a period of splendour lasting 250 years it passed to the Catholic Monarchs in 1491 under the treaty of Santafé and thereafter remained in Christian hands. During the Renaissance it had further prosperity, but the bloody repression of a Moorish rising in 1569 was followed by a decline. The town's recovery began with the renewal of the irrigation system in the vega and the introduction of new crops at the beginning of the 20th c.

SIGHTS. – The hub of Granada's traffic is *Plaza Isabel la Católica*, where the wide *Gran Vía de Colón* meets Calle de los Reyes Católicos at right angles. In the square is a monument commemorating the Santafé agreement between Isabella the Catholic and Columbus in 1492.

Going W along Calle de los Reyes Católicos, we come (on left) to the little *Plaza del Carmen*, in which is the *Ayuntamiento* (Town Hall), built in 1858. Opposite it Calle Príncipe runs into the *Plaza de Bib-Rambla*, with the *Palacio Arzobispal* (Archbishop's Palace), mostly dating from the 18th c. On its E side is the *Alcaicería*, originally the Moorish bazaar, destroyed by fire in 1843 but now again lined by colourful little shops.

Beyond the Archbishop's Palace, to the NE, is the *Cathedral (Santa María de la Encarnación)*, a memorial to the victory of Christian Spain and the country's finest Renaissance-style church. It was begun in 1523, in Gothic style, continued in 1525 by Diego de Siloé (d. 1563) in Plateresque style and consecrated in 1561, while still unfinished. The imposing W front (1667) was built by Alonso Cano and his successors. Over the main doorway (*Puerta Principal*) is a large relief of the Incarnation by José Risueño (1717).

On the N side are the *Puerta de San Jerónimo* (sculpture by Siloé, Maeda and others) and the richly decorated *Puerta del Perdón* (completed 1537).

The INTERIOR of the Cathedral was not completed until after 1703. With double lateral aisles and a transept, it is richly furnished with sculpture and pictures, mostly by Alonso Cano and Juan de Sevilla. Particularly magnificent is the domed *Capilla Mayor*, 47 m high, with beautiful stained glass (16th c.) and bronze statues of the Apostles (1614). In the *Choir* are two large Baroque organs and the tomb of Alonso Cano (d. 1667). – Adjoining the Cathedral on the S side is the *Sagrario* (Baroque), built 1705–59 on the site of Granada's principal mosque. – In the S aisle of the Cathedral is the entrance to the *Capilla Real*, built 1506–17 in late Gothic style as the mausoleum of the Catholic Monarchs. A beautiful grille encloses the richly decorated *royal tombs*: to the right Ferdinand (d. 1516) and Isabel (d. 1504), by the Florentine sculptor Domenico Fancelli (1522); to the left Philip the Handsome (d. 1506) and Joan the Mad (d. 1555), by Bartolomeo Ordóñez. Steps lead down to the *Crypt*, which contains lead sarcophagi. Beyond the royal tombs is a large and beautifully carved *retablo* by Felipe Vigarní; on either side are finely carved and richly decorated *relicarios* (side altars) by Alonso de Mena (1623). – In the adjoining **Sacristy** are the valuable cathedral treasury and a notable collection of

Granada

200 m

pictures by Dutch masters, including Dierick Bouts, Roger van der Weyden and Memling. From the **N tower** there are very fine views.

A short distance NE of the Cathedral is the busy *Plaza Neuva*, in which is the *Audiencia* (Law Court), formerly the Real Cancillería (Royal Chancellery), built between 1531 and 1587, with a beautiful arcaded courtyard. From the square the Cuesta de Gomérez runs up to the Alhambra, high above the town to the E.

At the NE end of the Plaza Nueva the Río Darro emerges from underground. Here too is the Renaissance church of **Santa Ana** (1541–48), with a Plateresque doorway and a minaret-like tower (1563). – Along the N side of the Río Darro runs the *Carrera del Darro*, one of the oldest streets in Granada, with views of the Alhambra. Going along this street, we pass on the left (No. 31) the *Bañuelo*, an old Moorish bath. Farther along, on the right, is the church of *San Pedro y San Pablo*, and opposite this, on the left, is the Renaissance **Casa de Castril**, which now houses the *Museo Arqueológico*. The Carrera del Darro then joins the *Paseo de los Tristes*, with a view of the Alhambra and the Generalife on the hill to the right (steep ascent); to the left is the Albaicín quarter.

Turning left up the *Cuesta del Chapiz* and then right up the steep *Camino del Sacro Monte* (fine views), we pass large numbers of cave dwellings once occupied by the gipsies (*gitanos*) whose presence in Granada is attested since 1532. From the former Benedictine monastery of *Sacro Monte* footpaths (sometimes steep) lead up through deeply cut gullies (loose stones) to the hermitage of **San Miguel de Alto**, from which there are magnificent views extending to the Sierra Nevada.

From the Cuesta del Chapiz *Calle del Salvador* runs into the narrow lanes of the **Albaicín** quarter, parts of which still have a Moorish character. Passing the church of *San Salvador*, on the site of an earlier mosque, we come to the church of **San Nicolás** (1525), the heart of Albacín, with a splendid *view, frequently painted, of the Alhambra and the Sierra Nevada. From the nearby *Puerta de los Estandartes* a well-preserved stretch of Moorish walls, the *Muralla árabe*, runs W (best seen from the *Cuesta de la Alhacaba*). The street finally runs into the *Paseo del Triunfo*, in which is the Arco Elvira. From here it is 1 km N to the **Cartuja** (Charterhouse), a former Carthusian house dating from the 16th c.

To the SW of the Paseo del Triunfo is the **Hospital of San Juan de Dios**, founded in 1552, with the richly decorated tomb of St John of God in the church. A short distance SW is the former monastery of **San Jerónimo**, founded in 1492, with an 18th c. church, the interior of which is completely covered with wall paintings. In the splendid Capilla Mayor is the tomb of the "Gran Capitán", Gonzalo Fernández de Córdobe (d. 1515); on either side of the high altar (after 1570) are the kneeling figures of Gonzalo and his wife.

From San Jerónimo the Calle de la Duquesa leads SE to the **University**, founded in 1531 and transferred to its present building, the former Jesuit College (18th c., with Baroque façade), in 1759. Beyond the Plaza de la Trinidad, reached by way of Calle de Mesones, is the square called the *Puerta Real*, in which is the Head Post Office. From here the *Carrera del Genil*, runs SE. Off to the left is the *Castillo de Bibatuabín* (1752–64), now occupied by the Diputación Provincial. – Farther along, to the right, is the church of *Nuestra Señora de las Angustias* (1664–71), with an image of the Virgen de las Angustias, patroness of Granada. In the E of the town is a *museum* devoted to the Spanish composer *Manuel de Falla* (1876–1946), who lived in Granada for many years (Antequeruela).

The **Alhambra Hill** is reached from the Plaza Nueva by taking the *Cuesta de Gomérez*, which climbs 250 m to the *Puerta de las Granadas*, the main entrance to the Alhambra Park. On **Monte Mauror**, above the road on the right, are the *Torres Bermejas*, part of a 13th c. Moorish fortification. – From the Puerta de las Granadas we continue through the *Alhambra Park, which extends for some distance along a valley between the Alhambra Hill and Monte Mauror. Pedestrians take the steeper route up the *Cuesta Empedrada* to the *Puerta de la Justicia*; cars must take the longer way round by the wide road to the *Fuente del Tomate* and then up to the *Puerta de los Carros*, where one road goes right to the Parador and the other left to the *Plaza de los Aljibes* ("Cistern Square"), with fine views of the Darro valley, Albaicín and Sacro Monte.

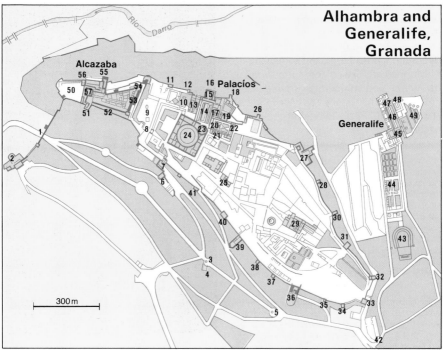

Alhambra and Generalife, Granada

1 Puerta de las Granadas (Gate of Pomegranates)	15 Sala de Embajadores (Hall of the Ambassadors)	31 Torre de las Infantas (Tower of the Infantas)
2 Torres Bermejas (Red Towers)	16 Torre de Comares	32 Torre del Cabo de la Carrera (Tower at the End of the Race-Track)
3 Fuente del Tomate (Tomato Fountain)	17 Apartments of Charles V	
4 Monument to Ángel Ganivet	18 Tocador de la Reina (Queen's Dressing Room)	33 Torre del Agua (Water Tower)
5 Fuente del Pimiento (Pepper Fountain)	19 Sala de las Dos Hermanas (Hall of the Two Sisters)	34 Torre de Juan de Arce
6 Pilar de Carlos V (Charles V's Pillar)	20 Patio de los Leones (Court of Lions)	35 Torre de Baltasar de la Cruz
7 Puerta de la Justicia (Gate of Justice)	21 Sala de los Abencerrajes	36 Puerta de los Siete Suelos (Gate of Seven Storeys)
8 Puerta del Vino (Wine Gate)	22 Sala de los Reyes (Hall of Kings)	37 Torre del Capitán (Captain's Tower)
9 Plaza de los Aljibes (Square of the Cisterns)	23 Crypt	38 Torre de las Brujas (Witches' Tower)
10 Patio de Machuca	24 Palacio de Carlos V (Charles V's Palace)	39 Torre de las Cabezas (Tower of Heads)
11 Torre de las Gallinas (Tower of the Hens)	25 Baños (Baths)	40 Torre de los Abencerrajes
12 Torre de los Puñales (Tower of the Daggers)	26 Torre de las Damas (Ladies' Tower)	41 Torre de los Carros (Tower of the Carts: exit)
13 Mexuar	27 Torre de los Picos	42 Entrance to Generalife
14 Patio de los Arrayanes (Court of Myrtles)	28 Torre del Cadí (Judge's Tower)	43 Theatre
	29 Parador Nacional de San Francisco	44 Jardines Nuevos (New Gardens)
	30 Torre de la Cautiva (Tower of the Captive)	45 Pabellón Sur (South Pavilion)
46 Patio de la Acquia (Court of the Water Channel)		
47 Pabellón Norte (North Pavilion)		
48 Patio de la Sultana (Court of the Sultana)		
49 Jardines Altos (Upper Gardens)		
50 Baluarte (Bastion)		
51 Torre de la Pólvora (Powder Tower)		
52 Jardines de los Adarves (Gardens of the Wall-Walk)		
53 Torre Quebrada (Broken Tower)		
54 Torre del Homenaje (Tower of Homage)		
55 Torre de las Armas (Tower of Arms)		
56 Torre de los Hidalgos (Tower of the Noblemen)		
57 Torre de la Vela (Watch-Tower)		

On the W side of the square is the **Alcazaba**, the older royal castle begun in the reign of Mohammed I, of which only the outer walls with their massive towers still remain. The *Puerta de la Alcazaba* leads into the *Jardines de los Adarves*, from which there is a magnificent view. There are even more extensive views from the *Torre de la Vela* (26 m high) at the W end of the terrace.

On the E side of the Plaza de los Aljibes is the ***Palacio de Carlos V**, a massive square structure (63 m each way, 17·4 m high), begun in 1526 by Pedro Machuca. Although unfinished, it is the finest example of High Renaissance architec-

ture in Spain. Apart from the external façades the only part completed is the pillared inner courtyard, an open two-storey rotunda. In the palace are the *Museo Provincial de Bellas Artes*, with Spanish pictures and sculpture of the 16th–18th c., and the *Museo de la Alhambra*, among whose principal treasures is the *Alhambra Vase (1320), 1·3 m high, beautifully decorated with enamels.

N of Charles V's palace is the ****Palace of the Alhambra** (*Palacio Árabe*), residence of the Moorish rulers of Granada, begun in Yusuf I (1333–54) and largely completed by Mohammed V (1364–91).

Like all Moorish secular buildings, it is externally plain and unpretentious: it depends for artistic effect on its carefully contrived ground plan and its sumptuous decoration, one of the great achievements of Moorish art. The palace, surrounded by its walls and numerous towers, was known to the Arabs as *Medinat al-Hambra*, the "Red City", after the colour of the stone.

The INTERIOR is an outstanding example of Islamic palace architecture, with its careful articulation into three main sections – the Mexuar, used for the public administration of justice and for large assemblies; the royal palace proper, the Diwan or Serrallo; and the women's apartments or Harem, designed for the private and family life of the monarch. In each section all the rooms open off a central courtyard, as in the earlier Greco-Roman house; in the Diwan this has a long ornamental pond (Court of Myrtles), in the Harem a fountain (the Lion Fountain).

An antechamber leads into the **Mexuar**, originally the audience chamber and court room, later used as a chapel. Turning right from the antechamber, we pass through the *Patio del Mexuar* and the *Zaguán* into the ***Court of Myrtles** (*Patio de los Arrayanes* or *de la Alberca*), named after the myrtles (*arrayanes*) planted round the central pond (*alberca*). The court is 37 m long by 23 m across. At its N end, beyond the *Sala de la Barca* (Hall of Blessing), is the *Torre de Comares* (45 m high), in which is the ****Sala de los Embajadores** (Hall of the Ambassadors), formerly used as a throne room. 11 m square and 18 m high, it has a magnificent larch-wood dome, with some of the richest decoration in the Alhambra (152 different patterns).

From the SE corner of the Court of Myrtles we pass through the *Sala de los Mozárabes* into the ****Court of Lions** (*Patio de los Leones*), the central feature of the royal winter residence built by Mohammed V, with the Harem. In the centre of this spacious court (28 m by 15 m), surrounded by 124 columns, is the *Lion Fountain*, its basin supported by 12 black marble lions. – On the S side of the Court of Lions is the ***Sala de los Abencerrajes**, named after a powerful Moorish family, with a splendid stalactitic ceiling; in the centre

Court of Lions, Alhambra

of the room is 12-sided marble fountain. – On the E side of the Court of Lions is the ***Hall of Kings** (*Sala de los Reyes*, also known as the *Sala de la Justicia*), divided into seven sections, with high stalactitic domes. In its alcove-like recesses are well-preserved 15th c. ceiling paintings.

From the N end of the Hall of Kings we pass into the ****Hall of the Two Sisters** (*Sala de las Dos Hermanas*), which together with the succeeding apartments was probably the women's winter residence. Its decoration is the richest and finest in the Alhambra. The honeycomb dome, the largest of all stalactitic vaults, has some 5000 cells. – Beyond this, straight ahead, is the **Sala de los Ajimeces**, between the arched windows (*ajimeces*) of which is the entrance to the **Mirador de Daraxa* (or *de Lindaraja*), a charming little enclosed balcony looking down on to the Patio de Daraxa, with three windows reaching down almost to the floor. Looking back, there is a fine view of the Court of Lions.

From the Hall of the Two Sisters we pass along the W side of the Patio de Daraxa and through two other rooms on the N side of the palace into the *Tocador de la Reina* (Queen's Dressing Room), on the uper floor of the Torre del Peinador, from which there are magnificent views, particularly to the E of the Torre de las Damas and the Generalife. – From here we return along the gallery on the N side of the palace and along one side of the *Patio de la Reja*, down a staircase into this patio and then E into the beautiful ***Patio de Daraxa**, formerly the inner palace garden, planted with cypresses and orange-trees. On the S side is the entrance to the massive substructures of the palace, the Sala de los Secretos, with a whispering gallery. To the S of the Patio de la Reja are the ***Baths** (*Baños*), a series of rooms dating from the time of Yusuf I: first the *Sala de las Camas*, with a gallery for singing girls, then a children's bath, a steam bath and two women's baths.

Court of Myrtles, Alhambra

The Alhambra and Generalife are open daily, though on Sundays not all rooms are open. From May to September the buildings are splendidly illuminated every Saturday evening from 10 to 12.

On the E side of the Palacio de Carlos V is the church of **Santa María**, built between 1581 and 1618 on the site of the Alhambra mosque, in which the first mass was celebrated after the surrender of Granada. To the right of the main doorway is a pillar recording the death of two Christian martyrs in 1397.

It is also well worth while visiting the **towers** of the Alhambra. To the E of the Alhambra Palace is the *Torre de las Damas*, a defensive tower with an adjoining vaulted hall, a pond and a small mosque. Farther E, at the *Puerta de Hierro* or *del Arrabal* (path down to the Paseo de los Tristes), is the *Torre de los Picos* (named after its battlements). Beyond this is the *Torre del Candil*, with a view (to right) of the former *Convento de San Francisco*, Granada's oldest religious house, converted in 1495 from a Moorish palace, which is now a Parador Nacional. Then comes the *Torre de la Cautiva*, or Tower of the (female) Captive, with a small patio and a splendidly decorated principal apartment. The *Torre de las Infantas*, beyond this, has a richly decorated hall (wide views from the upper platform). At the E end of the Alhambra hill is the *Torre del Agua*, with the cistern which supplied the Alhambra with water. On the S side of the hill are two smaller towers, the *Torre de Juan de Arce* and the *Torre de Baltasar de la Cruz*, then the tower of the *Puerta de los Siete Suelos* ("Seven-Storey Gate"), two other small towers, the *Torre de las Cabezas* and finally the *Torre de los Carros*, near the exit.

To the E of the Alhambra, on the slopes of the Cerro del Sol, is the ***Palacio del Generalife***, the summer palace of the Moorish kings, completed in 1319. From the outer gate at the E end of the Alhambra a beautiful avenue of cypresses leads to the 16th c. *entrance building*. Beyond this is the *Patio de la Acequia* (49 m by 13 m), named after the water channel (*acequia*) which flows through it; it is planted with myrtle and laurel hedges and orange-trees. From the N side of the court we enter the *Sala de los Reyes* (Hall of Kings), adjoining which is a room with an enclosed balcony affording a magnificent view of the Alhambra and the Darro valley; from the belvedere above the hall there is a wide prospect. – To the E a beautiful *park* extends up the hill, reminiscent of the garden of an Italian Renaissance villa with its terraces, grottoes, fountains and carefully trimmed hedges.

SURROUNDINGS. – Within easy reach of Granada are many other tourist attractions, chief among them the *Sierra Nevada* (see p. 213), with the *Alpujarras* to the S. A number of other attractive trips are suggested below.

To the Costa del Sol. – Leave Granada on N 323, which runs S through the suburban district of *Armilla* and the fertile countryside beyond, with a fine *view of Granada to the rear and of the Sierra Nevada to the left. Then up to the **Puerto del Suspiro del Moro** (865 m), the "Pass of the Moor's Sigh", where the last Moorish king of Granada, Boabdil, is said to have wept as he took his last look at the city he was leaving.

The road runs gently down to *Padul* and through the fertile *Valle de Lecrín*, framed between hills, to *Dúrcal*; then on to *Beznar*, beyond which a road branches off on the left into the wild hill scenery of the *Alpujarras*. N 323 continues through the *Tunel de Izboa* and runs high above the *Río Guadalfeo* to **Vélez de Benaudalla**, on a terrace above the river, with an old hexagonal tower. – The road then winds its way up to the *Mesata de los Pelados* and descends to **Motril** (alt. 40 m; pop. 30,000; hotels: Costa Nevada, II, 52 r., SP; El Carmen (no rest.), P III, 26 r.; etc. camping site), a port beautifully situated at the foot of the coastal hills. Two fine churches, one of which, on a hill, occupies the site of a former Moorish castle (beautiful views).

The coast road (N 340) runs through the fishing village of *Calahonda* to **Castell de Ferro**, another straggling fishing village dominated by the tower of a Moorish castle. – The road then continues through *La Rábita* to the little port of **Adra** in the province of Almería.

To the W the coast road crosses the *Río Guadalfeo*, passes through the charmingly situated little town of *Salobreña* with its white houses and comes to **Almuñécar** (hotels: Carmen (no rest.), IV, 24 r.; Goya (no rest.), IV, 24 r., no rest.; camping site; Piccadilly restaurant, 3 km E), a picturesque little town and seaside resort, with a ruined Moorish castle and remains of a Roman aqueduct. – From here the road continues into the province of Málaga and comes to the little resort of **Nerja** (see p. 175).

Round the Vega de Granada. – At *Armilla*, 5 km S of Granada, turn off N 323 into C 340, which runs SW through *Gabia la Grande*, with the Moorish tower known as El Fuerte, to (54 km) **Alhama de Granada** (alt. 854–960 m; Hotel Balneario, II, 101 r., SP, closed in winter, an old Moorish stronghold lying high above the little Río Alhama, now an important spa (sulphur springs, 42–45 °C (108–113 °F)).

C 340 continues to *Ventas de Zafarraya* (alt. 907 m), in the *Sierra Tejada* near the boundary of Málaga province, and then climbs to the **Puerto de los Alazores** (1040 m), where the *Río Guadalhorce* rises. The road then descends into the valley of the *Río*

Landscape near Granada

Barracón and joins N 342, coming from Antequera, which runs E to **Loja** (alt. 475 m; pop. 35,000), with the towering ruins of a Moorish castle and two 16th c. churches (bypass with fine views above the town to the S).

N 342 winds E along the slopes of the broad fertile valley of the Río Genil, with a distant prospect of the Sierra Nevada, and then runs through the Vega de Granada to the historic little town of **Santafé** (alt. 580 m; pop. 10,000), with the regular layout of a Roman camp, built by Queen Isabella in 1491 as headquarters for the siege of Granada. Three of the town gates are protected national monuments. Here the surrender of Granada was signed in 1491, and here too, in the following year, the agreement on Columbus's voyages of discovery was concluded. – From here it is 12 km to Granada, with fine *views of the town. Total distance 175 km. NW of Santafé in *Fuente Vaqueros* can be seen the birthplace (now a museum) of the Spanish poet (*Federico García Lorca* (1899–1936).

Through the Sierra Harana. – Leave Granada on N 342 (the Murcia road), which runs NE over the *Puerto de la Mora* (1360 m), the highest point on the road, to (55 km) **Guadix** (alt. 949 m; pop. 20,000), an episcopal town on the river of the same name with a Moorish castle, a fine 18th c. Cathedral built on the foundations of an earlier mosque and with numerous *cave dwellings in the Barrio de Santiago. – 17 km S of Guadix by the Almería road (N 324), at the foot of the Sierra Nevada, is the little town of *La Calahorra* (alt. 1257 m; pop. 1500), which has an imposing castle with four massive round towers.

N 342 climbs by way of *Venta del Baul* (alt. 1259 m) and then runs down through the steppe country of the *Llanos de Cuquillo* to **Baza** (alt. 870 m; pop. 24,000), originally an Iberian settlement where the Iberian figure known as the "Lady of Baza" was excavated in 1971. Collegiate church (18th c.); Moorish baths (protected monument). – N 340 then continues E via *Cúllar de Baza* to enter the province of Almería, and on to **Lorca** (see p. 150), in the province of Murcia.

Through the Sierra de Alta Colomna. – Leave Granada on N 323 (the Jaén road), which runs N through the Jurassic limestone hills of the *Sierra de Elvira* and beyond *Venta de las Navas* climbs, with numerous bends and gradients of up to 12 per cent, to the *Puerto de Zegri* (1080 m), with *views of the Sierra Nevada. Then on to the **Puerto de Carretero** (1040 m), in the *Sierra de Alta Colomna*, on the boundary between the provinces of Granada and Jaén. From here it is 46 km to the provincial capital, **Jaén** (see p. 141).

Guadalajara

Province: Guadalajara (GU).
Telephone code: 911.
Altitude: 641 m. – Population: 55,000.
ⓘ **Jefatura Provincial de Turismo,**
  Travesía de Beladiez 1;
  tel. 22 06 98.

HOTELS. – *Pax*, km 57 on N II, II, 61 r., SP; *España* (no rest.), Teniente Figueroa 3, IV, 33 r.; Hostal *Arroyo* (no rest.), Gonzalo Herranz 2, P III, 25 r.; *El Reloj*, Doctor Mayoral 11, P III, 14 r.; *Venecia* (no rest.), Doctor Benito Hernando 12, P III, 12 r.

RESTAURANTS. – *Mesón Hernando*, Carretera de Circunvalación (Castilian style); *La Murciana*, Miguel Fluiters 21 (rustic style); *El Ventorren*, Alfonso López de Haro 2.

EVENTS. – *Autumn Fiesta* (Sept.), with a large agricultural show, exhibitions, sporting contests and bullfights.

Guadalajara, capital of the province of the same name, is situated above the left bank of the Río Henares, in a region of harsh winters and hot summers. Its name is derived from the Arabic Wad al-Hajarah ("river of stones").

Guadalajara: bird's-eye view

SIGHTS. – **Palcio del Infantado** (15th c.), with a late Gothic ceiling supported on arches, a patio famed for its beauty and notable works of art. – Church of **San Ginés** (begun 1557), with tombs of the Infantado and Tendilla families. 16th c. bas-reliefs on the high altar. – Church of *Santa María de la Fuente* (13th c.), with a minaret-like tower in Mudéjar style and 15th c. tombs. – Convent of *La Piedad*, now an Institute, with Plateresque door-ways and a cloister with double arcades; tomb of the foundress of the convent, Brianda de Mendoza.

SURROUNDINGS. – There are many places of interest in the area round Guadalajara, most of them only a few kilometres from the main roads.

Through the Montes de Encinas. – Leave the town on N II, which runs NE in long straight stretches over the Castilian plateau in the direction of Zaragoza. In 18 km it comes to **Torija** (alt. 964 m), with a 13th c. castle which was destroyed by Juan Martin el Empecinado in 1811 but later restored. The parish church contains fine examples of goldsmith's work. – From Torija an attractive secondary road (C 201) runs into the *Sierra de Megorrón.*

After a long straight stretch through the *Montes de Encinas* another attractive side road (C 204) goes off on the left to the little episcopal city of **Sigüenza** (see p. 214), situated above the left bank of the *Río Henares*. From here C 114 leads back to the N II (additional distance about 15 km).

From the turning for Sigüenza N II runs up through *Algora* (alt. 1116 m) on to the *Sierra Ministra*, from which there is a fine view of Sigüenza, and continues via *Saúca* (alt. 1200 m) to **Alcolea del Pinar** (alt. 1250 m), where the road from Sigüenza (C 114) returns to the main road. – Beyond Alcolea N II turns N, enters the province of Soria and continues over the pass of *Cuestas de Esteras* (1150 m) to **Medinaceli** (see p. 169), from which N II continues to Calatayud and Zaragoza and N 111 runs N to Soria. – At Alcolea N 211 goes off on the right and climbs over the *Puerto de Maranchón* (1250 m) to **Molina de Aragón** (pop. 2500), an ancient settlement dating from pre-Moorish times. On a hill above the village is an imposing fortress surrounded by walls and towers. The Torre de Aragón (11th c.) is protected as a national monument. Church of Santa Clara (12th c.), with the tomb of Doña Blanca, foundress of the convent to which it belonged.

Into the Sierra de Megorrón. – Follow N II as far as *Torija* (above), 18 km from Guadalajara; then turn right into C 210, which leads to the old fortified town of **Brihuega** (alt. 886 m; pop. 4300), situated above the valley of the *Río Tajuña*. Ruins of the 12th c. Castillo de Piedra Bermeja; parish church of Santa María de la Peña, with a beautiful retablo; a former royal cloth factory, the Real Fábrica de Paños, with interesting gardens.

C 201 continues to **Cifuentes** ("hundred fountains" – from the countless springs in the area), situated at the foot of the Sierra de Megorrón. Castle, built by Juan Manuel in 1324; parish church (12th–13th c.), with a late Romanesque doorway.

From Cifuentes we take C 204, which runs S into the *Zona de los Lagos* (Lake District), finally coming to the *Embalse de Entrepeñas*, which is crossed half way along its length. At *Sacedón* the road joins N 320: turn right in the direction of Guadalajara. Some 20 km along N 320 a secondary road on the left leads S to **Pastrana** (pop. 3000), with a beautiful Gothic parish church (14th c.). Retablo by John of Burgundy (16th c.); tomb of the Princess of Eboli; 15th c. *tapestries and other works of art. – S of Pastrana is *Zorita de los Canes*, with a Moorish castle and a Romanesque church. Return to Guadalajara on N 320. Total distance 170 or 200 km.

The Henares valley. – Leave Guadalajara on N II and in 5 km turn N into C 101, which runs via *Torre del Burgo* to the little medieval town of **Hita**, with old town walls and the remains of a castle. – From here a minor road runs N to *Cogolludo*, with the Renaissance palace of the Medinaceli family (15th c.) and the parish church of Santa María (16th c.).

C 101 continues from Hita by way of *Miralrío* to **Jadraque**, with the ruined Castillo de Osuna. In the 16th c. parish church is a picture by Zurbarán, "Christ after the Scourging". – Farther N a side road goes off on the left to the *Embalse de Palmaces*. After passing the *Sierra de la Bordera* C 101 comes to a junction, from which C 114 runs left to **Atienza** (alt. 1169 m), another little fortified medieval town, with several interesting Romanesque and Gothic churches and a ruined castle.

Guadalupe

Province: Cáceres (CC).
Telephone code: 927.
Altitude: 640 m. – Population: 4000.
ⓘ **Ayuntamiento** (Town Hall),
Plaza del Generalísimo;
tel. 36 70 06.

HOTELS. – *Parador Nacional Zurbarán*, Marqués de la Romana 10, II, 40 r., SP (16th c. mansion with a magnificent garden); *Hospedería Real Monasterio*, Plaza Juan Carlos I, III, 46 r. (in an old convent).

The village of Guadalupe is noted for its fortress-like *monastery (occupied by Hieronymites 1389–1832, by Franciscans since 1928), one of Spain's great religious centres (feast-days on 8 and 30 September and 12 October).

The Monastery of Guadalupe

SIGHTS. – The *church (17th c.) contains numerous works of art, including richly carved *choir-stalls* (1744), a magnificent *reja* (1524), a *retablo* (1618) with a much venerated 13th c. black Virgin whose head-dress contains more than 30,000 precious stones, two 17th c. *organs* by Churriguera, and numerous monuments, paintings, etc. In the *Camarín*, dedicated to the black Virgin, are nine good pictures by Luca Giordano, and in the splendid *Sacristy* eight by Zurbarán depicting scenes from the life of St Jerome; in the adjoining *Capilla de San Jerónimo* is a lamp from the Turkish flagship at the battle of Lepanto (1571). – There are two beautiful **cloisters**, the 14th c. *Claustro Mudéjar*, with a fountain surmounted by a miniature temple (1405), and the *Claustro Gótico* (14th–16th c.). – In the monastery are the **Museo de Bordados**, with a rich collection of vestments and altar frontals of the 15th–16th c., and the **Museo de Libros Miniados** in the old chapterhouse, with a collection of 86 choir-books (15th–18th c.) and miniatures.

Guernica y Luno

Province: Vizcaya (B).
Telephone code: 94.
Altitude: 4 m. – Population: 8000.
(i) **Ayuntamiento** (Town Hall),
    Plaza Fuero 3;
     tel. 6 85 05 50 and 6 85 11 64.

HOTEL. – *Bolina*, Barrencalle 3, IV, 17 r.

Guernica, in the beautiful valley of the Río Mundaca (also known as the Río de Guernica), the "holy city of the Basques", was once the capital of the fief of Vizcaya, which had its own charter of rights (fueros), and the seat of a parliament which met here every two years under an old oak-tree.

The stump of the old oak can still be seen in the courtyard of the Casa de Juntas.

In Guernica

During the Civil War the town was the target of the first terror bombing by German aircraft, in which 1654 people were killed. This massacre inspired Picasso to paint his famous accusatory picture "Guernica", which during the time of Franco was in the Museum of Modern Art in New York, but which is now in the El Carsón Museum which is part of the Prado in Madrid.

SIGHTS. – **Casa de Juntas**, with the remains of the historic oak-tree and the assembly hall, decorated with tiles and pictures. Near by is a statue by Eduardo Chillida commemorating the attack of 1937. – Church of **Santa María** (begun 1418), with works by contemporary sculptors like Inurria, José Capuz and Moisés Huerta.

SURROUNDINGS. – 4 km NE are the **Cuevas de Basondo** (Santimamiñe), stalactitic caves with rock paintings of the later Palaeolithic period.

Haro

Province: La Rioja (LO).
Telephone code: 941
Altitude: 470 m. – Population: 9000.
(i) **Ayuntamiento** (Town Hall),
    Plaza de la Paz 1;
     tel. 31 01 05–6.

HOTELS. – *Hostal Higinia*, Vega 31, P II, 21 r.; *Iturrimurri*, km 41 on N 232; P II, 24 r.

RETAURANTS. – *Terete*, Lucrecia Arana 17 (with Bodega); *Beethoven II*, Santo Tomas 3.

EVENTS. – *Fiesta de San Juan y San Pedro* (June), with pilgrimage to the Ermita San Felices de Bilibio and the curious "Batalla del Vino" (Wine Battle) in which the young men of the town spray wine from leather bottles (*botas*) on their opponents.

Haro, at the junction of the Río Tirón and the Ebro, is the second largest town in the Rioja wine-growing region. To the S of the town is the extensive Sierra de la Demanda, with the Cerro de San Lorenzo (2262 m).

SIGHTS. – Haro is a picturesque old town of narrow streets, fountains and handsome town houses. – **Palacio del Conde de Haro** (17th–18th c.). – 18th c. *Ayuntamiento* (Town Hall), with arcades and galleries. – Church of **Nuestra Señora de la Vega** (17th c.), with a fine retablo. – Church of *Santo Tomás*

(16th c.), with stellate vaulting. Behind the high altar is a tabernacle (1757), with statuettes.

SURROUNDINGS. – 3 km N is **Briñas**, the "gateway of the Rioja", with an important exhibition of wine. – There are numbers of *bodegas* in the area round Haro.

Huelva

Province: Huelva (H).
Telephone code: 955.
Altitude: 56 m. – Population: 110,000.

ⓘ **Oficina de Información de Turismo,**
Plus Ultra 10,
tel. 24 50 92.

HOTELS. – *Luz Huelva* (no rest.), Alameda Sumdheim 26, I, 105 r., SP, golf; *Tartessos* (no rest.), Avda Martín Alonso Pinzón 13–15, II, 112 r.; *Costa de la Luz*, José María Amo 8, III, 35 r.; *Andalucía*, Vázquez López 22, IV, 23 r. – CAMPING SITES: *Las Vegas* in Alijaraque (4 km W).

RESTAURANTS. – *Las Meigas*, Plaza América; *La Muralla*, San Salvator 17; *Napoli*, Avenida de Italia 79 (Italian); *Victor*, Rascón 35. – IN ALJARAQUE: *El Don Pepe*, Sargento Pino 54; *Las Vegas*, Carretera Punta Umbria.

CAFÉS. – *Antón Montana* and *Pelayo*, all in Plus Ultra *Las Esquinita*, Gravina 5; etc.

EVENTS. – *Fiesta del Descubrimiento de América* (Aug.), in honour of Columbus and the discovery of America, with a fair, cultural events, bullfights, and folk performances. – *Feria de Nuestra Señora de la Cinta* (Sept.), patronal festival, with procession.

The town of Huelva, known to the Romans as Onuba and now capital of its province and the seat of a bishop, lies near the Atlantic coast of Andalusia (the Costa de la Luz) on the left bank of the Río Odiel, here 4 km wide and navigable for seagoing ships.

The commercial port of Huelva is one of the largest in Spain in terms of the traffic handled, mainly as a result of the shipment of ores from the Río Tinto and Tharsis. The tunny and sardine fisheries also contribute to its economy. Refineries.

SIGHTS. – The town, laid out on a spacious scale, has few outstanding sights to offer the visitor. The only older buildings of any interest – survivors of the 1755 earthquake – are a number of churches: *San Pedro* (16th c.), built on the ruins of a mosque, restored after the earthquake; the *Concepción* (16th c.), with two small paintings by Zurbarán;

View of Huelva

Nuestra Señora de la Cinta, 2 km away, with a Mudéjar roof and an image of the town's patroness. – *Museo Provincial*, with a small collection of pictures.

SURROUNDINGS. – Though Huelva itself may lack major tourist attractions, there are many places of historical interest in the surrounding area.

Round trip via La Rábida. – Leave Huelva on the Seville road (N 431), and just beyond *San Juan del Puerto* (14 km) take a road to the right which crosses the *Río Tinto* and comes to the little town, 21 km from Huelva, of **Moguer** (alt. 51 m; pop. 8000), situated on a hill. In the 16th c. this was the starting point of many voyages to America. On the outskirts of the town is the once important Convento de Santa Clara (founded 1348), with beautiful alabaster tombs by Montañés and fine choir-stalls. There is a museum devoted to the poet and Nobel prizewinner Juan Ramón Jiménez, a native opf the town (born 1881).

The road continues SW, running close to the Río Tinto, to the old port of *Palos de la Frontera*, now silted up and decayed, with the interesting 15th c. church of San Jorge. Beyond this is the Franciscan monastery of **La Rábida**, attractively situated on a hill at the mouth of the Río Tinto. A cross erected in 1892 commemorates Columbus's stay here. After failing in his efforts to win the support of John II of Portugal for his plans (1485), Columbus was given a friendly reception in the monastery and found an advocate of his cause in Prior Pérez de Marchena, Queen Isabel's confessor. After long negotiations Isabel was persuaded by the prospect of spreading Christianity in the new lands to conclude an agreement with Columbus which was signed at Santafé, and on 3 August 1492 he was able to set out on his voyage of discovery with his three carvels from Palos de la Frontera, returning to the same port on 15 March 1493. Hernán Cortés also landed there on his return from Mexico in 1528. The 14th c. church of the monastery has a Mudéjar cloister and a small museum with relics of the Conquistadors.

The return is by way of the bridge over the Río Tinto, at the far end of which, on the *Punta del Cebo*, is the *Columbus Monument* (34 m high). Then back to Huelva on the Paseo de la Rábida. Total distance 40 km.

To the Portuguese frontier. – This route to the extreme SW of Spain offers a number of opportunities of reaching the beaches of the Costa de la Luz, the resort of *Punta Umbria* and the beaches of *La Antilla* and *Isla Cristina*. – The road runs via *Gibraleón*, on the left bank of the Río Odiel, and *Lepe*, the Roman strong point of *Leptis*, and comes in 60 km to the Spanish frontier town of **Ayamonte** (at sea level; pop. 13,000; hotels; Parador Nacional Costa de la Luz, El Castellito, II, 20 r.; Don Diego, Ramón y Cajal, II, 45 r.), a fishing port of Phoenician origin at the mouth of the Río Guadiana. Interesting churches, including Nuestra Señora de las Angustias (beautiful façade; Capilla Mayor, with Mudéjar ceiling). – Car ferry (hourly service) to Portugal.

To the Río Tinto copper-mines. – On N 431 to (14 km) *San Juan del Puerto*; then N on N 435 towards the *Sierra Aracena*, passing through *Trigueros*, with the interesting Dolmen de Soto (probably 2nd millennium B.C.), and *Valverde del Camino* (alt. 270 m; pop. 10,000), where the Río Tinto copper-mining area begins, a region almost without vegetation. Then on to *Zalamea la Real* (alt. 387 m; pop. 5000), and from there E on C 421 into the **Río Tinto area**, with the towns of *Río Tinto* and *Nerva*, surrounded by the famous *copper-mines* (pyrites lying close to the surface, with 85% sulphur and between $\frac{1}{2}$ and 2% copper), among the richest in the world, which were already being worked in Iberian and Roman times. Formerly in British ownership, since 1954 they have been 66% Spanish-owned.

Continue N either on N 435 or on a local road from Río Tinto, both of which join European highway E 52 (N 433), which links Lisbon with Seville. On this road, E of the junction with N 435 and at the end of the direct road from Río Tinto, is the little hill town of **Aracena** (alt. 682 m; pop. 9000), situated among plantations of olives, figs and almonds; it has an excellent climate which makes it a popular health resort. Convento de Santa Catalina, with a fine doorway. On the *Cerro del Castillo* are the ruins of a Moorish castle with a church (13th c.), originally a mosque (12th c. Mudéjar tower). In the hill are the *Cuevas de las Maravillas*, with magnificent stalactites and stalagmites and an underground lake.

To the Tharsis mines. – Leave Huelva on N 431 and at *Gibraleón* (14 km) turn left into C 433, which runs NW via *San Bartolomé de la Torre* to *Alosno* (pop. 6000), 47 km from Huelva, at the beginning of the mining region of **Tharsis**, the Greek *Tartessos* and the Biblical Tarshish (Andalusia). The mines (pyrites, barytes, etc.) were worked by the Iberians and Romans.

Huesca

Province: Huesca (HU).
Telephone code: 974.
Altitude: 488 m. – Population: 38,000.
(i) **Oficina de Información de Turismo,**
  Coso Alto 23,
  tel. 22 57 78.
  Servicio Provincial de Turismo,
  Avda Santo Grial 6;
  tel. 22 13 77.

HOTELS. – *Pedro I de Aragon*, Del Parque 34, II, 52 r.; *Montearagón*, km 208 on N 240, III, 27 r.; Hostal *Mirasol*, Paseo Ramón y Cajal 29, P II, 13 r.; *Niagra*, Paseo Ramón y Cajal 67, P II, 18 r.; *Sancho Abarca* (no rest.), Plaza de Lizana 15, P II, 50 r.; *El Centro*, Sancho Ramírez 3, P III, 24 r.; *Lizana* (no rest.), Plaza de Lizana 8, P III, 19 r.; *Muro* (no rest.), Ricafort 2, P III, 24 r.;

San Lorenzo, San Orencio 10, P III, 26 r.; *La Unión Chaure* (no rest.), Zaragoza 2, P III, 14 r. – CAMPING SITE: *San Jorge*, on N 123.

RESTAURANTS. – In the hotels; also *Circulo Oscense*, Plaza de Navarra 7.

EVENTS. – *Semana Santa* (Holy Week), with processions. – *Fiesta de San Jorge* (Apr.), with pilgrimage to the saint's chapel and passion plays. – *Fiesta de San Lorenzo* (Aug.), with bullfights, sporting contests, folk performances and parades of splendidly decorated carriages.

Huesca, situated on the slopes of a hill above the Río Isuela, is a typical Pyrenean town. Capital of its province and a bishopric, it is also an important market town for the surrounding agricultural region.

HISTORY. – The Iberian *Osca* became in the 1st c. B.C., during the Roman civil war, the headquarters of the rebel Quintus Sertorius, who defended the country for almost ten years against Roman authority. After the expulsion of the Moors, Huesca was capital of Aragon from 1096 to 1118. During the Napoleonic wars the town was occupied by French troops, and it was the scene of heavy fighting during the Spanish Civil War.

SIGHTS. – On the highest point of the town, occupying the site of an earlier mosque, stands the Gothic **Cathedral** (13th–16th c.), with a beautiful 14th c. *main doorway* (rich figural decoration). Fine interior, with an alabaster *high altar* by Damián Forment (1520–33) and Renaissance *choir-stalls* (*c.* 1590). In the *Sacristy* is the valuable cathedral treasury. In the adjoining *Parroquía* is the famous Retablo de Monte Aragón by Gil Morlanes (1495). – Opposite the Cathedral is the 16th c. *Casa Consistorial* (Town Hall), with a Renaissance façade. – To the N is the **Museo Provincial**, housed in the ormer University, with prehistoric and Roman collections, Gothic frescoes and pictures of the 15th to 19th c. This was the scene of the "Bell of Huesca", an occasion in 1136 when King Ramiro II summoned his rebellious nobles and had 16 of them beheaded; 15 of the heads were then laid on the ground in the shape of a bell, with the sixteenth suspended above them as the clapper. – In the Mercado Nuevo is the church of **San Pedro**, one of the earliest Romanesque buildings in the region, built on the remains of an abbey (12th–13th c.), with a hexagonal *tower*. In the cloister are a number of tombs, including that of Ramiro II. – In the church of *San Lorenzo* (17th c.) is a carved and gilded altar.

SURROUNDINGS. – There are numerous places of interest or natural beauty within easy reach of Huesca. The most notable among them are covered in the following itineraries.

2 km SW of Huesca on N 123 is the *Santuario de San Jorge* (above the road on the right), built in 1554 on the remains of earlier walls; fine view of the town.

Over the Puerto de Monrepós. – C 136 (good for most of the way, but hilly and winding) runs N up the valley of the Río Isuela towards the Pyrenees, with the *Sierra de Guarra* (2076 m) on the right. Beyond *Nueno* are a number of short tunnels. The road then passes the *Embalse de Argüis* and comes to **Argüis** (alt. 1200), a popular summer holiday resort, after which it continues uphill, with many bends and fine views, and through a tunnel to the **Puerto de Monrepós** (1262 m). Thereafter it winds its way down into the valley of the *Río Gállego* and eventually reaches **Sabiñánigo**. 2 km farther on, at a road junction, there is a choice of two routes, which are described below as routes A and B.

Route A: Continue N on C 136 up the valley of the Río Gállego to **Biescas** (alt. 865 m; pop. 2000), a little market town situated astride the Gállego. – From here C 140 runs E over the *Puerto de Cotefablo* (1423 m) to *Torla*, and from there on to the magnificent **Parque Nacional de Ordesa** (alt. 1320 m), an area of rich and varied vegetation with numerous gorges, waterfalls, etc., in the valley of the *Río de Ordesa* below *Monte Perdido* (3352 m); splendid walking and climbing country.

Continuing N from Biescas, C 136 ascends the valley through beautiful mountain scenery. Above the road on the right is the convent of *Santa Elena*, a pilgrimage centre. – 15 km from Biescas a road goes off on the right and runs NE to the spa (sulphurous water) of **Balneario de Panticosa** (alt. 1659 m; Arruebo, III, 14 r.; Escalar, IV, 27 r.), in a magnificent *situation on a lake in a rocky cirque of the High Pyrenees.

Beyond the turning for Balneario de Panticosa C 136 continues up the Gállego valley to **Sallent del Gállego** (alt. 1310 m; hotels: *Formigal, I, 119 r.; Eguzki-Lore, II, 32 r., closed in summer), in the centre of a climbing and winter sports region; frontier town, with Spanish customs-post. – The road then continues uphill (moderate gradients), past the winter sports resort of *El Formigal* (1500 m), to the **Puerto de Portalet** (1792 m), on the French frontier (closed November to May).

Route B: C 134 runs W from Sabiñánigo along the foot of *Monte Bolas* (1467 m) to **Jaca** (see p. 140), situated on a hill above the *Río Aragón*. From here N 330 runs N up the valley of the Río Aragón, through magnificent mountain scenery, to **Canfranc** (alt. 1195 m), a high-altitude resort and frontier town (Spanish and French customs), with a 16th c. castle. Farther up the valley is the international railway station, at the end of the Somport tunnel (7875 m long).

N 330 continues up through a popular winter sports region, passing through *Candanchú* (alt. 1600 m), to the **Puerto de Somport** (1631 m), near the *Pic du Midi* (2885 m), on the French frontier (closed at night in winter).

Towards Pamplona. – N 240 runs over the fertile plain of *La Hoya* and then climbs, with many bends, on to the Meseta (fine views of the Pyrenees to the right), and comes to **Ayerbe** (alt. 560 m; pop. 2500), with the 15th c. Palacio del Marqués de Ayerbe. – 8 km NE is *Loarre*, at the foot of the Sierra de Loarre, with a picturesque *ruined castle (16th c.).

Mallos de Riglos

Beyond Ayerbe N 240 crosses the *Río Gállego* and runs through a gorge, with the mighty rock masses of the *Mallos de Riglos* on the right, followed by the *Embalse de la Peña*. It then continues to a road junction at **Santa María de la Peña** (alt. 542 m), where N 330 branches off on the right and crosses the *Puerto de Oroel* (1080 m) to *Jaca*. N 240 continues up the valley of the *Río Asabón*, with the *Sierra de San Juan de la Peña* on the right, and runs over the *Puerto de Santa Bárbara* (wide views) into the valley of the *Río Aragón*, reaching the river at a road junction where C 134 diverges to the right to Jaca.

Towards Lérida. – On N 240, which leads E towards Lérida, there are a number of features of interest in the immediate neighbourhood of Huesca. At *Quincena*, to the left, are the ruins of the monastery of *Monte Aragón*, founded in 1085 and destroed by fire in the 19th c.

Soon afterwards a road on the left runs N to the village of *Loporzano* (church of San Salvador, with a tabernacle from the monastery of Monte Aragón) and on to *Santa Eulalia la Mayor*, with the ruins of the monastery of San Martín de la Val Onsera (12th c.).

Torla, in the Pyrenees

A few kilometres farther on another road on the left runs N to *Liesa*, with fine 13th c. frescoes in the church of Santa María del Monte, and *Ibieca*, with the beautifully situated church of San Miguel de Foces (13th c.), which also has wall paintings, as well as a 12th c. figure of the Virgin.

N 240 continues via *Angüés* (alt. 544 m) to **Barbastro** (alt. 215 m; pop. 13,000); Hotel Rey Sancho Ramírez, III, 78 r., SP), an old episcopal town on the *Río Vero*. Interesting late Gothic Cathedral (16th c.), with a retablo by Damián Forment (1588) and stellate vaulting. Beside the road from Huesca is the pilgrimage chapel of San Pueyo.

From Barbastro a road goes N into the Pyrenees (see description below). – N 240 continues SE to **Monzón** (alt. 276 m; pop. 14,000), a little town with two castles, once the meeting-place of the Aragonese and Catalan Cortes, which sat in the building known as the Juego de Pelota.

The road crosses the *Canal de Zaidín* and continues via *Binéfar* (alt. 286 m) to *Almacellas*, beyond the boundary between Aragon (province of Huesca) and Catalonia (province of Lérida).

Via Barbastro into the Pyrenees. – Follow the preceding route as far as Barbastro (51 km from Huesca), and from there take C 138, a narrow road which winds NE up the valley of the *Río Cinca* to *El Grado* (dam, forming a long artificial lake) and *Naval* (ruined castle). It then goes over the *Alto del Pino* (857 m), with another artificial lake, the *Embalse de Mediano*, below on the right.

After passing through *Ainsa*, with a 12th c. collegiate church, an imposing ruined castle and the remains of a 9th c. monastery, the road comes to **Boltaña**, in the valley of the *Río Ara*, and continues up the valley, with the *Sierra de Bolave* on the right. Beyond *Brotó* it joins

C 140, coming from Biescas, and follows this road N to the magnificent Parque Nacional de Ordesa.

To Fraga. – Leave Huesca SE on C1310, coming in 2 km to the *Santuario de Nuestra Señora de Salas* (12th c. Romanesque church). Then continue through *Alberto Alto* and down the valley of the *Río Guatizalema* to **Sariñena**, a little town situated on a hill in a fertile vega. 9 km S is the *Cartuja de Monegros* (1731), with a large Baroque church and frescoes by Francisco Bayeu in the cells.

C 1310 continues SE from Sariñena. At *Villanueva de Sigena* is the monastery of Sigena, with a Romanesque church (1188) which had a Plateresque altar in alabaster (16th c.) and interesting monuments; good frescoes (13th c.) in several rooms, Mudéjar ceiling (13th c.) in one room.

C 1310 then reaches the valley of the *Río Cinca* and runs into N II (Zaragoza–Lérida). To the left of the junction is **Fraga** (alt. 120 m; pop. 7000), in a picturesque *situation above the left bank of the Río Cinca, a favourite summer resort. Church of San Pedro, originally Romanesque (12th c.), later rebuilt.

Jaca

Province: Huesca (HU).
Telephone code: 974.
Altitude: 820 m. – Population: 10,000.
ⓘ **Oficina de Información de Turismo,**
Paseo Calvo Sotela;
tel. 36 00 98.

HOTELS. – *Gran Hotel* (no rest.), Paseo del General Franco 1, II, 98 r., SP; *Conde de Aznar*, Paseo del General Franco 3, III, 23 r.; *La Paz* (no rest.), Mayor

41, III, 34 r.; *Pradas* (no rest.), Obispo 12, III, 39 r.; *Mur*, Santa Orosia 1, IV, 68 r.; *Hostal El Abeto* (no rest.), Bellido 15, P II, 25 r.; etc. – CAMPING SITES: *Victoria*, E of the town; two other sites *Edelweiss* and *Pirineos*, in the vicinity.

RESTAURANT. – *Somport*, Avda Primo de Rivera 1.

EVENTS. – *Semana Santa* (Holy Week), with procession. – *Moros y Cristianos* (May), with mock battles commemorating the Christian victory over the Moors; also Romería de la Victoria (pilgrimage). – *Fiesta de Santa Orosia* (June), patronal festival, with procession. – *Courses for foreigners* run by the University of Zaragoza (July–Aug.).

Jaca, situated on a hill above the Río Aragón, once a staging point on the Way of St James (see p. 242), is the seat of a bishop and a branch of Zaragoza University (in summer).

SIGHTS. – Remains of the old *town walls* (10th c,). – *Castle* (begun 1571), to the N of the town. – Romanesque **Cathedral** (1040), later remodelled and decorated in Plateresque style. Square *tower; frescoes* by Manuel Bayeu (1792); under the high altar the remains of Santa Orosia; tomb of a 16th c. bishop. – 16th c. *Ayuntamiento* (Town Hall), with wrought-iron grilles on windows.

SURROUNDINGS. – **Over the Puerto de Oroel**: S on N 330 to the *Puerto de Oroel* (1769 m), on the western slopes of the *Peña de Oroel* (1769 m: rewarding climb, 3 hours from Jaca), with magnificent views. Then on to *Bernués*, from which a mountain road runs 11 km W to the 11th c. monastery of *San Juan de la Peña* (alt. 1115 m). – Continue on N 330 past the *Embalse de la Peña* to the road junction at **Santa María de la Peña**.

Apse of Jaca Cathedral

Jaén

Province: Jaén (J).
Telephone code: 953.
Altitude: 573 m. – Population: 95,000.
(i) **Oficina de Información de Turismo,**
Avenida de Madrid 10;
tel. 22 27 37.
Patronato Provincial de Turismo,
Plaza de San Francisco 2;
tel. 26 21 11.

HOTELS. – *Parador Nacional de Santa Catalina,* Castillo Santa Cataline, I 43 r.; *Condestable Iranzo,* Paseo de La Estación 32, II, 147 r.; *Xauen* (no rest.), Plaza Deán de Mazas 3, II, 35 r.; *Europa* (no rest.), Plaza de Belén 1, III, 36 r.; *Rey Fernando* (no rest.), Plaza de Coco de la Piñera 7, III, 36 r.; *Hostal Reyes Católicos* (no rest.), Avda de Granada 1, P I, 28 r.; *La Yuca* (no rest.) km 340 on N 323, P I, 23 r.

RESTAURANTS. – *Dover*, Maestro Cebrián 1; *Los Mariscos*, Nueva 2. – on N 323: *Ruta del Sol*, 2 km N.

EVENTS. – *Fiestas de la Patrona* (Apr.), pilgrimage in honour of Nuestra Señora de la Cabeza, one of the most important Marian festivals in Andalusia. – *Semana Santa* (Holy Week), with an impressive procession. – *Fiestas de la Virgen de la Capilla* (June). – *Fiestas y Ferias de San Lucas* (Oct.), the town's principal fiesta, with bullfights, exhibitions and riding events. – *Lumbres de San Antón* (Jan.), a typical popular fiesta at which the traditional fires (*lumbres*) are lighted. – *Festividad de Santa Catalina* (Nov.).

The provincial capital of Jaén, an old established bishopric, lies at the foot of the Sierra Jabalcúz and the Sierra de la Pandera, the slopes of which, to the S of the town, are covered with large plantations of olive-trees.

HISTORY. – The town was known to the Romans as *Auringis*, and the local silver-mines were worked during the Roman period. Under the Moors Jaén was capital of the kingdom of Jayyan, and after it was recaptured by Ferdinand III in 1246 it became an advanced base of the Reconquista.

SIGHTS. – On the town's highest point stands the massive **Cathedral** (16th–18th c.), a fine example of Spanish Renaissance architecture. Built on the site of an earlier mosque, it was begun about 1500 by Andrés de Valdelvira. The W front has twin towers and a relief carving by Pedro Roldán. Impressive interior, with fine 15th c. *choir-stalls*. A shrine by the high altar contains a "napkin of St Veronica". – In the separate *Sagrario* are a picture ascribed to Albrecht Dürer and a figure of Jesus Nazarenus by Montañés which is carried in the Easter procession.

NW of the Cathedral is the historic old *Arco de San Lorenzo* (national monument). on a hill NW of the town stands the *Castillo de Santa Catalina*, now a Parador Nacional, with parts of the old town walls. – At the foot of the hill is the church of *La Magdalena*, probably the town's oldest church, with a late Gothic doorway; it occupies the site of an earlier mosque. To the E is the *Santa Capilla de San Andrés* (1515), founded by Gutiérrez González Doncel, Pope Leo X's treasurer, probably built originally as a synagogue; in the Capilla de la Purísima are a statue of the Virgin (Andalusian school) and a picture of the Virgen del Pópulo. Close by is the *Real Monasterio de Santa Clara* (13th c.), the town's oldest monastery, with a beautiful cloister and a fine representation of the Cristo de Bambú. In Calle Santa Clara is the *Palacio del Obispo Sanmartín*. Numerous other palaces and patrician houses. – In the Avenida del Ejército Español, in the N of the town, is the **Museo Provincial** (archaeology, works of art, folk art).

SURROUNDINGS. – In the immediate neighbourhood of Jaén there are a number of places of interest, including the spa and summer resort of *Baños de Jabalcúz* (6 km S on C 3221); *La Guardia de Jaén* (11 km SE on a minor road), with the ruins of an old castle and an interesting parish church; and *Otiñar* (14 km S on the minor road to the artificial lake of Quiebrajano), at the foot of the Sierra de la Pandera, with a monument dating from the time of Charles III.

Ruta del Renacimiento ("Renaissance Highway"). – This is the road to Albacete (N 321), which runs NE from Jaén, crosses the Guadalquivir on the Puente del Obispo and continues to **Baeza** (see p. 62), 48 km from Jaén, which is bypassed by the road to **Úbeda**, 9 km farther on. Here N 321 joins N 322, coming from Bailén, which runs NE to **Villacarrillo** (alt. 810 m; pop. 20,000), with an imposing 16th c. church, one of the finest Renaissance buildings in the province (by Valdelvira), and a 17th c. monastery.

Farther along N 322 a road on the left goes up to the mountain village of **Iznatoraf** (alt. 1032 m), a short distance off the main road, with a parish church of 1602 and a magnificent view of the surrounding mountains and villages – N 322 continues NE through

Castillo de Santa Catalina, Jaén

the *Sierra de Alcaraz*, passing through the little town of **Alcaraz**, and then crosses the *Puerto de los Picicos* (2058 m) and runs down to **Albacete**, 267 km from Jaén.

Ruta de las Batallas ("Battle Highway"). – Leave Jaén on N 323, which runs N in the direction of Manzanares. The road winds down the valley of the *Río Guadalbullón* and comes in 24 km to *Mengíbar* (alt. 323 m), the ancient *Ossigi*, with a Moorish tower, and after crossing the Guadalquivir continues to **Bailén** (alt. 349 m; pop. 14,000; Parador de Turismo, II, 86 r., SP), at an important road junction. Here in 208 B.C. the Roman consul Scipio the Elder defeated the Carthaginian general Hasdrubal, and in 1808 Spanish troops fought a battle with a Napoleonic army. Church of the Encarnación (15th c.), with sculpture by Alonso Cano. – From Bailén E on N 322 to (15 km) **Linares** (alt. 418; pop. 60,000), an industrial town near the site of the important Iberian settlement of *Castulo*, in a mining area in the upper Guadalquivir valley. Church of Santa María la Mayor (12th–13th c., Gothic); church of San Francisco, with a beautiful retablo (16th c.). 5 km from the town are the remains of the ancient Castulo. – 30 km W of Bailén on N IV is **Andújar** (alt. 212 m; pop, 33,000), an old town on the right bank of the Guadalquivir near the site of the Iberian *Illiturgi* (Los Villares); it is noted for the manufacture of handsome water jars (*alcarrazas*, *jarras*). The Gothic church of Santa María has a "Christ in the Garden of Olives" by El Greco.

From Bailén the Ruta de las Batallas continues N on N IV. A side road on the left leads to *Baños de la Encina* (6 km), with an old castle. Then via *Guarromán* (alt. 349 m) to **La Carolina** (alt. 605 m; pop. 15,000), off the road on the left, with the ruins of once flourishing lead-mines is a town built by 18th c. German settlers. – A short distance farther on, to the right of N IV (2·5 km), is **Las Navas de Tolosa** (alt. 694 m), another attractive village, also settled by German immigrants, which was the scene of a victory by a Christian army of Castilians, Aragonese and Germans over the Almohades on 16 July 1212 (monument just before the town).

N IV now climbs slowly to **Santa Elena** (alt. 742 m), a trim little town on a hill with extensive *views, near the boundary between Andalusia and New Castile. This was another of the series of new settlements established during the reign of Charles III (1767–69) and occupied mainly by German immigrants, now completely absorbed into the Spanish population.

Ruta de la Reconquista. – Leave Jaén on N 321, which runs W to the road junction at *Torredonjimeno*, and continue on N 321, bearing left, to **Martos** (alt. 747 m; pop. 22,000), founded in the Ibero-Roman period, with the Castillo de la Peña and the church of Santa María, in which is the tomb of the Carvajal brothers. – 5 km away is *Baños de Martos*.

Continue SW on N 321 to *Alcaudete*, with an Arab castle and the Casa del Almirante. –From here N 432 runs SE to **Alcalá la Real** (alt. 900 m; pop. 22,000), the Moorish *Al-Kalaat be Zayde*, with towers and fortifications, the *Castillo de la Mota* (13th–15th c.), the church of Santa María (imposing tower) and a beautiful Plateresque fountain (16th c.). From here N 432 leads SE to Granada: the present itinerary, however, follows N 432 NW via **Baena** (see p. 108) to **Córdoba** (see p. 104), 138 km from Jaén.

Játiva

Province: Valencia (V).
Telephone code: 96.
Altitude: 110 m. – Population: 21,000.
ⓘ **Oficina Municipal de Turismo,**
Alameda Jaume I. 35;
tel. 2 27 55 61.

HOTELS: – *Vernisa* (no rest.), Académico Maravell 1,
III, 39 r.; *Murta*, Angel Lacalle 1, IV, 21 r.; *Hostal
Moreno*, San Francisco 36, P III, 7 r.

**The charming old town of Játiva, the
Roman Saetabis and the Moorish
Xateba, noted since ancient times
for its textiles, has a magnificent
situation on the N side of Monte
Bernisa, whose two peaks are
crowned by castles. It was the birthplace of the painter José de Ribera
(1588–1652).**

SIGHTS. – The **Colegiata** church, built
on the foundations of an Arab mosque,
contains fine altarpieces, including one of
Nuestra Señora de la Seo, the town's
patroness, on the high altar. Tower 60 m
high. – In the picturesque *Calle de
Moncada* are many old palaces and fountains. – Parish church of *San Pedro*, with
a fine Gothic retablo. – *Museo Municipal*,
with archaeological and historical collections, including a richly decorated
Moorish marble basin (11th c.). – Fine
views from the Calvary, planted with
cypresses, from the *Ermita de San Feliú*
(13th c.) and from the *Castillo Major*,
built on Iberian and Roman foundations,
in which many notable prisoners were
confined (designated national monument).

SURROUNDINGS. – SW of Játiva on C 3316,
reached by way of a minor road (8 km) is the village of
Canals, with a castle which was the birthplace of
Alfonso Borja (b. 1378), founder of the Italian Borgia
family, and of Pope Calixtus III (d. 1458).

Jerez de la Frontera

Province: Cádiz (CA).
Telephone code: 956.
Altitude: 55 m. – Population: 180,000.
ⓘ **Oficina de Información de Turismo,**
Alameda Cristina;
tel. 34 20 37.

HOTELS. – **Jerez,*, Avda Alcalde Alvaro Domecq 35,
L, 121 r., SP; *Capele* (no rest.), General Franco 58, II,
30 r.; *El Coloso* (no rest.), Pedro Alonso 13, IV, 25 r.;

A bodega in Jerez de la Frontera

Garaje Centro (no rest), Doña Blanca 10, IV, 23 r.;
Motel Aloha, km 637 on bypass, II, 27 r., SP; etc.

RESTAURANTS.– *El Bosque*, Avda Alcalde Alvaro
Domecq 26; *El Buen Comer*, Zaragoza 38; *Gaitán*,
Gaitán 3; *San Francisco*, Plaza de Esteve 2.

EVENTS. – *Feria del Caballo* (May), the "Fiesta of the
Horse". – *Feria del Vino* (Sept.), a wine festival with
flamenco dancing.

RECREATION. – Bullfights; Parque Zoológico Alberto
Durán.

BODEGAS. – Every visitor should make a tour of one
of the famous *bodegas (wine-cellars). The usual time
for visits is from 9.30 to 12.30, but some cellars are
also open in the afternoon. The best known are the
following: *Bodega Bobadilla*, on the bypass; *Bodega
Garvey*, Guadalete 14; *Bodega González Byass*, María
González 12; *Bodega Pedro Domecq*, San
Ildefonso 3; and *Bodega Sandeman*, Pizarro 10.

**Jerez de la Frontera, famous for
sherry – to which it has given its
name, lies near Cádiz in a fertile hilly
region on the southern edge of the
Andalusian plain.**

HISTORY. – The area between Jerez and Cape
Trafalgar was the scene of the decisive battle in 711
between Visigoths and Moors in which Christian
Spain was condemned to many centuries of subjection under alien peoples from the East. Another
great battle fought here in 1340 ended in a Christian
victory which prevented the final invasion from North
Africa. Jerez has borne the style "de la Frontera" ("on
the frontier") – along with other towns on the frontier
with the Moorish East – since 1379.

SIGHTS. – The main attractions of Jerez
are the famous bodegas or wine-cellars
(see above). – The main square, the
Alameda Fortún de Torres, planted with
gardens, is in the southern part of the
town. On its S side is the *Alcázar*, a
massive structure dating from the 11th c.,
with a Gothic church and Arab baths; from
the keep there are extensive views.

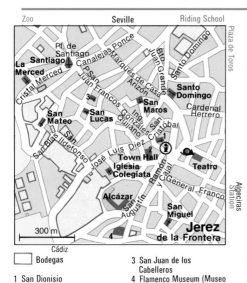

Bodegas

1 San Dionisio
2 Museo Arqueológico
3 San Juan de los Cabelleros
4 Flamenco Museum (Museo de Flamencología)

León (Town)

Province: Léon (LE).
Telephone code: 987.
Altitude: 837 m. – Population: 120,000.

ⓘ Oficina de Informatión de Turismo,
Plaza de Regla 4;
tel. 23 70 82.
Delegacion Provincial de Turismo
General Sanjurjo 15;
tel. 22 77 12

HOTELS. – *San Marcos*, Plaza de San Marcos 7, L, 258 r.;;*Conde Luna* (no rest.), Independencia 7, I, 154 r., SP; *Quindos* (no rest.), Avda José Antonio 24, III, 96 r.; *Riosol* (no rest.), Avda de Palencia 3, III, 141 r.; etc.

RESTAURANTS. – In the hotels, including *El Mesón* in Hotel Conde Luna; also *Novelty*, Independencia 4.

EVENTS. – *Fiesta de las Cabezadas* (second Sunday after Easter) in Basílica San Isidoro, a typical local fiesta with unique ceremonial. – *Fiestas San Juan y San Pedro* (June), with numerous contests, bullfights, and processions of carriages; partly combined with Festivales de España. – *Foro u Oferta* (Aug.) in cloister of the Cathedral, a colourful pageant play with folk singers (*cantaderas*). – *Pilgrimages* (Sept. and Oct.) to the chapel of the Virgen del Camino, with characteristic dances and costumes from all over the region.

To the NW of this is the Baroque *Colegiata* church (begun in 1695), built on the foundations of an earlier mosque; from the tower there are also good views. – NE of the Alcázar and the church are the *Ayuntamiento* (Town Hall) of 1575 and, in the Plaza de la Asunción, the *Museo Arqueológico*, now a national monument, with a Plateresque façade; rich collections and municipal library. To the E is the church of *San Dionisio* (1430), in Mudéjar style with a very fine Baroque retablo. – From here Calle San Cristóbal leads to the main square of the old town, the palm-shaded *Plaza General Primo de Rivera*, with a statue of the former head of the government, *Miguel Primo de Rivera* (1870–1930).

In the northern part of the old town are other notable churches including the 12th c. church of *Santo Domingo*, with a very fine cloister. To the W of this is the church of *San Marco* (begun 1613), another designated national monument. SE of the Alcázar is the church of *San Miguel* (1430–1512), with a W front built in 1672; the harmonious interior contains a retablo with carving by Montañés (1625) on the high altar.

SURROUNDINGS. – 4·5 km SE of Jerez is the **Cartuja**, a Carthusian monastery founded in 1477, which since 1876 has housed a stud farm, the Depósito de Caballos Sementals. It has a magnificent Renaissance gate (1571) and a Gothic church (richly decorated façade of 1667, beautiful *reja* of 1760). In the mid 18th c. Charles III presented the Empress Maria Theresa with a number of Cartuja stallions, sires of the Lipizzaner horses of the Vienna Riding School.

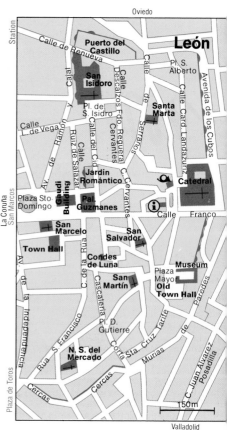

León Cathedral

León, capital of its province and the seat of a bishop, lies at the confluence of the Río Torío and the Río Bernesga in the north-western part of the Spanish inland plateau, the Meseta, on the S side of the Cantabrian Mountains.

The town owes its name to the Roman Seventh Legion, having developed out of the Legion's camp in the 1st c. A.D. Its heyday was from the 10th to the 12th c., when it was for a time capital of the kingdom of the same name, which extended from the Atlantic Ocean to the Rhône. It lost this status when the kingdoms of León and Castile were reunited in 1230. During the Middle Ages the town was also an important staging point on the Way of St James (see p. 242), the pilgrim route to Santiago de Compostela.

SIGHTS. – In the *Plazuela de San Marcelo,* the hub of the town's traffic, are a number of important buildings, including the church of *San Marcelo* (1588–1627), with a reliquary of the saint; the *Casa del Ayuntamiento* (Town Hall) of 1585; the adjoining *Theatre*; and the *Casa de Botines* designed by Antonio Gaudí (1894), a fine privately owned building. – On the NE side of the square is the *Diputación Provincial,* occupying a building reminiscent of an Italian palazzo, the Casa de los Guzmanes (1560), with wrought-iron balconies and an imposing façade.

From here the town's principal street, *Calle del Generalísmo Franco,* leads to the

Plaza de Regla, in which is the ****Cathedral** of *Santa María de la Regla* (13th–14th c.), the work of a number of different architects. It is an impressive structure, 91 m long, one of the great masterpieces of early Gothic architecture in Spain, showing close affinities to the cathedrals of Reims and Amiens. Particularly fine is the W front with its two imposing towers (65 m and 68 m high), the mighty rose window and the three doorways, richly decorated with sculpture. The similarly articulated S façade is also of outstanding quality.

The incomparable beauty of the harmonious INTERIOR is due particularly to the astonishing light effects produced by the tracery of the windows which are up to 12 m in height. The *stained glass* ranges in date from the 13th to the 20th c., the oldest glass being in the middle choir chapel and the rose windows on the W and N fronts. The *Choir* (15th–16th c.) has magnificent **choir-stalls.* The richly gilded alabaster *Trascoro* dates from 1575. The *Capilla Mayor* contains a Gothic retablo with 15th c. paintings (scenes from the life of San Froilán, bishop of Léon 900–905). – The chapels opening off the *ambulatory* contain numerous handsome monuments, notable among them the richly decorated tomb (early 14th c.) of Ordoño II (d. 924) on the rear wall of the Capilla Mayor. – On the N side of the Cathedral is the Plateresque *****Cloister**, which cannot be entered but can be seen from the adjoining **Cathedral Museum**.

S of the Cathedral, beyond the *Seminario Mayor* which now houses the *Diocesan Museum,* is the arcaded *Plaza Mayor,* on the W side of which is the imposing twin-towered *Consistorio Viejo* (Old Town Hall) of 1677. Behind it is the 13th c. church of *San Martín.*

From the E end of the Cathedral the line of the old **town walls,** partly dating from the 3rd c. A.D., with numerous round towers (*cubos*), runs N and then W to one of the old town gates, the *Puerta del Castillo* (1759). A little way SW via the Plaza del Castillo is the *****Colegiate de San Isidoro** (completed 1149), with a massive Romanesque tower and two richly decorated S doorways; the late Gothic Capilla Mayor contains a 16th c. retablo and the remains of San Isidoro. – Adjoining the church is the **Panteón,* the old royal burial vault, with remarkable Romanesque ceiling paintings (*c.* 1160–80) and several Romanesque reliquaries in the treasury.

In the NW outskirts of the town, on the Río Bernesga, is the former *****Convento de San Marcos** (now a hotel), the main (S) front of which (E half 1533–41, W half, with doorway, 1708–16) is unsurpassed in the richness and delicacy of its Plateresque decoration. – On the E side of the Convento is the church of *San Marcos* (consecrated 1541), with beautiful choirstalls (1543). The sacristy, the cloister and the adjoining chapter rooms house the *Museo Arqueológico Provincial*; outstanding among the museum's many treasures is an 11th c. ivory figure of Christ.

SURROUNDINGS. – The area round León, like other parts of Spain which have been the scene of great events, is rich in monuments of the past, many of them within easy reach of the main roads.

Over the Puerto de Pajares. – The route runs N through the Cantabrian Mountains on N 630, which follows the *Río Bernesga* and eventually climbs to the *Alto del Rabizo* (1160 m). Beyond this is *La Robla*, with coal-mines. The road then continues along the Bernesga valley to *La Pola de Gordón*, also with coalmines, and through a picturesque gorge to **Villamín** (alt. 1129 m), a village in the Cantabrian Mountains, from which an excursion can be made to the ruined monastery of *San Antón*, with the Romanesque Capilla de Poladura.

N 630 then climbs to the summit ridge of the Cantabrian Mountains and the **Puerto de Parjares** (1364 m; Parador Nacional, II, 28 r.), on the boundary between León and Asturias, with magnificent views. The road then runs down the northern slopes of the hills by way of *Mieres* to Oviedo (see p. 178), 120 km from León.

To Valladolid. – N 601 leaves León by way of the Avenida de Madrid and crosses the Meseta to *Río Porma* (13 km), where a road goes off on the left to *Mellanzos* and the important Mozarabic church of *San Miguel de la Escalada* (10th c.), now designated as a national monument.

The main road continues over the *Río Esla* to the little walled town on *Mansilla de las Mulas* and past the *Montes del Payuelo* (965 m), to the left of the road. A short distance farther on N 120 goes off on the left to (28 km) the old town of *Sahagún* (alt. 836 m; pop. 2600), with four brick-built Romanesque churches (12th–13th c.). – Soon afterwards N 601 enters the province of Valladolid and continues by way of **Medina de Rioseco** to **Valladolid** (see p. 236), 134 km from León.

To Benavente. – N 630 runs S down the valley of the *Río Bernesga* and later the *Río Esla* to *Villamañán* (32 km), where C 621 goes off on the left to **Valencia de Don Juan**, on the Río Esla, with the 15th c. castle of the Counts of Oñate, surrounded by walls and a moat, and the interesting church of San Pedro. N 630 then continues into the province of Zamora and comes to **Benavente** (see p. 80).

Over the Puerto del Manzanal. – N 120 runs SW over the *Río Bernesga*, beyond which a road goes off to the pilgrimage church of the *Virgen del Camino* (1960). – Thereafter N 120 crosses the *Canal del Páramo* and the *Río Orbigo* and comes to **Hospital de Orbigo** (camping site). From here a road runs S to the 30-arched bridge of *Veguellina* (2·5 km), where Suero de Quiñones and nine fellow-knights fought a famous battle lasting 30 days in 1434.

N 120 continues through an agricultural region to **Astorga** (see p. 57), where it joins N VI. – N VI runs NW into the *Maragatería* (p. 56) and through a moorland region, goes over a pass (1105 m) and climbs, passing through *Rodrigatos*, to the **Puerto del Manzanal** (1230 m), in the *Montañas de León* (restaurant, petrol station). It then winds its way down through a beautiful mountain valley (fine views) to *Torre del Bierzo* (alt. 656 m), on the Río Tremor, and continues through a coal-mining area, with pithead gear and spoil heaps, to **Bembibre**, with a ruined castle and a former synagogue (15th c.), now the church of San Pedro. – The road then descends the gradually widening valley of the *Río Boeza* to the industrial town of **Ponferrada** (see p. 187), where N 120 and N VI separate again.

León (Region)

Provinces: León, Zamora and Salamanca.

The three provinces which constitute the historic region of León are now regarded as belonging geographically and for administrative purposes to Castile-León. They include most of the northern part of the Meseta, bounded in the N by the Cantabrian Mountains and in the S by the Sierra de Gredos. The central part of the region is occupied by the Duero basin, interlaced by the Río Duero and its various tributaries.

On the higher ground the poor soils and unfavourable weather conditions allow only a limited amount of crop-farming in addition to stock-farming (cattle, including fighting bulls, and sheep) on the upland pastures (*dehesas*), usually planted with a scatter of cork-oaks. In the valleys of the rivers – which are increasingly being harnessed by the building of dams to provide irrigation and hydro-electric power – wheat and rye are grown (the former in Zamora, the latter in León). The people of this inhospitable region are tough and tenacious. The older generation hold steadfastly to their traditional way of life, while younger people leave the land in large numbers to seek employment in the towns and in other parts of Spain; only a few emigrate.

León has a glorious history going back to the Visigoths (who have left remains of their art and architecture). After the establishment of the kingdom of Asturias by Pelayo following his victory over the Moors, Alfonso III (866–910) pushed its frontier S to the Duero and moved the capital from Oviedo to León, which now gave its name to the kingdom. The union with Aragon and Navarre was followed by a period of splendour, but the kingdom was repeatedly weakened by conflicts with Castile, now strengthened by the Reconquista. Under Alfonso VI (1065–1109), whose vassal Rodrigo Díaz del Vivar became famous as El Cid, even Castile became subject to the crown of León, and the king now claimed the title of emperor. In 1230, however, under Ferdinand III, son of Alfonso IX of León and a daughter of Alfonso VIII of Castile, León finally lost its independence.

Lérida

Province: Lérida (L).
Telephone code: 973.
Altitude: 154 m. – Population: 102,000.
ⓘ **Oficina de Información de Turismo**,
Arc. del Pont s/n;
tel. 24 81 20.
Conserija de Turismo,
Avenida Blondell 1;
tel. 26 74 15.

HOTELS. – *Condes de Urgel II* (no rest.), Avda de Barcelona 17, I, 105 r.; *Sansi Park*, Alcalde Porqueres 4, II, 26 r.; *Llerda*, km 467 on Barcelona road III, 110 r.; *Jamaica*, km 462·5 on the Madrid road III, 24 r.; *Principal* (no rest.), Plaza de la Pahería 8, III, 53 r.; *Ramón Berenguer IV* (no rest.), Plaza Ramón Berenguer IV 3, IV, 60 r.; *Rexi* (no rest.), Avda. Blondel 56 IV, 25 r.; Hostal *España*, Rambla-Ferrán 20, P II, 30 r.; *Estación Renfe*, Estación Renfe, P II, 9 r.; *Goya* (no rest.), Alcalde Costa 9, P II, 19 r.; *Peninsular*, Plaza Berenguer IV 5, P II, 20 r.; *Santiago*, Alcalde Costa 15, P II, 19 r.; etc. – 2 km SW ON THE ZARAGOZA ROAD Hostal *Bimba*, P III, 29 r., SP; *La Jamaica* (no rest.), P III, 29 r. – CAMPING SITE: *Les Basses*, 6 km NW.

RESTAURANTS. – In the hotels; also *La Rada*, Avda Blondel 40; *Estación Colavidas*, at railway station. – ON N II: *Palermo*, 1·5 km SW. – ON C 1313: *Molí de la Nora*, 10 km SE.

EVENTS. – *Semana Santa* (Holy Week), with processions. – *Fanalets de* Sant Jaime (July), with a children's procession and a pilgrimage. – *Feria* (Sept.), a large fair and agricultural show.

Lérida, capital of the province of the same name, lies on the Río Segre in western Catalonia, between Barcelona and Zaragoza; it is dominated by a castle on a hill. It has been the seat of a bishop since 1149, and between 1300 and 1717 had a university (founded by Jaime II).

HISTORY. – The town was originally an Iberian foundation, which became Roman in the 2nd c. B.C. under the name of *Ilerda*. Between 713 and 1117 it was mostly under Moorish rule, and in the 12th and 13th c. was a residence of the kings of Argon.

SIGHTS. – There is a good general view of the town from the bridge over the Río Segre. Near the bridge, at the foot of the castle hill, is the central feature of the town, the *Plaza de España*, on the N side of which is the church of *San Juan*. – W of this square is the arcaded *Plaza de la Pahería*, from which the *Calle Mayor* (closed to cars) runs W. At the rear end of this street, on the left, is the *Ayuntamiento* (Town Hall), with a beautiful façade, originally Romanesque but several times rebuilt or altered; it houses a museum. At the end of the street, on the right, is the neo-classical **New Cathedral** (*Catedral Nueva*), built in 1781, with a Corinthian portico; the *Cathedral Museum* contains liturgical utensils, tapestries, etc. Facing the Cathedral is the *Hospital de Santa María* (15th–16th c.), with an impressive inner courtyard; it now contains an *archaeological museum* and a modern *picture gallery*.

A short distance NW of the New Cathedral, adjoining the modern *Bishop's Palace*, is the little church of *San Lorenzo*, built 1270–1300, which is believed to incorporate an earlier mosque converted from a Roman temple. The church has an octagonal tower and contains a number of retablos of the 14th and 15th c. – W of the Bishop's Palace, in the Rambla de Aragón, is the *Seminario* with the *Diocesan Museum* (sculpture, pictures, liturgical utensils).

Cloister of the Old Cathedral, Lérida

Viella, in the Pyrenees

From the Bishop's Palace the Calle de Tallada and a stepped path lead up to the 12th c. **Castillo**, a massive fortress with four towers on the summit of the hill. Within the walls is the **Old Cathedral** (*Seo Antigua*), originally built in the 13th c. but much the worse for 18th c. alterations. It still preserves its beautiful doorways, the octagonal domed tower over the crossing and a tall bell-tower (1416) adjoining the Gothic *cloister. The whole castle, including the Cathedral, is now designated as a national monument.

SURROUNDINGS. – Lérida is a good centre for excursions into the valleys of the Pyrenees and into Andorra.

Into the Pyrenees by way of Tremp. – Leave Lérida on C 1313 and in 27 km turn left into C 148, which crosses the Río Segre and comes to **Balaguer** (alt. 235 m; pop. 12,000; hotels: Conde Jaime de Urgel, I, 60 r., SP; Mirador del Segre, III, 33 r.), a little town situated in a fertile agricultural region, with the church of San Almater. – 8 km W is *Castelló de Farfaña*, with a ruined castle and an interesting Gothic church. – From Balaguer the C 147 along the left bank of the Segre is still under construction, and until it is completed it is necessary to take the existing secondary road on the right bank which runs over the Puerto de Ager and joins the completed section of C 147 near the Embalse de Terradets. The old road runs NW from Balaguer through the *Sierra de Montroig* to the village of *Las Avellanas*. ON a hill to the right of the road is a Premonstratensian monastery founded in 1166, once the burial place of the Counts of Urgel, with a Romanesque cloister. – After passing through *Font de Pou* the road climbs to the *Puerto de Ager* (912 m) and then runs down to **Ager**, an old town with the remains of Roman walls and the ruined collegiate church of San Pedro (12th c.). It then descends the slopes of the *Sierra de Montsech* (1677 m) into the valley of the *Río Noguera Pallaresa*, with the *Embalse de Camarasa*, an artificial lake formed by a dam 151 m long and 92 m high (hydro-electric power station, 700,000 kW). On the far side of the river the completed section of C 147 comes in on the right. Continuing on this, we go through the tunnels of the *Portell dels Terradets*, between the hills

of the Sierra de Montsech, and continue along the *Embalse de Terradets* to **Tremp** (alt. 459 m; pop. 4000), a busy little industrial town on a hill above the right bank of the Río Noguera Pallaresa, with remains of old fortifications and a hydroelectric station (300,000 kW) below the dam, 206 m long, 82 m high, which forms the large artificial lake along the W side of which the town now extends.

Then on through the little medieval town of *Talarn* to **Pobla de Segur** (alt. 540 m; pop. 3000), at the junction of the *Río Flamisell* and the *Río Noguera Pallaresa*, a good climbing and fishing centre. Here the road divides, offering two alternative routes.

Route A: From Pobla de Segur take the left-hand road (C 144), which winds its way via Senterada up to the *Puerto de Perves* (1350 m), with the *Siera de San Gervás* (1839 m) on the left. Then over the *Puerto de Viu* (1325 m) and down into the valley of the *Río Noguera Ribagorzana*, here dammed to form the 8 km long *Embalse de Escalas*, with **Pont de Suert**, where C 144 runs into N 230 from Lérida (see below). – Continue up the valley on N 230, passing through *Villaller* and running to the E of *Maladeta (Pico de Aneto, 3404 m), the highest peak in the Pyrenees; then through the *Tunel de Viella* to **Viella** (alt. 975 m; pop. 1000; hotels Tuca I, 118 r.; Parador Nacional Valle de Arán, II,135 r.; SP), the chief place in the Arán valley. Beautiful 13th c. church with a 16th c. tower.

From Viella N 230 continues up the Garona valley to *Bosost* (alt. 765 m), with a well-preserved Romanesque church (12th c.). Then via the little spa of *Lés* (alt. 635 m), with the Spanish frontier control, to the *Pont de Rey* (alt. 580 m), on the French frontier. The road then runs down the Garonne valley to Toulouse.

Route B: From Pobla de Segur the right-hand road (C 147) runs up the valley of the *Río Noguera Pallaresa*, passing numerous waterfalls, and through a wild gorge, the *Desfiladero de Collegats*, with the *Bou Mort* (2082 m) on the right. It then comes to **Gerri de la Sal**, with a former Benedictine monastery (12th c.), and traverses another large gorge to **Sort** (alt. 692), with a ruined castle. 12 km NW of the village is the winter sports resort of *Llesúy* (alt. 1400 m), with a ski-lift on to the Loma de Sauri.

After another narrow defile (tunnel) the *Río Cardós*, which rises on the *Pica d'Estax* (3141 m), the highest peak in Catalonia, flows into the Noguera Pallaresa on

Gerri de la Sal

the right. The road then continues to *Escaló*, with the ruins of the 10th c. monastery of Sant Pere del Burgal (Romanesque wall paintings). Beyond this, on the right, is an artificial lake almost 4 km long, the *Embalse de la Torrasa*. 6 km off the road on the left is the winter sports resort of **Espot** (alt. 1340 m), with a chair-lift and ski-lift. *Ermita de San Mauricio* (with lake). The village lies at the E end of the *Parque Nacional Aigües Tortes*.

C 147 continues through *Esterri de Áneu* (alt. 1000 m; hotels) into the valley of the *Río Bonaigua*, and then climbs again, passing the *Parador Farga de los Abetos* (closed in winter) and the *Santuario de los Ares* (alt. 1728 m; inn), to the **Puerto de la Bonaigua** (2072 m), on the watershed between the Mediterranean and the Atlantic. The road then runs down, with many bends and gradients of up to 9 per cent, into the *Valle de Arán*, a popular winter sports area, with *views of the High Pyrenees, and continues to **Tredós** (alt. 1295 m), off the road on the left, with a 12th c. church (Gothic altarpiece) which belonged to the Templars. – Then a further winding stretch down to *Salardú* (alt. 1265 m), where the road enters the *Garona* (Garonne) valley. To the left is the little spa of *Artiés* (sulphur spring), then on the right the village of *Betrén*, with a chair-lift to the La Tuca winter sports centre (1560 m). Finally at *Viella* C 147 joins N 230, coming from Lérida.

Into the Pyrenes via Benabarre. – The new road which runs N from Lérida (N 230), following the *Río Noguera Ribagotzana* for most of the way, is shorter than the road via Tremp described in the preceding itinerary, but much less interesting and varied.

25 km from Lérida N 230 cuts across C 148 at *Alfarrás*. 13 km W along this road, beyond the provincial boundary, is **Tamarite de Litera** (alt. 357 m; pop. 4500), with a number of interesting churches. Among them are the collegiate church of San Nicolás (12th c.), with a 14th c. tower, a Baroque W doorway and an alabaster statue of the Virgin (1504), and the Romanesque church of San Miguel (13th c., with later alterations), with good altarpieces.

N 230 continues beyond Alfarrás into Huesca province and runs through the *Sierra de Coscollá* to **Benabarre** (alt. 701 m; pop. 1200), a hill village on the E side of the *Sierra de Carrodilla*. Castle of the Counts of Ribagorza; interesting modern hospital church, with 15th c. altarpiece. – N 230 crosses the *Río Cagigar*, runs E to rejoin the valley of the Río Noguera Ribagorzana and continues N along its W bank, passing two artificial lakes, the *Embalse de Sopeira* and the *Embalse de Escalas*, to **Pont de Suert**, where it is joined by C 144 coming from Pobla de Segur.

Towards Barcelona. – Leave Lérida on N II, which crosses the *Río Segre* and runs E through steppe-like upland country via *Mollerusa* to the old-world little country town of **Bellpuig** (alt. 373 m; pop. 4000), off the main road to the right. It has a ruined castle and a number of notable churches, including the parish church, with the magnificent Renaissance tomb (by Giovanni da Nola, 1525) of Don Ramón de Cardona, Viceroy of Naples. The former Franciscan convent has a three-storey cloister of the 16th–17th c.

N II crosses the *Canal de Urgel* and continues to **Tárrega** (alt. 358 m; pop. 8000), an old town with a number of notable buildings, including the 13th c. Palacio Sobiés. – N II then descends the valley of the *Río Cervera*, which flows through an irrigated plain,

the *Llano de Urgel*, to **Cervera** (alt. 565 m; pop. 6000), another old-world little town which had a university from 1718 to 1842. It lies on a hill crowned by the church of Santa María (12th–13th c.), through which the road is carried in a tunnel. Fine 17th c. Town Hall on the Río Cervera. – The road then climbs up to the *Puerto de Panadella* (702 m), near which is the boundary between the provinces of Lérida and Barcelona.

To the Sierra de la Llena. – N 240 branches off N II immediately beyond the *Río Segre* and runs SE over an area irrigated by water from the river, skirting the Canal de Urgel for part of the way, to **Borjas Blancas** (alt. 296 m; pop. 7000), an old town, the ancient *Borgiarum Albarum*, with beautiful public gardens and typical arcaded streets. The road then runs into the *Sierra de la Llena*, where it crosses the boundary between the provinces of Lérida and Tarragona.

Logroño from the air

Logroño

Province: La Rioja (LO).
Telephone code: 941
Altitude: 384 m. – Population: 110,000.
(i) **Oficina de Información de Turismo,**
Miguel Villanueva 10;
tel. 25 54 97.
Consejería de Turismo,
Gran Vía 41;
tel. 22 76 54.

HOTELS. – *Los Bracos* (no rest.), Bretón de los Herreros 29, I, 72 r.; *Carlton Rioja* (no rest.), *Gran Vía* 5, I, 120 r.; *Gran Hotel* (no rest.), General Vara de Rey 5, II, 69 r.; *Murrieta*, Marqués de Murrieta 1, II, 113 r.; *El Cortijo*, km 2 on the Cortigo road, III, 40 r.; SP; *Isasa* (no rest.), Doctores Castroviejo 13, IV, 30 r.; Hostal *La Numantina* (no rest.), Sagasta 4, P I, 17 r.; *Marqués de Vallejo* (no rest.), Marqués de Vallejo 8, P II, 28 r.; etc. – CAMPING SITE: El *Ruedo* in Nájera, SW of the town.

RESTAURANTS. – *Dólar*, Marqués de Murrieta 50; *Milán*, General Vara de Rey 16; etc.

EVENTS. – *Fiesta de San Bernabé* (June), patronal festival. – *Fiestas de la Vendimia Riojana* (Sept.), a vintage festival, with bullfights, folk events, cavalcades of riders and battles of flowers.

Logroño, situated on the banks of the Ebro in the wine-producing La Rioja region, has textile and metal factories.

SIGHTS. – Church of *Santa María del Palacio* (11th c.), with a high altar by pupils of Berruguete and a 45 m high tower, the Aguja del Palacio. – Church of *Santa María de la Redonda* (15th–18th c.), with Baroque towers and beautiful carved altars. The name refers to its former circular ground-plan. – Church of *San Bartolomé* (12th c.), with a Romanesque and Gothic doorway, one of the finest examples of its kind in the Rioja.

SURROUNDINGS. – Logroño and its province are closely associated with the *Way of St James* (see p. 242), which runs through Logroño itself and a number of other towns and villages in the province. 16 km S of Logroño on a minor road via *Alberite* is **Clavijo**, which also has associations with St James. Below the walls of the *Castillo de Clavijo* Ramiro I defeated the Moors in 844, in a battle at which St James is traditionally supposed to have appeared in his role as Matamoros ("Moor-Slayer"). The *Basílica del Monte Laturce* has a large picture of the battle.

On the Way to St James. – The pilgrims' route to Santiago runs W from Logroño (N 120) via *Navarrete*, with an old equestrian statue of the Apostle, to **Nájera** (alt. 481 m; pop. 4000), on the *Río Najerilla*, the ancient capital of the Rioja. Monastery of Santa María la Real (11th c.), with the interesting Royal Pantheon, containing the tomb of Queen Blanca of Navarre, and a Gothic cloister (1522) in which historical pageant plays are performed in June. – 16 km S of the town is another station on the pilgrims' route, **San Millán de la Cogolla** (alt. 738 m), on the northern slopes of the *Sierra de la Demanda*. It is noted for its two monasteries, both designated as national monuments. The monastery of *San Millán de Yuso*, known as the "Escorial of the Rioja", is a large building dating from 1053, with several cloisters and valuable reliquaries containing the remains of San Millán and San Felice. *San Millán de Suso* has a small Mozarabic church (11th c.), the tombs of seven infantes and an effigy of San Millán. – Then return to N 120 and continue W to **Santo Domingo de la Calzada**.

Towards Zaragoza. – N 232 runs E down the Ebro valley to (49 km) **Calahorra** (alt. 322 m; pop. 15,000), an old episcopal city situated above the *Río Cidacos*, with remains of a Roman circus and aqueduct. On the high altar of the richly furnished and decorated Cathedral (originally Visigothic, rebuilt 1485) are two urns containing the remains of SS. Emeterius and Celedonius, who were beheaded here. The church of San Andrés (14th–15th c.) has a Churrigueresque retablo on the high altar.

N 232 continues SE, passing on the left the ruined castle of *Milagro*. Beyond the Ebro, to **Alfaro** (pop. 8000), an old town situated in a wine- and wheat-growing region which was once the key to Navarre. It has a number of monasteries and fine churches, including the collegiate church of San Miguel (17th c.), in monumental style.

Towards Vitoria. – N 232 runs W up the Ebro valley, which gradually becomes narrower, into the *Alta Rioja* wine-growing region. On the right is the massive bulk of the *Sierra de Cantabria* which forms the boundary of the Álava plateau, on the left the *Sierra de la Demanda*, with the Cerro de San Lorenzo (2262 m). The road then continues past *Cenicero* (pop. 3000) and *Briones*, built on terraces above the Ebro, with a ruined castle, to **Haro** (see p. 136).

Lorca

Province: Murcis (MU).
Telephone code: 968.
Altitude: 327 m. – Population: 65,000.
ⓘ **Oficina de Información y Turismo,**
Palacio Guevara, López Gisbert 12;
tel. 46 61 57.

HOTELS. – *Alameda* (no rest.), Musso Valiente 8, II, 43 r.; *La Hoya*, 146 km on N 340, III, 36 r.; Hostal *La Alberca* (no rest.), Plaza de Juan Moreno 1, P II, 21 r.; *Félix* (no rest.), Avda Fuerzas Armadas 146, P II, 28 r.

EVENTS. – *Semane Santa* (Holy Week), with an impressive procession.

Lorca, lying astride the Río Guadalantín, was a bishopric as early as the Visigothic period. It was known to the Romans as Illurco and to the Moors as Lurka.

SIGHTS. – The town has many old churches and palaces. Above the old town, huddled on the slopes of the hill, is a partly preserved Moorish *castle* (alt. 465 m), from which there are very fine views. – In the more recent lower town are the church of *San Patricio* (16th–17th c.), with a tower of 1772 and a handsome Baroque doorway, and the *Casa Consistorial* (Town Hall), of the 17th–18th c., with a battle picture by Miguel Muñoz (1723). – In the hillside to the N of the town are cave dwellings.

Lugo

Province: Lugo (LU).
Telephone code: 982.
Altitude: 465 m. – Population: 68,000.
ⓘ **Oficina de Información de Turismo,**
Plaza de España 27;
tel. 23 13 61.
Delegación Provincial de Turismo,
Doctor García Portela 7;
tel. 22 20 70.

HOTELS. – *Gran Hotel Lugo*, Avda Ramón Ferreiro s/n, I, 168 r., SP; *Méndez Núñez* (no rest.), Reina 1, II, 94 r.; *España* (no rest.), Villalba 2 bis, IV, 17 r.; Hostal *Buenos Aires* (no rest.), Plaza Comandante Manso 17, P II, 15 r.; *Rivera* (no rest.), General Sanjurjo 94, P II, 13 r.

Town walls, Lugo

CAMPING SITE: *La Parada*, 3 km away on the Orense road.

RESTAURANTS: – *Portón do Recato*, La Compiña; *La Barra*, San Marcos 27; *Casa Paco*, Tolda de Castilla; *Covadonga*, Cruz 20; *Verruga*, Cruz 12; *Mesón de Alberto*, Cruz 4; etc.

EVENTS. – *Semana Santa* (Holy Week), with procession. – *Fiestas de San Froilán* (Oct.), with literary competitions and the Feria del Pulpo, during which tasty dishes of *pulpos* (octopuses) are eaten.

Lugo, situated on the upper Miño (Portuguese Minho), in the Galician upland region of NW Spain, is capital of the province of the same name and the seat of a bishop. It was the Roman town of Lucus Augusti, and preserves most of its Roman circuit of walls and towers.

SIGHTS. – There is a very attractive walk (45 minutes) round the old **town walls*, built in the 3rd c. A.D. and renewed in the 14th c. They have a total length of 2131 m and an average height of 11 m, with four gates and 85 towers. Access to the walls at the Puerta Nueva and opposite the Cathedral. From the top of the walls there are extensive views. They can also be followed on the road which runs round the old town immediately outside the walls.

In the town's principal square, the *Plaza de España* or Plaza Mayor, is a fountain with a figure of Hispania. On the E side of the square is the *Ayuntamiento* (Town Hall), built about 1700, with a beautiful Rococo façade.

On the W side of the Square is the **Cathedral**, a fine 12th c. building frequently altered and extended from the 15th c. onwards, with an imposing twin-towered 18th c. façade. Richly decorated choir-stalls (1625); Rococo retablo in the Capilla Mayor, with the Host always exposed. Beautiful Baroque cloister (18th c.) by Gabriel and Fernando Casas y Novoa.

From the Plaza de España the Calle de la Reina leads to the Plaza de Santo Domingo with church of *Santo Domingo* (begun in 1280): beautiful Romanesque doorway; Churrigueresque retablos. To the W is the *Museo Provincial* (Galician handicrafts, coins, pottery).

SURROUNDINGS. – Lugo lay close to the Way of St James (see p. 242), the pilgrims' route to Santiago, and accordingly there are a number of stations on the road within reach of the town. 31 km S, on a minor road, is the village of *Puertomarín*; the original site of the pilgrim station was drowned in the waters of a new reservoir, the Embalse de Belesar, but the village with its historic old buildings was re-erected nearby. Fortified church of San Juan (12th c.). – 16 km W of Lugo is the church of *Santa Eulalia de Bóveda*, originally a Roman nymphaeum; Pre-Christian catacombs with wall paintings (national monument).

To Monforte de Lemos. – Leave Lugo on N VI, going SE and at *Nadela* take a road on the right which leads to **Sarría** (pop. 16,000), 31 km from Lugo. Now a modern little town, it was the Roman *Flavia Lambrio* and in the Middle Ages a station on the pilgrim road. Church of San Salvador (13th c.). Close by is the little spa of *Celticos*. – 12 km SE is the *Monasterio de Samos*, founded in the 8th c., later also a pilgrim staging point, with an 18th c. church.

From Sarría C 546 S over the *Gural* pass (412 m) to **Monforte de Lemos** (alt. 384 m; pop. 22,000), an old town on an eminence above the *Río Cabe*, still partly surrounded by walls and dominated by the tower of a castle belonging to the Counts of Lemos. In the lower town, near the river, is the former Jesuit College (Colegio de la Compañía), with a church containing a magnificent retablo by Francisco Mouro (17th c.) and three pictures by El Greco. Former Benedictine monastery of San Vicente del Pino, with fine Renaissance doorways (16th c.).

The road now climbs up the gorge-like valley of the Río Cabe on to the *Sierra de San Payol* and then winds its way down to the *Embalse de los Peares*, entering the province of Orense at the southern tip of the lake. At the village of *Peares*, on a hill above the road on the left, stands the abandoned monastery of *San Esteban de Ribas de Sil*, with a 10th c. cemetery chapel, a Gothic church and two beautiful cloisters.

To Orense. – N 640 leads SW over the Miño, crosses the *El Picato* pass (660 m) and comes to *Guntín* (20 km from Lugo). From here C 547 runs 15 km W to the old pilgrim station of *Palas del Rey*, with the interesting church of Vilar das Doñas and a 14th c. castle. – The road to Orense continues beyond Guntín on N 540, coming in 8 km to a side road on the left leading to *Puertomarín*. N 540 goes on to **Chantada**, an ancient little town with a number of notable churches in the immediate vicinity, among them San Salvador de Asma (2 km), with a Romanesque doorway, and San Esteban de Ribas de Miño (7 km), originally belonging to a Benedictine monastery. Other features of interest are *Celtic tombs* (6 km) and a *Roman bridge* over the Miño (6 km). – N 540 then crosses the *Río Bubal*, enters the province of Orense and continues to the town of **Orense** (see p. 176), 95 km from Lugo.

To La Coruña. – N VI runs NW up the Miño valley to *Rabadé*, where C 641 goes off on the right to *Villalba* (see below), and continues via *Begonte* to **Baamonde** (alt. 409 m), lying off the road to the right, with a Romanesque church. Here N634 diverges on the right to *Villalba* and *Mondoñedo*.

The road continues between areas of pasture and stony arable land to **Guitíriz** (alt. 460 m; Hostal La Casilla, P III, 38 r.), a small spa with a thermal spring (mainly effective in liver complaints) and an open-air swimming pool. – Then over moorland (good road) to the low pass of *Portobello* (510 m), the boundary between the provinces of Lugo and La Coruña. N VI continues via **Betanzos** (see p. 81) to **La Coruña** (p. 109), 98 km from Lugo.

To the Atlantic via Villalba. – Leave Lugo on N VI and at Rabadé turn right into C 461, which runs N to **Villalba** (alt. 480 m; pop. 21,000), chief town of the region known as the *Terra Cha*, with the Castillo de los Condes de Villalba, surrounded by walls and towers (Hotel Parador Nacional, II, 6 r.).

From Villalba take N 634, which goes NE through an area of pasture and arable land to the *Puerto de la Xesta* (590 m), and then gently descends, with magnificent views straight ahead, to **Mondoñedo** (alt. 200 m; pop 9000), an old episcopal town with a Cathedral of the 13th–16th c. (fine Plateresque choir). Monastery and seminary for priests, both 17th c.

The road continues via *Lorenzana*, with the imposing Benedictine church of San Salvador, traverses a beautifully wooded upland region and then descends into the fertile valley of the *Río Masma* to reach *Bareiros*, where the coast road from El Ferrol (C 642) comes in on the left. Then on to *Ribadeo* (alt. 150 m; pop. 9000; Hotels, Parador Nacional, II 47 r.; Eo, II, 20 r., SP), a port at the mouth of the Ría de Ribadeo which ships large quantities of iron ore. – N 634 then crosses the Ría de Ribadeo on the 'Puente de los Santos', which leads to Figueras, and continues to **Ovieda** (see p. 178).

The coast road to Vivero. – The coast road (C 642) branches off N 634 and runs NW over the *Río Masma*, which here opens out into the *Ría de Foz*. It then follows the ría to the pretty little fishing village and seaside resort of *Foz*, crosses the *Río Oro* and runs along the Galician coast to **Vivero** (pop. 14,000; Hotel Las Sirenas, II, 29 r.; Orfeo, III, 27 r.), an old port on the Ría de Vivero with a Romanesque church. – The road then continues to the *Ría del Barquero* (boundary between Lugo and La Coruña provinces), which is crossed by a railway bridge, and from there via **El Ferrol** (see p. 110) to **La Coruña** (p. 109).

Madrid

Autonomous Region.
Organ of Government: Consejo de Gobierno de la Comunidad Autónoma de Madrid.
Province: Madrid (M).
Telephone code: 91.
Altitude: 655 m. – Population: 3,188,000.

(i) **Oficina de Turismo de la Comunidad de Madrid,**
Barajas Airport: tel. 2 05 86 56.
Plaza de España.
Torre de Madrid; tel. 2 41 23 25.
Calle Duque de Medinaceli 2; tel. 4 29 49 51.
Oficina Municipal de Información,
Plaza Mayor 3;
tel. 2 66 54 77.

HOTELS. – BETWEEN THE HEAD POST OFFICE AND THE SOUTH STATION: **Ritz*, Plaza de la Lealtad 5, L, 156 r.; **Palace*, Plaza de las Cortes 7, L, 517 r.; *Carlton*, Paseo de las Delicias 26, I, 133 r.; *Inglés* (no rest.), Echegaray 8, II, 58 r.; *Mercator* (no rest.), Atocha 123, II, 90 r.; *Reyes Católicos* (no rest.), Ángel 18, II, 38 r.; *Sur*, Paseo de la Infanta Isabel 9, III, 49 r.; *Mediodía* (no rest.), Plaza del Emperador Carlos V 8, IV, 161 r.

BETWEEN THE HEAD POST OFFICE AND THE NORTH STATION: **Eurobuilding*, Padre Damián 23, L, 420 r., SP; **Meliá Madrid*, Princesa 27, L, 266 r.; **Princesa Plaza*, Serrano Jover 3, L, 406 r.; *Alcalá* (no rest.), Alcalá 66, I, 153 r.; *Emperador* (no rest.), Gran Vía 53, I, 232 r., SP; *Liabeny* (no rest.), Salud 3, I, 158 r.; *Mayorazgo* (no rest.), Flor Baja 3, I, 200 r.; *Menfis* (no rest.), Gran Vía 74, I, 122 r.; *Suecia*, Marqués de Casa Riera 4, I, 67 r.; *Capitol* (no rest.), Gran Vía 41, II, 95 r.; *Carlos V* (no rest.), Maestro Vitoria 5, II, 67 r.; *Cortezo* (no rest.), Doctor Cortezo 3, II, 90 r.; *Gran Vía* (no rest.), Gran Vía 25, II, 163 r.; *Moderno* (no rest.), Arenal 2, II, 98 r.; *Opera* (no rest.), Cuesta Santo Domingo 2, II, 81 r.; *Principe Pío*, Cuesta de San Vicente 14, II, 157 r.; *Regente* (no rest.), Mesonero Romanos 9, II, 124 r.; *Regina* (no rest.), Alcalá 19, II, 142 r.; *Rex* (no rest.), Gran Vía 43, II, 147 r.; *Victoria*, Plaza del Angel 7, II, 110 r.; *Francisco I*, Arenal 15, III, 58 r.; *París*, Alcalá 2, III, 114 r.; etc. – Apartment-Hotel *Eurobuilding*, Juan Ramón Jimenez 8, I, 154 r., SP.

NORTHERN DISTRICTS: **Villa Magna*, Paseo de la Castellana 22, L, 194 r.; **Luz Palacio*, Paseo de la Castellana 67, L, 182 r.; **Meliá Castilla*, Capitan Haya 43, L, 936 r., SP; **Miguel Angel*, Miguel Angel 31, L, 304 r., SP; **Mindanao*, Paseo San Francisco de Sales 15, L, 289 r., SP; **Wellington*, Velázquez 8, L, 261 r., SP; *Aitana* (no rest.), Paseo de la Castellana 152, I, 111 r.; *Castellana Inter-Continental* (no rest.), Paseo de la Castellana 57, I, 313 r.; *Cuzco*, Paseo de la Castellana 133, I, 330 r.; *Emperatriz* (no rest.), Lopez de Hoyos 4, I, 170 r.; *Florida Norte* (no rest.), Paseo de la Florida 5, I, 399 r.; *Los Galgos-Sol*, Claudia Coello 139, I, 359 r.; *Gran Versalles* (no rest.), Covarrubias 4, I, 96 r.; *Sanvy* (no rest.), Goya 3, I, 141 r.; *Velázquez*, Velázquez 62, I, 130 r.; *San Antonio de la Florida* (no rest.), Paseo de la Florida 13, II, 96 r.; *Tirol* (no rest.), Marqués de Urquijo 4, II, 93 r.; etc.

EASTERN DISTRICTS: *Colón*, Doctor Esquerdo 117, I, 389 r., SP; *Pintor* (no rest.), Goya 79, I, 176 r.; *Claridge* (no rest.), Plaza del Conde de Casal 6, II, 150 r.; etc.

UNIVERSITY QUARTER: **Monte Real*, Arroyo Fresno 17 (Puerta de Hierro), L, 77 r., SP; etc.

SOUTHERN DISTRICTS: *Puerta de Toledo* (no rest.), Glorieta Puerta de Toledo 4, II, 152 r.; *Finisterre* (no rest.), Toledo 111, IV, 97 r.; etc.

AT BARAJAS AIRPORT: *Barajas*, Avda. Logroño 305, L, 230 r., SP; *Alameda*, Avda Logroño 100, I, 145 r., SP.

CAMPING SITES. – *Aterpe Alai*, about 7 km N of the city centre, near the N 1 (Burgos–Madrid); *Osuna*, 7·5 km NE (near Barajas Airport). Others in the neighbourhood.

RESTAURANTS. – In the hotels, also *Aymer*, Fuencarral 138 (fish and seafood); *Basque*, Alcalá 66; *Cabo Major*, Juan Hurtado de Mendoza 11; *Edelweiss*, Jovellanos 7; *El Amparo*, Alvarez de Baena 4; *El Bodegon*, Pinar 15; *El Pescador*, Jose Ortega y Gasset 75 (fish and seafood); *El Viejo 1*, Ribera del Manzanares 123 (game); *Esteban*, Cava Baja 36; *Fass*, Rodríguez Marin 84 (German); *Guria*, Huertas 12 (Basque); *Horcher*, Alfonso XII 6; *Jockey*, Amador de los Ríos 6; *Korynto*, Preciados 36; *L'Alsace*, Doménico Scarlatti 10; *La Dorada*, Orense 60; *La Fuencisla*, San Mateo 17; *La Marmite*, Plaza de San Amaro 9 (French); *O'Pazo*, Reina Mercedes 20 (Galician specialities); *Zalacain*, Alvarez de Baena 4.

SHOPPING. – Madrid's principal shopping street is the Gran Vía but the most elegant is Calle Serrano. There are also many large shops in Calle Preciados and Calle Fuencarral.
Department stores: Arias, Montera 29 and Plaza del Carmen 7; Aurrera, Doctor Fléming 31 and Velázquez 136; Bobo y Pequeño, Atocha 20; Cortefiel, Gran Vía 27 and 76 and Preciados 13; Drug-Store, Fuerncarral 101; El Corte Inglés, Preciados 20 and Goya 76; Eleuterio, Fuencarral 14; Flómar, Gran Vía 52 and Preciados 20; Galerías Preciados, Preciados 28 and Carmen 29 and 31; Iregua, Carretas 10; Los Sótanos, Gran Vía 55; Mazón, Fuencarral 103 and Esparteros 5; Prats, Atocha 24 and Plaza de Cascorro 4; Progreso, Plaza Tirso de Molina and Alcalá 123; Rodríguez, Gran Vía 19 and Goya 20; Ruiz, Hortaleza 19 and Montera 12; San Mateo, Fuencarral 70 and 72; Sarma, Conde de Peñalver 38 and Fuerncarral 158; Sears, Serrano 47 and Paseo de la Castellana 86; Sederías Carretas, Carretas 6; Sepu, Gran Vía 32 and Virgen del Sagrario 6; Simago, Ronda de Valencia 9 and Avda de la Alburfera 9; Simeón, Plaza Santa Ana 14 and Avda de Aragón 1.

Antiques: in Calle del Prado, Plaza de las Cortes and Carrera de San Jerónimo. – *Flea market* on Rastro (S of San Isidro el Real): best time Sunday morning. – *Coin and stamp exchange:* under N arcade of Plaza Mayor, Sunday 11 to 1.

EVENTS. – As might be expected, Madrid offers a full and varied programme of events. In addition to the Carnival, Holy Week, Easter and Christmas, however, only the following celebrations have preserved something of their former splendour; *Fiesta de San Antonio* (Jan.), with procession of animals at the church of San Antonio Abad. – *Romería de San Isidro Labrador* (May), in honour of the city's patron saint; *Fiesta* (May), with comprehensive programme of bullfights. – *Corpus Christi*, with procession, best seen at Puerta del Sol. – Madrid has several bullrings. – Authentic flamenco performances in *Tablao del Flamenco Zambra*, Ruiz de Alarcón 7.

CASINO. – *Casino de Juego Gran Madrid*, Torrelodones.

The Spanish capital lies in the heart of Spain, on a pleateau to the S of the Sierra de Guadarrama, 80 m above

the **Río Manzanares, a small stream with a meagre flow of water and now partly canalised. With a population of about 3,200,000 in an area of 531 sq. km, it is the country's largest city. The seat of the government and a royal residence, it is also a university town and the see of an archbishop.**

Madrid was a political creation of the Spanish kings, lacking the natural advantages which might have promoted its rapid development. It was not until the coming of the railway and the construction of modern roads, making Madrid the focal point of the country's communications, that the city was able to forge ahead in the 19th and 20th c. It is now Spain's second largest industrial centre, after Barcelona. – The international airport at Barajas is 14 km NE, with bus connection to the town.

Situated at a relatively high altitude, Madrid shows considerable temperature variations (up to 17 °C (63 °F) during the day). The summers are hot (reaching 43 °C (109 °F)), the winters fairly cold (down to −12 °C (10 °F)). The air is so sharp and light, that, as a Spanish saying has it, it will kill a man but not put out a candle. Visitors should beware of catching a chill: "Hasta el cuarenta de Mayo no te quites el sayo." ("Until the 40th of May do not cast off your cloak.")

HISTORY. – In the 10th c. the site of the present Royal Palace was occupied by the little Moorish town and fortress of *Majrit*, which was captured by King Alfonso VI in 1103. In 1239 Ferdinand IV summoned the first Cortes to meet in Madrid, which thereafter became a frequent residence of the king. It was only in the time of the Emperor Charles V, however, that the old Alcázar was converted into a palace. In 1561 Philip II finally moved the court from Toledo to Madrid, which then had a population of some 30,000. This was the period that saw a great flowering of Spanish literature and art; and *Miguel de Cervantes Saavedra* (1547–1616) wrote the second part of "Don Quixote" in Madrid, while *Lope de Vega* (1562–1635), *Diego Velázquez* (1599–1660) and *Pedro Calderón de la Barca* (1600–81) lived for varying periods in the new capital. During the reign of Joseph Bonaparte (1808–13) numerous convents and whole districts were demolished in order to create more space in the town. The city suffered a heavy bombardment by Franco forces during the Spanish Civil War (1936–39).

Museums and Monuments

The opening times of museums, palaces and churches are very variable, and may change from time to time. They are likely to be closed during the long afternoon siesta, and most museums are also closed on Mondays.

The official public holidays, on which almost all institutions are closed, are 1 January (*Año Nuevo*); 6 January (*Reyes Magos*: the Three Kings, Epiphany); 19 March (*San José*); 1 May (*Día del Trabajo*, Labour Day); 15 May (*San Isidro*, Madrid's patron saint); 29 June (*San Pedro y San Pablo*); 18 July (*Día del Alzamiento Nacional*, the Falangist National Day); 25 July (*Santiago*, St James); 15 August (*Asunción*, Assumption); 12 October (*Día de la Hispanidad*, commemorating the discovery of America); 1 November (*Todos los Santos*, All Saints); 8 December (*Immaculada Concepción*, Immaculate Conception); 25 December (*Navidad*, Christmas); together with the movable festivals of *Viernes Santo* (Good Friday) and *Corpus Christi*.

MUSEUMS AND ART GALLERIES

Academia de Bellas Artes de San Fernando,
Calle Alcalá 13;
10–2.

America, Museum of.
See Museo de América.

Archaeological Museum.
See Museo Arqueológico Nacional.

Armería.
See Palacio Real.

Army Museum.
See Museo del Ejército.

Biblioteca Nacional,
Paseo de Recoletos 20.
(Palacio de la Biblioteca y Muses Nacionales)

Botica Real.
See Palacio Real.

Bullfighting Museum.
See Museo Taurino.

Carriage Museum.
See Palacio Real.

Casa Lope de Vega
(reconstitution of Lope de Vega's house and garden),
Calle Cervantes 11;
Tues.–Thurs. 11–2.
(closed 15 July–15 Sept.).

El Casón
(paintings),
Calle Filipe IV;
Tues.–Sat. 9–6.45; Sun. 9–1.45.

Colleccion Municipal,
Plaza de la Ville 4 and 5;
(mornings by arrangement).

Estudio de Zuloaga
(the painter's studio).
See Museo Español de Arte Contemporáneo.

Ethnological Museum.
See Museo Etnológico y Antropológico.

Fábrica de Tapices
(Tapestry Manufactory),
Calle Fuenterrabía 2.

Mint and Stamp Printing House.
See Fábrica Nacional de Moneda y Timbre.

Municipal Museum.
See Museo Municipal.

Museo Arqueológico Nacional,
Calle Serrano 13;
Tues.–Sun. 9.30–1.30.

Museo de África,
Paseo de la Castellana 5.

Museo de América,
Avenida de los Reyes Católicos 6;
(Ciudad Universitaria)
Tues.–Sun. 10–2.

Museo de Bebidas
(Museum of Drinks),
Calle de Fuencarral.

Museo de Carruajes.
See Palacio Real.

Museo de Cerralbo
(paintings etc.),
Calle Ventura Rodríguez 17;
Tues.–Sat. 10–2 and 4–7; Sun 10–2.
(closed in August).

Museo de Escultura al Aire Libre
(open-air museum; sculpture),
Pasea de la Castellana 38;
permanently open.

Museo de Figuras de Cera
(Wax Museum),
Paseo de Recoletos 41;
10.30–2 and 4–9.

Museo de Reproducciones Artísticas
(Museum of Casts),
Avenida de los Reyes Católicos 6;
(Ciudad Universitaria)
Mon.–Fri. 10–5; Sun. 10–1.

Museo de la Academia de la Historia,
Calle León 21;
at present closed.

Museo de la Fábrica Nacional de Moneda y Timbre
(coins and stamps),
Calle de Jorge Juan 106;
(morning visits by arrangement).

Museo del Ejército
(Army Museum),
Calle Méndez Núñez 1;
Tues.–Sat. 10–3; Sun. 10–2.

Museo Español de Arte Contemporáneo,
Avenida Juan de Herrera 2;
(Ciudad Universitaria)
Tues.–Sat. 10–6; Sun. 10–3.

Museo Etnológico y Antropológico,
Calle Alfonso XII 86;
Tues.–Sun. 10–2.
(closed in August).

◄ **Monument to Alfonso XII in the Parque del Retiro, Madrid**

Museo Lázaro Galdiano,
Calle Serrano 122;
Tues.–Sun. 10–2.

Museo Municipal,
Calle de Fuencarral 78;
(Hospicio de San Fernando)
Tues.–Sat. 10–2 and 5–9; Sun. 10–2.30

Museo Nacional de Arte del Siglo XIX.
See Museo Español de Arte Contemporáneo.

Museo Nacional de Artes Decoratives,
Calle de Montalbán 12;
Tues.–Fri. 10–5; Sat. and Sun. 10–2.

Museo Nacional de Cincias Naturales,
Paseo de la Castellana 82;
Mon.–Sat. 9–2; Sun. 10–2.

Museo Nacional de Etnologia,
Calle Alfonso XII 68;
Tues.–Sat. 10–2 and 4–7; Sun. 10–2.

Museo Nacional del Parado,
Paseo del Prado;
Summer – Tues.–Sat. 10–6;
Winter – Tues.–Sat. 10–5 and Sun. 10–2.

Museo Nacional Ferroviario,
Paseo de la Delicias 61;
Tues.–Sat. 10.30–1.30 and 4.30–7.30; Sun. 10.30–2.

Museo Naval,
Calle de Montalbán 2;
Tues.–Sun. 10.30–1.30.

Museo Pedagógico de Arte Infantil
(children's art),
Ciudad Universitaria;
Mon.–Thurs. (by prior arrangement).

Museo Romántico,
Calle de San Mateo 13;
Tues.–Sat. 10–6; Sun. 10–2.

Museo Sorolla
(the painter's studio),
Paseo General Martínez Camps 7;
Tues.–Sun. 10–2.

Museo Taurino
(Bullfighting Museum),
Plaza Monumental de las Ventas;
Tues.–Sun. 9–3.

National Library.
See Biblioteca Nacional.

Natural History Museum.
See Museo de Ciencias Naturales.

Naval Museum.
See Museo Naval.

Observatorio Astronómico,
Calle Alfonso XII 3;
Mon.–Sat. 9–2.

Palacio Real
(Royal Palace),
Calle de Bailén s/n;
conducted tours only (some with English-speaking guides); summer 10–12.45 and 4–5.45, winter 10–12·45 and 3·30–5·15. Sundays and public holidays 10–1.30. Permanent special exhibitions are the

Armería (Armoury, with a collection of weapons), *Museo de Carruajes* (Carriage Museum), *Botica Real* (a historic old pharmacy), Coin Cabinet and an exhibition of porcelain, glass and pictures.

Panteón de Hombres Ilustres
(famous people),
Calle de Julian Gayarre 3;
Mon.–Sat. 9.30–1.30.

Prado.
See Museo Nacional del Prado.

Queen Sophia Cultural Centre,
Ronda de Atoche.

Tapestry Manufactory.
See Fábrica de Tapices.

Wax Museum.
See Museo de Figuras de Cera.

CHURCHES AND CONVENTS
Most churches in Madrid have no fixed opening hours. The best times to see them are in the later part of the morning, after the morning masses, and in the afternoon between about 4 and 7.

Almudena,
Calle Mayor 92.

Basílica de Atocha,
Avenida Ciudad de Barcelona 1.

Capilla del Obispo,
Plaza Marqués de Comillas 9.

Convento de las Benedictinas de San Plácido,
Calle San Roque 9.

Convento de Concepcionistas.
See Convento de Santa Isabel.

Convento de las Descalzas Reales,
Plaza de las Descalzas;
Mon., Wed., Sat. 10–1.30 and 2–6; Fri. 10–1.30; Sun 11–2.

Convento de la Encarnación,
Plaza de la Encarnación.

Convento de las Madres Mercedarias,
Calle Valverde 15.

Convento de Santa Isabel,
Calle de Santa Isabel.

Ermita de San Antonio de la Florida
(frescoes by Goya),
Paseo de la Florida;
closed Wednesdays.

Ermita Virgen del Puerto,
Paseo Virgen del Puerto.

Esuelas Pías de San Antón,
Calle Hortaleza 63.

Iglesia de las Calatravas,
Calle Alcalá 25.

Iglesia del Carmen y San Luis,
Calle Carmen 10.

Iglesia de las Comendadoras de Santiago,
Plaza Comendadoras 11.

Iglesia de las Mercedarias Descalzas,
Calle Góngora 5.

Iglesia de Montserrat,
Calle San Bernardo 79.

Iglesia del Sacramento,
Calle Sacramento 7.

Iglesia de las Salesas Nuevas,
Calle San Bernardo 72.

Oratorio del Caballero de Gracia,
Calle Caballero de Gracia 5.

San Andrés,
Plaza Marqués de Comillas 9.

San Andrés de los Flamencos,
Calle Claudio Coello 89.

San Antonio de los Alemanes,
Calle Puebla 22.

San Antonio de los Pobres,
Calle San Pablo 16.

San Cayetano,
Calle Embajadores 15.

San Francisco el Grande,
Plaza San Francisco;
Tues.–Sun. 11–1 and 4–7.

San Ginés,
Calle Arenal 13.

San Jerónimo el Real,
Calle Moreto 4.

San José,
Calle Alcalá 41.

San Luis de los Franceses,
Calle Tres Cruces 8.

San Marcos,
Calle San Leonardo 10.

San Miguel,
Calle Sacramento 4.

San Nicolás,
Plaza San Nicolás.

San Pedro,
Calle Nuncio 12.

Santa Bárbara,
Calle General Castaños 2.

SIGHTSEEING IN MADRID. – Since there is so much to see in the Spanish capital it is advisable to divide it up for sightseeing purposes into smaller sections, as in the following itineraries.

The traditional centre of the city, and now the main junction of the underground railway system, the Metropolitano, is the *Puerta del Sol*, a square (named after the E town gate, demolished in 1570) from which ten streets radiate, including those leading into the six trunk roads which run to the country's frontiers. On the N side of the square are hotels and banks; on the S side is the *Police Headquarters*, built (by Jacques Marquet, 1786) as the General Post Office, with a clock-tower added in 1847.

East towards the Prado. – From the Puerta del Sol the *Calle de Alcalá*, the broadest street in the city centre, lined with banks and clubs, runs NE to the Plaza de la Cibeles (see below). At the near end, on the left, is the *Ministry of Finance*, and beyond it the *Academia de Bellas Artes de San Fernando*, with a notable collection of pictures (Spanish paintings, including works by Goya and Zurbarán, and Italian and Dutch pictures). Farther along, still on the left, is the *Iglesia de las Calatravas* (17th c.), the church of the knightly Order of Caltrava. Almost

opposite it, on the right, are the *Ministry of Education* (1928) and the monumental building, crowned by a tall tower, of the *Circulo de Bellas Artes* (1926: art exhibitions). Then on the left, at the end of the Gran Vía, is the church of *San José* (1742). – At the end of the inner section of the Calle de Alcalá, on the right, is the *Banco de España* (1891), with its main front facing on to the Paseo del Prado. On the left, in a large garden, is the *Palacio de Buenvista*, built in 1782 for the Duchess of Alba and occupied from 1805 to 1808 by Godoy, the "Prince of the Peace"; it now houses the *Ministry of Defence*.

The inner section of the Calle de Alcalá runs into the **Plaza de la Cibeles*, the city's busiest traffic intersection, with the 18th c. *Fuente de Cibeles*, a marble fountain with a figure of the goddess Cybele. At the SE corner of the square is the imposing *Head Post Office* (Correos), built in 1918. A short distance E, at Calle de Montalbán 12, is the interesting *National Museum of Decorative Art* (Museo Nacional de Artes Decorativas), with a rich collection of furniture, china and folk art. – From the Plaza de la Cibeles the Calle de Alcalá continues to the Plaza de la Independencia (see below), the Paseo de Recoletos runs N and the Paseo del Prado runs S.

View of the Plaza de la Cibeles, Madrid

The *Prado ("Meadow") is a beautiful tree-lined promenade flanked by wide carriageways. In the northern section of the Paseo del Prado is the imposing *Admiralty* (Ministerio de Marina, 1928), with an interesting *Naval Museum*. Farther along is the *Fuente de Apolo* (1780), and almost opposite this is the *Monumento del Dos de Mayo*, erected in 1840 to commemorate the "martyrs of freedom" who were killed during a rising against the French on 2 May 1808. At the NE corner of the Plaza de la Leaitad is the *Exchange* (1893). – At the S end of the N part of the Paseo is the *Plaza Cánovas del Castillo*, with the 18th c. *Fuente de Neptuno* and two luxury hotels. To the right extends the long *Plaza de las Cortes*, on the N side of which stands the *Palacio de las Cortes Españolas* (1850), the Spanish Parliament. A little way S of this square, at Calle Cervantes 11, is the *Lope de Vega Museum*, a reconstitution of the great Spanish playwright's house. – On the southern continuation of the *Paseo*

Head Post Office, Madrid

del Prado are the Prado Museum and the Botanical Gardens. The latter were laid out to the plans of the architect Juan de Villaneuva.

The ****Prado Museum** (*Museum del Prado*), in a building erected between 1785 and 1819 and enlarged and extended since then houses one of the oldest, most famous and most conprehensive picture galleries in the world, as well as an important collection of sculpture.

The ****Picture Gallery** displays over 2500 pictures out of a total stock of some 5000. The most important works are on the first floor. The gallery is notable particularly for its magnificent collection of works by Spanish painters, including 50 by *Velázquez*, 34 by *El Greco* and 60 by *Ribera*. Other important Spanish painters represented are *Murillo, Goya, Berruguete, Morales, Ribalta, Zurbarán, Cano* and *Coello*. There

Prado Museum

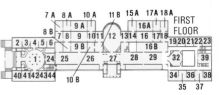

Because air-conditioning plant is being installed, some rooms of the Prado are at present closed; others have a temporary lay-out. The precise location of particular paintings can not therefore be given. Among the principal artists and schools represented are:

El Greco: Rooms 10 and 11	**Rubens:** Room 1 (Rotunda)
Veláquez: Rooms 12 and 27	**Rembrandt:** Room 55B
Goya: Rooms 53, 54, 55, 55A, 56, 56A and 57A (the "Majas")	**French painters:** Room 54

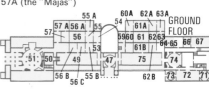

are also numerous works by 15th c. Italian masters, including *Fra Angelico, Raphael, Tintoretto, Tiepolo* and *Titian*; the early Dutch masters; the German school, especially *Albrecht Dürer* and *Lucas Cranach*; the Flemish school, notably *Rubens* (86 pictures), *van Dyck* and *Jan Brueghel*; later Dutch masters, among them *Rembrandt*; and much else besides. – The *Sculpture Collection is on the ground floor. In the nearby "El Cason" Museum can be seen Picasso's painting "Guernica".

Behind the Prado Museum is the church of *San Jerónimo el Real*, built in the 16th c. and restored in 1882. This was the meeting-place of the Cortes from 1528 to 1833, and here too the heir to the throne, the Prince of the Asturias, took the oath. – N of the church is the *Spanish Academy*, founded in 1713 to promote the study of

The Puerta de Alcalá, Madrid, at night

Spanish language and literature; it has been housed in its present premises since 1893. Nearby, to the N, is the *Army Museum* (Museo del Ejército), with a collection of weapons and models.

To the S of the Prado Museum is the **Botanic Garden** (*Jardín Botánico*), with large glasshouses on the N and E sides. – To the E, on higher ground, is the beautiful **Parque del Retiro**, originally laid out round a summer palace built by Philip II which was destroyed by fire in 1734. In the centre of the park is an artificial lake, the *Estanque Grande*, on the E side of which is a large *statue of Alfonso XII*, surrounded by a colonnade. On the N side of the Estanque are a restaurant, music pavilion and summer theatre. SE of the pond stand the two exhibition buildings Palacio de Velázquez and Palacio de Cristal. On the E side of the park is the *Zoological Garden*.

North to the Salamanca district. – At the NW corner of the Parque del Retiro is the busy *Plaza de la Independencia*, in which is the **Puerta de Alcalá**, a massive triumphal arch erected in 1778. From here an elegant shopping street, *Calle de Serrano*, runs N through the select **Salamanca** district. A little way along the street, on the left, is the *National Archaeological Museum* (see p. 160). 1·5 km N, at the end of Calle María de Molina (on

left), is the **Museo Lázaro Galdiano**, the finest private collection in Spain, bequeathed by its owner to the State. In addition to porcelain, ceramics and 12th c. bronzes it contains the richest collection of British pictures outside Britain and many works by Spanish, Italian and Dutch masters, including El Greco, Goya, Velázquez, Murillo, Zurbarán, Cano, Coello, Tiepolo, Leonardo da Vinci and Rembrandt. – At the E end of Calle María de Molina is an imposing tower block, the *Edificio María de Molina*.

Farther along Calle de Serrano, on the left, are the modern premises of the *Science Research Council* (Consejo Superior de Investigaciones Científicas), with the *National Archives* (Archivo Histórico Nacional: 20,000 documents), and the church of *Espíritu Santo* (1946), an example of contemporary Spanish church architecture.

Parallel with Calle de Serrano on the W, running N from the Plaza de Cibeles, is the *Paseo de Recoletos*, once Madrid's most aristocratic avenue, lined by noble palaces. In Calle de Doña Bárbara de Braganza, which goes off the Paseo on the left, is the *Palacio de Justicia* (Law Courts), built in 1758 as a convent of Salesian nuns. In the adjoining church of the *Salesas Reales* is the marble tomb of Ferdinand VI. To the NW, at Calle de San

Mateo 13, is the *Museo Romántico*, with furniture, pictures and other items dating from the second third of the 19th c.

At the end of the Paseo de Recoletos on the right, is the *Palacio de la Biblioteca y Museos Nacionales*, built 1866–94 to house the National Library and Museums. In the W part of the building is the **National Library*, founded by Philip V in 1711, one of the great libraries of Europe, with some 2 million printed volumes, including some 800 editions of "Don Quixote", as well as numerous manuscripts, documents, drawings and wood-cuts and more than 100,000 prints. In the E half of the building is the **National Archaeological Museum* (Museo Arqueológico Nacional), with prehistoric material and works of art and craftsmanship from antiquity to modern times: Iberian antiquities, including the famous "Lady of Elche" of the 4th or 3rd c. B.C. and the "Lady of Baza"; Egyptian, Etruscan, Phoenician, Greek, Visigothic, Roman and East Asian antiquities; a collection of coins; reproduction of the Altamira Caves. – Immediately N of the Museum is the *Plaza de Colón*, with a 17 m high statue of Columbus, in which are the *Mint* (Casa de la Moneda, 1861) and two tall office blocks. Close by, at Paseo de Recoletos 41, is the *Wax Museum* (Museo de las Figuras de Cera), with more than 300 figures and 28 set pieces.

From the Plaza de Colón the 2·5 km long *Paseo de la Castellana*, with an open-air exhibition of modern sculpture, runs N through the Salamanca district to the extensive group of buildings known as the **New Ministries**, with the offices of three government departments. On high ground to the SE is the **Natural History Museum**, founded 1771, with comprehensive collections including a number of large meteorites. To the N of the New Ministries is **Chamartín Station**, terminus of the main lines to northern Spain, which is linked with the Southern Station by a fast local line. 1·5 km N of the New Ministries, in the grandiose N section of the Paseo de la Castellana (on right), is the huge *Bernabeu Stadium*.

North-west to the University City. – From the Puerta del Sol the busy *Calle de la Montera* runs NE past the church of *San Luis* (1689) to the **Gran Vía*, Madrid's principal shopping and business street, lined with tall hotels and department stores, theatres, banks and offices. Immediately on the left, at the corner of *Calle de Fuencarral*, the northward continuation of Calle de la Montera, is a 16-storey tower block, the *Telefónica* building (1928). A short distance E is the *Museum of Drinks* (Museo de Bebidas), with 23,000 bottles from many different periods. At Calle de Fuencarral 78 is the old *Hospicio de San Fernando* (1729), with a magnificent Plateresque doorway, which now houses the *Municipal Museum* (fine Baroque doorway by Ribera).

From the Telefónica building the Gran Vía runs W to the busy *Plaza de España*, with many tower blocks, chief among them the 26-storey ***Edificio de España** (107 m high; café with magnificent views; swimming pool at a height of 96 m). On the NW side of the square is the 35-storey **Torre de Madrid** (1959), a block 124 m high which contains offices, flats, a cinema and a three-level underground car park for 350 vehicles. In the centre of the square is the *Cervantes Monument* (1928), with figures of Don Quixote and Sancho Panza. In Calle Ventura Rodríguez, which leaves the SW side of the square, is the interesting *Museo de Cerralbo*, with a fine collection of pictures, including particularly works by Spanish, Italian and Flemish old masters. – W of the Museum, in the Parque de la Montaña, is the Egyptian **Temple of Debod** (1st c. B.C.), from a site on the Nile 22 km S of Aswan, presented to Spain by President Nasser in 1972 and re-erected on this site, with extensions (beautiful wall reliefs, some of them reflecting the cult of Isis).

A short distance NE of the Plaza de España is the old **University**, moved from Alcalá de Henares to Madrid in 1836 with the title *Universidad Central de España* and housed from 1842 in a former Jesuit house for novices.

From the Plaza de España the Calle de la Princesa runs NW to the *Plaza de la Moncloa* (or Plaza de los Mártires de Madrid), with the massive premises of the *Air Ministry*, built from 1950 onwards. – On the far side of the square is the prominent *Arco de la Victoria* or Arco del Triunfo (39 m high), erected in 1956, westward from which extends the large **Parque del Oeste** (Western Park); in the southern part of the park an international rose show is held every spring. To the NE

Plaza de España, Madrid

of the Arco de la Victoria is the *Museo de América*, an excellent ethnographical collection covering the early cultures of Mexico and Central and South America. In the same building is the *Museo de Reproducciones Artísticas*, with plaster and bronze casts of fine sculpture of the past. – Farther NW is the circular *Plaza de la Ciudad* (officially Glorieta del Cardenal Cisneros), to the N and S of which extends the ***University City** (Ciudad Universitaria), with its impressive complexes of buildings. To the right, in the Avenida Complutense, the wide main avenue of the University City, is the *Gran Plaza* (officially the Plaza de Ramón y Cajal), in which is the *Faculty of Medicine*; at the N end of the avenue is the *Paraninfo* (Great Hall) of the University. In Avenida Juan de Herrera, which branches off SW from the Plaza de la Ciudad, stands the **Spanish Museum of Contemporary Art** (*Museo Español de Arte Contemporáne*), with works by Dali, Miró, Gris, Rusiñol, Solana, Tapiès, Saura, etc.

West to the Royal Palace. – From the S corner of the Plaza de España *Calle de Bailén* runs S past the former *Senate* and the *Museo del Pueblo Español* (a museum of Spanish folk traditions) to the *Plaza de Oriente*, the largest square in central Madrid, laid out in the reign of Joseph Bonaparte, with beautiful gardens and 44 statues of Visigothic and Spanish kings. In the centre is an **equestrian statue of Philip IV*, cast in 1640 by the Florentine sculptor Pietro Tacca to the design of I. M. Montañés. At the NE corner of the square is the former Augustinian *nunnery of the Encarnación*, now an art museum. On the E side of the square is the *Teatro Real*,

which has also been a Conservatoire since 1966. Behind the theatre is the Plaza de Isabel II, from which *Calle del Arenal* runs E past the church of *San Ginés* to the Puerta del Sol.

On the W side of the Plaza de Oriente is the ***Royal Palace** (*Palacio Real*), built for Philip V between 1738 and 1764 by Giovanni Battista Sacchetti to the design of F. Juvara (d. 1735), on the site of the old Alcázar and an older palace which was burned down in 1734; the projecting S wings were added in 1845. In the square inner courtyard are statues of the four Spanish-born Roman Emperors (Trajan, Hadrian, Theodosius and Honorius). The sumptuous interior is notable in particular for some 2500 tapestries (mainly Flemish products which belonged to Philip V), the richest collection of tapestries in the world outside Vienna. In the NE corner of the palace is the *Royal Library* founded by Philip V in 1716 (300,000 volumes, 4000 manuscripts, 3500 maps). Between the S wings of the palace is the *Plaza de la Armería*; from the colonnade on the W side are magnificent views of the palace gardens, the Manzanares depression and the Sierra de Guadarrama. In the SW wing of the palace is the ****Armería** (Armoury), the world-famous royal collection of weapons founded by Charles V, with numerous outstanding examples of the work of weaponsmiths of many different countries.

Facing the Plaza de la Armería on the S is the twin-towered **Catedral de Nuestra Señora de la Almudena**, with a neoclassical façade, which has been under construction since 1895. – Just N of the palace is the *Carriage Museum* (Museo de Carruajes). W of the palace, extending to the Paseo de la Virgen del Puerto, are the *palace gardens*, known as the *Campo del Moro* in memory of the Moorish siege of the Alcázar in 1109. From the Paseo de la Virgen the *Puente del Rey* crosses the canalised *Río Manzanares* into the **Casa de Campo**, a large recreation and amusement park with ponds, a hall for functions, an open-air theatre, a zoo, a bullring and cafés and restaurants (cableway from the Paseo del Pintor Rosales). – At the N end of the Paseo de la Virgen is the **Northern Station** (*Estación del Norte* or *Príncipe Pío*). From here the Paseo de la Florida runs NW alongside the Manzanares to the **Ermita de San**

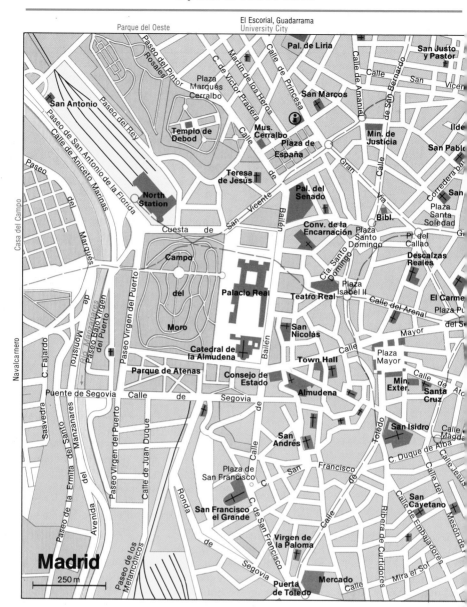

Madrid

250 m

Antonio de la Florida, a chapel built by J. Villanueva in 1792, with *ceiling paintings by Goya (1799); in the choir is Goya's tomb. – From here it is only a few minutes' walk to the Parque del Oeste.

Round the Plaza Mayor. – From the Puerta del Sol the Calle Mayor runs SW to the *Plaza Mayor* (pedestrian precinct), on the left. This is a large square of remarkable architectural unity laid out in 1619 and frequently used for ceremonial occasions, tournaments, horse-races and bullfights. In the centre is an *equestrian statue of Philip III*, modelled by Giovanni Bologna and cast in 1613 by his pupil Pietro Tacca in Florence. On the N side of

the square is the *Casa de la Panadería* (1672), with a frescoed façade, originally a bakehouse, now occupied by municipal offices. Opposite it on the S side of the square is the *Casa Consistorial*, also used as municipal offices. On Sundays a coin and stamp market is held under the N arcades of the square. – From the SW corner of the square the picturesque Arco de los Cuchilleros and Calle de los Cuchilleros lead into a crowded part of the old town. – A short distance SE of the Plaza Mayor in the little *Plaza de Jacinto Benavente* is the *Foreign Ministry*, built in 1643 as a prison. From here the busy *Calle de Atocha* leads to the Southern (Atocha) Station.

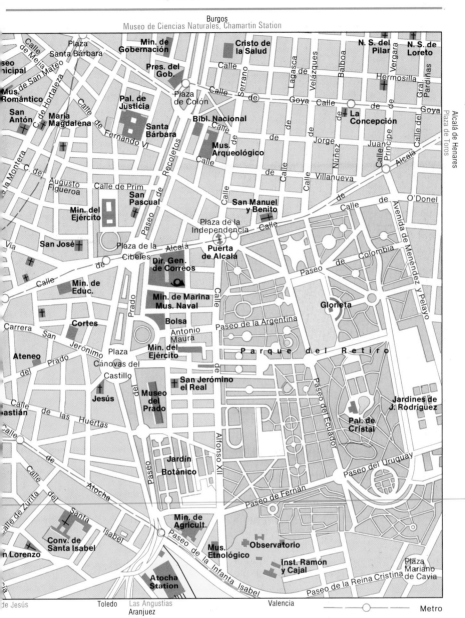

Burgos
Museo de Ciencias Naturales, Chamartin Station

W of the Plaza Mayor is the *Plaza de la Villa*, in which is the **Casa del Ayuntamiento** (Town Hall), with three towers, built in 1644 and several times enlarged since then. E of the Town Hall is the old *Torre de los Lujanes* (16th c., restored). – S of the Plaza de la Villa is the *Capilla del Obispo*, built in 1520 over the original tomb of St Isidore, with a Plateresque retablo (1547). Adjoining it is the domed church of *San Andrés* (17th c.). From here the Carrera de San Francisco runs SW to the church of *San Francisco el Grande*, a domed structure built in 1784 which was declared a National Pantheon in 1869; since 1881, however, it has not been used for that purpose. Sumptuous

interior in Doric style; in the first chapel on the left is an altarpiece by Goya (1782).

Calle de Toledo, one of the main arteries of the southern part of the old town, runs S from the Plaza Mayor. On the left is the church of **San Isidro el Real**, an imposing granite structure built 1622–51 and dedicated in 1769 to Madrid's patron saint, St Isidore the Ploughman (San Isidro Labrador, d. 1170), which serves as the city's cathedral pending the completion of the Almudena Cathedral. The saint's remains are in a shrine in the choir. – 300 m S is the beginning of the **Rastro**

Royal Palace, Madrid

district, a flea-market (also selling antiques) which is particularly busy on Sunday mornings. – Calle de Toledo continues beyond San Isidro to the **Puerta de Toledo**, an arched gateway begun during the Napoleonic period and completed in 1827. From here we reach the Ronda de Toledo and the *Ronda de Atocha*; the *Ronda de Atocha* ends at the *Glorieta de Atocha* (officially the Plaza del Emperador Carlos V). On the S side of the square is the **South Station** and opposite the **Centro de Arte Reina Sofia**, the newest centre of contemporary art in Madrid. – From the Glorieta the broad *Paseo de la Infanta Isabel* runs SE past the *Ethnological Museum* to the *Basílica de Nuestra Señora de Atocha*, begun in 1890 on the site of an old *ermita* but unfinished apart from the tower and a Pantheon for famous Spaniards.

SURROUNDINGS. – **To El Pardo:** Leave on N VI, going NW, and at the *Puerta de Hierro* (6 km) turn right into C 601, which runs through a former royal *deer-park*, noted for its holm-oaks, to **El Pardo**, a little town in the middle of the park, with a *palacio* (built 1543, enlarged 1772) which was for long the summer residence of the Spanish kings and in which General Franco lived until his death. Near the palace are the beautifully decorated and furnished Casita del Príncipe and the court church, both dating from the late 18th c. – To the W is the convent church of *Santo Cristo*, with an "Entombment" in carved and painted wood.

Via Colmenar to the Sierra de Guadarrama. – Leave on N I, going N, and just beyond Fuencarral (9 km) turn left into C 607 (of motorway standard),

which runs past the former royal deer-park to **Colmenar Viejo** (alt. 885 m; pop. 8500), a picturesquely situated little town with a 14th c. parish church containing a fine Plateresque retablo of 1579.

From Colmenar continue N on a minor road. In 8 km a road goes off on the left to the *Embalse de Santillana*, an artificial lake formed by a dam 800 m long and 28 m high. From here it is possible to continue to **Manzanares el Real**.

If we continue N on the minor road beyond the turning we come to **Miraflores de la Sierra** (alt. 1150 m; pop. 2500), a little town on the S side of the *Sierra de Guadarrama* which is much frequented in summer by the people of Madrid. – From here the road winds up to the *Puerto de la Morcuera* (1796 m) and then down to *Rascafría* (alt. 918 m) and through the beautiful valley of the Río Lozoya to the **Monasterio del Paular** (alt. 1153 m), a Carthusian house founded in 1930, with a beautiful cloister and a church rebuilt in Baroque style after the 1755 earthquake: richly furnished Capilla del Tabernáculo (1724), 15th c. marble high altar of Dutch workmanship.

From here C 604 runs SW, with fine views, to the *Puerto de Navacerrada*, from which it is possible to continue S on N 601 and so back to Madrid. Round trip 170 m.

To San Lorenzo del Escorial. – Leave on N VI, going NW, and after the separation of the motorway and the ordinary road bear left into C 505, which runs via *Las Rozas* (alt. 717 m; garden restaurants) and later over the *Embalse de Granjilla II* to the magnificent palace-monastery of **El Escorial** (see p. 118). N of Escorial a road goes off on the left to the memorial for the fallen in the *Valle de los Caídos* (13 km).

To the Montes Carpetanos. – N I, which runs N from Madrid, is the main road to Burgos and San Sebastián. It passes through the Madrid suburb of

Chamartín and continues via San Sebastián de los Reyes (alt. 678 m), off the road to the left, and San Agustín de Guadalix (alt. 684 m), also to the left of the road, and then past the Jarama race circuit (3·4 km) to the little spa of **El Molar** (alt. 817 m), where a road branches off on the right to (15 km) the little walled town of Torrelaguna (alt. 774 m), the birthplace of Cardinal Jiménez, below the S side of the Sierra de Guadarrama; it has a fine parish church (13th–15th c.).

Continue on N I, which winds its way up to a pass (1140 m) and then runs down to **Buitrago del Lozoya** (alt. 977 m), an ancient little town on the W side of the many-branched Embalse de Lozoya, with walls and towers, a 14th–15th c. castle and a 15th c. church.

Beyond the village of Somosierra the road climbs up to the **Puerto de Somosierra** (1404 m), where Napoleon fought his way over the Sierra de Somosierra in 1808. This range, part of the Montes Carpetanos in the Guadarrama mountains, forms the boundary between Old and New Castile. Fine views of the Sierra de Aylón on the right and the vast plateau of New Castile to the S.

Towards Cuenca. – Leave Madrid on N III (motorway standard), which runs through the suburban district of Vallecas and past Vaciamadrid, crosses the Río Jarama and comes to **Arganda del Rey** (alt. 618 m), with the beautiful Renaissance church of San Juan Bautista (1525), a castle (1400) and the Casa del Rey, a country house surrounded by gardens, which formerly belonged to the Spanish royal family.

The road winds its way through the rolling Meseta of New Castile, with views of the Sierra de Guadarrama to the rear. Beyond Perales de Tajuña (alt. 583 m) N III climbs up over the Peñas Gordas (794 m) and comes to Villarejo de Salvanés (alt. 758 m), which has a 13th c. church and the tower of an old castle. It then passes through a lowland stretch in the valley of the Río Tajo, continues through Fuentidueña de Tajo (alt. 563 m), with a ruined 11th c. castle, over the river and into the province of Cuenca. Soon afterwards N 400 branches off on the left for Cuenca.

To Aranjuez. – Leave Madrid on N IV, the main road S (with N 301 branching off it for Albacete and Murcia). After 14 km on the motorway a side road goes off on the left to the Cerro de los Ángeles, a conical hill (670 m) in the geographical centre of Spain, with the prominent Monumento al Corazón de Jesús, topped by a 9 m high figure of Christ, and a church. Beautiful *views of Madrid and the Sierra de Guadarrama to the N and the Castilian plain to the S.

A few kilometres farther S on N IV a minor road goes off to Pinto, with an old castle, in which the Princess of Eboli, notorious for her court intrigues during the reign of Philip II, was confined from 1578 to 1581. N IV then crosses in succession the Canal del Jarama, the Río Jarama and the Río Tajo and comes to Aranjuez (see p. 56).

To the Puerto de Guadarrama. – N VI, which runs NW through the Sierra de Guadarrama, is the main road to Galicia and La Coruña. It leaves Madrid as a motorway and after passing through Las Rozas (alt. 717 m) comes to **Torrelodones** (alt. 845 m), much favoured as a summer resort by the people of Madrid.

8 km N, in the upper valley of the Manzanares (extensive views), is the high-level resort of Hoyo de Manzanares (1000 m; hotels).

Some 10 km beyond Torrelodones N 601 goes off on the right and runs N over the Puerto de Navacerrada to **Segovia**. – N VI continues to **Guadarrama** (alt. 965 m), where it cuts across the road coming down from the Navacerrada pass on the right and leading (left) to the Escorial. From here a detour can be made to the memorial to the fallen in the *Valle de los Caídos.

The road then climbs up, with many bends and gradients of up to 12 per cent, to the *Puerto de **Guadarrama** (1511 m; tunnel, with toll), which takes the road over the ridge of the Sierra de Guadarrama. The pass, officially called the Alto de los Leones de Castilla (after the stone lions set up here in 1749, during the reign of Ferdinand VI, to commemorate the building of the road), marks the boundary between New and Old Castile: magnificent *views.

Málaga

Province: Málaga (MA).
Telephone code: 952.
Altitude: 8 m. – Population: 503,000.
ⓘ **Oficina de Información de Turismo,**
Calle Marqués de Larios 5;
tel. 21 34 45.
Delegación Provincial de Turismo,
Avenida de la Aurora s/n;
tel. 34 73 00.
Oficina de Turismo,
Airport;
tel. 31 20 44.

HOTELS. – *Málaga Palacio (no rest.), on the Parque, L, 228 r.; SP; Guadalmar, Apdo de Correos 568, I, 195 r., SP; Parador Nacional de Gibralfaro, on Gibralfaro, extensive views, II, 12 r. (good cuisine); Bahía Málaga (no rest.), Somera 8, II, 44 r.; Casa Curro, Sancha de Lara 7, II, 105 r.; Husa Las Vegas, Paseo de Sancha 22, II, 73 r., SP; Los Naranjos (no rest.), Paseo de Sancha 35, II, 41 r.; California, Paseo de Sancha 19, III, 26 r.; Lis (no rest.), Córdoba 7, III, 53 r.; Olletas (no rest.), Cuba 1–3, III, 66 r.; Astoria (no rest.), Avda del Comandante Benitez 3, IV, 61 r.; Lynda Mar, Canales 6, IV, 30 r.; Niza (no rest.), Larios 2, IV, 52 r.; etc. – CAMPING SITE: Balneario del Carmen, at Torre de San Telmo on the Almería road (N 340).

RESTAURANTS. – In most hotels; also Gibralfaro on Gibralfaro; La Alegria, Marin Garcia 1; Cortijo de Pepe, Plaza de la Merced 2; La Espuela, Trinidad Grund 14; Baños de Carmen, in Pedregalejo, Torre de San Telmo; Casa Pedro, Playa de El Palo, 5 km E; etc.

EVENTS. – Semana Santa (Holy Week), great celebrations, with particularly impressive and colourful processions at night and bullfights on Easter Day. – Corpus Christi, with solemn procession, bullfights and fireworks. – Fiestas de la Virgen del Carmen (July), with sea procession. – Feria, with traditional celebrations (Aug.). – Festivales de España (Aug.–Sept.), with international musical and theatrical performances. – Rallye Costa del Sol (Dec.), car

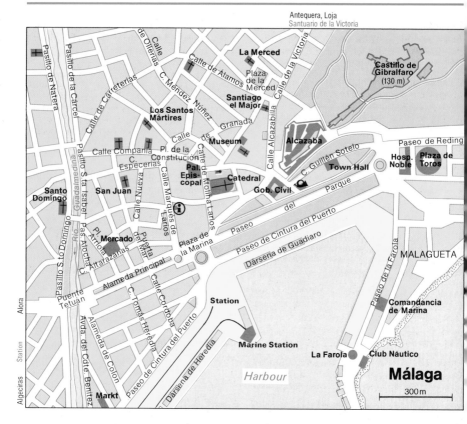

race through the provinces of Málaga, Granada and Almería.

BULLRING (*Plaza de Toros*, with seating for 11,000) in Paseo de Reding in the Malagueta district.

WATER SPORTS. – Large boating harbour; beaches of Baños del Carmen, El Palo, Acacias, Pedregalejo and El Chanquete, with fine sand, in immediate vicinity of town; San Andrés (beach 6 km long).

SPORT and RECREATION on land. – Bullfights, golf (several courses), tennis, riding; sports facilities and swimming pools in various parts of the town; shooting in surrounding area and in Coto Nacional de Sierra Blanca (Ojén); river and sea angling; flying (Aero Club).

*Málaga, picturesquely situated on the S coast of Spain at the foot of the Montes de Málaga, in a region of luxuriant subtropical vegetation, is one of the oldest Mediterranean ports, capital of its province and the seat of a bishop.

The wide sweep of Málaga Bay is bounded on the E by the *Punta de los Cántales* and on the W by the *Torre de Pimentel*. Half way round the bay is the hill of *Gibralfaro*, crowned by its castle.

To the W of the town extends the *Vega* or *Hoya de Málaga*, in which oranges, figs, bananas, sugar-cane, cotton and other crops flourish. Málaga is particularly famous for its raisins (*pasas*, Lat. *uvae passae*) and its excellent wines, already well known in Moorish times, among the best known of which are the sweet Pedro Ximenes and the Dulce and Lágrimas muscatel wines. On account of their magnesium phosphate content the wines are also used for medicinal purposes. Málaga's proverbially mild climate has made it the chief centre of the Costa del Sol, a popular resort in winter as well as in summer. It is also of some consequence as an industrial town and a port.

HISTORY. – Málaga was founded by the Phoenicians as a settlement for the trade in salt fish, and its name seems to be derived from the occupation of its first settlers (*malac*=to salt). It later became a Carthaginian stronghold, and long retained its Punic character. The Romans established a colony here, and were followed by the Visigoths (571–711) and then by the Moors, who regarded Málaga as a paradise on earth. In 1487 the town was recaptured by the Catholic monarchs, and thereafter many churches were built there. In May 1931 more than 40 churches were set on fire and destroyed, and the town also suffered severely during the Civil War. – Málaga was the birthplace of the painter Pablo Picasso, and the 17th c. sculptor Pedro de Mena lived and died in the town.

SIGHTS. – Málaga's main traffic artery is the *Alameda Principal*, 420 m long and 42 m wide which extends from the *Plaza de la Marina* in the old town to the *Puente de Tetuán* over the *Río Guadalmedina* and is continued into the western suburbs by a wide modern extension. A little way N of the Alameda is the *Market Hall* (Mercado), with a very lively and interesting morning fish market.

To the E of the Plaza de la Marina the *Paseo del Parque* extends along the harbour, with lush tropical vegetation and beautiful promenades shaded by palms and plane-trees. On the N side are the *Gobierno Civil*, the *Aduana* (Custom House), the *Post Office* and the **Ayuntamiento** (Town Hall, 1911–19). At the E end is the *Fuente de Neptuno* (Neptune Fountain, 1560). – The Paseo del Parque joins the Paseo de Reding, on the right-hand side of which is the *Plaza de Toros* (Bullring, 1874).

N of the Paseo del Parque in the old town, reached from Plaza Queipo de Llano by way of Calle Molina Larios, is the **Cathedral**, on the site of an earlier mosque. A massive limestone structure begun in 1538 to the design of Diego de Siloé; it was partly destroyed by an earthquake in 1680. Building was resumed in 1719. W front with two towers; from the N tower (86 m high) there are extensive views.

The splendidly proportioned INTERIOR, with laterial aisles, is 115 m long. The *Choir* (1592–1631) has beautiful stalls (1658), with carved wooden *statues of saints and other figures by Pedro de Mena and Giuseppe Micaelo. In the *Capilla del Rosario* (3rd chapel in S aisle) is a "Virgin with Saints" by Alonso Cano. On the left-hand wall of the *Capilla de los Reyes* (first chapel in S choir aisle) are kneeling figures of the Catholic monarchs by Pedro de Mena and a statuette of the Virgin which Ferdinand and Isabella are said always to have taken with them on their crusades. In the *Capilla Mayor* is a modern altar with scenes from the Passion (1580).

A little way N of the Cathedral, in Calle San Agustín, is the *Museo de Bellas Artes*, with a collection of antiquities and a small picture gallery containing early works by Picasso and other pictures of the 16th–20th c.; specialist library on the work of Picasso. – Then along Calle Granada, past the church of *Santiago el Mayor* (1490), to the large *Plaza de la Merced*, with the modest *birthplace of Pablo Picasso* (small commemorative tablet; museum planned). – Farther N, reached by way of Calle de la Victoria, is the church of *Nuestra Señora de la Victoria*, a handsome Baroque building

erected on the site of Ferdinand V's camp. It contains the 15th c. Virgen de la Victoria, patroness of the town, and two pieces of sculpture by Pedro de Mena.

From the Plaza de la Merced the Calle del Mundo Nuevo climbs up the saddle known as the *Coracha* ("leather bag") and the **Alcazaba** ("Fortress"), built on the site of the earliest settlement. It has been much restored, but there are still some remains of the original stronghold of the Moorish kings, including the *Torre de la Vela* and the *Arco de Cristo*. There is an interesting *Archeological Museum*, with finds from the site and a collection of Spanish-Arab pottery; beautiful *gardens in the courtyards. On the N side of the hill are remains of a *Roman theatre*. – From the Coracha we continue NE, between walls, up **Gibralfaro** (170 m: Arabic *jebel*, "hill", and Greek *pharos*, "lighthouse"), with fortifications dating from the 13th c. From the old walls there are magnificent *views of the town, the harbour and the surrounding area. On the S side of the hill is the Parador de Gibralfaro.

Roman theatre, Málaga

From the Plaza de la Marina *Calle Marqués de Larios*, Málaga's principal shopping street (on right, Tourist Information Office), runs N into the *Plaza de la Constitución* with a fountain and the handsome *Casa del Consulado* (17th c. doorway of white and grey-green marble), now the headquarters of the *Sociedad Económica de Amigos del País*.

SURROUNDINGS. – Málaga, situated on the beautiful and popular *Costa del Sol, offers a variety of excursions to the many tourist centres along the coast, with their beaches and their busy international life; but inland too there is a wide choice of interesting trips into the mountains.

Towards Granada. – Leave Málaga by way of the Paseo del Parque and Paseo de Reding, and continue on N 340, through sugar-cane plantations, to (10 km) **Rincón de la Victoria** (alt. 5 m; pop. 5000), a prettily situated fishing village. In a park above the village is a large cave with Neolithic rock drawings which in later periods provided a refuge for both Christians and Moors. Beach 3 km long.

After another 21 km along the coast we reach the little port and seaside resort of *Torre del Mar*, near which the remains of a Greek settlement destroyed by the Carthaginians (*Mainake*) were discovered. – From here C 335, a hilly road with many bends, runs up to the old Moorish town of *Vélez Málaga* (alt. 115 m; pop. 45,000) and through the *Sierra Tejada* to *Ventas de Zafarraya* (alt. 907 m), on the boundary of the province of Granada; then via *Alhama de Granada* to **Granada** (see p. 127), 109 km from Málaga.

Through the hills to Ronda. – Leave Málaga on the Paseo de los Tilos, and continue W through the Vega de Málaga. 5 km off the road on the left, beyond the old Moorish township of *Cártama*, the Roman *Cartima*. The road then traverses the Guadalhorce valley to *Pizarra* (alt. 80 m). Just beyond this turn left into a minor road which crosses the *Sierra de la Robla*, and near *Alozaina* turn right into C 344, which passes *Yunquera* and the picturesque *El Burgo*, then through the *Serranía de Ronda* to **Ronda** (see p. 189), 96 km from Málaga.

Marbella

Province: Málaga (MA).
Telephone code: 952.
Altitude: 14 m. – Population: 65,000.
ⓘ **Oficina de Información de Turismo,**
Avenida Miguel Cano 1;
tel. 77 14 42.

HOTELS. – *El Fuerte*, Llano de San Luis, I, 146 r., SP; *San Cristóbal* (no rest.), II, Ramón y Cajal 18, 102 r.; *Lima* (no rest.), Avda Antonio Belon, III, 64 r. – ON THE MÁLAGA ROAD: *Don Carlos*, Urb. Elviria, 10 km E, L, 236 r., SP; *Los Monteros*, 7 km E, L, 171 r., SP; *Artola*, 12 km E, II, 19 r., SP; *Bellamar*, 2·5 km E, II, 66 r., SP; *Las Charpas*, 10·5 km E, II, 117 r., SP; *Estrella del Mar*. 10 km E, II, 98 r., SP. – ON THE CADIZ ROAD: *Meliá Don Pepe*, Finca Las Merinas, 1 km W, L, 218 r., SP; *Puente Romano*, 3·5 km W, L, 198 r., SP; *Marbella Club*, 3 km W, I, 76 r., SP; *Marbella Dinamar Club 24*, 6 km W, I, 117 r., SP; *Guadalpin*, 1·5 km W, II, 103 r., SP. – *Club Mediterranée "Don Miguel"*, SP. – CAMPING SITES. *La Buganvilla*, km 188·8 on N 340. *Marbella Playa*, at 192·9 km on N 340.

RESTAURANTS. – *El Cenador*, Urb. La Merced, 1 km W opposite Hotel Meliá Don Pepe; *Beach Club*, 3 km W in Hotel Marbella Club; *Chez Charlemagne*, 8 km E; *Derby*, Torre de Marbella, Avda del Fuerte; *El Faro*, Paseo Marítimo; *La Hacienda*, 11 km E; *Metropol*, Avda Ricardo Soriano, Edificio Globus; *Siete Puertas*, Avda Ricardo Soriano 33; *Kai-Alde*, Avda Ricardo Soriano (Basque specialities); *Marisquería Santiago*, Avda Antonio Belón 1 (seafood); etc.

The beach, Marbella

EVENTS. – *Fiesta del Sol* (Jan.), with various sporting contests and exhibitions. – *Pilgrimage* to La Cruz de Juaná (May). – *Fiestas de San Bernabé* (June), with market, procession to the Cruz del Humilladero and bullfights. – *Pilgrimage* to Guadalpín (June). – *Semana del Sol* (Aug.), with pageants, sporting events and traditional ceremonies. – *Rallye Costa del Sol*, car race (Dec.).

CASINO. – *Casino Nueva Andalucía Marbella*.

WATER SPORTS. – Facilities for all kinds of water sports on beautiful long beaches: Las Chapas (8 km), El Ancón (2 km), La Fontanilla (1·5 km), El Fuerte (5 km), etc. Three boating harbours in Marbella, Nueva Andalucía (Puerto José Banus) and at Cabo Pino. Sea angling (boats and equipment available for hire). Sailing.

SPORT and RECREATION on land. – Bullfights (three bullrings), golf (several courses), tennis, riding, shooting (partridges, quails, rabbits) in the Sierra Blanca.

Marbella is a busy port and an internationally renowned seaside resort on the Costa del Sol, between Málaga and Algeciras; a residential and tourist town, with extensive hotel and apartment developments in the surrounding area, it has become one of the principal centres of the Spanish tourist trade in the Mediterranean, with beautiful large bathing beaches and every facility for shopping and entertainment.

Lying in the shelter of the Sierra Blanca, Marbella has a mild climate throughout the year. The old town with it white-washed houses still preserves remains of its medieval defensive walls, with two battlemented towers. Above the town are well-preserved remains of a Moorish castle (walls, patio, keep).

Medinaceli

Province: Soria (SO).
Telephone code: 975.
Altitude: 1160 m.
ⓘ **Centro de Iniciativas y Turismo,**
   Plaza Mayor;
   tel. 50.

HOTELS. – *Nico Hotel 70* km 151 on N II, II, 22 r.; *Duque de Medinaceli* (no rest.), km 150 on N II, IV, 12 r.; *Hostal Catalán* km 150 on N II, P II, 9 r., *Medinaceli*, Del Portillo 1, P II, 7 r.; *Torremar*, km 154 on N II, P III, 22 r.

RESTAURANT: in *Hotel Duque de Medinaceli*.

The picturesque little town of Medinaceli, known to the Romans as Ocilis and to the Moors as Medina Selim, was an important Moorish frontier stronghold and later the seat of the ducal family of Medinaceli. It has Roman remains dating from the 1st to the 3rd c. A.D.

SIGHTS. – **Roman triumphal arch** with three openings. – Remains of an old *Moorish fortress* in the N of the town. – Many patrician houses, including the *Palacio de los Duques de Medinaceli* (18th c.). – Churches and convents, among them the 16th c. church of *Santa María*, with the tombs of the ducal family.

SURROUNDINGS. – 11 km W is the prehistoric settlement of *Ambrona*, with an interesting museum. – 27 km NE, under the *Cerro de la Cruz*, is **Santa María de la Herta**, with the 12th c. Real Monasterio (national monument), a Cistercian house of fortress-like aspect, surrounded by walls (Gothic refectory, Plateresque cloister), and the Palacio de los Marqueses de Cerralbo.

Medina del Campo

Province: Valladolid (VA).
Telephone code: 983.
Altitude: 721 m. – Population: 15,000.
ⓘ **Ayuntamiento** (Town Hall),
   Plaza de España;
   tel. 80 00 01 and 80 02 27.

HOTELS. – *La Mota* (no rest.), Fernando el Católico 4, III, 40 r.; *San Roque* (no rest), km 157 on Coruña road, III, 40 r.; *Medina*, Isabel la Católica 3, IV, 14 r.; Hostal *Europa*, Padilla 40, P II, 33 r.

EVENTS. – *Semana Santa* (Holy Week), with a solemn procession in which splendid statues are carried through the streets. – *Summer Festival* (June).

The little town of Medina del Campo, on the Río Zapardiel, is an important railway and road junction on the N VI, which links Madrid with La Coruña.

SIGHTS. – Above the town stands the **Castillo de la Mota** (15th c.), one of the finest castles in Spain. It was a favourite residence of Isabella the Catholic who died here in 1504. César Borja was confined in the castle from 1504 to 1506. – The collegiate church of *San Antolín* (1503) has a number of fine retablos, one of them partly by Berruguete. – The Renaissance *Casa de las Dueñas* has a beautiful inner courtyard.

Melilla

Province: Málaga (ML).
Telephone code: 952.
Altitude: at sea level. – Population: 47,000.
ⓘ **Oficina de Información de Turismo,**
   General Aizpuru 20;
   tel. 68 40 13.

HOTELS. – *Parador Nacional Don Pedro de Estopiñán* (no rest.), Apartado Correos 312, II, 35 r.; *Anfora* (no rest.), Pablo Vallesca 8, III, 145 r.; *Rusadir San Miguel* (no rest.), Pablo Vallesca 5, III, 27 r.

BOAT SERVICES. – Car ferries daily from Málaga and Almería; the crossing takes about 8 hours in each case.

The town of Melilla, a Spanish "plaza de soberanía" on the North African coast, is a modern city, with interesting remains of the past in the old part of the town, which has been a free port since 1863. The climate, as elsewhere on the Mediterranean coast, is of notable mildness.

SIGHTS. – The old town, *El Pueblo*, is made up of three separate walled sections cut off from each other by deep moats which are crossed by drawbridges. The *Puerta de Santiago* and the bridge of the same name, with the coat of arms of Charles V, gave access to the most interesting part of the town. – Melilla's oldest church is the **Purísima Concepción** (16th c.), with a Baroque retablo. Under the church are the so-called Cuevas del Conventico.

Mérida

Province: Badajoz (BA).
Telephone code: 924.
Altitude: 196 m. – Population: 50,000.
ⓘ **Oficina de Información de Turismo,**
   Calle El Puente 9;
   tel. 31 53 53.

HOTELS. – *Parador Nacional Vía de la Plata*, Plaza de la Constitución 3, I, 44 r.; *Las Lomas*, km 338 on Carretera N-V, I, 139 r., SP; *Emperatriz*, Plaza de Espagña 19, II, 41 r.; *Nova Roma* (no rest.), Suarez Somonte 42, III, 28 r.; *Zeus* (no rest.), km 341 on Carretera N-V, III, 44 r. – CAMPING SITE: on Lago Prosérpina.

EVENTS. – *Feria* (Sept.), with a fair and a large cattle market. – *Fiesta de Santa Eulalia* (Dec.).

*Mérida, the Spanish town which is richest in remains of the Roman period, lies on a flat-topped hill on the right bank of the Río Guadiana, on the sparsely populated plateau of Extremadura which adjoins the Portuguese frontier.

HISTORY. – Founded about 25 B.C., the Roman town of *Augusta Emerita* rose to prosperity as capital of Lusitania, and maintained its position during the Visigothic period. It was captured by the Moors in 713. After its reconquest by Alfonso IX of León in 1229 it was granted to the Order of Santiago, but thereafter it declined in importance.

SIGHTS. – The hub of the town's traffic is the arcaded *Plaza de España* or Plaza Mayor, on the NW side of which is the church of *Santa María* (13th–15th c.). – To the NW stands the **Arco de Trajano** or *Arco de Santiago*, a Roman triumphal arch almost 13 m high, with four tiers of columns, which was the N gate of the Roman town.

S of the Plaza de España on the banks of the Río Guadiana is the old **Alcazaba**, originally built by the Visigoths, enlarged

Roman theatre, Mérida

by the Moors in 855 and converted into a monastery by the Knights of Santiago. In the garden is a Visigothic cistern. To the W of the Alcazaba is one of Mérida's principal tourist attractions, the **Roman bridge** (*Puente romano*) over the Guadiana, 792 m long, with 64 granite arches. It was probably built in the time of

Augustus but repaired or renewed several times in subsequent centuries.

In the NE of the town, near the railway station, is the *Convento de Santa Eulalia*, with a church which is said to have been founded in the 4th c. From here Calle Teniente Coronel Yagüe runs E to the **New Aqueduct** (*Acueducto moderno*), with 140 arches, dating from the Moorish period. Close by is the little Gothic church of *San Lázaro* and remains of the imposing Roman *Circus Maximus*. From the aqueduct we go S, past fragments of a Roman aqueduct, to the excavated remains of the *Roman amphitheatre* (Anfiteatro romano, with seating for 15,000), which dates from 8 B.C., and the ***Roman theatre** (*Teatro romano*), built by the Roman general Agrippa in 16 B.C. and rebuilt after a fire in the time of Hadrian, with well-preserved seating and stage wall (partly rebuilt). From the top of the rows of seats (which could accommodate an audience of 6000) there is a very fine view. In the immediate neighbourhood are other remains of late Roman buildings and the town walls. W of the Teatro Romano stands the new **Museum of Roman Art** with archaeological exhibits from Roman, western Gothic and Moorish times, as well as sculptures, mosaics and inscriptions.

To the NW of the town, with the railway line cutting across it, is the mighty ***Roman aqueduct** (*Acueducto romano*), also known as *Los Milagros*, the "Marvel", of which 37 piers and ten arches up to three high have been preserved. A short distance W the little Río Albarregas is crossed by another Roman bridge 125 m long, the *Puente de Albarregas*.

SURROUNDINGS. – There are other Roman remains in the surrounding countryside – e.g. two Roman reservoirs, the *Pantano Cornalvo* (10 km NE) and the *Pantano de Prosérpina* (10 km NW). The latter has a dam 426 m long and two 17th c. towers with steps leading down to the water.

N 630 runs S from Mérida over the almost treeless plateau of the *Tierra de los Barros* and comes in 29 km to **Almendralejo** (alt. 336 m; pop. 30,000), a picturesque Andalusian-style town. In the Palacio del Marques de Monsalud is a widely renowned collection of Roman antiquities.

N 630 continues S to *Villafranca de los Barros*, 12 km beyond which a road goes off on the right to **Los Santos de Maimona** (alt. 545 m; pop. 10,000), the Roman *Segeda Angurina*, with remains of a fort dating from the time of Trajan. Nearby is the hermitage of *Nuestra Señora de la Estrella*, with a picture by Zurbarán.

Montserrat

**Montserrat (1241 m), the "jagged mountain", and to the Catalonians Montsagrat, the sacred mountain, 60 km NW of Barcelona, is one of Spain's major tourist attractions by virtue both of its scenic magnificence and its famous monastery, situated at an altitude of 721 m.

This great massif, 22 km long, rears out of the Catalonian upland plain on the right bank of the *Río Llobregat* in splendid isolation, with steep rock faces on almost every side, looking from the distance, with its fantastically eroded crags and terraces, like some gigantic fortress. Not surprisingly, therefore, it has in the past been associated with the Castle of Monsalvat in the Grail legend.

HISTORY. – Legend has it that the monastery was founded in 880 in honour of a wonder-working image of the Virgin. In 976 it was granted to the Benedictine order and occupied by monks from Ripoll. In 1410 Pope Benedict XIII raised it to the status of an independent abbey, but later it became subject to the bishop of Barcelona. Most of its enormous wealth was dispersed during the Wars of Liberation (1808–14) and during its closure (1835–60) in consequence of the Carlist wars. Since the 15th c. the monks of Montserrat have run a school of church music.

ACCESS. – Coming from Barcelona, take either N II, which runs through the city's western industrial suburbs, or the motorway to Martorell. – At the village of *Collbató* (alt. 380 m) follow a signpost to the right. The road runs round the head of a valley, passing the *Cuevas del Salitre* ("Saltpetre Caves"), and continues under the steep rock face of Montserrat, over 400 m high, to a high bridge over the *Río Llobregat*, beyond which is the lower station of the cableway up to the monastery (7½ minutes).

The road up to the monastery passes the hamlet of *Colonia Gomis* and the village of *Monistrol* (alt. 145 m), surrounded by vineyards and olive-groves, and then winds its way up the sides of the *Valle de Santa María*, with magnificent views and gradients of up to 16 per cent, and joins the broad road which leads to the monastery car park.

TOUR OF THE MONASTERY. – From the end of the road we turn right into the monastery courtyard. On the left are a few remains of the *old monastery*, with one restored wing of the Gothic *cloister* of 1460. Along the E side of the courtyard is the *new monastery*, begun in 1765 but left unfinished on account of the Carlist wars and finally completed (including the tower) only shortly after the end of the Second World War. Passing through an

Montserrat Monastery

arcaded courtyard (*claustro*), we enter the imposing **Basilica**, built 1560–92 in Renaissance style and restored in the 19th c., with a neo-Romanesque apse of 1860 and a façade of 1901. In the dark interior, above the high altar, is a wooden image of the Virgin, black with age (probably 12th c.), known as the "Santa Imagen" (in Catalan "S. Imatge"). The legend is that the image was made by St Luke, brought to Spain by St Peter and found in the Santa Cueva in 880.

The monastery has a large *library* of over 200,000 volumes and contains a number of *museums* (Museum of the Bible, Museum of Prehistory, Museum of Egyptology, Natural History Museum, Musem of Decorative Art, a picture gallery, etc.).

SURROUNDINGS. – Access to Montserrat for walkers and climbers is facilitated by various paths and four mountain railways: **Cableway** (1·5 km) from lower station (railway from Barcelona) to monastery (7½ minutes). – **Funicular** (0·5 km) from monastery in 6 minutes to *San Juan* ridge (970 m). 10 minutes W are restaurants and an observation terrace. Nearby, among the rocks, are the remains of many hermitages. Good walk on footpath to *San Jerónimo* (3·5 km). – **Funicular** (800 m) down from monastery (2 minutes), then 20 minutes' walk along a path (Stations of the Cross) below a cliff to the *Santa Cueva*, in which the sacred image of the Virgin, concealed during the Moorish period, is said to have been found. Above the cave is the *Santuario de la Cueva* (17th c.). – *Cableway* (680 m long, difference in height 535 m), the oldest in Spain,

3·25 km NW of the monastery near the *Ermita Santa Cecilia* (founded 872), with restaurant: from there 9 minutes to the upper station near the *Ermita San Jerónimo* (in Catalan, Sant Jeroni), 5 minutes below the *Turó de San Jerónimo* (1241 m), the highest peak in the whole massif, with panoramic *views of the mountains and plains of Catalonia, extending in the N to the Pyrenees, and in the SE (in absolutely clear weather) as far as the Balearics. From the Ermita it is an hour's walk, between rock pinnacles known as the "Guardians of the Holy Grail" or the "Fingers of God", to *San Juan*. – The best general view of the monastery is from the *Mirador* viewpoint (781 m), 20 minutes SE, near which is the *Capilla de San Miguel* (821 m).

17 km N on the C 1411 lies the ancient and highly industrialised town of **Manresa** (234 m.; population 60,000); one of the finest of its Gothic churches is Santa Maria de la Seo (14th–15th c.).

Apostles' Doorway, Murcia Cathedral

Morella

Province: Castellón (CS).
Telephone code: 964.
Altitude: 1004 m. – Population: 2500.

ⓘ **Ayuntamiento** (Town Hall),
Segura Barreda 58;
tel. 16 00 34.

HOTELS. – *Cardenal Ram*, Cuesta Súñer 1, III, 19 r.

The old frontier stronghold of Morella lies high in the uplands of the Maestrazgo region on a conical hill within a rocky depression, on the boundary between Aragon and Valencia.

In the little walled town is the Gothic church of **Santa María la Mayor** (13th c.), with beautiful doorways, a 15th c. choir and a Churrigueresque Capilla Mayor; it contains a fine picture by Ribalta. – From the ruined *castle* there are magnificent panoramic views. – 15th c. *aqueduct*. Truffles are found in the district.

Murcia

Province: Murcia (MU).
Telephone code: 968.
Altitude: 43 m. – Population: 289,000.

ⓘ **Oficina de Información de Turismo,**
Alejandro Séiquet 4;
tel. 21 37 16.
Dirreción Regional de Turismo,
Isidoro de la Cierva 10;
tel. 21 37 10.

HOTELS. – *Siete Coronas Meliá*, Ronda de Garay 5, I, 122 r.; *Conde de Floridablanca* (no rest.), Corbalán

7, II, 60 r.; *Fontoria* (no rest.), Madre de Dios 4, II, 120 r.; *Hispano II*, Radio Murcia 3, II, 35 r.; *Rincón de Pepe* (no rest.), Apóstoles 34, II, 122 r.; etc.

RESTAURANTS. – *Rincón de Pepe*, Apóstoles 1 (Castilian style); *Hispano*, Lucas 7 (rustic style); *Zarauz*, Plaza Luxmarina 1; etc.

EVENTS. – **Semana Santa** (Holy Week), famous celebrations with impressive night processions in which the *pasos* by Salzillo (see below) are carried through the streets. Particularly striking is the procession on the morning of Good Friday, also with Salzillo's figures. After Easter there are battles of Flowers, cavalcades, etc. – *Nuestra Señora de la Fuensanta* (Sept.), fiesta with pilgrimage and fair.

Murcia, situated in the hot coastal plain of SE Spain, is capital of its province, a university town and the seat of a bishop. The old town lies on the left bank of the Río Segura, the newer districts on the right bank.

HISTORY. – From 1224 Murcia was an independent Moorish kingdom, which was conquered by Castile in 1243. During the War of the Spanish Succession the huerta was flooded to defend the town against Austrian forces. In 1936, during the Civil War, most of the churches, which contained many works by the Murcia-born sculptor Francisco Salzillo or Zarcillo (1707–83), were severely damaged.

SIGHTS. – At the N end of the *Puente Viejo* (Old Bridge) which leads to the newer part of the town is the *Plaza de*

Martínez Tornel, from which Murcia's main traffic artery, the *Gran Vía Escultor Salzillo*, runs N. Immediately W of the Plaza de Martínez Tornel is the *Plano de San Francisco*, and beyond this square is the *Paseo del Malecón*, a riverside promenade (*malecón*=embankment, quay) which affords fine views but no protection from the sun. – To the E of the Plaza de Martínez Tornel an attractive public garden, the *Glorieta de España*, extends along the river, with the **Ayuntamiento** (Town Hall) and the *Bishop's Palace* (18th c.). There is a bridge over the river opposite the Bishop's Palace, and farther down-stream is another, the *Puente Nuevo* (New Bridge).

Behind the Bishop's Palace is the ***Cathedral** (*Santa María*), an imposing Gothic structure built in 1358 on the site of a mosque and altered in the 16th c., with a mid 18th c. W façade. There are two fine side doorways, richly decorated. – the Gothic Portada de los Apóstoles (Apostles' Doorway) in the S transept, the 16th c. Portada de las Cadenas in the N transept. The Capilla Mayor has a fine *reja* of 1497 and a gilded retablo (19th c.); in a recess on the left is a sarcophagus containing the entrails of Alfonso the Wise, and in a recess on the right the remains of St Fulgentius and St Florentina. The choir has beautiful Plateresque stalls (1571); in the ambulatory are a number of richly furnished chapels, particularly notable being the fourth chapel (Capilla de los Vélez). – The *Diocesan Museum* is housed in the cloister and chapterhouse. From the 95 m high tower (16th–18th c.: entrance on N side of Capilla Mayor) there are magnificent views of the town and its huerta.

From the Cathedral the Trapería (Calle del Príncipe Alfonso), formerly Murcia's main street, runs N through the old town. Together with the Platería which branches off on the left it forms the core of the bustling pedestrian precinct with its numerous shops. The Trapería ends in the *Plaza de Santo Domingo*, with the imposing twin-towered church of *Santo Domingo* (17th–18th c.). To the W, behind the church, is the *Theatre*; a little way E along Calle de la Merced is the *University*. From here it is only a few minutes' walk to the *Museo de Bellas Artes* in Calle Obispo Frutos, which contains frescoes and paintings by a Murcia-born pupil of Velázquez, Nicholá Villacís (1616–94). – N of the Plaza de Santo Domingo is the *Museo Arqueológico* (Casa de Cultura), with prehistoric, Iberian and Roman material; pottery.

The most interesting of the numerous churches in the western districts of the town are the Baroque church of *San Nicolás*, with sculpture by Alonso Cano,

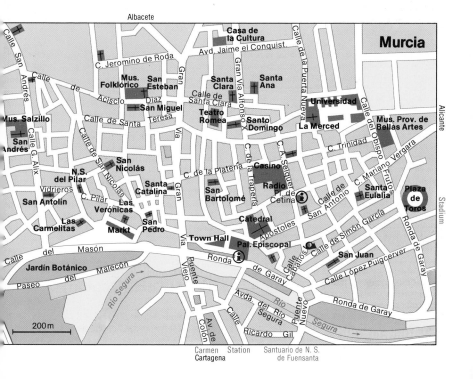

La Manga on the Mar Menor

Pedro de Mena and Salzillo, and *San Miguel*, with several altar figures by Salzillo and the sculptor's workshop. Opposite San Miguel, in Calle Acisto Díaz, is the former convent of San Esteban, which houses the *Museo Internacional del Traje Folklórico*, with traditional costumes from all over Spain. Farther W, in the Plaza de San Agustín, in the round *Ermita de Jesús* (Baroque, 1777), is the *Museo Salzillo*, which contains the famous processional figures (*pasos*) by the 18th c. sculptor Francisco Salzillo and his Nativity group with numerous figures.

SURROUNDINGS. – There are a number of interesting places to visit in the immediate vicinity of Murcia. – 5 km W of the town is the Baroque monastery of **San Jerónimo** (1578, rebuilt in the 18th c.), with a church containing a fine figure of St Jerome by Salzillo (1755). – 5 km N, on **Monteagudo**, are remains of a Roman fort; on the summit of the hill is a 15 m high statue of the *Sagrado Corazón* (Sacred Heart), from which there are fine views. – 6 km S is the 17th c. convent of **La Fuensanta**, a place of pilgrimage with a fountain of 1577. – From *Alcantarilla*, 7 km W of Murcia, C 415 continues W to **Mula** (33 km from Murcia), a picturesque little town in the Huerta, with the church of San Miguel (1618) and other interesting churches; S of the town is the *Ermita del Niño*.

To the Mar Menor. – Leave Murcia on N 301, going S, and turn left into C 3319, which runs E to (45 km) **Santiago de la Ribera** (pop. 3000), on the *Mar Menor*, a large lagoon (area 180 sq. km) cut off from the sea by a narrow spit of land, *La Manga* 22 km long. The water of the lagoon (average depth 7 m; water sports, with bathing almost all year round) has a high salt and iodene content. On both sides of La Manga are numerous bathing beaches and tourist centres, with holiday bungalows, hotels and tall blocks of flats. At its S end is the precipitous *Cabo de Palos* (lighthouse).

To Almería. – Leave Murcia on N 340, which runs almost due W, crosses the *Río Segura* and comes to **Alcantarilla** (alt. 66 m; pop. 18,000; bypass), an industrial suburb of Murcia at the beginning of the luxuriant huerta, with a Huerta Museum. Here N 340 turns SW and follows the left bank of the *Río Sangonera*, at some distance from the river, to *Librilla*, situated on both sides of a gorge and surrounded by orange- and lemon-groves. The road then leads in a straight line through a corn-growing region to **Alhama de Murcia** (alt. 176 m; pop. 12,000), with warm sulphur springs emerging at the foot of a crag crowned by the tower of a Moorish castle.

Farther along, on a hill to the right of the road, is the little town of *Aledo* (alt. 604 m), famous for its wine, with a ruined castle which in the 11th c. was an important Castilian base in the fighting with the Moors. N 340 then comes to **Totana** (alt. 233 m; pop. 10,000; bypass), a little town of Moorish aspect at the foot of a southern outlier of the *Sierra de España* (1584 m).

The road now enters the *Huerta de Lorca*, which owes its fertility to irrigation from the large *Embalse de Puentes* (30 million cu. m), 14 km W. The dam was built in 1789, but burst in 1802 and was rebuilt in 1884.

The road towards **Lorca** is almost dead straight, with the *Sierra de Almenara* on the left and the *Sierra del Caño* on the right. It then continues to **Puerto Lumbreras** (alt. 466 m; pop. 7000), attractively situated on the slopes of a valley. Thereafter it enters the province of Almería and runs into the "Ruta de los Acantilados", continuing via *Sorbas* and *Tabernas* to *Almería* (see p. 52), 219 km from Murcia.

Over the Sierra de las Cabras. – This is the Albacete road (N 301, running NW from Murcia). 10 km from Murcia is **Molina de Segura** (alt. 34 m; pop. 15,000), on the left bank of the *Río Segura*, with salt-pans and canning factories. – Soon afterwards a road goes off to the left to (4 km) the spa of *Archena* (alt. 122 m), on the Segura (sulphurous water).

N 301 continues through the Segura valley, known as the *Valle de Ricote*. Below the road on the left is *Blanca*, at the foot of the Peña Nigra, with the ruins of a Moorish castle. The road now comes to **Cieza** (alt. 180 m; pop. 25,000; bypass), picturesquely situated on the left bank of the *Río Segura*. Nearby are the remains of a Roman fort. – The road then climbs to the *Sierra de las Cabras* and continues via *Hellín* to **Albacete** (see p. 46), 143 km from Murcia.

Murcia (Region)

Autonomous Region.
Organ of Government: Consejo de Gobierno de la Region de Murcia.
Province: Murcia.

Although the soil in the Region of Murcia, which bestrides the Río Segura in the SE of Spain, is naturally dry (summer temperatures up to 45 °C; less than 300 mm precipitation per annum), nevertheless it has been turned by artificial irrigation into a fruitful horticultural area (Huerta) where fruit and early vegetables thrive. The heart of the region is the town of Murcia (see entry).

Navarre

Autonomous Region.
Organ of Government: Diputación Floral de Navarra.
Province: Navarre.

Navarre, with a landscape patterned by the southern outliers of the Pyrenees, is a region of great scenic variety. In the NW it borders on Guipúzcoa, reaching almost to the sea, with scenery resembling that of the higher parts of the Cantabrian Basque country, while in the E it is bounded by Aragon, its configuration determined by the rivers flowing down from the Pyrenees. From the valley of the Ebro – the Ribera – the land rises towards the main western ridge of the Pyrenees, with rainfall and forest cover increasing with altitude.

From the dry and dusty Logroño plateau, resembling the landscape of Aragon, the region extends into the green valleys in which the old kingdom of Navarre, formerly reaching far into France, had its origin as a state controlling the Pyrenean passes.

The Puerto de Erro

For many centuries these valleys, so important for the defence of Spain's northern frontier, enjoyed a large measure of self-government as semi-independent *universidades* or *repúblicas*; and evidence of these embattled days is still to be seen in the trim and prosperous Navarrese villages, in the form of numerous mansions bearing the arms of noble families and in the old armouries in which the men of Navarre kept their weapons. The Navarrese, who are mostly of Basque origin, are still notable for the spirit of independence they have inherited from their martial past. The most interesting of the valleys of upland Navarre are the steep-sided *Baztán* valley (named after the River Baztanzubi or Baztán – the local name of the Bidasoa), which lies on the French frontier to the N of the provincial capital of Pamplona in its treeless basin, and, E of Pamplona, the valleys, running from N to S, of *Roncesvalles* (continued S by the Irati valley), *Salazar* and *Roncal*.

In Navarre are some of the most important pilgrim stations on the *"Way of St James"* (see p. 242), here known as the *"Camino francés"*, among them Roncesvalles, Leyre, Yesa, Javier, Sangüesa, Monreal, Puente la Reina, Estella and Los Arcos – all rich in Romanesque architecture and in memories of the great days of the pilgrimage to Santiago.

Nerja

Province: Málaga (MA).
Telephone code: 952.
Altitude: 21 m. – Population: 11,000.
(i) Ayuntamiento (Town Hall),
General Franco 29;
tel. 52 04 00 and 52 04 04.

HOTELS. – *Parador Nacional*, El Tablazo, I, 60 r., SP; *Monica*, Playa Torecilla s/n, I, 234 r., SP; *Balcón de Europa*, Paseo Balcón de Europa 1, II, 105 r., beach; *Cala-Bella*, Puerta del Mar 10, IV, 9 r.; *Portofino*, Puerta del Mar 2, IV, 12 r; etc.

RESTAURANTS. – *Cueva de Nerja*, 4·5 km NE (view of sea); *Rey Alfonso*, Balcón de Europa.

EVENTS. – *Fiestas de San Isidro* (May), pilgrimage with parade of carriages and fireworks. – *Fiestas de la Virgen del Carmen* (July), with procession on the sea. – *Festivales de España* (Aug.), in the Cueva de Nerja, with music and dancing. – *Patronal festival* (Oct.).

SPORT and RECREATION. – Facilities for all kinds of water sports on the beaches at Burriana (1 km long), in the surrounding area and at El Playazo (2 km long), with picturesque cliff-fringed bays; rowing, scuba diving. Walking and climbing in the hills.

This little fishing port, now a popular resort, lies at the mouth of the Río Chillar on a steeply sloping site under the Sierra de Mijara. The coast road along the Costa del Sol (N 340)

The Costa del Sol at Nerja

Orense

Province: Orense (OR).
Telephone code: 988.
Altitude: 125 m. – Population: 80,000.

(i) **Oficina de Información de Turismo**,
Curros Enríquez 1;
tel. 23 47 17.
Delegación Provincial de Turismo,
Avenida Habana 105,
tel. 22 80 90.

HOTELS. – *San Martin*, Curros Enríquez 1, 60 r.; *Sile*
Avda de la Habana 61, II, 64 r.; *Padre Feijoo* (no rest.
Eugenio Montes 1, III, 53 r.; *Barcelona*, Avda c
Pontevedra 13, IV, 47 r.; *Parque* (no rest.), Parque c
San Lázaro 24, IV, 57 r.; *Hostal Riomar* (no rest.
Accesos Puente Novísimo 15, P II, 39 r.; *La Confianz*
(no rest.), Juan XXIII 4, P III, 40 r.; *Lido*, Mateo c
Prado. Juan XXIII 6, P II, 66 r.; etc.

RESTAURANTS. – *Sanmiguel*, San Miguel 12. – On
120: *Caracoles*, in La Derrasa (10 km E).

The provincial capital of Orense, i
southern Galicia, has long bee
famed for its sulphur springs. It wa
the Roman town of Aurium, a nam
probably derived from the legendar
gold of the Río Miño. In the 6th an
7th c. it was the residence of th
Suevian kings. It is the seat of
bishop.

SIGHTS. – The hub of the town's life is th
Plaza Mayor, with the Romanesque *Bish*
op's Palace (national monument), in th
arcaded courtyard of which are th
Archaeological Museum and the *Provin*
cial Archives. Nearby, in an old-world par
of the town, is the **Cathedral** (*Sar*
Martín), built in the 12th and 13th c. an
restored in the 16th and 17th c. afte
severe damage by earthquakes and war. I
is particularly notable for the rich Roman
esque sculptured decoration of the porcl
(El Paraíso, "Paradise") and the sid
doorways, particularly the 13th c. S
doorway. Features of the interior are th
fine Plateresque grille in the presbytery
with an equestrian figure of St Martin; the
tomb of Bishop Vasco Mariño (1333–43)
in the N aisle; beautiful 16th c. choir-stall
and a large Gothic retablo in the Capilla
Mayor; and an old crucifix in the Capilla
del Cristo (1567–74), traditionally believed to have been washed ashore on the
Galacian coast in 1330. The *Diocesar*
Museum in the chapterhouse contains
valuable 13th c. enamels.

In the southern part of the town is the
Romanesque church of the *Trinidad* (13tr
c.), with two round towers and a Gothic

runs through the town. The name
(meaning "abundant spring") is of
Arabic origin.

SIGHTS. – *Balcón de Europa*, a viewpoint on a promontory rising high above
the sea near the town centre, with
magnificent views of the varied coastal
scenery; attractive walks in the neighbourhood. Photograph, p. 114.

SURROUNDINGS. – 7 km E is the *Cuerva de Nerja*,
a stalactitic cave with prehistoric cave paintings. At
the entrance are a restaurant and a small archaeological museum. The Festivales de España are held here in
summer.

Oña

Province: Burgos (BU).
Telephone: via operator.
Altitude: 559 m. – Population: 1700.
(i) **Diputación Provincial**,
Plaza de Santorio Convento;
tel. Oña 200.

HOTEL. – *Hostal Morales*, km 99 on N 232, P III, 6 r.

The village of Oña lies in the N of
Burgos province on the beautiful
road (N 232) which runs from San-
tander to Logroño.

SIGHTS. – The principal attraction is the
famous Benedictine abbey of **San Sal-**
vador, founded in the 11th c. Richly
furnished interior, with 15th c. stalls,
many royal tombs and a Romanesque
figure of Christ (12th c). – Interesting
museum in the sacristy, with a charming
17th c. Virgin. Gothic *cloister* (15th c.).

doorway. – In a public garden SW of the Plaza Mayor, at the foot of the hill, are three hot thermal springs (66–68 °C) known as *Las Burgas*, which were frequented in Roman times and are still much visited in summer.

N of the Plaza Mayor in the direction of the station is the *Puente Viejo* (Old Bridge) over the Miño, originally constructed in 1230 but several times rebuilt since then; the central arch is 38 m high and has a span of 43 m. Farther upstream is the *Puente Nuevo* (New Bridge). SW of the old bridge is the *Campo de los Remedios*, with a pilgrimage chapel containing a much venerated image of the Virgen de los Remedios.

SURROUNDINGS. – **To Ribas de Sil:** 30 km NE of Orense (by a minor country road or C 546), on a hill beside the village of *Peares*, is the abandoned monastery of *San Esteban de Ribas de Sil*, with a 10th c. cemetery chapel, a Gothic church and two beautiful cloisters. – At the S end of the *Embalse de Los Peares* the road enters the province of Lugo.

To Ponferrada and Astorga. – N 120, going E, comes in 19 km to *Esgos*, with the rock-built church of *San Pedro de Rocas*, on a hill. The road then continues through *La Iglesia* and over the Río Arnoya and winds its way up to a pass, the **Alto de Rodicio** (949 m), from which there are extensive views. From the pass it runs down, past the *Embalse del Mao*, to the little summer resort of *Castro Caldelas*, with a sulphur spring and a 14th c. castle. It then follows a twisting course with many undulations, to the **Alto de Cerdeira** (890 m), and thereafter winds down into the gorge of the *Río Navea*, passing on the right the *Embalse de Guistolas*. After climbing again to 790 m it comes to **Puebla de Trives** (alt. 746 m), a popular summer resort in a beautiful setting, surrounded by a number of artificial lakes and dominated on the S by the well-wooded Cabeza de Manzaneda (1778 m).

Beyond Puebla de Trives the road descends, with many bends, to the *Codos de Laroco*, where N 120 follows the line of a Roman road. On the left are the *Embalse de Montefurado* and beyond this the village of *Petín*, where the *Río Sil* (with a dam at this point) is crossed on a Roman bridge. The road then continues up the Sil valley to **El Barco de Valdeorras** (alt. 324 m; pop. 9000), a coal-mining town noted for its wine. – N 120 runs along the right bank of the Río Sil, through a valley which in places narrows into a gorge. At the *Embalse de Pumares* the road enters the province of León and continues via *Carucedo*, on a lake of the same name, to **Ponferrada** (see p. 187), and from there via **Astorga** to **Léon** (p. 144).

To the Portillo de la Canda. – Leave on N 525, the road to Zamora, which runs SE from Orense. After crossing the railway it winds its way up the valley of the *Río Barbaña* and through an upland region, with large areas of forest, towards the mountains. 24 km from Orense is **Allariz** (alt. 470 m; pop. 10,000), an old-world little town still partly enclosed by walls, with a Romanesque parish church. – The road continues steadily uphill through a fertile region, crosses the *Río Limia* to reach *Ginzo de Limia*, and then follows the valley of the *Río Támega* to **Verin**,

(alt. 612 m; pop. 9000; Parador Nacional de Monterrey, 4 km distant, II, 23 r., SP), attractively situated at the meeting of several valleys, with thermal springs. – N 525 continues E through hilly country and goes over the *Alto de Fumaces* (855 m), with the bare summit of *Peña Nofre* (1548 m) to the left. It then winds up to *la Gudiña* (alt. 980 m) and soon afterwards goes over the *Alto de Cañizo* (1067 m), beyond which, off the road on the right, is *Pereiro*, with a Romanesque church. Thereafter N 525 climbs, with many bends, to the **Portillo de la Canda** (1262 m), on the boundary between Galicia (Orense province) and Castile (Zamora province). – From here there is a beautiful road via Puebla de Sanabria to **Zamora** (see p. 243).

Into Portugal. – Leave Orense on N 540, which runs S to (26 km) **Celanova** (alt. 645 m; pop. 2500), a little market town with a famous Benedictine monastery founded in 936: a Baroque church with a magnificent façade, a beautiful cloister and panelled staircases. – 12 km W of Celanova is *Mosteiro*, with a Romanesque and Gothic church.

N 540 crosses the *Alto de Vieiro* (850 m) in the Montes de Bande and comes to *Bande*, the Roman *Aquis Querquinnis*. In *Baños*, on the *Embalse de las Conchas*, is the interesting Visigothic church (7th c.) of Santa Comba de Bande. – The road then continues via *La Herdadiña* to the Portuguese frontier.

To Vigo. – N 120/N 541 runs W to a road junction (13 km from Orense) where N 541 branches off and runs NW to the health resort of *Carballino*, surrounded by forest. – N 120 continues W through *Razamonde* and down the beautiful Miño valley to **Ribadavia** (alt. 180 m; pop. 7000), an old-world little town with a number of interesting churches, including the Romanesque San Juan (13th c.) Santiago (early Gothic) and Santo Domingo (Gothic, with interesting tombs). Beyond Ribadavia the road leaves the Río Miño, enters the province of Pontevedra and continues via *Puenteáreas* to **Vigo** (see p. 239), 106 km from Orense.

Orihuela

Province: Alicante (A).
Telephone code: 965.
Altitude: 24 m. – Population: 48,000.
ⓘ **Oficina de Información de Turismo,**
Francisco Diez 25,
tel. 30 27 47.

HOTELS. – *La Zenia*, Urbanización la Zenia, I, 220 r., SP; *Montepiedra*, Dehesa de Campoamor, II, 64 r.; SP; *Hostal Casa Corro* (no rest.), Avda teodomiro 1, P II, 16 r.; *Rey Teodomiro*, Avda Teodomiro 10, P II, 30 r.; etc.

RESTAURANT. – *Venta de Martin*, 5 km N on N 340 (accommodation also available).

The old episcopal town of Orihuela lies on the left bank of the Río Segura at the foot of the Cerro de Oro, surrounded by beautiful orange-groves. It was known to the Romans as Aurariola. Above

the town is a large seminary for the training of priests, from which there are fine views.

SIGHTS. – *Cathedral* (14th c.), with a beautiful N doorway; fine retablos (16th c.), including one dedicated to Santa Catalina. – *Diocesan Museum*, with the "Temptation of St Thomas Aquinas" by Velázquez. Two cloisters. – Church of Santiago (late Gothic, 15th c.), with a fine doorway and sculpture by Salzillo.

SURROUNDINGS. – 15 km SE, in the *Sierra del Cristo*, is the *Embalse de la Pedrera*.

Ovieda

Province: Asturias (O).
Telephone code: 985.
Altitude: 228 m. – Population: 182,000.

(i) **Oficina de Información de Turismo,**
Plaza de Alfonso II El Casto 6,
tel. 21 33 85.
Fomento del Turismo,
Hermanos Pidal 32,
tel. 23 05 33.

HOTELS. – *La Reconquista*, Gil de Jaz 16, L, 139 r., SP; *Gran Hotel España*, Jovellanos 2, I, 89 r.; *La Jirafa*, Pelayo 6, I, 89 r.; *Ramiro I* (no rest.), Calvo Sotelo 13, I, 83 r.; *Regente*, Jovellanos 31, I, 88 r.; *La Gruta* (no rest.), Alto de Buenavista s/n, II, 55 r.; *Principado*, San Francisco 6, II, 55 r.; *Barbón* (no rest.), Covadonga 7, III, 40 r.; *Ramos* (no rest.), Carta Puebla 6, IV, 40 r.; *Tropical* (no rest.), 19 de Julio 6, IV, 44 r.; etc.

RESTAURANTS. – In hotels; also *La Ronda Jirafa-Club*, Pelayo 4; *Pelayo*, Pelayo 15; *Marchica*, Dr Casal 10; *Casa Fermin*, San Francisco 8; *La Goleta*, Covadonga 32 (fish dishes).

CAFÉS. – *Arizona*, Gles. Beseda 57; *Café de Alfonso*, P. Valdés 15; *La Paloma*, Argüelles 25; *San Remo*, Avda Galicia 7; etc.

EVENTS. – *Fiesta de la Ascensión* (May), with ferias. – *Fiesta de San Mateo* (Sept.), with ferias, riding and other sporting events, bullfights and folk dancing.

Oviedo, once capital of the kingdom of Asturias, is now the chief town of the province of the same name, the seat of a bishop and a university town. It lies on the slopes of a hill some 30 km from the N coast of Spain, on a fertile plateau enclosed by the foothills of the Cantabrian Mountains.

HISTORY. – The town grew up in the 8th c. around a monastery on the site of the ancient *Ovetum*. From 810 to 924 it was capital of the kingdom of Asturias, which held out against the Moors but was later united with León and Castile. In modern times it has become

an industrial town. It suffered heavy damage during the rising of the Asturian miners in 1934 and in a siege lasting almost two years during the Civil War (1936–37). Since then a whole new district has been developed to the SW of the town.

SIGHTS. – The central feature of Oviedo is the large *Parque de San Francisco*, at the NE corner of which is the *Plaza de la Escandalera*, with the *Diputación Provincial* (the provincial government headquarters). From here the busy *Calle de Fruela* runs SE to the arcaded *Plaza Mayor*, in which are the former Jesuit church of *San Isidoro* (1578) and the *Casa Consistorial* (Town Hall) of 1662.

From the Plaza Mayor *Calle la Rúa* leads to the **Cathedral* (*Basílica del Salvador*), on the N side of the old town. This is an impressive Gothic structure (begun 1388, interior completed 1498), with a fine central doorway (Baroque relief of the Transfiguration) and a tower 82 m high (completed in 1539) which is one of the finest church towers in Spain (fine panoramic view from the top). It has a harmonious interior, with a number of notable features: the Capilla de Santa Eulalia in the N aisle, with an 11th c. silver gilt casket containing the saint's remains; the Capilla Mayor, with a retablo of 1520 on the high altar and the Gothic monument of Archbishop Arias de Villar (*c.* 1500); the Capilla del Rey Casto adjoining the N transept, which Alfonso II (d. 842) made the Panteón de los Reyes, the burial place of the Asturian kings (8th c. royal sarcophagus). From the S transept steps lead to ante-chapel, beyond which is the *Cámara Santa*. The rear chamber contains the Cathedral's magnificent treasury of *reliquaries (Cruz de los

View of Oviedo Cathedral

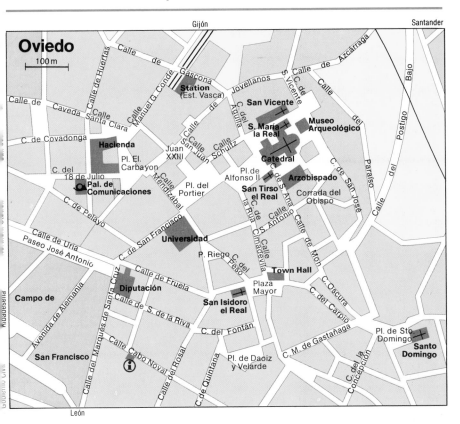

Ángeles, the 9th c. Cruz de la Victoria, an agate shrine of 910: conducted visits). Adjoining the S transept is a beautiful *cloister* (9th–15th c.), with a number of monuments and pilgrims' gravestones.

Near the cathedral can be seen several notable buildings; to the S stand the *Bishop's Palace* (16th–18th c.) and the 9th c. Church of *San Tirso*. In the Palacio de Velarde, near the church, is the *Museum of Art*, housing Renaissance and Baroque works as well as pictures by the contemporary painters of Asturia.

N of the Cathedral is the church of *San Pelayo*, also dating from the 9th c. and founded by Alfonso II, but rebuilt in the 18th c. In this area too is the church of *Santa María la Real*, a late Renaissance building (1592) which contains the tombs of notabilities of the past.

W of the Cathedral are several palaces, including the 17th c. Palacio del Marqués de Camposagrado, now housing the *Audiencia* (Provincial Court). Farther W is the *University*, founded in 1608 by Archbishop Fernando Valdés Sala, with a bronze statue of the founder in the courtyard.

From the Plaza de la Escandalera the town's main traffic artery, *Calle de Uría*, which is particularly busy in the afternoon and evening, runs NW to the *Northern Station* (Estación del Norte). – In the Plaza del Progreso, immediately N of the Plaza de la Escandalera, is the *Theatre*.

SURROUNDINGS. – 2 km NW of Oviedo, on the slopes of the *Sierra de Naranco* (1233 m), is the little town of **Naranco**, with two historic old churches – *Santa María de Naranco, with a barrel-vaulted roof and a Mozarabic altar, which was originally a reception room in the palace of the kings of Asturias, and *San Miguel de Lillo (9th c.), formerly the palace church (with later restoration and alteration). From the top of the hill there are magnificent views.

To Santander by the direct road. – Leave Oviedo by way of Calle de Azcárraga and N 634, which runs E to *Colloto* (fine view back to Oviedo) and **Pola de Siero**, in a coal-mining area, which is noted for its Fiesta de los Huevos Pintos (Fiesta of Painted Eggs) at Easter, with a traditional parade and groups in folk costumes.

N 634 continues to the ancient little town of *Nava*, with a Romanesque church which originally belonged to a Benedictine monastery. From here a road runs N to the *Monasterio de Valdediós*. Farther on, off the road to the right (1·5 km), is the little spa of *Baños de Fuensanta*, with hot sulphur springs. N 634 then comes to **Infiesto** (alt. 150 m; pop. 16,000), a small town with the Santuario de la Virgen de la Cueva; some 27 km E, near Cangas de Onís, is a Roman arched bridge.

The Visigothic chapel of San Miguel de Lillo

The road now passes the ruins of the 12th c. monastery of Santa María and down the Piloña valley via *Villamayor* to **Arriondas** (alt. 261 m; pop. 1000), at the junction of the *Río Piloña* with the *Río Sella* (salmon, trout and eel fishing). – From Arriondas a rewarding excursion can be made to the **Picos de Europa* (see p. 185) and the pilgrimage centre and holiday resort of Covadonga. – N 634 then descends the beautiful valley of the *Río Sella* between ranges of hills with large areas of forest, to *Llovio*, where the coast road from Gijón and Ribadesella (N 632) comes in on the left. It then continues E, passing through a number of small places; then, to the left, it passes the remains of an 11th c. Benedictine monastery and *San Antolín de Bedón*, with a small sandy beach, the Playa de San Antolín. Then on via *Celorio* to the old-established port, off the road to the left, of **Llanes** (pop. 21,000; hotels: Don Paco, ii, 42 r., closed in winter; Montemar, II, 40 r.), with remains of the town walls (on the N side), a 13th c. castle and the 15th c. church of Santa María (16th c. Flemish altarpiece). Iron and copper from the nearby mines are shipped from here.

N 634 continues through wooded uplands, out of sight of the sea, passing numerous dolmens (pre-historic chambered tombs), to *La Franca*. On a hill to the left is *Pimiango*, near which is the Cueva del Pindal, with important Palaeolithic cave paintings.

At *Unquera*, where another road goes off on the right to the Picos de Europa, N 634 enters the province of Santander and continues via *San Vicente de la Barquera* to **Santander** (see p. 198), 213 km from Oviedo.

To Santander by the coast road. – Leave Oviedo on the road which runs NE through the suburban district of *Santullano*, with the 9th c. Basílica de San Julián de los Prados (wall paintings in primitive Romanesque style). Then either on the motorway (A 66) or N 630 through attractive hilly country to **Gijón** (27 km), and from there E on the coast road (N 632). This follows a hilly and winding route, with beautiful views of the mountains on the right, over the *Alto del Infanzón* to **Villaviciosa** (alt. 5 m; pop. 3000), an old-world little port and fishing town on the Ría de Villaviciosa. Church of Santa María (Gothic, 13th c.), with a richly decorated doorway. – From here a detour can be made to the old Cistercian monastery

of *Santa María de Valdediós*. To the N of the principal church is the pre-Romanesque church of San Salvador (originally consecrated 893), built during the reign of Alfonso III, which shows clear Mozarabic influence.

The coast road then goes over the *Alto de Buenos Aires* (170 m) and comes to the handsome village of *Colunga*, situated on rising ground. The road now comes in sight of the sea and runs through the resorts of *La Isla* and *Caravia*, both with beaches and accommodation for visitors, to **Ribadesella** (alt. 27 m; pop. 8000; hotels: *Gran Hotel del Sella, I, 74 r., SP; Playa, III, 12 r. – both closed in winter), a little port at the mouth of the *Río Sella* (good fishing), with a semicircular bay which offers good bathing and facilities for water sports, including sub-aqua diving. Near the town are the **Tito Bustillo Caves*, with paintings of animals dating back between 15,000 and 20,000 years. – At *Llovio* the coast road joins the direct road to Santander, N 634 (see preceding route).

Over the Puerto de Pajares. – On N 630, which goes S through the Cantabrian Mountains to León. The road first climbs to a point from which there is a fine view of Oviedo and then runs steeply down (12%) to *Olloniego*, where it crosses the *Río Nalón*, and continues to **Mieres** (alt. 207 m; pop. 68,000), an industrial town in the centre of the Asturian mining country, with iron, sulphur and other mines and many blast furnaces, steelworks and zinc works.

Continuing in the direction of the Cantabrian Mountains, N 630 comes to *Pola de Lena*, in a beautiful wide valley, birthplace of Gonzalo Bayón, the conqueror of Florida (1565). 4 km beyond Pola, on a hill to the left of the road, is the Visigothic *Ermita de Santa Cristina de Lena* (9th c.). The road then climbs, with gradients of up to 15%, via *Pajares* to the **Puerto de Pajares** (1364 m; Hotel Parador Nacional, III, 28 r.), on the main summit ridge of the Cantabrian Mountains, which forms the boundary between Asturias and León. Magnificent views; winter sports (ski-lift). – N 630 then descends the southern slopes through *La Pola de Gordón* to **León** (see p. 144), 120 km from Oviedo.

Over the Puerto de la Espina. – Leave Oviedo by way of the Avenida de Galicia and N 634, going W. Just outside the town there is a view (on right) of *Naranco*, with two important Visigothic churches (see above). The road then winds its way through attractive hill scenery, with the hills round the Puerto del Aramo (1715 m) on the left. Soon afterwards a side road goes off to the spa of *Caldas de Oviedo*, on the Río Nalón.

N 634 crosses the *Río Nalón* and skirts the little industrial town of *Trubia*, off the road to the left, with a gun foundry and small-arms factory. Then down-stream via Peñaflor to **Gradö** (pop. 14,000). 12 km N is the *Candamo Cave*, with prehistoric paintings. – Beyond Grado the road climbs steeply (10%) and then drops down again, crosses the *Río Narcea* and comes to *Cornellana*, with a former monastic church (12th–17th c.). Then through the foothills of the Cantabrian Mountains to **Salas** (alt. 241 m; pop. 14,000), with the collegiate church of Santa María, which contains the tomb of Grand Inquisitor Fernando de Valdés (by P. Leoni, 1568).

Beyond Salas the road climbs again (10%) and continues to *La Espina*, from which there are winding mountain roads (on left) through the Cordillera Cantábrica to Lugo (153 km) and Ponferrada (151 km). – N 634 then runs steeply down again into the beautiful valley of the *Río Ore*, which it follows to the coast at *Canero*.

N 634 now continues W along the coast above a beautiful cliff-fringed beach. It then runs down, with a picturesque view of Luarca and the high railway viaduct over the *Río Negro*, passes under the viaduct and comes to **Luarca** (alt. 6 m; pop. 25,000; Hotel Gayosa, II, 26 r.; Hostal Casa Consuelo, P II, 26 r.), an old-world town with a ruined castle and a beautiful beach.

The road winds gradually uphill on to a plateau, with the *Sierra de Ranadoiro* on the left, and then winds its way down again, with beautiful views of the *Río Navia* and the town of **Navia** (pop. 9000), charmingly situated on the right bank of the Ría de Navia, bordered by wooded hills.

Beyond Navia the road climbs again, with picturesque views to the rear, and continues via *Valdepares* to the little port of *Tapia*, near the cliff-fringed bay next to *Cabo Cebes*. Thereafter it goes downhill again, with a charming *view of Castropol (characteristic tower) and the little town of Ribadeo on the opposite side of the *Ría de Ribadeo*; then soon afterwards turns sharp right over a narrow bridge and climbs up the high E bank of the ría, on which is **Castropol** (pop. 7000), a small port which ships the local timber. From *Figueras*, to the N, the Puente de los Santos bridge, following the N 634, crosses the bay to the port of *Ribadeo* (alt. 150 m; pop. 9000). The N 634 first runs parallel to the coast, then turns SW, crosses the N 641 (the Lugo road) at Villalba and joins the N VI at Baamonde. From here it continues NW to **La Coruña** (see p. 109).

Palencia

Province: Palencia (P).
Telephone code: 988.
Altitude: 700 m. – Population: 75,000.
ⓘ **Oficina de Información de Turismo,**
Calle Mayor 105;
tel. 72 00 68.
Delegación Territorial de Turismo,
Jardinillos de la Estación s/n;
tel. 74 01 87.

HOTELS. – *Castilla la Vieja* (no rest.), Casado del Alisal 26, II, 87 r.; *Rey Sancho de Castilla* (no rest.), Avda Ponce de Leon s/n, II, 100 r.; *Colón-27*, Colón-27, IV, 22 r.; *Los Jardinillos*, Eduardo Dato 2, IV, 33 r.; Hostal *Monclus* (no rest.), Menéndez Pelayo 3, P 1, 40 r.; *Roma* (no rest.), Alonso Fernández de Madrid 8, P II, 23 r.

RESTAURANTS. – *Mesón del Concejo*, Martínez de Azcoitia 5 (Castilian style); *La Rosario*, General Franco 3; *Carlos V*, Don Sancho 2; *El Zaguán*, Teniente Velasco 8; *Casa Damián*, Martinez de Azcoitia 9; *Lorenzo*, Casado del Alisal 10; etc.

EVENTS. – *Semana Santa* (Holy Week), with a colourful procession. – *Romería del Santo Cristo del Otero* (Apr.), pilgrimage to the Ermita del Cristo del Otero, N of the town, with folk events and dances in traditional costume. – *Feria* (May), with a large cattle market. – International canoe trip on the Río Pisuerga and Canoe Festival of Palencia at Alar del Rey (usually in Aug.).

The old town of Palencia, in ancient times Pallantia, belonging to an Iberian tribe, the Vaccaei, is now capital of its province and the seat of a bishop. It lies between Burgos and Valladolid on the Meseta of Old Castile, on the left bank of the Río Carrión.

HISTORY. – The heyday of Palencia was in the 12th c., when it was the residence of the kings of Castile and the seat of the Castilian Cortes. In the 13th c. Alfonso VIII of Castile founded Spain's first university in the town.

SIGHTS. The main street of Palencia is the Calle Mayor, which cuts through the middle of the town from N to S. To the W of this street, in the little *Plaza de San Antolín*, is the ***Cathedral** (*San Antolín*), one of the finest late Gothic churches in Spain (1321–1516), from whose unfinished S tower there are extensive views. Notable features of the exterior are the doorways – the Puerta del Obispo (15th c., by Diego Hurtado de Mendoza), the Puerta de los Novios (16th c.) and in the N transept, the Plateresque Puerta de los Reyes, with fine sculpture decoration.

The INTERIOR (130 m long. 28 m high) contains fine sculpture decoration by Simon de Cologne and Gil de Siloé and a Plateresque staircase leading down to the crypt. – **Capilla Mayor**, with a beautiful *reja* (1520), a magnificent Plateresque *high altar* and 12 pictures by Juan de Flandes. The *Capila Mayor Vieja* contains the tombs of Inés de Osorio (1492) and Queen Urraca of Navarre (12th c.). – The **Choir** has a fine *reja* of 1555 and *choir-stalls* of 1519. In the *Trascoro*, richly decorated with late Gothic reliefs and sculpture, is an altarpiece by Juan de Holanda (1505). – In the S transept is an interesting clock. The *Capilla del Sagrario* has a Plateresque retablo (16th c.). – The **Treasury** contains, among much else, a silver *custodia by Juan de Benavente (16th c.) and a painting of Charles V by Lucas Cranach. – In the **cloister** and chapterhouse is a *museum*, with Flemish tapestries, pictures by El Greco, Zurbarán and Cerezo, sculpture and monuments.

Palencia, on the Río Carrión

S of the Cathedral, in the little *Plaza Isabel la Católica*, is the modest church of *Nuestra Señora de la Calle* (16th c.), which contains the Virgen de la Calle, the town's patroness; Baroque altars. – Farther S is the Gothic parish church of *San Miguel* (13th–14th c.), with a massive battlemented tower. The Spanish national hero, El Cid, was married in this church. – In Calle San Bernado, on the far side of the Calle Mayor, is the *Capilla de San Bernardo*, with an imposing façade (national monument). – In Calle de Burgos, to the NE, is the *Convento de Santa Clara* (late 14th c.); the church has a beautiful doorway and contains an impressive recumbent figure of Christ. Also in Calle de Burgos is the *Diputación Provincial*, with the *Museo Arqueológico*, which has fine collections of Iberian and Roman material.

In the N of the town, near the staton, is the 15th c. church of *San Pablo*, with a 17th c. façade. The Capilla Mayor has a large Plateresque retablo and contains tombs of the Rojas family (16th c.). In the choir is a late Gothic carved altar.

SURROUNDINGS. – N of the town is the little **Ermita del Cristo del Otero**, the scene of the great pilgrimage in April. Outside the church, built by Juan de Tordesillas, is a 20 m high statue of Christ the King by Victorio Macho (d. 1966).

To Santander. – N 611 runs N past the Ermita del Cristo del Otero and *Fuentes del Valdepero* (off the road to the right), which has a historic old castle, to **Monzón de Campos**, with the Castillo de Monzón (now a Parador Nacional, II, 10 r.). Near the town is the old royal Palacio de Altamira.

N 611 continues N over the *Canal de Castilla* to **Frómista**, an old pilgrim station on the Way of St James. Of a former Benedictine house founded in the 11th c. there remains the church of San Martín (1066), now protected as a national monument, and an important example of Spanish Romanesque architecture. The church of Santa María has a large 15th c. retablo.

The road continues through the *Tierra de Campos*, a fertile corn-growing region, passing *Marcilla de Campos* and through *Santillana de Campos* (40 m high medieval watch-tower), to **Osorno**, close to the border of Burgos province, where N 611 cuts across N 120.

Still going N, N 611 runs through *Herrera de Pisuerga* (alt. 840 m), with a ruined castle, and *Alar del Rey* to **Aguilar de Campóo** (see p. 46). It then enters the province of Cantabria and continues over the *Puerto de Pozazal* (987 m) and through *Reinosa* to **Santander** (see p. 198), 203 km from Palencia.

To Valladolid. – N 611, going S from Palencia, soon joins N 620, coming from Burgos, near the railway junction and industrial town of **Venta de Baños**.

2·5 km E is the spa of *Baños de Cerrato*, the water of which cured the Visigothic king Recceswinth of a stone. The little church of *San Juan Bautista, one of the oldest in the Iberian peninsula, was founded by Recceswinth in 661 and rebuilt in the 9th c.

N 620 continues S down the valley of the *Río Pisuerga*, passing on the left the Trappist monastery of *San Isidro de Dueñas*. founded in the 10th c., with a fine domed church (Romanesque) containing a carved retablo (16th c.). Adjoining the church is a Roman villa (*mosaic) which was destroyed by fire in 1963. – After crossing the *Canal de Castilla*, constructed in the 18th c., the road comes to **Dueñas**, with the Romanesque and Gothic church of Santa María (13th c.), which has a 15th c. Flemish retablo. – The road then crosses the provincial boundary and continues S to **Valladolid** (see p. 236), 47 km from Palencia.

Up the valley of the Río Carrión. – There are a number of places of interest on C 613 and C 615, which runs NW from Palencia. C 613 leads to **Paredes de Nava**, which was the seat of a count in the time of John II. Its most important architectural monument is the Romanesque tower of the church of Santa Eulalia, which houses a parish museum with a fine collection of paintings. – C 615 follows the valley of the Río Carrión to **Carrión de los Condes**, a pilgrim station on the Way of St James. Benedictine monastery of San Zoilo (11th c.), with a fine Plateresque *cloister; church of Santa María del Camino (11th c.), with sculptured bulls' heads on the façade. – 7 km SE is *Villalcázar de Sirga*, with a 12th c. Templar church.

Pamplona

Province: Navarre (NA).
Telephone code: 948.
Altitude: 449 m. – Population: 186,000.
(i) **Oficina de Información de Turismo**,
   Duque de Ahumada 3;
   tel. 22 07 48.
   Servicio de Turismo,
   Arrieta 11;
   tel. 22 72 00.
   Dirección Provincial de Turismo,
   Paseo de Sarasate 9.

HOTELS. – *Los Tres Reyes, Jardines de la Taconera s/n, I, 168 r., SP; *Ciudad de Pamplona* (no rest.), Iturrama 21, II, 117 r.; *Nuevo Hotel Maisonnave*, Nueva 20, II, 160 r.; *Orhi* (no rest.), Leyre 7, II, 55 r.; *Yoldi* (no rest.), Avda de San Ignacio 11, II, 48 r.; *Eslava* (no rest.), Plaza Virgen de la O 7, III, 28 r.; *La Perla* (no rest.), Plaza de Castillo 1, IV, 67 r.; *Hostal Sancho Ramírez*, Sancho Ramírez 11, P I, 82 r.; etc. – CAMPING SITE: *Ezcaba*, near Eusa on N 121 (8 km N).

RESTAURANTS. – In the hotels, also *Hostal del Rey Noble*, Paseo Sarasate 6; *Josetxo*, Plaza Príncipe de Viana 1; *Grill Don Pablo*, Navas de Tolosa 19; *Rodero*, Arrietta 3; *Vista Bella*, Jardines de la Taconera; etc.

CAFÉS. – *Iruñaberri*, Avda Pío XII 7; *Tres Reyes*, Jardines de la Taconera; *Koppo*, Plaza del Vínculo 5; *Ibiza 5*, Avda Pío XII 5; *Reta*, Plaza Conde de Rodezno 8; *Shanti*, González Tablas 4; etc.

Fiesta de San Fermín, Pamplona

From the Plaza del Castillo the *Paseo de Sarasate*, the town's principal promenade, runs SW past the *Monumento de los Fueros* (commemorating the town's charter of rights) to the fortress-like church of *San Nicolás* (13th c., originally Romanesque) with an interesting figure of Christ and beautiful altars. The Paseo runs into the *Parque de la Taconera*, from which there are fine views. In the park are numerous monuments and the church of *San Lorenzo*, a notable feature of which is the Capilla de San Fermín.

From the S side of the Plaza del Castillo the *Avenida de Carlos III*, lined with modern buildings, runs SE, crossing the broad Avenida de la Baja Navarra, to the large *Plaza del Conde de Rodezno*, with the *Monumento de los Muertos*, a memorial church crowned by a massive dome decorated with frescoes, which was erected in 1959 to commemorate those who died in the Civil War. To the E of the church is the *Museo de Sarasate*, housed in a room in the Conservatorio de Música.

EVENTS. – *Semana Santa* (Holy Week), with a famous and impressive procession on Good Friday, the Santo Entierro. – **Feria y Fiesta de San Fermín** (July), the "Sanfermines", with the unique parades of "Gigantes" (Giants) and "Cabezudos" (Bigheads), a procession in honour of St Firmianus on 7 July, and bullfights, before which the young men of the town run through the streets between barriers, pursued by the bulls (the "Encierros"). – *Chiquita* (Sept.), with picturesque parades, a cattle market and fireworks.

A short distance NW of the Plaza del Castillo, in the little *Plaza Consistorial*, is the **Ayuntamiento** (Town Hall), a 17th c. building (restored 1953) with a Baroque façade. To the W of this is the Gothic church of *San Saturnino* (13th–14th c.), the oldest church in the town, with two Romanesque towers; fine N doorway; retablo in baptistery. – NW of the Town Hall, housed in a former hospital, is the interesting *Museo de Navarra*, with a Plateresque façade (1556); the museum contains Roman mosaics, Romanesque capitals and Gothic wall paintings.

Known in Roman times as Pompaelo (the "city of Pompey"), Pamplona was from the 10th to the beginning of the 16th c. capital of the kingdom of Navarre. It is now the chief town of the province of the same name and the seat of an archbishop. It is attractively situated on a hill on the left bank of the Río Arga, at the western end of the Pyrenees.

SIGHTS. – The central point of the town, which is still partly surrounded by its old walls, is the large *Plaza del Castillo*. At the SW corner of this square is the *Diputación Foral* (built 1847, enlarged 1932), seat of the provincial government. In the splendid Throne Room are two portraits by Goya, of the *Marqués de San Adrián (1804 – one of his finest works) and Ferdinand VII. – Adjoining the Diputación on the S is the interesting *Archivo General de Navarra*, with a valuable collection of manuscripts. Close by is the little church of *San Ignacio* (1694).

NE of the Plaza del Castillo, just inside the town walls, is the massive *Cathedral, mostly dating from the 15th c., with a classical-style façade and towers of 1780. In the nave is the tomb of Charles III and his wife Eleanor of Castile, with alabaster statues by a Flemish master (*c.* 1420). The choir has splendid choir-stalls by Miguel de Ancheta (1530) and the Capilla Mayor has a retablo of 1507. From the S aisle a richly gilded doorway with a beautiful tympanum (14th c.) depicting the death of the Virgin leads into the 14th c. *cloister, one of the most beautiful in Spain. The Diocesan Museum is housed in the cloister and the adjoining rooms. On the E side of the cloister is the Capilla

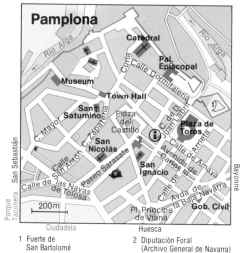

Pamplona

Catedral
Pal. Episcopal
Museum
Town Hall
San Saturnino
Plaza del Castillo
San Nicolás
San Ignacio
Plaza de Toros
Gob. Civil
Pl. Príncipe de Viana
200m
Río Arga
C. Mayor
Calle San Antón
Calle de las Navas de Tolosa
Paseo Sarasate
Calle Dormitalería
C. de Juan de Labrit
Calle de Amaya
Avenida de Carlos III
Avda. de la Baja Navarra

Parque Taconera
San Sebastián
Bayonne

Ciudadela   Huesca
1 Fuerte de   2 Diputación Foral
  San Bartolomé   (Archivo General de Navarra)

Barbazona, with the monument of its founder (d. 1355); on the S side is the 14th c. doorway of the Sala Preciosa, the former meeting-place of the Cortes of Navarre; adjoining it the old refectory; rich treasury.

To the E of the Plaza del Castillo, in Calle de Amaya, is the *Plaza de Toros* (Bull-ring). In front of it stands a *monument to Ernest Hemingway* (1899–1961), author of "Fiesta".

SURROUNDINGS. – **Over the Puerte de Velate:** N 121 runs through *Villava*, where C 135 branches off and runs NE to the Puerto de Roncesvalles (see below), and continues up the valley of the *Río Ulzama*, over the *Puerto de Matacola* (662 m) and on the **Puerto de Velate** (847 m), from which there are extensive views. Thereafter the road winds is way down, with beautiful views, into the valley of the little river *Bidasoa* to reach **Mugaire**, where the road forks.

Route A: From Mugaire N 121 continues NE up the picturesque Basque valley of the *Baztán* to **Elizondo** (alt. 196 m; pop. 2000; Hotel Baztán, II, 84 r., SP), which has houses decked with coats of arms, handsome palaces and the Palacio-Ayuntamiento. – N 121 then winds its way up to the *Puerto de Otsondo* (602 m) and continues to the French frontier at the *Puente de Dancharinea*, from which the road continues via Espelette and Ustaritz to Biarritz.

Route B: From Mugaire C 133 runs NW down the beautiful valley of the *Bidasoa*, passes through *Oyerequi* and comes to **Santesteban** (alt. 125 m), a picturesque little place and a popular holiday resort, lying off the main road.

There follows a beautiful stretch of road, with many bends, down the valley, which is flanked by wooded hills and in places by rugged crags, to **Vera de Bidasoa** (alt. 56 m), in a particularly beautiful part of the valley.

Beyond *Endarlaza* the valley narrows, with the river (on right) marking the French frontier. The road continues to the Spanish frontier town of *Behobía*,

beyond which is the international bridge over the Bidasoa into France. Within France the road continues via St-Jean-de-Luz to Biarritz.

Over the Puerto de Roncesvalles. – From *Villava* C 135 runs NE up the valley of the *Río Arga*, passes through *Zubiri* and goes over the *Puerto de Erro* (801 m: photograph, p. 175), from which there are beautiful views. It then runs through *Erro* into the beautiful valley of the *Río Urrobi* and comes to **Burguete** (alt. 910 m), an old market town which is now a summer holiday resort. – Then to **Roncesvalles** (alt. 981 m), at the entrance to the Pyrenean pass made famous by the heroic death of Charlemagne's paladin Roland. Here there is an Augustinian abbey founded in the 12th c., with a *church (13th c.) containing magnificent gilded retablos, a rich treasury and a carved wooden figure of the Virgin (13th c.) on the high altar. Near the church is a much-visited pilgrimage chapel, the Capila del Espíritu Santo, traditionally believed to have been built by Charlemagne to house Roland's tomb.

The road then continues over the *Puerto de Roncesvalles (1057 m), the gateway through which invaders from Northern Europe made their way into Spain during the early Middle Ages, and the scene, according to the "Chanson de Roland", of the battle in 778 in which the rearguard of Charlemagne's army, then returning from Zaragoza, was defeated by the Moors, and Roland, commander of the rearguard, and his companions were killed. On the pass, from which there are fine views, is a column commemorating Charlemagne and his paladins. – The road then winds down through the gorge to the Spanish frontier post at *Valcarlos*, crosses the frontier at the little river *Nive* and continues via St-Jean-Pied-de-Port to Biarritz.

To the Monasterio de Leyre. – A rewarding trip on N 240, the road from Pamplona to Huesca. – Leave Pamplona on the road (of motorway standard) which runs S to *Noain*, from which N 240 runs SE via *Salinas*

Roncesvalles Abbey

de Ibargoiti, at the foot of the Peña de Izaga (on left), to Liédena. Shortly before this little town a road branches on the right to (5 km) **Sangüesa** (alt. 404 m; pop. 4600), an ancient little town with some notable remains of the past: Romanesque church of Santa María la Real (11th–13th c.); church of the Virgen del Carmen; church of San Francisco, with a Gothic cloister; Castillo del Príncipe de Viana; several palaces. – The road then continues over a plateau to **Yesa** (alt. 492 m), at the W end of the reservoir, Embalse de Yesa (500 million cubic metres), with a Club Náutico. – Here a road goes off on the left to the **Monasterio de Leyre**, 4 km NE on a hill at the foot of the Sierra de Leyre. The monastic buildings are mainly 17th and 18th c. Romanesque church (9th–11th c.), with a crypt which was the burial place of the kings of Navarre; richly decorated W doorway (11th c.).

4 km S of Yesa is Javier (alt. 476 m), with a 14th c. castle which was the birthplace of San Francisco Javier (St Francis Xavier). – Beyond Yesa N 240 crosses the boundary between Navarre and Aragon and follows the N side of the Embalse de Yesa, 11 km long, to Tiermas (thermal spring); then via Berdún into the province of Huesca.

To Tudela. – The section of motorway S of Pamplona to Noain joins N 121, which continues past Tiebas (on left), with a ruined castle, and over the Puerto del Carrascal (591 m) to **Tafalla** (see p. 216), on the W bank of the Río Cidacos.

A few kilometres farther S is the old-world little town of **Olite** (alt. 388 m; pop. 3000; Hotel-Parador Nacional Príncipe de Viana, II, 48 r.), with old walls, the Castillo-Palacio of the kings of Navarre (15th c.) and the 13th c. church of Santa María la Real, which has a richly sculptured main doorway and a 16th c. retablo.

The road then continues S, past the little town of Caparroso (pop. 3000), off the road on the right, with a ruined castle, runs through Arguedas, with the monastery of Nuestra Señora del Yugo, and crosses the Ebro to enter **Tudela** (see p. 230).

To Logroño. – N 111 goes SW from Pamplona along the old pilgrims' road to Santiago de Compostela. It soon begins to wind its way up (fine views) to the Puerto del Perdón (679 m), in the sierra of the same name. Beyond the pass it descends into the valley of the Río Arga and comes to **Puente la Reina** (alt. 347 m; pop. 2000), at the meeting of pilgrim routes from northern and central Europe. Former Templar church (11th c.), with a famous crucifix (c. 1400); five-arched pilgrims' bridge over the Arga; handsome patrician houses in the Calle Mayor.

N 111 now runs W through hilly country to **Estella** (see p. 121). In the southern outskirts of the town it crosses the Río Ega and after passing through a short tunnel continues through hilly country to Los Arcos, passes Sansol and comes to **Viana** (alt. 469 m; pop. 3000), an old town with many handsome fortified mansions. In the church of Santa María is the tomb of César Borja (Cesare Borgia), the most violent member of the Spanish-Italian Borgia or (in Spanish) Borja family. Born in 1475, son of the future Pope Alexander VI, he was killed in 1507 in the service of the king of Navarre. There is a monument to him in the town. – N 111 then runs down into the Ebro valley and comes to **Logroño** (see p. 149), 92 km from Pamplona.

Over the Puerto de Aspiroz. – N 240 runs NW from Pamplona over a plain, with views to the right of the western Pyrenees, where here merge into the Cantabrian Mountains, and comes to a road junction at **Irurzun** (alt. 461 m), where N 240, to the right, crosses the Alto de Olagain (613 m) to the high-level resort of **Lecumberri**, situated between the ridges of the Cantabrian Mountains, with beautiful views. It then goes over the **Puerto de Aspiroz** (616 m), from which there are extensive views, and winds its way down, with gradients of up to 18 per cent, to the little village of Betelú, in a beautiful elevated woodland setting. Thereafter the road enters the province of Guipúzcoa and comes to Tolosa, from which N 1 runs N to **San Sebastián** (see p. 194), 92 km from Pamplona.

Picos de Europa

ⓘ **Federación Española de Montañismo** (Spanish Climbing Federation), Alberto Aguilera 3, Madrid 15; tel. (91)–2 23 47 82.

HOTELS. – IN ARENAS DE CABRALES: Fonda Picos de Europa, 6 r.; IN CANGAS DE ONÍS: Hotel Ventura, III, 22 r.; Eladia, P IV, 24 r.; etc. – IN COVADONGA: Hotel Pelayo II, 55 r. – IN FUENTE DÉ: Parador Nacional Río Deva, I, 78 r. – IN PANES DE PEÑAMELLERA: Hostal Covadonga, P II, 10 r.; Lama, P III, 7 r. – IN POTES: Hotel la Cabaña (no rest.), 24 r., SP; Picos de Valdecoro (no rest.), II, 24 r.; Hostal Picos de Europa (no rest.), P II, 26 r.; Rubio, P II, 16 r.

The Picos de Europa

The *Picos de Europa are a wild and majestic range of mountains, with steeply scarped peaks and deeply slashed valleys, lying between the rivers Deva and Sella near the N coast of Spain. The Torre de Cerredo (2648 m) is the highest point in the Cantabrian Mountains, which continue the line of the Pyrenees to form the northern boundary of the Castilian Meseta. This highland barrier, extending parallel to the coast for a distance of almost 40 km, is

separated from the sea by the lower Sierra de Cuera, reaching to within 20 km of the Bay of Biscay at its nearest point.

TOUR. – The Picos de Europa, which lies within the three provinces of Asturias, Cantabria and León, are traversed by a number of roads. Accommodation is available not only in the places mentioned in the following itinerary but also in various mountain huts which offer varying facilities and services.

From **Oviedo** take C 634, which runs E to *Arriondas*: from here turn right into C 637, which runs up the valley of the Río Sella to the old town of **Cangas de Onís** (alt. 195 m; pop. 10,000), 68 km from Oviedo. This was the starting point of the Reconquista, the recovery of Spain from the Moors. *Puente Romano*, spanning the picturesque gorge of the Río Sella; handsome old noble mansions.

From Cangas de Onís a road follows the N side of the Picos de Europa via *Arenas de Cabrales* (see below) to Santander. From *Soto de Cangas*, 4 km along this road, a side road runs SE up a beautiful mountain valley to the popular pilgrimage centre of *Cova-donga* (alt. 260 m), situated on a projecting spur, with a church founded in the 11th c., the Santa Cueva and the famous image of the Virgin of Covadonga. – From the Hotel Pelayo a magnificent road, with gradients of up to 18 per cent, winds steeply uphill to the *Mirador de la Reina* (8 km), from which there are splendid views of the mountains and the sea; then downhill for 5·5 km to the *Lago Enol*, and another 1·5 km to the *Lago de la Encina*, in the beautiful Montaña de Covadonga nature reserve.

The road from Cangas de Onís continues E beyond the turning for Covadonga, runs into the valley of the *Río Cares* and follows this down to **Arenas de Cabrales** (alt. 120 m), 31 km from Cangas de Onís, a little town noted for its cheese. From here a steep and narrow mountain road (tunnel) ascends the Cares valley to *Poncebos* (6 km), from which the Torre de Cerredo can be climbed (10 hours; guide necessary). The route is by way of the mountain village of *Bulnés* and from there on strenuous mountain paths via the *Refugio de Camburero* (1375 m).

The road then runs down the Cares valley and comes to **Panes de Peñamellera** (30 km), at the junction of the Río Cares and the Río Deva. Panes is on C 621, which, coming from Santander, runs into the eastern part of the Picos de Europa. Following this road S up the Deva valley, we pass through *La Hermida*, with thermal springs (49 °C – 120 °F), and comes to **Potes** (27 km from Panes, 115 km from Santander), an attractive little place which is a good base for exploring the Picos de Europa, 3 km SW is the monastery of *Santo Toribio de Liébana*, which claims to possess the largest piece of the True Cross. – From Potes a road goes W through the Picos de Europa to *Espinama* (*fonda*) and *Fuente Dé* (25 km from Potes), with a Parador Nacional and the starting point of a cableway to the *Balcón del Cable* (1840 m). From the upper station of the cableway a mule track runs E (1½ hours) to *Áliva* (1780 m), a good base for climbers (guide required). – C 621 continues from Potes up a side valley of the Río Deva over the *Vega de Liébana*, and climbs, with many bends, to the *Puerto de San Glorio* (1609 m). From here it runs down the valley of the Río

Lechada to *Portilla de la Reina*, from which a secondary road runs N over the Puerto de Pandetrave into the Picos de Europa. C 621 continues down the Lechada valley and comes to **Riaño** (alt. 1040 m), 56 km from Potes, a little town in the upper Esla valley, in the province of León. From here C 637 runs N over the *Puerto del Pontón* (1292 m) and so back to Cangas de Onís.

Plasencia

Province: Cáceres (CC).
Telephone code: 927.
Altitude: 316 m. – Population: 27,000.
ⓘ **Oficina Municipal de Información,**
Trujillo 1,
tel. 41 27 66.

HOTELS. – *Alfonso VIII*, Alfonso VIII 32, II, 56 r.; Hostal *Mi Casa* (no rest.), Maldonado 13, P II, 40 r.; *Real*, km 128 on the Salamanca road, P II, 32 r.; *Rincón Extremeño* (no rest.), Vodrieras 6, P II, 30 r.; etc.

The old-world episcopal town of Plasencia, situated on a hill en-circled by the deep gorge of the Río Jerte, was founded in 1189 under the name of "Ut Deo placeat" ("May it please God").

SIGHTS. – Medieval **aqueduct** (53 arches). – Fine **Cathedral**, the earliest parts dating from the 13th–14th c.; continued from 1498 onwards but never completed. Plateresque N front, with the beautiful Puerta del Enlosado in the N transept. The most notable features of the interior are the Capilla Mayor (by Juan de Álava, Diego de Siloé and Alonso de Covarrubias), a magnificent *reja* (1604), the choir-stalls (1520) and a retablo (by Gregorio Hernández, 1629) with a relief of the Assumption. 15th c. cloister. Above the sacristy is a museum (pictures by Ribera, etc.). – The town is surrounded by its original double ring of walls, with 68 towers. A promenade affording extensive views, particularly on the NE side, runs round the walls.

SURROUNDINGS. – 46 km NE on C 501 is the old Hieronymite monastery of *Yuste* (San Jerónimo de Yuste), founded in 1404, devastated by the French in 1809 and later partly restored. It is famous as the last retreat of the Emperor Charles V, who withdrew here in 1566 after abdicating in favour of his son Philip II, and who died in the monastery in 1558. The interior of the palace is of great interest, and from the covered terrace there is a fine view of the fertile surrounding country extending as far as the Sierra de Guadalupe. – Near Yuste is **Jarandilla** (Parador Nacional Carlos V, II, 53 r.).

Ponferrada

Province: León (LE).
Telephone code: 987.
Altitude: 543 m. – Population: 52,000.
ⓘ **Oficina Municipal de Información,**
Avenida de la Puebla 1,
tel. 41 22 50.

HOTELS. – *Del Temple* (no rest.), Avda Portugal 2, II, 114 r., SP; *Conde Silva* (no rest.) Avda de Astorga 2, III, 60 r.; *Madrid*, Avda José Antonio 46, III, 54 r.; *Hostal Lisboa*, Jardines 3, P II, 16 r.; *Marán* (no rest.), Antolín Lopez Peláez 29, P II, 24 r.; *Santa Cruz* (no rest.), Marcelo Macías 4, P II, 32 r.; etc.

RESTAURANTS. – In hotels; also *Rugantino*, Fueros de León 12.

EVENTS. – *Patronal festival* (Sept.) in honour of the Virgin of the Oak, with folk events, exhibitions and contests, music, battles of flowers and fireworks; also Día del Bierzo.

The industrial town of Ponferrada, which may have been the Roman Interamnium Flavium, lies on high ground between the Río Sil and Río Boeza, with panoramic views. Above the town is a large 13th c. castle, once held by the Templars.

SIGHTS. – Fine Gothic church, *Santa María de la Encina*, with a 17th c. retablo and a statue of the Magdalene by Gregorio Fernández. – *Casa Consistorial* (Town Hall), 1692. – Outside the town is the church of **San Tomás de las Ollas** (c. 930), in Mozarabic style. Nearby are the ruins of a 10th c. monastery.

SURROUNDINGS. – **To Peñalva de Santiago:** A country road runs S over the *Río Boeza*, passes through the villages of *San Lorenzo* and *San Esteban* and comes to the **Santuario de Santiago de Peñalva**, in a hill setting, with a Mozarabic church of 930.

Over the Puerto de Piedrafita del Cebrero. – N VI runs NW from Ponferrada, climbs a hill (510 m) and continues past *Pieros*, with old defensive walls, to **Villafranca del Bierzo** (alt. 504 m; pop. 6000; Parador Nacional, II, 40 r.), the chief place of the Bierzo district, an ancient little town which was a pilgrim station on the Way of St James (p. 242). Interesting Jesuit church of Santa María (1726); Castillo del Marqués de Villafranca (15th–16th c.), with four round towers. – 4 km S is *Corullón*, with a ruined castle and the church of San Esteban (12th c.).

The road continues NW through the charming Bierzo district, a region of great fertility thanks to its mild climate (chestnut-trees, cherries, acacias, maize). it then runs up the valley of the *Río Valcárcel* to the **Puerto de Piedrafita del Cebrero** (1109 m) in the *Sierra de Ancares*, on the boundary between León and Galicia, with the *Peña Rubia* (2214 m) to the right. – N VI then continues to **Lugo** and **La Coruña** (see p. 109).

Pontevedra

Province: Pontevedra (PO).
Telephone code: 986.
Altitude: 19 m. – Population: 60,000.
ⓘ **Oficina de Información de Turismo,**
General Mola 3;
tel. 85 08 14.

HOTELS. – *Parador Nacional Casa del Barón*, Marceda, II, 47 r.; *Rías Bajas* (no rest.), Daniel de la Sota 7, II, 100 r.; *Virgen del Camino* (no rest.), Virgen del Camino 55, II, 53 r.; *Comercio* (no rest.), A González Besada 3, IV, 26 r.; *Mexico* (no rest.), Andrés Murvais 8, IV, 28 r.; etc. – CAMPING SITE: *Paxariñas*, W of the town, near Sangenjo (about 22 km).

RESTAURANTS. – In hotels, particularly the *Parador Nacional*; also *Calixto*, Benito Corbal; *El Castaño*, Rúa de la Paja; *Los Robles*, Padre Luis; *Titón*, García Camba; *Pub Lord Nelson* (cafeteria), Peregrina.

EVENTS. – *Fiesta de la Virgen de la Peregrina* (Aug.), the start of a programme of events throughout the month, including a feria with folk celebrations and battles of flowers and a festival of dancing, music and drama. – *Pilgrimages* in May and on Corpus Christi.

CASINO. – *Casino Isle de la Toja* in El Grove, 34 km W on C 550.

WATER SPORTS. – Bathing on the sandy beach of Placeres; scuba diving, sea angling, water skiing. Club Marítimo and Yacht Club.

SPORT and RECREATION on land. – Tennis, climbing, fishing (trout, salmon), game shooting, target shooting, etc.

The lively town of Pontevedra, capital of its province, is attractively situated on the Ría de Pontevedra, estuary of the rivers Lérez, Alba and Tomeza. It was once a major port, and preserves remains of town walls dating from that period.

SIGHTS. – The *Casa de los Monteagudos* (1760) houses the *Museo Provincial*, which has a fine collection including Celtiberian precious stones, processional crosses of the 13th–19th c. and pictures by Zurbarán, Giordano, Veronese and other artists. – Church of *Santa María Mayor* (Gothic, 16th c.), with a magnificent façade by Cornelis de Holanda. Cristo del Buen Viaje on S doorway. Several Gothic monuments. – Church of *San Francisco (14th c.), with an earlier (13th c.) doorway; Gothic monuments. – Chapel of *La Peregrina*, on an unusual circular ground-plan (1776): one of the finest examples of Galician Baroque, with slender towers. – The ruined church of *Santo Domingo*, with tall 14th c. apses, now houses the *Museo Arqueológico* (Roman and medieval material, particularly lapidary).

Pontevedra

SURROUNDINGS. – Pontevedra offers a wide range of possible excursions, particularly to the resorts on the much indented W coast and its rías.

Round trip to the south (70 km). – Take C 550 (motorway standard), which runs SW to the port and seaside resort of *Marín*, with the beautiful church of Santa María del Puerto and the Escuela Naval Militar (Naval College). The road then continues past numerous bathing beaches to **Bueu**, on the Ensenada de Bueu, with a bathing beach, maritime museum and lighthouse.

From the village of *Beluso* the promontory of *Cabo Udra*, with wide views, can be reached. The road then follows a winding course along the coast, passing through a number of small places and past more beaches, to **Cangas**, on the Ría de Vigo (ferry to Vigo on the opposite side). – Then return to Pontevedra via *Moaña* and C 550.

Round trip to the north (120 km). – This road is also numbered C 550. Immediately W of Pontevedra it passes the monastery of *San Juan de Poyo*, with a neo-classical church, and then follows the Ría de Pontevedra, passing a number of bathing beaches and running through *Sangenjo* and *Portonovo*, to **El Grove** (34 km from Pontevedra), a developing seaside and health resort with an international casino, linked by a bridge with the island of *La Toja*, C 550 then skirts the bay in a wide curve to **Cambados**, a typical coastal village with interesting old mansions, a beautiful beach and restaurants offering a rich variety of crustaceans and shellfish (Parador Nacional, II, 63 r.). From Cambados there are boats to La Toja.

The road now passes through *Villanueva de Arosa* and comes to **Villagarcia de Arosa** (pop. 22,000), a port and popular seaside resort, also with a number of fine old mansions and an abundance of excellent seafood. – Then back to Pontevedra either via C 550 to *Puentecesures* or via *Caldas de Reyes*.

To Vigo and Túy. – N 550 runs S from the Alameda through the suburbs of Pontevedra and then through a hilly region with many vineyards. Soon, from a hill, there is a magnificent view of beautiful Vigo Bay. The road then winds downhill, with further attractive *views, to **Redondela** (alt. 10 m; pop. 17,000), an old fishing town with bathing beaches on the *Ría de Vigo*. After passing under a railway bridge (318 m long) the road comes to a fork.

Route A: Bearing right at the fork, we continue along the Ría de Vigo, running close to the shore, through beautiful scenery to **Vigo** (see p. 239).

Route B: Keeping straight ahead at the fork, we pass *Monte Sallir* (on left) and come to **Porriño** (alt. 10 m; pop. 9000; bypass), a small industrial town where the road from Vigo joins N 550. From here it continues uphill, with many bends, and then runs down through wooded hills and vineyards to **Túy** (see p. 231).

To Santiago de Compostela. – N 550 goes N over the *Río Lérez* and then winds its way uphill, with fine views looking back to the Ría de Pontevedra. Then through an attractive garden landscape and over the *Río Umia* to **Caldas de Reyes** (alt. 40 m), a spa with suphur springs (up to 60 °C (140 °F)) which were already frequented in Roman times. 8 km NE on N 640, the Orense road, is another little spa of similar type, *Cuntis O'Baño*. – Beyond Caldas de Reyes N 550 continues to *Puentecesures* (bypass), with an imposing church, crosses the *Río Ulla* into La Coruña province and runs NE via Padrón to **Santiago de Compostela** (see p. 200), 54 km from Pontevedra.

paces to musical accompaniment. Performances are at the Royal Andaluz Equestrian School (Recreo de las Cadenas, Avenida Duque de Abrantes s/n; tel. 956-31-11-11), owned by the Domecq family, which also owns one of the most prestigious sherry businesses. Call ahead for reservations.

Two major annual events can both add color to a visit to Jerez—and make it extremely difficult to find a hotel room. The **May Horse Fair** is described by the Spanish Tourist Office as "a traditional Andalusian spring festival with a Spanish-style rodeo in a wine-country setting." The **Vendimia,** or September harvest festival, is a commercial fair as much as it is a tourist event. Exact dates change each year.

The "White Towns" of Andalucía

Visiting some of the *pueblos blancos,* or "white towns," offers yet another perspective on the complex phenomenon that is Andalucía. This excursion is both rural and urban. Rural because it takes you through a landscape alternatively steep, craggy, and mountainous and one of fertile fields carpeting low, flat plains and rolling hills. Urban because it revolves around a network of small towns that dot the scenic mountains and valleys located between Sevilla and the Mediterranean coast to the south.

Several of these towns include the term "de la Frontera" (of the Border) in their names because portions of this region of Cádiz province, between Sevilla and the Mediterranean coast, were passed back and forth between Muslims and Christians over a period of several hundred years, before the defeat of the Moors by the Christian kings at Granada in 1492.

This trip can be planned as a circuit from either Sevilla or Jerez or an inland trip from Cádiz or any town on the Costa del Sol. Although it's possible to visit several towns in a day's trip from Jerez, you'll get a better feeling for the areas by staying overnight in one or more towns en route. (See Accommodations in Jerez, below.)

Jerez de la Frontera, while too big to be considered a "white town," is a good jumping-off point for a circuit starting at **Arcos de la Frontera,** where the *parador,* which seems to cling precariously to the mountainside, offers both rooms and a restaurant with a spectacular view of the patchwork of the valley below.

Almost any road you take in this region will offer a variety of scenery as it weaves in and out of the mountains and carries you to towns such as **El Bosque,** nestled peacefully at the bottom of the mountains; **Grazalema,** known for its blankets and woodworking; **Ubrique,** noted for its leather crafts; the well-preserved medieval towns of **Castellar de la Frontera** and **Vejer de la Frontera;** and **Zahara,** at the bottom of a hill topped by a medieval castle and watchtower. (Contact the Spanish Tourist Office, listed in Travel Arrangements, to request its excellent guide "The Route of the White Towns.")

Although an explosion of tourism has disrupted it to the point that it's hard to include it in the same category, **Ronda**—about twenty circuitous miles (32 kilometers) east of Grazalema—has traditionally been considered one of the "white towns." Located on a plateau more than two thousand feet above sea level, the city's most striking features are the 18th-century arched bridge, or Puente Nuevo, near-ly three hundred feet high, which spans a gorge carved out of the precipitous rock by the Guadalquivir River.

The bridge connects the old San Francisco Quarter with the new, more modern Ronda. On the new side are the Plaza de España, with its tourist shops, tourist office, parking lot, nearby restaurants, and the two-hundred-year-old bullring. Across the bridge in the San Francisco district are a number of structures—among them Arab baths and the Renaissance Mondragon Palace—that represent the Muslim and Christian history of the town.

Ronda is now on the tour-bus circuit, so if you decide to visit, be prepared to encounter lots of traffic and tourists.

The **Pileta Cave** (Cueva Pileta), site of red, yellow, and black rupestrian paintings believed to date back twenty-five thousand years, is 15 miles (24 kilometers) from Ronda, reached by a left turn off the road to Jerez just past the town of La Quinta. For information on how to visit the cave and other nearby sites, check in at the tourist office on the Plaza de España in Ronda.

📖 ACCOMMODATIONS IN JEREZ

Capele, Gral. Fsauco 58, 11402; tel. (956) 34-64-00, telex 75032. Thirty rooms. Located in the town center, an older three-star hotel where all rooms are clean and well kept; those in the new wing are decorated in a more modern style. Public areas include a large arched marble lobby, bar, and a restaurant popular with local residents for its fresh fish. No garage, but parking in subterranean garage available down the street. Doubles 6,930–10,320 ptas. Air-conditioned. All cards.

Jerez, Av. Alc. Alvaro Domecq 35, 11405; tel. (956) 30-06-00, telex 75059. One hundred twenty-one room, five-star hotel. Garden, swimming pool, tennis, and all the other five-star amenities. Doubles run 13,125–16,590 ptas. Air-conditioned. All cards.

Royal Sherry Park, Av. Alc. Alvaro Domecq 11, 11405; tel. (956) 30-30-11, telex 75001. This crisply modern four-star, 173-room hotel, set in an acre of lawns, is run by English-speaking management and staff. Near the Royal Andaluz Equestrian School and across the street from the Sandeman *bodegas*. Accommodations, including direct-dial telephones and TVs with satellite reception, are attractive, as are the public rooms—but the flavor here is international rather than local. Parking in front. Double room, 12,000–15,000 ptas. Air-conditioned. All cards.

☕ RESTAURANTS IN JEREZ

El Bosque, Av. de Alvaro Domecq 26; tel. (956) 30-33-33. Considered the best in town, El Bosque is a well-appointed, professionally operated restaurant. Begin with a *fino* aperitif (sherry) and consider trying the *arroz a la marinera,* a rice and seafood casserole flavored with seafood broth and saffron. A meal will cost about 3,000 ptas. Closed Sun. AE, DC, V.

El Gaitan, Gaitan 3; tel. (956) 34-58-59. In this centrally located restaurant, owner and chef Juan Hurtado serves authentic local fare with a modern creative touch. Specialties include sole Vendimia and sea bass Bellavista, both made with sherry; oxtail, steaks, and roasts; cream of artichoke and other cold Andalusian soups. Tasting the incredibly rich *tocino del cielo,* a dessert made from egg yolks and sugar, is a must on any trip to Andalucía. Here's a place to do it. Free parking in the Plaza Mamelón. A meal runs 2,500 ptas. and up. Closed Sun. and Aug. 5–20. AE, DC, V.

Reus

Province: Tarragona (T).
Telephone code: 977.
Altitude: 190 m. – Population: 80,000.
ⓘ Centro de Iniciativas y Turismo,
San Juan 36;
tel. 31 00 61.

HOTELS. – *De Francia*, Vicaría 8, III, 39 r., SP; *Hostal Gaudí*, Arrabal Robuster 49, III, 71 r.; *Olle* (no rest.), Paseo de Prim 45, P II, 32 r.; *Giralt*, Carretera Tarragona, P III, 36 r.; *Simonet*, Arrabal de Santa Ana 18, P III, 45 r.

RESTAURANTS. – *San Remo*, Carretera Saloú 3–5; *Alpino*, Paseo de Prim 34; *Llanes*, Generalísimo 80; etc.

The industrial and commercial town of Reus, at the foot of the Sierra de la Musara, is an important market for dried fruit and poultry, and was the birthplace of the Catalan architect Antonio Gaudí (1852–1926).

SIGHTS. – Church of *San Pedro*, with an octagonal tower 66 m high (fine views of the sea). – *Museo Municipal*, with a collection of archaeological material, a picture gallery and a section devoted to local industry and crafts.

Romanesque church in Berguedá

La Rioja

Autonomous Region.
Organ of Government: Gobierno de la Comunidad Autónoma.
Province: La Rioja.

In the upper course of the Ebro stretches the region of La Rioja, a well-known wine producing area.

Capital of the region, in which there are many monasteries and ruined castles, is Logroño (see p. 149).

Ripoll

Province: Gerona (GE).
Telephone code: 972.
Altitude: 679 m. – Population: 10,000.
ⓘ Centro de Iniciativas y Turismo,
Plaza de l'Abat Oliba 3;
tel. 70 23 51.

HOTELS. – *Monasterio*, Plaza Gran 4, IV, 40 r.; *Payet* (no rest.), Plaza Nueva 2, IV, 22 r.; *Hostal Canaulas* (no rest.), Puente de Olot 1, P II, 15 r.; *Ripollés*, Plaza Nuava 11, P III, 13 r. – ON THE N 152 (2 km S): *Solana del Ter*, III, 28 r., SP.

The little industrial town of Ripoll (ironworking, arms manufacture) lies at the junction of the Río Freser with the Río Ter, to the E of the Sierra de San Marcos.

SIGHTS. – The town is notable for its **Benedictine monastery of Santa María**, founded in 874. The *church* (restored in the 19th c.) has within a narthex a richly decorated W front covered with 12th c. Romanesque carving; beautiful interior (16th c. choir). Adjoining the church are a fine Romanesque *cloister and a tower 40 m high. There is a small *museum* of folk art.

SURROUNDINGS. – 46 km W of Ripoll on C 149 is the town of *Berga* (alt. 720 m; pop. 11,000), in the valley of the Río Llobregat. To the S is the idyllic district of **Berguedá**, with several Romanesque churches dating from the 10th, 11th and 12th c.

Ronda

Province: Málaga (MA).
Telephone code: 952.
Altitude: 850 m. – Population: 30,000.
ⓘ Oficina de Información de Turismo,
Plaza de España 1;
tel. 87 12 72.

HOTELS. – *Reina Victoria*, Jerez 25, I, 89 r., SP; (on the W side of the town, with fine views); *Polo* (no rest.), Mariano Soubiron 8, II, 33 r.; *Hostal Royal* (no rest.), Virgen de la Paz 42, P I, 25 r.; etc.

EVENTS. – *Fiesta de la Reconquista*, with bullfights and cattle market (May). – *Fiesta*, with fair (Sept.).

Ronda, in the Andalusian Mountains, owes its great attraction as one of the leading tourist sights in southern Spain to its extraordinary **situation.

1 Puente Nuevo Mesón
2 Convento
  Santo Domingo
3 Puente Romano
4 Puente Árabe

5 Puerta Felipe V
6 Palacio Salvatierra
7 Baños Árabes
8 Casa del Gigante
9 Iglesia de la Caridad

The town is built on a triangular plateau, with its point towards the S. It rears out of a fertile vega at the foot of the *Serranís de Ronda* (Torrecilla, 1919 m), with almost vertical rock faces on the W side, and is divided into two by the gorge of the *Río Guadalevín*, between 40 and 90 m wide and up to 150 m deep. On the southern tip of the plateau is the old town (Ciudad), occupying the site of the Roman *Arunda*, with the outer district of San Francisco below it to the S; on the northern part is the new town (Mercadillo), founded by the Catholic monarchs, who recovered Ronda from the Moors in 1485.

SIGHTS. – The main shopping and commercial street of the **New Town** is the *Carrera de Espinel* (pedestrian precinct), which runs into *Calle Virgen de la Paz*. Just off this street is the *Plaza de Toros* (1785), the second oldest bullring in Spain. Calle Virgen de la Paz leads to the *Alameda de José Antonio*, an attractive promenade. From projecting spurs of rock, protected by railings, there are magnificent *views of the river valley, almost 200 m deep, and of the vega and the hills beyond. From here we go past the church of the *Merced* to the Hotel Reina Victoria, in which the poet Rainer Maria Rilke stayed in 1912–13 (mementoes in Room 208); in the hotel garden is a statue of the poet by the sculptor N. Díaz Piquero (1966).

Higher up the hill, above the gorge, is the **Old Town** (*Ciudad*). Crossing the bridge, we go along Calle del Teniente

Gordo to the *Plaza de la Ciudad*, in which is the church of **Santa María la Mayor**. This was originally a mosque, and still has four Moorish domes; after the Reconquista the Gothic aisles and the tall Plateresque Capilla Mayor were added. It has fine Renaissance stalls and an old Moorish mihrab. From the tower – a former minaret – there are far-ranging views. – Near the church is the **Alcazaba**, the castle of the Moorish kings, which was destroyed by the French in 1808. From here the Paseo de San Francisco leads down to the district of *San Francisco*, with a Moorish gate, the Puerta Árabe.

From the Plaza de la Ciudad it is a short distance to the *Plaza del Campanillo*, above the gorge, with views of the hills to the N. From here footpaths lead down to the ruined *mills* on the Río Guadalevín – either on the main path which winds down to the lower mills ($\frac{1}{2}$ hour), or on a path which branches off on the right through a small Moorish gate and descends the slope to the power station (20 minutes), or to the upper mills, with magnificent views of the waterfalls and the Puente Nuevo.

From the Puente Nuevo the Calle del Comandante Linares (to left) leads to the *Casa del Rey Moro*. a beautifully furnished old mansion with terraced gardens affording beautiful views; flight of 365 steps cut through the rock leading down to the river. – Calle del Comandante Linares runs down from here through an arched gateway to the lower bridges over the river, the *Puente Viejo* (or *Puente de la Mina*) and *Puente de San Miguel*.

SURROUNDINGS. – There are a number of interesting excursions in the area round Ronda which should be included in every visitor's programme.

*Cuevas de la Pileta. – C 339 (the Jerez road) runs NW over the river and comes in 12 km to a side road on the left which leads via *Montejaque* to *Benaoján*. near

Moorish gate, Ronda

which are the very interesting Cuevas de la Pileta: stalactitic caves with realistic paintings of animals, like those of Altamira, dating from the Stone Age (*c.* 10,000 and 25,000 years B.C.).

To the Mediterranean. – C 339 follows a winding course SE to the *Sierra de las Nieves*, with the nature reserve of the *Coto de la Serranía de Ronda* (ibexes), and continues to meet the coast road (N 340) along the Costa del Sol at the resort of **San Pedro de Alcántara** (see p. 194), 54 km from Ronda.

Sagunto

Province: Valencia (V).
Telephone code: 96.
Altitude: 46 m. – Population: 55,000.
ⓘ **Oficina Municipal de Turismo,**
   La Autonomia 2;
   tel. 2 46 12 30.

HOTELS. – *Azahar*, Avda Pais Valencia 8, III, 25 r.; *Bergantín*, Plaza del Sol s/n, IV, 27 r.; Hostal *Teide*, Nueve Octubru 53, P II, 28 r. – CAMPING SITE.

RESTAURANT. – *Los Valles*, 6 km N on N 340.

CASINO. – *Casino Monte Picayo*, Puzol.

Sagunto, with the imposing remains of the ancient fortress of Saguntum, founded by the Iberians, on a steep-sided crag (170 m) above the town, lies near the Mediterranean coast on the right bank of the Río Palancia 25 km N of Valencia, in the centre of a large agricultural region.

HISTORY. – The destruction of Sagunto, which was in league with Rome, by the 28-year-old Punic general Hannibal sparked off the Second Punic War in 219 B.C. It was recovered by the Romans in 214. The importance of the town in Roman times is demonstrated by the remains of the theatre and other buildings. Under the Moors (who were temporarily driven out of the town by El Cid in 1099) it was known as *Murbiter* (from *Muri veteres*, "old walls"). This became *Murviedro* until 1877, when it reverted to its ancient name of Sagunto. The remains of the old town have been restored in recent years.

SIGHTS. – In the arcaded *Plaza Mayor*, in the centre of the town, is the Gothic parish church of *Santa María* (begun 1334), which has alabaster windows and a gilded 18th c. altar with a mother-of-pearl cross.

From the Plaza Mayor *Calle del Teatro Romano* runs up SE to the well-preserved *****Roman theatre**, half way up the castle hill. It has a diameter of 50 m and could seat 8000 spectators.

From the Roman theatre a road winds up (fine views) to the *****Castillo de Sagunto**, which extends for 800 m along the hilltop and contains considerable remains of Iberian, Carthaginian and Roman structures. The long circuit of walls, from which there are attractive views of the town and the coast, dates mainly from the Arab and later periods. Near the entrance is a small *Museo Arqueológico*, with material from Roman and Phoenician Sagunto.

SURROUNDINGS. – 6 km E on C 237 is **Grao de Sagunto**, the port of Sagunto and a considerable industrial town, with orange-groves and a bathing beach.

To the N of Sagunto, extending to around Vinaroz, is the popular holiday region known as the *****Costa del Azahar** ("Orange-Blossom Coast": see p. 114).

Salamanca

Province: Salamanca (SA).
Telephone code: 923.
Altitude: 802 m. – Population: 135,000.
ⓘ **Oficina de Información de Turismo,**
   Gran Vía 41;
   tel. 24 37 30.
   Delegación Territorial de Turismo,
   España 39;
   tel. 24 66 93.
   Oficina Municipal de Información,
   Plaza Mayor 10;
   tel. 21 83 42.

HOTELS. – *Parador Nacional de Salamanca*, Teso de la Feria 2, I, 108 r., SP; *Gran Hotel* (no rest.), Plaza del Poeta Iglesias 5, I, 100 r.; *Monterrey* (no rest.), Azafranal 21, I, 89 r.; *Alfonso X* (no rest.), Toro 64, II, 66 r.; *Castellano III* (no rest.), San Francisco Javier 2, II, 73 r.; *Ceylán*, San Teodoro 7, III, 32 r.; *Condal* (no rest.), Santa Eulalia 3, III, 70 r.; *Emperatriz*, Compañía 4, III, 37 r.; *Pasaje*, Espoz y Mina 23, III, 62 r.; *Castellano* (no rest.), Avda de Portugal 29, IV, 22 r.; *Clavero*, Consuelo 21, IV, 26 r.; *Las Torres*, Plaza Mayor 26, IV, 33 r.; Hostal *Barcelona* (no rest.), Paseo San Vicente 24, P II, 36 r.; etc. – *Hotel Regio y Mesón Lazarillo de Tormes*, km 204 on N 501, I, 118 r., SP. – CAMPING SITES: *Regio*, 4 km E on N 501; *Don Quijote*, 4 km NE on the Aldealengua road; *El Cruce*, 55 km SW on Ciudad Rodrigo road.

RESTAURANTS. – In hotels; also *Candil Nuevo*, Plaza de la Reina 1 (Castilian style); *Chez Victor*, Espoz y Mina 16; *Venecia*, Plaza del Mercado 5 (first floor); *Rio de la Plata*, Plaza del Peso 1; *La Posada*, Aire y Azucena 1, *El Mesón*, Plaza del Poeta Iglesias 10; etc. – ON N 620: *El Quinto Pino* (2·5 km).

CAFÉS. – *Feudal*, Plaza del Poeta Iglesias 3; *Las Torres*, Plaza Mayor 45; *Altamira*, Plaza Mayor 21; etc.

EVENTS. – *Semana Santa* (Holy Week), with a solemn procession. – *Patronal festival* (June) in honour of the town's patron saint San Juan de Sahagún, with bullfights and traditional ceremonies. – *Ferias y Fiestas* (Sept.), with bullfights, an international riding contest, an art exhibition, etc.

Plaza Mayor, Salamanca

The ancient and famous university town of *Salamanca, capital of its province and a bishopric, lies in southern León on the right bank of the Río Tormes, on an almost tree-less plateau.

With its many old and historic buildings, including some particularly fine examples of Plateresque architecture, the whole town has been declared a national monument. The climate shows sharp contrasts: the winter is almost as severe as at Burgos or Ávila, while the summer can sometimes be quite hot. Salamanca is noted for its filigree work.

HISTORY. – Salamanca, the Roman *Salmantica*, was captured in 217 B.C. by Hannibal and in the 8th c. by the Moors. During the long wars between Christians and Moors the town was almost completely destroyed, and only recovered some measure of importance around 1100, under the rule of King Alfonso VI of Castile. The international reputation of Salamanca, however, was established by the University founded by Alfonso IX of León (d. 1230), which vied with the universities of Bologna, Paris and Oxford and transmitted Arabic science and learning to the rest of Europe. In the 16th c. the University had over 7000 students. The establishment of a bishopric in Valladolid (1593), which had previously been within the diocese of Salamanca, and the expulsion of the Moriscos in 1600 led to the decline of Salamanca, from which it has recovered only in recent times.

SIGHTS. – The central feature of Salamanca is the **Plaza Mayor (begun by Alberto de Churriguera in 1720), a regular square of arcaded buildings in uniform architectural style, a splendid setting for ceremonial occasions and one of the finest squares in Spain in its unity of conception and execution. On the N side is the *Ayuntamiento* (Town Hall), in the style of José de Churriguera (1650–1723), with a belfry added in 1852.

Just off the Plaza Mayor to the SW is the late Romanesque church of **San Martín**

(12th c.), with a relief of St Martin (13th c.) on the N doorway. It has a retablo by Alberto de Churriguera (1731) and contains a number of Gothic tombs. – From here the *Rúa Mayor* continues SW. In a little square on the right is the **Casa de las Conchas** (House of Cockle-Shells), built in 1514, so called from the shells on its façade and window grilles. It has a beautiful courtyard and a fine coffered ceiling over the staircase. – Opposite it is the **Clerecía** (1617), a spacious domed Baroque church, with an impressive twin-towered façade. Adjoining it is the *Universidad Pontífica* (theology, philosophy, canon law), with a handsome Baroque courtyard. – The Rúa Mayor ends in the *Plaza de Anaya* (1811), bounded on the W by the University and on the S by the New Cathedral.

The ***New Cathedral** (*Catedral Nueva*) is an imposing building, begun by Juan Gil de Hontañón in 1513 but not completed until 1733, with late Gothic, Plateresque and Baroque features. Particularly notable are the richly decorated Plateresque doorways, including the tripartite *W doorway and the N doorway, with a relief of the Entry into Jerusalem. The 110 m high tower, with a beautiful dome (probably by J. de Churriguera), has reinforcement walls round its lower storeys, built in 1755 as a protection against earthquakes. The richly furnished interior (104 m long, 48 m wide) achieves an effect of spaciousness and height

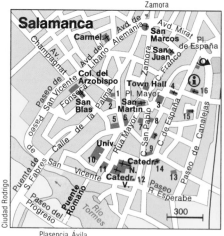

1	Palacio de Monterrey	9	Convento de Dueñas
2	Convento de Augustinas	10	Escuelas Menores
3	Mercado	11	Palacio Episcopal
4	San Julián	12	Puerta de San Pablo
5	Clerecía	13	Seminario Diocesano
6	Casa de las Conchas	14	San Esteban
7	Palacio de la Salina	15	San Cristóbal
8	Torre del Clavero	16	Espíritu Santo

(38 m) in spite of the insertion of the choir which has beautifully carved Baroque stalls and Baroque sculpture by Alberto de Churriguera. The chapels contain numerous works of art, including the tomb of Sánchez de Palenzuela in the Capilla Dorada (of which he was the founder) and the Virgen de la Cueva (patroness of Salamanca) in the Capilla del Mariscal. Other notable features are the sacristy and the relicario.

Adjoining the S side of the New Cathedral and entered from its S aisle, is the Romanesque *Old Cathedral (Catedral Vieja or Santa María de la Sede), founded about 1100 and probably completed before 1200, one of the most splendid achievements of Spanish Romanesque architecture. From the Patio Chico, a little square on the S side of the New Cathedral, there is a view of the chancel and the magnificent high dome over the crossing, known as the Torre del Gallo from the figure of a cock which surmounts it. In the principal apse is a retablo with 53 scenes from the life of Christ and the life of the Virgin, painted, like the large fresco of the Last Judgment, by Nicolás Florentino (1445 onwards); in the centre of the retablo is the 12th c. Virgen de la Vega. In the cloister (1178, altered 1785) are a number of large memorial chapels and the Cathedral Museum (15th c. triptychs).

SW of the Old Cathedral, on the far side of the Plaza del Puente, is the Puente Romano over the Río Tormes, of whose 27 arches the 15 at the near end are still Roman. From the far side of the river there is a very fine view of the town. – A short distance upstream is the Puente Nuevo (New Bridge), starting point of the roads to Madrid, Plasencia and Ciudad Rodrigo.

NE of the Puente Nuevo is the Puerta de San Pablo, from which Calle San Pablo runs N to the Plaza Mayor. Off this street to the E is the Dominican church of *San Esteban (1524–1610), with a richly decorated Plateresque façade. It has a gilded high altar by José de Churriguera (1693) and three other altars by pupils of his. On the W wall above the raised choir is a large fresco by Antonio Palomino, "The Triumph of the Church" (1705). Adjoining the church are the cloister, sacristy and chapterhouse. – Facing San Esteban, to the N is the Convento de Dueñas (1533), with a beautiful two-storey Renaissance *cloister.

From the SW corner of the Plaza Mayor Calle del Prior runs W to the imposing Palacio de Monterrey (c. 1540), with a long gallery along the S side and two elaborate low towers. – Facing the palace, to the SW, is the Convento de las Agustinas (1598–1636), with some fine pictures by Ribera in the church, including the "Conception" on the high altar, one of his finest works. – Farther W is the former Colegio Mayor Arzobispo Fonesca (1527–78), with a Plateresque doorway. The church has a retablo by Alonso de Berruguete and a number of paintings from his studio. The two-storey courtyard has beautiful capitals and roundels containing busts. – S of the Convento de las Agustinas via Calle de Cervantes, on the E side of the Patio de las Escuelas, is the University, originally a plain building erected 1415–33, with a later W front covered with a profusion of Plateresque decoration. Notable features are the cloister-like courtyard, the chapel and the central hall (conducted visit). On the first floor is the University Library, founded in 1254, with more than 250,000 volumes, 3500 manuscripts and 350 early books. – A little way N of the University is the Museo Provincial (antiquities, pictures). – In the Patio de las Escuelas is a statue of Luis de León (1528–91), a famous university teacher of his day. On the S side of the square are the Escuelas Minores (Lesser Schools), now housing the Rectorate of the University, with two charming Plateresque doorways.

N of the Plaza Mayor is a Romanesque round church, San Marcos (c. 1200). E of the square stands the 16th c. Espíritu Santo church, with a Plateresque doorway, a remarkable high altar of 1659 and a fine Capilla del Sacramento, 13th c. cloister. Farther SE is the Plaza de Colón, with a monument to Columbus, the Torre del Clavero (1480) and the Palacio de la Salina or de Fonseca (1516; beautiful courtyard), which now houses the Diputación Provincial.

SURROUNDINGS. – In the area round Salamanca there are numerous historic buildings and charming old towns and villages which are well worth a visit.

28 km N of Salamanca on N 630 (the Zamora road), a little way off the main road, is Villanueva de Cañedo, with the fine 13th c. Castillo de Buen Amor, which has round towers, a handsome inner courtyard and a magnificent interior (Mudéjar coffered ceiling).

34 km NW on a minor road is Ledesma, a little walled town on the Río Tormes which is a popular spa.

Church of Santa María (13th–16th c.), with fine monuments. – Near the town is the Fortaleza built by Beltrán de la Cueva.

Ruta de los Embalses. – This route round a number of artificial lakes (reservoirs), also known as the Ruta de los Arribes del Duero, runs through the western part of Salamanca province. From Salamanca C 517 runs W to *Vitigudino*, to the NW of which is **Aldeadávila de la Ribera**, on the banks of the Río Duero, which here describes a series of large bends (*arribes*). Near the town is the *Embalse* or *Pantano de Aleadávila*, formed by a dam. Within the town itself are two old churches and the Palacio del Marqués de Caballeros (18th c.), with coats of arms on the façade.

From here we continue on minor roads running close to the Duero, to *Saucelle*, where there is another large dam, and **La Fregeneda**, surrounded by almond-, orange- and lemon-groves. The Fiestas del Almendro are celebrated here in March. – From here it is only a few kilometres on C 517 to *Lumbrales*, to the S of which is the little town of **San Felices de los Gallegos**, the whole of which is protected as a national monument (old town walls, ruined castle, patrician houses).

The road continues S to **Ciudad Rodrigo** (see p. 104), from which N 620 runs NE to Salamanca through the *Montañas de Caraza*, entering the city by the Roman bridge over the Río Tormes.

To Béjar. – N 630 runs S across the Huerta de Salamanca, which ends at *Mozárvez*. Soon after this a side road goes off on the left to **Alba de Tormes** (see p. 47). The main road continues to *Guijuelo* and then winds its way up through rugged country to the **Puerto de Vallejera** (1200 m), from which there are magnificent views of the plateau and the surrounding sierras. The road then runs down to **Béjar** (see p. 79), in a beautiful setting. Beyond this is the **Puerto de Béjar** (980 m), on the western slopes of the *Sierra de Béjar*.

To Ávila. – Leave Salamanca by way of the Roman bridge and continue on N 501, which runs E over a plateau which at first is entirely treeless, passing through *Calvarrasa de Abajo*, to **Peñaranda de Bracamonte** (alt. 900 m; pop. 6000), a little town lying off the main road (bypass), which has an imposing church with a fine high altar. Soon afterwards the road leaves León (Salamanca province) and enters Old Castile (Ávila province). It then continues through the *Moraña*, an outlier of the *Sierra de Ávila*, to **Ávila**, well-known for its association with St Theresa (see p. 58), 97 km from Salamanca.

San Pedro de Alcántara

Province: Málaga (MA).
Telephone code: 952.
Altitude: 20 m. – Population: 4000.
ⓘ **Oficina de Información de Turismo,**
Avenida Miguel Caño 1, Marbella;
tel. 77 14 42.

HOTELS. – *Golf Hotel Guadalmina*, Hacienda Guadalmina, I, 80 r.; golf, SP; *El Pueblo Andaluz*, km 179 on N 340, III, 172 r., SP; *Alcotán*, km 179 on Urbanización Cortijo Blanco, IV, 84 r., SP. – IN URBAN AREA OF NUEVA ANDALUCIA; *Golf Hotel Nueva Andalucía*,

Campo de Golf, L, 22 r., golf, SP; *Andalucia Plaza*, km 180 on N 340, I, 424 r., golf, SP. – *Las Fuentes del Rodeo* (apartment hotel), km 180 on N 340, II, 85 r., SP.

RESTAURANTS. – *Benamara*, 4 km W on N 340; *Pepe Romero*, on N 340 (seafood).

EVENTS. – *Fiestas* (Oct.), with fair, concerts and sporting contests.

SPORT and RECREATION. – Several golf-courses; riding club; water sports of all kinds; tennis; clay-pigeon shooting. Sports facilities in the new residential developments.

A picturesque little place on the Costa del Sol, situated in the beautiful foothills of the Sierra Bermeja and Sierra de Tolox.

SIGHTS. – In the little township, which is named after St Peter of Alcántara (1499–1562), can be seen the remains of a Roman settlement, including a circular building with five arches; there is also an early Christian basilica with a font in the form of a fish (both are national monuments). Between Marbella and San Pedro de Alcántara lies the tourist centre of *Nueva Andalucía*, with villas, bungalows, golf courses and swimming pools.

From San Pedro de Alcántara a mountain road leads through the Sierra Bermeja in 54 km to **Ronda** (see p. 189).

San Sebastián

Province: Guipúzcoa (SS).
Telephone code: 943.
Altitude: at sea level. – Population: 167,000.
ⓘ **Oficina de Información de Turismo,**
Miramar/Calle Andría;
tel. 42 62 82.
Centro de Atracción y Turismo,
Reina Regente;
tel. 42 01 02.
Oficina de Información,
at the International Bridge, Irún;
tel. 62 22 39.

HOTELS. – *María Cristina*, Paseo República Argentina s/n, L, 139 r.; *Costa Vasca*, Avda Pío Baroja 15, 203 r., SP; *Londres y Inglaterra*, Zubieta 2, I, 120 r.; *Monte Igueldo* (no rest.), Monte Igueldo, I, 125 r., SP; *Orly* (no rest.), Plaza de Zaragoza s/n, I, 63 r.; *San Sebastián* (no rest.), Avda de Zumalacárregui 20, I, 94 r., SP.; *Avenida* (no rest.), Subida al Igueldo, II, 47 r., SP; *Gudamendi*, Barrio de Igueldo, II, 20 r.; *Niza* Zubieta 56, II, 41 r.; *Arana* (no rest.), Vergara 7, III, 56 r.; *Parma* (no rest.), General Jáuregui 11, III, 21 r.; *Codina*, Avda Zumalacárregui 21, III, 77 r.; *Pellizar* (no rest.), Barrio de Intxaurrondo, III, 33 r.; *Isla*, Miraconcha 17, IV, 38 r.; Hostal *Buena Vista* (no rest.), Barrio de Igueldo s/n, P I, 12 r.; *José Mari*, San Bartolomé 3, P I, 30 r.; *Alameda*, Alameda del Boulevard 23, P II, 30 r.; *Bahia* (no rest.), San Martin 54, P II, 60 r.; *La Estrella* (no rest.), Plaza de Sarriegui 1, P II, 27 r.; *Lasa*, Vergara 15, P II, 33 r.; *Terminus*, Avda de Francia s/n, P II, 20 r.;

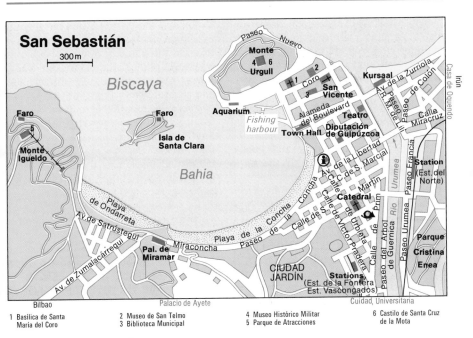

San Sebastián

300 m

Biscaya

Bilbao

Faro

Monte Igueldo

Av. de Zumalacárregui

Pal. de Miramar

Av. de Satrústegui

Playa de Ondarreta

Bahia

Isla de Santa Clara

Faro

Aquarium

Fishing harbour

Playa de la Concha

Miraconcha

Paseo de la Concha

Paseo Nuevo

Monte Urgull

4 6

San Vicente

1 2

Coro

3

Alameda del Boulevard

Town Hall

Diputación de Guipúzcoa

Teatro

Kursaal

Av. de la Zurriola

Paseo de Colón

Irún

Casa de Oquendo

Calle Miracruz

Av. de la Libertad

C. de S. Marcial

Catedral

Calle de Martín

Calle de Prim

Calle de Víctor Pradera

Calle de Urbieta

Calle de S

Río Urumea

Paseo del Árbol de Guernica

Paseo Urumea

Paseo Francia

Station (Est. del Norte)

Parque Cristina Enea

CIUDAD JARDÍN

Stations, (Est. de la Fontera Est. Vascongados)

Palacio de Ayete

Cuidad, Universitaria

1 Basílica de Santa María del Coro
2 Museo de San Telmo
3 Biblioteca Municipal
4 Museo Histórico Militar
5 Parque de Atracciones
6 Castilo de Santa Cruz de la Mota

Bahía, San Martin 54, P II, 60 r., beach; *La Estrella,* Plaza de Sarriegui 1, P II, 27 r., beach; *Lasa,* Vergara 15, P II, 24 r.; *Terminus,* Avda de Francia, P II, 20 r.; etc. – Numerous pensiones. – CAMPING SITE: *Iqueldo,* at the foot of Monte Igueldo (W side).

RESTAURANTS. – In hotels; also *Casa Nicolasa,* Aldamar 4 (first floor); *Alta Mari,* Puerto 23; *Monte Igueldo,* on Monte Igueldo (striking situation); *Monte Ulía,* on Monte Ulía; *Arzac,* Alto de Miracrus 21, 3 km E; *Azaldegui,* Paseo de Miraconcha 23; *Barandiarán,* Alameda del Boulevard 26; *Equía,* Fermin Calbetón 28; *Echeverría,* Iñigo 8; etc.

CAFÉS. – *Dover,* Avda de la Libertad 21 and Loyola 4; *Gaviria,* Avda de la Libertad 40; *Ondarreta,* Avda Zumalacárregui 20; *Orly,* Triunfo 2; *Kansas,* Alameda del Boulevard; *Avenida 3,* Avenida 3; *California,* Hernani 17; *California 27,* Avda de la Libertad 27; *Madrid,* Avda de la Libertad 35; etc.

EVENTS. – Few towns in Spain are more given to fiestas and other celebrations than San Sebastián, which has a full programme of events throughout the year. – *Tamborada* (Jan.), a parade of drummers and

masks; also the fiesta of the town's patron saint. – *Semana Santa* (Holy Week), with a procession, a programme of festivities and a series of recitals of church music. – *Semana Grande* (Aug.), with bullfights, sporting events, summer festival, summer courses for foreigners, Basque folk celebrations, a film festival and a festival of music and folk traditions; also *Fiesta de la Asunción* (Assumption).

CASINO. – *Nuevo Gran Casino,* Kursaal.

WATER SPORTS. – Bathing on beaches of fine sand at Playa de la Concha, Playa de Ondarreta and Playa de Gros; sailing regattas run by Real Club Náutico; whaler races.

SPORT and RECREATION on land. – Handball, basketball and volleyball; rugby and tennis; pelota; riding, golf, clay-pigeon shooting.

San Sebastián (in Basque, Donostia), situated on the Bay of Biscay near the French frontier, is capital of the Basque province of Guipúzcoa and the seat of a bishop.

It is Spain's most fashionable seaside resort and in the late summer becomes the seat of the Spanish government and the residence of the Diplomatic Corps. The town is attractively situated on alluvial land between the canalised *Río Urumea* and the oval **Bahía de la Concha,* bounded on the E by *Monte Urgull* and on the W by *Monte Igueldo* and sheltered on the seaward side by the island of *Santa Clara,* a water sports centre.

SIGHTS. – The hub of the town's life is the tamarisk-shaded *Alameda del Boulevard,*

In San Sebastián harbour

which is lined with shops, restaurants and cafés. At its western end are the fishing harbour and the *Casas Consistoriales* (Town Hall), in the former Gran Casino, the W front of which overlooks the wide bay and the Playa de la Concha. – To the S of the Town Hall is the *Parque Alderdi-Eder* ("beautiful square"), with the tourist information office. From the park the *Paseo de la Concha* runs in a semicircle half way round the bay to the large bathing station of *La Perla* and the royal bathing pavilion, the *Caseta Real*. From here it is a short distance NW to Monte Igueldo.

To the E of the Paseo de la Concha is the **New Town**, with the busy *Avenida de la Libertad* and *Plaza de Guipúzcoa*. On the W side of this square is the imposing *Palacio de la Diputación* (1885), which has busts of notable figures on the façade and contains pictures by Ignacio Zuloaga (1870–1945). – A short distance NW, at the end of the Puente del Kursaal, is the *Teatro Victoria Eugenia*. – In the southern part of the new town, beyond another busy street, *Calle de San Martín*, is the neo-Gothic *Catedral del Buen Pastor* (1897), with a spire 75 m high which dominates the town.

N of the Alameda, extending to Monte Urgull, is the **Old Town**, the central feature of which is the arcaded *Plaza de la Constitución*, formerly used as a bullring. – To the E of this square is the *Fish Market* (Pescadería), to the NE the Gothic church of *San Vicente* (1507), the town's oldest church, with a richly carved retablo of 1584. NW of the church, in the former convent of **San Telmo**, a 16th c. Renaissance building, are the *Municipal Library* and the *Museo de la Ciudad*, with historical and ethnographical collections and a fine gallery of pictures by Spanish artists, including both old masters and modern painters. – SW of San Telmo is the Baroque church of *Santa María* (1764), with a richly decorated Churrigueresque façade; altarpiece with side-wings painted by Robert Michel, sculpture.

From Santa María a stepped path (pedestrians only) climbs up **Monte Urgull** (135 m), a sandstone hill which was formerly an island. On the top is the *Castillo de la Mota*, with a museum of military history and a chapel dedicated to the Sacred Heart crowned by a 12 m high statue of Christ. – On the S side of Monte Urgull and the W side of the old town is the **harbour**, from which a boat can be taken to the island of *Santa Clara* (lighthouse). W of the harbour is the interesting *Museo Oceanográfico*, with model ships and an *aquarium*. – From here the *Paseo Nuevo runs round the seaward side of Monte Urgull (fine views) to the mouth of the Río Urumea and crosses the river on the *Puente del Kursaal*. Beyond the bridge, on the left, is the *Gran Kursaal*, from which a seafront promenade runs E almost to Monte Ulía.

To Monte Igueldo. – From the W end of the Paseo de la Concha the Miraconcha continues through a tunnel under the *Palacio de Miramar*, formerly a royal summer residence, to the district of *Antiguo* and the beautiful *Playa de Ondarreta*. – From here a funicular (3 minutes) and a winding road (2 km; 4·5 km from the town centre; small toll) lead up to the top of *Monte Igueldo (184 m), with a good terrace restaurant, an amusement park, a radio transmitter, an observatory and an outlook tower (lift), from which there are magnificent views of the town, the sea and the Basque uplands. On the N side of the hill is a lighthouse (alt. 120 m).

To Monte Ulía. – 7 km E of the town, rising above the outlying district of Gros, is *Monte Ulía (230 m: winding road to top), with an aerial mast, a garden restaurant (alt. 200 m) and three observation terraces; best view of the town and the coast from the *Peña del Águila*.

SURROUNDINGS. – **To the French frontier:** The motorway and N I run E over the Río Urumea and through the suburban district of *Pasajes de San Pedro* (with a busy harbour, to left) to **Rentería** (alt. 10 m; pop. 18,000), an industrial town on the *Río Oyarzun*. 3 km N, in a beautiful land-locked bay which has something of the air of an Alpine lake, is the little port of **Pasajes de San Juan*, from which Lafayette sailed to America in 1776.

From here the road runs through the Basque hills, with the *Alto de Jaizquibel* (584 m) on the left and the *Peña de Aya* (816 m) on the rght, to *Irún* (alt. 20 m; pop. 30,000; Hotel Alcázar, II, 48 r.), the Spanish frontier town. Church of *Nuestra Señora del Juncal* (16th c.) and Ayuntamiento (Town Hall, 17th c.) in Plaza de San Juan. – 3 km N, in the bay at the mouth of the *Río Bidasoa*, is the old Basque town of *Fuenterrabía (pop. 10,000), once an important strong point and now a popular seaside resort, with picturesque little streets and old-world houses. Church of Nuestra Señora de la Asunción (Gothic, enlarged in 16th c.). From the 12th c. Palacio del Rey Carlos V, now the Parador Nacional El Emperador (II, 16 r., open all year), there are very fine views. – 4 km farther on is *Cabo Higuer* (lighthouse; views),

In Fuenterrabía

2 km beyond the pass N I enters the province of Navarre and continues through *Alsasua* to the junction with N 240, which runs E to Pamplona.

Over the Puerto de Aspiroz. – On N I to **Tolosa** (see p. 227), and from there SE on N 240, which leads through *Lizarza* and enters the province of Navarre. It then climbs steeply (gradients of up to 18 per cent) via *Betelú* to the **Puerto de Aspiroz** (616 m), from which there are extensive views. Then on to **Pamplona** (see p. 182), 92 km from San Sebastián.

Along the Cantabrian coast. – Leave on N I and after passing through the Antiguo district turn right (at access road to the Bilbao motorway) into N 634, which runs W through the Basque uplands. After passing through *Usúrbil* (alt. 45 m), with a handsome church and the old mansion of the Soroa family, it enters the valley of the *Río Oria*, which is quite wide at this point, and comes to **Orio** (alt. 34 m), a little fishing town and port on the right bank of the fjord-like estuary of the river. The road then goes over the *Col d'Orio*, with a view of the Bay of Biscay, and descends to **Zarauz** (alt. 3 m; pop. 11,000; hotels: La Perla, II, 72 r.; Zarauz, II, 82 r.; Paris, III, 28 r.; Hostal Alameda, P II, 26 r.; two camping sites), an attractive little town on the flat and sandy coast at the W end of a plain surrounded by hills. This quiet little resort, with a beautiful beach and a golf-course, is much favoured by Madrid society during the summer. In the 16th c. it was famous for its shipyards; the "Victoria", in which Juan Sebastián Elcano (d. 1526), the companion of Magellan, carried out the first circumnavigation of the globe in 1519–22, was built here. In the picturesque little streets of the town are a number of handsome old mansions, including the Casa Consistorial (18th c.), the Palacio del Marqués de Narros (15th c.), with a beautiful park, and the Torre Lucea (15th c.: national monument). Above the town rears the *Monte de Santa Bárbara*.

At Zarauz begins the magnificent ****Cornisa Cantábrica** (Cantabrian Corniche), which runs close to the rocky coast, with a fine view of ***Guetaria** (alt. 2 m), a fishing port picturesquely situated on a promontory sheltered by the fortified island of San Antonio, which is connected with the mainland by a breakwater. A road runs up to the lighthouse, from which there are beautiful views. By the main road stands a monument (erected 1922) to the navigator Juan Sebastián Elcano, who was born here. In the Town Hall are frescoes by Zuloaga (1922) depicting Elcano's voyage round the world. Under the Gothic church of San Salvador (13th c.) are tunnels leading down to the harbour.

From here the beautiful coastal road, with views of Guetaria to the rear, continues to **Zumaya** (alt. 2 m; pop. 6000), a little town and seaside resort at the foot of *Monte Santa Clara*, with a Gothic church. At the near end of the town is the Villa Zuloaga (formerly the 12th c. convent of Santiago Echea), a museum founded by the painter Ignacio Zuloaga, with pictures by El Greco, Goya and Zuloaga himself and a collection of ceramics. – N 634 continues, with many bends, past *Iciar* (alt. 160 m), with the 12th c. pilgrimage church of Nuestra Señora de Iciar, to the little resort of **Deva** (alt. 3 m; pop. 5000; Hotel Miramar, II, 60 r.), at the mouth of the Río Deva, with the beautiful church (14th and 17th c.) of Nuestra Señora de la Asunción (13th c. doorway, 13th c. Romanesque bas-reliefs) and the ruined monastery of San Antonio. – From Deva C 6212

probably the site in antiquity of a temple of Venus. – From Fuenterrabía there is a very attractive road up the bare sandstone ridge of Jaizquibel, with the pilgrimage church of *Nuestra Señora de Guadalupe* and the Hostal Provincial de Jaizquibel (alt. 448 m), from which there are extensive views.

From Irún it is a short distance to the Spanish frontier post at *Behobía* and the international bridge over the *Río Bidaso*, which here forms the frontier with France. From Behobía C 133 runs S to Pamplona.

Over the Puerto de Echegárate. – N I, a broad modern road, runs inland from the district of Antiguo to *Lasarte* (alt. 30 m; pop. 1000), 4 km E of which, high above the right bank of the *Río Urumea*, is **Hernani** (pop. 14,000), with handsome balconied houses and a Town Hall of 1874 in the beautiful Plaza Mayor. The large parish church, famous for its wood-carving, contains the tomb of Juan de Urbieta (d. 1553).

N I continues S via *Andoaín* and *Irura* to **Tolosa** (see p. 227), from which N 240 runs SE to Pamplona. Then up the valley of the *Río Oria*, with the Sierra de Aralar and the rocky cone of *Aralar* (1427 m), one of the highest peaks in the Basque country, on the left, and via *Icazteghuetta* (alt. 92 m) and *Legorreta* (alt. 115 m), with a 16th c. church, to **Villafranca de Oria** (alt. 165 m), a town of picturesque narrow streets. Then on past the little industrial town of *Beasín* to *Idiazabal*, with a handsome church.

The road then winds its way up through beautiful *scenery, with magnificent views of the Basque mountains to the rear, to the **Puerto de Echegárate** (658 m), an important pass through the eastern *Cantabrian Mountains*, with a small restaurant and magnificent views of the Navarre plateau ahead. To the right is the *Sierra de San Adrián*, to the left the *Sierra de Aralar*.

continues along the coast into the province of Vizcaya and on via *Lequeitio* to **Guernicay y Kuno** (see p. 136).

To Bilbao by the direct road. – From Deva the motorway and N I runs up the valley of the *Río Deva* to *Alzola* (alt. 70 m), with thermal springs, and **Elgóibar** (alt 82 m; pop. 7000), founded in 1346, with small-arms factories.

At *Málzaga* (alt. 95 m), a railway junction, N I leaves the Deva valley. Beyond the river, on a hill to the right, is the *Ermita de Nuestra Señora de Arrate* (alt. 532 m), from which there are extensive views. Then on to **Éibar** (alt. 120 m; pop. 17,000), rebuilt after severe destruction during the Civil War, with large arms factories. From here there is a road up to the Ermita (8 km).

The route then follows a winding course into the province of Vizcaya and up a wooded valley to the *Puerto de Areitio* (625 m). Then on via *Durango* to **Bilbao** (see p. 82), 119 km from San Sebastián.

Over the Puerto de Descarga. – From just beyond *Zumaya*, on the Cantabrian Corniche, C 6317 runs S through the Urola valley, between wooded heights, to the health resort of *Cestona* and **Azpeitia** (alt. 85 m; pop. 11,000), an industrial town with handsome old patrician houses. Gothic church of San Sebastián, in which St Ignatius of Loyola was baptised; fine portico by Ventura Rodríguez (1767). – From Azpeitia there is an attractive excursion (13 km E) on C 6324 up the beautiful Régil valley to the *Alto de Vidania* (532 m), from which the road continues to Tolosa (see p. 227).

C 6317 continues up the Urola valley to the monastery (off the road to the left) of **Loyola** (*Monasterio de San Ignacio de Loyola*, alt. 115 m), an extensive range of buildings, erected between 1689 and 1888 to the design of Carlo Fontana, which houses a Jesuit college. The domed *church, 55 m high and richly decorated with marble, is one of the finest of its kind in Spain; it was completed only in the mid 18th c. In the left wing of the monastery is the Santa Casa, the house in which St Ignatius of Loyola, who founded the Jesuit order in 1534, was born (Iñigo López de Recalde, *c.* 1491–1556).

After passing through *Azcoitia* (alt. 130 m), an old market town in a beautiful situation, the road continues on a winding course to **Zumárraga** (alt. 357 m; pop. 3500), prettily situated on the right bank of the *Río Urola*, a road and railway junction and the birthplace of 1569 of Miguel López de Legazpi, conqueror of the Philippines (monument, erected 1897).

From here C 6322 winds its way up to the **Puerto de Descarga** (487 m), from which there are extensive views. The road then descends to **Vergara** (alt. 145 m; pop. 13,000), at the junction of the Río Anzuola with the Río Deva. Church of San Pedro, with a statue of Christ by Montañés (1657); Palacio Jáuregui (16th c.), with a very individual façade.

From here S on C 6213 to **Mondragón** (alt. 210 m; pop. 21,000), a developing industrial town at the foot of the *Peña Udala* (1092 m). In the main square are the old church of San Juan and the Town Hall (1746).

Santander

Province: Cantabria (S).
Telephone code: 942.
Altitude: 15 m. – Population: 184,000.

(i) **Patronato de Turismo,**
Plaza de Velarde 1; tel. 21 24 25.
Oficina de Información de Turismo,
Plaza Porticada 1; tel. 31 07 08.

HOTELS. – IN THE TOWN: *Bahía* (no rest.), Avda de Alfonso XIII 6, 181 r.; *Rex* (no rest.), Avda Calvo Sotelo 9, II, 54 r.; *México* (no rest.), Mendez Nuñez 2, III, 35 r.; Hostal *Arenal* (no rest.), Emilio Pino 7, 63 r.; *Ignacia* (no rest.), General Mola 5, P II, 57 r. IN SARDINERO (most hotels closed in winter): *Real*, Paseo de Pérez Galdós 28, standing high, with fine views (1 km from the beach), L, 124 r.; *Santemar* (no rest.), Avda Joaquín Costa 28, I, 350 r.; *María Isabel* (no rest.), Avda de Manuel García Lago s/n, II, 63 r.; *Sardinero* (no rest.), Plaza de Italia 1, II, 113 r.; *Roma* (no rest.), Avda de los Hoteles 5, III, 52 r.; *Castilla* (no rest.), Avda de Joaquín Costa 43, IV, 30 r.; *Colón* (no rest.), Plaza de las Brisas 1, IV, 33 r.; Hostal *París* (no rest.), Avda de los Hoteles 6, P II, 71 r.; etc. – CAMPING SITE: *Bella Vista*, on the Faro road (lighthouse).

RESTAURANTS. – In hotels; also *Cañadio*, Gomez Oreña 15; *Casa Valentin*, Calle de Isabel II, 19; *Iris*, Castelar 5; *Posada del Mar*, Juan de la Cosa 3 (rustic atmosphere); *Puerto*, Hernán Cortés 63 (1st floor); *Vivero*, Puerto Pesquero (fish dishes).

CAFÉS. – *Arenal*, Emilio Pino 7; *Dover*, Paseo de Pereda 13–14; *Kansas*, Calvo Sotela 23; *Mónaco*, Calvo Sotela 3; *Suizo*, Paseo de Pereda 29; etc.

EVENTS.– *Fiesta de Santiago* (July–Aug.), with a night procession of riders and a large programme of celebrations in honour of St James. – *Semana Grande* (Aug.), an international festival of drama and music.

CASINO. – *Gran Casino del Sardinero*.

WATER SPORTS. – Facilities for bathing and all kinds of water sports on the beaches round Santander – in Sardinero Bay (3 km from the town centre) and at Castañeda (beach 1800 m long), Sardinero (900 m) and Concha (200 m), which are joined up at low tide; also, at Cabo Mayor, the picturesque beach of Mataleñas and the Magdalena beach. Real Club Marítimo in Puerto Chico.

SPORT and RECREATION on land. – Climbing and winter sports in the Picos de Europa (see p. 185), on the Alto Campóo, etc.; tennis, golf, polo, hockey, riding (racecourse), fishing, shooting, flying (Aéro Club); bullfights.

The port of Santander in Old Castile, capital of the Province of Cantabria and the seat of a bishop, lies in a beautiful bay on the N coast of Spain, ringed by hills and within easy reach of the highest peaks in the Cantabrian Mountains, the Picos de Europa.

Santander was a considerable port in Roman times, and is still one of the leading ports of northern Spain, handling a large export and import trade. With a magnificent beach and mild climate, it is also a popular seaside resort.

SIGHTS. – The central artery of Santander is the *Avenida de Alfonso XIII*, a little way W of which, on the edge of the old town, is the Gothic **Cathedral** (13th c.; restored after a fire in 1941). In its large crypt (the Iglesia del Cristo) of about 1200 are the remains of the martyred SS. Celedonius and Emeterius. In the cloister is the tomb of the writer Marcelino Menéndez y Pelayo (1856–1912). – SW and E of the Avenida de Alfonso XIII, alongside the *Muelle de Maliaño* and farther SW, is the **Harbour**, with the Custom House and ramps for the loading of iron ore, etc. In clear weather there is a view of the Picos de Europa from here.

From the Avenida de Alfonso XIII the *Avenida de Calvo Sotelo*, rebuilt after the fire and now the town's main shopping street, runs W, leading to Calle Rubio, in which is the **Museo Municipal de Bellas Artes**, which contains among much else a portrait of Ferdinand VII by Goya and a rich collection of works by Italian, Flemish and Spanish artists of the 17th and 18th c. In the same building is the *Biblioteca Menéndez y Pelayo*, a library of 40,000 volumes with Menéndez y Pelayo's study, preserved as it was in his day. Separated from the library by a garden is the house in which he worked and died. – From the W end of the Avenida de Calvo Sotelo a tunnel runs through the hill on which the old town is built to the stations.

On the E side of the Avenida de Alfonso XIII are the beautiful gardens flanking the *Paseo de Pereda*, which extends to the *Puerto Chico* (Small Harbour). At its E end is the *Estación de Biología Marítima* (Marine Biological Station), with an interesting museum and aquarium (exhibition of preserved specimens of marine fauna). N of the Small Harbour is the *Diputación Provincial* (provincial government offices), with the *Museo de Prehistoria*, one of the most important in its field in Europe (numerous finds from prehistoric caves, including Altamira).

The line of the Paseo de Pereda is continued by *Calle Castelar*, the Avenida de la Reina Victoria and the Paseo de Ramón Pelayo, which lead to the beautiful

bathing beach of ***El Sardinero**, NW of the town centre, with seafront terraces, the Gran Casino and numerous hotels. From the E end of the Avenida de la Reina Victoria a road runs on to the peninsula of *La Magdalena*, with a palace built in 1912 as a royal summer residence.

SURROUNDINGS. – 3 km N of El Sardinero is the *Cabo Mayor*, with a lighthouse and the *Puente Forado*, a large natural bridge in the lcoal limestone rocks.

To the Cuevas de Altamira. – N 611 runs inland, with views of the Picos de Europa (partly snow-capped), to *Barreda*, from which C 6316 runs W to **Santillana del Mar** (see p. 202). From here it is 2 km (turn left, then in 300 m right) to a car park near the famous ***Cuevas de Altamira**. (As the breath of very many visitors has affected the wall painting over a long period, only about 35 persons are now admitted on any one day.) In these caves, at a depth of 270 m, are lifelike paintings of the animals hunted by Palaeolithic man (*c.* 13,000–25,000 years old; restored 1974). The quality of the painting is such that the caves have been called the "Sistine Chapel of rock painting". Adjoining the caves is a small museum. Nearby is another cave with fine stalactites and stalagmites.

2 km farther W on C 6316 is a hill from which there is a view of the sea and a road down to *Suances*, with beautiful pine-fringed beaches. C 6316 continues through *Oreña* and follows a winding course to the little town of **Comillas** (pop. 4000; hotels: *Casal del Castro, II, 45 r.; Paraíso, II, 36 r.), perched like a fortress on a hill above the sea, with a beautiful beach, overlooked by a large seminary for the training of priests.

C 6316 finally joins N 634, which continues via *La Revilla* to **San Vicente de la Barquera** (pop. 4000), an old-world little port and popular resort with a large beach. It preserves part of its old battlemented walls, a ruined castle and the imposing church of Santa María de los Ángeles (13th–16th c.), with fine 15th and 16th c. monuments.

To Bilbao. – N 634 runs S from Santander and then round the *Bahía de Santander* in a wide curve to **Solares** (alt. 50 m), a health resort (also noted for its table water) attractively situated on the Río Miera.

An excellent stretch of road then runs E through hilly country. A few kilometres beyond *Praves* C 629 branches off on the left to **Santoña** (pop. 11,000), a port situated on a small peninsula. In earlier days the town was fortified, and Napoleon planned to make it a northern Gibraltar. Romanesque collegiate church (12th–13th c.), with a 16th c. retablo. In the convent of San Sebastián de Anó is the tomb of Barbara Blomberg of Regensburg, who died at Colindres in 1597. She was the mother of Don John of Austria, a natural son of the Emperor Charles V, and the victor of Lepanto in 1571. – 2 km N is the beach of *Playa Berria*.

N 634 continues through the fertile delta of the *Río Asón* to *Colindres* (alt. 30 m), where a road goes off on the right and runs up the Asón valley to the pilgrimage centre of *Limpias* (7 km). In the parish church is the miracle-working image of Santo Cristo de la Agonía (17th c.). – N 634 runs on to **Laredo** (alt. 35 m; pop. 8000; hotels: El Ancla, II, 25 r., Cosmopol,

II, 60 r., both with a beach), a popular seaside resort attractively situated in Santoña Bay (holiday centre; beach 5 km long), with the interesting 13th c. church of Nuestra Señora de la Asunción (16th c. doorway) and handsome old houses and villas.

Beyond Laredo the road begins to climb, with beautiful *views to the rear of the town and the wide sweep of Santoña Bay. Thereafter it follows a winding course to the *Punta de Sonabia*, after which there is a magnificent stretch along the rocky coast to *Castro Urdiales* (alt. 2 m; pop. 13,000; hotels: Las Rocas, II, 61 r.; Miramar, III, 33 r.), a picturesquely situated little port, now also a quiet seaside resort, which is probably the oldest settlement on the Cantabrian coast (the Roman *Flaviobriga*). It has a notable Gothic church, Nuestra Señora de la Asunción (13th–15th c.), with a fine Puerta del Perdón and a valuable treasury. Castillo de Santa Ana (lighthouse), on a rocky promontory from which there are fine views. – Beyond *Mioño* the road enters the province of Vizcaya and continues via *San Juan de Somorrostro* to **Bilbao** (see p. 82), 110 km from Santander.

To Burgos. – Leave Santander on N 623, which runs S via *Muriedas* through hilly country, with the *Peña Gabarga* on the left and *Monte Garona* on the right. At *Renedo* it enters the valley of the *Río Pas* and runs uphill to **Vargas**, where it cuts across N 634 (Bilbao–Oviedo). 1·5 km off the road to the SE is *Socobio*, with a domed Romanesque church (12th c.)

The Burgos road continues up the Pas valley to **Puente Viesgo** (alt. 62 m), an attractively situated little spa (35 °C – 95 °F). In the vicinity are several caves with prehistoric rock paintings, including the *Cueva del Castillo* (discovered 1903) and the *Cueva de la Pasiega* (discovered 1911), both of them well worth a visit.

Then on to *Ontaneda* (alt. 170 m) and *Entram-basmestas* (alt. 192 m), where the road leaves the Río Pas and climbs up to the **Puerto del Escudo** (1011 m), flanked by Alpine meadows on the summit ridge of the Cantabrian Mountains. Here the road crosses into the province of Burgos and continues over the *Puerto de Carralas* and the *Puerto de Párama de Masa* to **Burgos** (see p. 85), 156 km from Santander.

To Palencia. – N 611 runs SW via *Barreda* to **Torrelavega** (alt. 16 m; pop. 40,000), an industrial town and the principal ironworking centre in the province of Santander. The road then continues S up the valley of the *Río Besaya* through the beautiful *Cantabrian Mountains*, mostly covered with forest, to **Las Caldas de Besaya**, a picturesquely situated spa (alt. 65 m) with thermal springs at a temperature of 37 °C (99 °F).

The road continues to *Bárcena del Pie de Concha* (alt. 287 m), runs through a wild gorge, the *Hoces de Bárcena*, and climbs steeply up, with many bends, to **Rienosa** (alt. 847 m; pop. 12,000), an ancient little town, now a summer holiday resort, in the high valley of the *Río Ebro*, which rises at *Fontibre*, 4 km W, and to the E is dammed to form the large *Pantano del Ebro*. From Reinosa C 6318 runs along the N side of this artificial lake to *Corconte*.

N 611 then leads S to *Cervatos*, which has an important Romanesque collegiate church (12th c.: national monument), crosses the summit ridge (987 m) and descends to the central Meseta, entering the province of Palencia and continuing via *Aguilar de*

Campóo and *Frómista* to **Palencia** (see p. 181), 203 km from Santander.

To the Picos de Europa. – There are two possible routes to the wild and majestic *Picos de Europa (see p. 185). One is the coast road via *Santillana del Mar* and then N 621 from *Unguera*, on the provincial boundary, SW to *Panes*. The alternative is by N 611 via *Torrelavega* to *Cabezón de la Sal*, then on C 625 SW to *Canuérniga*, and from there W on the winding C 6314 to *La Hermida*.

Santiago de Compostela

Province: La Coruña (C).
Telephone code: 981.
Altitude: 260 m. – Population: 90,000.

Oficina Municipal de Turismo,
Plaza del Obradoiro s/n;
tel. 58 29 00.
Oficina Archicofradía del Apóstol Santiago
(Arch-Confraternity of the Apostle St James),
Plaza de la Quintana;
tel. 58 16 30.

HOTELS. – *Los Reyes Católicos*, Plaza de España 1, L, 157 r.; *Araguaney*, Alfredo Brañas 5, L, 57 r., SP; *Compostela* (no rest.), Hórreo 1, I, 99 r.; *Peregrino*, Avda Rosalía de Castro s/n, I, 148 r., SP; *Gelmírez* (no rest.), Hórreo 92, II, 138 r.; *Santiago Apóstol*, La Grela 6, II, 91 r.; *Rey Fernando*, Fernando III El Santo 30, III, 24 r.; *Universal* (no rest.), Plaza de Galicia 2, III, 54 r.; Hostal *Windsor* (no rest.), República de El Salvador 16, P I, 50 r.; *Alameda* (no rest.), San Clemente 32, P II, 20 r.; etc. – CAMPING SITE. – *Puente Sionilla* about 7 km N on N 550.

RESTAURANTS. – In the hotels; also *Alameda*, Avda Figueroa 15, first floor; *Anexo Vilas*, Avda Villagarcía 21; *Chitón*, Rua Nueva 40; *Don Gaiferos*, Rua Nueva 23; *El Caserío*, Baudizados 13, first floor; *La Trinidad*, San Clemente 6; *Retablo*, Nueva 13; *Don Quijote*, Galleras 20; etc.

EVENTS. – Under a special privilege granted by Pope Calixtus II, every year in which the feast of St James (25 July) falls on a Sunday ranks as a *Holy Year*, marked by special celebrations beginning with the opening of the Puerta Santa on the preceding New Year's Eve. The next Holy Year is 1993. – *Fiestas de Santiago Apóstol* (July), with a great procession and the swinging of the huge censer known as the Botafumeiro. – *Ascension, Corpus Christi* and *31 December* are celebrated with particular festivity in Santiago de Compostela.

Santiago de Compostela, traditionally known in English as Compostella, once capital of the kingdom of Galicia and now the seat of a metropolitan archbishop and an ancient university, lies in NW Spain some 35 km from the Atlantic coast. NW of the town – which has one of the highest rainfalls in Spain – is Monte Pedros (735 m).

Santiago is Spain's most celebrated place of pilgrimage, with a magnificent Cathedral which is one of the country's outstanding tourist attractions. According to legend the bones of the Apostle St James the Great (Santiago), brother of the Evangelist John, were transported to Spain after his martyrdom in A.D. 44 and found on the site of the present Cathedral in the year 813. Thereafter St James became the patron saint of Spain, and pilgrims from all over Europe flocked in their thousands along the Way of St James (see p. 242) to visit his shrine.

The Cathedral, Santiago de Compostela

SIGHTS. – The objective of all visitors to Santiago is the *Plaza del Obradoiro (also known as the Plaza de España), surrounded by handsome buildings, with the Cathedral on the E side. The square, which lies in the western part of the old town, with its old-world arcaded streets and its numerous churches and convents, is one of the finest and best preserved old squares in Spain.

On the S side of the square is the former Colegio de San Jerónimo, now occupied by the Institute of Galician Studies, with a beautiful sculptured doorway of 1490. Behind it is the Colegio Fonseca (1544), now the Faculty of Pharmacy, with a two-storey patio. – On the W side of the square is the **Palacio de Rajoy** (1777) or Palacio Consistorial (Town Hall). – The N side of the square is occupied by the *Hospital Real (now the Hotel de los Reyes Católicos), founded by the Catholic monarchs in 1489, with a Plateresque doorway bearing coats of arms, four courtyards of the 16th–18th c. and a Gothic chapel (beautifully carved piers at the crossing, grille of 1556. – On the E side of the square, to the left of the Cathedral, is the Palacio del Arzobispo (Archbishop's Palace), a plain building on the site of the Palacio de Gelmírez (12th–13th c.). To the right of the Cathedral is the Cloister, with open pillared galleries.

The **Cathedral**, one of the supreme achievements of early Romanesque architecture, was built between 1060 and 1211 on the site of an earlier 9th c. church and remodelled externally in Baroque style in the 16th and 17th c. The *W front, facing the Plaza del Obradoiro is one of the most impressive façades in Spain, a lavishly decorated piece of Baroque architecture (by Fernando Casas y Novoa, 1738–47), with a statue of St James on the central gable, flanked by two richly articulated towers 76 m high. Of the doorways the most notable are the Puerta de la Azabachería (1769), the N doorway, in the Plaza de la Inmaculada; the Puerta Santa, the E doorway (opened only in Holy Years), in the Plaza de los Literarios, with 12th c. sculpture; and the oldest, the *Puerta de las Platerías, on the S side adjoining the 75 m high Torre de la Trinidad (view). The entrance on the W side is opened only for important ecclesiastical and lay dignitaries. – The admission ticket covers also the Cathedral treasury and museums.

The most impressive view of the Romanesque INTERIOR (94 m long, nave 24 m high, dome 33 m) is from the S doorway. The dominant feature is the Capilla Mayor, built over the Apostle's tomb. The high altar consists of a superstructure of jasper, alabaster and silver with numerous figures (1665–69) and the actual altar (by Figuera, 1715), with a statue of the Apostle (head 13th c.) richly decked with silver, gold and precious stones. – Under the high altar is the Crypt, with the tombs of the Apostle and his two disciples; the silver casket containing the Apostle's remains is modern. – In the dome over the crossing is a device (installed in 1604) for swinging the huge Botafumeiro or censer (2 m high). – The chapels in the transepts and apse contain Baroque sculpture and retablos and a number of notable tombs. – In the Relicario (first chapel in S aisle) are the tombs of kings and queens of the 12th–15th c. – In the Capilla de San Fernando is the Cathedral Treasury, with a silver custodia by Antonio de Arfe (1545). – Within the W doorway is the *Pórtico de la Gloria, a tripartite porch with a profusion of sculptured decoration (originally coloured), one of the largest surviving complexes of Romanesque sculpture (by Mateo, 1166–88). – In the S transept of the Cathedral, adjoining the Puerto de las Platerías, is the entrance to the Plateresque *Cloister (conducted tours), one of the largest and finest in Spain (each side 35 m long by 5·8 m wide). In the adjoining Sala Capitular (chapterhouse) are 17th c. tapestries by Raés. In the upper storey of the Cloister is a Tapestry Museum, with tapestries from Flanders and others made in Madrid after cartoons by Teniers, Rubens, Goya, Bayeu and other artists. When not in use the Botafumeiro is kept in the Library. On the intermediate storey of the Cloister is a small *Archaeological Museum.* – The interesting *Lower Church* (Catedral Vieja), dating from the 12th c., is entered from the staircase outside the W entrance.

N of the Cathedral, in the *Plaza de la Immaculada,* is the former Benedictine monastery of **San Martín Pinario** (founded 899), now a seminary, with an imposing pillared doorway (begun 1590), a handsome courtyard and a church completed in 1645 (fine choir-stalls of 1644). – To the NW is the Faculty of Medicine, and near this the convent of San Francisco (13th c., remodelled 1618–1783), with a twin-towered church and a Gothic cloister.

To the S of the Cathedral are two parallel arcaded streets, the *Rúa del Villar* and the *Rúa Nueva,* the town's principal traffic arteries. In the Rúa Nueva is the 12th c. Romanesque church of *Santa María Salomé.* Farther E, in the *Plaza del Instituto,* is the late 18th c. building of the **University** (founded 1532), with a classical façade and an external flight of steps. The Library contains valuable 16th c. and other works.

On the SW side of the old town, off the broad *Alameda,* is the *Paseo de la Herradura,* in a park from which there is a general *view of the town. In the park is the church of *Santa Susana* (begun 1105). To the S is the University City.

SURROUNDINGS. – There are a number of features of interest in the immediate vicinity of the town. In the *Barrio de Sar* (1 km SE) is the 12th c. church of *Santa María de Sar,* the pillars and walls of which are far from vertical, probably because of an unstable site. Fine 13th c. cloister, partly preserved, with rich sculptured ornament by Maestro Mateo.

In *San Lorenzo,* 2 km W of the town, is the early 13th c. church of *San Lorenzo de Transouto,* with a marble altar of 1525 and figures by Montañés.

To Cape Finisterre. – An attractive trip, either via *Padrón* and the *Cabo Carreiro* or the more direct route via *Noya.* Continue, if desired, to *Carballo* and **La Coruña** (see p. 109).

To the Sobrado de los Monjes. – C 547 runs E past the airport to *Arzúa,* a former pilgrim station on the Way of St James; then NE on a minor road to the **Sobrado de los Monjes** (national monument), a monastery, originally Romanesque, with several cloisters of the 17th and 18th c., a Renaissance sacristy and an elegant Baroque façade.

To Pontevedra. – N 550 runs S along the Alameda and then through attractive hilly country to the pilgrimage church of *Nuestra Señora de la Esclavitud* (16 km). Then on a long causeway over the valley of the *Río Ulla* to *Padrón* (alt. 6 m; pop. 9000), the Roman *Iria Flavia,* at the confluence of the *Río Sar* and

the Ulla. Old noble mansions; collegiate church of Santa María, founded in the 11th c., with many bishops' tombs; ruined castle. – On the far side of the Río Ulla begins the province of Pontevedra. The road continues via *Caldas de Reyes* to the provincial capital, **Pontevedra** (see p. 187), 54 km from Santiago de Compostela.

Santillana del Mar

Province: Cantabria (S).
Telephone code: 942.
Altitude: 100 m. – Population: 4000.

ⓘ **Oficina de Turismo de Santilana,**
Plaza de Ramón Pelayo;
tel. 81 82 51.

HOTELS. – *Parador Nacional Gil Blas,* Plaza de Ramón Pelayo 11, II, 28 r.; *Los Infantes,* Avda Le Dorat 1, II, 30 r.; *Altamira,* Cantón 1, III, 30 r.; *Santillana,* Santo Domingo 1, III, 38 r.; *Conde-Duque* (no rest.), Campo de Revolgo s/n, IV, 14 r.; *Los Hildalgos* (no rest.), Campo de Revolgo s/n, IV, 18 r.; Hostal *Castillo* (no rest.), Plaza de Ramón Pelayo 6, P III, 4 r.; etc.

The charming and historic little town of Santillana del Mar, now protected as a national monument, grew up about the 6th c. round the Monasterio de Santa Juliana.

SIGHTS. – With its old mansions flaunting their old coats of arms, Santillana – now bearing the marks of a thriving tourist trade – gives a unique picture of the life of the old country nobility of Spain. It is also noted as the home of Gil Blas, hero of the French picaresque novel "Gil Blas de Santillane" by Alain-René Lesage (1668–1747). Its most notable building is the 12th c. **collegiate church** of the monastery, an outstanding work of Cantabrian architecture. It has a *retablo* painted by Jorge Inglés (1453) and contains the *tomb* of Santa Juliana. On the N side is a magnificent Romanesque *cloister* (late 12th c.).

SURROUNDINGS. – The *Cuevas de Altamira* (see p. 199) are within easy reach. – 10 km N are the pine-fringed beaches of *Suances.*

Collegiate church, Santillana del Mar

Santa Domingo de la Calzada

Province: La Rioja (LO).
Telephone code: 941.
Altitude: 638 m. – Population: 5000.
ⓘ **Oficina de Información de Turismo,**
Plaza del Beato Hermosilla.

HOTELS. – *Parador Nacional*, Plaza del Santo 3, II, 27 r.; *Hostal Santa Teresita*, General Mola 2, P II, 78 r., no rest.; *Río* (no rest.), Etchegoyen 2, P III, 12 r.

RESTAURANT. – *Mesón El Peregrino*, Zumala-cárregui 18 (rustic style).

The little town of Santo Domingo de la Calzada, on the Río Oja, lies on the famous pilgrim road to Santiago de Compostela, the Way of St James. The old 24-arched stone bridge was built by the local hermit Domingo de Viloria, who is also remembered as the builder of this section of the pilgrims' road (calzada).

SIGHTS. – The Romanesque and Gothic **Cathedral** (1180) stands on the site of an earlier church built by Domingo de Viloria; it has a Baroque tower added in 1767. Splendid high altar with a retablo by Damián Forment; tomb of a knight in the Capilla de Santa Teresa; burial place of Santo Domingo in the crypt. – The oldest church in the town is the Romanesque chapel of *Nuestra Señora de la Plaza*. – Convent of *San Francisco*, with a 16th c. church containing a retablo (also 16th c.) with rich sculptured decoration.

SURROUNDINGS. – 14 km S is the old pilgrim station of *Ezcaray*, now a picturesque little summer resort near *Monte San Lorenzo* (2262 m), surrounded by extensive pine forests.

Saragossa

See Zaragoza.

Segovia

Province: Segovia (SG).
Telephone code: 911.
Altitude: 1000 m. – Population: 40,000.
ⓘ **Oficina de Información de Turismo,**
Plaza Mayor 10;
tel. 43 03 28.
Dirección Provincial de Turismo,
Plaza de San Facundo 1;
tel. 43 27 11.

1 Convento de San Juan de la Cruz
2 Moneda
3 Palacio del Marqués del Arco
4 Casa de Hércules
5 La Trinidad
6 San Nicolás
7 San Agustin
8 Corpus Christi
9 San Juan de los Caballeros (Museo Zuloaga)
10 Torreón de los Lozoya
11 Palacio de los Condes de Alpuente
12 Casa de los Picos
13 San Sebastián
14 Academia de Artilleria

HOTELS. – *Parador Nacional, Apartado de Correos 106, I, 80 r., SP.; *Acueducto*, Avda. del Padre Claret 10, II, 73 r.; *Los Linajes* (no rest.), Doctor Valesco 9, II, 55 r.; *Victoria*, Plaza Mayor 5, IV, 30 r.; *Hostal Las Sirenas*, Juan Bravo 30, P I, 3 r. – ON THE CARRETERA N 110 (to Soria): *Puerto de Segovia*, II, 118 r., SP.

RESTAURANTS. – *Mesón de Cándido*, Plaza del Azoguejo 5, *Casa Duque*, Cervantes 12, *La Oficina*, Cronista Lecea 10 (all Segovian style); *Solaire*, Santa Engracia 3; *El Cordero*, Carmen 4; – IN CUELLAR: *Florida*, Las Huertas 4. – IN SEPULVEDA: *Cristóbal*; Conde Sepúlveda 9. – IN SAN ILDEFONSO: *Mesón Mariben*, Cuartel Nuevo 2.

EVENTS. – *Semana Santa* (Holy Week), with procession. – *Fiestas de Santa Águeda*, the festival of St Agatha, celebrated all over the province; particularly impressive at Zamarramala (4 km NW), with the election of *alcaldesas* ("mayoresses") and folk dancing.

Segovia, capital of its province and the seat of a bishop, is built on a rocky hill almost 100 m high, encircled by the little rivers Eresma and Clamores, on the northern slope of the Sierra de Guadarrama. It is a picturesque and attractive town with numbers of old medieval buildings and a unique Roman aqueduct.

HISTORY. – Originally an Iberian foundation, the town was for several centuries a place of considerable importance. Under the Romans it lay at the junction of two military roads, and during this period the magnificent aqueduct was built. After the Visigothic and Moorish periods the town was resettled by the Counts of Castile, and it was for long a favourite residence of the kings of that province. Isabel the Catholic was proclaimed Queen of Castile here in

1474. Segovia enjoyed further periods of splendour under the Trastamara dynasty, and after falling into oblivion for a time rose to fresh brilliance under the Bourbons in the 18th c., when its greatness was celebrated by many artists.

SIGHTS. – The hill on which the town stands is ringed by an almost complete circuit of walls, built by the Romans on Iberian foundations and restored in the 11th and 12th c., with 86 semicircular towers (*cubos*) and three imposing town gates.

The hub of the city's traffic is the *Plaza del Azoguejo*, below the E side of the upper town. This is traversed by the magnificent ****Roman aqueduct**, probably built in the late 1st c. A.D. in the reign of Trajan, which ranks with the walls of Tarragona as one of the two largest surviving Roman structures in Spain. The water channel, still bringing water from the Sierra de Fuenfría 17 km away, is carried over the deep valley, now occupied by the outlying districts of the town, on 118 arches of granite blocks laid without mortar or metal cramps, with a total length of 818 m. The arches range in height between 7 m and 28·5 m, and 43 of them, covering 276 m of the total length, are double-tiered. The aqueduct conveys the water to the upper town, ending at the Alcázar in an underground channel.

From the Plaza del Azoguejo a road to the NE ascends to the upper town. In Plaza Colmenares is the church of *San Juan de los Caballeros*, once the burial place of the leading families of Segovia, now deconsecrated and occupied by the *Museo Zuloaga*, containing works by the painter Ignacio Zuloaga and the potter Daniel Zuloaga. In Calle San Agustín is the *Museo Provincial de Bellas Artes* (pictures, engravings).

From the Plaza del Azoguejo the Calle Cervantes leads to the *Casa de los Picos* (so called after the faceted stones of which it is built), the palace of Pedro López de Ayala (15th c.); from the terrace there is a fine view of the Sierra de Guadarrama. Then along Calle Juan Bravo to a picturesque little square on the right, with two figures of mermaids and the 16th c. *Torreón de los Lozoyas*. Beyond this is the Romanesque church of **San Martín** (12th c.), with pillared Romanesque galleries on the S and W sides; museum, with pictures, sculpture and Baroque altars. A short distance W,

outside the town walls, is the *Paseo del Salón*, a promenade affording extensive views.

NW of San Martín, past the *Convento del Corpus Christi*, is the *Plaza Mayor*, the centre of the old town, with the tourist information office. On the N side of the square is the *Ayuntamiento* (Town Hall), a plain 17th c. building. On the SE side is the church of *San Miguel* (1558), with a fine high altar of 1572 and a number of tombs.

On the highest point in the town stands the late Gothic ***Cathedral**, built by Juan and Rodrigo Gil de Hontañón between 1525 and 1593, of impressive effect with its vigorously articulated exterior and its tower 100 m high (1558).

The spacious INTERIOR (105 m long) has rich stellate vaulting, vivid stained glass and fine sculpture and altars. Marble high altar with a 14th c. ivory figure of the Virgen de la Paz. On the S side of the ambulatory is the Capilla del Santísimo Sacramento, with a richly decorated altar. In the 5th chapel in the N aisle, the Capilla de la Piedad, is a polychrome wood "Lamentation" by Juan de Juni (1571). Opposite this chapel is the Capilla del Consuelo, with a richly carved doorway and the tombs of two bishops, Raimundo de Losana (1249–59) and Diego de Covarrubias (1564–77).

From the Capilla del Consuelo we continue into the Cloister, built 1524–30, mostly with material from the cloister of the old cathedral (destroyed in the 16th c.), which stood near the Alcázar. In the rooms opening off the cloister and in the Archive Room on the upper floor is the Museo Catedralicio, with valuable church furnishings, including pictures and Brussels tapestries (16th–17th c.). The Sala Capitular (chapterhouse) has a fine artesonado ceiling.

From the Plaza de la Catedral we go NW along *Calle Marqués del Arco*, past the Romanesque church of *San Andrés* (12th c.) and along Calle de Daoiz to the *Plaza del Alcázar*, from which there are far-ranging views. The ***Alcázar**, standing on a steep-sided crag between the narrow valleys of the Eresma and the Clamores, is a magnificent example of Old Castilian architecture, built in the 12th c. and later enlarged and embellished. The *Torre de Juan II*, ringed by ten semicircular turrets, on the E side (with wide views of the town and the Sierra de Guadarrama), and the *Torre del Homenaje* on the W side both date from the 14th c. The interior of the Alcázar is of great interest, with two inner courtyards, a terrace and a series of fine rooms containing old furniture, tapestries, weapons and armour.

The Alcázar, Segovia

A little way N of the Cathedral is the *Plaza San Esteban*, in which are the unpretentious *Palacio Episcopal* (Bishop's Palace) and the 13th c. Romanesque church of **San Esteban**, famous for its tall six-storey tower with a pyramidal roof. Close by is the *Plaza de la Trinidad*, with the *Torre de Hércules* and the church of *La Trinidad*.

Outside the walls. – From the Plaza del Azoguejo the Avenida de Fernández Ladreda runs SW to the Romanesque church of *San Clemente* (13th c.), with a Baroque interior and an interesting apse. Beyond this is the church of **San Millán**, also Romanesque, built between 1111 and 1124 and thus one of the oldest churches in the town, with a beautiful interior. – In the southern outskirts of the town, at the end of the aqueduct, is the *Convento de San Antonio el Real*, founded by Henry IV (15th c.). The church has a beautiful artesonado ceiling and Flemish retablos.

To the NE of the Plaza del Azoguejo is the San Lorenzo district, with the church of *San Lorenzo*, the tower of which is an outstanding example of Mudéjar architecture. From here we go W below the town walls, past the *convent of Santa Cruz*, and cross the Río Eresma to reach the **Monasterio del Parral**, on the hillside to the right. This Hieronymite house, founded by the Marqués de Villena in 1459, has a church with a huge 16th c.

retablo and two alabaster tombs (1528), one of them being that of the founder. Opposite the monastery, on the left bank of the Eresma near the bridge, is the old *Moneda* (Mint), in which the Spanish coinage was minted until 1730. On a hill W of El Parral, reached by way of Calle Marqués de Villena, is the church of **Vera Cruz** (national monument), a Templar church built in 1208–17 on the model of the Church of the Holy Sepulchre in Jerusalem; it contains 13th c. wall paintings. Farther W, lower down, is the *Convento de Carmelitas Descalzos* (house of the 'Barefoot' Carmelite Friars), founded in 1588 by the mystic St John of the Cross, who was prior here and is buried in the convent. Nearby is the 17th c. pilgrimage church of the *Virgen de la Fuencisla*.

SURROUNDINGS. – If the town is rich in churches, the province of Segovia is no less rich in majestic old castles and palaces. Two castle tours are described below, together with a visit to the palace of La Granja.

Castles Tour 1. – N 601 runs NW from Segovia via Carbonere el Mayor to (61 km) **Cuéllar** (alt. 775 m; pop. 7000), an interesting little town which was taken by the Romans in 96 B.C. (*Colenda*), and in later centuries was a frequent residence of the kings of Castile. It has well-preserved town walls, a 15th c. castle and many old palaces and brick-built Romanesque churches which are among the oldest examples of this style.

From here a narrow country road runs 32 km SW to the ancient little town of **Coca** (alt. 790 m; pop. 2000), at the confluence of the Río Eresma and the Río Voltoya. Originally a settlement of the Vaccaei, an Iberian tribe, under the name of *Cauca*, it was the birthplace (A.D. 346) of the Roman Emperor Theodosius. Imposing town gate, the Arco de la Villa; Castillo de Fonseca (15th c.), one of Spain's finest castles; church of Santa María, with four tombs belonging to members of the distinguished Fonesca family.

Then SE via *Nava de la Asunción* to *Santa María la Real de Nieva* (17 km), with a church which has a very beautiful cloister. From here return to Segovia on C 605. Total distance 145 km.

Castles Tour 2. – Leave Segovia on N 601 and in 9 km turn right into C 603, which runs NE to (34 km) **Turégano** (alt. 936 m), a little episcopal town with an arcaded Plaza Mayor, under a partly ruined castle (13th–15th c.): battlemented walls and keep, enclosing the Romanesque church of San Miguel.

Continue on C 603 to *Cantalejo* (15 km). 24 km N is *Fuentidueña*, with the ruins of two Romanesque churches and a powerful castle. – From Cantalejo a minor road runs 15 km NE to the picturesque little town of **Sepúlveda** (alt. 1032 m; pop. 2000), situated high above a loop of the Río Duratón. This was the Roman *Septempublica*, and still has well-preserved remains of Roman fortifications. Several Romanesque churches, including El Salvador (11th c.), in a commanding situation, with a galleried portico and a free-standing tower (exceptional panoramic views). Castle founded by Fernán González.

From the crossroads called Las Cuatro Carreteras take a minor road which runs S past the castle of Castilnovo (12th–13th c., originally Moorish), on left, to **Pedraza**, an old-world little town which claims to be the birthplace of the Emperor Trajan. Massive castle on a huge crag of rock; attractive Plaza Mayor; Torre San Juan (Romanesque); Casa de la Inquisición, now an inn.

Another 10 km brings us to N 110, which runs SW to Segovia via *Collado Hermoso*. Total distance 135 km.

To La Granja. – N 601 runs SE, with fine views of the Sierra de Guadarrama, to (12 km) **San Ildefonso** or **La Granja** (alt. 1156 m; pop. 5000), in a beautiful situation at the foot of the massive *Peñalara* (2430 m), famous for the splendid palace, with beautiful gardens and fountains, which was built in the 18th c. in imitation of Versailles. Conducted tours of the palace, including the Throne Room and a magnificent collection of tapestries. Palace church, with the tomb of Philip V and his wife Isabella Farnese. Gardens, with fountains and cascades. – From here it is possible to continue through the Sierra de Guadarrama, going over the *Puerto de Navacerrada* (1860 m), to Madrid.

To Ávila. – N 110 runs SW, crosses N VI and comes to **Villacastín** (alt. 1040 m; pop. 1700; Hosteria del Pilar, IV, 21 r.), on the western slopes of the Sierra de Guadarrama, with a number of old noble mansions and an interesting parish church (15th–17th c.) containing a handsome retablo and various tombs. – Beyond Villacastín the road, now numbered N 501, crosses the provincial boundary and continues via *Aldeavieja* (alt. 1215 m), off the road on the right, to **Ávila** (see p. 58), 65 km from Segovia.

To Soria. – N 110 runs NE along the *Sierra de Guadarrama* and at *Santo Tomé del Puerto* joins N I, follows this road 3 km N and then branches off and runs NE to **Riaza** (alt. 1200 m), a little town and winter sports resort beautifully situated among the wooded hills of the *Sierra de Ayllón*, with well-preserved town walls and the extensive ruins of a castle. Near the town is the convent of *Nuestra Señora de Hontanares*. – N 110 then continues to *Ayllón*, crosses the provincial boundary and goes over the *Altos de Ayllón* (1100 m); then via *El Burgo de Osma* (see p. 85) to **Soria** (p. 215), 194 km from Segovia.

Seo de Urgel

Province: Lérida (L).
Telephone code: 973
Altitude: 700 m. – Population: 10,000.
ⓘ **Oficina Municipal de Turismo,**
  Paseo de José Antonio;
  tel. 35 00 10.

HOTELS. – *El Castell*, Carretera Lleida s/n, I, 39 r., SP; *Parador Nacional*, Santo Domingo s/n, II, 84 r., SP; *Nice* (no rest.), Avda. Pau Clarís 4, III, 50 r.; *Andría*, Paseig Brudieu 24, IV, 25 r.; *Cadi*, Duque de Seo de Urgel 4, IV, 42 r.; *Mundial*, San Dot 2, IV, 69 r.; etc.

EVENTS. – *Fiesta de San Odón* (July), patronal festival with famous dances in traditional costume and other folk celebrations. – *Retaule de Sant Ermengol* (July–Aug.), a mystery play performed on Sundays in the cloister of the Cathedral.

Seo de Urgel lies near the frontier of Andorra, magnificently situated in the wide valley of the Río Segre, framed by the Pyrenees. The town, usually known simply as "La Seo", is the seat of a bishop.

SIGHTS. – The town's finest building is the Romanesque **Cathedral** (11th c. with later restoration and alteration). In the 12th c. cloister is the *Diocesan Museum*. Gothic high altar; shrines containing relics. – Gothic *Bishop's Palace*, with chapel of San Miguel (11th c.). – Other medieval buildings, including the 15th c. *Ayuntamiento* (Town Hall).

SURROUNDINGS. – Seo de Urgel is the southern gateway to the Pyrenean republic of **ANDORRA** (see p. 54), and lies on C 1313, which runs SW down the valley of the *Río Segre* to Lérida (with side roads leading to Barcelona).

Seville

Province: Seville (SE).
Telephone code: 954.
Altitude: 10 m. – Population: 654,000.
ⓘ **Oficina de Información de Turismo,**
  Avenida de la Constitución 21;
  tel. 22 14 04.
  Oficina Municipal de Turismo,
  Paseo de las Delicias s/n;
  tel. 23 44 65.
  Delegación Provincial de Turismo,
  Avenida de la Constitución 21;
  tel. 22 89 90.

HOTELS. – *Alfonso XIII*, San Fernando 2, L, 149 r.; SP; *Colón*, Canalejas 1, I, 262 r.; *Doña María* (no rest.), Don Remondo 19, I, 61 r., SP; *Gran Hotel Lar*, Plaza de Carmen Benitez 3, 137 r.; *Inglaterra*, Plaza Nueva 7, I, 120 r.; *Los Lebreros*, Luis Morales 2, I, 439 r., SP; *Macarena*, San Juan Ribera 2, 305 r., SP; *Pasarela* (no rest.), Avda de la Borbolla 11, I, 82 r.; *Porta Coeli* (no rest.), Avda Eduardo Dato 49, I, 246 r.; *Alcázar* (no rest.), Menendez Pelayo 10, II, 96 r.; *América* (no rest.), Jesus del Gran Poder 2, II, 100 r.; *Bécquer* (no rest.), Reyes Católicos 4, II, 126 r.; *Corregidor* (no rest.), Morgado 17, II, 69 r.; *Don Paco*, Plaza Jerónimo de Córdoba 4, II, 220 r., SP; *Fernando III* (no rest.), San José 21, II, 156 r.; *Giralda*, Sierra Nevada 3, II, 90 r.; *Monte Carmelo* (no rest.), Turia 9, II, 68 r.; *Reyes Católicos* (no rest.), Gravina 57, II, 26 r.; *Venecia* (no rest.), Trajano 31, 24 r.; *Virgen de los Reyes*, Luis Montoto 131, II, 80 r.; *Ducal* (no rest.), Plaza de la Encarnación 19, II, 51 r.; *International* (no rest.), Aguilas 17, III, 26 r.; *Montecarlo*, Gravina 51, III, 25 r.; *Murillo* (no rest.), Lope de Rueda 7, III, 61 r.; *Niza*, Reyes Católicos 5, III, 56 r.; *La Rábida*, Castelar 24, III, 87 r.; *Sevilla* (no rest.), Daoiz 6, III, 32 r.; *Lyon*, Vidrio 15, IV, 33 r.; *Simón*, García de Vinuesa 19, IV,

Seville: Plaza de Espana and Palacio Central

47 r.; Hostal *Itálica* (no rest.), Antonio de la Peña Lopez 5, P I, 27 r.; *Madrid* (no rest.), San Pedro Martir 22, P I, 23 r.; *El Paraíso*, Gravina 27, P I, 29 r.; *Sierpes*, Corral del Rey 22, P III, 39 r.; *Zaida* (no rest.), San Roque 26, P I, 27 r.; *Central* (no rest.), Zaragoza 18, P II, 22 r.; *Duque*, Trajano 15, P II, 35 r.; *Jentoft* (no rest.), Benidorm 2, P II, 58 r.; *Los Naranjos* (no rest.), San Roque 11, P II, 25 r.; *Prado* (no rest.), Avda de Málaga 6, P II, 43 r.; *Zahira*, San Eloy 43, P II, 19 r.; etc. – CAMPING SITES. *Sevilla*, Carretera N–IV, 6 km E; *Villsom*, Dos Hermanas, 12 km S.

RESTAURANTS in the hotels; also *El Burladero*, José Canalejas 2; *Río Grande*, Betis s/n, on Guadalquivir, Blick auf Torre del Oro; *Méson del Moro*, Méson del Moro 6; *La Dorada*, Virgen de Aguas Santas 6; *El Figón de Cabildo*, Plaza del Cabildo; *Hostería del Laurel*, Plaza de los Venerables 5; *Rincón de Curro*, Virgen de Luján 45; *Or-Iza*, San Fernando 41; *San Marco*, Cuna 6 (Italian cuisine), *Maitre*, Avenida San Francisco Javier 7; *Jamaica*, Jamaica 16; *Venta de los Reyes*, Carretera Aeropuerto, 5 km E, on road to airport, etc.

CAFÉS. – *Huerta del Rey*, Avda Eduardo Dato 10; *Via Veneto*, Avda de la Constitución 32; *Catunambu*, Ronde de Capuchinos 3; *La Reja*, Santa María de Gracia 15; etc.

EVENTS. – **Semana Santa** (Holy Week), one of the most impressive festivals in Spain, particularly the processions of the confraternities (*cofradías* or *hermandades*) from the different quarters of the town, beginning on Palm Sunday, in which richly decked figures of saints (*pasos*) are carried through the streets, and the main processions on the night before Good Friday and on Good Friday morning; ceremonies in the Cathedral. – *Feria de Abril*, Seville's principal secular fiesta, lasting six days. – *Festivales de España* (autumn), with ballet and concerts by artistes of international standing. – *Fiesta del Santísimo Corpus* (Corpus Christi), a brilliant procession from the Cathedral by way of the Plaza de San Francisco Española to the church of San Salvador, preceded by

the *Danza de los Seises* in the Cathedral. – *Fiesta de la Virgen de los Reyes* (Aug.), patronal festival. – *Feria de San Miguel* (Sept.), with bullfights and fights with young bulls (*novilladas*). – *Romería del Rocío* (Whit week), one of the most famous pilgrimages in Spain, in which groups of pilgrims travel on horseback, muleback or ox-carts from Seville, Huelva, Cádiz, Jerez and other areas to pay honour to the Virgen de Rocío in the presence of the Archbishop of Seville.

SPORT and RECREATION. – Seville has a modern stadium, a racecourse, a golf-course and a Club Náutico, as well as flying, tennis and judo clubs, a sub-aqua club and a shooting range. Bullfights; fishing in the Guadalquivir and other rivers, shooting in the sierra by arrangement with the Sociedad de Caza Deportiva and local shooting clubs.

*Seville (in Spanish Sevilla), capital of Andalusia and of Seville province, the seat of an archbishop and a university town, is Spain's fourth largest city (after Madrid, Barcelona and Valencia); it is situated on the left bank of the Río Guadalquivir in a fertile plain.

Here the Guadalquivir emerges into the Andalusian lowlands, and at high tide – the effect of which is felt for over 100 km up the river – it is possible for seagoing ships of some size to reach the river port of Seville, 87 km from the sea, using a canal which bypasses the last bend on the river before the town. In 1948–49 the main channel of the Guadalquivir was diverted round the W side of the town; the port installations, however, are still on the old course. The *Huerta de Sevilla* begins N of the city beyond the outer districts which ring the old town.

The climate of Seville is one of the hottest in Europe, with temperatures rising as high as 48 °C (118 °F). Accordingly the houses usually have patios, decked with flowers and a plashing fountain, often tantalisingly glimpsed from the street, which provide a cool retreat in the heat of summer. – With the abundance of art and architecture which it has inherited from the many centuries of its past, the lively and bustling activity of a southern Mediterranean town which is also a port, Seville is a fascinating and exciting city to visit, fully justifying the old saying, "Quien no ha visto Sevilla, no ha visto maravilla". ("Those who have not seen Seville have missed a marvel.")

HISTORY. – When the Romans arrived here about 205 B.C. they found a town which they called *Hispalis*, perhaps an Iberian or Phoenician foundation. Under Caesar it became an important port, with the name of *Colonia Iulia Romula*. In the 5th c. A.D. it became successively the capital of the Vandals (411) and the Visigoths (441). In 712 the Moors captured the town, which they called *Ihbiliya*. Subsequently it was ruled by the Umayyads (from 913), the Almoravides (from 1091) and the Almohades (from 1147). Under *Yusuf Abu Yakub* (1163–84) and *Yakub ibn Yusuf* (1184–98) many splendid buildings were erected in Seville, and for a time the city exceeded even Córdoba in size. In 1248 *Ferdinand III* of Castile recaptured the town and made it his residence. The king who features most prominently in the legendary history of Seville is *Pedro I*, the Cruel (1350–69). On August 3rd, 1492 the seafarer Christopher Columbus of Palos, a place on the SW coast of Spain, set sail in his carvel and discovered, among other places, Cuba and Haiti. On his return on March 31st 1493 he was received with great acclamation in Seville. Thereafter Seville gained a monopoly in overseas trade and developed into the principal port of Spain. When later the importance of the town had declined, the improvement of the Río Guadalquivir brought seagoing trade back to Seville. In 1992 a world exhibition – "Eppo 92" is to be staged in Seville; and at the same time the 500th anniversary of the discovery will be celebrated.

Seville was the birthplace of two famous painters, *Diego Velázquez* (1599–1660) and *Bortolomé Esteban Murillo* (1617–82). Numerous tablets in the streets commemorate scenes from Cervantes's writings, and Seville is also the setting of a number of famous operas. The action of Mozart's "Don Giovanni" and "Marriage of Figaro" and Bizet's "Carmen" takes place in the town, while several streets claim the honour of having the shop which features in Rossini's "Barber of Seville".

SIGHTS. – The central point of the town is the *Plaza de San Francisco*, formerly the scene of tournaments, bullfights, etc. On the W side of the Square is the **Ayun-

Seville Cathedral

1	Puerta Mayor	25	Tomb of Fernando Colón
2	Puerta del Bautismo	26	Coro
3	Sagrario	27	Capilla Mayor
4	Puerta del Perdón	28	Sacristía Alta
5	Biblioteca Colombina	29	Capilla del Bautisterio
6	Puerta de Oriente	30	Capilla de Escalas
7	Capilla de la Granada	31	Capilla de Santiago
8	Puerta del Lagarto	32	Capilla Sacramental
9	Giralda	33	Capilla de San Francisco
10	Puerta de los Palos	34	Capilla de las Doncellas
11	Sala Capitular	35	Capilla de los Evangelistas
12	Capilla Real	36	Capilla del Pilar
13	Sacristía	37	Capilla de San Pedro
14	Puerta de las Campanillas	38	Capilla de la Concepcion Grande
15	Contaduría Mayor		
16	Sala Capitular	39	Capilla del Mariscal
17	Antecabildo	40	Antesala
18	Sacristía Mayor	41	Capilla de San Andrés
19	Sacristía de los Cálices	42	Capilla de Dolores
20	Puerta de San Cristóbal	43	Tomb of Columbus
21	Dependencias de la Hermandad Sacramental	44	Capilla de la Antigua
		45	Capilla de San Hermenegildo
22	Capilla de Santa Ana	46	Capilla de San José
23	Capilla de San Laureano		
24	Puerta del Nacimiento o Portal de San Miguel		

tamiento (Town Hall), a handsome Renaissance building (1527–64), the E front of which ranks as one of the finest achievements of the Plateresque style. To the W of the Ayuntamiento extends the spacious *Plaza Nueva*, shaded by palms and surrounded by banks and offices.

A short distance S of the Ayuntamiento, on a site occupied in Moorish times by the principal mosque, is the ****Cathedral** (1402–1506), one of the largest and richest Gothic cathedrals in Christendom, unmatched in its impressive spatial effect and its abundance of artistic treasures. The finest of its doorways, all richly decorated with statues and reliefs, are the Puerta Mayor (the central doorway on the W front), the Puerta de San Cristóbal (also known as the Puerta de la Lonja) in the S transept, and the Puerta de las Campanillas and the Puerta de los Palos, both on the E side. – Between the Puerta de los Palos and the Puerta de Oriente, which leads into the Patio de los Naranjos, at the NE corner of the Cathedral, is the **Giralda**, the 93 m high tower which is Seville's most prominent landmark. It was built in 1184–96 as the minaret of the Great Mosque; the bell-chamber added in 1568 is topped by a weathervane 4 m high, the *Giraldillo*, in the form of a female figure carrying the banner of Constantine who represents Faith. From the first gallery, with 24 bells, there are wide views of the city and surrounding area, particularly fine in the evening. Above this gallery is the Matraca (not open to the public), a timber structure 70 m from the ground containing the rattles which are used during Holy Week instead of bells.

The INTERIOR (117 m long, 76 m wide, 40 m high, with five aisles) is one of the most impressive among the Gothic churches of Spain, notable for the clarity of its proportions and the beauty of its lines as well as for the abundance of art treasures it contains (only a selection of which can be mentioned here). Of the 75 stained glass windows (16th–19th c.) the oldest are those by Cristóbal Alemán (1504) and Arnao de Flandes (1525–57). Particularly notable among the numerous *altarpieces* are two by Murillo, the "Guardian Angel" to the right of the Puerta Mayor and another in the second chapel in the N aisle, with the "Baptism of Christ" and *"The Infant Christ appearing to St Antony of Padua". At the W end of the nave is the *tombstone of Fernando Colón*, Columbus's son (d. 1539). – The Choir has a beautiful grille (1519) and Gothic stalls (1475–79). – In the adjoining **Capilla Mayor**, which also has a large and richly decorated grille (16th c.), is a magnificent *retablo* (*c.* 1550), a masterpiece of Gothic wood-carving; in the centre is a silver image of the Virgen de la Sede, surrounded by 45 carved wood scenes from the life of Christ and the life of the Virgin.

In the *S transept*, just inside the Puerta de San Cristóbal, is the *monument of Columbus* (by Arturo Mélida), originally erected in Havana Cathedral in 1892 but moved to Santiago after Cuba declared its independence in 1898. In the *Sacristía de los Cálices* is a famous *crucifix by Montañes, together with numerous paintings, including works by Goya and Zubarán. – The **Sacristía Mayor** (entered through an antechamber: charge), a splendid structure (begun 1532) with a beautiful domed ceiling, contains a number of excellent pictures and the rich *Cathedral treasury* (Relicario y Tesoro), including the key of Seville (1248). – In the SE corner of the Cathedral is the Plateresque *Sala Capitular* (chapterhouse), built between 1530 and 1592.

At the E end of the Cathedral is the **Capilla Real**, a Renaissance structure 38 m long with a high dome (1551–75) built on the site of an earlier royal funerary chapel. Behind the grille (1773) are the tombs of King Alfonso the Wise (d. 1284) and his mother Beatrice of Swabia. In the apse are two altars: one in front with a silver *shrine* containing the remains of St Ferdinand (1729), and one to the rear with the Virgen de los

Reyes (13th c.), patroness of the town. Adjoining the front altar is a flight of steps leading down to the *Panteón*, with the tombs of Pedro the Cruel, his wife María de Padilla and a number of infantes. To the left of the Capilla Real is the Puerta de los Palos.

On the N side of the Cathedral, to the left, is the **Sagrario**, a fine Baroque structure (1618–62), now used as the parish church, which is entered through the Puerta del Sagrario; retablo with a "Deposition" by Pedro Roldán. – Adjoining the Sagrario, entered through the beautiful Puerta de los Naranjos, is the *Patio de los Naranjos** ("Court of Orange-Trees"), originally the courtyard of the mosque. The octagonal Visigothic fountain in the centre is a remnant of the Muslim *midha*, the fountain for religious ablutions. On the N side of the courtyard is the imposing *Puerta del Perdón*, the main entrance from outside, which dates from the Moorish period. In the SE corner of the courtyard is the *Capilla de la Granada*, with horseshoe arches, another relic of the old mosque. – On the E side is the **Biblioteca Colombina**, a library founded in the 13th c. but enriched by a bequest from Columbus. It contains rare works on the discovery of America and valuable manuscripts.

S of the Cathedral is the *Plaza del Triunfo*, with a monument to the Immaculate Conception (1917). On the SW side of the square is the **Casa Lonja**, the former Exchange, a High Renaissance building by Juan de Herrera (1583–98), on the first floor of which is the *Archivo General de Indias* (General Archives of the Indies), founded in 1781, with 46,000 files (*legajos*) of documents relating to the discovery, conquest and administration of America and the Philippines (autographed documents of Magellan, Pizarro, Cortés and Columbus). Nearby, to the E, is the Museo de Arte Contemporáneo.

Street scene, Seville

On the SE side of the Plaza del Triunfo is the *Alcázar, the stronghold of the Moorish and later of the Christian kings; the present building, still with the aspect of a medieval fortress, was built for Pedro the Cruel in the second half of the 14th c. by Moorish architects. The entrance, on the SE side of the square, leads into the *Patio de las Banderas*, planted with orange-trees, and through the *Jardín del Crucero* into the *Patio de la Montería*, the courtyard of the royal bodyguard, on the S side of which is the richly articulated *main front of the main Alcázar building.

The *INTERIOR is entered through the *Puerta Principal*, which leads along a passage into the Patio de las Doncellas (Court of the Maids of Honour), built 1369–79, with magnificent cusped arches and open-work upper walls borne on 52 marble columns. Beyond these are the *Salón de Carlos V*, the *Apartments of María de Padilla* and the *Salón de Embajadores* (Hall of the Ambassadors), with three handsome doorways and a splendid dome (1420). Beyond the long *Comedor* (Dining Room) is the *Patio de las Muñecas* (Court of the Dolls), the upper part of which is modern. Adjoining are the *Dormitorio de Isabel la Católica* (the Queen's Bedroom), the *Cuarto de los Principes* and the *Dormitorio de los Reyes Moros*. – On the upper floor there are very fine tapestries. – The *Alcázar Gardens, laid out by Charles V, are divided into two halves by a rocaille wall. Among their many features are underground *Baños* (Baths) and the *Pabellón de Carlos V*, built by Juan Hernández in 1540.

From the N side of the Plaza de San Francisco the narrow *Calle de las Sierpes* ("Street of the Snakes"), the town's principal shopping street (pedestrian precinct), runs N, lined by shops, cafés and clubs. Off to the right is the 16th c. church of **San Salvador**, rebuilt at the end of the 18th c. and decorated in Churrigueresque style. In Calle de la Cuna, which runs N from Plaza San Salvador, is the *Palacio Lebrija*, with a small private museum of Roman sculpture. Farther N, off this street to the right, is the **University** (Old University), founded in 1502, with the 16th c. *University Church*, which has a large retablo and paintings by Roelas, Alonso, Cano, Pacheco and others. – 500 m E of San Salvador, at the far end of Calle de Águilas, is the Plaza de Pilatos, with the 16th c. *Casa de Pilatos*, built by Christian and Moorish architects, which is popularly believed to be a copy of Pilate's house in Jerusalem. It reveals a variant of the Mudéjar style, modified by Gothic and Renaissance features. In the beautiful patio are a number of pieces of ancient sculpture. – From Plaza de Pilatos the Calle de Caballerizas runs NW to the twin-towered Baroque church of *San*

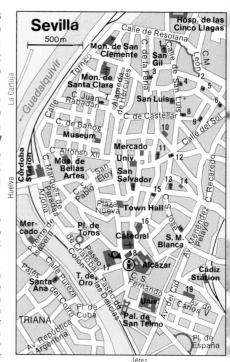

1   Puerta Macarena
2   Puerta de Córdoba
3   Omnium Sanctorum
4   Santa Marina
5   San Julián
6   Santa Lucia
7   San Lorenzo
8   San Marcos
9   Convento de Santa Paula
10   Palacio de las Dueñas

11   San Pedro
12   Santa Catalina
13   San Ildefonso
14   Casa de Pilatos
15   San Isidoro
16   Palacio Arzobispal
17   Hospital
      de la Caridad
18   Casa Lonja
19   Bus station

Ildefonso, from which the Calle de los Descalzos leads to the *Plaza del Cristo de Burgos*. On the NW side of this square is the Gothic church of **San Pedro** (14th c.), with a beautiful Mudéjar tower and a fine interior ("St Peter Freed from Prison" by Roelas). A short distance E of San Pedro is the church of *Santa Catalina*, with a tower which was originally a minaret. To the NW is the *Palacio de las Dueñas*, with a beautiful Mudéjar *patio.

The line of Calle de las Sierpes is continued N, past the *Plaza del Duque*, to the *Alameda de Hércules*, a fine promenade laid out in gardens, at the S end of which are two tall granite columns from a Roman temple, erected here in 1574, bearing statues of Hercules and Julius Caesar. To the W is the church of **San Lorenzo**, with a beautiful high altar and a much venerated figure of "Nuestro Señor del Gran Poder" in a side chapel. – On the N side of the old town, between the *Puerta de Córdoba* and the *Puerta de la Marcarena*, is a considerable stretch of the old *town walls*, built on Roman foundations. Against the Puerta de la Macarena stands the church of *San Gil*, with the popular Virgen de la Macarena.

In the western part of the old town, reached from the Plaza del Duque by way of Calle de Alfonso XII, is the 17th c. *Convento de la Merced*, which now houses the ***Museo de Bellas Artes**, with 20 rooms displaying a magnificent collection of Spanish painting, particularly of the 17th c.

In Room IV is *El Greco's* portrait of his son Jorge Manuel. In Rooms VI, VII and VIII (in the convent church) are works by *Juan de Roelas, Zurbarán* (including his "Apotheosis of St Thomas Aquinas", 1631) and *Murillo*, who is well represented with three Immaculate Conceptions and the 'Vision of St Francis". In the cloister are works by other Andalusian Baroque painters, and on the upper floor are several works by Valdés Leal and pictures by 19th c. Spanish artists.

Along the SW side of the old town, on the left bank of the Guadalquivir, extends the *Paseo de Cristóbal Colón*, beginning at the *Puente de Isabel II*. From here the port installations run S to the Paseo de las Delicias. On the left is the *Plaza de Toros* (Bullring), and beyond this the Plaza de Jurado, laid out in gardens. On the E side of this square is the **Hospital de la Caridad** (1661–64), founded by Miguel de Mañara, who is supposed to have been the prototype of Don Juan. From a pillared courtyard we enter the *church*, the façade of which is decorated with fine azulejo panels. In the church are pictures by Valdés Leal (at the entrance) and six *paintings by Murillo (in the nave). – S of the Plaza Jurado, on the river, is the **Torre del Oro** (1220; in part 1760), a Moorish

defensive tower which was originally covered with gold azulejos. Later used by Pedro the Cruel as a treasury and prison, it now houses a *Maritime Museum*, with an *aquarium and a good view from the top.

On the long *Paseo de las Delicias*, near the *Puente de San Telmo*, is the **Palacio de San Telmo**, built in 1734 as a naval college, with a tall Baroque doorway: it is now occupied by the *Universidad Pontífica*, a seminary for the training of priests. To the E, in Calle de San Fernando, is the former *Fábrica de Tabacos* (Tobacco Factory), a Baroque building erected in 1757, now used as lecture rooms of the University. – Calle de San Fernando runs into the busy *Plaza de Juan de Austria*, to the N of which are the extensive Alcázar Gardens. Beyond the gardens, to the left, is the picturesque ***Santa Cruz** quarter, which during the Moorish period was the Jewish quarter (*Judería*), with squares and streets gay with flowers, beautiful courtyards and the church of *Santa Maria la Blanca*, which until 1391 was a synagogue (ceiling paintings of 1659).

To the S of the Plaza de Juan de Austria is the main entrance to the large ***Parque de María Luisa**, laid out by the Infanta María Luisa Fernanda de Borbón. The Ibero-American Exhibition was held in the park in 1929–30, and a number of buildings still remain – the *Palacio Centrale*, with two towers 82 m high at the corners, in the semicircular *Plaza de España* and the *Pabellón Mudéjar*, the *Pabellón Real* and the *Palacio del Renacimiento* in the *Plaza de América*. The last of these now houses the **Museo Arqueológico**, with prehistoric and Roman antiquities, including a statue of Diana and material from Itálica (see p. 212).

On the right bank of the Guadalquivir is the **Triana** district, mainly a working-class and gipsy quarter, which has been the home of many famous bullfighters. It has also been from time immemorial the potters' quarter of Seville, producing the best azulejos in the city. To the left of the Puente de Isabel II is the Mudéjar-style church of *Santa Ana*, built by Alfonso the Wise, which contains a "Virgen de la Rosa" by Alejo Fernández. – Farther upstream is the **Cartuja**, a former Carthusians house founded in 1401. Its church of *Nuestra Señora de las Cuevas* has an interesting cloister.

In the Judería, Seville

SURROUNDINGS. – As the ancient capital of Andalusia, Seville lies in the centre of a region which has been the scene of great events over the centuries, and there are many places of historical interest within easy reach of the town.

To Itálica. – From the motorway which runs W from Seville over the Guadalquivir turn right into N 630, leading N to (8 km) the village of **Santiponce** (alt. 18 m), with the much dilapidated monastery of San Isidoro del Campo, founded in 1298 by Guzmán el Bueno. The church has a beautiful Gothic altar of carved wood and contains the tombs of the founder and his wife. – 1 km farther on, to the left of the road, is *Itálica, the site of a Roman town founded by Scipio Africanus the Elder in 205 B.C., with the interesting remains of an amphitheatre and traces of houses and fountains. The fine mosaics found here are now in the Archaeological Museum in Seville. The town was the birthplace of the Emperors Trajan (A.D. 53) and Hadrian (A.D. 76).

To Sanlúcar la Mayor. – N 431 (the Huelva road) runs W to *Castilleja de la Cuesta* (pop. 3500), where Hernán Cortés, conqueror of Mexico, died in 1547. Beyond this, 20 km from Seville, is **Sanlúcar la Mayor** (alt. 145 m; pop. 6000), situated on a hill: a former Moorish settlement with a ruined castle and the church of Santa María (1214), the tower of which was originally a minaret.

To Córdoba. – N IV (motorway for the first stretch) runs NE past the airport and through a fertile hilly region to (30 km) **Carmona** (alt. 215 m; pop. 30,000), the Roman *Carmo* and the Moorish *Karmuna*, an old-world country town situated on a bare ridge rising above the rich Vega de los Corbones and dominated by its Alcázar (from which there are extensive views). On the right-hand side of the main road through the town is the church of San Pedro, with a tower resembling the Giralda in Seville. To the left (signposted "Necrópolis Romana") is a *Roman cemetery* with more than 900 tombs, some of them having an atrium and triclinia (couches) for the funeral meal; the most notable of these is the Triclinio del Elefante. Notable also is the large Tumba de Servilia. From the terrace of the small museum (material from the site, collection of vases) there is a very fine view.

Farther along the road there is a good *view back to Carmona. N IV continues E to the straggling settlement of *La Luisiana* and through a gently rolling region known as the "frying-pan (*sartén*) of Andalusia" on account of its torrid summers to *Écija (see p. 117: bypass). It then crosses the Río Genil and runs NE via *La Carlota* to **Córdoba** (se p. 104), 139 km from Seville.

To Antequera. – N 334 (motorway) runs SE over the fertile Andalusian plain to (16 km) **Alcalá de Guadaira** (alt. 37 m; pop. 35,000), on the right bank of the Río Guadaira (bypass). Ruins of a Moorish castle with underground corn-stores; church of San Miguel, originally a mosque; old Moorish mills in the vicinity.

The road continues over the plain, with its extensive cornfields, flanked on the N by the Sierra Morena and on the S by the *Serranía de Ronda*, to the ancient little town of *El Arahal*. Beyond this a road goes off on the left to (7 km) *Marchena* (alt. 103 m; pop. 20,000), situated on a hill, with old town walls, the palace of the Dukes of Arcos and the interesting church of San Juan (retablo of 1500). – N 334 continues via *La Puebla de Cazalla* to **Osuna** (alt. 450 m; pop. 25,000), the Roman *Urso* and the Moorish *Oxuna*, picturesquely situated on the slopes of a hill. Remains of the palace of the Dukes of Osuna; collegiate church (1534), with a "Christ on the Cross" by Ribera. The former University, with four towers (1549–1824), which is mentioned in "Don Quixote", is now a school. Near the town is a *Roman cemetery*.

N 334 crosses the Río Blanco and continues via *Aguadulce* to **Estepa** (alt. 604 m; pop. 10,000), with several churches lies at the foot of the Sierra de Estepa.

At the railway junction of *La Roda de Andalucía* the road reaches the plateau of the *Sierra de Yeguas*, crosses the boundary of Málaga province and continues to **Antequera** (alt. 510 m; pop. 40,000; Parador Nacional, II, 55 r.), situated in the fertile valley of the *Río Guadalhorce* at the foot of the *Sierra del Torcal*. Above the town are the ruins of a Moorish castle. Church of Santa María la Mayor which has an interesting façade; the little Arco de Santa María (1585), with Roman inscriptions; Palacio Nájera, with a museum on the history of Antequera. – Near the town are the *dolmens* of Menga, Vera and El Romeral.

To Cádiz. – On the motorway or N IV, which run together for the first 13 km. – At the point where the two roads separate, off on the left, is **Dos Hermanas** (alt. 42 m; pop. 35,000), the scene of a famous pilgrimage on the third Sunday in October. – Farther S is *Los Palacios*, where a road branches off on the left to (13 km) **Utrera** (alt. 6 m; pop. 36,000), a prosperous little town with several Gothic churches, including Santa María de la Asunción (14th c.). On the outskirts of the town is the church of Nuestra Señora de la Consolación, with a miracle-working image of the Virgin, the object of a great pilgrimage in September. – Then on via **Jerez de la Frontera** to **Cádiz** (see p. 90), 133 km from Seville.

Sierra de Gredos

Federación Española de Montañismo (Spanish Climbing Federation), Alberto Aguilera 3, Madrid 15; tel. (91) 2 23 47 82.

The *Sierra de Gredos thrusts across the Castilian plateau like a mighty rock wall, dividing it into two. With the lower heights of the neighbouring Sierra de Guadarrama and Sierra de Béjar it forms the central Spanish mountain chain.

The central massif of the Sierra de Gredos, with its peaks covered by perpetual snow, is a region of magnificent scenery and one of the most popular climbing areas in Spain. The highest peak is *Almanzor* (2592 m). At the foot of the N face of this mountain is the *Laguna de Gredos*, reached from the Club Alpino hut (no services) by a beautiful and well-marked path. From the Laguna de Gredos there are poorly way-marked paths (caution

El Barco de Ávila

Sierra Nevada

ⓘ Estación de Esquí Sierra Nevada,
Plaza de Pradollano s/n (Sierra Nevada),
Granada;
tel. (958) 48 10 00

HOTELS. – IN SOLYNIEVE: *Meliá Sierra Nevada*, I, 221 r.; *Meliá Sol y Nieve* (no rest.), II, 178 r; *Nevasur*, III, 50 r. – ON THE PICO DE VELATA ROAD: *Parador Nacional Sierra Nevada*, II, 32 r. – ON THE GRANADA ROAD (km 21): Hostal *El Nogal*, P I, 37 r.

The *Sierra Nevada is a massive mountain chain extending for a distance of almost 110 km between the Río Almería and the Valle de Lecrín, with the highest peaks in the Iberian peninsula, the Cerro de Mulhacén (3481 m) and the *Pico de Veleta (3428 m).

From November to June the Sierra Nevada offers magnificent facilities for winter sports and as the most southerly winter sports region in Europe usually has a blue sky and brilliant sunshine as well as snow. Throughout the area much effort has been devoted to improving the available facilities, with ski-lifts and ski schools: the existing pistes are constantly supervised and are being extended. In addition to hotels there are numerous mountain huts provided by various skiing and climbing organisations.

required) to five picturesque mountain lakes, the *Cinco Lagunas*, and Almanzor, rearing above them to the S.

The Sierra de Gredos lies mostly within the southern part of Ávila province, and can be reached from Ávila by way of the *Puerto de Menga* (1570 m), in the Sierra de la Paramera, and the little township of *Venta del Obispo*. On C 500, which runs along the N side of the sierra through the high valley of the *Río* Alberche, is the ***Parador Nacional de Gredos** (alt. 1650 m; 62 km from Ávila), a popular winter sports resort magnificently situated in the wooded foreland of the sierra, with beautiful views of the mountains. Much of this region, which is well stocked with wild life (ibexes), is now a national park.

To the Pico de Veleta. – An enchanting trip (which can be made by bus) into the glorious mountain world of the Sierra Nevada on a good asphalt road which climbs from 640 m to a height of 3392 m, making it one of the highest mountain roads in Europe. This continuous ascent of almost 35 km, without any shelter from the sun, calls for an early start, and warm clothing should be taken for protection from the cold and the wind on the top. A striking feature of the run is

Among places of interest in the Sierra de Gredos are:
El Barco de Ávila (alt. 1014 m), attractively situated on the right bank of the Río Tormes, with a Gothic church and a 14th c. castle.
Mombeltrán, with another beautiful Gothic church and the 14th c. castle of the Dukes of Alburquerque, one of the most typical of Castile's old medieval castles.
Arenas de San Pedro (alt. 510 m), a health resort and a good climbing centre. Gothic parish church (14th c.); convent of San Pedro de Alcántara (17th c.), with a pretty chapel; Castillo de la Triste Condesa ("Castle of the Sorrowful Countess").

In the extreme SW of the Sierra, 64 km from Arenas, is the ***Monasterio de Yuste** (*San Jerónimo de Yuste*), founded in 1404, devastated by the French in 1809 and later partly restored, which is famous as the last retreat of the Emperor Charles V, who abdicated in favour of his son Philip II in 1556 and retired here in 1557, dying in the monastery in the following year. The *palace* which he occupied is interesting, and there are beautiful views from the covered terrace of the fertile landscape which extends to the Sierra de Guadalupe.

The Sierra Nevada in summer

Granada

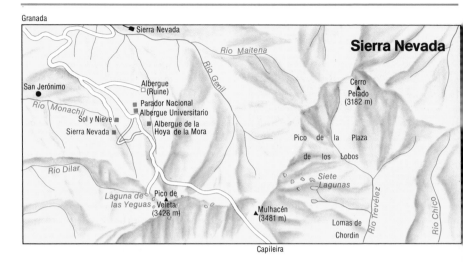

the contrast between the lush southern landscape of the Vega de Granada and the snow-capped peaks of the mountains.

From Granada the road runs E along the slopes above the right bank of the *Río Genil* to (6 km) *Cenes de la Vega* (alt. 737 m). Farther up the valley the road crosses the river, passes a side road on the left to *Pinos Genil* and winds its way uphill, with gradients of 8–12 per cent, between slopes which are still covered with olive-groves; magnificent views down the valley, extending in some places as far as Granada. After 20 km or so the road reaches the 1500 m contour, and soon afterwards the trees disappear. In another 8 km the 2000 m contour is reached. This is the beginning of the winter sports region of **Solynieve** (Sol y Nieve="Sun and Snow", at an altitude of between 2000 and 2600 m, with hotels, chalet colonies and blocks of flats, mountain huts, ski-lifts and cableways. – From Solynieve there is a road (4 km) to the hotel village of *Pradollano* (alt. 2100 m), from which there is a chair-lift E to the *Parador Nacional* (2500 m) and also a cabin cableway S to the hotel village of *Borreguiles* (2600 m): change here for the Pico de Veleta.

It is also possible to drive round the Solynieve region, remaining on the main road and bearing left to reach the *Parador Nacional Sierra Nevada*, beyond which,

off the road to the left, is the *Residencia Universitaria* (alt. 2550 m). The road to the Pico de Veleta continues through rugged mountain scenery and comes to a side road on the right which leads in 2 km to a beautiful mountain lake, the *Laguna de las Yeguas* (alt. 2970 m; mountain hut). After another 5 km the road ends at an altitude of 3392 m on a rocky platform, with a revolving restaurant, only a short distance below the ***Pico de Veleta** (3428 m), the second highest peak in the Sierra Nevada.

From the Pico de Veleta a narrow unasphalted road winds up round the summit and then descends down in hairpin bends on the S side of Mulhacén to the picturesque village of *Capileira* (alt. 1436 m), 37 km from the Pico de Veleta, in the wild mountain region of the **Alpujarras**. From here there is a good road to (20 km) the beautifully situated little town of *Órgiva* (alt. 417 m; pop 6000), with the Palacio de los Condes de Sástago. The road continues W via the popular spa of *Lanjarón* (alt. 687 m; chalybeate water) to join N 323, which runs N to Granada and S through beautiful scenery to the Mediterranean (53 km from Órgiva).

Sigüenza

Province: Guadalajara (GU).
Telephone dialling code: 911.
Altitude: 982 m. – Population: 6000.
ⓘ **Oficina de Información de Turismo,**
Cardenal Mendoza 2;
tel. 39 12 62.

HOTELS. – *Parador Nacional Castillo de Sigüenza*, Plaza del Castillo, I, 77 r.; *Hostal El Doncel*, General Mola 1, P II, 16 r.; *Elías*, Alfonso VI 6, P III, 15 r.; *El Mesón*, Román Pascual 14, P III, 12 r.; *Venancio*, San Roque 1, P III, 17 r.

RESTAURANT. – *El Motor*, Calvo Sotelo 12.

The little episcopal town of Sigüenza, on the left bank of the Río Henares, can look back on a long history. As Segontia it was a Celtiberian base in 195 B.C. during the

The Sierra Nevada in winter

conflict with Rome, and under the Visigoths it became the seat of a bishop.

SIGHTS. – The ***Cathedral** (12th–14th c.) is one of the finest late Romanesque buildings in Spain. It has the appearance of a fortress and has elements of both Romanesque and Gothic-Plateresque architecture. Magnificent interior: Capilla de Santa Librada, with the tomb of the town's patron saint; Capilla del Doncel, with the tomb of a young nobleman named Vázquez de Arce (d. 1486); Capilla Mayor (retablo by Giraldo de Merlo, 1619); fine sacristy; chapterhouse, with an "Annunciation" by El Greco; Gothic cloister. – S of the Cathedral is the *Plaza Mayor*, with the *Ayuntamiento* (Town Hall), built in 1511. – From the Plaza Mayor we go past the church of *San Vicente* and the *Arco de San Juan* to reach the Castillo (12th c.) (now a Parador Nacional), from which there are very fine views.

Parador National "Castillo de Sigüenza"

Sitges

Province: Barcelona (B).
Telephone code: 93.
ⓘ Oficina de Informacíon de Turismo,
  Paseo Vilafranca;
  tel. 8 94 12 30.

HOTELS. – *Calipolis* (no rest.), Paseo Marítimo s/n, I, 163 r.; *Terramar* (no rest.), Paseo Marítimo s/n, I, 209 r., SP; *Antemare*, Avda Verge Montserrat 48, II, 72 r., SP; *Galeón*, San Francisco 44, II, 47 r., SP; *Los Pinos*, Paseo Marítimo s/n, II, 42 r., SP; *Arcadia* (no rest.), Socias 22, III, 38 r.; *Bahía*, Parelladas 27, III, 37 r.; *Caramelles* (no rest.), Francisco Guma 22, III, 28 r.; *Londres*, Juan Maragall 3, III 20 r.; *Picadilly* (no rest.), Espalter 29, III, 20 r.; *Platjador*, Paseo Ribera 35, III, 44 r.; *Sitges Park Hotel*, Jésus 12, III, 87 r., SP; *Subur*, España 1, III, 95 r.; *Alexandra* (no rest.), Pasaje Termes 1, IV, 26 r.; *Bertrán* (no rest.), Marqués de Montroig 11, IV, 67 r.; *Don Pancho* (no rest.), San José 2, IV, 85 r.; *Romantic*, San Isidro 23, IV, 55 r.; *San Francisco*, Santiago Rusiñol 8, IV, 48 r.; *Sitges* (no rest.), San Guadenci 5, IV, 52 r.; Hostal *La Reserva*,

Paseo Marítimo 62, P I, 24 r.; *Casa Munich*, Enrique Morera 16, P II, 29 r., SP; etc.

RESTAURANTS. – In hotels; also **El Greco*, Paseo de la Ribera 72 (English style); **Fragata*, Paseo de la Ribera 1; *Mare Nostrum*, Paseo de la Ribera 60, *Vivero*, Paseo Balmins. – ON THE ROAD TO SAN PEDRO DE RIBAS: **Vallpineda* (with garden and terrace).

CAMPING SITES. – Several sites in and around Sitges, including *El Rocá*, *Sitges* and *Garraf*.

WATER SPORTS. – 4 km long beach of fine sand, with calm sea; boating harbour.

The attractive little port of Sitges, now a popular seaside resort, is also noted for its wine (Malvasía). – It lies on the Costa Dorada between Barcelona and Tarragona.

SIGHTS. – On the Playa, in a house once occupied by the painter Santiago Rusiñol, is the *Museo Cau Ferrat*, with Spanish metalwork, pottery, pictures by El Greco and others, drawings by Picasso, etc. – From the 18th c. Baroque *church*, which stands on high ground, there are beautiful views. – The *Museo Romántico Provincial*, in an old patrician house, displays decorative art, furniture, dolls, etc.

Soria

Province: Soria (SO).
Telephone code: 975.
Altitude: 1063 m. – Population: 28,000.
ⓘ Oficina de Información de Turismo,
  Plaza Ramón y Cajal;
  tel. 21 20 52.
  Delagación Territorial de Turismo,
  Alfonso VIII 1;
  tel. 22 48 55.

HOTELS. – *Parador Nacional Antonio Machado*, Parque del Castillo, II, 34 r.; *Alfonso VIII*, Alfonso VIII 10, II, 103 r.; *Caballeros* (no rest.), Eduardo Saavedra 4, II, 84 r.; *Mesón Leonor*, Paseo de Mirón, II, 32 r.; *Las Heras*, Plaza Ramón y Cajal 5, IV, 24 r.; *Hostal Cadosa*, km 146 on N 122, P I, 76 r.; *Comercio*, Plaza de los Jurados, P II, 30 r.; *Casa Diocesana Pio XII*, San Juán 5, P III, 51 r.; etc. – CAMPING SITE: *Fuente de la Teja*, 1 km S on N 111.

RESTAURANTS. – *El Arco*, Zapatería 23; *Casa Garrido*, Vicente Tutor 8; *Mesón Castellano*, Plaza Mayor 2; etc. – ON N 122: *Cadosa*, 6 km E.

EVENTS. – *Fiestas de San Juan* (June), in honour of St John and the Virgin; bullfights, in which each *cuadrilla* of the town supplies a bull.

Soria, a provincial capital in the bleak upper valley of the Río Duero, on the right bank of the river, is an

San Juan de Rabanera, Soria

old-world town with many fine Romanesque buildings.

HISTORY. – The origins of the town are obscure. Alfonso el Batallador, king of Aragon, recovered it from the Arabs, and soon afterwards it became part of the kingdom of Castile. A number of noted Spanish writers lived in the town, including the great lyric poet Antonio Machado.

SIGHTS. – Outstanding among the town's many churches is the 13th c. **San Juan de Duero**, outside the town on the left bank of the river. It originally belonged to a house of the Templars and has a very individual *cloister* (Romanesque and Gothic). Small *Museo Celtibérico*. – From here we cross the river to reach the *Cathedral of San Pedro* (12th–16th c.), with a beautiful Plateresque doorway and a Romanesque cloister (12th c.). In the Capilla de San Saturio is a Flemish triptych (1559) with a representation of the Crucifixion. – From San Pedro the Calle Obispo Augustín leads W to the grandiose *Palacio de los Condes de Gómara*, a 16th c. Renaissance building with an elegant square tower. Close by is the church of **San Juan de Rabanera** (12th c., Byzantine-Romanesque), with a *tympanum* from the church of San Nicolás; *retablo* by Juan de Baltanás and Francisco de Ágreda. – To the N is the church of **Santo Domingo** (second half of 12th c.), with a richly decorated Romanesque *façade*; imposing retablo, interesting sculpture. – In Plaza General Yagüe is the *Museo Numantino*, an archaeological museum with Iberian and Roman material from nearby Numancia (see below). – On top of the hill are the ruins of a castle (fine views), with the Parador Nacional.

SURROUNDINGS. – There are many Celtiberian and Roman sites in the area round Soria. On a steep hill 8 km N of the town are the remains of **Numancia**, marked by an obelisk 17 m high. This was the site of a fortified Celtiberian town, noted for its heroic resistance to the Romans for many years until its final destruction by the consul P. Cornelius Scipio Aemilianus in 133 B.C. Excavations were carried out between 1905 and 1912 by Professor Schulten of Erlangen University.

To Ágreda. – The road E from Soria comes in 5 km to a fork, from which N 122 runs NE over the *Puerto del Madero* (1140 m) to **Ágreda** (alt. 950 m; pop. 4000), an ancient little town on a rocky crag on the frontiers of Castile and Aragon, with many fine old buildings. Above the town is the Castilo de la Muela. Churches of Nuestra Señora de la Peña, with Gothic panel paintings; San Miguel, with a Renaissance painting; Nuestra Señora de los Milagros (16th c.), with a 15th c. Gothic retablo. Near the town is a medieval watch-tower.

Towards Madrid. – N 111 runs S, at first following the course of the *Río Duero*, and then over the fairly monotonous plateau of the *Pinares de Almazán*, then crosses a bridge of 13 arches, 163 m long, and enters **Almazán** (alt. 950 m; pop. 5000), on the left bank of the Duero, with the remains of its old walls and gates, the 16th c. Palacio Hurtado de Mendoza and several old churches, originally Romanesque. Among them is the church of San Miguel (national monument), with reliefs depicting the martyrdom of St Thomas Becket on the front of the altar. – The road then continues via *Adradas*, in the *Sierra de Ontalvilla*, and over the *Puerto de Radona* (1150 m) to **Medinaceli** (see p. 169). Here N 111 runs into N II, which continues towards Madrid, going over the *Cuestas de Esteras* pass (1150 m) to enter the province of Guadalajara.

To Segovia. – N 122 runs W from Soria and almost immediately branches off to run SW, climbs to the *Altos de Villaciervos* (1200 m) and runs down to **Calatañazor** (off the road to the right), a little medieval town on a hill with its old town walls, charming half-timbered buildings and a ruined castle.

The road continues SW to **El Burgo de Osma** (see p. 85). At *San Esteban de Gormaz* N 110 goes off on the left, crosses the Duero and climbs up to the *Altos de Ayllón* (1100 m). Soon after the pass it crosses the provincial boundary and continues towards **Segovia** (see p. 203), 194 km from Soria.

Tafalla

Province: Navarre (NA).
Telephone code: 948.
Altitude: 426 m. – Population: 8000.
(i) **Ayuntamiento** (Town Hall),
    Plaza Navarra 7;
    tel. 70 00 92.

HOTELS. – *Tafalla*, on the Pamplona–Zaragoza road, P II, 30 r. – IN OLITE: *Parador Nacional Príncipe de Viana*, II, 48 r.; *Hostal Castillo*, P III, 8 r.

RESTAURANT. – *Tubal*, Plaza de Navarra 2 (first floor).

EVENTS. – *Ferias de Ganado* (Feb.), with an agricultural show. – *Patronal festival* (Aug.), the town's principal festival, with folk performances and bullfights with young bulls.

Tafalla lies on the W bank of the Río Cidacos, dominated by the ruins of a 14th c. royal castle.

SIGHTS. – The town has a number of old palaces and interesting churches, including the Romanesque church of **Santa María**, with a splendid *retablo* by Juan de Anchieta (16th c.). In the *Monasterio de la Oliva* (*c.* 1740) is a high altar by the Flemish artist Roland de Moys.

SURROUNDINGS. – 8 km E on C 132 is **San Martín de Unx**, with a fine 12th c. fortified church. – 6 km S on N 121 is the old-world title little town of **Olite** (see p. 185).

Talavera de la Reina

Province: Toledo (TO).
Telephone code: 925.
Altitude: 351 m. – Population: 60,000.
(i) **Ayuntamiento** (Town Hall),
General Primo de Rivera;
tel. 80 53 00.

HOTELS. – *Beatriz*, Avda Madrid 1, II, 161 r.; *León*, km 119 on the Estramadura road, II, 30 r.; *Perales* (no rest.), Avda Pío XII 3, 65 r.; *Talavera*, Avda Gregorio Ruiz 1, III, 80 r.; *Auto-Estación*, Avda de Toledo 1, IV, 40 r.; Hostal *Edán*, Avda General Yague, P II, 12 r.; *Sierra* (no rest.), Ronda del Cañillo 31, P III, 11 r.

Talavera de la Reina, known to the Romans as Caesarobriga, lies on the Río Tajo (Tagus), S of the Sierra de Gredos. It is noted for its embroidery and its pottery.

SIGHTS. – Notable features of the town are the *Torres Albarranas*, square Moorish towers with remains of the triple wall system of the Arab period and of the original Roman walls. – Gothic collegiate church of *Santa María la Mayor* (13th–15th c.), in Mudéjar style, with a Gothic rose window. – To the N is the old convent church of **Santo Domingo** (14th c.), with an interesting façade and Renaissance tombs. – To the E of the town is the *Ermita de la Virgen del Prado*, faced with Talavera tiles of the 16th–18th c.; retablo of 1571. – The **Museo Ruiz de Luna** displays pottery of the 15th–19th c. – 15th c. bridge over the Tajo (35 arches).

Tarazona

Province: Zaragoza (Z).
Telephone code: 976.
Altitude: 475 m. – Population: 12,000.
(i) **Ayuntamiento** (Town Hall);
tel. 64 01 00.

HOTELS. – *Brujas de Becquer* (no rest.), km 44 on N 122, III, 60 r.; *Hostal María Cristina* (no rest.), Carretera Castilla 3, P III, 5 r.

The little episcopal town of Tarazona is picturesquely situated on the Río Queiles to the N of the Sierra de Moncayo, which rises to over 2300 m.

SIGHTS. – Notable *Cathedral** (12th–13th c.), with a beautiful N doorway; fine retablos and tombs. Large *cloister* in Mudéjar style (14th c.). – *Palacio Episcopal* (Bishop's Palace) of the 14th–15th c., once a palace of the kings of Aragon, with an artesonado ceiling. – *Ayuntamiento* (Town Hall, 16th c.), with a high-relief carving on the façade. – Several old churches, including *San Francisco* (16th c.), *La Magdalena* (Mudéjar tower) and *La Merced* (17th c.).

Tarragona

Province: Tarragona (T).
Telephone code: 977.
Altitude: 60 m. – Population: 100,000.
(i) **Oficina Municipal de Turismo,**
Calle Mayor 39;
tel. 23 48 12.
Servicio Territorial de Turismo,
Rambla Nova 25;
tel. 20 30 34.

HOTELS. – *Imperial Tarraco*, Rambla Vella 2, I, 170 r., SP; *Astari*, Vía Augusta 95, II, 83 r., SP; *Lauria* (no rest.), Lauria 4, II, 72 r., SP; *París* (no rest.), Maragall 4, III, 45 r.; *Sant Jordi* (no rest.), Vía Augusta s/n, III, 40 r.; *España* (no rest.), Rambla Nova 49, IV, 42 r.; *Marina* (no rest.), Vía Augusta 151, IV, 26 r.; *Nuria*, Vía Augusta 217, IV, 61 r.; *Urbis* (no rest.), Reding 20, IV, 58 r.; Hostal *El Callejón* (no rest.), Vía Augusta 213, P III, 18 r.; etc. Several CAMPING SITES.

RESTAURANTS. – In hotels; also *Roger de Lauria*, Rambla Nova 20 (first floor); *Iruña*, Caragena 1 (rustic style); *La Puda*, Muelle Pescadores 25 (view of harbour; fish dishes); *Club Náutico*, Muelle de Costa (on harbour); *Las Palmeras*, Paseo del Milagro (below the Balcón Mediterráneo); *Mesón del Mar*, Playa Large (4 km E); etc.

EVENTS. – *Fiesta de San Magín* (Aug.), procession with "holy water" in decorated carriages; folk

Tarragona

200 m

Mon. Santes Creus

	Ibero-Roman walls	A	Vaulting of circus	C	Amphitheatr
	Ancient remains (some underground)	B	Remains of ancient buildings	D	Forum

celebrations. – *Fiesta de Santa Tecla* (Sept.), patronal festival, also with procession and folk celebrations.

WATER SPORTS. – Swimming on the *Playa del Milagro*, below the Balcón del Mediterráneo, and on other beaches extending NE by way of *Rabasada* and *Sabinosa* to the *Punta de la Mora*; to the SE on the *Playa de la Pineda* and the neighbouring *Salou*.

The old port of Tarragona, famous for its wine, is capital of the Catalan province of the same name and the see of an archbishop. It is picturesquely situated, 100 km SW of Barcelona, on a hill rising 160 m above the sea which is crowned by the Cathedral, on the site of an ancient fortified settlement.

As an important centre of the wine trade Tarragona has numbers of large *bodegas* in which the wine grown in the Campo de Tarragona, the Campiña de Reus and the Priorato is stored. When the monks of the

Grande Chartreuse near Grenoble were expelled from their monastery they came to Tarragona and made their excellent liqueur here between 1903 and 1929.

HISTORY. – The origins of the ancient fortress on this rocky hill go back to the 3rd millennium B.C. The first town walls were built by an Iberian tribe, the Cerretani. After its conquest by the Romans in the second Punic War (218 B.C.) the town became the main Roman base in Spain, and in the time of Augustus it was made capital of the whole province of Spain. The remains of splendid buildings still testify to the wealth of ancient *Tarraco*. In later centuries the town was frequently destroyed – by the Visigoths in 475, by the Moors in 713 and most recently by the French in 1811.

SIGHTS. – The town's principal traffic artery is the broad tree-lined *Rambla Nova*. At the S end of this street is the **Balcón del Mediterráneo*, with panoramic views of the sea and the coast. From here a series of promenades, also affording fine views, extend eastwards, high above the sea, to the beaches. From the Balcón steps lead down to the *railway station* and the *harbour*, which is sheltered by the Dique de Levante, a breakwater 1700 m long (lighthouse). Below the Balcón is the *Parque del Milagro*, a municipal park containing the remains of a *Roman amphitheatre* of the Augustan period (excavated 1952). To the E is the beautiful *Paseo de las Palmetes*, laid out in terraces. At its far end, on the left, is the *Rambla Vella*, Tarragona's other main street, with the Baroque church of *San Agustín* and the church of *San Francisco*.

Half way along the Rambla Vella a street runs E into the elongated *Plaza de la Fuente*, on the site of the Roman circus; there are remains of foundations and vaulting in the adjoining houses. At the N end of the square stands the early 19th c. **Casa Consistorial** (Town Hall).

From the Plaza de la Fuente the *Bajada de la Misericordia* and its continuation, the narrow *Calle Mayor* (the main street of the ancient town), climb to the **Cathedral*, built on a site previously occupied by a Roman temple of Jupiter and a Moorish mosque. Mainly built in the 12th and 13th c., it is one of the most splendid examples in Spain of the transition from Romanesque to Gothic. On the W front (begun 1278; upper part left unfinished) is a deep *Gothic doorway* with rich sculptured decoration, flanked by massive buttresses, and above it is a magnificent rose window. The side doorways are also very fine.

Doorway of Tarragona Cathedral

The INTERIOR of the Cathedral creates an impression of great austerity. The *Choir* (14th c.) has carved stalls (1478–93) and an organ of 1563. The richly ornamented side altars are of various periods. Over the crossing is an octagonal dome, and the rose windows in the transepts have fine stained glass of 1574. – The *Capilla Mayor* has a *high altar with statues of the Virgin and Child, St Thecla and St Paul; delicate alabaster reliefs by Johan de Valfogona (1434). To the right of the altar is the *tomb of Archbishop Juan de Aragón (d. 1334). – At the E end of the N aisle is the *Capilla de los Sastres* (14th c.), with wall paintings and an early Gothic altar dedicated to the Virgin. To the left of the chapel is the entrance to the ***Cloister** (13th c.), one of the finest in Spain. – In the NE corner is the **Diocesan Museum**, with pictures, vestments, 52 *tapestries of the 15th–17th c. and ancient and medieval sculpture. – In the adjoining little church of **Santa Tecla** (12th c.) is the Museum's collection of tombstones and sculpture.

Just N of the Cathedral in the *Plaza del Palacio* is the early 19th c. *Palacio Arzobispal* (Archbishop's Palace), with an old defensive tower, the Torre del Paborde, which occupies the highest point in the town, on the site of the Roman *castrum* (fine views). In the courtyard of the palace are a number of tombstones.

The Paseo Arquelógico (Archaeological Walk). – From the N end of the Rambla Vella the Vía del Imperio runs E to the *Puerta del Rosario* (6th or 5th c. B.C.), the starting point of the *Paseo Arqueológico*, an interesting archaeological walk along the massive ****ancient cyclopean walls** (*murallas ciclópeas*). The walls, enclosing the highest part of the town, are preserved almost without interruption for a length of 1000 m, standing to heights of between 3 and 10 m. The lowest level, representing the remains of the Iberian town walls of about the 6th c. B.C., is built of huge irregular blocks up to 4 m long. Above this lie the Roman walls built by the Scipios from 218 B.C. onwards; native workmen were employed in the construction, and many of the stones bear Iberian masons' marks. Higher still are the remains of the Augustan walls. The six surviving gates date from the earliest period. In Plaza Pallol, inside the walls at the Puerta del Rosario, is the *Municipal Museum* (Museo de la Ciudad), containing Roman and medieval material. W of the Puerta del Rosario is a section of Moorish wall, built with blocks of rammed earth. – The Paseo Arqueológico, which is pleasantly shaded by cypresses and affords extensive views at each end, passes a bronze *statue of Augustus* (presented by Italy in 1934), the Torre del Paborde, and a *seminary* for the training of priests to the E end of the hill. From here the *Paseo Torroja* and *Paseo de San Antonio* lead past the *Puerta de San Antonio* (1757) to the ***Museo Arqueológico**, which with the adjoining *Pretorio Romano* (Praetor's Palace; also known as the Torreón de Pilatos) contains one of the finest collections in Spain of ancient and medieval material. Particularly notable items are a number of mosaics, pottery and an ivory doll of the 4th c., 23 cm (9 in.) long, which was found in a child's grave. NE on the Santa Ana road is the *Museum of Modern Art*.

From here, going SW, it is only a short distance to the SE end of the Rambla Vella. – Another attractive drive is N from the Puerta del Rosario past the *Campo de Marte*, a park containing an open-air theatre, and round the old town to the Puerta de San Antonio.

The western districts. – W of the Rambla Nova is the *Plaza Corsini*, near which are the remains of the *Roman forum* (entrance from Calle Lérida) and numerous Roman houses, dating from the time when Tarragona was capital of the province of Spain.

W of the town beyond the *Plaza de Toros* (Bullring, with seating for 17,500 spectators; magnificent views from top gallery), in the grounds of a tobacco factory, is an **early Christian cemetery** (3rd–6th c.), with the *Early Christian Museum* (Museo Paleo-Cristiano), which contains lead and marble sarcophagi, urns, mosaics, ornaments and jewellery, etc.

SURROUNDINGS. – 1·5 km NE of the Puerto del Rosario, past the cemetery, is the ruined fort of *Alto del Olivo*, with magnificent *views of the town and the coast. – 6 km NW of the town centre on the Constantí road is the late Roman **Mausoleum of Centcelles**, probably built for Constans, son of the Emperor Constantine. Carefully restored by German archaeologists, it has a well-preserved mosaic dome.

To Barcelona. – Either by motorway or on N 340, a good road which forks just before entering the province of Barcelona, continuing over the Cruz de Ordal while C 245 runs along the coast.

N 340 runs E from Tarragona, with extensive views, and then passes through a coastal zone with beaches and camping sites. 6 km from Tarragona, to the left, is the **Torre de los Escipiones** (Tower of the Scipios), a square structure 8 m high dating from the 1st c. A.D. There is no basis for the association with the two Roman generals of that name, the brothers Gnaeus and P. Cornelius Scipio, who were killed in the battle

of Amtorgis. 2 km farther on a road on the left leads to the *Roman quarry* (*cantera romana*) or *El Medol*.

Continuing along a pleasant avenue flanked by lemon-groves, we come to **Tamarit**, off the road to the right, close to the sea. It is an old-world little place with remains of its 14th c. town walls, a Romanesque church and the Castillo de Tamarit (12th–13th c.; museum). – Beyond this is **Torredembarra** (alt. 16 m), a fishing town and seaside resort near *Cabo Gros* (bypass) with a tall church tower. The road continues through a fertile area (wheels for raising water) and runs past a prominent Roman monument, the *Arco de Bará*, a triumphal arch 12 m high dating from the 2nd c. A.D., dedicated to Lucius Licinius Sura, a wealthy friend of the Emperor Trajan. A short distance away is *Roda de Bará*, with a *Pueblo Español* (Spanish Village) on the beach. – Road on right to the popular beaches of *Comarruga*.

N 340 now runs inland to **Vendrell** (alt. 50 m; pop. 9000), attractively situated on a hill in a famous wine-growing region, with a prominent belfry. It was the birthplace of the cellist Pablo Casals (1876–1973).

Beyond Vendrell the road forks: C 245 returns to the coast and continues along the Costas de Garraf, while N 340 goes over the Cruz de Ordal (see p. 78). Total distance from Tarragona to Barcelona by either route 99 km.

Roman aqueduct near Tarragona

To Lérida. – N 240 runs N, crosses the motorway and 4 km from Tarragona reaches a footpath to the **Roman aqueduct of Las Ferreras**, popularly known as the Puente del Diablo or Devil's Bridge, which carried water from the *Río Gayá* over a side valley of the Río Francolí. Probably dating from the early Empire, this is one of the most impressive Roman remains in Spain. It is a two-tier structure (lower tier 73 m long, upper tier 217 m), with 25 arches. The water channel had a total length of 35 km.

The road continues up the Francolí valley to **Valls** (alt. 215 m; pop. 13,000), with a parish church containing a much venerated image of Nuestra Señora de la Candela. From here a side road runs 18 km NE to the **Abbey of Santes Creus**, a Cistercian house founded in 1157 which ranks with Poblet as one of the most important monasteries in Catalonia. It has a fine Romanesque church (completed 1254), with a fortress-like façade and an octagonal dome over the crossing, which contains the tombs of Pedro III of Aragon and Jaime II. *New and Old Cloisters; chapterhouse, dormitory and Palacio Real.

From Valls the road winds its way through the *Sierra de Cogulla*, and over the *Puerto de Lilla* (581 m) to

Montblanch (alt. 310 m; pop. 5000), with old walls, gates and towers, a Gothic church and a municipal museum.

N 240 now turns W, passing (off the road to the left) the little radium spa of *Espluga de Francolí*. From here a detour (strongly recommended) can be made to the *Monastery of Poblet* (Santa María), founded by Benedictines in 1151 and substantially completed by the end of the 14th c., destroyed in the early 19th c. and reoccupied by Cistercians in 1940 (conducted tour). The monastery, famed as the burial place of the kings of Aragon, is still highly impressive. The most notable features within its precincts, which are completely surrounded by walls, are the Romanesque church, with an alabaster *high altar (16th c.) and the marble tomb of King Jamie I of Aragon (d. 1276); the early Gothic *cloister and the beautiful chapterhouse which adjoins it, with the tombs of many abbots; the library and dormitory; and the royal palace (14th–15th c.).

N 240 then runs to the *Sierra de la Llena* and enters the province of Lérida; then via *Borjas Blancas* to **Lérida** (see p. 147), 93 km from Tarragona.

To Zaragoza. – N 420 goes W over the coastal plain, the *Campo de Tarragona*, with its vineyards and its plantations of olives, almonds and walnuts, to **Reus** (see p. 189). It then follows a winding course over a number of passes to **Falset** (alt. 362 m; pop. 2500), in a beautiful valley under Monte Mola (919 m), the chief place in the rich wine-growing district of *Priorato*, with a ruined castle and remains of a palace which belonged to the Dukes of Medinaceli.

Then through a well-cultivated upland region, with the *Sierra de Montsant* (1071 m) on the right, to the River *Ebro*, here cutting through the coastal hills. After crossing the river N 420 continues via *Mora de Ebro* (alt. 200 m) to **Gandesa** (alt. 368 m; pop. 3000), which suffered severe destruction during the Civil War but was later rebuilt. – 6 km beyond the little town C 221 goes off on the right to Caspe and Zaragoza; alternatively continue on N 420 into the province of Teruel to join N 232, and then via *Alcañiz* to **Zaragoza** (see p. 245), 238 km from Tarragona.

To Castellón de la Plana on the coast road. – For this journey through the southern part of the *Costa Dorada* ("Golden Coast") there are two routes out of Tarragona – either on N 340, going W, or on the short stretch of motorway which runs SW, crosses the Río Francolí and comes (7 km from Tarragona) to **Salou** (pop. 9000; hotels: Salou Park, I, 102 r., SP; Cala Font, II, 318 r., SP; Calaviña, II, 70 r., SP; Europa Park, II, 325 r., SP), a port and popular seaside resort in a bay sheltered by *Cabo Salou*, with holiday chalets, tall hotels and blocks of flats and a boating harbour. King Jaime I sailed from here in 1229 on his conquest of Majorca.

From Salou a road of motorway standard runs to the road junction of *Cuatro Carreteras*, where it meets N 340 coming from Tarragona. 6 km N is **Reus** (see p. 189). – N 340 leads SW to **Cambrils** (pop. 7000), a fishing village with a fortress-like church tower and the bathing station of *Cambrils Playa* (Hotel Augustus I, II, 243 r., SP; Centurión Playa, II, 233 r., SP).

The road continues SW, close to the coast. It passes several camping sites, through *Miami Playa* and past a series of other beaches to **Hospitalet del Infante**, with an old pilgrims' hospice, situated close to the sea.

N 340 then runs past the *Castillo de Balaguer*, on a hill, and the fishing villages of *La Atmella de Mar* and *Ampolla* (both with hotels and camping sites), and along the W side of the Ebro delta. At *Amposta-Aldea* C 235 branches off on the right to *Tortosa*, 14 km W. Soon afterwards N 340 crosses the Ebro and comes to **Amposta** (alt. 8 m; pop. 12,000), a little town (bypass) noted for its rice. The *Ebro delta* in which it lies, a marshy area with countless little waterways and pools, is well suited for the growing of rice. The river has two mouths, the Gola del Norte and the Gola del Sur, with the island of Buda between them; the area is a paradise for birds.

On the S side of the Ebro delta N 340 comes to the port of *San Carlos de la Rápita*, on the extensive *Puerto de los Alfaques* ("harbour of the sandbanks"). It then crosses the provincial boundary at *Alcanar* and continues via *Torreblanca* to **Castellón de la Plana** (see p. 100), 190 km from Tarragona.

Tarrasa

Province: Barcelona (B).
Telephone code: 93.
Altitude: 277 m. – Population: 160,000.

(i) **Oficina de Información de Turismo,**
Gran Vía de les Cortes Catalanes 658; Barcelona; tel. 3 01 74 43.

HOTEL. – *Hostal Egara* (no rest.), Onésimo Redondo 1, P II, 22 r.

RESTAURANT. – *Burrull-Hostal del Fum*, Carretera de Moncada 19 (closed Aug.).

The industrial town of Tarrasa, notable for the production of silk, lies in the fertile Vallés district on the right bank of the Río Palau. It was formerly the episcopal see of Egara, founded in 450.

SIGHTS. – On a hill SE of the railway station are three famous early Christian churches. The church of *Santa María*, originally a Visigothic basilica, was enlarged in the 12th c. in Catalan Romanesque style; remains of a 4th c. mosaic; museum. The church of *San Miguel*, built in the 6th century as a baptistery, shows Byzantine and Visigothic influences, with later restoration work; the crypt has 7th c. paintings. The church of *San Pedro*, originally a funerary chapel, has a Byzantine apse, ancient columns, a Romanesque nave (12th c.), Visigothic, Romanesque and early Gothic frescoes and magnificent retablos (15th c.) by Jaime Huguet, Luis Borrassá, Jaime Cirera and Guillermo Talarn. – *Textile Museum*, with old looms, etc.

SURROUNDINGS. – 23 km NE on C 1415 is *Caldas de Montbuy* (or *Mombuy*), a health resort with a Roman bath (restored).

Teruel

Province: Teruel (TE).
Telephone code: 974.
Altitude: 915 m. Population: 24,000.
ⓘ **Oficina de Turismo,**
Tomás Nogués 1;
tel. 60 22 79.
Servicio Provincial de Turismo,
Tomás Nogués 1;
tel. 60 20 62.

HOTELS. – *Parador Nacional,* 2 km outside the town,
II, 60 r.; *Reina Cristina,* Paseo Generalísmo 1, II, 62 r.;
Civera (no rest.), Avda Sagunto 37, III, 73 r.; *Goya,*
Tomás Nogués 4, IV, 24 r.; *Orienté* (no rest.), Avda de
Sagunto 5, IV 31 r.; *Hostal Utrillas,* Rondo Dámaso
Torán 23, P III, 41 r.

**The provincial capital and seat of a
bishop, Teruel stands on a hill sur-
rounded by the gorges of the Río
Turia. A town of Iberian origin
(Turba), it was devastated by the
Romans in 218 B.C. It retained its
Moorish inhabitants long after the
Reconquista: the last mosque was
closed only in 1502.**

Mudéjar church tower, Teruel

SIGHTS. – Teruel's numerous Mudéjar
buildings and towers dating from the
Moorish period give the town its very
distinctive aspect; it also preserves many
remains of its medieval walls. – The 16th c.
Cathedral has a tower with a dome of
brightly coloured tiles (1538); magnificent retablo (1535) on the high altar;
two elaborate silver monstrances, 3 m
high, in the sacristy. – Two 12th c.
churches, *San Salvador* and *San Martín,*
with handsome Mudéjar towers. – The
church of **San Pedro** (13th c.) has a
beautiful 16th c. retablo and houses the

glass coffins containing the mummified
bodies of the famous "Lovers of Teruel"
(13th c.). – To the N of the town is an
aqueduct, **Los Arcos,** built in 1558 on the
Roman model, which also serves as a
footbridge.

SURROUNDINGS. – An attractive run of some 40 km
through the *Sierra de Albarracín,* W of the town, leads
to **Albarracín** (alt. 1182 m; pop. 2000), still partly
surrounded by its old walls, with picturesque little
streets and a fine collegiate church containing
valuable 16th c. Brussels tapestries. The whole town
is protected as a national monument. – S of the town
(respectively 4 and 6 km) are the caves of *El Callejón
de Plou* and *Cueva del Navazo* (access roads), with
interesting prehistoric paintings (hunting scenes).

To Valencia. – N 234 runs S and winds its way up
and over the *Puerto Escandón* (1242 m) to *La Puebla
de Valverde,* with old town walls. Beyond *Sarrión*
(pop. 2000) it enters Castellón province and continues to *Barracas* (alt. 980 m), on the plateau of the
same name, where the sea comes into sight, and then
down through the fertile valley of the *Río Palacia* to
Jérica (alt. 490 m; pop. 3000), an ancient little town
picturesquely situated on the slopes of a steep
limestone hill, with the ruins of a Moorish castle and
two interesting churches.

11 km farther on, S of the *Embalse del Regajo,* is
Segorbe (alt. 362 m; pop. 8000), the Iberian and
later Roman *Segobriga,* a little episcopal town
magnificently situated between two hills crowned by
castles. Cathedral (15th–16th c., with later alteration
and restoration), with a Gothic cloister; it contains
pictures by Vicente Macip. In the 17th c. church of
San Martín de las Monjas is one of Ribalta's finest
paintings "Christ in Limbo". Near the town is a *Roman
aqueduct.*

N 234 now enters the province of Valencia and joins
N 340, the coast road along the Costa del Azahar, S of
Sagunto; then on to **Valencia** (see p. 231), 145 km
from Teruel.

To Zaragoza. – N 234 runs NW via *Torrelacárcel* to
Monreal del Campo (alt. 940 m; pop. 3500), at the
foot of the *Sierra Menera,* in which are the rich iron-
mines of *Ojos Negros.* From here N 211 runs W to
Molina de Aragón and Madrid. – N 234 then
continues N to **Calamocha** (alt. 884 m; pop. 3000),
situated in a wide plain, with the ruins of a Moorish
castle. On a nearby hill is the *Ermita de Bárbara.*

The road then descends the valley of the *Río Jiloca* to
Báguena, in a beautiful vega; ruined castle near the
town. After entering Zaragoza province it comes to
Daroca and then continues N (N 330) to **Zaragoza**
(see p. 245), 181 km from Teruel.

Toledo

Province: Toledo (TO).
Telephone code: 925.
Altitude: 529 m. – Population: 53,000.
ⓘ **Oficina de Información de Turismo,**
Puerta de Bisagra;
tel. 22 08 43.
Dirección General de Turismo,
Cuesta de Carlos V 10,
tel. 21 09 00

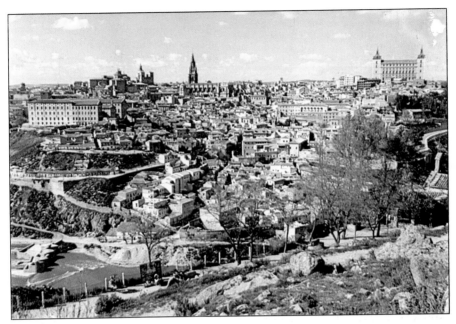

Toledo

HOTELS. – *Parador Nacional Conde de Orgaz,
2·5 km SE, Paseo de los Cigarrales, I, 57 r., SP; Alfonso
VI (no rest.), General Moscardó 2, II, 80 r.; Cardenal
(no rest.), Paseo de Recaredo 24, II, 27 r.; Carlos V,
Trastamara 1, II, 55 r.; María Cristina, Marqués de
Mendigorria 1, II, 43 r.; Almazara (no rest.), Carretera
Toledo – Arges y Guerva, km 3·4, III, 21 r.; Maravilla,
Barrio Rey 7, III, 18 r.; Imperio (no rest.), Cadenas 7,
IV, 21 r.; Lino, Santa Justa 9, IV, 12 r.; etc. – CAMPING
SITES: E: Greco (open all year); Toledo and Circo
Romano (all close to the town).

RESTAURANTS. – In hotels (the Carlos V being
particularly well spoken of); also Aurelio, Plaza del
Ayuntamiento 8; La Cubana, Paseo de la Rosa 2;
Hostal del Cardenal, Paseo Recaredo 24; El Mirador,
Nuñez de Arce 11; Chirón, Paseo Recaredo 1; Plácido,
Santo Tome 6; Siglo XIX, Cardenal Tavera 10;
Trocadero, Avda de la Reconquista 10; San Antonio,
Avda de América 6; Venta de Airez, Circo Romano 25,
NW outside the Puerta Vieja de Bisagra; etc.

EVENTS. – Semana Santa (Holy Week), with solemn
processions on Good Friday and Easter Day. – Fiesta
del Olivo (Apr.), with a pilgrimage to the Ermita de la
Cabeza (Mora de Toledo); parade with carriages,
decorated floats and folk groups. – May Festival, with
a pilgrimage to the Ermita de la Virgen del Valle. – Feria
(Aug.), with a fair, bullfights and a great firework
display.

**Toledo, capital of the province of the
same name in New Castile and seat
of the Primate of Spain, is one of
the country's most attractive tourist
centres, notable for its magnificent
*situation, its picturesque old town
and the *treasures of art and architecture it contains.**

The town is situated on a granite hill
surrounded on three sides by the deep
gorge of the Río Tajo. With its ring of
Gothic and Moorish walls, its towering
Alcázar and its splendid Cathedral, it
presents a picture of incomparable effect.

The layout of Toledo, with its irregular
pattern of narrow streets and numerous
blind alleys, reflects its Moorish past. The
blank walls, the windows with their iron
gratings and the open courtyards of the
houses also betray Oriental influence. The
architecture of the Christian period is
represented by numerous churches, convents and hospices. Thus the city as a
whole is a kind of open-air museum
illustrating the history of Spain. Since
1970 much work has been done on the
restoration of its historic buildings, and
this process is continuing. – Toledo is also
famous for its swords ("Toledo blades")
and its gold and silver inlay work.

HISTORY. – Toledo is one of the oldest towns in
Spain. The capital of an Iberian tribe, the Carpetani, it
was captured by the Romans in 192 B.C. and given the
name of Toletum. Under the Visigoths, between 534
and 712, it again enjoyed the status of a capital and
was the meeting-place of many councils. During
the Moorish period (712–1085) it was known as
Tolaitola, and until 1035 was the seat of an emir
subject to the Caliph of Córdoba. Thereafter it became
an independent kingdom and rose to prosperity
through the manufacture of weapons and its silk and
woollen industries. Science and learning were also
eagerly cultivated in the town. The Christian inhabitants, known as Mozarabs ("servants of the
Arabs" or "pseudo-Arabs"), adopted the Arabic
language, which remained in use together with
Spanish for centuries and was not finally prohibited
until 1580. In 1087 the town became the residence of
the kings of Castile and the ecclesiastical centre of the

whole of Spain, and the Cardinal-Archbishops of Toledo – Mendoza, Jiménez, Albornoz and others – were involved in all the great events of the period. The revolt of the Comuneros also began in Toledo. With the transfer of the court to Madrid by Philip II (who returned to stay in Toledo for a period in 1559–61) the town lost political importance. During the Civil War (1936–39) Toledo became famous for the defence of its Alcázar.

SIGHTS. – It is impossible to list all there is to see in Toledo, or to do justice even to the main sights in one excursion. The best plan is to start from the triangular *Plaza de Zocodover* (familiarly known as *Zoco*), Toledo's busiest traffic intersection, and explore the city in three directions – S to Cruz (museum including paintings by El Greco) and N to the nearby Miradero.

From the Plaza de Zocodover the busy *Calle del Comercio* runs SW to the real centre of Toledo, the *Plaza Mayor*, on the NW side of which is the plain *Palacio Arzobispal* (Archbishop's Palace). On the SW side of the square is the **Ayuntamiento** (Town Hall), built in 1618, with two handsome corner towers and a beautiful tiled frieze of 1595 in the Sala Capitular.

On the E side of the Plaza Mayor stands the ****Cathedral**, the *Catedral primada* of Spain and the country's finest Gothic cathedral after Burgos. It was built between 1227 and 1493 on the site of the

North tower of Toledo Cathedral

Moorish Great Mosque. In the N tower (90 m high: view), built 1380–1440, is the famous bell known as the Campana Gorda, cast in 1753, which weighs 17,515 kg. The S tower, which was left unfinished, has a Baroque dome. On the W front are three imposing Gothic doorways (1418–50), richly decorated with sculpture and reliefs; the central doorway, the Puerta del Perdón, was the work of Juan Alemán. Of the beautiful side doorways the most notable is the richly decorated Gothic Puerta de los Leones (1458–66), at the end of the S transept; on the inside of this are fine 16th c. *woodcarvings, and above it is the "Imperial Organ" (1594, restored), with a stone sounding-board. There are also two fine doorways on the N side of the Cathedral, opening off the Cloister. The Cathedral is entered from the Cloister (to the left of the N tower).

The INTERIOR of the Cathedral (110 m long without the Capilla de San Ildefonso), with its 88 richly articulated clustered columns, is highly impressive. Magnificent 16th c. *stained glass*. The richly gilded *Capilla Mayor has a beautiful Plateresque *reja* of 1548. The huge *retablo* of gilded and painted larchwood (1504) has four tiers of New Testament scenes with lifesize figures; in the centre is a magnificent pyramidal *custodia*. On either side of the high altar are *royal tombs* (*sepulcros reales*) of 1289. Behind the Capilla Mayor, the walls of which are decorated with numerous figures of saints and reliefs, is the tomb of Cardinal Diego de Astorga, with the *Transparente*, a huge marble altar dedicated to the Virgin, surmounted by a painted openwork dome (1722). The Choir has a *reja* of 1548 and *Sillería (choir-stalls) of walnutwood – the lower stalls (1495) with 54 carved scenes from the war with Granada, which had recently ended, and the richly carved upper stalls (1543), the *S side by Berruguete, the N side by Felipe Vigarní. On the free-standing altar in the Choir is a stone figure of the "Virgen Blanca" or White Virgin (*c.* 1300), now black with age. – Immediately to the right of the main entrance, in the S tower, is the **Capilla Mozárabe** (1504), in which mass is celebrated every morning about 9.45 according to the Visigothic (Mozarabic) rite.

A doorway in the ambulatory leads into the *Sala Capitular (1512), with a superb artesonado ceiling, 13 frescoes and a series of likenesses of archbishops. The *Capilla de San Ildefonso*, the central chapel in the ambulatory, contains numerous tombs. Adjoining it is the **Capilla de Santiago*, in rich Gothic style, with fine marble tombs (1488), the most ornate of which are the tombs of the founder, Álvaro de Luna, and his wife. Next to this chapel is the entrance to the **Capilla de Reyes Nuevos*, with magnificent Plateresque decoration. – To the left is the entrance to the **Sacristy** (1592–1616), with an elaborately decorated doorway. On the altar is El Greco's "Disrobing of Christ" (1579); to the right of the altar is Goya's "Betrayal of Christ" (1788); and on the walls are 16 figures of Apostles by El Greco. – Immediately W of the Sacristy is the *Ochavo*, an octagonal chamber with a high dome (ceiling paintings by F. Ricci and Carreño, 1670), in which there is a collection of some 400 relics. The adjoining *Capilla de la Virgen del*

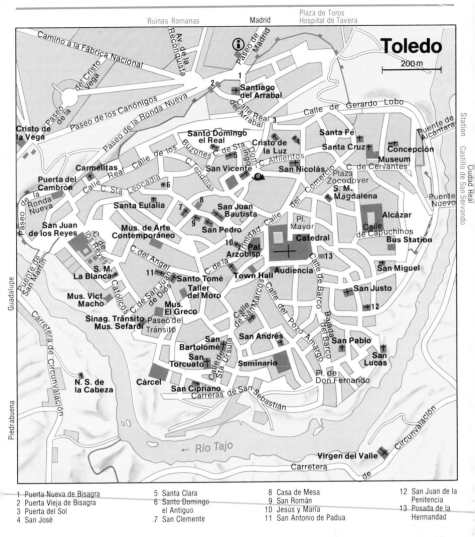

Toledo
200 m

Sagrario houses a much venerated image of the Virgin enthroned (c. 1200), covered with valuable jewellery. – The **Capilla de San Juan** under the N tower contains the *Cathedral Treasury* (Tesoro Mayor), the chief treasure of which is the famous *custodia* by Enrique de Arfe (1524), almost 3 m high and 172 kg in weight, with 260 silver-gilt statuettes. – On the N side of the Cathedral is the **Cloister** (begun 1389). The lower cloister (*claustro bajo*) has frescoes by Francisco Bayeu and Maella (1776) on the S and E walls. In the NE corner is the *Capilla de San Blas* (not open to the public), with Florentine ceiling paintings of the early 15th c. In a room opening off the upper cloister (*claustro alto*), entered from Calle Hombre de Palo, are the *gigantones*, the huge figures some 6 m high, clad in 18th c. costume, which are carried in procession during the fiestas.

W of the Cathedral, in *Plaza Santo Tomé*, is the church of **Santo Tomé**, originally a mosque, rebuilt by the Count of Orgaz in Gothic style in the 14th c., with a beautiful Mudéjar tower. In an annex, is the famous ***"Burial of Count Orgaz" (1586), one of El Greco's finest works. – To the S of the church is the *Taller del Moro* building which contains a small *Museo de Arte Mudéjar*. – From Santo Tomé the *Calle de Ángel* leads W to the Franciscan convent of ***San Juan de los Reyes**, founded in 1476 as the burial-place of the Catholic monarchs and their descendents but not completed until the 17th c. The church (begun 1553) has a richly carved main doorway, and round the outer walls are the fetters once borne by Christian prisoners of the Moors. The *cloister* (1504), to the SE, is one of the finest achievements of late Gothic architecture in Spain. From the terrace in front of the main doorway there are extensive views. – NW of the church, lower down, is the *Puerta des Cambrón* ("Gate of the Thorn-Bush"), an imposing double gate built in 1102, from which a road leads downhill to the *Ermita del Cristo de la Vega* (originally 4th c. but remodelled in Mudéjar style), in the *Vega Baja*.

SW of the church of San Juan and the Puerta del Cambrón, reached by way of the town walls (fine views), is the **Puente de San Martín** (30 m high), built in 1212 and repaired in 1390, from which there is a magnificent prospect of the gorge of the Río Tajo.

SE of San Juan stands the church of ***Santa María la Blanca**, in Mudéjar style, built as a synagogue in the 12th–13th c. and converted into a Christian church in 1405. It has magnificent arte-sonado ceiling, 28 horseshoe arches and pine-cone capitals. – SW of Santa María by way of the *Plaza de la Judería*, once the centre of the Jewish quarter, is the Mudéjar ***Sinagoga del Tránsito** (1366), which after the expulsion of the Jews in 1492 was given to the Order of Calatrava. Adjoining it is the *Museo Sefardí*, with a collection illustrating the history and culture of the Jews in Spain, including the Sarcófago de Tarragona, with a trilingual inscription in Hebrew, Latin and Greek. – NE of the Synagogue is the **Casa El Greco**, in which the Cretan-born painter Domenikos Theotokopoulos, – know as El Greco, lived and died (1614). It contains period furniture, paintings by El Greco, etc. Adjoining the house to the N is the **Museo El Greco**, which contains 20 pictures by El Greco, in-cluding a "View of Toledo" and "Christ with Apostles" (photograph, p. 34. – S of the Synagogue is the *Paseo del Tránsito*, from which there are very fine views, and beyond this is the *Calvario*, standing high above the Tajo.

There are a number of notable churches NW of the Cathedral. Calle del Nuncio Viejo leads into *Calle Alfonso X*, in which stands the church of *San Ildefonso*, with an imposing Baroque façade and two towers; it contains two pictures by El Greco. A short distance W is the 13th c. church of *San Román* (deconsecrated), with a Moorish tower, which now houses the *Museo Concilios* (13th c. frescoes; collection of Visigothic antiquities), and farther NW the church of *Santo Domingo el Antiguo* (completed 1576); altarpieces by El Greco, who was buried in the church. – NE of San Ildefonso in the *Plazuela de San Vicente* is the (deconse-crated) church of San Vicente, now a *Museum of Religious Art* (17th c. works of art, liturgical vessels). From here the steep *Cuesta del Seminario* leads down to the **Ermita del Santo Cristo de la Luz**,

formerly a small mosque, with nine domes and columns from a Visigothic church; the choir (remains of wall paintings) was added in Christian times. – Lower down are the *Puerta del Cristo de la Luz* and the Mudéjar ***Puerta del Sol** (14th c.), a massive structure with two towers. To the right is the *Paseo del Miradero*, a promenade with a high terrace from which the Sierra de Gredos can be seen in clear weather.

From the Puerta del Sol the *Calle Real del Arrabal* runs down NW to the outer district (*arrabal*) of **Santiago**, in which is the Mudéjar church of *Santiago del Arrabal*, with a Moorish tower. Beyond this is a double gateway, the **Puerta Nueva de Bisagra** (repaired 1550). A short distance SW along the town walls is the Moorish ***Puerta Vieja de Bisagra**

Puerta Vieja de Bisagra, Toledo

(9th c.). – From the Puerta Vieja the attractive *Paseo de Merchán* (views from the W side) leads to the outlying district of **Las Covachuelas**, in which is the **Hospital de Tavera** (1541), with a Plateresque façade: rooms furnished in the style of the 17th c., paintings by El Greco, Tintoretto, Zurbarán and other artists, and an exact reproduction of a 16th c. pharmacy (not open to the public). In the church, under the dome, is the tomb (by Berruguete, 1561; can be seen on request) of the founder, Archbishop Juan de Tavera.

From the Plaza de Zocodover the *Cuesta del Alcázar* runs S to the **Alcázar**, the old citadel of Toledo, built on the site of an earlier Roman fort on the highest point in the town. In 1882 it became a military cadet school, and during the Civil War the Nationalist garrison held out for 68 days against Republican attacking forces. It has now been restored as a national memorial, with a beautiful arcaded court-yard. Exhibition rooms to house a military collection are in course of construction.

Going E from the Plaza de Zocodover, we pass through the Moorish *Arco de la Sangre* and come to the ***Hospital de Santa Cruz**, a Renaissance building designed by Enrique de Egas (15th–16th c.), with a fine early Plateresque doorway. It now houses the ***Museo Santa Cruz*, with prehistoric, Roman and Visigothic material, Brussels tapestries and pictures, including more than 20 pictures by *El Greco as well as works by Ribera, Murillo and other artists. – Below the Hospital, to the E, is the ***Puente de Alcántara** (no cars) over the Río Tajo. Originally a Roman structure, this was completely rebuilt by the Moors in 866, and in its present form dates mainly from the 13th–14th c. At the W end is a gate tower, the *Puerta de Alcántara* (1484), at the E end a Baroque gate (1721). From the bridge there is a magnificent view of the town, rising steeply up from the river, and the Alcázar. Upstream are the *Puente Nuevo* (1933) and remains of a *Roman aqueduct*. High above the left bank of the river stands the 11th c. *Castillo de San Servando*, now a school (views).

SURROUNDINGS. – There is a very attractive ****circuit round the town** (6·5 km): from the *Puerta del Sol* to the *Puerta de Bisagra*, then SW on the Paseo de Recaredo past the *Puerta Vieja de Bisagra* and the *Puerta del Cambrón* to the *Puente de San Martín*; over the bridge and up the hill to the **Ermita de Nuestra Señora de la Cabeza** (magnificent *views); then left along the Carretera de Circunvalación, above the Tajo valley and the town, to the **Ermita de la Virgen del Valle**; down to the *Puente Nuevo* and along the E bank of the river to the *Puente de Alcántara*; from here back to the Puente Nuevo, over the river, past the *Puerta de Alcántara* and along Calle Gerardo Lobo to return to the Puerta del Sol.

Ruta de la Mancha Toledana. – This route runs through a region once travelled by Don Quixote. Leave Toledo through the outer district of *Las Covachuelas* and continue on N 401 (the Madrid road) to (34 km) **Illescas** (alt. 588 m; pop. 2000), which is bypassed by the main road. In the church of the Hospital de la Caridad are five *pictures by El Greco.

N of Illescas a side road goes off on the right to *Esquivias*, with the church of Santa María in which the Marrige of Cervantes is recorded in the register. The road then continues via *Aranjuez* (see p. 56) to **Ocaña** (alt. 730 m; pop. 7000), an old town with the dilapidated remains of its walls but with a glorious history. It has a trim 18th c. Plaza Mayor, a number of interesting churches, including San Juan, San Martín and Santa María, and the place of the Dukes of Frías. – From here SE on N 301 to *Villatobas* (alt. 723 m) and over the *Río Cigüela* to **Quintanar de la Orden** (alt. 691 m; pop. 7700), a little town, formerly held by the

Order of Santiago, in the corn- and wine-growing district of La Mancha which Cervantes depicts so faithfully in "Don Quixote". 9 km S on a minor road is the village of *El Toboso*, home of Don Quixote's Dulcinea, with a museum and library.

From Ocaña N IV runs S over the steppe-like plateau of the New Castilian Meseta, past *La Guardia* (alt. 665 m), situated on a low hill, to **Templeque** (alt. 635 m), a typical little La Mancha town, with an attractive Plaza Mayor, the Baroque Palacio de las Torres and an interesting Gothic parish church. – The road then continues, passing three windmills, to **Madridejos** (alt. 674 m; pop. 10,000), a little town of low houses. From here N IV runs on via *Puerto Lápice* to **Manzanares** (see p. 103), while the Ruta de la Mancha turns W on C 400 and comes in 8 km to **Consuegra** (alt. 704 m), once held by the Order of St John, with a ruined castle and 13 windmills (*view). In one of these is a Windmill Museum.

C 400 now runs NW past the Montes de Consuegra to **Mora** (alt. 717 m; pop. 4000), with a fine Gothic church and interesting Roman remains.

From here C 402 goes SW to (10 km) **Orgaz** (alt. 744 m; pop. 4000), with a massive 14th c. castle, a Roman bridge and a typical Plaza Mayor. – Then return to Toledo on N 401.

Ruta de los Castillos. – Toledo is a land of castles, and this route introduces the visitor to the martial past of this region.

N 403 runs NW from Toledo, crosses the *Río Guadarrama* and comes to **Torrijos** (alt. 526 m; pop. 5000), a picturesque little town with a late Gothic church (fine Plateresque doorway) and the Palacio de Altamira. – Shortly before the town a road goes off on the right to *Barcience*, with an unusually tall 15th c. castle.

The road then crosses N V and comes to **Maqueda** (alt. 483 m), an old-world little town. Church of Santa María (15th–16th c.), with a carved wooden retablo (1554); Moorish *castle* with battlements and wall-walk. – A few kilometres N is *Escalona*, with the ruins of a 15th c. Alcázar.

From Maqueda N V runs SW via *Santa Olalla* to **Talavera de la Reina** (see p. 217) and **Oropesa** (alt. 420 m; pop 5000), a little town with a medieval atmosphere, noted for its embroidery. The magnificent Castillo de los Duques de Frías (14th c.) is now the Parador Nacional Virrey de Toledo (l, 44 r.): fine views. – S of Oropesa is *El Puente del Arzobispo*, which has a parish chruch with a beautiful Capilla Mayor.

Tolosa

Province: Guipúzcoa (SS).
Telephone code: 943.
Altitude: 79 m. – Population: 18,000.
ⓘ **Centro de Iniciativas Turísticas**,
   Calle San Juan;
   tel. 67 40 19.

HOTELS. – Hostal *Atxondo* (no rest.), Poligono Arkante 8, P III, 5 r.; *Oyarbide*, Plaza de Gorriti 1, P III, 19 r.

RESTAURANTS. – *Mesón Idiaquez*, Plaza Idiaquez l (in a 16th c. mansion); *Venta Aundi*, 1·5 km S on N I.

Tolosa, beautifully situated in the green valley of the Río Oria, which is joined at this point by the Río Azpiroz, was capital of the province from 1844 to 1854. It is now a busy little industrial town.

SIGHTS. – In the town centre, which is bypassed by the main road, is the fine church of *Santa María*, with a colossal statue of John the Baptist on the main façade. – On the Madrid road is the 16th c. church of *San Francisco*, with a retablo by Bengoechea. – Interesting 16th c. *Armería* (Armoury).

Tordesillas

Province: Valladolid (VA).
Telephone code: 983.
Altitude: 702 m. – Population: 6000.
ⓘ **Ayuntamiento** (Town Hall);
   Plaza Mayor I,
   tel. 77 00 61.

HOTELS. – *Parador Nacional* km 151 on N-620, II 73 r.; SP; *El Montico*, km 145 on N-620, II, 34 r., SP; *Jambrina*, km 320 on N-132, IV, 15 r., etc.

RESTAURANT: in *Parador Nacional* (Castilian style: well spoken of).

EVENT. – *Summer Festival* (June), a typical fiesta with traditional celebrations.

The old Castilian market town of Tordesillas, situated on a hill above the Río Duero, is an important road junction and was a frequent residence of the kings of Spain. Queen Joan the Mad (Juana la Loca) lived here after her husband's death. During the rebellion of the Comuneros it was the headquarters of their "Junta Santa" ("sacred league").

SIGHTS. – The church of *San Antolin*, with a graceful tower, has a fine retablo and contains the tomb of Gaspar de Tordesillas (1550). – The **Monasterio de Santa Clara** (14th–18th c.), originally built as a royal palace, has a number of courtyards in Mudéjar style and a Gothic *church* with a superb artesonado ceiling and a 15th c. altar. The **Treaty of Tordesillas**, which, after arbitration by Pope Alexander VI, laid down the colonial spheres of influence of Spain and Portugal, especially in S America, was signed in the monastery in 1494.

Toro

Province: Zamora (ZA).
Telephone code: 988.
Altitude: 754 m. – Population: 10,000.
ⓘ **Ayuntamiento** (Town Hall),
   Plaza de España;
   tel. 69 01 00.

HOTEL. – *Juan II*, Plaza del Espolón 1, II, 42 r., SP; *Hostal Doña Elvira*, Antonio Miguelez 47, P III, 19 r.

The little town of Toro, picturesquely situated on a plateau which slopes down to the River Duero, is surrounded by vineyards and orchards. In Toro, which was captured by Hannibal in 220 B.C. are a number of fine buildings.

West doorway, Santa María la Mayor, Toro

SIGHTS. – Collegiate church of **Santa María la Mayor** (12th–13th c.), with a beautiful dome and magnificent doorways, the *Pórtico de la Gloria* on the W front being particularly notable. It contains a picture of the "Virgen de la Mosca" and a valuable treasury. – Church of *San Lorenzo*, brick-built (12th c.), with fine tombs and a retablo by Fernando Gallego. – Convent of *Sancti Spiritus*, founded 1316, with the alabaster tomb of Beatrice of Portugal, widow of John I of Castile (d. 1432). – *Palacio de las Leyes* (or *de las Cortes*), in which the Cortes met in 1505, with a fine doorway. – Other features of interest include the old town gates, various secular buildings and churches and the Town Hall (1778).

Torremolinos

Province: Málaga (MA).
Telephone code: 952.
Altitude: 40 m. – Population: 29,000.
(i) **Oficina de Información de Turismo.**
Bajos de la Nogalera 517;
tel. 38 15 78.

HOTELS (mostly with a beach). – *Meliá Torremolinos*, L, 283 r., SP; *Parador Nacional del Golf*, I, 40 r.; *Al Andalus*, I, 164 r., SP; *Cervantes*, I, 393 r.; SP; *Don Pablo*, I, 443 r., SP; *Pez Espada*, I, 149 r., SP; *Tropicana*, I, 86 r., SP; *Alta Vista*, II, 107 r.; *Camino Real*, II, 144 r., SP; *Lago Rojo*, II, 144 r., SP; *Nautilus*, II, 116 r., SP; *Las Palomas*, II, 294 r. SP; *Principe-Sol*, II, 577 r., SP; *Los Arcos*, III, 51 r., SP; *Piscis* (no rest.), III, 49 r., SP; etc. – Apartment Hotels *Aloha Puerto-Sol*, I, 418 r., SP; *Meliá Costa del Sol*, I, 540 r., SP; and many others. – CAMPING SITE: *Torremolinos*, km 235 on the Cádiz road.

RESTAURANTS. – ON THE MÁLAGA ROAD: *La Parrilla*, Urb. La Colina; *Chez Lucien (Casa París)*, Carretera Cádiz (French cuisine). – IN THE TOWN CENTRE: *Las Rejas*, Urb. Playamar; *La Chalana*, Paseo Marítimo, Playamar-Lido: *La Tortuga*, San Miguel 14 (rustic style); *Chipén*, San Miguel 3; *Cantón*, Plaza de la Gamba Alegre; *Montmartre*, Avda de Palma de Mallorca; *El Bodegón*, Cauce (French): *Hong Kong*, Cauce (Chinese); *La Taberna Roja*, Cauce; *Saghora*, Carretera de Benalmádena 1 (Moroccan style); *Molina de la Torre*, Mirador San Miguel (rustic style; view of sea). – IN LA CARIHUELA: *Siete Mares*, Galerías

Eurosol; *Portofino*, Casa Marco, Playa Montemar (seafood; terrace); *Mesón de la Pimienta*, Bulto; *Prudencio*, Carmen 43 (terrace); etc.

EVENTS. – *Fiesta de San Miguel* (Sept.), with pilgrimage, traditional fiesta and bullfights. – *Rallye Costa del Sol*, car race (Dec.). – Torremolinos has a modern congress and exhibition centre.

WATER SPORTS. – All kinds of water sports, including fishing and sub-aqua diving (boats and equipment available for hire); sailing.

SPORT and RECREATION on land. – Golf (several courses), tennis, riding, shooting (partridges, hares, rabbits); bullfights; Wine Museum, Wax Museum.

Torremolinos is a popular seaside resort on the coast road between Málaga and Algeciras, particularly favoured by the large travel operators. Lying in a wide bay with a beach almost 9 km long, sheltered by the Sierra Tejada to the N and the Sierra Nevada to the W, it enjoys an excellent climate.

In the 19th c. a mere village which had grown up round the towers and the mills referred to in its name, Torremolinos is now a busy little town with numerous hotels, blocks of flats and places of entertainment. The life of the town centres on the old Calle San Miguel, while the old fishermen's quarters of *La Carihuela* and *El Bajondilla* have developed into flourishing tourist centres, with accommodation and facilities for large numbers of visitors. Round the town are a whole series of new developments with holiday flats and chalets.

Torremolinos

Tortosa

Province: Tarragona (T).
Telephone code: 977.
Altitude: 10 m. – Population: 46,000.
(i) **Oficina Municipal de Turismo.**
Calle de la Rosa 10;
tel. 44 19 23.

HOTELS. – *Parador Nacional Castillo de la Zuda*, I, 82 r., SP; *Berenguer IV*, Cervantes 23, III, 54 r.; *Hostal Siboni*, Calle del Ángel 6, P III, 35 r.

RESTAURANTS. – In *Parador Nacional*; also *Rosa*, Marqués Bellet 4; *Bodegón Bartolomé*, Lonja 16; *La Rambla*, Rambla Cataluña 66; etc.

Tortosa is an old episcopal town on the Ebro, situated between high hills. It lies within easy reach (15 km

on C 235) of the coast road (N 340) along the *Costa Dorada ("Golden Coast").

SIGHTS. – Gothic **Cathedral** (1347) with a Moorish tower, choir-stalls of 1588 and a 14th c. cloister. – The town also has a number of interesting *churches*, a *Bishop's Palace* dating from the 14th c., handsome *palaces* of the 15th and 16th c., considerable remains of its old walls and a ruined castle. – The convent of *San Luis* (16th c.) has a beautiful inner courtyard.

Trujillo

Province: Cáceres (CC).
Telephone code: 927.
Altitude: 485 m. – Population: 15,000.
ⓘ **Oficina Municipal de Turismo,**
   Plaza de España s/n;
   tel. 32 06 53.

HOTELS. – *Parador Nacional de Trujillo, Plaza*, Plaza Santa Clara, I, 46 r., SP; *Las Cigüeñas*, 1 km NE on N V, III, 78 r., *Hostal Emilia*, General Mola 26, P III, 29 r.; *La Estacion* (no rest.), km 252 on N V, P III, 28 r.; *Pizarro*, Plaza Mayor 13, P III, 5 r.; etc.

RESTAURANTS. – In *Hotel Parador Nacional* and *Las Cigüeñas*; also *Mesón Pillette*, Plaza Mayor; *El Túnel*, General Mola; *Figón Luciano*, Sillería 8.

EVENTS. – *Domingo de Gloria* (Apr.), at Easter. – *Fiesta de la Patrona* (Sept.).

The old town of Trujillo, dominated by a Moorish castle, has preserved much of the atmosphere of the period of the Conquistadors.

HISTORY. – Originally a Roman town (*Turgalium*), Trujillo was the birthplace (1475) of Francisco Pizarro, the conqueror of Peru, and of other conquistadors, who employed the wealth they had acquired in America in erecting large palaces in their native town.

SIGHTS. – The central feature of the old town is the *Plaza Mayor*, in which stands

Trujillo

an *equestrian statue of Pizarro* (photograph, p. 122). Round the square are the *Palacio de los Marqueses de la Conquista*, a Plateresque building with a large coat of arms on the façade and elaborate gratings on the window; the *Palacio de los Duques de San Carlos*, in Renaissance style, with a two-storied patio; the *Palacio de Santa María* (16th c.); the *Casa Piedras Albas*, and other handsome mansions. – In the 13th c. Gothic church of *Santa María la Mayor* is the tomb of Diego García de Paredes, the "Samson of Extremadura", born in Trujillo in 1466. – In the church of *Santiago* are a statue of St James, the town's patron saint, and a Gothic retablo. – There are many other *noble mansions* in the town, some of them with coats of arms decorating the doorway. Outside the town is an old Hieronymite *monastery* with a tall belfry.

Tudela

Province: Navarre (NA).
Telephone code: 948.
Altitude: 275 m. – Population: 20,000.
ⓘ **Oficina de Información de Turismo,**
   Plaza de los Fueros;
   tel. 82 15 39.

HOTELS. – *Santamaria*, San Marcial 14m III, 51 r.; Hostal *De Tudela*, on carretera N-232, P. I, 16 r.; *Navarra*, Avda. Zaragoza 29, P II, 39 r.; *Remigio*, Gaztambide 4, P II, 39 r.; etc.

EVENTS. – *Fiestas de Santa Ana* (July), with bullfights, sporting events and traditional celebrations.

Tudela is an old-world episcopal town on the right bank of the Río Ebro which in the course of its long history has been captured and plundered many times.

SIGHTS. – The town has numerous old palaces and churches, but its most notable building is the **Cathedral** (1135–68), which has a beautiful *W doorway* with a magnificent sculptured Last Judgement. It contains a painting by Diego Ortiz of Oviedo (1489–94), remains of Romanesque wall paintings and several chapels with very fine retablos. – Church of *La Magdalena* (13th–16th c.), with a 12th c. doorway; fine 16th c. retablo. – Church of *San Nicola's* (12th c.), brick-built, with a Romanesque doorway; it contains the tomb of King Sancho el Fuerte (d. 1234).

Túy

Province: Pontevedra (PO).
Telephone code: 986.
Altitude: 45 m. – Population: 13,000.
ⓘ **Oficina de Información de Turismo,**
Puente de Tripes;
tel. 60 17 85.

HOTELS. – *Parador Nacional San Telmo*, Carretera de
Túy (1 km), II, 16 r.; *Hostal Generosa*, P III, 16 r.

EVENTS. – *Fiesta de San Telmo* (Apr.). – *Fiesta de San
Julián* (July).

The old Spanish frontier town of Túy, the seat of a bishop, is picturesquely situated on a hill above the right bank of the Río Miño (Portuguese Minho). There was a fortress here in Roman times (Tude), and in the 8th c. it was the residence of the Visigothic kings.

SIGHTS. – The town is dominated by its fortress-like **Cathedral** (11th–13th c.), begun in Romanesque style but much altered in later centuries. It has a porch with a fine Gothic *W doorway* (14th c.), and contains several tombs and choir-stalls with interesting carving; cloister of the 14th and 15th c. – Several other notable churches.

S of Túy is the Spanish frontier control post (passports and customs), and beyond this the 333 m long international bridge over the Miño (Minho), which forms the frontier between Spain and Portugal.

Úbeda

Province: Jaén (J).
Telephone code: 953.
Altitude: 757 m. – Population: 30,000.
ⓘ **Oficina de Información de Turismo,**
Plaza de los Caídos;
tel. 75 08 97.

HOTELS. – *Parador Nacional Condestable Dávalos*, II,
26 r.; *Consuelo* (no rest.), III, 39 r.; Hostal *La Paz* (no
rest.), P II, 53 r.; *Casa Castillo*, P III, 24 r.

RESTAURANT. – *Méson Pintor*, V. de Guadalupe 4.

The little Renaissance town of Úbeda, situated near the upper Guadalquivir amid large olive plantations, has preserved its ancient Iberian name. Its numerous historic

buildings have earned it the title of the "Andalusian Salamanca".

SIGHTS. – Church of **El Salvador**, in Renaissance style, built by Diego de Siloé (16th c.). On the high altar is a "Transfiguration" by Alonso Berruguete; other altars of the Flemish school. – In the attractive Plaza de Vázquez de Molina is the church of **Santa María** (13th c., later remodelled), with richly decorated Gothic chapels and a fine choir screen by Maestro Bartolomé (16th c.). – Church of **San Pablo**, in the N of the town, dating from the period of the Reconquista, with an apse of 1380 and an interesting fountain (1559) built into the church wall. – *Palacio de los Marqueses de Mancera*, once the property of the Viceroy of Peru. – Other old palaces; remains of town walls, with towers.

SURROUNDINGS. – 8 km NE is the charming little town of **Sabiote**, with a large Moorish castle, a 16th c. church designed by Vandaelvira and a Carmelite convent. – 9 km SW is the old-world town of **Baeza** (see p. 62). – 50 km SE by way of *Peal de Becerro* is the typical little hill town of **Cazorla** (alt. 790 m; pop. 14,000), a good base for walks and climbs in the *Sierra de Cazorla* (Parador Nacional El Adelantado, II, 33 r.), a range of hills some 70 km long and almost 20 km across, with the *Coto Nacional de Cazorla* (nature reserve). – S of Cazorla is the typical Andalusian village of *Quesada*, with the Zabaleta Museum, which contains the largest collection of works by that name. – N of Cazorla is the village of *La Truela*, with a castle on the edge of a precipitous cliff.

Valencia (Town)

Province: Valencia (V)
Telephone code: 96.
Altitude: at sea level. – Population: 752,000.
ⓘ **Oficina de Información de Turismo,**
Plaza del País Valenciano 1, (Town Hall),
tel. 3 51 04 17.
Calle de la Paz 46,
tel. 35 22 87.
Asociación Provincial de Promoción del Turismo,
Gregorio Mayans 3;
tel. 3 34 16 02.

HOTELS. – *Astoria Palace*, Plaza Rodrigo Botet 5, I,
208 r.; *Dimar* (no rest.), Gran Via Marqués del Turia
80, I, 95 r.; *Reina Victoria*, Barcas 4, I, 92 r.; *Rey Don
Jaime*, Avda Baleares 2, I, 314 r.; SP; *Excelsior* (no
rest.), Barcelonina 5, II, 65 r.; *Expo Hotel*, Avda Pio XII
4, II, 396 r., SP; *Feria Sol*, Avda de la Feria 2, II, 136 r.;
Inglés, Marqués de Dos Aguas 6, II, 62 r.; *Lehos* (no
rest.), General Urrutia s/n, II, 104 r., SP; *Llar* (no rest.),
Colón 46, II, 50 r.; *Metropol* (no rest.), Játiva 23, II,
108 r.; *Oltra* (no rest.), Plaza del Pais Valenciano 4, II,
93 r.; *Recati*, km 18 on the Valencia-Oliva road; II,
44 r., SP; *Renasa* (no rest.), Avda Cataluña 5, II, 73 r.;
Sorolla (no rest.), Convento Santa Clara 5, II, 50 r.;

Bristol (no rest.), Abadía San Martín 3, III, 40 r.; *Continental* (no rest.), Correos 8, III, 43 r.; *La Marcelina* (no rest.), Playa de Levante 72, III, 40 r.; *Patilla* (no rest.), Pinares 10, II, 28 r.; *Alcázar*, Mesón Femades 11, IV, 18 r.; *Europa*, Ribera 4, IV, 81 r.; *Internacional* (no rest.), Bailén 8, IV, 55 r.; *La Pepica* (no rest.), Avda de Neptuno 2, IV, 53 r.; *Valencia* (no rest.), Convento San Francisco 7, IV, 59 r.; Hostal *Florida* (no rest.), Padilla 4, P I, 45 r.; *Londres* (no rest.), Barcelonina 1, P I, 57 r.; *Mediterráneo*, Avda Barón de Cárcer 45, P I, 30 r.; etc. – CAMPING SITES: *Voramar*, In Meliana, 6 km N; *El Saler* and *Valencia*, both 8 km S; *El Palmar*, 13 km S; other sites, S on the Carretera Alicante.

Fallas, Valencia

Burning of the *fallas*

RESTAURANTS. – In most hotels; also *Los Viveros*, Jardines del Real; *Les Graelles*, Plaza Galicia 10; *La Hacienda*, Avda de Navarro Reverter 12; *Mesón del Marisquero*, Félix Pizcueta 7; *Siona*, Pizato 9; etc. – AT PLAYA DE LEVANTE: *Las Arenas*; etc.

EVENTS. – **Fallas** (Mar.), a fiesta in honour of San José and also a spring festival, during which large structures known as *fallas*, with figures made of papier mâché and rags (*ninots*) are set up in the streets an burned at midnight on the last day of the fiesta. *Fiesta de la Virgen de los Desamparados* (May) an *Corpus Christi*, both with processions. – *Feria de Sa Jaime* (July), with bullfights, a literary contest i the Teatro Principal and a battle of flowers (*juego florales*) in the Alameda at the end of the fiesta. *Iberflora* (flower show) in autumn, and numerou trade fairs throughout the year.

CASINO. – *Casino Monte Picayo*, Puzol.

WATER SPORTS. – Several bathing beaches near th town (bus services); *Playa de Levante*, to the left o the harbour, with Las Arenas bathing station; *Play de la Malvarrosa*, next the Playa de Levante, wit restaurants and cafés; *Playa de Nazaret*, to the right o the harbour, with Benimar bathing station, restaurant and cafés. There is a Club Nautico.

SPORT and RECREATION on land. – Shooting an fishing at La Albufera; golf, tennis, riding, targe shooting; bullfights; walks, organised by the Centr Excursionista.

BOAT SERVICES. – Car ferries to the Balearics (Ibiza Palma de Mallorca). – Information: Compañia Tras mediterránea, Avenida Manuel Soto 15, and Estació Marítima (at the port).

The old capital of the kingdom o Valencia, now the chief town of it province, the see of an archbishop, university town and Spain's thir largest city, lies close to the Medi terranean on the right bank of th Río Turia (known to the Arabs a the Guadalaviar, the "White River") in the fertile Huerta de Valencia.

Valencia, described in an ancient saying as "a piece of heaven fallen to earth", is typically southern town with its bustling streets and the brightly coloured tiles (*azulejos*) on the domes of its many churches. The climate is unusually mild and predominantly dry. Its port of *El Grao* 4 km E of the city centre, is mainly engaged in shipping the agricultura produce of the huerta (oranges, wine raisins, oil and rice). With its extensive suburban districts Valencia is a lively modern city fully in tune with the world o today.

HISTORY. – Originally a Greek settlement, Valenci later fell into the hands of the Carthaginians, and in the 2nd c. B.C. became the Roman colony of *Valentia* which rose to prosperity in the time of Augustus. I 413 it passed to the Visigoths and in 714 to the Moors who called it *Medina bu-Tarab* ("city of joy"). Afte the fall of the Caliphate of Córdoba Valencia and the adjoining coastal region became an independen kingdom, which was conquered by the Almoravide in 1092. Two years later it was recovered by El Cid, bu in 1102 it again fell into Moorish hands. Unde Mohammad ibn Said it became capital of a powerfu Moorish kingdom until its reconquest by Jaime I o

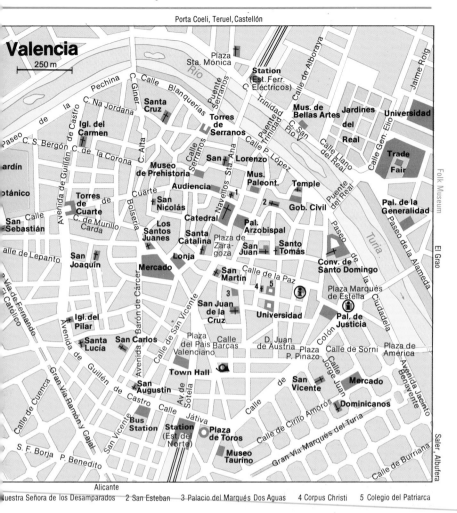

Porta Coeli, Teruel, Castellón

Valencia

250 m

Río

Pechina · C. Giner · Calle · Blanquerías

Plaza Sta. Mónica

Station (Est.Ferr. Eléctricos)

Calle de Alboraya

Jaime Roig

C. Na Jordana · Santa Cruz

Torres de Serranos

Mus. de Bellas Artes · Jardines del Real · Universidad

Igl. del Carmen

Paseo · de · la · Avenida de Guillén de Castro · C. de la Corona · C. Alta

C. S. Bergón · C. de la Corona

jardín

Calle · P. López

Calle Gen. Elío

Trade Fair

Folk Museum

botánico

Museo de Prehistoria · Audiencia

San Aña · Lorenzo

Mus. Paleont. · Temple

Gob. Civil

Pal. de la Generalidad

San Sebastián · Torres de Cuarte · Calle · de · Cuarte · C. de Murillo · Carda

San Nicolás

Catedral

Pal. Arzobispal

El Grao

alle de Lepanto

Los Santos Juanes · Santa Catalina

Plaza de Zaragoza · San Juan · Santo Tomás

Conv. de Santo Domingo

Turia

San Joaquín

Mercado

Lonja

San Martín · Calle de la Paz

Paseo de la Alameda

Vía de Fernando el Católico

Igl. del Pilar

San Juan de la Cruz

Universidad

Plaza Marqués de Estella

Pal. de Justicia

Santa Lucía · San Carlos

Plaza del País Valenciano

Calle Barcas

D. Juan de Austria · Plaza P. Pinazo

Calle de Sorni

Plaza de América

Avenida Jacinto Benavente

Saler, Albufera

Gran Vía Ramón y Cajal

Avenida de Guillén de Castro

Town Hall

San Agustín

Calle · Játiva

de · San Vicente · Mercado

Dominicanos

Calle de Cuenca

Bus Station

Station (Est. del Norte)

Plaza de Toros

Museo Taurino

Calle de Cirilo Amorós

Gran Vía Marqués del Turia

Calle de Burriana

S. F. Borja · P. Benedito

Alicante

1 Nuestra Señora de los Desamparados   2 San Esteban   3 Palacio del Marqués Dos Aguas   4 Corpus Christi   5 Colegio del Patriarca

ragon (Jaime el Conquistador) in 1238. In 1702 the ingdom lost its special privileges; from 1936 until 1937 Valencia was the seat of the republican overnment.

IGHTS. – The hub of the city's life and affic is the elongated *Plaza del País Valenciano*, with a fountain; it is surrounded by hotels, cafés and offices. On the W de of the square is the **Ayuntamiento** or *Palacio Consistorial* (Town Hall), containing the *Municipal Library* and the *Municipal History Museum* (pictures, valuable books, etc.) In the basement is a tourist information office – To the S, in alle Játiva, one of the streets which encircle the old town, is the *Estación del Norte* (Northern Station), and next to this the *Plaza de Toros*, one of Spain's largest bullrings (18,000 seats), with an interesting *Museo Taurino* (Bull-fighting Museum).

at a tall office block at the N end of the Plaza País Valenciano we cut across *Calle an Vicente*, Valencia's principal street,

the northern section of which is particularly busy, and continue along a new street, *Calle María Cristina*, into another large elongated square, the busy *Plaza del Mercado* (underground car park), once the scene of tournaments and public ceremonies. On the left is the *Mercado Central* (Central Market), built in 1928 and lavishly decorated with azulejos, which has some 1300 market stalls. Adjoining the Market is the church of the *Santos Juanes* (1368), with a beautiful façade and a ceiling painting by A. Palomino, both dating from about 1700. Opposite the Market is the *Lonja de la Seda* (Silk Exchange), a magnificent late Gothic building, erected in 1498 on the site of a Moorish alcázar, with richly decorated doorways and window tracery and fine gargoyles (*gárgolas*). The main hall has rich stellate vaulting borne on twisted columns. From the tower (144 steps) there are fine views of the town. – N of the Plaza del Mercado is the church of **San Nicholás**, also built on the site of an earlier mosque, with fine frescoes and pictures.

At the N end of Calle San Vicente is the *Plaza de Zaragoza* (considerably enlarged in recent years), the central square of the old town. On the left is the Gothic church of *Santa Catalina*, with a richly ornamented hexagonal tower. On the N side of the square is the ***Cathedral** (*La Seo*), built between 1262 and 1482 on the site of a mosque. It is an imposing building with a predominantly Gothic exterior but a Baroque façade. At its SW corner is the 68 m high bell-tower (unfinished) known as the **Torre del Miguelete* (or *Micalet*), containing the bell of the same name (baptised on Michaelmas Day 1418) which formerly regulated the irrigation of the huerta with its chimes; from the outlook platform (50 m, 207 steps; entrance from N aisle) there are magnificent views. – In the N transept is the Gothic *Puerta de los Apóstoles*, richly decorated with sculpture, and above it is a 14th c. rose window; in the S aisle is the Romanesque *Puerta del Palau*.

In Valencia

The INTERIOR (98 m long) was completely remodelled in the 18th c. It contains many fine pictures, including works by Goya and Palomino. – The Choir has beautiful 16th c. stalls. Over the crossing is a majestic octagonal dome (*cimborio*). – The **Capilla Mayor** has a magnificent 15th c. high altar, with side panels painted by two pupils of Leonardo da Vinci (1509). – The *Sala Capitular* (1482) contains a valuable collection of pictures, including works by Ribera and Macip. – In the S aisle is the ***Capilla del Santo Cáliz**, built as the chapterhouse in 1369, with Gothic stellate vaulting. In this chapel is the *Santo Cáliz* (Holy Chalice), set with rubies and pearls, which is believed to be the chalice of the Last Supper, the Holy Grail itself. Until the 15th c. it was kept in the Pyrenean monastery of San Juan de la Paña. – The **Cathedral Museum** contains paintings by Zurbarán, Juan de Juanes, Goya and other artists.

On the N side of the Cathedral, joined to it by an arch, is the *Capilla de Nuestra Señora de los Desamparados* (Our Lady of the Helpless), built in 1667. On the high altar is a carved wooden figure of the Virgin (1416), the much venerated "Sagrada Imagen", patroness of the city. – NE of the chapel, in the old public granary, the Almudín, is the *Museo Paleontológico*, with a collection of prehistoric animal remains from South America.

NW of the Cathedral in *Calle de Caballeros* is the **Palacio de la Generalidad** (*Audiencia*), built 1510–79 to house the parliament of the kingdom of Valencia,

now occupied by the Diputación Provincial. On the first floor are the **Salón d' Cortes*, in which the Cortes met, and th Sala Dorada, with splendid artesonado ceilings.

On the N side of the old town are th ***Torres de Serranos**, the old N gate built (on Roman foundations) in 139 and restored in 1930; from the massiv towers there are fine views. N of the gat is the *Puente de Serranos* over the Rí Turia (which is dry for most of the year, and on the far side of the river is the churc of *Santa Mónica*.

Calle de Caballeros and its continuatio Calle de Cuarte lead W to the **Torres d Cuarte** (or *Puerta de Cuarte*), which i similar to the Serranos gate (1440–90). short distance away, on the far side of th ring of streets round the old town, is th *Jardín Botánico*, a botanic garden con taining thousands of species of plant Particularly notable among the sub tropical flora are *Polygala grandiflora* an speciosa, with purple flowers (March, NW in Calle de la Corona are the *Museo de Ethnología y Prehistoria*.

S of the Plaza de Zaragoza in Calle Sa Vicente, is the Gothic church of *Sa Martín* (1372), with a bronze statue of S Martin on horseback above the doorwa A little way E is the imposing 18th *Palacio del Marqués de Dos Aguas*, wit an elaborately decorated alabaster doo way by Ignacio Vergara. It now houses th *Museo Nacional de Cerámica*, Spain leading ceramic museum, with more tha 5000 examples of traditional potter mainly from Valencia and the surroundin

ea (azulejos, faience; also modern
eces by Benlliure and Picasso). – S of
e palace is the church of *San Andrés*,
uilt in 1686 on the site of an earlier
osque, with numerous pictures by local
tists and hand-painted azulejos from
anises. – E of the church is the **Colegio
el Patriarca**, a Renaissance mansion
ith an arcaded courtyard built between
586 and 1610 for Juan de Ribera,
rchbishop and Viceroy of Valencia. The
apilla de la Concepción contains 16th c.
emish tapestries. On the first floor is the
ector's House, with a valuable collection
f old masters (Dierick Bouts, van der
Weyden, Juanes, Ribalta, Morales, El
reco, etc.) and some superb Brussels
pestries. At the S corner of the building
ands the church of *Corpus Christi*
586), with a *Last Supper (1606) by
ibalta on the high altar. The Miserere
rvice (every Friday about 10) is an
npressive occasion, during which
ibalta's picture disappears and a curtain
suddenly pulled aside to reveal a
ooden crucifix (believed to be of 16th c.
erman workmanship). –Across the street
om the Colegio is the **University**
present building 1830), with a valuable
rary of some 87,000 volumes, including
umerous incunabula and manuscripts.

E of the University is the *Paseo de la
Jorieta* (gardens), to the N of which is
e church of *Santo Domingo*, also called
e *Capilla San Vicente Ferrer* (re-
odelled at the end of the 18th c.), which
entered through a fine doorway adjoin-
g the uncompleted tower. In the 15th c.
apilla de los Reyes (on right) is the tomb
Rodrigo Mendoza (d. 1554).

the N of the church the *Puente del Real*
598), with statues of St Vincent the
artyr and St Vincent Ferrer (17th c.),
osses the Río Turia to the *Jardines del
eal* (also known as the *Viveros Muni-
pales*), with numerous modern monu-
ents. Adjoining the gardens is the Trade
ir building, from which the Paseo de la
ameda runs alongside the river, down-
ream, to the Puente de Aragón.

ust W of the gardens, near the river, is the
Museo Provincial de Bellas Artes, in
former convent. On the first floor are
ctures by the great artists of the past
Ribalta, Ribera, Macip, Espinosa, Veláz-
uez, Murillo, El Greco, Goya, Morales,
nturicchio, Andrea del Sarto, etc.), on

the second floor works by Valencia
painters of the 19th and 20th c.

SURROUNDINGS. – E of Valencia, reached by way of
the Puente de Aragón, is **El Grao**, the port of Valencia
since medieval times and still one of Spain's leading
seaports. From the E breakwater there is an attractive
view of the bay, with the *Sierra de Cullera* to the S and
the *Castillo de Sagunto* to the N. On both sides of the
harbour are popular bathing beaches. To the S of the
Playa de Pinedo, on the spit of land between the sea
and the Albufera lagoon, is the resort of **El Saler**, with
hotels, a golf-course and a long beach (hotels: Sidi
Saler Palace-Sol, L, 272 r., SP, beach; Parador
Nacional de Luis Vives, I, 58 r.).

NW of Valencia (Puente San José, then a minor road)
is the little town of *Burjasot* (pop. 12,000), a summer
holiday resort with cave dwellings and underground
grain-stores (16th–18th c.). Beyond this the road
continues through the picturesque little town of
Bétera (pop. 7000) to the beautifully situated
Cartuja de Porta Coeli, a Carthusian house with
three cloisters and a handsome church (beautiful
chapels and ceiling paintings). From the hills above
the monastery there are magnificent views.

8 km W of Valencia via the Avenida del Cid is the old
potters' village of **Manises**, still producing its
traditional pottery

The coast road to Alicante. – The *road from
Valencia to Alicante along the coast (N 332) is one of
the most beautiful roads in southern Spain. Leave the
city either by the road (motorway standard) which
runs close to the coast via *El Saler* or by the more direct
N 332 via *Sueca* to **Cullera** (pop. 15,000), an old
town on the slopes of the *Monte del Oro*, below a
castle and a church containing a much venerated
image of the Virgen del Castillo, patroness of the town.

The route then continues over the Huerta de Gandía,
passes the *Castillo de San Juan*, above the road on the
right, and comes to **Gandía** (see p. 123). Soon
afterwards it enters the province of Alicante, passes
minor roads on the left to *Denia* and *Jávea* and reaches
the international resort of **Benidorm** (see p. 80); then
via *Villajoyosa* to **Alicante** (see p. 50), 185 km from
Valencia.

Over the Puerto de Albaida to Alicante. – N 340
runs S to **Alberique** (alt. 30 m; pop. 8000), lying off
the road to the left, which has a Baroque church with
a fine retablo. Then on to **Játiva** (see p. 143), and
from there over the *Puerto de Albaida* (628 m) into the
province of Alicante and via *Alcoy* to **Alicante**,
168 km from Valencia.

Over the Puerto de Almansa to Albacete. – Leave
Valencia on N 340/430, and at the fork where N 340
continues to Játiva bear right on N 430, which runs
SW past *Montesa*, with a castle (destroyed in an
earthquake in 1748) which gave its name to the Order
of Montesa, founded in 1318 to replace the Templars.
– Then on through *Mogente* (alt. 358 m), a little town
established by the Moors, and up to the *Puerto de
Almansa* (692 m), on the provincial boundary, after
which the road continues to **Almansa** and through
the Montes de Chinchilla to **Albacete** (see p. 46),
188 km from Valencia.

Over the Puerto de Contreras. – N III runs W
through the well-cultivated Huerta de Valencia to the

township of **Chiva** (alt. 282 m; pop. 4000), off the road to the right, with a ruined Moorish castle and an 18th c. parish church (1733–81). SW of the town, in a beautiful and fertile valley known as the "Valencian Switzerland", is the little spa of *Buñol* (alt. 300 m), with the ruins of a Moorish stronghold.

The road continues through an upland region in the *Sierra de la Cabrillas* to **Requena** (alt. 292 m; pop. 21,000), beautifully situated on two hills above the *Río Magro*, with a ruined castle and several Gothic churches, including Santa María, which has a magnificent late Gothic doorway, and the 13th c. church of San Nicolás. In the castle is the *Museo del Vino* (Museum of Wine), with more than 2000 bottles of wine up to 400 years old.

N III then ascends the fertile valley of the Río Magro to **Utiel** (alt. 700 m; pop. 15,000), an old-world little town with a 16th c. church, 32 km N (dust-free road) is an artificial lake in a very beautiful setting, the *Pantano del Generalísimo*.

The road now climbs via *Villagordo del Cabriel* (alt. 855 m) to the **Puerto de Contreras** (890 m), with a bridge over the Río Cabriel, the boundary between the provinces of Valencia and Cuenca and between the Levante and Castile. Immediately N is the reservoir, the *Embalse de Contreras*.

Along the Costa del Azahar. – N 340 leads N from Valencia along the *Costa del Azahar*, the "Orange-Blossom Coast", passing (to the right) *Puig*, with a ruined castle and, at the foot of the hill, a former Carthusian monastery (Gothic tombs and frescoes in the church). The road then continues via *Puzol* (fine church) to **Sagunto** (see p. 191), in a large agricultural area.

Valencia (Region)

Autonomous Region.
Organ of Government: Consell de la Comunidad Valenciana.

Provinces: Alicante, Castellón de la Plana and Valencia.

In the Valencia region the rivers flowing down from the interior, such as the Río Turia and the Río Júcar, which at certain times – in spring, when the snow melts, or

The huerta, near Valencia

after thunder showers – surge tem pestuously down their valleys and i the course of time have built u areas of fertile alluvial land alon the coast, are harnessed to suppl water to irrigate the hot lands lyin in the rain-shadow of the hills, th "campo de regadío". These irriga tion systems, first constructed b the Romans and later developed b the Moors, make the Valencia regio one of the most fertile in Spain, wit melons, tomatoes and a variety o vegetables growing in the shadow c the orange-, apricot-, almond- an fig-trees. On the unirrigated lan the "campo secano", olives, vine and carobs flourish.

The region extends along the coast in narrow strip from the Ebro delta to th mouth of the Río Segura; but the souther part of Alicante province, beyond Cabo c la Nao, belongs to Murcia. Here th treeless reddish-grey plateaux of th *Meseta* come close to the Mediterranea terminating – in a steep rocky coa slashed by narrow gorges.

The Catalan population of this regio created the attractive landscape pattern c the **huertas**, often laid out on a geometr plan, in which the fruit orchards ar planted on terraces, with groups c slender palms or cypresses adding vertical note. The white houses (*barracas of the peasants (*hortelanos*) are even distributed over the green landscape c the huertas. The creaking water-whee (*norias*) of the Moors, worked by mule are increasingly giving place to electrical operated pumps. An ancient court, th *Tribunal de las Aguas*, operates under well-conceived code of law to ensure th equitable distribution of the preciou water, which is fed to the thirsty lan through an intricate network of canals an water-channels.

Valladolid

Province: Valladolid (VA).
Telephone code: 983.
Altitude: 694 m. – Population: 330,000
ⓘ **Oficina de Información de Turismo,**
Plaza de Zorrilla 3;
tel. 35 18 01.
Delegación Territorial de Turismo,
Divina Pastora 6 and 8;
tel. 30 60 11 and 30 61 22.

HOTELS. – *Felipe IV* (no rest.), Gamazo 16, I, 130 r.; *Olid Meliá*, Plaza de San Miguel 10, I, 226 r.; *Meliá Parque*, García Morato 17, II, 306 r.; *Imperial*, Peso 4, III, 80 r.; *Roma*, Héroes del Alcázar de Toledo 6, III, 38 r.; *Enara* (no rest.), Plaza de España 5, IV, 26 r.; Hostal *Burgalesa*, Plaza Santa Ana 7, P II, 16 r.; *París* (no rest.), Especeria 2, P II, 24 r.; etc. – ON THE BURGOS ROAD, km 120: *Hostal Covatra*, P II, 18 r. – CAMPING SITE: *El Plantío*, on the N 620 Salamanca road about 12 km SW.

RESTAURANTS. – In the hotels; also **Feria de Muestras*, Avda de Ramón Pradera; *El Atrío*, Atrío de Santiago 7; *El Cardenal*, Plaza Tenerias 18; *Mesón de Cervantes*, El Rastro 6; *Mesón La Fragua*, Paseo de Zorilla 10; *Oscar*, Ferrari 1, *Panero*, Recoletos 3; etc.

EVENTS. – *Semana Santa* (Holy Week), with processions (a particularly impressive one on Good Friday, when large statues are carried through the streets). – *International Film Week* (Apr.), devoted particularly to religious and humanitarian films. – *Ferias y Fiestas* (Sept.) in honour of San Mateo, with bullfights, sporting and traditional events; may be associated with the Regional Trade Fair for Old Castile and León. – *Festivales de España* (Oct.–Nov.), with dramatic and operatic performances, concerts and lieder recitals. – Courses for foreign students (summer).

Valladolid, situated on the Río Pisuerga just above its junction with the Duero, on the fertile plateau of Old Castile, is an industrial city, capital of its province, the see of an archbishop and a university town.

HISTORY. – There was a settlement here in the time of the Arabs, who called it *Velad-Olid* ("town of the governor") or *Balad-Walid* ("town of the *walid*"). In 1469 the Catholic monarchs, Ferdinand and (Isabel), were married in Valladolid, and in 1504–06 Columbus, an ailing and disappointed man, spent the last two years of his life in the town. For brief periods during the 16th and 17th c. in the reigns of Philip II and III, Valladolid was the seat of the Spanish court.

SIGHTS. – The hub of the city's traffic is the arcaded *Plaza Mayor*, on the N side of which is the *Ayuntamiento* (Town Hall), built in 1908. – A short distance NW of the Town Hall is the church of *San Benito* (1499–1504), with a large open porch in front of the tower; beautiful wrought-iron choir screen (1571). – Immediately W of the Plaza Mayor, in the former church of the Pasión, is a *picture gallery*, with works by Spanish masters of the 16th and 17th c. In the nearby church of *Santa Ana* are paintings by Goya and Bayeu.

From the Plaza Mayor the *Calle de Santiago* runs S to the church of *Santiago*, with a fine retablo by Berruguete and a figure of Christ by Francisco de la Mata (in a side chapel). Farther S is the *Plaza*

de Zorilla, and adjoining this the *Paseo del Campo Grande*, a wide park-like promenade at the S end of which is a large *monument to Columbus* (1905). Off this avenue branches the *Avenida de los Filipinos*, in which is the Augustinian convent, *Real Colegio*; housing the Oriental Museum with Chinese and Philippino works of art. – To the E of the Plaza de Zorilla, in the short Calle del Rosario, is the *Casa de Cervantes*, in which Cervantes lived in 1603–06 and where he probably wrote the first part of "Don Quixote". In this and two adjoining houses is the *Cervantes Museum*, with a library.

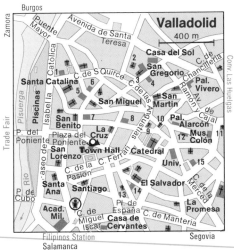

1 Palacio de los Condes de Benavente	7 Casa de Berruguete
2 Convento de Santa Teresa	8 Palacio Arzobispal
3 Convento de San Pablo	9 Iglesia de las Angustias
4 Casa del Marqués de Villena	10 Santa Maria la Antigua
5 Palacio de los Marqueses de Valverde	11 La Magdalena
6 Museo Arqueológico	12 Palacio de los Zuñiga
	13 Porta Coeli church
	14 Palacio Capicholatro
	15 Colegio de Santa Cruz

Some 500 m E of the Plaza Mayor is the **Cathedral**, begun by Juan de Herrera in 1580 on an ambitious scale, continued by Alberto Churriguera from 1730 onwards but never completed. Of the four corner towers which were planned only the S tower was built (restored in 1885 after its collapse in 1841). In the spacious interior (122 m long, 62·5 m wide) are a high altar by Juan de Juni (1561), originally in Santa María la Antigua, beautiful Renaissance choir-stalls and an "Assumption" by Velázquez. The adjoining *Diocesan Museum* contains among much else a silver *custodia* in the form of a temple, 2 m high, Juan de Arfe's masterpiece (1590).

To the E of the Cathedral, in *Plaza de la Universidad*, is the **University** (founded 1346), with an imposing Baroque façade (by Diego and Narciso Tomé), 1715). – SE of the University is the former **Colegio de Santa Cruz** (1492), in early Plateresque style, with a richly sculptured façade and a beautiful patio; it now houses the *Colegio Mayor* of the University, with a valuable *library* of 52,000 volumes. – From here *Calle del Cardenal Mendoza* runs NE into Calle de Colón, with the *Casa de Colón*, in which Columbus died on 31 May 1506; there is a small museum in the adjoining house. Opposite, to the E, is the church of *La Magdalena* (16th c.), with fine roundels containing coats of arms on the façade. Adjoining is the *Convento de las Huelgas*, with a 16th c. church.

NW of the University is the church of *Santa María la Antigua* (12th–14th c.), the oldest church in the town, with a Romanesque tower and an elegant nave with lateral aisles. Close by is the church of *Las Angustias* (1597–1604), with a chapel containing the much venerated Virgen de los Cuchillos, a carved wooden figure by Juan de Juni (1560). – Calle de las Angustias runs N to the *Plaza de San Pablo*, with the church of **San Pablo** (founded 1276), whose soaring *façade (by Simon of Cologne, 1492), flanked by plain towers, vies in decorative richness with San Gregorio (below). Features of the interior are the beautiful doorways in the transepts and a statue of Santo Domingo by Gregorio Hernández. – Opposite San Pablo is the former *Palacio Real* (Royal Palace), now the *Capitanía General*, with a beautiful arcaded courtyard. – Next to San Pablo is the former *Colegio de San Gregorio** (1488–96), with a late Gothic façade overloaded with statues, coats of arms and naturalistic ornament. It has two courtyards, the second being particularly fine. On the first floor is the **Museo Nacional de Escultura* (National Museum of Sculpture), with a magnificent collection of Spanish sculpture (mostly polychrome) of the 16th and 17th c., including works by Gregorio Hernández (1566–1636), Alonso Berruguete (*c.* 1482–1561), Pedro de Mena (1664) and Juan de Juni ("Entombment of Christ", 1544). – A little way SW of the former Royal Palace is the *Palacio de Fabio Nelli*, a handsome Renaissance palace (1594), with a beautiful pillared courtyard, which now houses the *Museo Arqueológico Provincial*.

SURROUNDINGS. – The part played by the Valladolid region in the history of Spain has left it with numerous castles, many built for defence; some will be seen on any excursion in the surrounding area.

The Pisuerga and Duero route. – This is the road for Zamora or Salamanca. Leave Valladolid on N 620, which runs SW, close to the right bank of the *Río Pisuerga*, to (11 km) **Simancas** (alt. 725 m; pop. 6000; Hotel Simancas, IV, 24 r.), with the formidable Castillo de Simancas, now housing the Spanish national archives (more than 30 million documents, in 52 rooms). – Then on to **Tordesillas** (see p. 228), near the junction of the Pisuerga with the *Río Duero*, where N 620 cuts across N IV. – From Tordesillas continue on N 122 via *Toro* (see p. 228) to **Zamora** (p. 243), 96 km from Valladolid; or alternatively on N620 to *Alaejos*, with an interesting 16th c. church, and then over a fertile plain to **Salamanca** (p. 191), 114 km from Valladolid.

The Duero route. – N 122 runs E up the Duero valley to *Quintanilla de Onésimo*. From here an excursion can be made to **Valbuena de Duero**, on the N bank of the river, to see the monastery of Santa María, with the ruins of a 12th c. Cistercian church and a fine late Gothic cloister. – Then back to N 122, or along a minor road on the N bank of the Duero, to **Peñafiel**, with a castle (12 round towers and a keep 24 m high) built by the Counts of Castile in the 12th c. and the Convento de San Pablo, in Mudéjar style.

To Madrid. – N 403 runs S over the low-lying land between the Pisuerga and the Duera to **Olmedo** (alt. 787 m; pop. 5000), an ancient little walled town, once the seat of noble families and a formidable stronghold, containing numerous convents. Romanesque church of San Miguel (13th c.), with a picturesque domed lower church; church of Santa María (retablo of 1550). – 7 km beyond Olmedo a road turns off on the left via *Fuente de Santa Cruz* and *Ciruelos de Coca* to the little town of *Coca* (15 km). – The main road continues via *Montuenga*, where a road branches off on the right to (8 km) **Arévalo** (see p. 57), to **Martín Muñoz de las Posadas**, with a palace built by Juan Bautista de Toledo in 1572 for the Inquisitor Diego de Espinosa (whose tomb is in the parish church). – Soon afterwards N 403 joins N VI, coming from La Coruña, which continues to Madrid, bypassing the little town of *Villacastín*.

Towards Segovia. – Take N 601, which runs SE, crosses the Canal de Castilla and comes to *El Arrabal del Portillo*. Off the road to the left is **Portillo**, with a strongly walled castle, formerly a state prison for political offenders in which Don Álvaro de Luna was confined.

Towards León. – N 601 runs NW across the wide valley of the Duero and up to **Villanubla** (alt. 843 m), lying off the road to the left. From here a minor road leads W to *Wamba*, with the church of Santa María, which incorporates part of a 12th c. Mozarabic church. The Visigothic king Recceswinth died at Wamba in 672. Beyond Wamba on the same minor road is *Torrelobatón*, dominated by a well-preserved 13th c. castle with massive round towers and an imposing Torre del Homenaje. – On the secondary road running E from N 601 is the village of *Fuensaldaña*, with the 15th c. Castillo de Vivero.

N 601 continues through an upland region in the *Montes de Torozos* to **Medina de Rioseco** (alt. 735 m; pop. 5000), an old-world little town with six notable churches dating from the 15th–17th c. Among them is Santa María de Mediavilla, which has two fine *rejas* (1532, 1554), an altar by Esteban Jordán (1590) and the Plateresque Capilla de los Benavente (1546).

SURROUNDINGS. – 6 km E is *San Julián de Vilatorta*, with a Romanesque church. From here the road continues to the *Embalse de Sau* (reservoir).

Vich

Province: Barcelona (B).
Telephone code: 93.
Altitude: 485 m. – Population: 28,000.
ⓘ Oficina Municipal de Turismo,
Ciutat I;
tel. 8 86 20 91.

HOTELS. – *Parador Nacional*, 14 km from the town, I, 31 r., SP; *Ausa*, Plaza de Caudillo 4, III, 26 r.; *Colón*, Rambla Paseig 1, IV, 38 r.; Hostal *Cal-U*, Rambla Santa Teresa 7, P III, 30 r.

RESTAURANTS. – In the *Parador Nacional*; also *Anec Blau*, Verdaguer 21.

EVENTS. – *Mercat del Ram* (Palm Sunday), with a large market and folk celebrations. – *Fiesta* (July).

The old episcopal town of Vich, the Roman Ausa, lies on a plateau N of Barcelona at the confluence of the Río Meder and the Río Gurri. It is now a busy little industrial town.

SIGHTS. – The fine **Cathedral**, founded in 1040 and restored 1803–21, has a Romanesque tower (11th c.), a beautiful 14th c. cloister, a 15th c. marble altar and modern frescoes by Sert (scenes from the lives of Apostles and Evangelists). In the ***Archaeological Museum** are pictures, sculpture, liturgical utensils and vessels and Iberian tombs. – *Roman temple* (2nd c. A.D.), restored.

Vigo

Province: Pontevedra (PO).
Telephone code: 986.
Altitude: 28 m. – Population: 259,000.
ⓘ Oficina de Información de Turismo,
Jardines de las Avenidas s/n,
tel. 43 05 77.
Delegación Local de Información,
Colón 30 (first floor);
tel. 21 10 51.

HOTELS. – *Bahía de Vigo*, Avda Cánovas del Castillo 5, I, 110 r.; *Ciudad de Vigo* (no rest.), Concepción Arenal 4, I, 101 r.; *Coia* (no rest.), Sangenjo s/n, I, 126 r.; *Gran Hotel Samil*, Playa de Samil, I, 127 r., SP; *Ensenada*, Alfonso XIII 35, II, 109 r.; *Ipanema* (no rest.), Vázquez Varela 31, II, 60 r.; *Lisboa*, Urzaiz 50, II, 93 r.; *México* (no rest.), Vía Norte 10, II, 112 r.; *Niza*, María Berdiales 32, II, 102 r.; *Almirante* (no rest.), Queipo de Llano 13, III, 31 r.; *América* (no rest.), Pablo Morillo 6, III, 56 r.; *Celta* (no rest.), México 22, III, 45 r.; *Galicia* (no rest.), Colón 13, III, 53 r.; *Junquera*, Uruguay 27, III, 35 r.; *Nilo* (no rest.), Marqués de Valladares 26, III, 52 r.; etc. – CAMPING SITE: *Samil*, about 6 km SW of Vigo on the shores of the bay.

RESTAURANTS. – In the hotels; also *Las Bridas*, Ecuador 58; *El Castillo*, Monte del Castro; *El Castro*, Manuel Olibie 31; *El Mosquito*, Plaza Villavicencio 4 (fish and seafood); *Mendikea*, Avda del Aeropuerto 151 (Basque dishes); *Puesto Piloto Alcabra*, Atlántida 194; etc.

EVENTS. – *Fiesta del Carmen* (July), with procession of boats. – *Feria del Cristo de la Victoria* (Aug.). – *Pilgrimage* to Monte de Santa Tecla (Aug.), usually with folk events and traditional costumes.

BOAT SERVICES. – Regular connections with the Canaries, northern Spain, Hamburg, London, Rotterdam and overseas ports.

WATER SPORTS. – Numerous bathing beaches in the surrounding area, the nearest being *Playa de Samil*

Vigo

(5 km SW), *Playa de la Meda* (6 km NE), *Playa de Rande* (8 km NE) and *Playa del Bao* and *Playa de Canido* (8 km SW).

SPORT and RECREATION on land. – Facilities for a wide range of sports, including fishing, tennis, golf, pelota; horse-races; bullfights. Several sports clubs. Aero Club based at Peinador airport.

An important naval and commercial port and one of Europe's principal centres of the sardine fisheries, Vigo is situated in the extreme NW of Spain on the S side of the *Ría de Vigo, a long inlet which penetrates 30 km inland.

In 1702, at the beginning of the War of the Spanish Succession, a British and Dutch fleet attacked the Spanish silver fleet in Vigo harbour, captured part of the treasure it was carrying and sank many of the ships in the deep waters of the bay, from which they were never recovered.

SIGHTS. – Vigo surrounds a hill on which are two castles, the *Castillo de San Sebastián* (alt. 55 m) and the *Castillo del Castro* (125 m), from which there are extensive views in clear weather. – To the E of the hill extends the **New Town**, with tall modern buildings, fine wide avenues and beautiful parks. Its main traffic arteries are the Avenida de García Barbón and its continuation Calle de Policarpo Sanz, half way up the hill, the Avenida de José Antonio above this which leads towards the old town, *Calle del Príncipe*, Vigo's principal business and shopping street. – Below Calle de Policarpo Sanz is the *Plaza de Compostela* or Alameda, with numerous monuments, from which the *Avenida de Felipe Sánchez* runs E past the *Commercial Harbour* (Puerto Comercial).

NW of the new town, between the hill and the sea, is the **Old Town**, with narrow and mostly steep and winding streets. In the centre is the neo-classical *Colegiata Santa María* (early 19th c.). Nearby, below the wharf, is the *Fish Market* (Pescadería), the scene of lively activity when a fish sale is in progress. On the *Muelle de Viajeros*, a pier reaching out into the ría, are the Marine Station (Estación Marítima) and the mooring berths. To the SW is the old-world fishermen's quarter of **Berbés**, with the *Dársena del Berbés*, the busy fishing harbour. Along the slope above this runs the *Paseo de Alfonso XIII*, from which there are fine views of the town, the harbour and the bay.

SURROUNDINGS. – Close to the town (1 km NE) is the *Mirador de la Guía*, with the Ermita de la Guía, another fine viewpoint overlooking the town and the sea.

Along the coast to La Guardia. – C 550 runs past the little fishing port of *Bouzas* and continues SW, running close to the shores of the Ría de Vigo. A side road on the right leads to the seaside resort of *Panjón*, with a monument to the dead of the Spanish merchant navy on an adjoining promontory. C 550 then crosses a bridge over the *Río Muiño* and comes to **Bayona** (pop. 7000; Hotel-Parador Nacional Conde de Gondomar, I, 66 r., SP), a prettily situated little port which is also a popular seaside resort. Romanesque and Gothic collegiate church (12th–13th c.); Castillo Monte Real (16th c.).

From here there is a beautiful stretch of road along the coast, which is rocky in places, to *Oya*, which has a Benedictine monastery in a style transitional between Romanesque and Gothic; 16th c. cloister, façade of 1740. Then on to **La Guardia** (pop. 8000), a small port near the mouth of the Río Miño (Portuguese Minho). To the S is *Camposancos*, on a point between the sea and the Miño, above which rises *Monte Tecla (360 m: extensive views), with a pilgrimage chapel and the remains of a pre-Roman settlement (small museum).

NE of La Guardia, near the N bank of the long estuary of the Miño (the S side of which is in Portugal), is **Túy** (see p. 231).

To Orense. – Leave Vigo by way of Calle José Antonio and continue SE on N 120, which winds its way up the slopes, partly forest-covered, of *Monte Ferreira* and then runs down into the valley of the *Río Louro* and comes to **Porriño** (alt. 10 m; pop. 9000), a small industrial town where N 120 cuts across the Pontevedra–Túy road (N 550). It then pursues a twisting course, with many undulations, through a region of wooded hills to **Puenteáreas** (alt. 50 m; pop. 15,000), on the *Río Tea*, from which a side road runs N up the Tea valley to the popular health resort of *Mondariz-Balneario* (alt. 121 m).

N 120 continues E, goes over the *Alto de Fuentefría*, with the *Faro de Avión* (1155 m) to the left, and runs down to *La Cañiza* (alt. 570 m). It then goes over another wooded ridge, enters Orense province and continues via *Ribadavia* to **Orense** (see p. 176), 106 km from Vigo.

Villanueva y Geltrú

Province: Barcelona (B).
Telephone dialling code: 93.
Altitude: 23 m. – Population: 35,000.
(i) **Oficina de Información de Turismo,**
Paseo de Ribes Roges;
tel. 8 93 59 57

HOTELS. – *César*, Isaak Peral 4, II, 30 r., SP; Hostal *Mar del Cal Ceferino*, Paseo de Ribes Roges s/n, P II, 28 r.; *Mare Nostrum*, Rambla de la Pau 66, P II, 20 r.; *Solvi 70*, Paseo de Ribes Roges 1, P II, 30 r.; *Burcet*, Rambla Castillo 46, P III, 18 r.; *Can Gatell*, Puigcerdá 12, P III, 63 r.; *Costador*, Passeo Maritimo 49, P III, 22 r.; etc.

Villaneuva y Geltrú

CAMPING SITES: *Vilanova Park*, about 3·5 km outside the town; *Platja Vilanova*, off the C 246 km 48·3 towards the sea.

RESTAURANTS. – *Bernardo y Margarita*, Ramonlull 4 (French cuisine); *Peixerot*, Paseo Marítimo 56 (fish dishes); *Xenius*, Paseo Marítimo (fish dishes).

WATER SPORTS. – Beach of fine sand 3 km long extending on either side of the harbour; boating marina; good sports facilities.

The industrial town and resort of Villanueva y Geltrú lies on the Costa Dorada near the boundary between Barcelona and Tarragona provinces.

SIGHTS. – Picturesque fishing quarter; 13th c. *castle* with a square inner courtyard. Near the station is the **Museo Balaguer**, founded by the Catalan writer and statesman Victor Balaguer (d. 1901): antiquities, paintings by El Greco and other artists, ethnographical collection, library.

Vitoria

Province: Álava (VI).
Telephone code: 945.
Altitude: 525 m. – Population: 193,000

ⓘ **Oficina de Información de Turismo,**
Parque de la Florida;
tel. 13 13 21.
Delegación Territorial de Turismo,
General Alava 10;
tel. 23 30 95.

HOTELS. – *Canciller Ayala* (no rest.), Ramon y Cajal 5, I, 185 r.; *Gasteiz* (no rest.), Avda de Gasteiz 19, I, 150 r.; *General Alava* (no rest.), Avda de Gasteiz 53, II, 105 r.; *Desiderio* (no rest.), Colegio San Prudencio 2, III, 21 r.; *Páramo* (no rest.), General Alava 11, III, 40 r.; *Bilbaína*, Prudencio María de Verástegui 2, IV, 29 r.; *Dato 28* (no rest.), Dato 28, IV, 14 r.; Hostal *Achuri*, Rioja 11, P II, 40 r. – ON THE MADRID–IRUN ROAD,

km 361: *Parador Nacional Argomaniz*, II, 54 r.; etc. – CAMPING SITE: *Ibaya* in Zuazo, SW of the town.

RESTAURANTS. – *Portalón*, Correría 151 (in a 15th c. house); *Carey*, Manuel Iradier 20 (modern style); *Dos Hermanas*, Madre Vedruna 10; *Naroki*, Florida 24 (Basque rustic style).

EVENTS. – *Fiestas de San Prudencio* (Apr.); beating of the retreat on the eve of the festival. – *Feria de la Virgen Blanca* (Aug.), patronal festival, with the "Bajada de Celedón", a traditional performance by the village people of the province. – *Pilgrimage* to Olárizu (Sept.), with dancing and a splendid procession afterwards. – *Musical festival* (autumn). – At *Christmas* a large Nativity scene is set up in the Parque de la Florida.

Vitoria, capital of the Basque province of Álava and the seat of a bishop, lies in a plain on the N side of the Montes de Vitoria near the Río Zadorra, a tributary of the Ebro.

HISTORY. – This was probably the Visigothic settlement of *Gasteiz*. It was given its present name in the reign of Sancho the Wise to commemorate the Navarrese victory over the town. It was the scene of a British victory during the Peninsular War (1813).

SIGHTS. – In the centre of Vitoria, on the S side of the **Old Town** (many picturesque old houses with oriel windows), is the arcaded *Plaza de España*, built in 1791 on the model of the Plaza Mayor in Salamanca. On the N side of the square is the *Casa Consistorial* (Town Hall). To the N are two Gothic churches, *San Vicente* (14th c.) and *San Miguel* (also 14th c.). San Miguel has a figure of the "Virgen Blanca" (White Virgin) on the façade and a retablo by Juan de Velázquez and Gregorio Hernández on the high altar. – To the W of the Plaza de España is the *Plaza de la Virgen Blanca*, with a

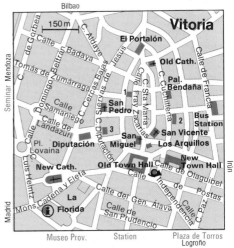

monument commemorating the decisive British victory over French forces on 21 June 1813. NW of the square is the Gothic church of **San Pedro** (14th c.), with a beautiful doorway; in the *Capilla Mayor* are tombs of the Álava family. – From the lower end of the square it is a short distance NW to the *Palacio de la Diputación* (1858), the provincial government headquarters.

In the New Cathedral, Vitoria

In the northern part of the old town, which is built on a hill, is the **Old Cathedral** of *Santa María* (14th–15th c.), with a magnificent tripartite doorway decorated with statues, a Baroque portico and an inner doorway which was separated from later work in 1962. The *Capilla Mayor* has an "Assumption" in high relief by Valdivielso; the *side chapels* contain a number of fine paintings, including works by Rubens and van Dyck. – To the N, in the Plaza Santo Domingo, is the *Provincial Museum of Arms and Archeology*. Opposite it is the *Casa del Portalón* (12th c.), a half-timbered house which also forms part of the museum, with relics of the battle of Vitoria and a small bullfighting museum.

The southern part of Vitoria consists of the spaciously planned **New Town**. On the W side of this, adjoining the *Parque de la Florida*, is the **New Cathedral** (*Cathedral Nueva*), begun in 1907, and consecrated in 1969. To the SW, in the *Paseo de Fray Francisco*, is the **Casa de Álava** (1916), in which are the *Museo Diocesano*, the *Museo de Arqueología y Armas* and the *Museo Provincial* (pictures by Ribera, Alonso Cano, etc.).

SURROUNDINGS. – There are many places of interest within reach of Vitoria, several of them lying off the main traffic routes and reached by minor country roads.

Over the Puerto Azáceta to Pamplona. – Leave Vitoria on C 132, which runs SE to (9 km) the village of **Argandoña**, with a Romanesque parish church. From here it is a 20-minute climb to the well-preserved Romanesque basilica of *Estibaliz* (12th c.), with a statue of the Virgin, patroness of Álava. The church has interlace ornament on the S front and a notable font. Wide-ranging views.

C 132 then climbs up to the **Puerto de Azáceta** (890 m), beyond which is *Azáceta*, venue of the Basque summer games. The road eventually crosses the provincial boundary and continues via *Estella* (see p. 121) to join N 111, which runs E to **Pamplona** (p. 182), 111 km from Vitoria.

To Pamplona by the direct road. – There are a number of places of interest on and near the main road E to Pamplona (N I). Soon after leaving Vitoria the church of Estibaliz can be seen on a hill to the right. Then a side road goes off on the right to **Alegría**, near which is the *Capilla de Nuestra Señora de Ayala*, on a route leading to the Way of St James (see below).

N I then continues over the fertile Álava plateau, with views ahead of **Salvatierra** (alt. 542 m), a picturesque little town, mostly lying away from the main road, with two Gothic churches. From here a minor road runs 3 km to *Ocáriz*, with Romanesque architectural fragments, Roman tombstones and pieces of medieval sculpture in the parish church.

To the left of N I is the *Dolmen of Eguilaz*, a prehistoric chambered tomb built of massive slabs of stone. In the nearby village of *San Román* and at *Araya*, a short distance away to the N, are Roman tombstones.

After entering the province of Navarre the road continues via *Alsasua* to **Pamplona** (p. 182), 93 km from Vitoria.

Towards Burgos. – N I (motorway standard) runs SW from Vitoria to 2·5 km) **Armentia**, traditionally the birthplace of San Prudencio, patron saint of Álava, with the Romanesque church of San Prudencio (12th c., much altered in the 18th c.).

The road then continues along a wide valley between mountain ranges: to the right the *Sierra de Aroto* (Oteros, 1042 m), to the left the *Montes de Vitoria* and the *Sierra de Cantabria*. Beyond *Ariñez*, off the road to the right, is the Roman site of *Iruña*, with the remains of two bridges and a ruined 13th c. monastery. – After passing the little walled town of *La Puebla de Arganzón* the road forks: N I (to right) continues via *Miranda de Ebro* to **Burgos** (see p. 85), 117 km from Vitoria, while N 232 (to left) runs S to *Haro* and **Logroño** (p. 149), 86 km from Vitoria.

Way of St James (Camino de Santiago, Ruta Jacobea)

ⓘ **Oficina Archicofradía del Apóstol Santiago**
(Arch-confraternity of the Apostle St James), Plaza de la Quintana, Santiago de Compostela; tel. (981) 58 16 30.

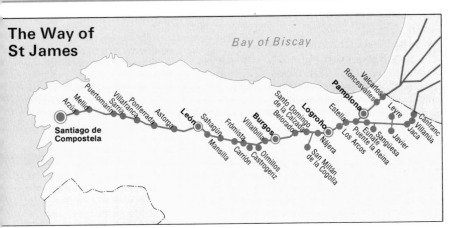

The Way of St James

Bay of Biscay

The ***Way of St James** was the old route followed by pilgrims from northern and central Europe on their journey to the tomb of the Apostle at Santiago de Compostela in Galicia. The route was lined by monasteries and religious houses, churches and chapels, hospices and hostels for the pilgrims, provided and maintained by the Benedictines as well as by various secular orders and by local bishops.

HISTORY. – The pilgrimage to Santiago was initiated by the discovery of the Apostle's tomb in western Galicia about the year 813. In the mid 10th c. the first pilgrims from central Europe began to travel through France and over the Pyrenees to join the road to Santiago, but the great days of the pilgrimage were in the 11th and 12th c., the most prolific period of Romanesque art and architecture and left a scatter of beautiful old buildings still to be seen along the pilgrim route.

The main pilgrim stations on the Way of St James are shown on the map. But the route was by no means a straight and narrow way as the map might suggest: rather it was a broad strip extending from E to W, leaving room for variations from the main highway. Most pilgrims entered Spain by *Roncesvalles* or the *Somport Pass*; these two routes met at *Puente de la Reina* and then continued W on the Camino de Santiago, almost 740 km long, which led by way of *Logroño, Santo Domingo de la Calzada, Burgos* and *Astorga* to *Santiago de Compostela* (see the entries on these various places).

Zamora

Province: Zamora (ZA).
Telephone code: 988.
Altitude: 649 m. – Population: 52,000.
ⓘ **Oficina de Información de Turismo,**
Santa Clara 20;
tel. 51 18 45.

Patronato Provincial de Turismo,
Plaza de Cánovas;
tel. 51 43 29.

HOTELS. – *Parador Nacional Condes de Alba y Aliste*, Plaza de Cánovas 1, I, 19 r., SP; *Dos Infantes* (no rest.), Cortinas de San Miguel 3, II, 68 r.; *Cuatro Naciones*, Avda José Antonio 11, III, 40 r.; Hostal *Rey Don Sancho*, km 276 on the Villacastín Vigo road, P I, 86 r.; *El Sayagues*, Plaza Puentica 2, P II, 56 r.; *Trefacio*, Alfonso de Castro 8, P II, 36 r.; etc.

RESTAURANTS. – *Rueda*, Ronda de la Feria 19 (Castilian style); *Pozo*, Ramón Álvarez 3; etc.

EVENTS. – *Semana Santa* (Holy Week), celebrated with great ceremony, with a procession and a solemn religious service. – *Feria de San Pedro* (June), with folk events and traditional customs; associated with the *Feria del Ajo* (Garlic Market).

The old-world provincial capital of **Zamora**, the seat of a bishop, lies on a rocky hill above the Río Duero, which reaches the Portuguese frontier 50 km downstream, in the southern part of the old kingdom of León. It has been called a museum of Romanesque art, with numerous churches of the 12th and 13th c.

HISTORY. – The town, originally a Moorish foundation, was the object of long and bitter conflicts between Christians and Moors, in which the Spanish national hero, El Cid, played a part, before Zamora was granted the style of "most noble and most loyal city" by Henry IV. While Sancho II was laying siege to the town he was treacherously murdered – an event still commemorated by the Portillo de la Traición ("Gate of Treason").

SIGHTS. – In the southern part of the **Old Town**, still surrounded by its walls and gates, is the **Cathedral**, near the right bank of the Duero. It is mainly Romanesque (1151–74), with a square tower, a handsome dome and splendid doorways, particularly notable being the *Puerta del Obispo*, with sculptured decoration. Fine

Zamora: view over the Duero

choir-stalls by Rodrigo Alemán (1480); *Capilla Mayor*, with a beautiful retablo by Fernando Gallego (1467) and a number of tombs. In the 17th c. *Cloister* is a museum (late Gothic custodia, 1515; valuable Flemish tapestries of the 15th–17th c.). – NW of the Cathedral is the *Castillo* (magnificent views of the town and the river from the keep). – S of the Cathedral, outside the town walls on the banks of the Duero, is the 11th c. church of *San Claudio de Olivares*, with an aisleless nave.

From the Cathedral *Rúa de los Notarios* runs NE to the little Romanesque Templar church of **Santa Magdalena** (12th c.), which has a splendid arched doorway with figures of lions and dragons, surmounted by a rose window; it contains a richly decorated 13th c. tomb. – S of the Magdalena is the church of *San Ildefonso* (13th c., with later alteration); in the Capilla Mayor are the relics of the town's patron saints, San Atilano and San Ildefonso. – From here *Calle Ramos Carrión* runs NE to the little Plaza de Cánovas and the Romanesque church of **San Cipriano** (12th c.), with remarkable relief carving on the exterior; the church contains an interesting *reja*, probably the oldest in Spain.

Farther NE is the *Plaza Mayor*, in which are the *Ayuntamiento* (Town Hall) of 1622 and the late Gothic church of *San Juan*, with a fine painted altar (figures). – W of San Juan is the church of *Santa María la Nueva*, with Romanesque wall paintings. Opposite it is the *Museo de la Semana Santa*, with a large collection of *pasos*, the figures which are carried through the streets by various con-

fraternities in the Holy Week processions. – SE of the Plaza Mayor is the church of **Santa María de la Horta** (12th c.), with a handsome tower, a beautiful doorway and a Gothic retablo. – NE of the Plaza Mayor, in the Plaza de Sagasta, is the 16th c. *Palacio de los Momos*, named after the *momos* (wild men) who support the coat of arms on its Renaissance façade; it is now occupied by the *Audiencia* (Law Courts). – Farther NE again is the Romanesque church of *Santiago del Burgo* (12th c.), with a square tower and fine doorways. – There are numbers of other interesting Romanesque churches, palaces and mansions, including the house of the Counts of Alba y Aliste, now a Parador Nacional. – From the old bridge over the Duero, the Puente Viejo, there is an attractive view of the town.

SURROUNDINGS. – It is well worth while making a short trip (20 km NW: leave on N 122 and beyond Venta del Puerto turn into a minor road) to *El Campillo*, on the shores of an artificial lake formed by the damming of the *Río Esla*, with the Visigothic church of **San Pedro de la Nave**, transferred here in 1931 when its original site, some kilometres away, was submerged by the reservoir. The importance of the church, probably built about 681, lies in its carved *capitals, perhaps the finest sculpture produced in Christian Spain before the Moorish period.

To the Valle de Sanabria and Orense. – Leave Zamora on N 630, which runs NW to the southern end of the reservoir, Embalse del Esla (21 km), where N 525 branches off on the left. This passes the remains of a large 13th c. bridge, the *Puente de la Estrella*, and comes to *Tábara*, with an interesting church (1132). The road then climbs to the **Portillo de Sazadón** (820 m), on an outlier of the *Sierra de Culebra*. Near the village of *Rionegro del Puente* N 525 is joined by C 620, coming in from Benavente on the right, and continues NW via *Mombuey*, with a 15th c. tower, to **Puebla de Sanabria**, in the *Valle de Sanabria*.

N 525 now ascends the valley of the *Río Castro*, passes through *Requejo* and climbs, with many

ends, to the **Portillo de Padornelo** (1329 m), a
pass between the *Sierra de la Gemoneda* on the left
and the *Sierra Segundera*, over 2000 m high, on the
right. It then continues via *Lubián* (alt. 979 m) to
the **Portillo de la Canda** (1262 m), which marks
the boundary between Castile (province of Zamora)
and Galicia (province of Orense). Then via *Verín* to
Orense (see p. 176), 282 km from Zamora.

Zaragoza (Saragossa)

Province: Zaragoza (Z).
Telephone code: 976.
Altitude: 200 m. – Population: 591,000.
(i) **Oficina de Información de Turismo**,
   Plaza de Sas 7; tel. 23 11 17.
   Servicio Provincial de Turismo,
   Alonso I 6;
   tel. 22 26 73.

HOTELS. – *Corona de Aragón*, Avda César Augusto
13, L, 249 r., SP; *Gran Hotel*, Costa 5, L, 138 r.;
Palafóx, Casa Jiménez s/n, L, 184 r., SP; *Don Yo*,
Bruil 4, I, 181 r.; *Goya*, Cinco de Marzo 5, I, 150 r.; *Rey
Alfonso I* (no rest.), Coso 17, I, 117 r.; *La Romareda*
(no rest.), Asin y Palacios 11, I, 90 r.; *El Cisne* (no
rest.), km 309 on N II, 61 r., SP; *Conquistador*, Herman
Cortes 21, II, 44 r.; *Europa* (no rest.), Alfonso I 19, III,
54 r.; *Oriente*, Coso 11, II, 87 r.; *París*, Pedro María Ric
14, II, 62 r.; *Ramiro I*, Coso 123, II, 105 r.; *Zaragoza
Royal*, Arzobispo Domenech 4, II, 92 r.; *Conde Blanco*
(no rest.), Predicadores 84, III, 83 r.; *Gran Vía* (no
rest.), Gran Vía 38, III, 41 r.; *Los Molinos* (no rest.),
San Miguel 28, III, 40 r.; *Avenida* (no rest.), Avda
César Augusto 55, IV, 48 r.; *Lafuente* (no rest.),
Valenzuela 7, IV, 65 r.; *Patria* (no rest.), Hermanos
Ibarra 8, IV, 41 r.; *Posada de las Almas*, San Pablo 22,
IV, 30 r.; *La Salle*, San Juan de la Cruz 22, IV, 81 r. SP;
etc. – CAMPING SITE: *Casablanca*, on N II towards
Madrid.

RESTAURANTS. – *Parilla Albarracín*, César Augusto
(rustic style); *Cafetería Savoy*, Coso 42; *Costa Vasca*,
Coronel Valenzuela 13; *Casa Tena*, Plaza San Francisco 6; *Chalet Suizo*, Avda Tenor Fleta 46; *Goyesco*,
Manuel Lasala 44; *La Mar*, Plaza de Aragón 12 (fish
and sea-food); *Mesón de Tomás*, Avda de las Torres
92; *Mesón del Carmen*, Hernán Cortés 4; *Paris*, Paseo
de las Damas 11; *Rogelio's*, Eduardo Ibarra 10. ON
N 232: *Cachirulo*, 4½ km. W. – ON N 11: *Venta de los
Caballos*, 8 km W.

EVENTS. – *Fiesta de Nuestra Señora del Pilar* (Oct.),
with "Rosario de Cristal", procession, accompanied
by numerous pilgrims. The celebrations usually last
several days, with folk events and bullfights (hotel
tariffs increased). – *Semana Santa* (Holy Week), with
a splendid procession. – *Fiesta de Primavera* (May),
Spring Festival, with exhibitions of Spanish painting
and sculpture, in alternate years.

CASINO. – *Casino Montesblancos*, in Alfajarín.

**Once the residence of the kings of
Aragon, Zaragoza (traditionally in
English Saragossa) is now capital of**
its province and the see of an archbishop, and it has a large university.
It lies in the Ebro basin, on the right
bank of the river, and has been from
time immemorial the principal
crossing point for traffic from the
Pyrenees into Castile.

The *Huerta de Zaragoza*, watered by the
Canal Imperial and the rivers Ebro, Huerva
and Gállego, is a region of great fertility,
and Zaragoza is accordingly an important
agricultural centre, as well as possessing
considerable industry.

HISTORY. – The old Iberian settlement of *Salduba*
was renamed by Augustus *Colonia Caesaraugusta*,
from which its present name is derived. It fell into the
hands of the Suevi in 452, of the Visigoths in 476 and
of the Moors in 712. After its capture by Alfonso I of
Aragon in 1118 it became the residence of the kings of
Aragon and rose to considerable importance; in the
15th c., however the seat of the court was transferred
to Castile, and Zaragoza's importance declined. It put
up a heroic defence against the French in 1808–09,
half of the population being killed before the
honourable surrender of the town. After the expulsion
of the Carlists, who captured the town in a surprise
attack in March 1838, Zaragoza was known by the
style "siempre heróica e inmortal" ("always heroic
and immortal").

SIGHTS. – The main traffic artery of
Zaragoza is the wide *Calle del Coso*,
which runs round the SE of the old town
to the Puente del Pilar. Halfway along the
Calle de Coso is the *Plaza de España*,
from which the Paseo de la Independencia runs S, while the busy *Calle de
Don Jaime I* and *Calle de Alfonso I*,
running parallel to it on the W, lead N to
the Plaza del Pilar.

At the E end of the wide *Plaza del Pilar*,
part of which is laid out in gardens, is the
little Plaza de la Seo, in which stands the
Gothic *Cathedral (La Seo,* dedicated to
San Salvador), built between 1119 and
1520 on the site of the Great Mosque,
with double lateral aisles, a main doorway
of 1795, a dome over the crossing (1520)
and a slender tower (1686).

INTERIOR. – The *Choir* has a superb grille and a large
alabaster retablo by a German master known as Hans
de Suabia (1477). The *Capilla de San Bernado* (to the
left of the SW entrance) contains the Plateresque
tombs of Archbishop Fernando and his mother Ana
Gurrea (1552), both by Diego Morlanes. In the
Capilla de San Miguel (to the left of the main
entrance), now used as a parish church, is the tomb of
Archbishop Lópe Fernández de Luna (d. 1382). In
the *Capilla de San Pedro Arbués* is the tomb of the
Inquisitor of that name who was murdered in the
Cathedral in 1485 (canonised 1867). The Cathedral
has a rich *Treasury* (Tesoro), and on the first floor is a

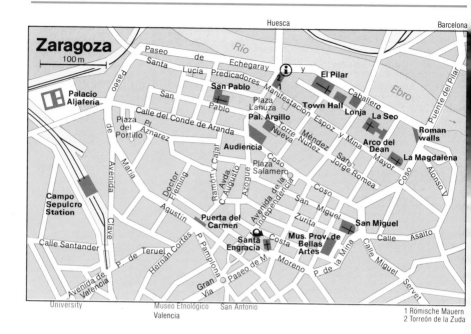

Zaragoza
100 m

Huesca   Barcelona

Rio   Ebro

Paseo de Echegaray
Santa Lucia   Predicadores
San Pablo   Manifestación
Palacio
Aljaferia
San   Plaza
Pablo   Lanuza
Calle del Conde de Aranda   Pal. Argillo
Plaza   Torre
del   Nueva   Méndez
Portillo   Aznarez
Audiencia   Coso
Plaza
Salamero
Avda   Azogue
Campo   C. Augusto   Avenida de la
Sepulcro   Agustin   San   Miguel
Station
Clave   Puerta del   Zurita
Calle Santander   Carmen   Santa   Costa
Engracia
P. de Teruel   Hernán Cortés   P. Pamplona   Moreno
Avenida de   Gran   Paseo de M.
Valencia   Via
University   San Antonio
Museo Etnológico
Valencia

El Pilar
Caballero
Town Hall   Lonja
Espoz y Mina   La Seo
Arco del   Roman
Dean   walls
Sarb   La Magdalena
Jorge Romea   Mayor   Coso
Coso
San Miguel   Alonso V
Mus. Prov. de   Calle   Asalto
Bellas
Artes   Calle Miguel Servet

1 Römische Mauern
2 Torreón de la Zuda

Tapestry Museum containing some 30 valuable tapestries, some dating from the 15th c.

Between the Plaza del Pilar and the Ebro is Zaragoza's second cathedral, the pilgrimage church of ***Nuestra Señora del Pilar**, a square structure with a large central dome, ten smaller domes faced with azulejos and four tall corner towers. The church (132 m long, 67 m wide), on the site of an earlier chapel, was begun in 1681 by Francisco Herrera the Younger, continued by V. Rodríguez in 1753 but not completed until the end of the 19th c.

The INTERIOR is in neo-classical style. The *Choir* has a fine grille of 1574, Plateresque stalls (1548) and a Gothic *retablo (1484–1515), partly of alabaster, by Damián Forment and others. At the E end of the church is the *Capilla de Nuestra Señora del Pilar*, with fine ceiling paintings by Goya (1771) and Bayeu (1781); on the W wall is a small early 15th c. alabaster figure of the Virgin on the marble pillar, now faced with silver, at which she is said to have appeared to the Apostle St James (statue above the altar, to the left) on 2 January in the year 40 when he was on his way to Compostela. There are other ceiling paintings by Goya in the domes. The Sacristía Mayor and Sacristía house the *Cathedral Treasury. – From the NW tower (lift) there are wide views.

Between the two cathedrals, in Plaza del Pilar, is the former ***Lonja** (Exchange), a handsome Renaissance building (1551) with a single large hall, and also the *Ayuntamiento* (Town Hall) of 1954, with an interesting interior (Roman statue of Augustus). – N of the Lonja is a seven-arched 15th c. bridge, the **Puente de Piedra**, which crosses the Ebro to the northern suburb (*Arrabal*) of the town.

Downstream is the *Puente del Pilar*, upstream the modern *Puente de Santiago*. From the left bank of the Ebro there is a famous *view of the town with the two Cathedrals.

At the W end of the Plaza del Pilar is a large *War Memorial* to the dead of the Civil War (1936–39). Beyond it, in the little *Plaza de César Augusto*, are the *Torreón de la Zuda*, a 14th c. tower in Mudéjar style, and the church of *San Juan de los Panetes* (18th c.), with a leaning tower. Adjoining the S side of the Torreón are considerable remains of the *Roman town walls*. To the N is the Puente de Santiago.

In the W part of the old town is the Romanesque and Gothic church of **San Pablo** (c. 1259), with an interesting octagonal Mudéjar tower (14th c.); fine interior, with a magnificent high altar by Damián Forment (1511). – In the western outskirts of the town is the **Castillo de la Aljafería**, built by the Moors in the 11th c. and which later became the residence of the kings of Aragón, which was largely destroyed in 1809. It contains a number of fine rooms with beautiful artesonado ceilings. – SE of San Pablo, at the end of Calle del Coso, is the **Audiencia** (Court of Appeal), with a beautiful pillared courtyard. Built in 1537 as the palace of the powerful Counts of Lara, it is popularly known as the *Casa de los Gigantes*, after the two huge guardian figures at the entrance.

The *Paseo de la Independencia*, which runs S from the Plaza de España, half way along Calle del Coso, is a magnificent avenue with arcades along the W side. Near the end of this street, on the left beyond the Post Office, is the former convent of **Santa Engracia**, an elaborately decorated Plateresque building (15th–16th c.) which was almost completely destroyed in 1809 and restored in 1898; only the alabaster doorway is original. In the crypt are two Early Christian marble sarcophagi. – To the E, in the Plaza de José Antonio, is the **Museo de Bellas Artes**. On the ground floor is the *department of archaeology* (Roman mosaic of Orpheus), on the first floor a picture gallery, with works by both earlier and contemporary Spanish painters (including Ribera and Goya). – At the S end of the Paseo de la Independencia is the oval *Plaza de Aragón*, a short distance W of which is the *Puerta del Carmen*. Some 2 km S, to the right of the Paseo de Fernando el Católico, is the **Ciudad Universitaria** (University City). Farther S, on the Paseo de Isabel la Católica, is the *Trade Fair Building*, in which the National Trade Fair is held annually in October. To the E is the beautiful *Primo de Rivera Park*, with a *Museum of Ethnology and Natural History*.

SURROUNDINGS. – There are many places of historical and artistic interest within easy reach of Zaragoza, most of them not far from the main road.

Towards Tarragona. – N 232 runs SE from Zaragoza along the edge of the green Ebro basin, following the line of the **Canal Imperial de Aragón**, a ship canal 90 km long begun by Charles V in 1528 which is now used only for industrial purposes and for irrigation. After passing an old Carthusian monastery on the left the road runs through *El Burgo de Ebro* (alt. 185 m), beyond which, on the banks of the Ebro to the left, is the *Ermita de Nuestra Señora de Zaragoza la Vieja*, and comes to *Fuentes de Ebro* (alt. 196 m), at the end of the Canal Imperial, with the palace of the Counts of Fuentes. The road then continues to **Quinto** (alt. 150 m; pop. 3000), with brine springs. 20 km beyond Quinto a minor road branches off on the left and crosses the Ebro to *Escatrón*, near which is the **Monasterio de Rueda**, founded in the 13th c., with an interesting church and a Byzantine-Gothic chapterhouse. The road then enters the province of Teruel and comes to *Azaila*, from which C 221 runs E to **Caspe**, near two large artificial lakes on the Ebro, the *Embalse de Caspe* and the *Embalse de Moros*; 13th c. Cistercian church.

Then SE from Caspe on C 221 (or from Azaila on N 232) to join N 420, which continues to **Tarragona** (see p. 217), 238 km from Zaragoza.

Over the Puerto de Paniza to Teruel. – N 330 runs SE from Zaragoza up the valley of the *Río Huerva* to the little village of *Muel*, which carries on an old tradition of pottery-making. Then via *Longares*, with a beautiful parish church containing an impressive "Ecce Homo", to **Cariñena** (alt. 410 m; pop. 3000), a little town famous for its wine, with origins going back to Neolithic times. Old town walls; Baroque church, built on the foundations of an earlier Gothic one. – 24 km E of Cariñena is the village of *Fuendetodos*, birthplace of the painter Francisco Goya (1746–1828), with a small museum in the house in which he was born (restored).

Beyond Cariñena N 330 climbs up to the *Puerto de Paniza* (925 m), from which there are extensive views. It then continues SW and, soon after the junction with

Nuestra Señora del Pilar, Zaragoza

N 234 from Calatayud (on right), enters **Daroca** (alt. 769 m; pop. 6000), picturesquely situated in a deep gorge on the *Río Jiloca* below the *Pico de Almenara* (1421 m), in the Sierra de Santa Cruz. Originally founded by the Iberians, this little town has preserved a circuit of walls 3 km long, with 114 towers. Moorish fort built in the rock (Kalat Daruka); collegiate church of Santa María (13th–15th c.), with good 15th c. altarpieces and a parish museum. – Beyond Daroca N 234 crosses the provincial boundary and continues via *Monreal del Campo* to **Teruel** (see p. 222), 181 km from Zaragoza.

Over the Puerto de Cavero. – N II: a route for those interested in Mudéjar architecture. The road (first section of motorway standard) runs SW to the limestone hills of the *Plana de la Muela* and the little town of *La Muela*, winds its way downhill and then heads, in a dead straight line, for **La Almunia de Doña Godina** (alt. 218 m; pop. 5000), where it leaves the green basin of the Ebro. N of the town is the chapel of *Nuestra Señora de Cabañas*.

The road then goes over a series of passes – first the *Puerto de Morata* (708 m), closely followed by the *Puerto del Frasno* (785 m), and finally, after passing through *Aluenda*, the **Puerto de Cavero** (765 m), in the bare uplands of the *Sierra de Vicort*, with beautiful views. – From the top of the pass the road runs down to **Calatayud** (see p. 94).

Beyond Calatayud is *Ateca* (pop. 3500), with Moorish towers and a castle which was taken by El Cid in 1073. N II then continues, via *Bubierca*, to **Alhama de Aragón** (alt. 648 m; hotels: Parque, II, 108 r., SP; Termas II 35 r., SP), a spa with thermal springs (24–33 °C – 75–91 °F), known to the Romans as *Aquae Bilbilitanae*. Its present name comes from the Arabic *al-Hamma* ("hot spring"). In the grounds of the spa is an impressive gorge on the Río Jalón. – From here an interesting excursion can be made to the *Monasterio de ta*, 18 km SE.

N II continues past the castle of *Campillo* (on left) and comes to *Ariza* (alt. 717 m), built on the slopes of a rocky hill; then crosses the boundary between Aragon (province of Zaragoza) and Castile (province of Soria), just beyond which is **Santa María de Huerta** (Hotel Parador Nacional, II, 40 r.), with the Monasterio de Santa María, founded in the 12th c. (beautiful choir-stalls, Gothic refectory, Plateresque cloister).

The road then runs on to *Arcos de Jalón* and **Medinaceli** (see p. 169).

To Tarazona. – N 232 runs NW up the wide green valley of the Ebro, with the Pyrenees to the N and the *Sierra de Moncayo* to the W, to *Alagón*, which has a Jesuit church with a prominent dome faced with azulejos and a parish church with the octagonal tower so common in Aragon. After crossing the Canal Imperial it continues to a junction where the road to Tarazona branches off on the left (N 122).

In another 13 km N 122 comes to the little town of **Borja** (pop. 5000), in the valley of the *Río Huecha*. Originally the Iberian settlement of *Bursao*, it is now the centre of a large wine-growing region, with the ruins of the ancestral castle of the Borja (Borgia) family. This is a good base from which to explore the

Sierra de Moncayo (2316 m), a range of craggy sandstone hills which separates the Ebro basin from the Castilian plateau.

Beyond Borja a minor road runs S from N 122 into the Sierra de Moncayo; then at the village of *Vera de Moncayo* a side road leads to the picturesque **Monasterio de Veruela** (12th–15th c.), now a Jesuit college, surrounded by massive battlemented walls, with an interesting church. The monastery contains mementoes of the visit of Gustavo Adolfo Bécquer, the 19th c. poet. – From the monastery a footpath leads up to the pilgrimage church of *Nuestra Señora del Moncayo* (alt. 1621 m), with a 13th c. image of the Virgin. – N 122 then goes over the *Puerto de Lanzas Agudas* (681 m) and comes to **Tarazona** (see p. 217).

Towards Pamplona. – There are two alternative routes to Pamplona. The first is on N 232, as in the previous route, continuing to Tudela, in Navarre, and from there on N 121. The other, running through the north of Zaragoza province, leaves N 232 beyond *Pedrola* and turns N into a minor road which leads to **Tauste**, a small village on the *Río Arba* with a fine Mudéjar parish church (begun 1243): handsome tower, fine carved retablo (16th c.) on high altar.

From Tauste C 127 runs N to **Ejea de los Caballeros**, at the junction of the *Río Arba de Luesia* and the *Río Arba de Biel*. Romanesque fortified church (13th c.: national monument), with an imposing defensive tower; church of Santa María, with a Romanesque doorway; 13th c. statue in the church of Nuestra Señora de la Oliva, patroness of the little town.

From Ejea C 124 runs NW to *Sádaba* and over the *Puerto de Sos* (856 m) to **Sos del Rey Católico**, a little fortified town of medieval aspect. Ferdinand of Aragon, "el Rey Católico", was born in 1452 in the 12th c. Palacio de Sada. Fine Romanesque parish church (11th–12th c.) with interesting 14th c. wall paintings. – 24 km SE of Sos, also reached direct from Sádaba (16 km), is *Uncastillo*, with a massive 12th c. castle built on a rocky crag. Also of interest is the church of San Juan, built above a 7th c. cemetery hewn from the rock, with a Romanesque-Byzantine painting (12th c.).

To Huesca. – The main road (N 123) runs N along the W bank of the *Río Gállego* to *Zuera*. The alternative is a minor road which runs up the E bank and comes in 12 km to the **Cartuja de Aula Dei**, a Carthusian monastery founded in 1564 by Ferdinand II. In the cloister are scenes from the life of St Bruno by Antonio Martínez. The church has a beautiful doorway and frescoes by Goya depicting scenes from the life of the Virgin (1772). Fine views from the Mirador. – Beyond Zuera the two roads join, and N 123 crosses the provincial boundary and continues on an excellent stretch of road to **Huesca** (see p. 138), 72 km from Zaragoza.

To Lérida. – There are two roads, the motorway and N II, which cross the Ebro, offering a fine *view of Zaragoza to the rear, and continue E along the Ebro basin via *Alfajarín*, with a ruined castle, and *Osera*, with a long aqueduct, towards the plateau of the *Montes de la Retuerta*, in the middle of which is the little town of *Bujaraloz*. N II then crosses the provincial boundary and continues via *Fraga* to **Lérida** (see p. 147), 140 km from Zaragoza.

Practical Information

Warning

Visitors to Spain should be very careful to look after their property. Particularly in the larger towns and conurbations and in the popular seaside resorts theft, including snatching of handbags and even luggage, cameras, binoculars, watches, jewellery and other valuable articles is commonplace. Breaking into and stealing from vehicles, especially caravans and minibuses, are everyday occurrences.

It is important, therefore, to carry all objects of value – papers, money, cheques, credit cards and keys – on your person and never to leave them in an unattended vehicle. The glove compartment – and if possible the boot as well – should be left empty and unlocked. Overnight your car should be kept in a lock-up garage, if one is available, preferably with a safety lock or similar device.

The Spanish police are always ready to help, but are virtually powerless in face of this type of crime. After a break-in or a robbery with violence they can often do little more than take particulars of the offence (which is in any case an essential part of the procedure of making a claim against your insurance company).

If you lose travellers' cheques, a bank card or a credit card you should at once inform the bank or issuing agency by phone or telegram, so that the account can be blocked.

Flamenco dancer

When to go

The best seasons for a visit to Spain are spring and autumn, from mid March to the beginning of June and from the beginning of September to the beginning of November (in northern Spain to the beginning of October). The most attractive time to go is spring; in the interior of the country the weather is even more settled in autumn, but much of the land is parched and arid after the blazing heat of summer. – The best time to visit the Atlantic coast of northern and northwestern Spain is summer, since visitors at other times of the year are likely to encounter a good deal of rain. The seaside resorts on the SE coast and in the Balearics and the hill resorts in the Pyrenees, the Sierra de Guadarrama and the Sierra Nevada are much frequented in summer; and the coastal resorts, with sea breezes mitigating the heat of summer, tend to be particularly busy during the school holidays (July–August). The months of July and August are almost unbearably hot in the interior of the country. – For winter sports and winter holidays on the S and SE coasts the best months are December, January and February. In recent years the Balearics and the Mediterranean coast have become popular with people able to take a long winter holiday of several weeks or even months. – The Canary Islands, with their mild and equable climate, can be visited at any time of year.

Weather

Central Spain – a plateau enclosed by ranges of mountains, has a markedly continental climate, with dry, hot summers and severe winters. In the coastal regions the moderating influence of the sea produces relatively cool summers and mild winters, with rain distributed throughout the year. This oceanic influence is strongest on the N Atlantic coast. – For a more detailed account of the climate in the different parts of mainland Spain and on the islands see pp. 20–21.

Time

Spain is in the Central European time zone, one hour ahead of GMT. From the beginning of April to the end of September *summer time* is in force, and Spain is then two hours ahead of GMT.

Travel documents

Visitors from the United Kingdom, the Commonwealth and the United States must have a valid *passport*. No *visa* is required by nationals of the United Kingdom, Australia, Canada and New Zealand for a stay of up to three months, or by United States nationals for a stay of up to six months, provided in each case that they are not taking up any employment. An extension of stay can be granted by the police authorities.

A national *driving licence* is acceptable in Spain, but only if accompanied by an official translation stamped by a Spanish consulate. It may be easier and cheaper to carry an international driving permit (which is required in any event for business trips). Cars must display an oval international distinguishing sign of the approved type and design. Failure to comply with this regulation is punishable by a fine. An *international insurance certificate* ("green card") is required, and a *bail bond* (issued by an insurance company together with the green card) should also be taken out, since in the event of an accident the car involved may be impounded pending payment of bail. – Foreign cars may not be driven by Spanish residents. If the driver of a car is not the owner he must be in possession of a document authorising him to drive it, validated by a notary public or a motoring organisation.

There is no free medical treatment for visitors to Spain: it is advisable, therefore, to take out short-term insurance providing cover for the cost of any medical attention required.

Customs regulations

No duty is payable on clothing, toilet articles and other personal effects (cameras, camping gear, etc.), or on small quantities of food and drink. Visitors from a country belonging to the European Community may import free of duty the following: – 300 cigarettes or 150 cigarillos or 75 cigars or 400 grammes tobacco; 3 litres wine and 1½ litres spirits over 22° Gay-Lussac (38·8° proof) or 3 litres fortified or sparkling wine up to 22° proof; 75 grammes perfume and 0·375 litres toilet water.

If any of the above have been bought in a duty free shop the permitted amounts are approximately one third less. These reduced concessions also apply to visitors from other countries including the United States and Canada.

Personal effects, etc., may be taken out without formality.

Heavy deposits against duty and taxes are likely to be required by the Spanish Customs for items such as portable television sets, cassette recorders, musical instruments, etc.

Currency

The unit of currency is the **peseta** (*pta*), centimos (1 peseta = 100 centimos) are no longer used.

There are banknotes for 200, 500, 1000, 2000, 5000 and 10,0000 pesetas, and coins in denominations of 1, 5, 10, 25, 50, 100 and 200 pesetas.

Visitors entering Spain may bring in up to 150,000 pesetas; the limit on leaving the country is 100,000 pesetas. There is no restriction on the import of foreign currency, but only the equivalent of 500,000 pesetas may be exported. Visitors are recommended to use Eurocheques, travellers' cheques or other credit cards.

Postal rates

Letters (up to 20 grammes) 19 pesetas within Spain, 48 pesetas abroad.
Postcards 14 pesetas within Spain, 40 pesetas abroad, 54 pesetas to the US and Canada.

Travel in Spain

Motoring

The Spanish *road system* is now generally good, thanks to the improvement of the main roads and the continuing development of **motorways** (*autopistas*). Tolls are charged on most stretches of motorway such as the Autopista del Mediterráneo (Figueras–Barcelona–Valencia–Alicante), Barcelona–Zaragoza–Pamplona/Bilbao and Cádiz–Seville.

The **national highways** (*carreteras nacionales*), numbered with the prefix N, are mostly good modern roads, with the little houses of the maintenance men (*peones camineros*) set at intervals along them. The best are the six main highways radiating from Madrid, identified by Roman numbers on red and white kilometre stones: N I to San Sebastián, N II to Barcelona, N III to Valencia, N IV to Cádiz, N V to Badajoz, N VI to La Coruña. – The

regional highways (*carreteras com-arcales*), numbered with the prefix C, are also, for the most part, reasonably good, at any rate on the main routes. Unnumbered minor roads may be in poor condition. – Road improvement works will often be encountered, though frequently little warning is given of work in progress (*obras*) or diversions (*desvíos*). Similarly stretches of particularly bad road or potholes are usually not signposted. Care is therefore always necessary, particularly after dark. Railway level crossings are sometimes inadequately guarded or signposted. In Extremadura and certain other parts of Spain a strip of grazing land, (*cañada*), for travelling flocks of sheep, runs alongside the road even at junctions.

Driving in Spain. – Traffic travels on the right, with overtaking on the left. – *Seat belts* must be worn; it is recommended that children sit in the back seat. – It is compulsory for visiting motorists to equip their vehicle with a set of replacement light bulbs.

At junctions and roundabouts traffic coming from the right has priority. This applies even to side streets in towns; exceptions are signposted. – When turning left off a road outside a built-up area a car must pull over to the right and wait until the road is clear. – Spanish cyclists and motorcyclists often indicate a change of direction by raising or lowering their arm, but this does not always make their intention clear: the right arm may be used to give warning of a left-hand turn, or vice versa.

When *overtaking*, the left-hand indicator must be flashing during the whole process and the right-hand one used when pulling back to the right. The horn must be sounded (or, after dark, the headlights flashed) before overtaking or before a bend, but unnecessary use is prohibited and the horn may not be used at all in urban areas except in cases of emergency. Side lights may be used alone on urban roads and single carriageway roads provided the public lighting is adequate. A watchful eye should be kept on overtaking trucks and lorries. Beware of cars without lights! – *Parking* is permitted in one-way streets only on the side with even numbers on even-numbered days and on the side with odd numbers on odd-numbered days.

Care is necessary in towns, particularly when the streets are crowded in the evenings, to avoid pedestrians, who are often reluctant to give precedence to cars on the roadway. Caution is also required on country roads with relatively little traffic, since country people often pay little heed to the rules of the road, and livestock are frequently an additional hazard. A powerful horn is therefore very desirable. – Foreign motorists in particular should observe strict driving discipline. The directions of the Policia Municipal in towns and the Guardia Civil de Trafico in the country should be immediately

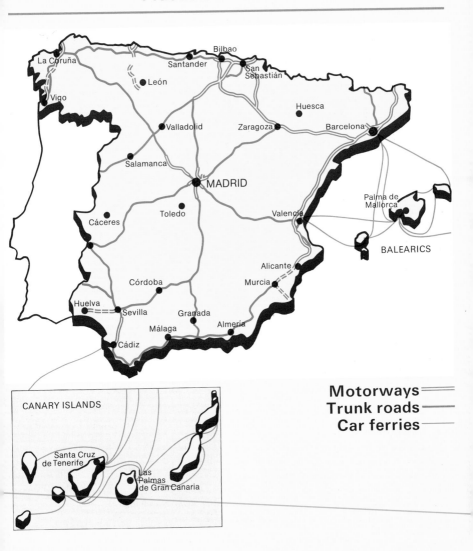

Motorways ═══
Trunk roads ────
Car ferries ────

complied with: if a driver fails to stop when signalled to do so the police may well make use of their revolvers, since they are not infrequently on the alert for terrorists. The fines for traffic offences must be paid on the spot, and are high. – The blood alcohol limit is 0·80% (8 milligrammes per millilitre).

An accident in Spain can have very serious consequences, including the impounding of the car and the occupants' property and the detention of the driver pending bail. It is very desirable, therefore, to have a bail bond (see above, p. 252). Any accident should at once be reported to your insurance company in accordance with the instructions on the green card. – The towing of broken-down vehicles by private cars is prohibited.

Speed limits are 120 km/h ($74\frac{1}{2}$ m.p.h.) on motorways, 100 km/h (62 m.p.h.) on dual carriageways, 90 km/h (56 m.p.h.) on other roads and 60 km/h (37 m.p.h.) in built-up areas. Trailer caravans are prohibited from overtaking on mountain roads.

Fuel is available in several grades – 92 octane (*normal* grade), 97 octane (*super*), 95 (lead free) and diesel (*gas-oil*). Fuel in cans is liable to customs duty.

Car Ferries

SERVICE	FREQUENCY	COMPANY
Spain–Balearics		
Barcelona–Mahón	6 times weekly	Trasmediterránea
Barcelona–Palma de Mallorca	daily	Trasmediterránea
Barcelona–Ibiza	daily	Trasmediterránea
Valencia–Palma de Mallorca	6 times weekly	Trasmediterránea
Valencia–Ibiza	3 times weekly	Trasmediterránea
Málaga–Palma de Mallorca	3 times weekly	Trasmediterránea
France–Balearics		
Sète–Palma de Mallorca/Ibiza	twice weekly (June–September)	Trasmediterránea
Italy–Balearics		
Genoa–Palma de Mallorca	weekly	Trasmediterránea
Balearics (domestic)		
Palma de Mallorca–Ibiza	3 times weekly	Trasmediterránea
Palma de Mallorca–Cabrera	weekly	Trasmediterránea
Palma de Mallorca–Ciudadela	weekly	Trasmediterránea
Ciudadela–Puerto de Alcudia	4 times weekly	Trasmediterránea
Spain–Canary Islands		
Malaga–Las Palmas	weekly	Trasmediterránea
Cádiz–Las Palmas/Tenerife	weekly	Trasmediterránea
Italy–Spain		
Genoa–Palma de Mallorca/Málaga	weekly	Trasmediterránea
Spain–Melilla–Ceuta		
Almeria–Melilla	three times weekly	Trasmediterránea
Málaga–Melilla	six times weekly	Trasmediterránea
Algeciras–Ceuta	daily	Trasmediterránea
Spain–Morocco		
Algeciras–Tangier[1]	daily	Comarit Ferry
	daily	Limadet Ferry
	daily	Trasmediterránea
Gibraltar–Morocco		
Gibraltar–Tangier	six times weekly	Transtour
Spain–Great Britain		
Santander–Plymouth	once or twice weekly	Brittany Ferries

[1] A passport is necessary to enter Morocco

Information and bookings

Brittany Ferries
Millbay Docks
Plymouth, PL1 3EF
(tel. 0752 21321)

Trasmediterránea
Melia Travel
12 Dover Street
London W1
(tel. 01–493 1985)

Ybarra
Townsend-Thoresen Car Ferries
127 Regent Street
London W1
(tel. 01–734 4431)

DFDS (UK) Ltd
Mariner House, Pepys Street
London EC3
(tel. 01–481 3211)

Fred Olsen Lines
229 Regent Street
London W1
(tel. 01–437 9888)

Transtour, Algeciras
Bland Lines, Gibraltar
Limadet Ferry, Tangier
Compagnie Nationale Algérienne de Navigation, Algiers

Air services

Spain is linked with the international network of air services by a number of airports, the most important of which are Madrid/Barajas, Barcelona and Palma de Mallorca.

The Spanish national airline, **Iberia**, flies both international and domestic services. Domestic services are also provided by *Aviaco* (Aviación y Comercio).

Scheduled services *between Britain and Spain* are provided by Iberia and British Airways, which fly from London direct to Alicante, Barcelona, Bilbao, Madrid, Málaga, Palma de Mallorca and Valencia. There are also services by Iberia to Almería, Santiago de Compostela, Seville, Minorca and Ibiza, Las Palmas and Santa Cruz de Tenerife. British Caledonian fly from London to the Canaries. There is also a weekly service between Dublin and Madrid.

Scheduled services *between North America and Spain* are provided by Iberia, TWA and Canadian Pacific Airlines (New York to Madrid, Montreal to Madrid, and also to Málaga, Barcelona and Palma, and Las Palmas).

There are also numerous charter flights, mainly serving the principal holiday areas.

Rail services

Although the Spanish railway system is not so well developed as those of some other Western European countries it is being continually improved and modernised. All the principal towns can be reached by rail on a network of lines radiating from Madrid (only partly electrified); but though the more densely populated regions in the N (Asturias, the Basque provinces) and E (Catalonia, Valencia) are relatively well served, large areas on the thinly populated central

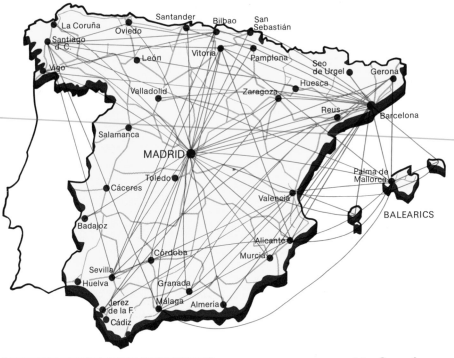

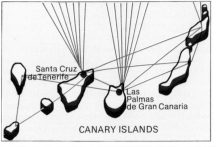

CANARY ISLANDS

Air Services

Iberia and Aviaco ————————

Railways

Main lines ————————
Branch lines ————————

plateau are without any railway services. – Since the Spanish main lines are wide-gauge (1674 mm, compared with the 1435 mm or 4 ft 8½ in. normal in the rest of Europe) it is necessary to change trains at the French–Spanish frontier except on certain international trains which change bogies at the frontier. Many branch lines are of narrow gauge.

The main-line services are run by the Spanish State Railways, **RENFE** (*Red Nacional de los Ferrocarriles Españoles*), which has travel offices in all the larger towns. There are also a number of privately run lines, with a narrower gauge, both on the mainland and in the islands.

Types of train: *Talgo*, a luxury air-conditioned diesel train. These are Spain's fastest trains (some operating as Trans-European Expresses, 1st class only), running daily between Madrid and Barcelona, Irún, Bilbao, Zaragoza, Valencia, Málaga, Seville and Cádiz. – *Electrotrén*, a luxury air-conditioned electric train. – *Ter*, a luxury diesel train. – *Taf*, a diesel train (2nd class only). – *Expreso*, express train; *rápido*, a (relatively) fast train; *semidirecto*, slower than a *rápido*. – *Automotor*, rail-car. – *Omnibus*, stopping train. – *Ferrobús*, diesel car. – *Tranvía*, local train. – Long-distance and express trains usually have 1st and 2nd class, stopping trains usually only 2nd.

Tickets (*billetes*) should be bought at least 24 hours before departure at a RENFE office. Although it is not obligatory to book a seat in advance, it is highly desirable to do so during the main holiday season and before major feast days; the seat ticket should be bought at the same time as the travel ticket. After the advance booking period tickets can be bought and seats booked (if available) only at the station, where the ticket windows open only an hour or half an hour before the departure of the train and usually close five minutes before departure; in consequence there is likely to be a considerable crowd at the ticket office. Rail tickets bought aboard must be stamped before each section of the journey, either in a RENFE office or at the station on the day of departure (unless the passenger has a seat card).

Motorail services

Motorists travelling from Britain can reduce their road mileage by using one of the motorail services which will take them at least part of the way to Spain; there are no services covering the whole distance from the Channel to Spain. The most convenient are the services from Boulogne to either Biarritz or Narbonne; alternatively there is a service from Paris to Madrid. Information from Sealink Car Ferry Centre, Grosvenor Gardens, London SW1, or French Railways, 179 Piccadilly, London W1.

Within Spain there are motorail services (*auto-expresos*) between Barcelona and Madrid, between Irún and Madrid, and from Madrid to Algeciras, Cádiz, Málaga, Santander, Seville, Valencia and Vigo. Information from railway stations and the larger travel agencies.

Rail services within Spain are supplemented by a dense network of **bus services**.

Language

As the mother tongue of over 220 million people Spanish is the most widely spoken of the Romance languages and, after English, the world's most important commercial language. Since it originated in the Castilian dialect, Spanish (*español*) is also referred to as *lengua castellana*. It incorporates many words of Arabic origin. – It adds greatly to the pleasure of a visit to Spain, and may avoid some problems, to have at least some acquaintance with the language. In the larger hotels and shops and in the popular tourist resorts English is widely understood, but visitors travelling on their own who want to get off the beaten track of tourism will find it a great help to have some idea of the pronunciation of Spanish, the basic rules of grammar and a few everyday expressions.

Pronunciation. – Vowels are pronounced in the "continental" fashion, without the diphthongisation practised in English. The consonants *f, k, l, m, n, p, t* and *x* are normally pronounced much as in English;

b has a softer pronunciation than in English, almost approximating to *v* when it occurs between vowels; *c* before *e* or *i* is pronounced like *th* in "thin", otherwise like *k*; *ch* as in English; *d* at the end of a word or between vowels is softened into the sound of *th* in "that"; *g* before *e* or *i* is like the Scottish *ch* in "loch", otherwise hard as in "go"; *h* is silent; *j* is the Scottish *ch*; *ll* is pronounced like *l* followed by consonantal *y*, i.e. like *lli* in "million" (in many areas like consonantal *y* without the *l*); *ñ* like *n* followed by consonantal *y*, i.e. like *ni* in "onion"; *qu* like *k*; *r* is strongly rolled; *z* is pronounced like *th* in "thin".

Stress. – The rule is that words ending in a vowel or in *n* or *s* have the stress on the second-last syllable; words ending in any other consonant have the stress on the last syllable. Any departure from this rule is indicated by an acute accent on the stressed vowel. Thus Granada and Estaban, with the stress on the second-last syllable, and Santander and Jerez, with the stress on the last syllable, are spelt without the acute accent: contrast Málaga, Alcalá, Sebastián, Alcázar, Cádiz, etc. For this purpose the vowel combinations *ae, ao, ea, eo, oa* and *oe* are regarded as constituting two syllables, all other combinations as monosyllabic: thus *paseo* has the stress on *e*, *patio* on *a*, without the need of an acute accent to indicate this. The acute accent is, however, required when the first vowel in the combinations *ia, ie, io, iu, ua, ue, ui, uo* and *uy* is to be stressed (e.g. *sillería, río*), and when the second vowel in the combinations *ai* or *ay, au, ei, or ey, eu, oi or oy and ou* is to be stressed (e.g. *paraíso, baúl*).

Numbers

0	cero
1	uno (una)
2	dos
3	tres
4	cuatro
5	cinco
6	seis
7	siete
8	ocho
9	nueve
10	diez
11	once
12	doce
13	trece
14	catorce
15	quince
16	dieciseis
17	diecisiete
18	dieciocho
19	diecinueve
20	veinte
21	veintiuno
22	veintidós
30	treinta
31	treinta y uno
40	cuarenta
50	cincuenta
60	sesenta
70	setenta
80	ochenta
90	noventa
100	ciento (cien)
101	ciento uno
153	ciento cincuenta y tres
200	doscientos
300	trescientos
400	cuatrocientos
500	quinientos
600	seiscientos
700	setecientos
800	ochocientos
900	novecientos
1000	mil
1 m.	un millón

Ordinals

1.	primero (primera)
2.	segundo
3.	tercero
4.	cuarto
5.	quinto
6.	sexto
7.	sétimo/séptimo
8.	octavo
9.	nono/noveno
10.	décimo
20.	vigésimo
100.	centésimo

Fractions

$\frac{1}{2}$	medio (media)
$\frac{1}{4}$	un cuarto
$\frac{1}{10}$	un décimo

Everyday expressions

Good morning!	¡Buenos dias!
Good afternoon!	¡Buenas tardes!
Good evening, good night!	¡Buenas noches!
Goodbye!	¡Adiós!
	¡Hasta luego!
Yes, no	Sí, no (señor, etc.)
Please!	¡Por favor!
Thank you (very much)!	¡(Muchas) gracias!
Not at all! (You're welcome!)	¡De nada!
	¡No hay de qué!
Excuse me! (for a mistake, etc.)	¡Perdón!
Excuse me! (e.g. when passing in front of someone)	¡Con permiso!
Do you speak English?	¿Habla Usted inglés?
A little, not much	Un poco, no mucho
I do not understand	No entiendo
What is the Spanish for . . . ?	¿Cómo se dice en español . . . ?
What is the name of this church?	¿Cómo se llama esta iglesia?
The Cathedral (of St John)	La catedral (San Juan)
Where is Calle . . . ?	¿Dónde está la calle . . . ?
Where is the road to . . . ?	¿Dóndo está el camino para . . . ?
To the right, left	A la derecha, izquierda
Straight ahead	Siempre derecho
Above, up	Arriba
Below, down	Abajo
When is it open?	¿A qué horas está abierto?
How far?	¿Qué distancia?
Today	Hoy
Yesterday	Ayet
The day before yesterday	Anteayer
Tomorrow	Mañana
Have you any rooms?	¿Hay habitaciones libres?
I should like . . .	Quisiera . . .

A room with private bath With full board	Una habitación con baño Con pensión completa
What does it cost?	¿Cuánto vale?
Everything included	Todo incluído
That is too dear	Es demasiado caro
Bill, please! (to a waiter)	¡Camarero, la cuenta (nota) por favor!
Where is the toilet?	¿Dónde está el retrete?
Wake me at six!	¡Llámeme Usted a las seis!
Where is there a doctor?	¿Dónde hay un médico?
Where is there a dentist?	¿Dónde hay un dentista?
Where is there a chemist/pharmacist?	¿Donde hay una farmacia?
I have pains here	Siento dolores aquí
I am suffering from . . .	Padezco de . . .
I need something for . . .	Necesito un medicamento contra . . .
How often must I take it?	¿Cuántas veces tengo que tomar esta medicina?

Road signs

Aduana	Customs
¡Alto!	Halt
¡Atención	Caution
Aparcamiento	Car park
Autopista	Motorway
Bifurcación	Road-fork
Cañada	Track for livestock
¡Ceda el paso!	Give way
¡Cuidado!	Caution
Desvío	Diversion
Dirección única	One way only
Grúa	Crane, two-away service
¡Lleva la derecha (la izquierda)!	Keep to the right (left)
Niebla	Fog
¡Obras!	Road works
¡Al paso!	Dead slow
Paso a nivel	Level crossing
Paso prohibido	No entry

Peatones	Pedestrians	Cartuja	Charterhouse,
¡Peligro!	Danger		Carthusian monastery
Playa	Beach	Casa Consistorial	Town hall
Prohibido el	No overtaking	Cementerio	Cemetery
adelantamiento		Cimborio	Dome over crossing
Prohibido aparcar	No parking	Ciudad	City, town
Sentido único	One-way street	Claustro	Cloister
Viraje peligroso	Dangerous bend	Colegio	College, seminary
		Convento	Monastery, convent

Travelling by train

		Coro	Choir
		Coto	(Nature) reserve
All aboard!	¡Viajeros al tren!	Cuesta	Slope, hill
All change!	¡Cambiar de tren!	Cueva	Cave
Arrival	Llegada	Cumbre	Summit
Departure	Salida	Custodia	Monstrance
Fare	Precio, importe	Diputación Provincial	Provincial Council
Halt	Apeadero		(Offices)
Junction	Empalme	Embalse	Reservoir, artificial lake
Luggage, baggage	Equipaje	Ermita	Small country church,
Non-smoking	No fumadores		pilgrimage chapel
compartment		Estrella	Rose window
Platform	Andén	Faro	Lighthouse
Smoking compartment	Fumadores	Fonda	Inn, small restaurant
Station	Estación	Fuente	Fountain, spring
Stop	Parada	Hostal	Inn, hostelry
Ticket	Billete	Huerta	Fertile irrigated area
Ticket-collector,	Revisor	Llano	Plain
conductor		Loma	Hillock
Ticket-window	Taquilla de billetes	Lonja	(Stock) exchange
Timetable	Horario de trenes	Mezquita	Mosque
Waiting room	Sala de espera	Mihrab	Prayer niche in a mosque
			(indicating the

At the post office

			direction of Mecca)
		Mirador	Enclosed balcony;
Address	Dirección		lookout point
Air mail	Por avión	Mudéjar	See p. 30
Express	Por correo urgente	Pantano	Reservoir, artificial lake
Letter	Carta	Parador	Tourist hotel
Letter-box, post-box	Buzón	Parroquia	Parish church
Postage	Porte, franqueo	Paseo	Avenue, promenade
Postcard	Tarjeta postal	Paso	Figure, group of saints,
Poste restante	Lista de correos		etc., carried in Easter
Postman	Cartero		procession
Post office	Correo	Patio	Courtyard
Printed matter	Impreso	Peña	Crag, cliff
Registered letter	Carta certificada	Picota	Pillory
Stamp	Sello	Plateresque	See p. 31
Telegram	Telegrama	Playa	Beach
Telephone	Teléfono	Portillo	Side gate; narrow pass
		Puerta	Door(way)

Geographical, architectural, etc., terms

		Puerto	Port, harbour; pass
		Punta	Point, headland
		Quinta	Country house
Alcazaba, alcázar	Moorish castle	Rambla	Watercourse (which
Arrabel	Outlying district of a		dries up during the
	town		summer); avenue,
Artesonado	Coffered (ceiling)		boulevard
Audiencia	Court of appeal	Reja	Grille, grating
Avenida	Avenue; spate (of river)	Retablo	Reredos, altarpiece
Ayuntamiento	Town hall	Ría	Tidal estuary of a river
Azulejos	Glazed tiles (originally	Río	River
	blue – azul)	Sagrario	Sacristy, chapel
Bahía	Bay	Sala capitular	Chapterhouse
Barrio	District, quarter (of a	Seo	Cathedral
	town)	Serranía	Range of hills
Cabo	Cape	Sierra	Mountain range
Calina	Heat-haze (in southern	Sillería	Choir-stalls
	Spain)	Taberna	Bar, tavern
Campiña	Flat stretch of cultivated	Torrente	Mountain stream
	land	Trascoro	Retrochoir
Capilla	Chapel	Trassagrario	Rear side of high altar
Capilla Mayor	Principal chapel,	Urbanización (Urb.)	Urban development,
	containing the high		housing development
	altar	Vega	Fertile irrigated plain
Carretera	(Main) road	Venta	Country inn

Accommodation

Hotels

Spanish hotels are officially classified in various categories according to their function and standard: *hoteles* (singular *hotel*), providing accommodation with or without meals, usually with their own restaurant; *hoteles-apartamentos*, apartment hotels, with facilities similar to hotels but with accommodation in flats or bungalows (chalets); *hostales* (sing. *hostal*), modest hotels or inns providing accommodation with or without meals; and *pensiones* (sing. *pensión*), pensions or guesthouses with a limited number of rooms, providing full board only. Hotels, apartment hotels and *hostales* may also be run as *residencias*, providing only accommodation and usually breakfast.

In major tourist centres there are also *Paradores Nacionales de Turismo* (sing. *Parador Nacional*), high-class hotels in old castles, palaces and convents, or sometimes purpose-built, excellently run and offering every comfort and amenity as well as an excellent cuisine. They are rather dearer than ordinary hotels in the same category, but provide a unique touristic experience. Advance booking is advisable.

Motels, on the main roads, offer accommodation for a restricted period of stay. – The simplest form of accommodation is provided by *fondas* or *casas de huéspedes*.

Under the official classification system hotels are divided into five price categories, *hostales* and *pensiones* into three, the categories being indicated by the number of stars. – Prices vary not only according to category but also according to situation and the size of the town. The dearest are hotels in large cities, bathing resorts and spas. – The prices shown in the following table are taken from the official Spanish hotel guide ("Guía de Hoteles"), but are liable to be increased.

Hotels in the top category are normally up to international standards of comfort and amenity. Single rooms are rare, particularly in the more modest establishments. Guests are usually expected to take their meals in the hotel so far as possible. Breakfast may be included in the charge for accommodation (no reduction if the guest does not take it). – During the main tourist seaon advance booking is advisable, particularly in the popular areas on the Mediterranean and Atlantic coasts and in the larger towns.

Parador Nacional San Telmo, Túy

Category		All prices in pesetas		
official	in this Guide	Double room per night (2 persons)	Breakfast	Lunch or dinner
Hotels				
*****	L	10000–35000	500–1000	2500–5000
****	I	4000–20000	400–700	1800–4500
***	II	3000–7000	250–650	1000–1600
**	III	2200–4700	220–500	700–1300
*	IV	2000–4200	200–300	600–1000
Hostales and pensiones				
***	P I	3000–6000	200–350	800–1100
**	P II	2000–3500	250–300	600–900
*	P III	1500–3000	150–280	550–850

The price for a single room is approximately 60 to 70% of that of a double

Youth hostels

There are youth hostels (*albergues juveniles* or *albergues para la juventud*) in towns all over Spain providing cheap accommodation for young people. They are listed in the annual International Youth Hostel Handbook (Vol. I, Europe and the Mediterranean) which can be obtained through national youth hostel associations. The hostels are open (usually July–September) to members of national associations. Hostellers are not allowed to spend more than three nights at a time in any particular hostel.

Camping and caravanning

There are more than 700 officially approved camping sites (*campings, campamentos*) in Spain, more than two-thirds of them on the coasts. They are listed in the annual "Guía de Campings" published by the Secretaría General de Turismo, Calle de María de Molina 50, Madrid 6, which contains illustrations and sketch maps and has an introduction in English.

Food and drink

Since visitors staying in hotels will normally eat there, they are likely to go to restaurants only in the larger towns and the seaside resorts. The Spaniards have always taken their meals much later than in other European countries, though with the development of the tourist trade it is now usually possible to get lunch or dinner a good deal earlier than in the past.

Spanish meals are usually substantial (hors d'œuvre, etc., followed by main dish, fruit and cheese). The best plan is to take the fixed-price menu (*comida*) of four or more courses: it costs more to eat à la carte. There is now a tourist menu, in three price ranges, consisting of three courses; the price usually includes ¼ litre of wine or beer, service and other charges. – Breakfast is usually a very simple meal.

Spanish cooking makes much use of olive oil (*aceite*) and garlic (*ajo*). Egg dishes, rice dishes and fish are particularly tasty and appetising. There are many restaurants specialising in seafood (*marisquerías*). – Ordinary table wine (*vino corriente* or *vino de mesa*) is frequently mixed with water or mineral water. A popular and refreshing drink is Sangría (made from red wine, brandy, mineral water and fruit juice). – Beer restaurants (*cervecerías*) see imported beers as well as the lighter Spanish beers, which are increasingly being drunk instead of wine. – A quick meal can be obtained in numerous snack bars and buffets in the towns.

Cafés (often with a billiard room) are mainly patronised by men. Coffee is drunk as *café solo* (black espresso coffee) or *café con leche* (with milk – taken at breakfast time). Good refreshing drinks can be had in summer in the *horchaterías*, which specialise in *horchata*, made from earth almonds (*chufas*) or real almonds with lemonade, iced water, etc. – Pâtisseries (*confiterías* or *pastelerías*) are found only in the larger towns.

Tobacco, cigarettes and cigars – a state monopoly – can be obtained in *estancos*, distinguished by their red-yellow-red markings.

Reading a Spanish menu
(*lista de comidas*)

Breakfast *desayuno*; lunch *comida*; dinner *cena*. – Table-setting *cubierto*; knife *cuchillo*; fork *tenedor*, spoon *cuchara*; teaspoon *cucharita*; plate *plato*; glass *vaso*; cup *taza*; napkin *servilleta*; corkscrew *sacacorchos*.

Hors d'œuvres (entremeses). – *Aceitunas* olives; *ensalada* salad; *ostras* oysters; *anchoas* anchovies; *sardinas* sardines; *rábanos* radishes; *mantequilla* butter; *pan* bread; *panecillo* roll.

Soups (sopas). – *Sopa de legumbres, de yerbas* or *de verduras* vegetable soup; *sopa con guisantes* pea soup; *sopa de lentejas* lentil soup; *sopa con tomates* tomato soup; *sopa de fideos* noodle soup; *sopa de arroz* rice soup; *sopa pescado* fish soup; *caldo* bouillon.

Egg dishes (platos de huevos). – *Huevo* egg (*crudo* raw, *fresco* fresh, *duro* hard-boiled, *pasado por agua* soft-boiled); *tortilla* omelette; *huevos revueltos* scrambled eggs; *huevos fritos* or *al plato* fried eggs; *huevos con tomate* eggs fried with tomato.

Fish (pescado). – *Frito* baked, *asado* roasted, *cocido* boiled, *ahumado* smoked. – *Anguila* eel; *arenque* herring; *atún* tunny; *bacalao* cod; *besugo* sea bream; *carpa* carp; *esturión* sturgeon; *gado* haddock; *lenguado* sole; *merluza* hake; *rodaballo* turbot; *salmón* salmon; *sollo* pike; *pescadilla* whiting; *trucha* trout. – *Almeja* clam; *calamar* squid; *cangrejo* crab, crayfish; *camarón, langostino* shrimp, prawn; *langosta* spiny lobster; *bogavante* lobster; *erizo de mar* sea-urchin; *ostras* oysters; *mariscos* seafood.

Meat (carnes). – *Asado* roast; *pierna* leg; *chuleta* chop, cutlet; *gordo, graso* fat. – *Carnero* mutton; *cerdo* pork; *cochinillo, lechón* suckling pig; *cordero* lamb: *ternera* veal; *vaca* beef; *bistec* steak; *rosbif* roast beef; *carne estofada* stew; *carne salada* salt meat; *carne ahumada* smoked meat; *tocino* bacon; *fiambre* cold meat; *jamón* ham (*serrano* smoked); *salchichón* salami-type sausage. – *Poultry (aves)*: *faisán* pheasant; *ganso* goose; *pato* duck; *perdiz* partridge; *pichón* pigeon; *pollo* chicken. – *Game (caza)*: *ciervo* venison (red deer); *corzo* roe-deer; *jabalí* wild boar; *liebre* hare.

Vegetables (verduras). – *Patatas* potatoes, *patatas fritas* chips; *alcachofas* artichokes; *berza, col* cabbage; *col lombarda* red cabbage; *col de Bruselas* Brussels sprouts; *coliflor* cauliflower; *repollo* white cabbage; *acelgas* chards;

cebollas onions; *espárragos* asparagus; *espinacas* spinach; *guisantes* peas; *garbanzos* chick peas; *judias* beans; *tomates* tomatoes; *zanahorias* carrots. – *Ensalada* salad; *lechuga* lettuce; *pepino* cucumber; *apio* celery; *escarola* endive; *vinagre* vinegar; *aceite* oil; *pimienta* pepper (*molida* ground); *sal* salt (*salado* salted, salty); *mostaza* mustard.

Desserts (postres). – *Helado* ice (*de chocolate* chocolate, *de frambuesa* raspberry, *de vainilla* vanilla); *barquillo* wafer, cone; *pastel* cake; *bollo* bun; *compota* compote; *dulces* sweets; *nata batida* whipped cream; *tarta* tart; *torrijas* fritters. – *Fruit (frutas)*: *almendras* almonds; *cerezas* cherries; *brevas, higos* figs; *chumbos* prickly pears; *dátiles* dates; *fresas* strawberries (*con naranja* with orange-juice, *con nata* with whipped cream); *manzanas* apples; *melocotones, duraznos* peaches; *melones* melons; *naranjas* oranges (*mandarinas* mandarines); *nueces* nuts (*avelanas* hazelnuts, *cacahuetes* groundnuts); *pasas* raisins; *peras* pears; *piñas (de América)* pineapples; *plátanos* bananas; *uvas* grapes. – *Cheese (queso)*: *gruyère* Gruyère; *de Holanda* Dutch; *queso de nata* cream cheese; *queso de cabras* goat's milk cheese; *queso de ovejas* ewe's milk cheese; *requesón* curds; *queso blando* soft cheese, spreading cheese.

Special dishes. – *Cocido*, the national dish, also known as *puchero, olla podrido, pote* or *caldo*: chick peas with meat, bacon, potatoes and vegetables, the exact composition varying from one part of the country to another. – *Arroz* or *paella a la Valenciana*: rice steamed in oil with meat, sausage, seafood (shellfish, shrimps, snails, etc.) and red or green peppers. – *Empedrado*: rice with chick peas and beans. – *Gazpacho andaluz*: a kind of cold soup made of water, vinegar and oil with bread, gherkins, tomatoes, onions and garlic. – *Potaje*: chick peas with spinach. – *Jamón en dulce*: ham preserved in sugar (eaten cold). – *Butifarra*, a Catalan sausage. – *Chorizo*, red paprika sausage. – *Torreznos*, rashers of bacon. – *Media tostada*: half a roll, toasted (for breakfast). – *Gambas*: prawns.

Drinks (bebidas). – *Café con leche* coffee with milk, *café solo* black coffee, *café helado* iced coffee; *chocolate* chocolate; *té* tea (*con ron* with rum, *con limón* with lemon); *agua mineral* or *de Seltz* mineral water; *horchata*, a refreshing drink made

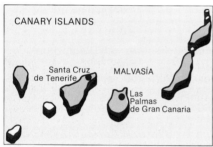

Wine-growing Areas in Spain

from almonds, lemonade, etc.; *leche de almendras* almond milk; *limonada* lemonade; *jugo (de naranjas)* (orange) juice; *agua helada* iced water; *sidra* cider; *cerveza* beer (*dorada* light, *negra* dark, *del pais* Spanish-made); *vino* wine (*dulce* sweet, *blanco* white, *tinto* red, *del año* of the current year, *añejo* older, *corriente* or *de mesa* table wine, drinking wine). – Bars (*tabernas, tascas*) serve a variety of appetisers (*tapas;* in Madrid *pichos*) with glasses of wine.

Some typical Spanish dishes

Hors d'œuvres (*entremeses*) include *sausage*(from Cantimpalos, Rioja, Burgos, Candelario, Vich); *ham* (jamón serrano, de Jabugo, de Trevélez, de Avilés, de Tineo); *seafood* such as shrimps, shellfish (scallops, *vieiras*, and barnacles, *percebes*, being particularly good) and spiny lobsters (*langostinos, cigalas*); and *olives* (particularly Manzanilla and Gordal olives).

Among Spanish **soups** (*sopas*) are *gazpacho* (see above) and other soups flavoured with garlic, such as the Castilian version made with eggs, *sopa al cuarto de hora* ("quarter of an hour soup"), *pote* and *caldo* in Galicia and Asturias, the Basque *sopa zarauztarra*, a soup made in the Levante with roasted rice, and *ajo blanco con uvas* (white garlic with grapes).

Venenciador at work, Jerez de la Frontera

The first **main course** (*plato fuerte*) is often *tortillas* (omelettes), in numerous variations both savoury and sweet. The various local dishes combining meat and vegetables, among them *cocido* (see above), are both nourishing and substantial. Other dishes of this kind are the Asturian *fabada*, a rich stew of beans, pork, etc., and *callos* (tripe), which is particularly tasty in Madrid. Also excellent when properly made is the well-known *paella*, a rice dish made with chicken, meat, fish, seafood, beans and peas for which Valencia is particularly renowned.

Fish (*pescado*) is served in many forms. *Zarzuela de mariscos* is a stew of different kinds of fish, highly seasoned; *merluza a la vasca* is hake with green sauce; *bacalao* (cod) is eaten in the Basque country with a tomato sauce or slowly simmered *al pil pil*; in Navarre trout are stuffed with ham. Fish are also served as *tapas* (appetisers), particularly eels (*anguilas*) boiled in oil with garlic and pepper. Any kind of fresh fish is excellent simply fried in oil.

In southern Navarre and Aragon poultry, lamb, rabbits and veal are cooked *a la chilindrón* in a sauce of onions and tomatoes stewed in oil with strong seasoning. In Castile and León sucking pig and roast lamb are popular.

Spain has a great variety of **desserts** (*postres*) – excellent cheeses and a wide range of sweets *Turrón* (a kind of nougat made with honey and almonds) and marzipan date from Moorish times; and in addition there are pastries, particularly on Majorca (*ensaimadas*), spiced cakes, egg jelly, flan (caramel custard), candied yolk of egg and magnificent fruit.

Wine   Map: p. 264

Galicia

Pontevedra (white and red); Ribeiro (mainly white); Albariño/Valle de Rosal (highest quality).

León

León (white and red).

Old Castile

La Nava, Roa, Peñafiel (white and red, fairly strong); Toro (red, heavy).

Navarre

Rioja (red and white: of high quality, the Spanish equivalent of burgundy): Rioja Alta (the best, light); Rioja Alavesa (full-bodied; *clarete*, a light-coloured red wine); Rioja Baja (heavy).

Aragon

Cariñera (white and red, sweet); Somontano (white and red).

Catalonia

Wines of high quality: Panadés, Marfil (white, dry; much sparkling wine); Sitges (white, Malvasía, muscatel); Tarragona (white and red, sweet; fortified); Priorato (red, dry, strong).

New Castile

La Mancha (the largest-wine-growing area): Valdepeñas (mainly red, strong); Cebreros (white and red).

Valencia

Utiel, Requena; Albaida, Jumilla, Monóvar (mainly red; heavy and sweet).

Extremadura

Almendralejo (white: a modest wine).

Andalusia

Jerez de la Frontera (wine of high quality; the best sherry); Carrascal, Macharnudo, Anina (white, full-bodied, heavy); Balbaina, Manzanilla (well-known brands Pedro Domecq, Sandeman, González Byass); Huelva (white only; best sorts used to make sherry); Sanlúcar de Barrameda, Miraflores (good sherry); Montilla, Moriles (quality wine; white; the inland equivalent of sherry); Málaga (mainly white; dessert wine).

Tenerife

Malvasía ("malmsey": white, strong, fairly sweet).

Manners and customs

The relaxed manner of the educated Spaniard and the native politeness which is common to all classes of the population make it easy for the visitor to get on with the people of Spain. But of course visitors must have regard to the customs of the country and behave with equal courtesy and discretion – remembering that, with his strongly developed sense of equality, every Spaniard of whatever class expects to be treated as a *caballero* (gentleman). Spanish national pride is easily offended, and visitors should therefore show tact in discussing politics or expressing any criticism of the Spanish way of life. And they should avoid showing impatience – an emotion alien to the Spanish temperament.

Great importance is still attached to correct **dress**. It is considered bad manners for a man to wear shorts in town, and Spaniards tend to cling to their tie, even in the heat of summer to a greater extent than in some other countries. A degree of tolerance is extended to foreign visitors in the popular tourist resorts, but they should not stretch this indulgence too far lest they attract a measure of ridicule. In Catalonia and the Balearics people are easier in matters of dress and behaviour than in the more conservative Castile or in inland Andalusia. There are no official facilities for nude bathing in Spain, though there are certain beaches on Formentera and in the Canaries where it is tolerated by the authorities. – Women should not enter churches in sleeveless garments, excessive décolleté, unduly short skirts or shorts.

Guides (*el guía*) usually lie in wait for visitors at the main tourist sights and in the large hotels; their charges tend to be high. **Interpreters** (*intérprete*) usually demand at least twice as much as the guides; before hiring one it is advisable to check his linguistic competence. A good guide, with a real knowledge of his subject, can add greatly to the interest and enjoyment of a visit; but it is necessary to beware touts whose only objective is to get their client to patronise some particular shop or place of entertainment.

Tipping. – A service charge (*servicio*) is usually added to the bill in hotels and restaurants, but it is normal to give a small additional tip (*propina*) to waiters (*camareros*), chambermaids (*camareras, muchachas*), porters (it is not usual to carry your own suitcase), pages (bellboys), life attendants, etc. A tip will also be expected by custodians of tourist sights and ushers or usherettes in cinemas, theatres, bullrings, etc. It is advisable, therefore, to be well

provided with small change. A note of appropriate size, discreetly offered, will sometimes help to solve the problems which may crop up for the traveller – when no rooms are available in a hotel, when some office is closed, when there are no tickets left for an entertainment, and so on.

In Spain there are no statutory **opening times** for shops, etc. Most shops are open from 9 to 1 and from 3 or 4 to 7, and in summer often much later (particularly food shops and tobacconists). In Madrid shops are open on Saturdays from 9 to 2 and from 5 to 8. Spanish banks are open only in the mornings. Tabernas are supposed to close at midnight, restaurants at 1 a.m.

The opening times of museums, castles, churches, etc., vary considerably and are subject to change. They will usually be closed during the long afternoon siesta.

Bathing beaches

Map: p. 268

⬤ **COSTA BRAVA**

The Costa Brava ("Wild Coast") is the most northerly stretch of the Spanish Mediterranean coast, extending from Port-Bou on the French frontier to Blanes. The coast is rugged, with many fringes of cliffs, between which are small coves and some longer expanses of beach. Many of the steeply scarped promontories cannot be reached by car; some are accessible only by boat.

The first real sandy beaches on the Costa Brava are in the *Bahía de Rosas*.

1 Rosas
Main beaches: *Playa Santa Margarita, Playa Rastrillo, Playa Salatá*, together 2 km long, up to 50 m wide, fine sand, flat. Bars and restaurants. Sewage disposal. To the E are *Playa Canyellas Petitas* (300 m long, up to 30 m wide) and *Playa Canyellas Grossas* (300 m long, about 10 m wide). Farther E, at Cabo Norfeu, are *Cala Montjoy* (200 m; dark-coloured stony beach; restaurant) and *Cala Joncols* (150 m; dark-coloured stony beach).

2 San Pedro Pescador
Several kilometres of open sandy beach; dunes.

3 San Martín de Ampurias
Three beaches, 200 m long below the ruins of Ampurias.

4 La Escala
Narrow beach of *Riells*, by harbour. To the SE is *Cala de Montgó* (150 m long, 30 m wide fine sand; bars, restaurants).

5 Estartit
5 km long beach of fine sand, 30–60 m wide; dunes on estuary of Río Ter and Río Daró. Bars, restaurants; sewage disposal; beach cleaning

within town. To the S is *Playa de Pals*, with only limited facilities.

6 Bagur
Several beautiful bays in area: *Sar Riera* (200 m; fine sand; bars and restaurants; fine views); *Sa Tuna* (quiet beach 100 m long; stony); *Cala Fornells* (Aigua Blava), a rocky cove with a bathing terrace and a small sandy beach.

7 Palafrugell
Within easy reach of *Tamariú*, a picturesque beach 100 m long and up to 30 m wide (to the N the Urbanización Aigua Gelida); *Llafranch*, a bay with a carefully tended beach 300 m long; and *Calella de Palafrugell* (six small bays, the largest of which is 50 m long).

8 Palamós
Beach 2 km long; to the S the Urbanización San Antonio de Calonge. To the N of Cabo Gros is *La Fosca*, a flat beach 400 m long, 10–60 m wide.

9 Playa de Aro
Main beach 2 km long, 70 m wide, coarse sand; beach cleaning. Several smaller bays (Playa de Roig, Cala del Pi, Cala Sa Cova, Playa d'en Rovira).

10 S'Agaró
San Pol (sandy beach 1 km long); *Cala del Pi; Sa Conca*, a bay with a beach 250 m long.

11 San Feliú de Guixols
The beach, 300 m long, is in the harbour, which is sheltered by a breakwater. On either side of the harbour are picturesque rocky coves.

12 Tossa de Mar
Main beach *Playa Mayor* (500 m long, 30–40 m wide, steep, coarse sand; crowded; showers, lavatories, bathing cabins). *Playa de la Palma* (200 m long, 10–30 m wide), and a number of small bays; *Playa de Llorell* and *Cala El Llevador* (both in the direction of Lloret) and *Es Codolar* (on Punta del Faro), *Cala Pola, Cala Giverola* and *Cala Salions* (in the direction of San Feliú).

The beach, Benidorm

13 Lloret de Mar
Main beach (shingle, steep), 1 km long, 30–50 m wide, crowded. *Playa de Fanals*, 500 m, sandy, all services; *Playa Canyellas*, 300 m long, 20–50 m wide, fine sand, restaurant and cafeterias; *Cala Santa Cristina*, 350 m long, 20–30 m wide, fine sand; sewage disposal; snack bars.

14 Blanes
Municipal beach, 300 m long, 10–40 m wide, all services; *Playa Sabanell*, over 2 km long, up to 80 m wide, coarse sand, steep.

○ COSTA DORADA

The Costa Dorada ("Golden Coast") extends along almost the whole coastal strip of Barcelona and Tarragona provinces from the mouth of the Río Tordera (Malgrat) to the mouth of the Ebro (San Carlos de la Rápita). It has gently sloping beaches of fine golden-yellow sand, often separated from the hinterland by the road and the railway.

15 Calella de la Costa
Main beach, 2 km long, 30–80 m wide, light-coloured coarse sand, steep; all beach facilities, bars and restaurants. At the lighthouse (on the Barcelona side) are beautiful cliff-fringed bays. Crowded.

16 Arenys de Mar
Steep beaches of coarse sand on either side of harbour; *Playa de Levante*, 500 m long, up to 60 m wide, all facilities.

17 Castelldefels
Along with *Gavamar* beach 7 km long, up to almost 100 m wide, showers, bathing cabins, lavatories, fresh-water pool. A villa suburb of Barcelona.

18 Sitges
Main beach *Playa de Oro*, fully 2 km long and up to 60 m wide; showers, bathing cabins, lavatories, beach cleaning. Overcrowded, water not clear. *Paya San Sebastián*, 100 m long, 25 m wide, sandy, rainwater gutters. Smaller bays to NE.

19 Calafell
Between San Salvador (to SW) and Cunit (to NE) is a 4 km long beach of fine sand, 40–80 m wide; all facilities, bars and restaurants.

20 Comarruga
Beach of fine golden-yellow sand 4 km long, 40 m wide. To the NE is San Salvador, with elegant villas; to the SW the Urbanización Bará.

21 Torredembarra
Beach of fine golden-yellow sand almost 4 km long, up to 90 m wide, with low dunes at NE end; bars and restaurants.

22 Tarragona
Beaches on the N side of the town: *Playa Larga, Playa de la Sabinosa, Playa de la Rabasadá, Playa del Milagro* (opposite the old town), with the usual facilities.

23 Salou
Playa Central, divided into Playa Poniente and Playa Levante by the boating harbour: 4 km within the town, 20–80 m wide, continuing SW to Vilafortuny; all facilities, bars and restaurants. *Playas de la Torre Alta*, consisting of Playa Larga (300 m long, up to 40 m wide) and other small rocky coves. *Playa de la Pineda*, about 4 km long, 40–60 m wide, continuing towards Tarragona.

24 Cambrils
Beach 7 km long, but of good quality only E of fishing harbour (in direction of Salou). *Playa de*

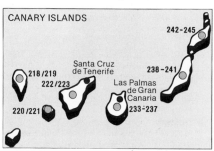

CANARY ISLANDS

218/219
220/221
222/223
Santa Cruz
de Tenerife
238-241
242-245
Las Palmas
de Gran
Canaria
233-237

Cambrils (1 km), *Playa Cavet* (400 m) and *Playa de Vilafortuny* (2 km), all 260 m wide.

25 Miami Playa

A tourist complex with two beaches: *Playa Cristal* (400 m long, 30 m wide, restaurants) and *Playa de Rifá*, which extends for some kilometres in the direction of Cambrils.

26 Hospital del Infante

Beach of light-coloured fine sand 2 km long, 15 m wide. To the S are a small bay (beach 100 m long) and *Playa de las Barcas*, 1 km long.

27 San Carlos de la Rápita

Poor beach in harbour. Boat services every hour over the Puerto de los Alfaques to *Punta Galacho*, at the W end of a long spit of land with a total of 24 km of open sandy beaches (100 m wide; dunes). Punta Galacho can also be reached by road (via Villa franca to Los Eucalyptus, then on sand tracks via Playa del Trabucador). On the N side of the Ebro delta is *Playa de la Marquesa*, 6 km long.

● COSTA DEL AZAHAR

The Costa del Azahar ("Orange-Blossom Coast") extends from Vinaroz, S of the Ebro estuary, along the coast of Castellón de la Plana province and the wide

open Gulf of Valencia to beyond Denia. It has large flat beaches, but is much polluted by industrial waste water.

28 Vinaroz

The town beach (300 m long, 10 m wide, steep large pebbles) is not to be recommended (pollution). To the N are small cliff-fringed bays

29 Benicarló

Short untidy beach; to the S open coast, at first shingle, then at Peñíscola sand.

30 Peñíscola

To the N is *Playa de Peñíscola* (2 km long within town, 10–40 m wide; clean, fine sand; all facilities). To the S, in the harbour, is another beach 200 m long and 30 m wide (pollution, no facilities).

31 Alcosebre

Beautiful flat beach of fine sand, 500 m long 50 m wide, without services. 1 km away is *Marina las Fuentes*, with a flat sandy beach 300 m long 30 m wide.

32 Oropesa

Playa Torre del Rey: flat beach 300 m long 20–30 m wide, ending in a rocky stretch of coast, all facilities.

33 Benicasím

Playa de la Villas, in the villa district to the N: 2 km long, 20 m wide; clean, fine sand; only limited services. The main beach, *Playa de Benicasím*, is 3 km long and 10–30 m wide; every facility including free showers. To the S, extending from the outskirts of the town to Castellón, are several kilometres of open beach, still undeveloped.

34 Valencia
5–10 km from the town are the overcrowded beaches of *Playa de Nazaret*, *Playa de Pinedo* and *Playa del Saler*, with all services (pollution). To the S of Playa del Saler, which is 1 km long, is *Playa del Recati* (18 km from Valencia), with dunes, extending along the Albufera lagoon; no facilities. Still farther S, 23 km from Valencia, is *Playa del Perelló*, with a long flat sandy beach and cleaner water; limited services.

35 Cullera
Sandy beach 10 km long, under various names – Mareny de San Lorenzo, Dosel, El Faro, Portet, San Antonio. Within the town is a much frequented beach 1 km long, 50 m wide, with all services. 12 km S is *Playa de Tabernes*, with a long sandy beach 40 m wide; some services.

36 Gandía
Well-run beach colony 3 km from the town. The town beach, Playa Dorada, 1 km long, 50 m wide, with all facilities.

37 Oliva
Sandy beach, untidy, 1 km long, 50 m wide; water not clear, few services.

● **COSTA BLANCA**

The Costa Blanca ("White Coast") extends from Setla (Punta de la Almadraba) to Cabo de Gata, taking in the coast of Alicante province and part of Murcia province. The beaches are mostly flat, with fine white sand. The winter in this region is very mild. Inland the country is rather featureless.

38 Denia
Playa de las Marinas, in the town: 500 m long, 50 m wide, fine grey sand, much of it left in its natural state (grass); seaweed; limited services. 2 km S is *Playa de las Rotas* (untidy, no services, seaweed).

39 Jávea
Two beaches in the town. At entrance to harbour 200 m of coarse shingle (deposits of bitumen, water dirty, no services); to the S a similar stretch of beach 500 m long, rather wider. On the southern outskirts of the town is *Playa de la Arena*, 300 m long, 80 m wide; clean fine sand; simple installations (only one shower).

40 Moraira
Playa del Castillo, 200 m long, 20 m wide, fine sand; clean water (shallow); marshy terrain inland from the beach (midges); limited services. 1 km N is the villa colony of *El Portet*, with a beach of fine sand, 100 m long, no facilities.

41 Calpe
E of the Peñón de Ifach is *Playa de Levante*, 500 m long, 20–30 m wide, fine sand, enclosed by cliffs; adequate services; seaweed often washed up. *Playa del Puerto*, near the town centre: 400 m long, 20 m wide; partly sand, partly shingle or flat rocks; limited services.

42 Benidorm
Playa de Levante: 3 km long, 30–40 m wide, clean fine sand; close to town. To the W of the old town is *Playa de Poniente*: 3 km long, 40–50 m wide, fine sand. Both beaches are regularly cleaned and have every facility; always over-crowded during the season. To the S, at a villa

colony, is *Playa de la Cala*, 100 m long, 50 m wide; clean fine sand.

43 Villajoyosa
A picturesque little town with rather untidy beaches but good cheap restaurants. Popular with day trippers.

44 Alicante
Formerly a popular winter resort, with elegant hotels and a beautiful promenade. *Playa de Postiguet*, under the Castillo de Santa Bárbara, close to town: 300 m long, 20–40 m wide, clean fine sand; excellent facilities; overcrowded. 3 km N in the direction of San Juan is *Playa de la Albufereta*: 200 m long, 20–30 m wide, clean fine sand, reasonably good services. 4 km farther N is *Playa de San Juan*: 4 km long, 20–30 m wide, flat, clean sand (occasional seaweed and tar deposits), good services. Immediately N of this is *Playa Muchavista*: 2 km long, 10 m wide, shingle; deep, clean water; no services.

45 Los Arenales del Sol
Beach (still relatively undeveloped) 1 km long, 40 m wide, limited services; heavy swell.

46 Aanta Pola
Ideal for non-swimmers (water shallow for at least 50 m). Several kilometres of beaches; the main one, *Playa de Levante*, is 500 m long and 30 m wide. Water calm, shallow, not clear. Good services.

47 Guardamar del Segura
Dunes, kept away from the town by pinewoods and avenues of eucalyptus trees. Beach 1 km long, 30 m wide, fine sand; high waves.

48 Torrevieja
Salt-pans; seaweed deposits; bleak country inland. In the developments to the N there are some fine uncrowded beaches with limited facilities. In the town itself the water is polluted. The coast to the S is mostly rocky.

49 Campoamor
Beach 200 m long, 40 m wide; clean, light-coloured, fine sand (seaweed is regularly removed); sometimes heavy swell. Inland are pools of brackish water (midges).

50 Santiago de la Ribera
On the Mar Menor, the largest lagoon in Spain (180 sq. km); water with high salt and iodine content, increasingly exposed to pollution. Noise from military aerodrome.
Playa de la Ribera: 10 m wide, clean fine sand; on account of overcrowding extended into the water by long wooden gangways. N of the Sailing Club there is another kilometre of similar narrow beach. Some services. To the S are extensive military training areas closed to the public. The villages beyond the town (Los Alcázares, Los Urrutias, Los Nietos, Mar de Cristal) have untidy and polluted beaches.

51 La Manga del Mar Menor
On both sides of this long spit of land (access via Cabo de Palos and Urmenor) are many kilometres of beaches 50 m wide, often fringed by dunes, which are still largely undeveloped. There are limited services in the centre of the holiday colony.

52 Puerto de Mazarrón
Several small sandy bays between 100 and 400 m long, well protected from wind and waves; water shallow and clean; little in the way of services.

53 Águilas
Beach 200 m long in harbour, polluted. 7 km SW is *Playa de Los Terreros*, several kilometres long, 30 m wide, very fine white sand; no services.

54 Mojácar
Beach 2 km from town, shingle and sand, very clean water; no services.

● **COSTA DEL SOL**

The Costa del Sol ("Sunshine Coast") comprises practically the whole Mediterranean coast of Andalusia from Cabo de Gata to Tarifa, Spain's most southerly point. It is now a densely populated tourist region which attracts an international crowd of visitors. The hinterland contains many places of artistic and historical interest as well as picturesque little Andalusian villages and a rich and varied flora. The coast, with its southern exposure, offers bathing from March to October.

55 Aguadulce
A large holiday colony with a beach 400 m long, 10 m wide, of large pebbles; seaweed deposits, sea-urchins. There is another similar beach 300 m long.

56 Roquetas
E and W of the town are some kilometres of beaches of coarse sand, still undeveloped.

57 Calahonda
Beach 500 m long, 10–30 m wide, of fine, dark-coloured pebbles; little in the way of services.

58 Torrenueva
Beach 2 km long, 20 m wide, steep, partly shingle; no services.

59 Motril
Water polluted by industry and the harbour. W of the town is an untidy dark-coloured beach 1 km long and up to 50 m wide; to the E a narrow strip of sand 1 km long. Practically no services.

60 Salobreña
Playa de Salobreña, 1 km from town: 1 km long, 50 m wide, no services. Beyond a cliff is a narrow shingle beach 500 m long in a beautiful bay: no services, but clean water.

61 Almuñécar
Playa Punta del Mar, 500 m long, up to 30 m wide, fine clean shingle; some facilities. To the E is a pretty little bay with a shingle beach 50 m long and 20 m wide; limited services. To the W is *Playa de San Cristóbal*, 1 km long, 40 m wide; little in the way of services. 9 km W is the beach of *La Herradura* (no services).

62 Nerja
Immediately below the Balcón de Europa is *Playa de Calahonda*, 50 m long and 20 m wide, fine shingle; restaurant. To the W is *Playa El Salón*, 50 m long and 10 m wide, coarse sand; facilities for hotel guests only.

Playa de la Torrecilla, 150 m long and 30 m wide, with a clean beach of coarse sand; all services. To the E *Playa de Burriana*, 800 m long, 40 m wide, clean sand with pebbles; good services. *Playa de Caraveo*, 40 m long and 10 m wide, a pebble beach between cliffs. No services but clean water.

63 Torre del Mar
Beach of sand and shingle 3 km long, 70 m wide; full range of services; restaurant in Balneario.

64 Málaga
Town beaches small and overcrowded. 12 km E is *Rincón de la Victoria*, with a beach 2 km long but only 10–20 m wide; fine dark-grey sand; some services; pollution.

65 Torremolinos
Shallow water with surf; sometimes tar and jellyfish; sewage disposal. Beach 3 km long, 40 m wide, well maintained; every facility and amenity. To the NE are open, uncrowded beaches. Torremolinos itself, much favoured by the package tours, is usually overcrowded.

66 Benalmádena Costa
This is still really part of Torremolinos. Beach under various names, 3 km long, of fine grey sand and rocks. Water not always clean.

67 Fuengirola/Mijas
Those who want to avoid the featureless blocks of flats of Fuengirola can find accommodation in the picturesque little hill town of *Mijas*, 8 km inland. *Playa de las Gaviotas*, in front of the tower blocks: 2 km long, 20–30 m wide, sand and shingle; pollution. SW of the harbour is *Playa Santa Amalia*: 1 km within the town, then 300 m of open beach, 30 m wide, fine sand, clean. All services.

68 Marbella
Once a fashionable society resort. Beach 1·5 km long, under various names, 20–30 m wide, fine clean sand; every service and amenity; overcrowded. Numerous groynes used for sunbathing. Many of the large hotels outside the town have their own sandy beaches, some of them fringed by dunes. Colonies of holiday bungalows round the boating harbour, Puerto José Banús, and inland (Nueva Andalucía).

69 San Pedro de Alcántara
Beach about 1 km long, 20–30 m wide, shingle and sand; only the central section is cared for and cleaned.

70 Estepona
Beach 2 km long, 30 m wide, fine grey sand, not always clean, with the usual services.

71 Buenas Noches/Bahía de Casares
Kilometres of open unfrequented beaches, developed only round the Bahía de Casares *urbanización*.

72 Algeciras
Pollution from industry and shipping. Main beach *El Rinconcillo*, 2 km long, narrow, artificially built up. 6 km S is the unfrequented *Playa de Getares*, 500 m long, 50 m wide; fine sand, clean.

73 Tarifa
Mediterranean coast rocky and inhospitable. On the Atlantic side beaches and fine sand many kilometres long and up to 200 m wide, fringed by dunes.

○ **COSTA DE LA LUZ**

The Costa de la Luz ("Coast of Light") takes in the southern Atlantic coast of Spain between the Tarifa promontory and the mouth of the Río Guadiana (the Portuguese frontier). It has fine long sandy beaches and unspoiled dunes, but the communications and services are often inadequate and communications with the hinterland difficult.

74 Barbate de Franco
Fine golden-yellow sand. *Playa de Barbate*, in the town, 500 m long, and *Playa de los Caños de Meca*, with caves and fresh-water springs.

75 Conil de la Frontera
A total of 15 km of fine sandy beaches, with dunes; *Playa de los Bateles*, *Playa Roche*.

76 Chiclana de la Frontera
5 km from the town is *Playa de la Barrosa*, 5 km long, fine sand, pines.

77 Cádiz
Playa de la Caleta, in the town. Near the town, at *Playa de Cortadura* and *Playa la Victoria*, are another 10 km of sandy beach.

78 El Puerto de Santa María
The port of Jerez de la Frontera. *Playa de Valdelagrana*, *La Puntilla*, *Playa Andalucía*, *Fuentebravía*, with the usual services.

79 Rota
Playa de la Costilla, in the town; *Playa la Almadraba*, in the outlying district of Arroyo Hondo.

80 Chipiona
Playa de Regla, with fine golden-yellow sand.

81 Sanlúcar de Barrameda
On the estuary of the Guadalquivir and the fine sandy beaches of *La Jara*, *Sanlúcar* and *Bajo de Guía*.

82 Torre de la Higuera
S of the town is the sandy beach of *Playa de Matalascañas*, several kilometres long, with dunes; services in the hotels.

83 Mazagón
A picturesque beach of fine white sand.

84 Punta del Sebo
A promontory at the mouths of the Río Odiel and Río Tinto. Industrial pollution.

85 Punta Umbria
On a promontory W of the Río Odiel estuary; fine white sand, pines.

86 El Rompido
An open sandy beach on a long promontory.

87 La Antilla
A much frequented beach of fine white sand; services.

88 Isla Cristina
Beaches of *Isla Canela* and *El Morral*, with services; other open beaches.

● **NORTH ATLANTIC COAST**

This long coastal stretch, extending along the Cantabrian coast from the Bay of Biscay to Cape Finisterre, Spain's most westerly point, and then S to the Miño estuary (Portuguese frontier), is relatively little visited by tourists from the rest of Europe; and yet, even if the climate is more severe than on the Mediterranean coast, it will well repay a visit. The beaches are mostly of fine sand, fringed by cliffs and rocky crags, and the hinterland is covered with fresh green vegetation: the coast of Asturias is well named the Costa Verde. In Galicia the rivers have long fjord-like estuaries, the so-called rías. There is excellent fishing both in the sea and in inland waters.

89 Fuenterrabía
A long beach of fine golden-yellow sand; all the usual services.

90 San Sebastián
A fashionable and cosmopolitan resort. The main beach, *La Concha*, is one of the most beautiful in Spain, with fine golden-yellow sand. Next to it is the beach of *Ondarreta*. Excellent services.

91 Orio
A fishing port, with a beach of coarse sand 2 km away.

92 Zarauz
A long beach of fine sand with good services.

93 Guetaria
A fishing port with a small beach of fine sand.

94 Zumaya
A picturesque little port. To the W is *Playa de San Telmo*, to the E *Playa de Santiago*.

95 Deva
A beautiful beach of golden-yellow sand at the mouth of the Río Deva.

96 Motrico
To the W is a small beach of fine sand, *Playa de Saturrarán*.

97 Ondárroa
A fishing port with a small beach of fine sand.

98 Lequeitio
Beach in town and 2 km E *Playa de Carraspio*, each 800 m long, fine sand.

99 Ibarranguelua
Playa de Laida and *Playa de Laga*, two beaches of fine sand, each 600 m long, on the right bank of the Ría de Guernica.

100 Pedernales
A picturesque little place on the left bank of the Ría de Guernica, with a beach of fine sand.

101 Mundaca
Also on the left bank of the Ría de Guernica, near the mouth. *Playa de Laidachu*.

102 Baquio
A large open bay with a beach of fine sand.

103 Gorliz
A large beach of fine sand in a sheltered bay.

104 Plencia
A small sheltered beach of fine sand.

105 Sopelana
Two wide, open sandy beaches, *Playa de Achiriribil* and *Playa de Larrabasterra*.

106 Algorta (Guecho)
Two beautiful long beaches, *Playa de Arrigunaga* and *Playa de Ereaga*, the latter with excellent services.

107 Las Arenas
A small sheltered beach.

108 Abanto y Ciérvana
Playa de la Arena, a long open beach of fine sand.

109 Castro Urdiales
Playa de Brazomar, in a small bay, 500 m long, fine sand. At the mouth of the Río Agüera is the *Playa de Oriñón*, 1·8 km long, fine sand, flat.

110 Laredo
Playa de la Salve, a very beautiful flat beach of fine sand, 5 km long, 500 m wide.
Santona
2 km NW is *Playa de Beria*, 2 km long, 250 m wide at high tide; flat, fine sand.

111 Isla
A beach of fine sand, with some rocks, in the Ría de Ajo, 350 m long; culture of crabs and spiny lobsters.

112 Ajo
W of the Ría de Ajo: beach of fine sand 900 m long.

113 Somo
On right bank of Ría de Cubas: beach 5 km long on a flat sandy promontory bounding the Bahía de Santander.

114 Santander
Playa de la Magdalena, on the Magdalena peninsula: 700 m long, fine sand. The famous *El Sardinero* beach, 900 m long, fine sand, all services. Other beaches in the area: *Playa de Castañeda* (of considerable length), *Mataleñas* (in a beautiful bay), *Puntal de la Bahía*.

115 Santa Cruz de Bezana
Playa de Soto la Marina, 500 m long, between meadowland and steep hillsides; *Playa de Valdearenas*, 3·5 km long, fine sand, pines.

116 Liencres
Beach 700 m long at the foot of a steep escarpment; meadowland.

117 Miengo
Playa de Mogro and *Playa de Usgo*. Rocky shore; in estuary of Río Pas sandy beach 1 km long, with dunes and pines.

118 Suances
On the right bank of the ría is *Playa de Cuchia* 800 m long (fine sand, with dunes). On the left bank is *Playa de la Concha*, 900 m long, flat, with fine sand; pinewood. W of the Punta del Dichoso is the little *Playa de los Locos*, 300 m long, with rocks and pines.

119 Cobreces
Beach 400 m long beside rocks; fine white sand; clump of eucalyptus trees.

120 Comillas
Gently sloping beach of fine white sand, 800 m long.

121 San Vicente de la Barquera
NE of the Ría de San Vicente, extending to the Cabo Oyambre, is the *Sable de Merón* beach, 3·4 m long and 100 m wide at high tide; fine white sand.

122 Pechón
On left bank of Ría de Tina Menor: beach 500 m long, very clean water, enclosed by cliffs.

123 Colombres
E of the estuary of the Río de las Cabras is the beautiful *Playa de la Franca*, with fine yellow sand.

124 Llanes
Fishing port with a beautiful cliff walk. 40 km of rugged coast, with some 30 small cliff-fringed beaches.

125 Ribadesella
Playa de Santa Marina, a horseshoe-shaped beach of fine sand on the right bank of the beautiful Ría de Sella (good fishing), with excellent services.

126 Colunga
Three beautiful sandy beaches at the foot of Monte Sueve – from E to W *Playa de la Isla*, *Playa Colunga* and *Playa de Lastres*.

127 Villaviciosa
A typical fishing village on the Ría de Villaviciosa. On the right bank are the beautiful *Playa de Rodiles* and *Playa del Puntal*, on a promontory.

128 Gijón
In the town is the beautiful *Playa de San Lorenzo*, bounded by rocky promontories: 2 km long, fine yellow sand, good services.

129 Luanco
A small sheltered bay; seafront promenade.

130 Salinas
W of the mouth of the Ría de Avilés. The town beach and *Playa de San Juan* are together more than 5 km long; pinewood, all services.

131 Cudillero
A picturesque fishing village with a beautiful beach of yellow sand.

132 Luarca
Beach of grey sand, with services. Slaty cliffs.

133 Tapia de Casariego
Beach of yellow sand enclosed by cliffs and meadowland.

134 Castropol
A beautiful fishing village on the left bank of the Ría de Ribadeo (Río Eo). 12 km NW is the sandy *Playa de Peñarronda*, enclosed by grassy cliffs.

135 Ribadeo
A port on the left bank of the Ría de Ribadeo.

Nearby are beaches of fine white sand – *Playa de los Castros*, *Playa de la Rochela*, *Playa Xuncos*.

136 Barreiros
On the right bank of the Ría de Foz. Beautiful beaches of white sand at *San Miguel de Reinante*, *San Pedro de Benquerencia*, *San Cosme de Barreiros* and *San Bártolo*.

137 Foz
A fishing port on the left bank of the Ría de Foz, with the *Playa de la Rapadoira*. Within easy reach are the beaches of *Yas*, *Arealonga* and *Areoura*, all with fine white sand.

138 Cervo
To the NE is *Playa de San Ciprián*, to the SE *Playa de Burela*, both sheltered and with fine sand.

139 Jove
Playa de Morás, with fine white sand.

140 Vivero
On the Ría de Vivero. *Playa de Covas*, a beautiful sandy beach with good services. 4 km away are *Playa de Area* and *Playa de Abrela*; at Cillero *Playa de Lavandeira* and *El Puerto*; *Playa de Sacido* (hotel beach).

141 Vicedo
On the estuary of the Río Sor. *Playa de Area Longa*, *Playa de Fomento*, *Playa de San Román del Valle*, *Playa de Xilloy*.

142 El Barquero
On the Ría del Barquero. *Playa de Vilela*, *Playa de Vares*: beautiful beaches of fine sand.

143 Ortigueira
Playa de Morouzos: 4 km of sand, sheltered by dunes, pines and eucalyptuses.

144 Cedeira
Playa de Area Longa, semicircular, 2 km long, with fine, firm sand.

145 Valdoviño
A long sandy bay, with a lagoon lying inland.

146 San Martín de Covas
Alternation of sandy beaches and cliffs; heavy surf.

147 El Ferrol
NW, towards Cabo Prior, is *Playa de San Jorge*; farther S *Playa de Doniños*, with a beautiful lake.

148 Cabañas
NE of the Ría de Ares at the mouth of the Río Eume: beautiful beach of firm sand, large pinewood.

149 Miño
SE of the Ría de Betanzos, on the estuary of the Río Lambre: long beach of fine sand, dunes.

150 Sada
On the left bank of the Ría de Betanzos: fine sandy beach, calm water.

151 Mera
A small fishing port on the NE shore of the Bahía de la Coruña, with a sandy beach 400 m long.

152 Santa Cruz
A series of small sheltered bays, separated by cliffs, on the Bahía de la Coruña.

153 Santa Cristina
A beach of very fine sand 1 km long and 100 m wide at high tide.

154 La Coruña
In the Bahía de Orzán, within the town limits, is *Playa de Riazor* (coarse sand).

155 Cayón
A typical fishing village on a small peninsula; beaches of fine sand nearby.

156 Malpica
Playa de Area Maor, 500 m long, fine sand. Boat trips to Islas Sisargas.

157 Lage
On the left bank of the Ría de Lage: beautiful beach of fine sand, 1·5 km long.

158 Camariñas
On the right bank of the Ría de Camariñas, S of Cabo Villano. Several beaches fringed by pines.

159 Finisterre
3 km N of Cape Finisterre: many sheltered beaches of fine sand, with pines.

160 Corcubión
A small beach of firm, fine sand on the Ría de Corcubión.

161 Carnota
A beautiful coastal area opposite Cape Finisterre. Several beaches with a total length of over 10 km.

162 Muros
A typical village on the large Ría de Muros. *Playa de San Francisco*, on the Punta de Louro.

163 Noya
Deep in the Ría de Noya. 2 km away is *Playa de Boa* (fine sand).

164 Puerto del Son
On the S side of the Ría de Muros y Noya. Many beautiful beaches.

165 Santa Eugenia de Ribera
On the N side of the Ría de Arosa. *Playa de Coroso*, a beautiful beach 2 km long.

166 Puebla del Caramiñal
A beautiful bay on the right bank of the Ría de Arosa. Several sandy beaches fringed by pines.

167 Rianjo
In a beautiful bay near the mouth of the Río Ulla: good beach 500 m long.

168 Villagarcía de Arosa
On the left bank of the Ría de Arosa. *Playa de Compostela*, in a park, with good services and a restaurant.

169 Villanueva de Arosa
Playa de las Sinas, a good beach over 1 km long, with services and pines. Other beaches on the *Isla de Arosa*.

170 Cambados

A fishing village (seafood); boat trips to La Toja peninsula.

171 El Grove

On a peninsula, with beautiful beaches – *Marisma del Bao*, *Terra do Porto*, *Playa del Son*, *Mexilloeira* and *Area Grande*; on the open sea *Playa de la Lanzada*.

172 Le Toja

A health and bathing resort with good services.

173 Sangenjo

Excellent beaches of fine sand: in Portonovo *Playa de Canelas* and *Playa de Caneliñas*, in Sangenjo itself *Playa de Silgar* and *Panadeira*; 1·5 km away *Playa de Areas* (pines).

174 Poyo

Many beautiful beaches, the best known being *Playa de Lourido* and *Playa de Campelo*.

175 Pontevedra

Within easy reach of the Poyo beaches (above); otherwise only *Playa de Placeres*, a small beach of coarse sand.

176 Marín

Several beaches of fine sand, including the long *Playa de Portocelo*, *Playa Mogor* and *Playa de Aguete*.

177 Bueu

Bueu shares with Marín the *Playas de Lapamán* (fine sand). *Playa de Beluso* and *Playa de Cela* have rather coarser sand but are clean and a considerable extent.

178 Cangas de Morrazo

To the NW, at Aldán, is *Playa de Menduiña*. To the W, at Hío, are *Playa de Pitens* and *Area Brava* (fine sand). In the Ría de Vigo is the *Barro de Limens* beach; in Cangas itself *Playa de Rodeira*, 1 km long.

179 Redondela

On the left bank of the Ría de Vigo: *Playa de Cesantes*, 3 km long, fine sand.

180 Vigo

An important port. *Playas de Bonzas*, *Alcambre* and *Samil*, the principal beach. At Corujo are *Playa del Bao* and *Playa de Canido*.

181 Nigrán

One of the leading beaches of the Rías Bajas is *Playa de América*, which with *Playa de Panjón* has 3 km of fine, firm sand. Also *Playa de Patos*, 300 m long, well maintained.

182 Bayona

A picturesque little town with the small beaches (fine sand) of *Concheira*, *Playa de Barbeira* and *Playa del Burgo*. 1·5 km away are *Playa de Santa Marta* and *Playa de Ladeira* (sheltered pines).

183 La Guardia

On the N side of the Miño estuary. *Area Grande* and *Playa de Fedoreto*, with fine white sand. The beach of *El Molino de Camposancos*, looking across the estuary towards Portugal, is renowned for its size, its fine sand and its sheltered situation in the lee of the Santa Tecla pinewoods.

◌ BALEARICS

Majorca. – The coastline of the island is as long as that of the Costa Brava (300 km). At some of the more popular places over-building has destroyed the scenery, and the communications and services have not always kept pace with the new developments; but there are still many bays of idyllic beauty, and the hinterland offers scope for interesting trips.

184 El Arenal/Ca'n Pastilla

Fully 5 km of sandy beach, narrow in places but up to 40 m wide elsewhere, extending from the Club Marítimo El Arenal to the Club Náutico in Ca'n Pastilla (rocky coast); all services.

185 Cala Mayor/San Agustín

On the main road from Palma to the W of the island. A little bay which cannot cope with its hordes of visitors, many of whom make for Paguera instead.

186 Illetas/Portals Nouse

Good situation, with a view of the beautiful bay, but not much sand on the little bathing beaches.

187 Palma Nova/Magaluf

Playa de Palma Nova consists of two beaches on a beautiful seafront promenade (pines, palms). To the S is a well-kept beach of fine, light-coloured sand, 200 m long, 25 m wide (part of it reserved for hotel guests; services).

N of the Torrenova *urbanización* is another beach 300 m long, varying in width and in quality. *Playa de Magaluf* has 400 m of clean light-coloured sand, up to 20 m wide.

188 Santa Ponsa

Flat beach of fine sand, 400 m long, up to 50 m wide.

189 Paguera

E of the town centre are two good beaches separated from one another by rocks, altogether 400 m long, up to 60 m wide, with pines. In the town itself there are only narrow strips of sand with concrete terraces. 1·5 km E is the beautiful little *Cala Fornells*.

190 Camp de Mar

A sandy beach 100 m long in one of the most beautiful settings on Majorca, between Puerto de Andraitx and Cala Fornells (much new building).

191 San Telmo

A beautiful quiet beach of rather dark-coloured sand opposite the Isla Dragonera; good services.

192 Puerto de Sóller

A wide, almost enclosed, bay on the rugged NW coast. Beach 150 m long at the fishing harbour (fine sand, then shingle). Another sandy beach 100 m long opposite the harbour entrance; good services.

193 Cala San Vicente

Four quiet bays, between 30 and 60 m of sand, stretches of rocky coast.

194 Puerto de Pollensa

N of the harbour is a sandy beach 1 km long, with pines, 3–15 m wide, interrupted by stretches of rocky coast. Sewage disposal. At the Hotel Formentor is the *Cala Pi* (boat service), 300 m long, up to 25 m wide; fine, light-coloured sand. All services. Other small bays in the direction of Cabo Formentor are *Cala Figuera* and *Cala Murta*. Towards Alcudia there is a sandy beach (no services) 5 km long.

195 Puerto de Alcudia
Almost 10 km of sandy beach, extending to beyond Ca'n Picafort. Ruined buildings; inadequate communications and services.

196 Ca'n Picafort
In the town is the busy *Playa de Santa Margarita*, 20–40 m wide. There is a quieter stretch of beach immediately NW in the direction of Puerto de Alcudia. At the E end of the town is the little *Playa de Son Bauló*, 100 m wide, and beyond this a stretch of rocky coast fringed by dunes, followed by another sandy beach.

197 Cala Ratjada
1 km from the town centre is the popular *Cala Guyá*, 400 m long, up to 40 m wide, with fine, light-coloured sand, edged by dunes. In the town itself is the crescent-shaped *Playa Son Moll* (sandy), 100 m long, up to 50 m wide. To the S, at the Artá caves, is *Playa de Cañamel*, 200 m long, up to 50 m wide. To the N is the beautiful *Cala Mezquida*, still relatively undeveloped.

198 Cala Bona/Cala Millor
Cala Bona is the old fishing village; Cala Millor has a sandy beach 1·5 km long, up to 50 m wide. To the N are the *Costa de los Pinos* and *Playa d'es Rivell*.

199 Porto Cristo
The town beach (150 m long, up to 25 m wide) is in the harbour. Two beaches, 50 m long and 50 m wide, in *Cala Anguila* (Porto Cristo Novo).

200 Calas de Mallorca
Six little bays on the E coast, only two of them with sandy beaches (80 by 80 m and 70 by 100 m).

201 Porto Colom
Cala Marsal, with a wide beach 80 m long enclosed by rocks.

202 Cala d'Or
A quiet little resort with 100 m of sandy beaches. Boats to *Cala Mondragó*, with two sandy beaches, one (150 m long) well kept, the other (200 m) without services; pines. *Cala Ferrara*: rocky coast, sub-aqua diving.

203 Cala Santanyi/Cala Figuera
At Figuera a deep fjord-like bay with a rocky coast; in Cala Santanyí a well-kept sandy beach 100 by 80 m.

204 Colonia de Sant Jordí
NW of Cabo Salinas. To the NW of the village are many kilometres of beaches with clear water, still largely undeveloped. To the SE are the lonely beaches of *Els Dols* and *Es Carbó*, accessible only by boat.

Minorca. – Although the second largest of the Balearics, Minorca is far less important for tourism than the third largest, Ibiza. This is due partly to its less agreeable climate and to its smaller and less

well protected beaches, but also to the fact that the authorities are anxious to avoid spoiling the countryside, which is principally used for agriculture, by permitting touristic development.

205 Round Mahón
To the N are the beautiful quiet bays, enclosed by cliffs, of *Cala Mesquida* and *Es Grao*. – To the S are the quiet resort of *S'Algar* (no sand) and *Alcaufar* (very small sandy beach). At the SE corner of the island is *Punta Prima*, with a flat sandy beach 100 m long and up to 40 m wide. – On the S coast is the region of the "White Villages", the names of which often begin with the Arabic prefix *bini* (Biniancolla, Binisafúa, Binidali). The most popular with tourists is *Binibeca*, with buildings skilfully adapted to the local architecture (small sandy beach, clear water).

206 Cala'n Porter
A sandy beach, 100 by 100 m, in a cove which cuts deeply into the rocks.

207 Playa de Son Bou
The longest beach on Minorca (over 2 km), 40 m wide, flat; dunes.

208 Santo Tomás
A long sandy beach with a hotel colony.

209 Cala de Santa Galdana
A wide semicircular bay with a sandy beach 500 m long and up to 40 m wide; pines, a large rocky crag and the mouth of a river at the W end. 1 km away, respectively E and W of the main bay, are *Cala Mitjana* and *Cala Macarella*, each with a sandy beach 200 m long.

210 Near Ciudadela
On the W coast near Ciudadela are a series of bays cutting into the rocky plateau, which is lower at this point: *Playa Bosch, Cala de Santandría, Cala en Blanes, Cala Forcat* and *Cala Blanca*. The little sandy beaches are no more than sufficient for the guests of the hotels built here.

211 Arenal d'en Castell
In a much indented bay on the N coast. Beach 600 m long, 40 m wide, at the foot of cliffs. To the W is the picturesque fishing village (spiny lobsters) of *Fornells*, on the bay of the same name.

Ibiza. – The island, formerly the preserve of artists, hippies and other individualists, has now been taken over by mass tourism, but still manages to preserve something of its characteristic atmosphere. It justifies the name of Pitiusas ("Pine Islands") given to the group, since the hills, particularly in the N and S, are still densely wooded. The large sandy beaches lie to the S of the capital, but those who prefer less frequented stretches of sand will do well to make the crossing to Formentera.

212 Ibiza Town
Separated from the harbour basin by a narrow promontory is the semicircular *Cala Talamanca*, 1 km in diameter, with a flat sandy beach; bars and restaurants. In the hotel district is *Playa de ses Figueretas*, with a stretch of rocky coast on the side nearest the town. Pollution. 5 km from the town centre is *Playa d'en Bossa*, 2 km long, 25 m wide (sand; dunes; rocks to S). 11 km from

Ibiza is *Playa Salinas* or Playa Sa Trincha, with a beach of fine sand 1·5 km long and up to 30 m wide. To the E of this is *Playa Es Cavalett*, with a beach 1 km long. SW of the airport is *Playa Godolá*, an open sandy beach 1·5 km long.

213 San Antonio Abad

Only a narrow strip of sandy beach on the S side of the bay. 2 km away is *Cala García*, a fjord-like inlet with two tiny sandy bays. 5 km away (reached by boat service, bus or car) is *Port de Torrent*, with a beach of fine sand 200 m long; pines; all services. 8 km away (reached by boat service or by road – last section unsurfaced) is *Cala Bassa*, with a beach of fine sand 200 m long and 20 m wide; pines; all services. Other small bays with beaches are *Cala Conta*, *Cala Tarida*, *Cala Molí* and *Cala Vadella*.

214 Portinatx

In the NE of the island, with a sandy beach 100 m long and a beautiful pinewood.

215 Cala San Vicente

A beautiful bay in the extreme NE of the island. Narrow beach of sand and pebbles, 300 m long; all the usual services.

216 Santa Eulalia del Rio

No sandy beaches worth the name in the town itself. 7 km S is *Cala Llonga*, a well-kept sandy beach 200 m long and up to 80 m wide in a deep cove; beautiful scenery inland. 4 km NE of Santa Eulalia is *Cala Pada*, a triangular sandy beach 60 m long, with a pinewood. 2.5 km father N is *Playa de'es Caná*, with a sandy beach 300 m long, and 1 km N again is *Cala Nova*, with a sandy beach 250 m long and dunes lying inland.

217 Formentera

In recent years tourism has increased considerably on Formentera, the smallest of the Balearic islands. Visitors are attracted by the great stretches of beach many kilometres long. The more remote beaches offer facilities for nude bathing.

W of Punta Prima is *Playa d'es Pujols*, at the beginning of a long series of beaches extending along the salt-pans to the N tip of the island.

In the S is the long *Playa de Mitjorn*.

● CANARY ISLANDS

The Canary Islands, with their very mild climate, are the "islands of eternal spring". The eastern group has a rather continental climate, with low rainfall and sharp variations between day and night temperature, particularly at higher altitudes. In the western group the climate is more oceanic, since the hills bring down the rain from the trade winds.

La Palma
218 Playa de Cancayo

4 km S of Santa Cruz de la Palma: beach of black volcanic sand, 600 m long.

Gomera
220 San Sebastián

Poor, exposed beach in harbour. The Club Náutico, below the Parador, has 80 m of reddish-brown sand and shingle.

221 Valle Gran Rey

A rocky valley on the W coast. Beach of black sand 800 m long; Playa del Inglés, dark brown.

Hierro

Not an island for bathers; the little sandy bays are difficult to reach by land.

Tenerife
222 El Médano

Beach 1 km long, sheltered by harbour breakwater; beyond Monte Roja a beach of light-coloured sand up to 200 m wide; various smaller sandy bays without services.

223 Costa de Silencio

A rocky bay with steps and a bathing platform. At *Tel Bel* is a large sea-water swimming pool; narrow sandy bay. Beyond Las Galletas two small sandy bays. To the E of the promontory are smooth flat rocks.

224 Los Cristianos

Beach of light-brown sand 400 m long, up to 100 m wide; no services.

225 Playa de las Américas

Three bays of brownish-black sand separated by rocks, each 100 m long; at high tide only a narrow strip is left above water.

226 Puerto de Santiago

A small bay with a beach of black sand 200 m long and up to 100 m wide; under the cliffs of Los Gigantes another sandy beach 500 m long.

227 San Marcos

A bay on the N coast near Icod, shut in by mighty rock walls, with a beach of dark-coloured sand 70 m long.

228 Puerto de la Cruz

A tourist metropolis with an exposed rocky coast and heavy surf. Only 300 m of black sandy beach at Hotel San Felipe. On the seafront promenade at the old town is a rock bathing pool with cabins. Many swimming pools, three of them with sea water.

229 Mesa del Mar

A bay with an artificial beach of light-coloured sand and a sea-water swimming pool. Heavy surf on the open sea. A tunnel through the rocks leads to a neighbouring bay, not yet developed, with a beach of black sand.

230 Bajamar

Three sea-water swimming pools with all services. Beautiful country inland.

231 Punta Hidalgo

A sheltered coast, with a gangway over the rocks. Many hotel swimming pools.

232 Playa de las Teresitas

An artificial sandy beach 1 km long and 100 m wide; pool services.

Gran Canaria
233 Las Palmas

Las Canteras, a beach of light-coloured sand 2 km long and up to 100 m wide; well kept and illuminated at night. To the S of the harbour is *Playa de Alcaravaneras*, 60 m long and up to 80 m wide.

234 Maspalomas
A 17 km long stretch of coast extending to the S tip of the island, backed by dunes. *Playa de San Agustín*: 600 m of fine greyish-brown sand. *Playa del Inglés*: sandy beach 6 km long, running into high dunes reaching far inland at the S end. At the southern tip of the island (lighthouse) is *El Oasis*, a flat beach of fine sand, 6 km long and up to 100 m wide, backed by high dunes.

235 Arguineguin
A small sandy bay (120 by 20 m) sheltered by high cliffs.

236 Puerto Rico
An artificial sandy beach 400 m long and 150 m wide, protected by breakwaters. Two large swimming pools; gardens; good services.

237 Puerto de las Nieves
A beach of stony black sand 100 m long; popular for day trips (beautiful views).

Fuerteventura
238 Puerto del Rosario
3 km S, near the Parador, is *Playa Blanca*, a quiet beach of light-coloured sand 600 m long and 40–80 m wide.

239 Taralejo Playa
Nearby is a sheltered bay with a beach of dark-brown lava sand.

240 Playa de Sotavento
A 15 km stretch of undeveloped coast, with sandy bays and dunes, on the E side (the lee side – *sotavento*) of the Jandia peninsula; popular with nude bathers.

241 Corralejo
12 km of white sandy beach extending S from the NE tip of the island, still undeveloped.

Lanzarote
242 Arrecife
Beach of light-coloured sand 200 m long; few services. 10 km W is *Playa de los Pocillos*, a sandy beach 2 km long and up to 80 m wide.

243 Playa Blanca
Situated at the southernmost tip of the island. Beach of light-coloured sand at the Hotel Los Fariones, 80 m long and 30 m wide. To the NE is a beach 2 km long, still in its natural state. In the fishing village a beach of light-coloured sand 100 m long.

244 Playa Famara
A sandy beach 800 m long and 80 m wide; stones and driftwood.

245 Isla Graciosa
On this little island N of Lanzarote there are beautiful unspoiled sandy bays but no services of any kind.

Spas

The mineral springs of Spain, many of them known to the Phoenicians, Romans and Arabs and still attracting an international public at the turn of the 19th and 20th c., have lost a good deal of their former importance. Something like a hundred spas are still operating, and some of them, open all year round, enjoy a considerable reputation – in the province of Barcelona *Caldas de Montbuy* and *La Garriga*, in Cádiz *Chiclana de la Frontera*, in Castellón *Benicasim*, in Gerona *Caldas de Malavella*, in Murcia *Archena* and *Fortuna*, in Portevedra *Cuntis* and *La Toya* (El Grove), in Zaragoza *Alhama de Aragón* and *Paracuellos*.

National Parks Map: p. 279

Spain's nine National Parks have a total area of some 395,360 acres. Only the parks of Covadonga, Ordesa and Coto de Doñana have regulations complying with international standards, and in the case of the Coto de Doñana it is doubtful whether the protective provisions can be enforced in practice. As in many other countries, therefore, much remains to be done if rare animals and plants are to be provided with conditions in which they can survive. Even in their present state, however, the Spanish national parks are of great interest and well worth a visit.

1 Parque Nacional de la Montaña de Covadonga o de Peña Santa
Province: Asturias.
Established 1918. Area 41,822 acres.

SITUATION and CHARACTER. – The Parque Nacional de Covadonga lies in the western part of the Picos de Europa range, between Asturias and León.

The principal rivers are the Río Cares and the Río Deje. The park contains two of Spain's few natural lakes, the picturesque Lagos de Covadonga – Lago de Enol (alt. 1070 m, area 121,500 sq. m) and Lago de Ercina (alt. 1108 m, area 121,000 sq. m).

The region is also of historical interest, since the valley of the Río Auseva was the scene of the first resistance to the Moors by the Christians of Asturias. The leader of this resistance, the Visigothic prince Pelayo (d. 737), had according to the legend found a miracle-working image of the Virgin in the Santa Gruta; the image has been preserved since 1901 in the church on the Cerro del Cueto.

FLORA. – Between 800 and 1500 m the hills are covered with extensive beech forests (*Fagus sylvatica* L.). There are also chestnuts (*Castanea sativa* Mill.) and oaks (*Quercus robur* L., *Q. pyrenaica* Willd., *Q. petraea* Liebl.). The underwood consists of yew (*Taxus baccata* L.), holly (*Ilex aquifolium* L.) and ivy (*Hedera helix* L.). Also very common are bracken (*Pteris aquilina* L.) and monkshood (*Aconitum napellus* L.).

FAUNA. – The commonest predators are the wild cat (*Felis sylvestris*), pine marten (*Martes martes*), fox (*Vulpes vulpes*), stoat (*Mustela erminea*) and polecat (*Putorius putorius*); the wolf (*Canis lupus*) also ranges up to the boundaries of the park. There are numerous badgers (*Meles meles*). The rivers are inhabited by trout (*Salmo trutta fario*), salmon (*Salmo salar*) and otters (*Lutra lutra*); there is also the mole-like Pyrenean desman (*Galemys pyrenaicus*), which is an excellent swimmer and diver and can leap up the rapids of the rivers. The birds include the golden eagle (*Aquila chrysaetos*), booted eagle (*Hieraaetus pennatus*), Bonelli's eagle (*H. fasciatus*), falcons, kites, hawks, eagle owls, the jay (*Garrulus glandarius*), magpie (*Pica pica*), chough (*Pyrrhocorax pyrrhocorax*) and Alpine chough (*P. graculus*). The capercailzie (*Tetrao urogallus*) nests in the forests. The higher slopes are inhabited by large herds of chamois (*Rupicapra rupicapra*) and by the edible dormouse (*Glis glis*).

2 Parque Nacional del Valle de Ordesa
Province: Huesca.
Established 1918. Area 38,817 acres.

SITUATION and CHARACTER. – The Vallee de Ordesa is a U-shaped valley in the Aragonese Pyrenees with a maximum width of 3 km. Unusually, it extends not from N to S but from E to W, from the cirque of Cotatuero (Soaso: alt. about 1000 m) to the Puente de los Navarros on the Pico de Diazas (2237 m). The park contains some 15 km of the course of the Río Araza, which rises at 1787 m and flows into the Río Ara at 1090 m. There are numerous waterfalls, particularly on the tributary streams, like the Gradas de Soaso, the Cascada de la Cueva, the Cascada de Arripas, the Cascada Tamborrotera, the Cascada del Arco Iris and the Cascada del Molinieto. The greatest flow of water is in May–June, the smallest in August. Typical features of the valley are the *fajas*, bands of rock formed by wind erosion; the best known are the Faja de Pelay on the S side of the valley and the Fajas de Mallo, de Mondarrugeo, de Luenga and de los Petrazales on the N side. In addition to the Vallee de Ordesa several other valleys are included in the park.

FLORA. – The commonest trees are pines, particularly on the N side of the valley (*Pinus sylvestris* L. *and P. uncinata* Mill.), but there are also numerous beeches (*Fagus sylvatica* L.) and firs (*Abies alba* Mill.). The underwood consists of yew (*Taxus baccata* L.), poplar (*Populus tremula* L.), hazel (*Corylus avellana* L.), birch (*Betula pendula* Rothm.), box (*Buxus sempervirens* L.), whin (*Genista horrida* L.), juniper (*Juniperus communis* L.) and Alpine buckthorn (*Rhamnus alpina* L.). There are also lilies (*Lilium*

pyrenaicum Gonan.) and edelweiss (*Leontopodium alpinum* Cass.).

FAUNA. – The commonest animals are the ibex (*Capra pyrenaica*) and chamois (*Rupicapra rupicapra*); others found in the park include the wild cat (*Felis sylvestris*), the genet (*Genetta genetta*), the fox (*Vulpes vulpes*), the polecat (*Putorius putorius*), the pine marten (*Martes martes*), the badger (*Meles meles*), the edible dormouse (*Glis glis*) and the garden dormouse (*Elyomis quercinus*). Among the water-dwellers are the trout (*Salmo trutta*), the otter (*Lutra lutra*), the kingfisher (*Alcedo atthis*) and the mole-like Pyrenean desman (*Desmana pyrenaica*), an excellent swimmer. The birds include the bearded vulture or lammergeier (*Gypaetus barbatus*), the golden eagle (*Aquila chrysaetos*) and the ptarmigan (*Lagopus mutus*). Two interesting smaller denizens of the park are the asp viper (*Vipera aspis*) and the midwife toad (*Alytes obstetricans*).

3 Parque Nacional de Aigües-Tortes y Lago de San Mauricio
Province: Lérida.
Established 1957. Area 55,341 acres.

SITUATION and CHARACTER. – The park lies in the Sierra de los Encantos to the S of the National Game Reserve of Alto Pallars-Arán (Pico Pinató, 2653 m), which is a kind of buffer zone protecting the park. It is bounded by two ranges of hills from E to W, between which are the valleys of the Río Sant Nicolau (reached by way of Bohí) and the Río Escrita (reached by way of Espot), linked by the Collado de Portarro de Espot. The area is a "glacier garden" with moraines, and the characteristic land-form is therefore the cirque.

Valle de Sant Nicolau. – This valley runs from the cirque of Bergús (several mountain lakes, including the Estany Bergús, 47 m deep) in the N to the rocky gorges of Gavatos-Cometes in the S. On both sides of the Río Sant Nicolau are glaciated rocky side valleys. On the right is the Circo de Contraig, a perfectly circular cirque between the Pico de Serrader (2941 m), the Pico de Contraig (2957 m) and the Gran Tuc de Colomers (2932 m), on the floor of which is the beautiful Lago de Contraig. On the left are the rocky gorges of Cortiselles (with two small lakes), the Valle de Delhú (divided) and the Valle de Morrano.

Valle del Río Escrito. – The valley of this river, a right-bank tributary of the Río Noguera Pallaresa, runs from W to E between the cirque of Ratera in the N and the smaller Valle de Subenulls in the S. The rivers in both valleys flow into the Lago de San Mauricio, with a waterfall on the N side. Here too there are side valleys – on the right-hand side the Valle de Monastero (four small gorges), with the peaks of Els Encantats (2747 m) towering over it, the Valle Estany Serrul and the Valle de Boteró, small U-shaped hanging valleys 400 m above the main valley. Finally there is the Circo de Peguera, with the largest tributary, fed by its 15 lakes. Other glacial lakes include the Lago de la Ratera, the Lago de Monastero, the Lagunas Negras, Las Llosas and Estany Llebreta.

FLORA. – Firs (*Abies alba* Mill.) and pines (*Pinus sylvestris* L., *P. uncinata* Mill.), poplar (*Populus tremula* L.) and juniper (*Juniperus communis* L.), birch (*Betula pendula* Rothm.), willow (*Salix caprea* L.) and rowans (*Sorbus aucuparia* L., *S. Chamaemespilus* Crantz); lilies (*Lilium martagon* L., *L. pyrenaicum* Gonan.), gentians (*Gentiana nivalis* L., *G. burseri*

National Parks
Mountain parks ◐
Water parks ◐
Island parks ◐

Game-shooting areas
Large game ▦
Small game ▢

CANARY ISLANDS

Santa Cruz de Tenerife

Las Palmas de Gran Canaria

Lapeyr.), saxifrages (*Saxifraga oppositifolia* L., *S. aizoides* L.), monkshood (*Aconitum anthora* L., *A. napellus* L.); and numerous species of fungi, mosses, lichens and algae.

FAUNA. – In the rivers are trout (*Salmo trutta*) and the interesting Pyrenean desman (*Galemys pyrenaicus*), a rare mole-like creature which is an excellent swimmer and can leap over rapids in the rivers. Amphibians and reptiles are represented by the Pyrenean brook salamander (*Euproctus asper*) and the yellowish-green western whip snake (*Coluber viridiflavus*). The birds include the golden eagle (*Aquila chrysaetos*), the red kite (*Milvus milvus*) and the ptarmigan (*Lagopus mutus*); in the forests are found the capercailzie (*Tetrao urogallus*), the black woodpecker (*Dryocopus martius*), the wall creeper (*Tichodroma muraria*), the citril finch (*Serinus citrinella*) and the rock bunting (*Emberiza cia*). Among mammals there are the edible dormouse (*Glis glis*), the pine marten (*Martes martes*), the stoat (*Mustela erminea*), wild pigs (*Sus scrofa*) and chamois (*Rupicapra rupicapra*).

4 Parque Nacional de la Tablas de Daimiel
  Province: Ciudad Real.
  Established 1973. Area 4477 acres.

SITUATION and CHARACTER. – This unusual national park lies in the La Mancha area of New Castile. *Tablas* are the shallow lagoons formed by rivers flooding out beyond their normal beds, linked by a network of channels which can be negotiated only by flat-bottomed punts. Scattered about in the water are numerous islands.

FLORA. – The waterways are covered by a dense mat of aquatic plants known as *ovas*. An unusual feature of the area is that the Río Cigüela brings in brackish water from the salt Parameras de Cabrejas, while the water of the Río Guadiana is fresh. Reeds (*Phragmites communis* Trin.) flourish in the fresh water, fen sedge (*Cladium mariscus* L. – the largest stand in Western Europe) in the salt water. Since the canalisation of the Río Guadiana has reduced the inflow of fresh water the salt content is increasing, and it is feared that this may lead to changes in the ecosystem. Recently it has been proposed to pump in additional fresh water. The only species of tree or shrub in the area is the tamarisk (*Tamarix gallica* L.), which grows on the islands.

FAUNA. – Formerly there were large numbers of crayfish (*Atlantostatus pallipes*), which provided the local people with a source of income, but stocks are now so much reduced that the fisheries are no longer economic. The pike (*Esox lucius*), formerly unknown in Spanish inland waters, has now established itself in the *tablas* and has almost completely exterminated the barbel (*Barbus barbus*) and carp (*Ciprinus carpio*) which were formerly numerous. It is now threatening the ducklings. Among the amphibians and reptiles found here are the tree frog (*Hyla arborea*), the European pond terrapin (*Emys orbicularis*), the grass snake (*Natrix natrix*) and the viperine snake (*N. maura*). The mammals include the polecat (*Putorius putorius*), the fox (*Vulpes vulpes*), the otter (*Lutra lutra*) and the weasel (*Mustela nivalis*). In recent years wild boar (*Sus scrofa*) have made their way into the area from the surrounding mountains and have greatly increased their numbers, living in the shelter of the reed-beds.

The principal denizens of this region, however, are the *birds*, for whose protection the national park was established. The resident species include the marsh harrier (*Circus aeruginosus*), the moorhen (*Gallinula chloropus*), the mallard (*Anas platyrhyncos*), the gadwall (*Anas strepera*) and the kingfisher (*Alcedo atthis*). Of the migrants which frequent the *tablas* the most notable are the purple heron (*Ardea purpurea*), the little egret (*Egretta garzetta*), the night heron (*Nycticorax nycticorax*), the bittern (*Botaurus stellaris*), the red-crested pochard (*Netta rufina*), the ferruginous duck (*Aythya nyroca*) and the hobby (*Falco subbuteo*). The marshy banks and shores are the haunt of the redshank (*Tringa totanus*), the avocet (*Recurvirostra avosetta*), the black-winged stilt (*Himantopus himantopus*) and the ruff (*Philomachus pugnax*). The reeds provide nesting-places for the fan-tailed warbler (*Cisticola jundicis*), Savi's warbler (*Locustella luscinioides*) and the bearded reedling (*Panurus biarmicus*).

5 Parque Nacional de Doñana
Province: Huelva.
Established 1969, Area 187,215 acres.

SITUATION and CHARACTER. – This is the largest of the Spanish national parks and perhaps the most interesting, with a fauna which includes many African species. It lies in the delta at the mouth of the Guadalquivir, on the very edge of Europe and on the route followed by migratory birds on their way to Africa. In spite of the protective statutory provisions it is in practice gravely threatened, since it is almost entirely private property. Plans to drain the land and to build a motorway have combined with pollution of the water and touristic development in the vicinity of the park to endanger the very rare species which live here. – There are two different ecosystems in the park – the wet area (*Doñana húmedo*), consisting of the *marisma* or fenland in the river delta and the lagoons (only a few hundred acres, within the national park), and the dry area (*Doñana seco*). The areas which are under water for most of the year (*almajales*) consist of the dead channels of the Guadalquivir (*caños*), the *ojos* (springs) and the *lucios* ("pikes – the long shallow lagoons); between these are the *paciles* (small circular hummocks) and the *vetas* or *vetones* (higher and longer expanses of dry land).

The fenland (marisma). – There are sharp differences in water level over the year. During the dry season (July to September, with the water reaching its lowest point in August) the area is arid and deserted; then at the end of September the first migrants (wild geese and ducks) make their appearance. The usual way of getting about is in flat-bottomed boats (*cajones*), which are either punted or drawn by horses.

FLORA. – Bulrushes (*Scirpus maritimus* L., *S. lacustris* L.), reed-mace (*Typha latifolia* L.).

A typical *marisma* landscape

FAUNA. – Many migratory birds spend the winter here or rest on their way to Africa – wigeon (*Anas penelope*), pintail (*A. acuta*), teal (*A. crecca*), shoveler (*A. clypeata*), pochard (*Aythya ferina*), etc. Among birds which nest here in spring are the coot (*Fulica atra*), the mallard (*Anas platyrhynchos*), the gadwall (*A. strepera*), the great crested grebe (*Podiceps cristatus*), the little grebe (*P. ruficollis*), the purple heron (*Ardea purpurea*), the gull-billed tern (*Gelochelidon nilotica*), the whiskered tern (*Chlidonias hybrida*) and the black tern (*C. niger*). There are also numerous shallow-water dwellers and the marsh harrier (*Circus aeruginosus*).

The lagoons. – These are distributed widely throughout the area, the larger ones lying parallel to the coast (Laguna de Santa Olalla, Laguna Dulce, Laguna del Taraje), the smaller ones farther inland (Laguna del Moral, de Navazo del Toro, del Sapo, del Brezo, del Caballo, del Pino, etc.).

FLORA. – The lagoons are fringed by groups of trees – cork-oaks (*Quercus suber* L.) and pines (*Pinus pinea* L.) – and by tree heaths (*Erica scoparia* L.), dwarf gorse (*Ulex minor*) and bracken (*Pteridium aquilinum* L.).

FAUNA. – Carp (*Cyprinus carpio*), eels (*Anguilla anguilla*), tree frogs (*Hyla arborea*), marsh frogs (*Rana ridibunda*), the European pond terrapin (*Emys orbicularis*) and the Caspian turtle (*Clemmys caspica leprosa*) are the principal water-dwelling species. All the species of duck mentioned above visit the lagoons which are also the last European refuge of a threatened species, the crested coot (*Fulica cristata*). Their shores are also visited by fallow deer, red deer and wild pigs, while otters (*Lutra lutra*) live in the water.

Cork-oak woods (alcornocal). – This biotope has become rare in many parts of the national park, but there is a swathe separating the *marisma* from the Monte de Doñana. In these cork-oaks (*Quercus suber*) are the famous nesting-places (*pajareras*) which house whole colonies of birds during the breeding season.

FAUNA. – Among birds which nest here are the grey heron (*Ardea cinerea*), little egret (*Egretta garzetta*), cattle egret (*Ardeola ibis*) and some white storks (*Ciconia ciconia*). A number of birds of prey also visit the colonies or nest there – the buzzard (*Buteo buteo*), the red kite (*Milvus milvus*), the kestrel (*Falco tinnunculus*) and many jackdaws (*Corvus monedula*), which are nest-robbers. Wild pigs (*Sus scrofa*) often come here, and the poisonous Lataste's viper (*Vipera latasti*) is commonly found.

Monte de Doñana. – *Monte* here means not hill but woodland or brush. This biotope consists of Mediterranean-type macchia with scattered cork-oaks.

FLORA. – *Halimium halimifolium* L., *Phyllirea angustifolia* L., heather (*Calluna vulgaris* L.), rosemary (*Rosmarinus officinalis* L.); at the higher altitudes juniper (*Juniperus phoenicea* L.), *Halimium commutatum* Pan., French lavender (*Lavandula stoechas* L.) and white thyme (*Thymus mastichina* L.).

FAUNA. – Reptiles and amphibians include the spur-thighed tortoise (*Tesudo graeca*), the ladder snake (*Elaphe scalaris*), the Montpellier snake (*Malpolon monspessulanus*) and the small but very poisonous Lataste's viper (*Vipera latasti*). In addition to the birds of prey mentioned above there are the magpie (*Pica pica*), the great shrike (*Lanius excubitor*), the red-necked nightjar (*Caprimulgus ruficollis*) and numerous red-legged partridges (*Alectoris rufa*). The commonest mammals are red deer (*Cervus elaphus*), fallow deer (*Dama dama*) and wild pigs (*Sus scrofa*); others include the weasel (*Mustela nivalis*), the polecat (*Putorius putorius*), the wild cat (*Felis sylvestris*), the fox (*Vulpes vulpes*) and – more rarely – the genet (*Genetta genetta*). Badgers (*Meles meles*) are very common, and there are large numbers of rabbits (*Oryctolagus cuniculus*), which provide an abundant food supply for larger predators.

Pinewoods (pinares). – This biotope is found mainly in the southern part of the national park.

FLORA. – The undergrowth between the pines consists mainly of tree heaths, cistuses, the broom-like *Osyris alba* L. and the mastic tree (*Pistacia lentiscus* L.).

FAUNA. – Wood pigeons (*Columba palumbus*), turtle-doves (*Streptopelia turtur*), blackbirds (*Turdus merula*), mistle thrushes (*Turdus viscivorus*), buzzards (*Buteo buteo*), red kites (*Milvus milvus*) and kestrels (*Falco tinnunculus*) are residents; visitors who return every year are the hobby (*Falco subbuteo*) and the short-toed eagle (*Circaëtus gallicus*). A very rare bird, found here but hardly anywhere else, is the azure-winged magpie (*Cyanopica cyanus*).

Dunes (dunas). – Along the coast extend long travelling dunes, which as they move inland enclose little islands (*corrales*) of pines. The trees eventually die, leaving groups of dried-up and contorted trunks which are known as *campos de cruces*.

FLORA. – Very sparse, consisting mainly of lyme grass (*Ammophila arenaria* L.) and a shrub called *camarina* (*Corema album* Don.), with sweet-tasting fruit which provides food for birds.

FAUNA. – A common species of lizard is the spiny-footed lizard (*Acanthodactylus erythrurus*); common snakes are Lataste's viper (*Viperi latasti*) and the Montpellier snake (*Malpolon monspessulanus*). These reptiles provide food for the short-toed eagle (*Circaëtus gallicus*) and the barn owl (*Tyto alba*). Predators are attracted by the large numbers of rabbits.

Rare species. – Found only in the Coto de Doñana are the pardel lynx (*Lynx pardinus*), spotted and smaller than the European lynx, and the snake-eating true ichneumon (*Herpestes ichneumon*), the only European representative of the family, which can frequently be seen trotting through the park in family

groups. Other species very rare in Europe are the imperial eagle (*Aquila heliaca*) and the greater flamingo (*Phoenicopterus ruber*). Here too is the only nesting colony in Europe of the purple gallinule (*Porphyrio porphyrio*). Rare species of duck which are protected here are the ferruginous duck (*Aythya nyroca*) and two species which winter in the park, the ruddy shelduck (*Tadorna ferruginea*) and the white-headed duck (*Oxyura leucocephala*).

The National Parks in the **CANARY ISLANDS** are notable for their interesting volcanic formations, but even more for their unique vegetation, including species which can be traced back to the Tertiary era and have been preserved here since the effects of the Ice Age on these islands were much less severe than on the mainland of Europe.

---

6 Parque Nacional de la Caldera der Taburiente

Province: Santa Cruz de Tenerife.
Established 1954. Area 11,440 acres.

SITUATION and CHARACTER. – Within this park, on the island of La Palma, is the Caldera de Taburiente, one of the largest volcanic craters in the world (circumference 28 km, greatest diameter 19 km). The highest point on the rim of the crater is the Roque de los Muchachos (2426 m). The floor of the crater has an average altitude of 800 m. The area is well supplied with water and accordingly has suffered severe erosion. The natural outlet for the spring water, which forms many waterfalls up to 50 m in height, is a gorge known as the Barranco de las Angustias. This was a sacred place to the Guanches (prehistoric inscriptions in the Cueva de Tajodeque) and the last refuge of the native population at the time of the Spanish conquest.

FLORA. – The most important tree is the Canary pine (*Pinus canariensis* DC). On the higher slopes are "Canary cedars" (*Juniperus cedrus* Webb-Berth.), growing in bizarre forms. From 2000 m up the *codeso* (*Adenocarpus viscosus* Webb-Berth.) is found. Also found at high altitudes are species of forget-me-nots (*Viola palmensis* Webb-Berth.) and cistus (*Cistus vaginatus* Ait.). On the crater floor there are beeches (*Myricca faya* Ait.), tree heathers (*Erica arborea* L.) and holly (*Ilex canariensis* Poir.). Here too there are clumps of laurels (*Laurus canariensis* Webb-Berth.), mixed with barbusanos (*Apollonias canariensis* Nees.), *Viñátigos* (*Persea indica* Spreng.) and *marmolanes* (*Myrsine canariensis* Spreng.). There are also many succulents, like *bejeques* (genus *Aeonium*), *tabaibas* (genus *Euphorbia*) and *verodes* (genus *Kleinia*).

FAUNA. – Rabbits, wild goats, pigeons (*Columba broley*), some passerines like the blackcap (*Sylvia atricapilla*), the Canary lizard (*Lacerta galloti*).

7 Parque Nacional de Garajonay

Province: Santa Cruz de Tenerife.
Founded 1979. Area 9820 acres.

SITUATION and CHARACTER. – The Garajonay National Park, situated in the Canaries on the island of Gomera, includes Mount Garajonay after which it is named. More than half the area of the park, ridges, chains of hills and gorges, is covered in forest. The park was originally created in order to protect the trees and plants of the island. – A road leads from San Sebastian to the national park, in which there are opportunities for forest walks.

FLORA. – Holly, heather, laurel and other bushes are characteristic of the landscape. Many of the tree trunks and branches are covered with moss and lichens.

FAUNA. – The Parque Nacional de Garajonay is mainly the home of birds: chaffinches, blue tits, wood pigeons, blackcaps and falcons.

8   Parque Nacional del Teide
Province: Santa Cruz de Tenerife.
Established 1954. Area 29,322 acres.

SITUATION and CHARACTER. – The park lies in a huge volcanic crater on the island of Tenerife at an average height of 2100 m. It is divided into two semicircular halves by the Roques de García, and is enclosed on the S, E and W by sheer rock faces, along the top of which the park boundary runs.

To the N the volcanic cone of the **Pico de Teide** towers up more than 1700 m above the old crater. On its slopes are three sharp projections, former subsidiary craters – to the SW the Pico Viejo or Montaña de Chaorra, which last erupted at the end of the 18th c.; to the E the Montaña Blanca, so called because of its whitish-yellow colour; and to the N the Pico Cabra. Just below the summit is the Pitón de Azúcar ("Sugar-Loaf"), cut off by an almost exactly circular crater (25 m deep, 70 m in diameter). On the summit itself (3717 m) is the wide crater of Teide, still emitting hot vapour. Between the summit and the old crater are the Cañadas del Teide, deep gashes and gullies caused by past eruptions. The whole area of the park is of volcanic origin, and much of it consists of the barren "*mal país*", in which the red or black lava flows stand out against a yellow ground composed of lapilli. The floor of the old crater is littered with volcanic "bombs" of all sizes. From Santa Cruz a road leads up to the Teide; from there a cable way goes up almost to the summit.

The climate, reflecting the southern latitude, is desert like, modified by altitude. During the winter the summit of Teide is covered with snow, and in the early morning the rocks and bushes in the Cañadas are covered with layers of crystalline ice up to 10 cm thick which sparkle in the sun (*cencellada*). The temperature variation between day and night is extreme, and the relative humidity of the air is very low (under 50 per cent, in June and July sometimes as low as 25 per cent).

FLORA. – In spite of the altitude and the unfavourable soil conditions the park is covered with luxuriant vegetation, the flowers standing out against the volcanic rock. On the steep rock faces there are "Canary cedars", junipers (*Juniperus cedrus*) growing in bizarre shapes and occasional Canary pines (*Pinus canariensis* DC). The most characteristic species, however, is the Teide broom (*Spartocytisus nubigenus* Webb-Berth.), the whitish-pink flowers of which are much sought after by the local bees. Other common species are two types of bugloss, *tajinaste rojo* (*Echium wildpretii* Pears.) and *tajinaste azul*

(*Echium auberianum* Webb-Berth.). Flowers found on the lava fields are the *hierba del Teide* (*Nepeta teydea* Webb-Berth.), the *alhelí de las Cañadas* (*Cheiranthus scoparius* Bro.), resembling the gillyflower, and the *hierba pajonera* (*Descurainia bourgaeana* Webb), which is endemic here. The Cañada de Diego Hernández is particularly notable for the number of rare species to be found there, like the "Teide daisy" (*Chrysanthemum anethifolium* Brouss.), the *hierba de la cumbre* (Scrophularia glabatra Ait.), rare mosses (*Polycarpea tenuis* Webb-Berth.) and *verode barbudo* (*Aeonium smithii* Webb-Berth.). Two species rarely seen are the "Guanche rose" (*Bencomia stipulata* Svent.) and the Teide violet discovered by Alexander von Humboldt (*Viola cheiranthyfolia* H.B. and K.).

FAUNA. – The range of animal species is less wide than that of the plants. Apart from rabbits and goats and cats which have gone wild the fauna consists almost entirely of birds – birds of prey such as the red kite (*Milvus milvus*), kestrel (*Falco tinnunculus*), sparrowhawk (*Accipiter nisus*) and the carrion-eating Egyptian vulture (*Neophron percnopterus*); the rock dove (*Columba livia*), the Barbary partridge (*Alectoris barbara*), crows (*Corvus tinginatus*) and the endemic blue Canary finch (*Fringilla teydea*). The Canary lizard (*Lacerta galloti*) lives on the lava fields.

9   Parque Nacional de Timanfaya
Province: Gran Canaria.
Established 1974. Area 12,620 acres.

SITUATION and CHARACTER. – This Spanish national park, in the NW of the island of Lanzarote, is a centre of volcanic activity. After numerous eruptions between 1730 and 1736 the last ones took place in 1824, when more than 25 volcanic orifices in the Macizo del Fuego or de Timanfaya poured out lava. The subsoil is still hot.

The lower part of the park consists of a large lava field out of which rise a series of cones and craters, like the Caldera Roja, near which is the only spring in this hot and very dry area, the Fuente de los Miraderos. These higher points, covered with volcanic ash, lapilli and "bombs", are a striking sight with their varied hues of black, yellow and red. Visitors can follow the Ruta de los Volcanes (14 km) through the park.

FLORA. – The inhospitable volcanic terrain is slow to acquire a fresh mantle of vegetation. The most resistant plants are the lichens, of which there are more than a dozen species. They are usually followed by succulents like *Aeonium lancerotense* Prager and members of the euphorbia family (*E. balsamifera* Ait., *E. obtusifolia* Poir.); also common is the *aulaga majorera* (*Zollikoferia spinosa* Boiss.), which the local people set on fire on the Montaña de Fuego for the benefit of tourists. A curious feature to be seen on the coast, where the lava has formed natural bridges, is the growth of rushes (*Juncus acutus* L.) in regular rows on the porous subsoil which stores up water.

FAUNA. – The only vertebrates are reptiles, the commonest and most interesting of which is the Atlantic lizard (*Lacerta atlantica*) or *lagarto de haria*, a species endemic in the Canaries.

Caves

Something like 10,000 caves have been found in Spain, concentrated mainly in the regions of karstic rock in the N, NE, E and S of the country. In many areas systematic prospecting and exploration have not yet been carried out.

The following list gives only a very small selection of caves which are of interest either for their prehistoric rock paintings or their stalactitic or other formations and can be seen without too much difficulty.

1 Cueva de Santimañiñe (*Cueva de Basondo*)
Province of Vizcaya;
in Mont Ereñusarre, 4·5 km NE of Guernica.
Beautiful coloured stalactites and stalagmites. Stone Age paintings and engravings in two small chambers (difficult of access) 150 m from the entrance.
Conducted tour.

2 Cueva de Covalanas
Province of Cantabria;
near Ramales, 36 km SE of Santander (guide in village).
Two long galleries; in the right-hand one (70 m long) paintings in red (stags, bisons).

3 Cueva del Castillo
Province of Cantabria;
in the Pico del Castillo, near Puerto Viesgo, 22 km SW of Santander.
Several galleries (total length 300 m; palaeontological finds (in Museo Prehistórico, Santander), 750 figures of animals.

4 Cuevas de la Pasiega
Province of Cantabria;
in Pico del Castillo, SW of Santander (guide at Cueva del Castillo, No. 3).
A maze of passages with well-preserved Paleolithic paintings (monochrome).

5 Cuevas de Altamira
Province of Cantabria;
2 km SW of Santillana del Mar.
A horizontal gallery (total length 270 m). Large painted ceiling in a chamber near the entrance with the famous polychrome figures of animals (bisons, stags, horses, wild pigs). Only 35 visitors are admitted each day.

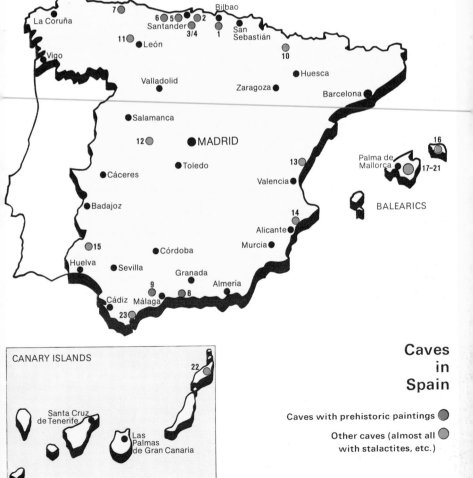

**Caves
in
Spain**

Caves with prehistoric paintings ⬤

Other caves (almost all ◯
with stalactites, etc.)

6 Cueva del Pindal
Province of Asturias;
59 km W of Santander, in the cliffs near Pimiango
(guide at San Emerito lighthouse).
A wide gallery 360 m long with figures of animals.

7 Cueva de Candamo (*Cueva de San Román*)
Province of Asturias;
at San Román, 20 km NW of Oviedo.
A series of chambers leading to a large hall; some
60 figures of animals (engravings and paintings).
Also fine stalagmites.

8 Cueva de Nerja
Province of Málaga;
near Nerja, 51 km E of Málaga.
A series of chambers of considerable size. The
lower passage (well arranged for visitors) is 800 m
long; upper passage about 2000 m. Numerous
stalactites and stalagmites, some very large (one
pillar 60 m high, diameter 18 m). Palaeolithic
paintings mainly in upper passage (stags, horses,
goats, dolphins). Important excavations (fragments of skulls).
Music, coloured lighting; frequent concerts, ballet
performances, etc.

9 Cueva de la Pileta
Province of Málaga;
at Benaoján, 11 km SW of Ronda.
Large main gallery with several chambers and side
passages; smooth white stalactites, pools of water.
Total length 1500 m. Palaeolithic engravings
(older than those of Altamira, No. 5) of horses,
bisons, stags, ibexes, a rhinoceros, fishes.

10 Cueva Vieja
Province of Huesca;
near Villanua, 12 km N of Jaca (guide).
Large stalactites and stalagmites.

11 Cueva de Valporquero
Province of León;
at Valporquero, 35 km N of León.
A large gallery 1·8 km long with numerous
branches and chambers. Numerous stalactites and
stalagmites in many colours; waterfalls, pools and
lakes.

12 Cueva del Águila
Province of Ávila;
about 60 km SW of Ávila, 6 km SW of Arenas de
San Pedro.
Numerous rock concretions of all kinds; only one
large hall (18,900 sq. m) open to the public.

13 Gruta de San José
Province of Castellón;
26 km SW of Castellón de la Plana near Val de Uxo.
A long gallery (about 800 m), with an underground river (boats). Many fine stalactitic and
other concretions.
Coloured lighting, music.

14 Cueva de Canalobre
Province of Alicante;
10 km ESE of Jijona, 3 km N of Busot, at 700 m on
N side of the Sierra de Cabeza de Oro.
Large sloping hall with numerous stalactites and
stalagmites.
Coloured lights, music, stage for folk performances and concerts. Good view of the coast from
the entrance.

15 Gruta de las Maravillas
Province of Huelva;
at Aracena, 75 km NW of Seville (entrance in a
house).
A system of passages and chambers up to 70 m
high, with lakes, many colourful stalactites and
stalagmites, crystals.
Illuminations, music. Conducted tour (1200 m;
1 hour).

16 Cueva de S'Aigu
Province of the Balearics;
on Minorca, 4 km S of Ciudadela at Cala Blanca.
Total length 215 m. Large lake of brackish water
(80 m long), in which the brightly coloured
stalactites and stalagmites are reflected.

17 Cueva de Génova
Province of the Balearics;
on Majorca, 4·5 km W of Palma at Génova
(entrance beside a house).
A series of halls with many delicate stalactites and
stalagmites in a variety of colours. Conducted
tour.

18 Cueva de Campanet
Province of the Balearics;
on Majorca, 37 km NE of Palma near Campanet.
A large cave with numerous rock concretions of
different kinds, in particular delicate needle-
shaped formations.
Conducted tour (1300 m); music.

19 Cueva de Artá
Province of the Balearics;
on Majorca, 70 km E of Palma, 9·5 km ESE of Artá
at Cabo Vermell; entrance on coast.
Huge halls with imposing stalagmites up to 22 m
high. Total length 450 m.
Conducted tour (1 km; 1 hour).

20 Cuevas del Drach
Province of the Balearics;
on Majorca, about 60 km E of Palma at Porto
Cristo; entrance on coast.
A series of four large halls with several lakes (one
177 m long and 12 m deep). Many brightly
coloured rock concretions. Total length about
2 km.
Coloured lighting, boat trips; classical concerts,
with the orchestra on illuminated boats.
Conducted tour (1 km; 2 hours).

21 Cuevas dels Hams
Province of the Balearics;
on Majorca, near Porto Cristo, 2 km NW of the
Cuevas del Drach (No. 20).
Beautiful chambers formed by an underground
river; several lakes. Varied rock concretions, in
particular delicate hook-shaped white stalactites
(*hams*="fish hooks").
Part of the caves arranged for concerts, etc.
Conducted tour.

22 Cueva de los Verdes
Province of Las Palmas de Gran Canaria;
on the N coast of Lanzarote 28 km NE of Arrecife,
at the foot of the Corona volcano.
Long galleries on several levels. Volcanic rock,
with no stalactites. Underground lakes. Total
length 6 km.
Large hall at entrance used for concerts, etc.
Conducted tour.

23 St Michael's Cave
Gibraltar;
on the W side of the Rock at a height of 300 m.
A series of halls running down to a depth of 76 m.
Many rock concretions of varied shape and colour;
small pools.
Illuminations in changing colours, music; con-
certs, etc.

Winter sports

There is excellent skiing to be had in the **Pyrenees** and the *Cantabrian Mountains* in northern Spain; the **Sierra de Guadarrama** in central Spain, at the very gates of Madrid; and the **Sierra Nevada** in the S, within easy reach of the Costa del Sol. In all these areas there are winter sports resorts at varying stages of development, with cableways and ski-lifts, practice slopes and pistes, hotels and other accommodation. The season usually lasts from November to May; at the higher altitudes skiing is also possible in summer.

The principal winter sports resorts in the **Pyrenees** are Rasos de Peguera/Ensija (up to 1700 m); Valle de la Molina (1436–2537 m), with La Molina and Super-Molina; Masella (1600 m up); Nuria (1964–2983 m); Baqueira/Beret (1500–2500 m) in the Valle de Arán (source of the Garonne); Sant Joan de l'Erm (1950–2150 m); Espot, with Super-Espot (1500 m up); Llesúy (1280–2900 m); Candanchú (1500–2240 m); Cerler/Benasque (1505–2858 m); Sallent

de Gállego, with El Formigal (1500–2350 m); Panticosa (1165–1865 m); and Burguete (1050 m up). Others include Camprodón (920–2300 m); Valle de Farreras, under the Pica d'Estax (3141 m); Port del Compte y del Vert (2000 m up); Tossa de Das (about 1500 m); and Isaba (about 1500 m).

In the **Cantabrian Mountains**: Pajares (1366–2100 m); Alto Campóo/Reinosa (1600–2222 m); and San Isidro (1520–2155 m); also Riaño/Maraña, San Emiliano and Peitariegos.

In the **Sierra de Guadarrama**: Navacerrada (1700–2230 m) and Valcotos (1774–2275 m); also Valdesqui and La Pinilla (1500–2273 m).

The **Sierra de Gredos** (Almanzor 2592 m) is primarily a touring area.

The **Sierra Nevada** is the most southerly skiing area in Europe. The principal hotels are Melia Sierra Nevada, Melia Sol y Nieve and the Parador Nacional Sierra Nevada.

There are also facilities for skiing in the **Sierra de Gúdar** (1600–2024 m), N of Valencia.

In most of these resorts there are ski schools run by the *Escuela Española de Esqui* under the auspices of the Federación Nacional de Esqui (headquarters in Madrid, Calle de Claudio Coello 32, tel. 91 2 75 05 76).

Folk traditions

The manifestation of Spanish folk art best known abroad is the Andalusian **flamenco**; but what is offered to tourists under that name, particularly outside Andalusia, is often no more than a colourful dance show to Andalusian rhythms. In the genuine *tablao* (from *tablado*, "stage") the virtuoso playing of the *tocadores* (guitarists) and the improvised words and melodies of the *cantaores* (singers) are more important than the dancing of the *bailaores*, which arises out of the elaborate rhythms of the music, accompanied by the cries of the participants and the spectators. The oldest and most authentic form of the flamenco is the *cante hondo* ("deep" or fervent singing), which shows evident Arab influence in its complicated rhythms and melodies (pentatonic chords). The *cante chico* ("small" song) seems lighter, more dance-like and more familiar to other European ears. Two melancholy types of song are the *soleá* (from *soledad*, "loneliness"), usually singing of unhappy love, and the *saeta*, formerly improvised by spectators of the great Holy Week processions commemorating Christ's Passion.

The national dance of *Catalonia* is the *sardana*, a sedate round dance which is

Folk dance, Gran Canaria

Dance group, Tolosa

very probably of Greek origin. It is accompanied by the rather nasal sounds produced by the *cobla*, an orchestra whose characteristic instruments are the oboe-like *tenora* and the *fluviol*, a flute played with one hand. In the *xiquets de valls* tall human pyramids are built up to the music of the *gralla*, a tapering oboe.

The folk music of the *Basque country* is quite different from anything found in the rest of Spain. The *aurresku* is a war-dance, performed by men, which ends with the turbulent *arin-arin*, accompanied by the piercing cries (*irrinchis*) of the dancers. The *zorzico* is a quite sedate dance in 5/8

time. There is also a popular sword dance, the *ezpata dantza*. All these dances are accompanied by the *silbotia*, a large flute, the smaller *chistuak*, which is played with only one hand while the other beats the *tiun-tiunak*, a small drum hanging from the player's sleeve, and the high-pitched drum called the *atabal*.

The Basques also have their own characteristic sports, which include, in addition to the fast ball game of *jai alai* or *pelota*, such tests of strength as lifting heavy stones, tossing tree-trunks, chopping wood and contests with ox-carts. On pelota see the next section.

Fiestas, bullfighting, games

Festivals and celebrations of various kinds – *fiestas, ferias* (fairs) and *romerías* (pilgrimages) – play a great part in the life of the Iberian peninsula and reflect ancient folk traditions. In addition to the traditional Catholic festivals (Epiphany, Easter, Corpus Christi, feasts of the Virgin and saints, All Saints, Christmas) almost every town has its own fiestas, which are celebrated with parades, bullfights, dramatic performances and fairs, but also with Passion plays, plays on the life of the Virgin and pigrimages (see under the various places in the body of this Guide). At certain times visitors travelling about the country will encounter some local

celebration every few days, involving the closing of shops and offices. Lists of fiestas are issued annually by the Spanish tourist authorities.

Bullfights (*corridas de toros:* seen at their best in southern Spain, e.g. in Seville) were held until the 16th c. as a form of weapon training as well as on the occasion of fiestas, the mounted *caballeros* being pitted against the bulls with their lances. At the beginning of the 17th c. bullfighting began to take a less hazardous form, and the present rules are attributed to Francisco Romero, born in Ronda about 1700. The building of the first large *plaza de toros* in Madrid in 1749 finally made it a public spectacle in which only professional toreros take part.

Bullfight

In central and southern Spain and in Barcelona bullfights are held on almost every Sunday and public holiday from Easter to November, and sometimes also on weekdays (particularly Thursdays). They take place between 4 and 6 or between 5 and 7 in the afternoon, but only in good weather ("si el tiempo lo permite"). During the dog days (July–August) and from mid October onwards only the lesser forms of bullfight known as *novilladas* are held, with less experienced bullfighters (*novilleros*) and young bulls (*novillos*). In northern Spain and Catalonia bullfights are usually held only on great feast days and during the summer fair (*feria*). – The bullring is exactly circular, with the expensive seats on the shady side (*sombra*) and the cheaper ones in the sun (*sol*). The black or brownish-red bulls (*toros*), which must not be older than six years, come mainly from breeding farms in Andalusia. The bullfighters, identifiable by the characteristic pigtails, are also mostly of Andalusian origin. There are something like 1000 registered toreros (the correct name of the bullfighter – not the traditional English "toreador"). A successful bullfighter can achieve great fame and considerable wealth.

The bullfight (*lidia*) has three main parts (*suertes*). After a brief prologue during which the *capeadores* tease the bull by playing it with their brightly coloured capes (*capas*) there follows the *suerte de picar* or *suerte de varas*, in which the mounted *picadores* provoke the bull to attack them, plunge their lances (*garrochas*) into its neck and withstand the charges of the infuriated beast as best they can. When the bull has been sufficiently weakened (*castigado*) by his wounds (*varas*) the second stage, the *suerte de*

banderillas, begins. The *banderilleros* run towards the bull carrying several *banderillas* and, skilfully eluding its charge at the last moment, stick them into its neck. The normal banderillas are sticks 75 cm (30 in.) long with barbed points and paper streamers; the *banderillas a cuarta* are only 15 cm (6 in.) long. Bulls which are too fierce or vicious are distracted by plays with a cloak (*floreos*). When three pairs of banderillas have been planted in the bull's neck the *suerte suprema* or *suerte de matar* begins. The *espada* or *matador*, armed with a red cloth (*muleta*) and a sword (*estoque*), begins by teasing the bull with the cloth and seeks to manoeuvre it into a position in which he can give it the death stroke (*estocada*) after which the coup de grâce is administered by a *punterillo* with a dagger. If the bull has shown itself courageous and aggressive it wil be loudly applauded. – The show is repeated six or eight times until the onset of darkness.

In recent years **football** (*fútbol*) has displaced bullfighting as the most popular spectator sport, particularly in large towns such as Madrid or Barcelona which have especially famous teams. – The Basque ball game and national sport of **pelota** is now played all over Spain, with many professional players. The court is 11 m wide and between 64 and 80 m long, and the game is played with a small solid ball which is hit against the high rear wall (*frontón*) with a hard curved glove.

Shopping and souvenirs

Spanish **handicrafts** have a long tradition, and many articles are still produced following old models, as well as new designs. Pottery can be bought almost everywhere, but particularly in Catalonia (La Bisbal), on Majorca (which gave us the name "majolica"), in Extremadura and in Talavera de la Reina (tiles). Good modern leather goods can be found in Catalonia and the Balearics (shoes particularly on Minorca), traditional work in Córdoba. Wrought-iron work is produced in Seville and Logroño, damascene steel articles in Toledo ("Toledo blades") and Éibar, small metal articles (knives, daggers) in Albacete. The main lace-making areas are *Camariñas* (pillow lace), Seville (mantillas), Granada, Almagro and the Canary Islands (drawn-thread lace). Copper mugs come mainly from Guadalupe and Granada. Murcia produces beautiful articles of esparto grass, the Balearics art glassware and artificial pearls (Manacor).

Spanish *sweets* are also a popular buy – the pastries (*ensaimadas*) and candied

Spanish pottery

fruit of Majorca, the *turrón* (nougat) of Alicante, the confections of Pamplona and Logroño, the truffle chocolates of Vitoria, the *yemas de Santa Teresa* (candied yolk of egg) of Ávila.

Other attractive souvenirs are records of Spanish folk music and illustrated books on Spain. Wines and spirits are also good buys – not only the native Spanish products but international brands, sold at very reasonable prices.

Calendar of events

January
1st
everywhere   Año Nuevo (New Year); much activity and excitement in the streets on New Year's Eve

2nd
Granada   Commemoration of the Reconquista (1492)

6th
many places   Reyes Magos (Epiphany): giving of presents to children; cavalcades, particularly in Aledo (Murcia)

17th
many places   San Antonio (St Antony's Day); blessing of domestic animals

February
5th
many places   Santa Águeda (St Agatha), particularly in Zamora, Segovia and Zamarramala

19th–25th
Santa Cruz de
Tenerife   Winter festival

25th
Sitges   International Veteran Car Rally

March
1st–19th
Valencia   San José (St Joseph); *fallas*

4th
Esparraguera
(Barcelona)   Passion play

1st–5th
Ulldecona
(Tarragona)   Passion play

Third week of Lent
Castelón de la
Plana   Santa Magdalena; bullfights, cavalcades

Holy Week
many places   Semana Santa processions, particularly in Seville, Córdoba, Granada, Málaga, Jerez, Jaén, Toledo, Cuenca, Gerona and Pollensa (Majorca); *pasos* in Valladolid and Murcia

First week after Easter
Murcia   Spring festival

April
15th
Cuenca   Canto de los Mayos

22nd–24th
Alcoy   San Jorge (St George); Moros y Cristianos

23rd
Barcelona   Book Festival

Sunday after 25th April
Tafalla/Ujué
(Navarre)   Romería de los Cruceros (pilgrimage)

End of April
Seville   Ferias de Abril

Last Sunday in April
Andújar   Pilgrimage to Virgen de la Cabeza

End of April/ beginning of May
Jerez de la
Frontera   Horse fair

May
Cádiz   Fiestas Típicas Gaditanas; processions, bullfights

3rd
Selva (Majorca)   Fiesta de la Santa Cruz (Finding of the Cross)

5th
Jaca (Huesca)   Romería de la Victoria; "Conde Aznar", pageant play

1st–12th
Córdoba   Competition for the most beautiful flower-decorated patio; Flamenco Festival

15th
Madrid   San Isidro (St Isidore); two-week programme of bullfights

30th
Aranjuez   Illuminations in gardens

End of May/ beginning of June
La Valga and
Torrona
(Pontevedra)   **Curros**: rounding up and branding of wild horses

Whitsun
El Rocío (Huelva)   Famous pilgrimage on horseback, with decorated carriages

Corpus Christi
many places   Magnificent processions over carpets of flowers, particularly in Granada,

Semana Santa

Barcelona, Sitges, Toledo, Cádiz, Valencia, Zaragoza, Seville and Burgos. Mystery play at Camuñas (Toledo)

une
1st–30th
licante | St John's Day (Midsummer), with the "Hogueras de San Juan" (bonfires)

3rd and 28th
arcelona | On the eves of St John's Day and St Peter's Day, Midsummer Festival in the Pueblo Español

3rd and 24th
iudadela (Minorca) | "Hogueras" (Midsummer bonfires)

4th–29th
eville | Folk dancing

9th
urgos | Feria in honour of San Pedro (St Peter)

9th
equeitio | St Peter's Day, with the Kaxarranka (fishermen's dance)

9th to 2nd July
ún | Alarde victory celebration; military parade

nd of June/ eginning of July
ranada | International Festival of Music and Dancing

uly
th–14th
amplona | San Fermín: feria, with the famous *encierros* (running of the bulls) and bullfights

3th
oncal (Navarre) | Handing over of three head of cattle as a tribute from France

6th
ort towns | Virgen del Carmen (Our Lady of Carmel); sea processions

5th–31st
antiago de ompostela | Festival in honour of Santiago (St James: 25th July); pilgrimage, fireworks

7th–31st
alencia | Feast of St James (in Catalan San Jaime: 25th July); battle of flowers, bullfights, *sardanas*

hroughout ugust
W coast | Semana Grande, with sporting and cultural events and bullfights, in San Sebastián, Bilbao, Gijón and La Coruña

ugust
st–9th
álaga | Feria, with bullfights

4th–9th
Vitoria | Fiesta of the Virgen Blanca (White Virgin)

13th–15th
Elche (Alicante) | Assumption; mystery play

15th
La Alberca (Salamanca) | Assumption; mystery play

14th–25th
Betanzos (La Coruña) | San Roque (St Roch); sea festival, guild dances

22nd to 2nd September
Requena (Valencia) | Feria and Vintage Festival

September
5th–9th
Jerez de la Frontera | Vintage Festival

5th–15th
Murcia | Feria

8th
many places | Romerís (pilgrimages) at Meritxell (Andorra), Utrera (Seville), La Peña de Francia (Salamanca), Andújar (Jaén), Ochagvía (Navarre), etc.

8th–22nd
Salamanca | Feria

First to second Sunday
San Sebastián | Basque Festival, with traditional celebrations and contests

19th
Oviedo | Día de las Américas (Day of the Americas)

19th–26th
Logroño | Rioja Vintage Festival

23rd
Tarragona | Santa Tecla (St Thecla); *sardanas* and *xiquets de valls* (see p. 218)

24th–28th
Barcelona | Santa María de la Merced (patroness of Barcelona); bullfights, traditional celebrations

25th–27th
Córdoba | Autumn Fair

29th
Albacín (Granada) | Pilgrimage and procession

October
7th–15th
Ávila | Santa Teresa

week including 12th
Zaragoza | Virgen del Pilar

December
24th/25th
many places | Midnight masses

Statutory public holidays

1 January	*Año Nuevo* (New Year's Day)
6 January	*Reyes Magos* (Three Kings, Epiphany)
19 March	*San José* (St Joseph)
1 May	*Día del Trabajo* (Labour Day)
24 June	*San Juan* (St John: the king's name-day)
29 June	*San Pedro y San Pablo* (SS. Peter and Paul)
25 July	*Santiago* (St James)
15 August	*Asunción* (Assumption)
12 October	*Día de la Hispanidad* (commemorating the discovery of America)
1 November	*Todos los Santos* (All Saints)
8 December	*Immaculada Concepción* (Immaculate Conception)
25 December	*Natividad del Señor* (Christmas)
Movable festivals	*Viernes Santo* (Good Friday) *Corpus Christi*

Information

Spanish National Tourist Office

57–58 St James's Street,
London SW1A 1LD;
tel. 01–499 0901–6.

665 Fifth Avenue,
New York, NY 10022;
tel. 759 8822.

180 North Michigan Avenue,
Chicago, IL 60601;
tel. 641 1842.

Suite 710, 209 Post Street,
San Francisco, CA 94108;
tel. (415) 986 2125.

Suite 201, 60 Bloor Street West,
Toronto 5, Ontario;
tel. 961 3131.

Within Spain tourist information is provided by the *Patronatos de Turismo* and by the *Delegaciónes Provinciales* which have their headquarters in the various provinces. In the larger towns information can be obtained from the *Oficinas de Información de Turismo*. In smaller places the visitor can often obtain help from the Town Hall (*Ayuntamiento*).

Real Automóvil Club de España (*RACE*),
José Abascal 10,
Madrid 3;
tel. 91–4 47 32 00.

Breakdown service in Madrid (open 24 hours): tel. (91) 4 41 22 22.

Branch offices in the larger towns.

Autoclub Turístico Español (*ATE*),
Calle P. Huidrobo s/n,
Madrid;
tel. 91–2 07 11 76.

Diplomatic and Consular Offices in Spain

United Kingdom

Embassy
Calle de Ferdinando el Santo 16,
Madrid;
tel. 91–4 19 02 00.

Consulates
Avenida de las Fuerzas Armadas II,
Algeciras;
tel. 956–66 16 00.

Plaza Calvo Sotelo 1–2 (1st floor),
Alicante;
tel. 965–21 61 90.

Edificio Torre de Barcelona (13th floor),
Diagonal 477,
Barcelona;
tel. 93–3 22 21 51.

Alameda de Urquijo 2–8,
Bilbao;
tel. 94–4 15 76 00.

Avenida Isidoro Macabich 45,
Ibiza;
tel. 971–30 18 18.

Consular Section of Embassy,
Calle de Ferdinando el Santo 16,
Madrid;
tel. 91–4 19 02 00.

Edificio Duquesa,
Calle Duquesa de Parcent 4,
Málaga;
tel. 952–21 75 71.

Plaza Mayor 30,
Palma de Mallorca;
tel. 971–21 20 85.

Edificio Hocasa (6th floor),
Calle Alfredo L. Jones 33,
Las Palmas de Gran Canaria;
tel. 928–26 25 08.

Edificio Mar. Suárez Guerra 40 (5th floor),
Santa Cruz de Tenerife;
tel. 922–24 20 00.

Plaza Nueva 8,
Seville;
tel. 954–22 88 75.

Santian 4,
Tarragona;
tel. 977–232502.

Plaza de Compostela (6th floor),
Vigo;
tel. 986–21 14 50.

United States of America

Embassy
Serrano 75,
Madrid;
tel. 91–2 76 34 00.

Consulates
Via Layetana 33,
Barcelona;
tel. 93–3 19 95 50.

Avenida del Ejército 11 (3rd floor),
Deusto, **Bilbao** 12;
tel. 94–4 35 83 08.

Paseo de las Delicias 7,
Seville;
tel. 954–23 18 85.

Canada

Embassy
Edificio Goya, Calle Núñez de Balboa 35,
Madrid;
tel. 91–2 25 91 19.

Consulate
Plaz de Toros Vieja 18A (4th floor),
Málaga;
tel. 952–31 81 45.

Airline offices in Spain

Iberia
Calle de Velázquez 130,
Madrid;
tel. 91–26 19 100 and 26 19 500.
Desks at all Spanish airports.

British Airways
Explanada de España 3,
Alicante;
tel. 965–20 05 94.

Paseo de Gracia 59,
Barcelona;
tel. 93–2 15 21 12.

Edificio Granada (4th floor), Gran Via 38,
Bilbao;
tel. 94–4 16 78 66.

Bethencourt 49,
Las Palmas;
tel. 928–36 01 11.

Avda José Antonio 68,
Madrid;
tel. 91–2 47 53 00.

José Pizarro 2,
Torremolinos;
tel. 952–38 68 00.

Airport,
Palma de Mallorca;
tel. 971–26 43 50.

c/o Iberia, Almirante Lobo 2,
Seville;
tel. 954–22 89 01 and 21 88 00.

Edificio Banco de Londres,
Plaza Rodrigo Botet 6,
Valencia;
tel. 96–3 21 50 21.

Cánovas del Castillo 22,
Vigo;
tel. 986–22 43 26.

International telephone codes

From Britain to Spain	010 34
From the United States or Canada to Spain	011 34
From Australia to Spain	0011 34
From Spain to Britain	07 44
From Spain to the United States or Canada	07 1
From Spain to Australia	07 61

Remember that in dialling an international call the 0 (in Spain the 9) in the local dialling code must be omitted. Some Spanish exchanges have not yet been connected to the subscriber trunk dialling network.

Radio messages for tourists

In cases of emergency the Spanish radio organisation, **Radio Nacional**, will transmit messages for tourists travelling in Spain. Information from motoring organisations.

Emergency telephone numbers

Fire, police, ambulance: in Madrid and Barcelona dial 091 for police and 2 32 32 32 for fire service; elsewhere call the operator.

Emergency telephones can be found almost everywhere on the motorways. Otherwise help can be obtained, in the event of a breakdown or accident through the *Guardia Civil de Trafico*, which maintains patrols on motorways and main roads; in towns assistance can be obtained from the *Police Municipal*.

Notes

Abbreviations for Provinces and Territories

A	Alicante	Álava	VI
AB	Albacete	Albacete	AB
AL	Almería	Alicante	A
AV	Avila	Almería	AL
B	Barcelona	Asturias	O
BA	Badajoz	Ávila	AV
BI	Vizcaya	Badajoz	BA
BU	Burgos	Balearics	PM
C	La Coruña	Barcelona	B
CA	Cádiz	Burgos	BU
CC	Cáceres	Cáceres	CC
CO	Córdoba	Cádiz	CA
CR	Ciudad Real	Cantabria	S
CS	Castellón	Castellón	CS
CT	Ceuta	Ceuta	CT
CU	Cuenca	Ciudad Real	CR
GC	Las Palmas de Gran Canaria	Córdoba	CO
GE	Gerona	La Coruña	C
GR	Granada	Cuenca	CU
GU	Guadalajara	Gerona	GE
H	Huelva	Granada	GR
HU	Huesca	Guadalajara	GU
J	Jaén	Guipúzcoa	SS
L	Lérida	Huelva	H
LE	León	Huesca	HU
LO	La Rioja	Jaén	J
LU	Lugo	León	LE
M	Madrid	Lérida	L
MA	Málaga	Lugo	LU
ML	Melilla	Madrid	M
MU	Murcia	Málaga	MA
NA	Navarre	Melilla	ML
O	Asturias	Murcia	MU
OR	Orense	Navarre	NA
P	Palencia	Orense	OR
PM	Balearics	Palencia	P
PO	Pontevedra	Las Palmas de Gran Canaria	GC
S	Cantabria	Pontevedra	PO
SA	Salamanca	La Rioja	LO
SE	Seville	Salamanca	SA
SG	Segovia	Santa Cruz de Tenerife	TF
SO	Soria	Segovia	SG
SS	Guipúzcoa	Seville	SE
T	Tarragona	Soria	SO
TE	Teruel	Tarragona	T
TF	Santa Cruz de Tenerife	Teruel	TE
TO	Toledo	Toledo	TO
V	Valencia	Valencia	V
VA	Valladolid	Valladolid	VA
VI	Álava	Vizcaya	BI
Z	Zaragoza	Zamora	ZA
ZA	Zamora	Zaragoza	Z